k-punk

Mark Fisher (1968 – 2017) was a co-founder of Zer0 Books and, later, Repeater Books. His blog, k-punk, defined critical writing for a generation. He wrote three books, *Capitalist Realism*, *Ghosts of My Life* and *The Weird and the Eerie*, and was a Visiting Fellow in the Visual Cultures department at Goldsmiths, University of London.

Darren Ambrose is a freelance writer and editor from the North-East of England.

Simon Reynolds is the author of *Retromania* and *Rip It Up and Start Again*.

k-punk

The Collected and Unpublished Writings of Mark Fisher

(2004-2016)

Edited by Darren Ambrose

Foreword by Simon Reynolds

Published by Repeater Books
An imprint of Watkins Media Ltd

19-21 Cecil Court
London
WC2N 4EZ
UK

www.repeaterbooks.com
A Repeater Books paperback original 2018
3

Distributed in the United States by Random House, Inc., New York.

Cover design: Johnny Bull
Typography and typesetting: Frederik Jehle
Typefaces: Meridien LT Std, Aleo

ISBN: 9781912248285
Ebook ISBN: 9781912248292

Printed and bound in Great Britain by TJ International Ltd, Padstow, Cornwall

CONTENTS

PART THREE

8

PART FIVE

foreword

The strange thing is that I encountered Mark's mind long before I actually met him. In a way, I knew him before I even knew *of* him.

Let me explain. In 1994, I wrote a piece for *Melody Maker* about D-Generation, a concept-laden outfit from Manchester whose line-up included Mark. But I only ever spoke on the phone with another member, Simon Biddell. Because I was so interested in D-Generation's ideas, it never even occurred to me to do the basic journalistic procedure of asking who else was in the group. So it was a full decade later that I learned I'd effectively written *about* Mark, when he shyly revealed this fact in an email to me. And sure enough, digging out the yellowing clip — D-Generation as "Pick of the Week" in the Advance section of *Melody Maker* — there was Mark right in the centre of the photo: his hair in a vaguely Madchester-style bob, his eyes staring out at the reader with a searching, baleful intensity.

D-Generation were one of those groups that are grist for the mill of the music press, catnip to a certain kind of critic: the conceptual framing was piquant and provocative, the sound itself lagged slightly behind the spiel. Rereading the piece and listening for the first time in many years to D-Generation's EP *Entropy in the UK*, it's fascinating just how many of Mark's signature fixations were already in evidence. There's the centrality of punk in his worldview: D-Generation described their music as "techno haunted by the ghost of the punk" (literally, in "The Condition of Muzak", which sampled Johnny Rotten's Winterland 1978 kiss-off "ever get the feeling you've been cheated?" and turned his bitter jeering laugh into a riff). There's the love-hate for Englishness: hating the hale 'n' hearty, artless and anti-intellectual side of the national character ("Rotting Hill" sampled "Merrie England? England was never merry!" from the film version of *Lucky Jim*),

13

loving a darkly arty deviant tradition that included the Fall, Wyndham Lewis, and Michael Moorcock (all referenced in D-Generation's press release). There's also early evidence of Mark's virulent contempt for retro: "73/93" targeted what D-Generation dubbed the "Nostalgia Conspiracy". And there's even flickering ectoplasmic portents of hauntology, that twenty-first century current of music and thought and sensibility that Mark championed so compellingly.

Beyond those specifics, though, it's the structure of the encounter itself that is revealing and prefiguring. Here's a music journalist (in this case, me) hungrily on the look-out for a group with ideas, and, having found one (in this case, D-Generation), forming a symbiotic alliance with musicians who themselves think like critics. That's how Mark would operate when he got to the other side of divide. In his fruitful relationships with Burial, the Caretaker, Junior Boys, and other artists, a mutually intensifying feedback loop between the music-theorist and the music-practitioner was set in motion. The borderline between the two fronts of activity dissolved. Both critic and artist contributed equally to the scene, pushing it ever forward in a dialectic of advance, counter-reaction, swerve, clash.

Raised on the British music press of the Eighties (primarily *NME*) and fuelled further by what survived of its approach and spirit into the Nineties (primarily *Melody Maker* and the *Wire*), Mark Fisher was possibly the last of a disappearing breed: the music critic as prophet. The primary mission was identifying the leading edge and proselytising on its behalf, while simultaneously directing laser beams of negativity to discredit the wrong paths being taken and to clear space for the true music of our time. But alongside weaponised praise in support of the new and radical, the messianic critic also set challenges for music — and for listeners and readers too.

Mark Fisher became the best music writer of his generation. But that is just one of his areas of achievement. Mark wrote brilliantly about the arts adjacent to popular music: television, science fiction, mainstream movies (particularly the pulp end of the spectrum — it always amazed me that he would routinely check out things like the CGI-bloated 2005 remake of *King Kong*, just on the off chance there was something salvageable there, something he could recruit to his "pulp modernism" concept). Mark wrote rivetingly about high culture too — visual arts, photography, literature, highbrow cinema. And he wrote penetratingly about politics, philosophy, mental health, the Internet and social media (the phenomenology of digital life — its peculiar affects of connected loneliness and distracted boredom). Often, and most crucially, Mark wrote about many — sometimes all — of these things at the same time. Making connections across far-flung fields, zooming in for vivid attention to aesthetic particulars and zooming out again to the widest possible scope, Mark would locate the metaphysics in a TV show like *Sapphire and Steel*, the psychoanalytic truths lurking in a Joy

Division song, the political resonances stitched into the fabric of a Burial album or Kubrick movie. His subject was all of human life (even though he would characterise himself as neither a humanist nor a vitalist). The ambition was vast; the vision was total.

The exciting thing about Mark's writing — in his blog k-punk, in magazines like the *Wire*, *FACT*, *Frieze*, and *New Humanist*, and in his books for Zer0 and Repeater — was the feeling that he was on a journey: the ideas were going somewhere, a gigantic edifice of thought was in the process of construction. You sensed, with mounting awe, that Mark was building a system. There was a feeling too that while the work was rigorous and deeply informed, it was not academic, either in terms of its intended audience or as an exercise done purely for its own sake. The urgency in Mark's prose came from his faith that words really could change things. His writing made everything feel more meaningful, supercharged with significance. Reading Mark was a rush. An addiction.

After that odd not-quite-encounter with D-Generation, the first time I came across the name "Mark Fisher" was a byline in the strikingly designed periodicals that emanated from an enigmatic entity known as Ccru. I can't recall whether they sent me their tracts or whether it was our mutual friend Kodwo Eshun who turned me on. Right from the start, Mark's work stood out. Much of the output of the Cybernetic culture research unit, a para-academic organisation loosely tethered to Warwick University's Philosophy Department, was wilfully hermetic, closer to experimental fiction than academic work. Practically writhing on the page, Mark's prose wasn't scholarly either, but it was always lucid. Oh, he was partial — as we all were in those days — to gnomic neologisms and portmanteau terms; there was an exuberant play with language in amidst the apocalyptic sobriety and urgency of the tone. But —and this would characterise his entire career as a writer — Mark hardly ever made his writing more dense or difficult than it needed to be. He had the zeal of the true communicator, someone who believes that the ideas and the issues being addressed are simply too important to be obfuscated. Why put obstacles in the way of understanding? I'm sure this is why Mark's work found a readership that extended beyond the narrow field of scholars and the university-educated that some of his more arcane and abstruse interests might have indicated. He didn't talk down to anyone, ever, but he always invited the reader in, pulled them along with him.

I met Mark for the first time in 1998, having persuaded the academic magazine *Lingua Franca* to assign me a lengthy piece about Ccru and its allies in renegade academia like O[rphan] D[rift>]. Compared with the deranging strangeness of their texts, Ccru in person were surprisingly mild and, well, British. But again, Mark stood out a little from his comrades, for his sheer intensity. I remember the way his hands shook with passion as he held forth acerbically on everything from the cyberpunk aesthetics of jungle to the decrepitude of socialism. Although soft-spoken, you could see already a distinct flair for public speaking, the aura of an orator in the making.

After that, Mark and I rubbed shoulders online as contributors to the post-rave music theory site Hyperdub, founded by Ccru member Steve Goodman, aka Kode9. But full-blown friendship really came when Mark hurled himself into the blogging fray in 2003, starting k-punk a few months after I launched my own Blissblog. With incredible speed, a rough equivalent to the old UK weekly music press reconstituted itself online. Or so I liked to think, anyway: that this was the music press in exile, a reactivation of all of its bygone best aspects that you could no longer find in the surviving print remnants (what passed for *NME* by then, monthlies like *Q*). Well, all except for the getting paid aspect. But on the early 2000s blog scene, the broader perspective that the golden-era rock press had — where music held a privileged status, but film, TV, fiction, politics bubbled in the mix too — was miraculously and unexpectedly resurrected.

"It wasn't only about music and *music* wasn't only about music", is how Mark put it, talking about what *NME* had meant to him growing up, a working-class boy with limited access to high culture. "It was a medium that made demands on you." The same applied to the blog circuit, whose population of autodidacts, independent researchers, disenchanted academics (like Mark) and assorted oddballs formulated theories and ransacked the works of famous thinkers for concepts and analytical tools to misuse. In compensation for not being able to make a livelihood off your ravings and rantings, the blogging platform afforded extra powers: incredible speed of response, flexibility of format (you could blog extensive think-pieces or miniature thought-bombs), and the ability to illustrate the writing using images, audio, video. Best of all, there was an interactive and collective aspect to blogging that had only ever been glimpsed in the music press (with the readers' letter page, writers arguing amongst each other week by week, and the regular uptake of malcontents from the fiery fanzines). The blog circuit was a true network.

Fizzing with fervour, k-punk soon became the hub of the community. Mark was a dynamo, hurling out provocations, ideas that demanded engagement. He became a cult figure. A catalyst. He was also the perfect host, convening a salon-style energy in the k-punk comments section, igniting debate and defusing dispute when things got a little testy (as they inevitably did). That amiably fractious spirit would then inform the message board Dissensus that Mark co-founded with Matthew Ingram (whose Woebot was our community's other hub). In some ways, it was in these comments sections and message board threads that Mark was in his truest element: arguing, sometimes agreeing, but always building on his interlocutor's point, pushing the conversation further along. Some of his best insights and lines emerged out of this back-and-forth: jewels that are hard to disentangle from the discursive thicket of their moment, countless brief exchanges and interactions in which his mind flexed itself most playfully and merrily.

During this whole period of the early-to-mid 2000s, I found myself in a pleasantly disorienting situation: someone whom I'd influenced became someone who influenced me. There was a certain edgy excitement to turning on the computer every morning and immediately checking to see what Mark had thrown down in terms of an ideas-gauntlet — a definite feeling of having to keep up. We would often operate as a long-distance double-act (with a five-hour delay, Mark being in London and me in New York). One of us would pick up on something the other had written. It was a complementary (and complimentary) relationship, like a baton being passed back and forth, but it also fairly frequently involved respectful disagreement. Others joined in as well, of course; it was an omnidirectional free for all.

As much as it was a cooperative endeavour, this blog circuit and in particular the dialogue between Mark and myself, there was also an undercurrent of competition. (No doubt this is the case with writers in many different fields). An unusual sensation, for me, of being outflanked and out-done, and having to repeatedly raise my game. In some of our exchanges, Mark had the advantage of seeing things in starker, more black-and-white terms, whereas I tended to see shades of grey, or recognise that there were things to be said in favour of the opposing view. That might be a virtue in real life, but in writing it definitely softens your attack.

Mark could access greater resources of "nihilation" — his term for a ruthless drive, on the part of a critic or an artist, to reject other approaches and condemn them to history's trashcan. (This dismissiveness was a feature of his print persona, I should add; in person, he was generous and open.) The improviser John Butcher described this mindset from an artist's point of view in a 2008 interview with the *Wire*:

> This music is here in opposition to other music. It doesn't all co-exist together nicely. The fact that I have chosen to do this implies that I don't value what you're doing over there. My activity calls into questions the value of your activity. This is what informs our musical thinking and decision making.

For Fisher and Butcher alike, severity towards "the opposition" is the mark of seriousness, a sign that something is at stake and that differences are worth fighting over. Above all, it is this negative capacity — the strength of will to discredit and discard — that keeps music and culture rattling along furiously in a forward direction, not wishy-washy tolerance and anything-goes positivity. If music-making can be a form of "active criticism", then criticism could equally be a sort of soundless contribution to music.

To gather my thoughts and clear my head before writing this, I went for a walk. There was something of an English feel to the bright and beautiful February morning in Southern California — a blustery breeze sent huge clouds skidding across the sky, their tufty whiteness shot through with piercing sunlight, creating that somehow crazed quality I associate with partly-cloudy summer days in the UK. I would love to have shown Mark around Los Angeles, shown him some of its other sides (he had some fixed ideas about the city, largely derived from Michael Mann's *Heat* and Baudrillard's *America*!). And I would love to have been shown around Suffolk, the coastal landscapes Mark loved.

But the amount of time we spent in each other's physical company was painfully small. It's possible that the number of meetings is in single figures. Mark and I lived on different continents most of the time we knew each other. That lent a kind of purity to the friendship, based as it was almost entirely on the written word: there was a lot of mental communing via email, inter-blog debate, message boards… but not much hanging out.

That means that what I've written here can only be a partial portrait of Mark, as both a public figure and as a man. We knew each other mostly as virtual colleagues and unofficial collaborators (we never co-wrote anything, but we formed a united front in various joint campaigns, like the hardcore continuum, hauntology, and a general anti-retro polemic). Above all, I knew him as a reader. (Again, the disconcerting thing was to become a fan of someone who had been a fan of me). But I know that there are many other Mark Fishers. Mark the teacher, Mark the editor, Mark the son and spouse and father. I encountered him almost entirely in the rarefied realms of discourse — usually fairly fevered discourse — and didn't get to see that much of him in more casual, everyday modes. I would love to have known better these other Marks — Mark at play, Mark having a laugh, Mark relaxing, Mark with his family.

The last time I saw Mark in the flesh was in September 2012, at the music festival Incubate in Tilburg, Holland. The theme of the festival was do-it-yourself. I gave the keynote, interrogating certain aspects of DIY ideology and wondering whether it had outlived its usefulness as a cultural ideal. Mark was set to follow and spontaneously decided to drop what he was going to say and improvise a new talk, building on my argument. It was like the old blog days, except this time happening in real-time and real-space. Where I had read from a pre-written text that I laced with the occasional ad lib, Mark spoke completely off the cuff, pulling riffs from the formidable arsenal in his brain, generating new thoughts and making electric connections. The performance was typical both of his collegiality and his mental agility. Mark likened it later to a stand-up routine — adding that it was becoming a problem that institutions and individuals were video-recording his talks and putting them up on YouTube, because people would become overly familiar with his material. But I can't imagine that was really ever going to be a problem: Mark was an inexhaustible font of insight and overview, bubbling over with fresh perceptions and original articulations, memorable maxims and acute aphorisms. He was never going to run out of things to say.

But then Mark ran out of time.

I feel his absence as a friend, as a comrade, but most of all as a reader. There are many days when I wonder what Mark would have had to say about this or that. I hadn't realised how dependent I had become on the surprises and challenges that Mark would throw out there at regular intervals: the spur and spark of his writing, the clarity he could bring to almost anything he shone his light upon. I miss Mark's mind. It's a lonely feeling.

Simon Reynolds, 2018

editor's introduction

"We have to invent the future."
— Mark Fisher[1]

Mark Fisher (k-punk) was not, and never wanted to be, a conventional academic writer, theorist or critic. His writing was too abrasive, polemical, lucid, unsentimental, personal, insightful and compelling for that. Despite displaying the most acute understanding of the physical, psychological, economic and cultural consequences of contemporary capitalism, his work was also optimistic and strategically operative. A great deal of his writing was undertaken in vehement opposition to the all-too evident PoMo dissociation and collective alienation around us, and as a response to what he termed the "boring dystopia" of our shared present, to the increasingly depthless present of this new millennium. Mark provided original, savage and stylish dissections of our moribund culture, and continually observed how popular modernist films, books, television and music that had had a lifelong effect on him continue to "haunt" our collective present.

In the 1990s Mark studied for a PhD in philosophy at the University of Warwick, successfully completing his thesis in 1999 titled "Flatline Constructs: Gothic Materialism and Cybernetic Theory-Fiction". Whilst at Warwick he was one of the founding members of the Cybernetic culture research unit (Ccru), along with others such as Nick Land, Sadie Plant, Kodwo Eshun, Steve Goodman (Kode9), Robin Mackay and Luciana Parisi. Several years later, whilst working as an FE teacher in Kent, he began his blog k-punk. k-punk emerged in the early days of blogging, where it quickly became an important part of a community of emergent bloggers, including music journalists Simon Reynolds, Ian Penman and David Stubbs, philosophers Nina Power, Alex Williams, Lars Iyer, Adam Kotsko, Jodi Dean and Steven Shaviro, writer and activist Richard Seymour, writers Siobhan McKeown and Carl Neville, and architecture critic Owen Hatherley. One of the most vital aspects of blogging for k-punk during those early days was the simple element of re-connection, of becoming involved in a new online collective at a time in his life, after Warwick, Ccru and the PhD, when he was perhaps at his most isolated. As he recalls in a 2010 interview:

> I started blogging as a way of getting back into writing after the traumatic experience of doing a PhD. PhD work bullies one into the idea that you can't say anything about any subject until you've read every possible authority on it. But blogging seemed a more informal space, without that kind of pressure. Blogging was a way of tricking myself back into doing serious writing. I was able to con myself, thinking, "it doesn't matter, it's only a blog post, it's not an academic paper". But now I take the blog rather more seriously than writing academic papers.[2]

And in a post written exactly a year after launching the blog, he writes:

> It's been my only connection to the world, my only outside line... It's reinvigorated my enthusiasm for so many things, and pricked my enthusiasm for things I'd never previously considered...[3]

The early years of the k-punk blog were ones marked by intensity and informality, with regular swathes of writing and numerous dialogues. k-punk traced the positive effects of regular writing, enabling Mark to access the depths of his own obsessions and interests and refine his own powerful style. As he developed he began to connect into a kind of thematic rhythm, and over the years, one begins to see his thoughts coalesce around the themes of hauntology, popular modernism and capitalist realism. As he acknowledges, k-punk was written as a way for him to escape from the imposed bonds and pointless strictures of academic writing. Dense, allusive, theoretically rich and abrasive posts were written in response to a consistent set of personal obsessions and external stimuli (a film, book or album to be reviewed; an event to be contextualised or theorised) and were often written with a real sense of urgency, by the need to participate in an ongoing dialogue, or by a self-imposed deadline. These k-punk posts encapsulated an intellectual moment of reflection on the world: they are responsive, immediate, and provide an affectively charged perspective. Some of his references and allusions are undoubtedly challenging and potentially intimidating

— Spinoza, Kant, Nietzsche, Marcuse, Adorno, Althusser, Deleuze and Guattari, Baudrillard, Jameson, Žižek, Zupančič, Berardi, Badiou, Lacan — but his writing is never marked by the zealous pedantry exhibited by so much academic writing in the theoretical humanities. Mark has faith in the intelligence and rationality of his readers; he trusts their capacity to be challenged by unfamiliarity, complexity and the new. He consistently displays the courage to take up a strong theoretical and practical position. His work rows against the tide of anti-intellectualism in the present which has tried so hard to flatten things out to a level of cretinous instrumentality and utilitarian stupidity.

For us, the readers of the k-punk blog, his writing always gives us reasons for continuing, against the odds, to hope for an alternative to the dystopian present. This is not just a consequence of the specific content of his writing, but is as much to do with the fact that he was there at all, for the persistence of his provocative and challenging voice. That voice — strident, angry, fiercely intelligent, sophisticated and enthusiastic, serious and animated — is so close to the way he actually spoke in person. There is always a real intimacy to his writing, and he possessed a unique and rare talent to be able to articulate his thoughts and ideas without the written words diminishing, softening or reducing them. Mark's voice is preserved in his work, and it is preserved online.

The first two k-punk posts in this collection, "Why K?" and "Book Meme", both written in 2005, offer us some precise insight into Mark's reasons for blogging as k-punk, together with an understanding of his operative objectives and ambitions.

One of these is the ongoing belief in simply grasping the new technological democracy of blogging and using it as a "kind of conduit for continuing trade between popular culture and theory". k-punk's belief in the importance of outsider forms of discourse never wavered. There is a consistent belief in the operative effectiveness of fugitive discourses which have been legitimated by neither the official channels of the establishment (via academia or mainstream media outlets) or traditional forms of publishing. In the early days of k-punk this was something he particularly came to associate with blogging:

> All that is lacking is the will, the belief that what can happen in something that does not have authorisation/legitimation can be as important — more important — than what comes through official channels.[4]

Another is his declared fidelity to the ideas of Kafka and Spinoza, along with his allegiance to a whole host of things which, by articulating and confirming his own perceptions, modernist sensibilities and thoughts of existential detachment, alternative possibilities and perspectives, he felt had first brought him to a degree self-awareness: Joyce, Burroughs, Ballard, Beckett, Selby. The early books, the music, the television, the films, the ideas, the events. The Miners' strike, the Falklands war, Thatcherism, Blairism, post-punk, Joy Division, the Fall, Scritti Politti, Magazine, acid house, jungle, Goldie, Deleuze and Guattari, Marx, Jameson, Žižek, Foucault, Nietzsche, the Ccru, Cronenberg, Atwood, Priest, M.R. James, Nigel Kneale, Marcuse, Penman, Reynolds, *Batman*, and in later years *The Hunger Games*, Burial, Sleaford Mods, the Caretaker and Russell Brand. The performativity of the k-punk blog was, at least in part, undertaken as part of a personal survival strategy, to regain and persistently re-state fidelity to those things in which he had discovered the original ideas that had animated and inspired him. He says as much in "Book Meme":

> The periods of my adult life that have been most miserable have been those in which I lost fidelity to what I discovered then, in the pages of Joyce, Dostoyevsky, Burroughs, Beckett, Selby...[5]

This fidelity is key, because it provides the animating fibre that underpins the vast collage which he somehow synthesises into an effective and operative worldview opposed to the tedious banalities of a present ruled by the merciless logic of what he came to term "capitalist realism", where alternative possibilities have become increasingly proscribed and reduced to almost nothing. His forensic attention was so brilliantly attuned to those often unnoticed traces of modernism in texts, music, films and television programmes, and he repeatedly worked out acute readings of popular culture as if piecing together, one by one, the fragmented pages of a lost manifesto of cultural alchemy necessary for challenging the disastrous tyranny of the present. For more than a decade, k-punk served as a critical epicentre for hauntology and counterculture, highlighting the latent radical potential of a lost and receding twentieth-century modernism. The k-punk blog warped the reality field by repeatedly and incisively piercing through the drab fabric of the early years of this new millennium. k-punk brought important, uncomfortable and original challenges to the present, interrupting it with shards of difference, elements of the past that remained out of joint with the present, that disrupted the inertial logic of our times. At its very best it served to effectively resist the tendency for things to settle into a hazy homogenous present where time equals capital, and where everything is flattened out into commodified and easily digestible consumables. It did this by keeping open a space for alternative possibilities, and by refusing to allow important things to become reduced to the mediocre, the banal, the downright stupid, and the boring.

Finally, there is his exemplary antipathy and negativity towards PoMo hyper-ironic posturing, dreary hopey-feely liberal leftism, delibidinised culture, upper-class superiority, vampiric trolls, vitalist positivity, and Deleuzo-creationism, which was always evident on the k-punk blog. The sentiments and positioning of his challenging and controversial piece "Exiting the Vampire Castle"[6] in 2013 is no less evident in earlier k-punk posts like "New Comments Policy"[7] in 2004 and "We Dogmatists"[8] in 2005. His savage, cold-rational polemics are often in full force throughout the life of the k-punk project. Take this for example from "Noise as Anti-Capital":

> THERE IS NO DIGNITY. Don't confuse the working class with the proletariat. Thatcher inhibits the emergence of the proletariat by buying off the working class with payment capital and the promise of owning your own Oed-I-Pod. The comforts of slavery. She gives the replicants screen memories and family photos. So that they forget that they were only ever artificial, factory farmed to function as the Kapital-Thing's self-replicating HR pool, and begin to believe that they are authentic human subjects. The proletariat is not the confederation of such subjectivities but their dissolution in globalised k-space. The virtual population of nu-earth... The heroism of the proletariat consists not in its dignified resistance to the inorganic-inhumanity of the industrialisation process... but in its mutative Duchamp-transformation of its body into an inhuman inorganic constructivist machine.[9]

In 2007, Mark left his teaching job in Kent and moved to Woodbridge in Suffolk, where he began working on what would become his first book, *Capitalist Realism: Is There No Alternative?*, published in 2009 with Zer0 Books, the alternative publisher he had helped to co-found with his friend Tariq Goddard.[10] This book, which synthesised some of his strongest early posts on k-punk, firmly established Mark's reputation as one of the important contemporary theorists. The publication of *Capitalist Realism* crystallised new forms of collective connection for Mark at the very point the original blogging community had begun to fragment and become a much more fractious and difficult space in which to operate. Although Mark continued to blog as k-punk, it became less and less frequent as he pursued his work, thought and activism in the form of invited lectures, talks and Q&As, as well as the pieces he wrote as a freelance writer having to earn a living. Mark's frustration with the direction that blogs and forums had taken is clearly evident in a number of charged and polemical k-punk posts regarding the etiquette of comments and discussion, as well as his numerous interventions found on online forums.

After a precarious period of freelance writing Mark began to teach again, teaching courses in philosophy for City Lit and the University of East London, and later had a permanent position at Goldsmiths. He went on to produce two further volumes of published work, *Ghosts of My Life* for Zer0 in 2014 and *The Weird and the Eerie* for his newly formed Repeater Books at the end of 2016. Both volumes cull work from k-punk and from his commissioned reviews and interviews for the *Wire*, a magazine he had acted as Deputy Editor for in 2008. During this period he also published significant amounts of writing for online and print publications in the form of book chapters, music reviews, film reviews, opinion pieces, pieces of activism and theoretical essays, as well as continued posts for k-punk. It is the aim of this volume to bring together for the first time a significant portion of this writing.

The editorial task of putting together this collection was, at times, akin to a peculiar form of digital archaeology and memento mori. It involved excavating a decade of digital layers, often confronting digital lacunae where the reconstruction of lost dialogues from online fragments, interlocutors having gone missing, became necessary. Sometimes the task was one of recovering lost memories from pages haunted by dead links, a task that felt oddly appropriate given Mark's emphasis on hauntology. It was accompanied by a strange melancholy, contemporary since it had been birthed by the first layers of the online age, but also weirdly resonant with previous forms of melancholy and memory associated with found photographs, diary fragments, carvings, etchings, paintings. I will confess that I had some trepidation that much of the writing by k-punk from the last decade, once excavated, would have lost something with the inexorable passing of time. But I quickly discovered that this is in fact not the case. There is so much here that remains vital, fascinating, inspiring and insightful, and a great deal of this writing is gathered together for this collection.

There were inevitably difficulties regarding the decision about what to include and exclude. It was immediately evident that there is a vast reservoir of writing, almost overwhelming in terms of its scale and scope. Yet, what also became sadly evident is its sheer finite quality. As one reads through Mark's collected writings one is simply led to the incredibly sad realisation that this is all there is, and all there ever will be. As David Stubbs wrote for the *Quietus*, Mark's death "leaves a gaping crater in modern intellectual life".[11] The loss of Mark's voice from the present situation is incalculable, let alone his companionship, camaraderie, and friendship. I will now provide a few words about the working criteria for inclusion that governed the assembly of this volume.

The first priority was to avoid any unnecessary repetition of previously existing published material in his three published books — *Capitalist Realism, Ghosts of my Life* and *The Weird and the Eerie* — together with his essays in the two edited and co-edited volumes on Michael Jackson and post-punk.[12] As was noted above, he had culled material for all of these publications from k-punk and his writings in the *Wire*, and therefore much of that material is excluded from this collection. Where there are exceptions it was felt necessary to include original posts which had been either significantly truncated or modified by Mark for subsequent publication in these volumes, and these pieces have been clearly indicated in the endnotes.

There was a clear need to reflect the full range of his k-punk writing on many different subjects from 2004-2016, rather than concentrate on just his music or film writing. The aim was always to provide as comprehensive a picture as possible of the blog throughout its lifetime by selecting pieces that reflect both its *eclectic* content, its theoretical *pluralism* and most of all its remarkable *consistency*. His earlier pre-k-punk writing, including that undertaken as part of the Ccru, is not included here. For this collection the decision was made to concentrate solely on his writing after the inception of the k-punk blog, and for his earlier work to be the province of another volume. A very small number of early k-punk posts, e.g. on antinatalism, were excluded by virtue of the fact that they seemed wildly out of step with Mark's overall theoretical and political development, and because they seemed to reflect a temporary enthusiasm for a dogmatic theoretical misanthropy he repudiated in his later writing and life. There was also a need to represent the sheer breadth of Mark's other writings — his freelance reviews, commissions and activism, including his writing for the *Wire*, *Frieze*, *New Humanist*, the *Visual Artists' New Sheet*, *Electronic Beats*, the *Guardian*, etc. Sometimes these resonate with and reflect on pieces he published on k-punk, but more often he wrote on a range of subjects and themes not found on the blog.

The pieces chosen for the collection needed be of sufficient length and depth to work in a published volume — there are so many insightful one or two paragraph blog posts on k-punk that are excluded for that reason. Their effectiveness is largely down to the context of the blog architecture and community, whether they are interventions in ongoing online conversations and dialogues, or immediate response pieces to something happening in the media, online, or in the everyday. There are, however, a few exceptions to this where it just seemed criminal not to include them, usually because they were exemplary bursts of critical savagery or brilliant pieces of brutal polemic.

For the purposes of this single-volume collection, there was a need to abstract k-punk posts, to a certain extent, from the old blog community architecture, and yet, at the same time, try to retain a certain flavour of that community of blog writing. In abstracting posts it was important not to completely lose sight of the fact that they were originally written as blog pieces, and to try and retain a sense of their immediacy, informality, collaborative qualities and the sense of them as being part of an ongoing online continuum. This was a delicate balance to achieve, sometimes necessitated by the simple fact that many of his online blog interlocutors have long disappeared from online or abandoned their blogs, leaving them like ghost ships in cyberspace. Where this balance was simply not possible or unworkable, pieces have been excluded. The advantage of a collection of writings such as this lies in the fact that it allows readers to access a vast range of Mark's work on a whole host of different topics and themes, all in one place. It allows for an appreciation of the sheer scale, depth and originality of his work. However, I have been conscious of the peculiar disadvantages of doing this with Mark's writing, the vast majority of which appears on his k-punk blog, in that it extracts and abstracts his work from the very specific context of the blog — its immediacy, its dialogic nature, its hyperlinked architecture and its sense of a holistic continuum. I have tried very hard to retain some important aspects of that particular quality of his writing in transposing it to a collection such as this, and where possible I took guidance from the way Mark himself carried this out when he culled his k-punk writing for his published books. All titles of the pieces are either Mark's own or those of the editors of the publications for which he wrote. Each piece includes a reference indicating when and in which publication it first appeared. The spelling and punctuation have, with some exceptions, been regularised and rendered consistent across the collection.

Rather than simply arrange the writing in chronological order, the decision was made to separate the work chronologically into several different themed sections. This decision clearly has the advantage of thematic coherence for the reader, but the disadvantage is that it obviously creates an artificial division between the k-punk posts, articles, reviews and essays, and breaks up the hyperlinked quality of much of his writing. As one reads across these pieces one will discover the clear theoretical resonances between pieces written on say film, music or political activism in 2006 or 2007, where Mark is weaving the operative influence of a particular theorist's ideas or set of principles between a range of different topics and themes at the same time. There is a slight tendency for this quality to be lost in the thematic arrangement of this volume, but efforts to mitigate this have been made in the footnotes where possible. However, despite arranging the writing thematically, the sheer consistency of his work across the different topics remains absolutely evident. These include Mark's ongoing fidelity to theory in order to provide different and challenging perspectives, alternative narratives, and for producing important truths. One also finds across all of the work a consistent concentration on the themes of class and collectivism, precarity and insecurity, depression and mental illness, dogmatism and purpose, attempts to trace post-capitalist forms of desire, the need to expose egregious forms of reality management, efforts to express forms of collective memory, and a nostalgia for popular modernism, hauntology and lost futures. I feel confident that the thematic arrangement of his work in this volume does nothing to diminish the sheer lucidity of his work in this regard.

It is also the case that one of the most significant qualities of online writing, namely the ability to embed shortcut hyperlinks to references and sources, is somewhat difficult if not downright impossible to reproduce in traditional published form in a book. However, where possible, every effort has been made to track down and reproduce in the footnotes all of the surviving hyperlinks contained in k-punk's posts and other online writing.

Finally, it was important to include any unpublished work. What is included here represents all that is considered unpublished, and takes the form of the final and sadly unfinished k-punk post "Mannequin Challenge", which addresses the US presidential election of 2016; a piece titled "Anti-Therapy", taken from a talk Mark gave in 2015, which was then translated into German and published as part of a collection by Matthes & Seitz and appears here in English for the first time; and the unfinished introduction to Mark's proposed book titled *Acid Communism*. The introduction to this final proposed work is extremely suggestive and significant. It is clearly the case that a great deal of Mark's work was written in response to Fredric Jameson, in particular Jameson's work on postmodernism (in *Postmodernism or, The Cultural Logic of Late Capitalism* and *A Singular Modernity*). Mark repeatedly notes Jameson's extraordinary prescience, back in 1991, in identifying and analysing the postmodern condition:

> Jameson [writes of] a depthless experience, in which the past is everywhere at the same time as the historical sense fades; we have a "society bereft of all historicity" that is simultaneously unable to present anything that is not a reheated version of the past.[13]

And:

> Could the only opposition to a culture dominated by what Jameson calls the "nostalgia mode" be a kind of nostalgia for modernism?[14]

What becomes evident in his late work on acid communism is how he became more and more drawn to a problematic identified by Jameson between Marcuse's cultural exceptionalism or the "semiautonomy" of the cultural realm — "its ghostly, yet Utopian, existence, for good or ill, above the practical world of the existent" — and the question of whether this semiautonomy of the cultural sphere "has been destroyed by the logic of late capitalism".[15] As Mark knew only too well, for Jameson this dissolution of an autonomous sphere of culture does not imply its disappearance. Rather, its dissolution is to be

> imagined in terms of an explosion: a prodigious expansion of culture throughout the social realm, to the point at which everything in our social life — from economic value and state power to practices and to the very structure of the psyche itself — can be said to have become

"cultural" in some original and yet untheorised sense... Distance in general (including "critical distance" in particular) has very precisely been abolished in the new sphere of postmodernism. We are submerged in its henceforth filled and suffused volumes to the point where our new postmodern bodies are bereft of spatial coordinates and practically (let alone theoretically) incapable of distantiation... It is precisely this whole extraordinary demoralising and depressing original new global space which is the "moment of truth" of postmodernism.[16]

And Mark, in his unfinished introduction to *Acid Communism*, insists upon revisiting the issue of the utopian vision that is the legacy of the Sixties, taught by Marcuse and raised here by Jameson:

The ultimate political coordinates of the problem of the evaluation of postmodernism is one of the Utopian impulses to be detected in various forms of the postmodern today. One wants to insist very strongly on the necessity of the reinvention of the Utopian vision in any contemporary politics: this lesson, which Marcuse first taught us, is part of the legacy of the Sixties which must never be abandoned in any reevaluation of that period and of our relationship to it.[17]

Here, towards the end of his life, in the unfinished introduction to *Acid Communism*, we find Mark reaching for "a new humanity, a new seeing, a new thinking, a new loving: this is the promise of acid communism".

Covering over a decade of writing, reading this collection is like taking a trip through recent cultural and political history with Mark as your guide. Hopefully these writings, together with his other published books, will serve as further reminder of Mark's own utopian vision, how vital, necessary and exciting k-punk was, his fidelity to the possibility of alternatives, and simply of how much we all have lost.

Darren Ambrose
Whitley Bay, February 2018

why k?[1]

1. Why I started the blog? Because it seemed like a space — the only space — in which to maintain a kind of discourse that had started in the music press and the art schools, but which had all but died out, with what I think are appalling cultural and political consequences. My interest in theory was almost entirely inspired by writers like Ian Penman and Simon Reynolds, so there has always been an intense connection between theory and pop/film for me. No sob stories, but for someone from my background it's difficult to see where else that interest would have come from.

2. Because of that, my relation to the academy has always been uh difficult. The way in which I understood theory — primarily through popular culture — is generally detested in universities. Most dealings with the academy have been literally — clinically — depressing.

3. The Ccru as an entity was developed in hostile conditions as a kind of conduit for continuing trade between popular culture and theory. The whole pulp theory/theory-fiction thing was/is a way of doing theory through, not "on", pop cultural forms. Nick Land was the key figure here, in that it was he who was able to hold, for a while, a position "within" a university philosophy department whilst dedicatedly opening up connections to the outside. Kodwo Eshun is key as someone making connections the other way — from popular culture INTO abstruse theory. But what we all concurred upon was that something like jungle was already intensely theoretical; it didn't require academics to judge it or pontificate upon it — the role of a theorist was as an intensifier.

31

4. The term k-punk came out of Ccru. "K" was used as a libidinally preferable substitution for the California/*Wired* captured "cyber" (the word cybernetics having its origins in the Greek, *Kuber*). Ccru understood cyberpunk not as a (once trendy) literary genre, but as a distributive cultural tendency facilitated by new technologies. In the same way, "punk" doesn't designate a particular musical genre, but a confluence outside legitimate(d) space: fanzines were more significant than the music in that they allowed and produced a whole other mode of contagious activity which destroyed the need for centralised control.

5. The development of cheap and readily available sound production software, the web, blogs means there is an unprecedented punk infrastructure available. All that is lacking is the will, the belief that what can happen in something that does not have authorisation/legitimation can be as important — more important — than what comes through official channels.

6. In terms of will, there has been an enormous retrenchment since 1970s punk. The availability of the means of production has seemed to go alongside a compensatory reassertion of spectacular power.

7. To return to the academy: universities have either totally excluded or at least marginalised not only anyone connected with Ccru but also many who were at Warwick. Steve "Hyperdub" Goodman and Luciana Parisi are both Ccru agents who have managed, against the odds, to secure a position within universities. But most of us have been forced into positions outside the university. Perhaps as a result of not being incorporated ("bought off"), many in the Warwick rhizome have maintained an intense connection and robust independence. Much of the current theoretical drift on k-punk has been developed via a collaboration with Nina Power, Alberto Toscano and Ray Brassier (co-organiser of the NoiseTheoryNoise conference at Middlesex University last year). The growing popularity of philosophers like Žižek and Badiou means there is now an unexpected if rogue and fugitive line of support within the academy.

8. I teach Philosophy, Religious Studies and Critical Thinking at Orpington College. It is a Further Education college, which means that its primary intake is sixteen to nineteen year-olds. This is difficult and challenging work, but the students are in the main excellent, and far more willing to enter into discussion than undergraduates. So I don't at all regard this position as secondary or lesser than a "proper" academic post.

PART ONE

METHODS OF DREAMING: BOOKS

book meme[1]

At least two people have asked me to do this, so here — at last — goes.

1) How many books do you own?

No way of knowing. Certainly can't count them and have no reliable way of calculating.

2) What was the last book you bought?

The Sex Appeal of the Inorganic, Mario Perniola.

3) What was the last book you read?

Read and finished: Michael Bracewell's *England is Mine* — disappointing and frustrating. There are flashes of insight but the organisation of the book seems to change from chapter to chapter; at one moment the narrative is historical, the next it is thematic, and then regional. There is a sense of always just approaching the time when things are happening or just having missed it. Can't help thinking that Bracewell will benefit from a more focused subject matter, which is why still I'm looking forward to his Roxy book, due out later this year. (And there's *way* too much attention paid to Eng Lit: *nothing* will ever interest me in W.H. Boredom, for instance.)

Finishing: Houllebecq's *Atmomised*. No wonder Žižek likes this one. Is there a better savaging of desolate hippie hedonism and its pathetic legacy in New Age zen bullshit?

4) Five books that mean a lot to me.

(I hate all those surveys of best films/books/LPs which have the Latest Thing at the top, so I have only allowed myself to select books that have meant something to me for *at least* a decade.)

Kafka: *The Trial, The Castle*

Is it possible to reproduce, later in life, the impact that books, records and films have between the ages of fourteen and seventeen? The periods of my adult life that have been most miserable have been those in which I lost fidelity to what I discovered then, in the pages of Joyce, Dostoyevsky, Burroughs, Beckett, Selby... Any of those could have been selected, but I choose Kafka, because of all of them, it is he who has been the most intimate and constant companion.

I actually encountered Kafka first in a Penguin compendium of *The Novels of Franz Kafka* that my parents, who knew very little about literature, bought me for Christmas because they thought "it looked like my kind of thing". So it proved.

It's difficult for me now to remember how I first received the text. Whether I initially enjoyed it or was frustrated by it I couldn't say. Kafka, after all, is a writer who doesn't waylay you. He invades subtly, slowly. I imagine that at the time I wanted and expected a more straightforward statement of existentialist alienation. Yet there was very little of that in Kafka. This was not a world of metaphysical grandstanding but a seedy, cramped burrow, whose ruling affect is not heroic alienation but creeping embarrassment. Physical force plays almost no role in Kafka's fictions — it is the ever-present possibility of social shaming that is the motive force of his winding non-plots.

Remember the pitiful scenes in *The Trial* when K, looking for the court in an office block, knocks in turn on each door, making the pathetic excuse that he is a "house painter"? Kafka's genius consists in banalising the absurdity of this: surprisingly, against all our expectations, it is indeed the case that K's hearing *is* taking place in one of the apartments in the building. Of course it is. And why is he late? The more absurd K thinks things are, the more embarrassed he becomes for failing to understand "the ways" of the Court or of the Castle. The bureaucratic convolutions appear ridiculous and frustrating to him, but that is because he "has not understood" yet. Witness the comedy of the opening scenes of *The Castle*, which are less an anticipation of totalitarianism than of call centres, in which K is told that the telephones "function like musical instruments". What kind of an idiot is he, if when he phones someone's desk, he expects *them* to answer? Is he so wet behind the ears?

It's not for nothing that Alan Bennett, the laureate of embarrassment, is an ardent admirer of Kafka. Both Bennett and Kafka understand that, no matter how absurd their rituals, pronunciations, clothes might appear to be, the ruling class are unembarrassable; that is not because there is a special code which only they understand — there is no code, precisely — but that *whatever they do is alright, because it is THEM doing it.* Conversely, if you are not of the "in-crowd", nothing you can do could EVER be right; you are a priori guilty.

Atwood: *Cat's Eye*

A while back, Luke asked me what an example of "cold rationalist" literature would look like. Atwood, with her reputation for coldness, is an obvious answer, but in truth, more or less all literature is cold rationalist. Why? Because it allows us to see ourselves as chains of cause and effect and thereby, paradoxically, to attain the only measure of freedom available to us. (Even Wordsworth, who admired Spinoza, described poetry as "emotion recollected in tranquility", i.e. not raw emotion expressed in some Dionysian ejaculation.)

Cat's Eye isn't my favourite Atwood novel — that would be the stark *Surfacing* — but it is the one that means most to me. I don't even remember all of the plot; what I will never forget are Atwood's horribly vivid descriptions of the pitiless Hobbesian cruelty of teenage "friendships". *They walk behind you so as they can criticise your shoes, the way you walk... They are worse than your worst enemies.* The long days, the breakfast toast *turning to cardboard* in your mouth, the anxiety so sharp and constant that you forget it is there, no longer even register it.

Are your most formative years those of your early childhood or your early teens? Reading *Cat's Eye* in my early twenties was a kind of auto-psychoanalysis, a way out of the legacy of misanthropy, suppressed rage and cosmic sense of inadequacy that had been the legacy of my teenage years. Atwood's icy analysis beautifully demonstrated that the humiliations of those teenage years were a structural effect of teenage relationships, not at all anything specific to me.

Spinoza: *The Ethics*

Spinoza changes everything, but gradually. There is no "road to Damascus" conversion to Spinozism, only a steady but implacable deletion of default assumptions. As with all the best philosophy, reading it is like running a *Videodrome* cassette: you think you are playing it, but it ends up playing you, effecting a gradual mutation of the way you think and perceive.

I'd been attracted to Spinoza as an undergraduate, but I only really read him at Warwick, under the influence of Deleuze. We spent over a year pouring over *The Ethics* in a reading group. Here was a philosophy that was at once forbiddingly abstract and immediately practical, pitched at both the largest conceivable cosmic scale and the minutiae of the psyche. The "impossible" bringing together of structural analysis and existentialism?

Ballard: *The Atrocity Exhibition*

If Spinoza and Kafka were slow-acting, Ballard's impact was instant. He connected immediately with an unconscious saturated in media signal.

That was partly because I had in effect encountered Ballard long before I had actually read any of his work: in Joy Division (though more in Hannett's *sound* than in many of the lyrics; the song "The Atrocity Exhibition", with its anguished pleading, couldn't be further from Ballard's dispassionate sobriety), in Foxx and Ultravox, in Cabaret Voltaire, in Magazine.

The Drowned World is the best of his disaster novels, inundated London as a literalised surrealist landscape coolly surveyed by a latter-day Conrad, but it is *The Atrocity Exhibition* that is indispensable. Much more than the better-known *Crash*, *The Atrocity Exhibition* provided a conceptual and methodological repertoire for approaching the twentieth century assembled from the century's own resources. It is austerely modernist, making little concession to either plot or character, more like a fictive sculpture than a story, an obsessively repeated series of patterns.

Yes, Ballard has been accepted into the review columns, become an elder statesman, but let's not forget how different his background was from the standard Oxbridge man of letters. Ballard rescued Britain from Eng Lit, from "decent" humanist certainties and Sunday supplement sleepiness.

Greil Marcus: *Lipstick Traces*

I've written before about the importance of this book to me. I read it when I had just finished university, no plans, the future collapsing into a grim attempt — bound to fail — to commensurate myself to the Thatcherite economic reality principle. Marcus' vast web of connections opened up an escape route. It was a description of a transhistorical Event, a break-out embracing anabaptists, situationists, dadaists, surrealists, punks. Such an Event was the exact opposite of the Grand Spectacles of the Eighties, the scripted and organised *Non* events which played out on global television with Live Aid at their epicentre. It was fugitive, secret, even when — necessarily — massively collective. *Lipstick Traces* was sure that pop can only have any significance when it ceases to be "just music", when it reverberates with a politics that has nothing to do with capitalist parliamentarianism and a philosophy that has nothing to do with the academy.

Lipstick Traces is itself best read as part of a textual rhizome which attempted to register, a decade or more on, the impact of punk. See also *Vague* magazine (if you are looking for one of the most powerful triggers for Ccru-style cyberpunk theory, check out Mark Downham's pieces in *Vague*), Savage's *England's Dreaming*. (This set not really complete until *Rip It Up* of course.)

5) Tag five people.

I can't think of one other blog that hasn't done this, so I'm stuck.

space, time, light, all the essentials — reflections on j.g. ballard season (bbc four)[1]

Like his admirer Jean Baudrillard,[2] Ballard has for a long time resembled a rogue AI, re-permutating the same few themes *ad infinitum*, occasionally adding a sprinkling of contemporary detail to freshen up a limited repertoire of fixations. Fixations, fixations. Appropriate, since, after all, Ballard's obsession is... obsession.

In the BBC Four profile — nothing new here, the old man gamely and tirelessly going over his favourite riffs, once again — Ballard repeated one of his familiar, but still powerfully sobering observations. People often comment on how extreme his early life was, Ballard said. Yet, far from being extreme, that early life — beset by hunger, fear, war and the constant threat of death — is the default condition for most human beings on the planet, now and in every previous century. It is the comfortable life of the Western Suburbanite which is in every way the planetary exception.

Thus *Home*, BBC Four's brilliant adaptation of Ballard's short story "The Enormous Space".[3] *Home* is the kind of thing the BBC used to excel at: drama that was genuinely, unsettlingly weird without being insufferably, unwatchably experimental. Not that *Home* has much hope of appealing to popular taste stuck away on BBC Four, of course. A sign of the times.

Home revealed itself to be a perverse cousin of the suburban drop-out situation comedy, *The Good Life* or *The Fall and Rise of Reginald Perrin* spliced with Polanski's *Repulsion*. (No surprise to see director Richard Curson-Smith name-checking Polanksi as an influence.) Anthony Sher was superbly, charmingly unhinged as Gerald Ballantyne, an accident victim who, instead of returning to work after his convalescence, decides to embark upon an experiment. "Decides" is no doubt too active a word; in every respect the typical Ballard character, Gerry *discovers* rather than initiates, finds himself drawn into a *logic* he is compelled to investigate. (In many ways a faithful

Freudian, Ballard has no doubt that obsession always has/is a logic.)

The experiment, it turns out, has a simple premise. Gerry will stay indoors, indefinitely, living off the supplies of his well-stocked larder and freezer until... until what? Well, that is what the experiment will establish. Can he survive by "using his front door as a weapon"? What unfolds is the descent into the maelstrom Ballard has explored since *High-Rise* and *Concrete Island*, a quest to the outer edges of the human that follows a well-defined sequence, whose stages can be readily enumerated:

A letting go of the old identity. This is given up easily. Ballard's twist on the disaster novel as far back as *The Drowned World* lay in the readiness of his characters to embrace rather than resist the new conditions which catastrophe had visited upon them. Ever since *High-Rise*, Ballard has seen characters going one-step further, actually initiating disaster as a revolt, not so much against conformity, as against air-conditioned comfort. Here, Gerry burns all his correspondence, his photographs, then his birth-certificate and — in the most sacrilegious act of all, which made mortified my Protestant soul — his money.

The loosening of the hold of civilisation [Bataille phase]. Ballard is endlessly rewriting *Civilisation and its Discontents*[4], and his fictions are attempts to imagine a libidinal utopia in which the pay-off between survival and repression spelled out by Freud's mordant pessimism is somehow circumvented. The return to savagery, even the experiencing of raw hunger pangs, are eagerly savoured opportunities to relax civilisation's impulse control and neutralising of affect. In *Home*, when Gerry's conventional food supplies are running low, he turns first to the flowers in his garden and then to his neighbours' pets. The scene in which Gerry's neighbour questions him — in that middle-class ever-so-slightly-insinuating way — about the disappearance of his dog "Mr Fred" and his wife's cat is a masterpiece of grisly comedy. "Perhaps they've eloped," Sher gibbers, by then constantly on the edge of all-but illegible hysteria. Laughter, a strange, snorting, sniffling chortle that he can barely contain: it is that laughter which signals, more than anything else, that Gerald has left polite society, never to return.

The exploration of the transcendental beyond [Kant/Blake phase]. I mean transcendental in its strict Kantian sense, of course. Ballard likes to refer to this as his exploration of inner space, but I have always found this to be a profoundly misleading description. Much more than astronauts floating in *empirical* space, it is the "Outer" which Ballard's suburban cosmonauts investigate: what they confront is time and space *themselves*, as preconditions of all perceptions and experiences, and what their explorations open up is an intensive zone beyond — outside — standard perceptual thresholds. Hence *Home* becomes an aberrant version of *The Incredible Shrinking Man*. Cut off from the world beyond his door — I refuse to call it the outside world — Gerry's sense of space massively expands. "The rooms are getting bigger." The attic becomes an antarctic "white world" of blank, freezer-burning vastness, the irruption of the transcendental outside into the empirical interior of the house, now a very cosmos, teeming with texture and previously unsuspected detail. "I feel like an explorer, or an astronaut."

Curson-Smith's use of the video-diary format gave the film a queasy intimacy and a suitably *unheimlich* relation to Pop TV now, something underscored by Gerry's sign-off remarks about undertaking the "ultimate home makeover." Yes, that's one way to make the most of your space.

The man whose head expanded. "Are you on drugs, Gerald?"

And self-denial, starving, the withdrawal from company, it's all very topical. I wonder — I hope — something Gerald-like is going on in David Blaine's head right now.[5]

why i want to fuck ronald reagan[1]

At the 1980 Republican Convention in San Francisco, pranksters reproduced and distributed the section of *The Atrocity Exhibition* called "Why I Want to Fuck Ronald Reagan",[2] without the title and adorned with the Republican Party seal. "I'm told," Ballard reports, "that it was accepted for what it resembled, a psychological position paper on the candidate's subliminal appeal, commissioned from some maverick think tank."[3]

What does this neo-Dadaist act of would-be subversion tell us? In one sense, it has to be hailed as the perfect act of subversion. But, viewed another way, it shows that subversion is impossible now. The fate of a whole tradition of ludic intervention — passing from the Dadaists into the Surrealists and the Situationists — seems to hang in the balance. Where once the Dadaists and their inheritors could dream of invading the stage, disrupting what Burroughs — still very obviously a part of this heritage — calls the "reality studio" with logic bombs, now there is no stage — no scene, Baudrillard would say — to invade. For two reasons: first, because the frontier zones of hypercapital do not try to repress so much as absorb the irrational and the illogical, and, second, because the distinction between stage and offstage has been superseded by a coolly inclusive loop of fiction: Reagan's career outstrips any attempt to ludically lampoon it, and demonstrates the increasing pliability of the boundaries between the real and its simulations. For Baudrillard, the very attacks on "reality" mounted by groups such as the Surrealists function to keep the real alive (by providing it with a fabulous dream world, ostensibly entirely alternative to but in effect dialectically complicit with the everyday world of the real). "Surrealism was still in solidarity with the real it contested, but which it doubled and ruptured in the imaginary."[4] In conditions of third (and fourth-order) simulacra, the giddy vertigo of hyperreality banalises a coolly hallucinogenic ambience, absorbing all reality into simulation. Fiction is everywhere — and therefore, in a certain sense, eliminated as a specific category. Where once Reagan's own role as actor-president seemed "novel", his subsequent career, in which moments from film history become montaged — in Reagan's own hazy memory and in media accounts — with Reagan's role in particular movies, the ludic becomes the ludicrous.

The apparent acceptance, by the Republican delegates, of the genuineness of the "Why I Want to Fuck Ronald Reagan" text, is both shocking and oddly predictable, and both responses are in fact a testament to the power of Ballard's fictions, which resides no more in their ability to mimetically reflect a pre-existing social reality than it does in their capacity to imaginatively overturn it. What Ballard achieves, rather, is what Iain Hamilton-Grant calls "realism about the hyperreal", a homeopathic participation in the media-cybernetisation of reality in late capitalism. The shock comes when we remind ourselves of (what would seem to be) the radical aberrance of Ballard's material. "Why I Want to Fuck Ronald Reagan", like many of the sections of *The Atrocity Exhibition*, particularly in the latter part of the novel, is presented as a report on experiments into audience responses to prepared media stimuli.

> Ronald Reagan and the conceptual auto-disaster. Numerous studies have been conducted upon patients in terminal paresis (G.P.I.), placing Reagan in a series of simulated auto-crashes, e.g. multiple pile-ups, head on collisions, motorcade attacks (fantasies of Presidential assassinations remained a continuing preoccupation, subjects showing a marked polymorphic fixation on windshields an rear-trunk assemblies). Powerful erotic fantasies of an anal-sadistic character surrounded the image of the Presidential contender.[5]

But this shock is counterposed by a sense of predictability arising from the cool elegance of Ballard's simulations. The technical tone of Ballard's writing — its impersonality and lack of emotional inflection — performs the function of neutralising or normalising the ostensibly unacceptable material. Is this simulation of the operations of hypercontrol agencies a satire on them, or do their activities — and the whole cultural scene of which they are a part — render satire as such impossible now? What, after all, is the relationship between satire and simulation? To begin to answer that question we need to compare Ballard's text with other, more definitively "satirical" texts. Before that, though, we need to bear in mind Jameson's comments on the eclipse of parody by pastiche, which we shall examine, briefly, now.

This is not the place to interrogate the differences between parody and satire; we shall proceed on the assumption that, whatever differences there are between parody and satire, they share enough in common so as to be jointly subject to Jameson's analyses. Parody, Jameson argues, depended upon a whole set of resources available to modernism but which have faded now: the individual subject, whose "inimitable" idiosyncratic style, Jameson wryly observes, could precisely gave rise to imitations; a strong historical sense, which has its necessary obverse a confidence that there is a genuinely contemporary means of expression; and a commitment to collective projects, which could motivate writing and give it a political purpose. As these disappear, Jameson suggests, so does the space of parody. Individual style gives way to a "field of stylistic and discursive heterogeneity without a norm", just as the belief in progress and the faith that one could describe new times in new terms wanes, to be replaced by "the imitation of dead styles, speech through all the masks and voices stored up in the imaginary museums of a new global culture". Late capitalism's "post-literacy", meanwhile, points to "the absence of any great collective project." What results, according to Jameson, is a depthless experience, in which the past is everywhere at the same time as the historical sense fades; we have a "society bereft of all historicity" that is simultaneously unable to present anything that is not a reheated version of the past. Pastiche displaces parody:

> In this situation, parody finds itself without a vocation; it has lived, and that strange new thing pastiche comes to take its place. Pastiche is, like parody, the imitation of a peculiar or unique, idiosyncratic style, the wearing of a linguistic mask, speech in a dead language. But it is a neutral practice of such mimicry, without any of parody's ulterior motives, amputated of the satiric impulse, devoid of laughter and of any conviction that alongside the abnormal tongue you have momentarily borrowed, some healthy linguistic normality still exists. Pastiche is thus blank parody, a statue with blind eyeballs...[6]

Despite what Jameson himself writes on Ballard,[7] one of the important differences between the Ballard text and pastiche as Jameson describes it is the absence of "nostalgia" or the "nostalgia mode" — an insistent presence in other postmodernist science fiction texts, as Jameson shows — in Ballard's work. Indeed, Ballard's commitment to striking textual innovations — as evidenced in the layout of the pages themselves in *The Atrocity Exhibition* — mark him as something of an anomaly in Jameson's terms; in this sense, at least, Ballard seems to be continuous with modernism as Jameson understands it. Yet in certain other respects — specifically in terms of the collapse of individual subjectivity and the failure of collective political action — Ballard is emblematic of Jameson's postmodernity. But, unlike Jameson's pastiche, Ballard does not imitate "a peculiar or unique idiosyncratic style". The style that Ballard simulates in "Why I Want to Fuck Ronald Reagan" — a style towards which the whole of *The Atrocity Exhibition* tends — is precisely lacking in any personality: if there are any idiosyncrasies, they belong to the technical register of (pseudo)scientific reportage, not to the characteristics of an individual subject. The fact that the text concerns a political leader draws attention to the lack of any explicit — or, more importantly when discussing satire or parody, implicit — political teleology in Ballard's writing. It is in this sense that "Why I Want to Fuck Ronald Reagan", like Jameson's pastiche, is "without any of parody's ulterior motives".

Certainly, this is one way in which "Why I Want to Fuck Ronald Reagan" differs greatly from a classical work of satire such as Swift's *A Modest Proposal* (1729). *A Modest Proposal* is a paradigmatic work of what Joyce called "kinetic" art, produced in particular political and cultural circumstances with a particular aim, to sway an audience into action. Swift's political purpose — his disparaging of the cruelty of certain English responses to the Irish potato famine — is marked by a certain stylistic and thematic excess (an excess that famously bypassed altogether certain of Swift's readers, who were able to take the text at face value), whereas Ballard's text — which emerged, no less than Swift's, from a very particular sociocultural situation — can be defined by its flatness. This marks a move on, (even), from Burroughs. For all their linguistic inventiveness, Burroughs' humorous "routines" such as "The Complete All-American Deanxietised Man"[8] remain in a classical tradition of satire through their use of exaggeration and their clear political agenda: using a series of excessive tropes, Burroughs mocks the amoral mores of American techno-science. By contrast, what Ballard's text "lacks" is any clear designs on the reader, any of Jameson's "ulterior motives"; the parodic text always gave central importance to the parodist behind it, his implicit but flagged attitudes and opinions, but "Why I Want to Fuck Ronald Reagan" is as coldly anonymous as the texts it imitates. Whereas we hear Burroughs' cackling at the absurd excesses of the scientists in "The Complete All-American Deanxietized Man", the response of Ballard to the scientists whose work he simulates is unreadable. What does "Ballard" want the reader to feel: disgust? amusement? It is unclear, and, as Baudrillard argues in relation to *Crash*,[9] it is somewhat disingenuous of Ballard the author to overcode his texts — in prefatory authorial remarks — with all the traditional baggage of "warning" that they themselves clearly elude. The mode Ballard adopts in "Why I Want to Fuck Ronald Reagan" is not that of (satirical) exaggeration, but is a kind of (simulated) extrapolation. The very genre of the poll or the survey, as Baudrillard shows, makes the question unanswerable, undecidable.

Despite what Ballard himself suggests, (see above), what matters is less the (possible) resemblance of "Why I Want to Fuck Ronald Reagan" to (possible) reports than the circulation of simulation to which such reports already contribute. Writing on pastiche, Jameson comes upon the concept of simulation, but attributes it to Plato rather than referring — here at least — to Baudrillard's reinvention of it. Yet Jameson's intuition about the relationship between pastiche and simulation is important. We could perhaps suggest a correlation between Baudrillard's third-order simulacra and Jameson's pastiche, on the one hand, and Ballard's text on the other. What simulation in Baudrillard's third-order sense entails is, as we have repeatedly insisted, the collapse of distance between the simulation and what is simulated. Satire, in its classical sense, we would probably want to locate as part of "first-order simulacra" — a simulation that resembles the original, but with certain tell-tale differences. Ballard simulates the simulation (the poll, the survey).

a fairground's painted swings[1]

Speaking of the pathology of amour, is it anywhere better exemplified than in the lyrics of "These Foolish Things" (the title track, significantly, of Ferry's first LP of covers).

What is fascinating about the song's litany of lost affects ("wild strawb'ries only seven francs a kilo... the sigh of midnight trains in empty stations... a fairground's painted swings") is that the lover features in them only as a series of absences ("a cigarette that bears a lipstick's traces... gardenia perfume ling'ring on a pillow") and is never directly invoked. This, of course, is because there is no "loved object itself". What is loved is the *petit objet a*, which is not a particular object, but the object as such, the "void presupposed by a demand". The physical and psychical "presence" of the lover is required only as that which allows the assemblage of affects to be given an apparent cohering centre. But, in the end, the lover is just that: the space, the canvas, on which the collage of memories and associations can be arranged.

Nevertheless, even though it is not the lover "herself" that is desired, the lover cannot be dispensed with altogether: otherwise we are in straightforward fetishism. Žižek illustrates the difference between "normal" pathology and fetishism by reference to that scene in *Vertigo* where Scotty is embracing Judy (re)made-over as Madeleine. The camera cuts away to show his pausing from kissing her to anxiously check that her hair colour is still blond. But this is NOT fetishism, since the fetishist would dispense with the woman altogether and derive his enjoyment from the lock of hair itself.

Vertigo's horror lies in its unstinting revelation of the artificiality of desire. Scottie can look into the void presupposed by his demands and still, grotesquely, make the demands. That is the difference between *Vertigo* and many of the film noirs it references, comments upon and surpasses: it

53

is not, in the end, that he is being deceived by a femme fatale, duped into believing that she is something that she is not. On the contrary, he knows full well that there is no Madeleine. But knowledge is nothing, and the explanation for his continued fixation upon a Madeleine that is not even a ghost is the one provided by Zupančič: for Scottie to give up his object would be for him to give up himself, to die.

There is no doubt a specifically male relationship to the *objet petit a* which *Vertigo* reveals. This goes some way to answering the question posed by I.T.[2] a while ago, after Žižek: namely, why would men, given the choice of sex with a monkey or sex with a robot always choose the robot? The more disturbing thought is that men would always in practice prefer a robot to an actual woman — and this is why the libidinal economics, if not yet the technical feasibility, of *The Stepford Wives* are horribly credible.

The text which most explicitly lays bare this male desiring mechanism is Villiers de l'Isle-Adam's *The Future Eve* (1877), which anticipates both *Vertigo* and *The Stepford Wives*, as well as *Metropolis* and *Blade Runner*.

The story concerns a dissolute decadent who is enchanted with his beloved, Alicia's, form, but who detests what he considers to be the frivolity and shallowness of her personality. He is persuaded by an inventor-mentor figure (given the name, in some versions, incredibly, of the then still-living Thomas Edison) that he should simply accept an automaton-copy of his lover, prepared by the inventor, which will be a perfect replica in every respect, except that it will be programmed to be a stimulating companion.

"Edison" couldn't be more forthright, more demystificatory, more Lacanian:

> the creature whom you love, and who for you is the *sole* REALITY is by no means the one who is embodied in this transient human figure, but a creature of your desire. [...] This illusion is the one thing you struggle against all odds to VITALISE in the presence of your beloved, depsite the frightful, deadly, withering nullity of Alicia. What you love is this *phantom* alone; it's for the phantom that you want to die. That and that alone is what you recognise as unconditionally REAL. In short, it is this objectified projection of your own mind that you call on, that you perceive, that you CREATE in your living woman, *and which is nothing but your mind reduplicated in her.*[3]

Of course, the "creative" force that really animates the loved object is not the freeplay of the Romantic imagination, but the implacable mechanism of the unconscious. *It's for the phantom that you want to die*: but such a "death" would mean that the desiring frame that makes sense of the world would survive. The only real death would be one in which that whole framework was destroyed, and the subject was confronted with the "white space" of pure potential.

This is what the subject slaved to the pleasure principle must avoid at all costs. The well-known tedium of Sadean desire is the inevitable consequence when this impasse is honestly confronted. If the object of Sadean desire is, as Žižek, says, the eternally beautiful undead victim, who can suffer all manner of privations and yet be magically renewed forever, then the *subject* of this desire is, as Burroughs knew very well, the vampire-junky. The vampire-junky must be insatiable and must pursue their desires *up to the point of self-destruction*, but must never cross the line into annihilation.

The empirical narrative would have it that the junkie is gradually "drawn into" addiction, lured into dependence by a chemical need. But it is clear that the junkie *chooses* to be addicted — the desire to get high is only the ostensible motivation for the drive, just as "winning money" is only the official alibi for the gambler's enjoyment.

Burroughs' paralleling of love with addiction is thus by no means cynical hyperbole. Burroughs understood very well that, if love is addiction ("If there's a cure for this, I don't want it"), then addiction is also a form of love ("It's my wife and it's my life"). There is always, as Gregory Bateson observed in his essay on alcoholism, a *meta* addiction to be dealt with: the addiction to addiction itself.[4] It is on this that Burroughs' "control addict" Bradley Martin is hooked: "I am not AN addict. I am THE addict."

The lyrical power of Burroughs' writing — especially in the early cut-up novels, which are consensually dismissed as difficult and boring — is often overlooked. But much of its mechanical melancholia is generated from its displaying of the "foolish things" of desire, the heroin-hacceities of train whistles, radio jingles, billboard images and sexual contact. Although initially random, these affect-collages, when repeated and remixed by memory and desire, become necessary. Thus only THAT shade of blue for Madeleine's suit, only THAT shade of lipstick on the cigarette tip, will do.

Yes, the painted swings of desire's cruel fairground…

what are the politics of boredom? (ballard 2003 remix)[1]

"Prosperous suburbia was one of the end states of history. Once
achieved, only plague, flood, or nuclear war could threaten its grip."
— J.G. Ballard, *Millennium People*[2]

"J.G. Ballard" is the name of a repetition.

That's very different from saying that Ballard repeats himself. On the
contrary, it is Ballard's formalism, his re-permutation of the same few
concepts and fixations — disasters, pilots, random violence, mediatisation,
the total colonisation of the unconscious by images — that prevent his name
being easily attributed to any self.

The obsessive quality of his preoccupations and his methodology is a sign
that Ballard has never lost faith with his earliest inspirations: psychoanalysis
and surrealism. In both, he found a rigorously depersonalised account of
the formations of the person. The so-called interior had a logic that could
be both exposed and externalised.

Ballard's career can be seen as a repeated rewriting of two texts of
Freud, *Civilisation and its Discontents* and *Beyond the Pleasure Principle*. The
environmental catastrophes in his earliest phase of novels (*The Drowned
World*, *The Drought*, *The Crystal World*) tend to be greeted by the characters
as opportunities, chances to shuck off the dull routines and protocols of
sedentary society. The second phase of his work, which began in the mid-
Sixties and to some extent continues to this day, follows this logic through
so that the catastrophes and atrocities that afflict the characters in these
fictions are actively willed by them. (Or is it that the humans seek to manage,
through repetition, the originary trauma of their being?) Disasters are now
the disasters of the media landscape — the space in which humans now
primarily live, and one which is both shaped by, and manufactured from,
their desires and drives. Once again, though, we must qualify this claim with

the further observation that human beings are not the "owners" of desires and drives — they don't "have" them. Rather, human beings are the playing out of these impulses, instruments through which trauma is registered.

Since *High-Rise* in 1975, Ballard has directed most of his attention to the hyper-affluent and bored denizens of closed communities. If Ballard's treatment of the mores of this population had begun to pall, it was refreshed by *Millennium People*, his latest and best rendition of this theme.

The world of *Millennium People* is ruled, "for the first time in history" (but not for the first time in Ballard's work), by a "vicious boredom", "interrupted by meaningless acts of violence". At first glance, the novel can look like a long overdue savaging of the middle class, in which the reader can revel in the brutal destruction of bourgeois sacred cows. Tate Modern... Pret A Manger... the NFT... all of them burn in Ballard's Bourgeois Terror.

> "I'm a fund raiser for the Royal Academy. It's an easy job. All those
> CEOs think art is good for their souls."
> "Not so?"
> "It rots their brains. Tate Modern, the Royal Academy, the Hayward...
> They're Walt Disney for the middle classes."[3]

The novel's middle-class insurgents seem, at first, to be merely the hard done-to whiners whose complaints about the rising expense of child care and school fees and the "inequity" of too high rents in their not quite luxurious enough apartments are the stuff of endless media columns. "Believe me, the next revolution is going to be about parking"[4], one character announces, echoing the petrol blockades of four years ago and anticipating the Ikea riots of 2005. Once their discontent is stirred up, however, the goals of this group of former professionals become less specific, less instrumentalist.

Like the Situationists, the insurgents of Ballard's fictional Chelsea Marina want to "destroy the twentieth century":

> "I thought it was over."
> "It lingers on. It shapes everything we do, the way we think...
> Genocidal wars, half the world destitute, the other half sleepwalking
> through its own brain-death. We bought its trashy dreams and now we
> can't wake up."[5]

Millennium People is in many ways Britain's answer to *Fight Club* (though, needless to say, the chances of Britain producing *Millennium People* as a film that would even remotely do the book justice are not even slight — precisely because the British film industry is under the control of the same militantly complacent whingers that it attacks). Like *Fight Club*, the novel begins with a rage against the bullet-pointed, brand-consulted hyper-conformity of modern professional life, but ends up in surfascism.

The most important figure in this respect is Richard Gould who, like most of Ballard's other characters, is little more than a spokesperson for the author's theories. (Which is fine, of course: we need more "well-drawn characters" like we need more "well-wrought sentences". The UEA Eng Lit mafia are as ripe for immolation as are any of the other cosily depressing targets of Ballard's pyromaniac prose.)

Gould reiterates essentially the same attack on the "air-conditioned totalitarianism" of contemporary securo-culture that had been essayed by Nietzsche, Mauss, Bataille, Dada, Surrealism, Situationist theory, Lettrism, Baudrillard and Lyotard:

> We're living in a soft regime prison built by earlier generations of inmates. Somehow we have to break free. The attack on the World Trade Centre in 2001 was a brave attempt to free America from the 20th century. The deaths were tragic, but otherwise it was a meaningless act. And that was its point. Like the attack on the NFT.[6]

Gould re-states the Nietzschean claim that human beings need cruelty, danger and challenge, but that civilisation gives them security. Gould, though, is as reminiscent of Fukuyama's rehearsal of Nietzsche's discontent with civilisation as he is of Nietzsche himself.

It is Fukuyama's Nietzsche — the scourge of bland egalitarianism and empty inclusiveness — that is the most relevant Nietzsche today. As you read the appalled invective with which Nietzsche blasts the herd-cult of managed security (which is so weak and insipid that it can never utter its real rallying cry: "long live mediocrity!") you can't help but think of Blair and the Millennium Dome, whose pallid, paradoxically self-deprecatory pomposity contrasts unhappily with the cruel opulence of the monuments erected in Nietzsche's beloved tragic and heroic aristocratic societies.

"Democratic societies," Fukuyama wrote in *The End of History and the Last Man*,

> tend to promote a belief in the equality of all lifestyles and values. They do not tell their citizens how they should live, or what will make them happy virtuous and great. Instead they cultivate the value of toleration, which becomes the chief virtue in democratic societies. And if men are unable to affirm that any particular way of life is superior to another, they will fall back on the affirmation of life itself, that is, the body, its needs, and fears. While not all souls may be equally virtuous, all bodies can suffer; hence democratic societies will tend to be compassionate and raise to the first order of concern the question of preventing the body from suffering. It is not an accident that people in democratic societies are preoccupied

with material gain and live in an economic world devoted to the myriad small needs of the body. According to Nietzsche, the last man has "left the region where it was hard to live, for one needs warmth".[7]

"We need to pick targets that don't make sense."[8]

If the characters in *The Atrocity Exhibition* wanted to re-stage the founding traumatic moment of the media Sixties — the assassination of Kennedy — then Gould and his allies want to re-stage the founding traumatic moment of the media Noughties — 9/11. But where Traven/Tallis/Travis wanted to kill Kennedy again, "but this time in a way that makes sense", Gould wants 9/11 to happen again, but in a way that *doesn't* make sense.

For Gould, the (post)modern world is oppressed by an excess of Sense, a surplus of Meaning. "Kill a politician and you're tied to the motive that made you pull the trigger. Oswald and Kennedy, Princip and the Archdukes. But kill someone at random, fire a revolver into McDonald's — the universe stands back and holds its breath. Better still, kill fifteen people at random."[9] Thus, the Jill Dando murder is more of a template for Gould's anti-political insurgency than is September 11th, whose violence was (still) too motivated, too freighted with Meaning. Dando's killing however — brutal, meaningless, and without any apparent motive — was a direct attack on the BBC's "regime of moderation and good sense"[10] and the "castle of obligations"[11] it protects. An action like this, whose only motive is an attack on the concept of motive itself, blows open an "empty space we could stare into with real awe. Senseless, inexplicable, as mysterious as the Grand Canyon."[12]

Gould is an elegant and eloquent salesman of the Deleuze-Guattari "line of abolition", the fascist drive to destruction which is ultimately a drive towards self-destruction. Ballard, who, to his credit has always refused to endorse facile moralising, would no doubt object to that characterisation, since to in any way condemn or censure Gould would be to confirm the very securocratic values he seeks to undermine.

However, the most compelling aspect of *Millennium People*, politically speaking, is not the in many ways familiar asignifying violence, but its punk theory of class revolt.

"Twickenham is the Maginot Line of the English class system. If we can break through here, everything will fall."
"So class systems are the target. Aren't they universal — America, Russia...?"
"Of course. But only here is the class system a means of political control. Its real job isn't to suppress the proles, but to keep the middle classes down, make sure they're docile and subservient."[13]

The moment at which Ballard's "new proletariat" ("furnished with private schools and BMWs") become real political actors is when they cease to pursue their own class interests. Only then can they come to the Marxist revelation that bourgeois class interests are in no one's interests.

> "They see that private schools are brainwashing their children into a kind of social docility, turning them into a professional class who will run the show for consumer capitalism."
> "The sinister Mr Bigs?"
> "There are no Mr Bigs. The system is self-regulating. It relies on our sense of civic responsibility. Without that society would collapse. In fact, the collapse may even have begun."[14]

Blairism has consolidated and outstripped the ideological gains of Thatcherism by ensuring the apparently total victory of PR over punk, of politeness over antagonism, of middle-class utility over proletarian art. It manages the tricky ideological dodge of reducing everything to instrumentality whilst at the same time dedicating all resources to the production of cultural artefacts of no possible use or function. From the Mayan codices to Mission Statements... Spin engenders a meaninglessness which, in the mandatory banality of its corrosive nihilism, makes Gould's grand poetics of asignifying rupture seem quaintly nostalgic.

Blair has made middle-class security the horizon of all aspiration. In this over-conscious, over-lit twenty-four-hour office of the soul, business, preposterously, is served up to us as the closest thing to anything animated by libido. Ballard knows that a break-out from this affective prison must involve the explicit de-cathexis of the "nice house, nice family" picture that bourgeois culture is still capable of projecting as ideal.

In histories of punk, much is made of the role of the middle classes, but the crucial catalytic role of that particular kind of middle-class refusal remains under-thought. The middle-class defection from reproductive futurism into scarification and tribalisation did nothing more than state the obvious — middle-class careers and the privileges they bring are empty, tedious and ennervating — but, now more than ever, it is this obviousness that cannot be stated.

> The interesting thing is that they're protesting against themselves. There's no enemy out there. They know that they are the enemy.[15]

let me be
your fantasy[1]

What Ballard, Lacan and Burroughs have in common is the perception that human sexuality is *essentially* pornographic. For all three, human sexuality is irreducible to biological excitation; strip away the hallucinatory and the fantasmatic, and sexuality disappears with it. As Renata Salecl argues in *(Per)Versions of Love and Hate*,[2] it is easier for an animal to enter the Symbolic Order than it is for a human to unlearn the Symbolic and attain animality, an observation confirmed by the news that, when an orangutan was presented with pornography, it ceased to show any sexual interest in its fellow apes and spent all day masturbating. The orangutan had been inducted into human sexuality by the "inhuman partner", the fantasmatic supplement, upon which all human sexuality depends.

The question is not, then, *whether* pornography, but *which* pornography?

For Burroughs, pornosexuality would always be a miserable repetition, a Boschian negative carnival in which the rusting fairground wheel of desire forever turns in desolate circles. But in Ballard, and in Cronenberg's version of Ballard's *Crash*, it is possible to uncover a version of pornography that is positive, even utopian.

Cronenberg's work can be seen as a response to the challenge Baudrillard posed in *Seduction*.[3] Hardcore pornography haunts late capitalism, functioning as the cipher of a supposedly demystified, disillusioned "reality". "A pornographic culture *par excellence*: one that pursues the workings of the real at all times and all places." Here, hardcore is the reality of sex, and sex is the reality of everything else. Hardcore trades on a kind of earnest literalism, a belief that there is some empirically specifiable "it" which = sex in/as the real. As Baudrillard wryly noted, this empiricist bio-logic is fixated on a kind of technical fidelity — the pornographic film must be faithful to the (supposed) unadorned, brute mechanism of sex. Yet, sign and ritual are inescapable: in hardcore, especially in bukkake, the function of semen is, after all, essentially semiotic. No sex without signs. The higher the resolution of the image, the closer you get to the organs, the more that the "it" disappears from view. There is no better image of this "orgy of realism" than the "Japanese vaginal cyclorama" Baudrillard described in the "Stereo-porno" section of *Seduction*. "Prostitutes, their thighs open, sitting on the edge of a platform, Japanese workers in their shirt-sleeves... permitted to shove their noses up to their eyeballs within the woman's vagina in order to see, to see better — but what?" "Why stop with genitalia?" Baudrillard asks, "Who knows what profound pleasure is to be found in the visual dismemberment of mucous membranes and smooth muscles?"[4]

Cronenberg's early work — from *Shivers* and *Rabid* through to *Videodrome* — is an answer to that very question. Cronenberg famously posed his own question, "why aren't there beauty contests for the *inside* of the body?", and *Shivers* and *Rabid* posit an equivalence between body horror and eroticism. The ostensible catastrophe with which both films conclude — the total degeneration of social structure into a seething, anorganic orgy — functions ambivalently. The disintegration of organismic integrity, the reversion to the condition of the pre-multicellular, is a kind of parodic-utopian riposte to Freud's *Civilzation and its Discontents*. If civilisation and unbound libido are incommensurate, it is implied, so much the worse for civilisation. The apartment block taken over by mindless sex zombies at the end of *Shivers* is the Sixties dream of liberated sex come true...

Crash is a sober retreat from all this, a model for a new mecho-Mascohistic mode of pornography in which it is no longer the so-called inside of the body that matters, but the body as surface — a surface to be adorned with clothes, marked by scars, punctured by technical machinery. Possessed by a mad passion to exchange biotic code, the sex plague victims in *Shivers* devolve beyond animality into a kind of bacterial replicator frenzy. By firm contrast, *Crash* is as passionless as a Delvaux dream. Sex here is entirely colonised by culture and language. All the sex scenes are meticulously constructed tableaux, irreducibly fantasmatic, not because they are "unreal", but because their staging and their consistency depend on fantasy. The film's opening scene, with Catherine Ballard in the aircraft hangar, is quite clearly an acting out of a fantasmatic scenario; it also functions, later, via its recounting, as a fantasmatic supplement to the first sexual encounter we see between Catherine and James. There is no "it" of sex, no brute, naked, definable moment when "it" happens, only a plateau that is (paradoxically) both dilated and deferred, in which words and memories reverberate more powerfully than any penetration.

Crash is so indebted to Helmut Newton that it often looks like little more than a series of animated Newton images. Or, better: in *Crash*, the bodies attain the near-inanimate stillness of Newton's living mannequins. The echoes of Newton are entirely fittingly, since Ballard regarded Newton as "our greatest visual artist",[5] a Surrealist image-maker whose vision shamed the mediocrity of those officially working in the fine arts. "In Newton's work," Ballard writes, "we see a new race of urban beings, living on a new human frontier, where all passion is spent and all ambition long satisfied, where the deepest emotions seem to be relocating themselves, moving into a terrain more mysterious than Marienbad."[6]

When Cronenberg talks about the future sexuality of the "new race of urban beings" in *Crash*, he tends to refer to it in negative terms:

The conceit that underlies some of what is maybe difficult or baffling about *Crash*, the sci-finess of it, comes from Ballard anticipating a future pathological psychology. It's developing now, but he anticipates it and brings it back to the past — now — and he applies it as though it exists completely formed.

The Ballards' marriage is to be understood as inherently dysfunctional:

Some potential distributors said, "You should make them more normal at the beginning so that we can see where they go wrong." In other words, it should be like a *Fatal Attraction* thing. Blissful couple, maybe a dog and a rabbit, maybe a kid. And then a car accident introduces them to these horrible people and they go wrong. I said, "That isn't right, because there's something horribly wrong with them right *now*. That's why they're vulnerable to going even further.[7]

Yet the Ballards' "pathology" in *Crash* seems oddly healthy, their marriage a model of well-adjusted perversity. Theirs is a utopian sexuality, where sexual contact is voided of all sentimentality, stripped of any reference to reproduction, and unfreighted by any guilt. The lack of face-to-face sex in the Ballards' marriage — which, again Cronenberg himself tends to talk of negatively, as if it were a deviation from some wholesome, facialised sex in which the partners achieve a harmonious oneness — points to an awareness that there is no sexual relationship. Yet, very far from being a difficulty for the Ballards' marriage, the lack of a direct rapport, the recognition that any sexual encounter has to go via fantasy, is the basis of all their erotic adventures. Compare the Ballards' marriage to that of the Harfords' in *Eyes Wide Shut*. The Ballards' using of their sexual encounters with others as a stimulus for their own — impassive, poised, oneiric — sex forms a clear contrast with the deadlock of the Harfords' marriage, which is exposed in Bill's failure to cope, or keep up, with Alice's fantasy. While Bill is scandalised by Alice's articulation of her fantasies, sex in the Ballards' marriage is governed by the "feminine" drive to talk; it is almost as if *all* of the physical encounters happen only so that they can be converted into stories to be recounted later.

The most charged scene in *Crash* takes place in the carwash, where James looks on through the rearview mirror at Catherine and Vaughan, who — in the words of Cronenberg's script — are "like two semi-metallic human beings of the future making love in a chromium bower". Deborah Unger, the film's real star, is particularly impressive here. A kind of feline automaton, she "acts with her hair, minor adjustments, tosses of the head that advertise the transit of small emotions."[8]

Who is using whom here? The answer is that all three of the characters are using each other. Catherine's encounter with Vaughan stimulates James, just as Catherine is stimulated by the thought that James is watching her with Vaughan. Vaughan is using the couple as subjects of his own libidinal experiments, while the Ballards are using Vaughan as the third figure in their marriage. A mis-en-abyme of desire...

Far from being some nightmare of mutual domination, this is Cronenberg/ Ballard's sexual utopia, a perverse counterpart to Kant's kingdom of ends. The kingdom of ends was Kant's ideal ethical community, in which everyone is treated as an end in themselves. Kant reasoned that, from the point of view of his ethics, sex was inherently problematic, because to engage in sexual congress entails treating the other as an object to be used. The only way in which sex could be commensurate with the categorical imperative — which in one of its versions maintains that one should never treat others as a means to an end — was if it took place in the context of a marriage, in which each partner has contracted out the use of their organs in exchange for the use of their partner's.

Desire is construed here in terms of simple appropriation (this equivalence is yet another way in which Kant is in tune with Sade). But what Kant — and those who follow him in condemning pornography because it "objectifies" — fails to recognise is that our deepest desire is not to possess an other but to be objectified by them, to be used by them in/as their fantasy. This is one sense of the famous Lacanian formula that "desire is the desire of the other". The perfect erotic situation would involve neither a dominance of, nor a fusion with, the other; it would consist rather in being objectified by someone you also want to objectify.

Crash, of course, follows Masoch and Newton in delocalising sex from genitality. Libido is invested in the mis-en-scene more than in the meat, which draws its attraction almost entirely from its adjacency to the decorous nonorganic — to clothes as much as cars. Clothes differentiate glam's cold and cruel cultivation of appearances from hardcore's passion for the real. Without suits, dresses and shoes, without fur, leather and nylon, pornography might as well be arranging meat in a butcher's window. Newton told Ballard that he "loved Cronenberg's *Crash*", but one thing bothered him. "The dresses," he whispered. "They were so awful." This strikes me as waspishly unfair to Denice Cronenberg's elegant wardrobe selections. (One major problem with Jonathan Weiss' version of *The Atrocity Exhibition*, however, is precisely the dreadfulness of the clothes.) *Crash* takes its cues from high fashion magazines, whose images are more sumptuously arty than fine art, more suffused with deviant eroticism than hardcore porn. Would it be impossible for there to be a pornography, sponsored by Dior or Chanel, scripted by a latter-day Masoch or Ballard, whose fantasies were as artfully staged as the most glamorous fashion photo shoot?

fantasy kits:[1] steven meisel's "state of emergency"[2]

A few weeks ago, I asked whether it would be possible "for there to be a pornography, sponsored by Dior or Chanel, scripted by a latter-day Masoch or Ballard, whose fantasies were as artfully staged as the most glamorous fashion photo shoot?"[3] Steven Meisel's *Vogue* photo-shoot, much more than Mike Figgis' drearily vanilla promotional films for *Agent Provocateur*, suggests that such a pornography is conceivable.

"State of Emergency" shows, once again, that it is left to high fashion to take up the role that fine art has all but abandoned. While much of fine art has succumbed to the "passion for the real", high fashion remains the last redoubt of Appearance and Fantasy.

The used tampons and pickled animals of Reality Art offer, at best, tracings of the empirical. Their quaint biographism reveals nothing of the unconscious. Meisel's elegantly-staged photographs, meanwhile, drip with an ambivalence worthy of the best Surrealist paintings. They are uncomfortable and arousing in equal measure because they reflect back to us our conflicted attitudes and unacknowledged libidinal complicities. (In this respect, they form a sharp contrast with the infinitely more exploitative image being used to front the American Express Red campaign[4], whose meaning is easily anchored to the coordinates of the currently dominant ideological constellation.)

Reframed as Art, the *Vogue* photographs would no doubt be described — in the all-too familiar terms of art-critical muzak — as "*negotiating with ideas* of violence/ terror/etc." As high fashion, they meet instead with a type of liberal denunciation that is no less familiar. In the *Guardian*, Joanna Bourke complained that, "It is no coincidence that the security forces are shown to be protecting us from a person who is neither male nor obviously Muslim".[5] Would Bourke have preferred it, then, if the images *did* feature a Muslim man?

Bourke continues:

> Instead, the terrorist threat is an unreal woman. In contrast to the security personnel depicted, she is placed beyond the realm of the human. Her skin is as plastic as a mannequin's; her body is too perfect, even when grimacing in pain. When the model is depicted as the aggressor, she remains nothing more than the phallic dominatrix of many adolescent boys' wet dreams. In both instances, the beauty of the photographs transforms acts of violence and humiliation into erotic possibilities.

Again, what would Bourke have preferred: simulated snuff in which "real-looking" women were roughed up by security staff? Bourke's hostility to the fantasmatic is oddly doubled by the aggression of the security personnel towards the "unreal" women. And what does it mean to substitute an "unreal woman" for an all-too-real Muslim male, in any case? What does the confusion of ontological levels — agents of reality conjoined with the waxy artificiality of Bellmer-doll fashion models — tell us? The photographs are fascinating and unsettling because there are no straightforward answers to these questions.

Needless to say, Meisel's photographs do find erotic possibilities in violence and humiliation, but this is not so much a "transformation" as a rediscovery. Two hundred years after Sade, a century after Bataille and Masoch, it appears that anything which publicly acknowledges that eroticism is inseparable from violence and humiliation is more unacceptable than ever. The issue is not how "healthy" sexuality can be purged of violence, but how the violence inherent to sexuality can be sublimated. Meisel's photographs — which, we should remember, appear in a magazine the vast majority of whose readership is not "adolescent males" but women — are "fantasy kits" which offer just such sublimations, providing scenarios, role-play cues and potential fantasmatic identifications.

"State of Emergency" demonstrates that, rather than simply retaining its capacity to shock, *The Atrocity Exhibition* is more disturbing than ever. The overt sexualisation and compulsory carnality of postmodern image culture distracts us from the essential staidness of its rendition of the erotic. As Baudrillard argues in *Seduction*, biologised sex functions as the reality principle of contemporary culture: everything is reducible to sex, and sex is just a matter of meat mechanics. Ours is an age of cynicism and piety, which, as Simon suggested in his initial post on "State of Emergency",[6] primly and pruriently resists the equivalences between eroticism, violence and celebrity that Ballard explored:

Entering the exhibition, Travis sees the atrocities of Vietnam and the Congo mimetised in the "alternate" death of Elizabeth Taylor; he tends the dying film star, eroticising her punctured bronchus in the over-ventilated verandas of the London Hilton; he dreams of Max Ernst, superior of the birds.[7]

To imagine the atrocities of September 11th and Abu Ghraib mimetised in the alternate death of Paris Hilton feels far more unacceptable, because contemporary piety has sacralised its atrocities in a way that the Sixties could not. In *Atrocity*, Dr Nathan's reminder that, at the level of the unconscious, "the tragedies of Cape Kennedy and Vietnam... may in fact play very different parts from the ones we assign them" is extremely timely. (As Burroughs tells us in his preface to *The Atrocity Exhibition*, "Surveys indicate that wet dreams in many cases have no overt sexual content, whereas dreams with an overt sexual content in many cases do not result in orgasm".) It is clear that the appalling Abu Ghraib photographs were *already* intensely eroticised stagings whose scenarios were derived from cheap American pornography. Love and Napalm: Export USA, indeed. Part of the reason that the Abu Ghraib images were so traumatic for a deeply conflicted American culture which combines religious moralism with hyper-sexualised commerce, and which is united only by a taste for mega-violence, is that they exposed the equation between military intervention and sexual humiliation that the official culture both depends upon and must suppress.

It's interesting to compare both *The Atrocity Exhibition* and "State of Emergency" to Martha Rosler's series of collages, "Bringing the War Home"[8]. "Sixties iconography: the nasal prepuce of LBJ, crashed helicopters, the pudenda of Ralph Nader, Eichmann in drag, the climax of a New York happening: a dead child": this typical section from *The Atrocity Exhibition* could almost be a gloss on Rosler's images, with their irruptions of war and atrocity amidst domestic scenes. But in Rosler's case, unlike in Ballard's, surrealist juxtaposition has a clear polemical purpose. *The Atrocity Exhibition*, like "State of Emergency", is devoid of any decipherable intent; the oneiric juxtapositions in Ballard's and Meisel's work seemed to be conceived of as neutral re-presentations of the substitutions and elisions made by the mediatised unconscious.

Meisel's fantasy kits, their narratives left implicit and mysterious, suggest ways in which Ballard might be adapted in future. Part of the problem with Weiss' film adaptation of *The Atrocity Exhibition* is that it subordinated the fragmentary mode of the novel to the duree — the lived time — of the feature film.[9] The most successful part of the film was perhaps the first few moments, where Ballard's text was intoned over still images in a style reminiscent of Marker's *La Jetee* (a film which Ballard adores, of course). That is partly because it is the profound stillness of the Surrealist paintings which

The Atrocity Exhibition describes and appropriates — their beaches drained of time — which sets the rhythm of the novel. The most successful adaptation of *The Atrocity Exhibition* would, precisely, be an exhibition — not only of photographs, but also of newsreel footage, mandalas, diagrams, paintings and notebooks. It would be left for the viewer-participant to assemble their own narratives from these fantasy kits.

the assassination of
j.g. ballard[1]

**They wanted to kill Ballard again, but this time in a way that made
sense.** The British know how best to kill something, softly. Assimilation is
sometimes the most effective kind of assassination.

"You say these constitute an assassination weapon?"

So here they come again — all the familiar profiles, all the old routines. All
that over-rehearsed musing about the supposed contrast between Ballard's
writing and his lifestyle and persona. All that central London cognoscenti
condescension: he lived in Shepperton, he wore a tie and drank gin and yet
he could come up with this — *imagine that*. As if it isn't obvious that English
suburbs are seething with surrealism. As if you could think for a minute
that *The Drowned World* or *The Atrocity Exhibition* were written by anyone
wearing jeans. Ballard mapped another America, another 1960s, one beyond
the pleasure principle of rock 'n' roll and its paraphernalia. (That was one
of the reasons that Ballard should have been so integral to post-punk's
unlearning of r and r and to electro's pursuit of a colder mechano-erotics
outside rock's passional regime.) As if Ballard's works could be mistaken
as anything other than the work of a bourgeois — Ballard's was to have
unashamedly fixated on the psychopathologies of his class (so no Keith
Talents here, only a litany of deranged professionals), a class which he had
a special insight into because he was always semi-detached from it.

You: Coma: Princess Diana

Assessing cultural figures by their alleged influence, their legacy, is an egregious postmodern tic — as if it reflected any merit to have inspired the Klaxons. Ballard is important precisely because it is completely unimaginable that any equivalent of his work could emerge from current conditions. As he made clear in his 1989 annotations to his most important work, *The Atrocity Exhibition*, he was a meta-psychologist of the pop age, his sensibility unsuited to the era of Reality, with its flattening fusion of celebrity and the hyper-banal.

> A unique collision of private and public fantasy took place in the 1960s, and may have to wait some years to be repeated, if ever. The public dream of Hollywood for the first time merged with the private imagination of the hyper-stimulated TV viewer. People have sometimes asked me to do a follow-up to *The Atrocity Exhibition*, but our perception of the famous has changed — I can't imagine writing about Meryl Streep or Princess Di, and Margaret Thatcher's undoubted mystery seems to reflect design faults in her own self-constructed persona. One can mechanically spin sexual fantasies around all three, but the imagination soon flags. Unlike [Elizabeth] Taylor, they radiate no light. [...] A kind of banalisation of celebrity has occurred: we are now offered an instant, ready-to-mix fame as nutritious as packet soup.[2]

Ballard's Sixties were inaugurated by the Kennedy assassination. The founding event of the media environment we live in now, in which consensual sentimentality has long since occluded Ballard's death of affect, was Princess Diana's car crash death in 1997. In his later novels, Ballard tried to get a grip on this mall-world of Ikea psychosis and shopping channel charismatics, but they never produced the same spinal charge as his encounters with the Sixties tele-cinematic arcades presided over by Elizabeth Taylor and Ronald Reagan. Ballard's most probing contributions in later years came in interviews and articles rather than in the novels: it was here that he identified retail parks and anonymous non-places as the authentic landscape of the twenty-first century, but he was not able to poeticise this hyper-banal terrain in the same way that he mythologised the brutalist concourses and high-rises of the Sixties and Seventies.

A Pulp Modernist Magus

What better way to destroy something than send in Martin Amis to praise it? Ballard was never a "good writer" in the way that Amis and his admirers and cronies in urbane Brit lit, with their handcrafted sentences, their well-drawn characters, their concerned social commentary, were. The significance of *The Atrocity Exhibition* was to have obsolesced this machinery of mediocrity, which he eviscerated in his 1964 profile of Burroughs.

To use the stylistic conventions of the traditional oral novel — the sequential narrative, characters "in the round", consecutive events, balloons of dialogue attached to "he said" and "she said" — is to perpetuate a set of conventions ideally suited to a period of great adventures in the Conradian mode, or to an overformalised Jamesian society, but now valuable for little more than the bedtime story and the fable.[3]

But Ballard's strategy in his best works was also opposed to that of another of his admirers and appropriators, Iain Sinclair. Whereas Sinclair transforms pop-cultural material into something opaque, obscure and hermetic, Ballard innovated a kind of pulp modernism in which the techniques of high modernism and the riffs of popular fiction intensified one another, avoiding both high cultural obscurantism and middlebrow populism. Ballard understood that collage was the great twentieth century artform and that the mediatised unconscious was a collage artist. Where are his twenty-first century inheritors, those who can use the fiction-kits Ballard assembled in the Sixties as diagrams and blueprints for a new kind of fiction?

a world of dread and fear[1]

"You couldn't sleep. You had to work.
Always light.
Head against the window, sun coming up —
The troops were gathering on the street below him. The Red Guard in good voice:
SCAB, SCAB, SCAB —
The dawn chorus of the Socialist Republic of South Yorkshire.
Another cup of coffee. Another aspirin"
— David Peace, *GB84*[2]

David Peace's *GB84* is typed in prose as stark and unforgiving as motorway service station strip-lights.

The harsh expressionist realism Peace honed over the course of the four books of the *Red Riding Quartet* is perfect for handling *GB84*'s subject matter, the events of the 1984-85 Miners' Strike. The *Quartet* counted forward — 1974-1977-1980-1983 — as if it is was approaching but would never reach the fateful date that will provide the title of *GB84*. From here we count backwards; *GB84* "is actually the last of an inverse post-war trilogy which will include UKDK, a novel about the plot to overthrow Wilson and the subsequent rise of Thatcher and another book, possibly about the Atlee Govt." From gothic crime to Political gothic...[3]

The fiercely partisan novel ends with the incantation: "the Year is Zero". But 1985, when both the strike and the book end, was very far from being a year of beginning or of possibilities for the novel's "us". (In fact, the very existence of that "us", the collective proletarian subject, is itself in question by then. At the same time, however, this is the first of Peace's novels in which the possibility of any sort of group-subject is raised. More typically, his characters are solipsistically alone, connected only by violence, their only shared project dissimulation.) On the contrary, it was a year of catastrophic defeat, the scale of which would not become apparent for a decade or more. (Perhaps it was only in the election of New Labour twelve years later that the defeat was both registered and finally secured.)

We now know — although this cannot enter into the present tension of the novel — that the strike was about a failed Proletarianisation. After the events the novel describes, what awaited was fragmentation, new opportunities for the few, unemployment and underemployment for the majority. The technique of flying picketing that Scargill had pioneered so successfully in the late Sixties and early Seventies (and which had contributed to the humiliation and collapse of the Heath government) was combatted by a comprehensive range of strategies (including a highly-organised counter-subversion operation run by MI5) that were designed while the Tories were still in opposition. The aim was to fragment miners' solidarity and to prevent support from sympathetic workers in other industries. In this, the creation of the Working Miners Committee and the Union of Democratic Mineworkers would prove crucial. The deterritorialisation of capital — its transmutation into "messages which pass instantaneously from one nodal point to another across the former globe, the former material world"[4] — was not to be met by a complementary deterritorialisation of labour. Miners were inveigled into identifying with their *own* terrirory rather than with the industry as a whole; hence the return to work of the Nottinghamshire and Derbyshire miners, who believed that they were safeguarding their future but in a satisfying irony found themselves no better off than miners from any other coalfield. Within a decade, the industry would be all but closed down in Britain, with members of the UDM no more likely to be in employment than those of the NUM.

Yes, we know all this, now. But Peace restores drama by excluding any of the knowledge hindsights brings. The events come at you as if they were happening for the first time, and without the emollient shield of an omniscient authorial voice. As Joseph Brooker identifies in a lengthy piece on GB84 in the current issue of *Radical Philosophy*,[5] the novel is bereft of any mediating meta-language. The tragic quality the novel possesses even in its earliest scenes comes courtesy of the knowledge we, the readers, bring — but which is, naturally, is denied to the protagonists — of the eventual course that the strike will take.

Counterfactuals are largely the preserve of the reactionary right, and Peace refuses the temptation to change the facts. He writes his retro-speculative fiction in the spaces between the recorded facts, extrapolating, inferring, guessing. Yet the question the reader cannot help but pose is: what would have happened if the miners *had* won? (A question that has added piquancy since subsequent revelations have shown that the government was much closer to defeat than was ever suspected at the time.) The narrative in which the strike is now embedded — the only narrative in town, the story of Global Capital — has it that it was part of a receding ebb tide of organised working-class insurgency. Defeat was inevitable, written into the historical passage from Fordism to post-Fordism. The hard left are outflanked, fighting under the banner of the Past for "the *history* of the Miner. The *tradition* of the Miner. The legacies of their fathers and their fathers' fathers."[6]

But such a narrativisation is question-begging, since the very credibility of this story relies upon the events of the strike unfolding as they did. What if they hadn't? Under the aspect of eternity, everything is inevitable and we are all Spinozists. But life has to be lived "forward", making us Sartreans. Reading the book now inevitably dramatises the tension between these two positions, between knowing that everything has already happened and acting as if it hasn't.

A gang of doppelgangers, near-duplicates, haunt the pages of *GB84*, this "fiction based upon a fact". Peace writes an occulted history of the present by constructing a simulation of the near-past. The dramatis personae do not bear the names of their real-life counterparts, and sometimes don't have names at all, merely titles designating their structural role: The President, The Chairman, The Minister. Sometimes, real world names are slightly altered; in *GB84* the NUM's Chief Executive Roger Windsor becomes the hapless Terry Winters. The relationship of these simulations to their real-life counterparts is complex. The President is not Scargill. But he's not *not* Scargill. No doubt Peace changed the names in part to avoid legal action, but in an odd way the extra imaginative latitude he is granted by not being compelled into fidelity to actual biography gives the characters more reality. He is able to get inside their heads in a way that would not be possible with actual biographical individuals.

The most controversial characterisation is that of Stephen Sweet, the professional strikebreaker based on Thatcher's right-hand man throughout the strike, David Hart. Hart was the driving force behind the creation of the Working Miners' Committee and the UDM. In the novel, Sweet is seen planning the crucial battle between police and pickets at the coking plant, Orgreave. (Devoting all its resources to Orgreave is now regarded as a major strategic error by the NUM.) Sweet is referred to throughout the novel as "The Jew". Although this designation remains uncomfortable — as it is intended to be, Peace has said — suspicions of anti-semitism are immediately rebutted by any sort of close reading of the novel. Everything we see of Sweet is focalised through his chauffeur-factotum, Neil Fontaine. (This distancing is significant, since Sweet's pomposity and grandiosity strike a slightly unconvincing note. It is almost as if Peace is unable to find the sympathy necessary for a convincing characterisation. On the other hand, perhaps Hart was the faintly absurd figure that Peace paints his fictional counterpart as. Peace does not make the mistake of portraying Sweet as a self-consciously evil figure; on the contrary, Sweet sees his efforts in a messianic light.)

Fontaine, presumably a co-opted member of the working class who has worked for the security services, is a blank slate of a figure, a man reduced to function (he is doubled in the novel by David Johnson, The Mechanic, who becomes an antagonist but who was clearly an ally in the past). It is Fontaine, a man with right-wing affiliations and connections but few passions, who will never stop seeing Sweet as "The Jew". That description foregrounds the provisional nature of the political alliance that Thatcher built: somehow, the Thatcher programme allowed fascists to consort with Jews, nationalists to find common cause with the agents of multinational capitalism.

Fontaine is also the connecting link between the overt and the covert counter-"subversion" operations undertaken by the state in *GB84*. It is in the unraveling of the MI5's role in proceedings that leads Peace into the territory of endemic corruption and betrayal that he staked out so viscerally in the *Red Riding Quartet*. Unusually for Peace, so skilled at putting himself (and therefore us) into the shoes of irredeemably corrupt power puppets, there is no major character in *GB84* who is a policeman. But there are state functionaries: Fontaine, Johnson, but, most vividly, Malcolm Morris, a man whose role is to be a shadow, a cipher, an expert phone-tapper who, in a Francis Baconoid delirium, fancies that his ears are always bleeding...

In *GB84*, MI5 are the key players in organising Terry Winters' spectacularly ill-judged trip to Libya. Who can forget the television images of Roger Windsor kissing Gadaffi in his tent? Winters/Windsor's Libyan visit — only a few months after the policewoman Yvonne Fletcher had been killed by Libyan agents — proved an important, perhaps decisive, PR defeat for the NUM. (The actual role of Libya in the strike was somewhat different: the Thatcher government had illicitly increased oil imports from the supposedly outlawed regime so as to see off the threat of power cuts.) Peace deliberately leaves the degree of Windsor/Winters' collusion with the security services unclear. He wanted the novel to be a "mess", like the strike itself.

The doubling of historical fact with Peace's version of it is internal to the novel's own structure, whose main fictional thread is cut through by a diary account of the strike by two miners, Martin and Peter. Martin and Peter's accounts, rendered in the Yorkshire dialect Peace captures so ably, were "not fictionalised", Peace has said. It is here that Scargill, Macgregor, Thatcher, McGahey and Heathfield appear in their own names. The first person accounts register the grim miseries of the strike, as well as its comaraderie, forming a contrast with the skullduggery, the corruption and the high-level meetings of the novel's central narrative.

Peace says that he first puts himself into the past, and then imagines. It's like method writing, or time travel. Peace has tried and tested tricks to get back. He uses jaundiced newsprint, books but most of all pop — not the stuff he would have listened to himself, then, and has listened to ever since, but the songs that, ubiquitous then, forgotten now, can function as audio-madeleines. Digging through the carboot sale detritus of 84 and 85 pop, Peace finds a coded history of the strike secreted beneath the dull sheen of thrownaway post-new pop. *GB84* begins with Nena's execrable "99 Red Balloons", which here becomes an apocalyptic carnival tune, bursting with all the hopes that will sag and bleed by the end of the novel's gruelling, long, long march. "Two Tribes" soundtracks the next phase, the confrontation between police and miner (both this and the Nena song, of course, played upon Cold War anxieties when they were released. Another reminder, and there are many in this novel, that 1984 was a world away). The exhilaration and adrenalin of out and out confrontation, Us and Them, gives way to suspicion (who is with us, and who is against us?) *"Two Tribes* — Must have heard that bloody song ten times a day now for weeks. Ought to make it National Anthem, said Sean."[7] The songs that Peace dredges up for the final phase of the strike are "Careless Whisper" ("guilty feet have got no rhythm") and, for the 84-85 winter that was cold, but not cold enough — the power cuts never come — Band Aid's "Do They Know It's Christmas". Characters speculate that Band Aid is a government-backed scheme to distract from the plight of the miners, and the line that Peace selects for sampling is, naturally, "There's a world outside your window, and it's a world of dread and fear."

Sampling is precisely the right term, since pop, much more than literature, film or TV (Peace actively distrusts these latter two) provides Peace with a methodology for drilling his words into the repetitions and refrains that are his stock-in-trade. Repetition is a hallmark of Peace's style; he has famously remarked that the strike was intensely repetitive and that the prose would reflect that. But in all of Peace's writing, repetition is what substitutes for both plot and character. His crime novels make no attempt to interest readers in the intrigue and enigma of plots; the plot of *GB84*, meanwhile, is given in advance, a kind of readymade. And one strange quality of Peace's writing that is not immediately evident is that, although it is unusually intimate — reading his novels is always like rifling through someone else's most secret places — his characters lack what is usually called "inner life". They are identified less by a reflexive vitality than by death-drive repetitions, riffs, echoes, habit-forms.

In *GB84* the result is more poetic than most poetry; it is, naturally, a poetry stripped of all lyricism, a harshly dissonant word-music. Peace is a writer particularly attentive to sound: the unsleeping vigilance of state power is signified by the "Click, Click" of the telephone tap, the massed ranks of the police by the *Krk, Krk* of boots and truncheons beaten against shields, both sounds repeated so much that they become background noise, part of the ambience of paranoia. The *Telegraph* review was right to observe that, "At times, the novel feels like an eardrum buzz, the literary equivalent of late-1970s Northern bands such as Throbbing Gristle and Cabaret Voltaire." It resembles even more closely the two great post-punk responses to the strike: Mark Stewart's *As the Veneer of Democracy Starts to Fade* (Keith Leblanc also produced the single "The Enemy Within") and Test Department's *The Unacceptable Face of Freedom*. Perhaps for this reason, Post-punk recedes as an explicit reference in *GB84*. It had been present in *Nineteen Eighty Three* in titles of sections of the novel: "Miss the Girl" (the Creatures) and "There are No Spectators" (the Pop Group). The tone for *GB84* is in every sense set by the title of the last section of *Nineteen Eighty Three*: "Total Eclipse of the Heart".

Part of the reason that 1985 seemed like the worst year for pop ever was that it was the beginning of the restoration. Up to 1984, British popular and political culture was still a battleground. 1985 was the year of Live Aid, the beginning of a time of the fake consensus that is the cultural expression of global capital. If Live Aid was the non-event that happened, the strike was the Event that didn't.

Swords and shields. Sticks and stones. Horses and dogs. Blood and bones—
The armies of the dead awoken, arisen for one last battle.
The windscreen of the Granada lit by a massive explosion—
The road. The hedges. The trees—
Fire illuminating the night. The fog now smoke. Blue lights and red—
Terry shook Bill's arm. Shook it and shook it. Bill opened his eyes—
"Where are we?" shouted Terry. "Where is this place?"
"The start and the end of it all," said Bill. "Brampton Bierlow. Cortonwood."
"But what's going on?" screamed Terry Winters. "What's happening? What is it?"
"It's the end of the world," laughed Bill Reed. "The end of all our worlds."[8]

82

ripley's glam[1]

"He hated becoming Thomas Ripley again, hated being nobody, hated putting on his old set of habits again, and feeling that people looked down on him and were bored with him unless he put on an act for them like a clown, feeling incompetent and incapable of doing anything with himself except entertaining people for minutes at a time."
— Patricia Highsmith, *The Talented Mr Ripley*[2]

We can learn a great deal about the glam impulse from these lines from *The Talented Mr Ripley*.

Significantly, Highsmith wrote the first Ripley novel in 1955 and only returned to the character in 1970. Tom Ripley was not a character that could fit into the rock and roll era, with its emphasis on teen desire, social disruption and Dionysiac excess. But Ripley's "hedonic conservatism", his snobbery and his facility with masks and disguise, mean that he would be perfectly at home in the Marienbad-like country estate of glam. If Sixties rock was characterised, on the one hand, by appeals made to the big Other (demands for social change and/or more pleasure) and, on the other hand, by the denial of the existence of the Symbolic order as such (psychedelia), then glam was defined, initially, by a hyperbolic/parodic identification *with* the big Other — by the return of Signs and/of Status.

In the sentence cited above, there are, evidently, two Toms — "Thomas Ripley" the performed social role, and the Tom who performs that role; Tom the speaking subject and Tom the subject of the statement. At the outset of *The Talented Mr Ripley* both these Toms are "nobodies" — as a speaking subject, like all speaking subjects, Tom is ontologically nothing; and as the subject of the statement is *socially* nothing. At this stage, Tom is very far from being the insouciant, poised figure he will appear to be later; he is capable of simulating confidence only when taking on the role of Other people.

It is not that Tom lacks status; it is that he has no place whatsoever in the social hierarchy. His status is *not even* low. His indeterminate social origins and his ability as a mimic and as a forger (skills upon which his anti-career as a fraudster are based) mean that he fits in nowhere (or anywhere). Tom experiences this nothingness in classic existentialist terms, feeling himself to be inchoate, a void, unresolved, unreal.

But the novel is a kind of existentialist picaresque by the end of which Tom has the (financial) means to create a Thomas Ripley he will not hate being. At the beginning of the next novel, *Ripley Under Ground*, it is immediately evident that Tom has created/become such a figure. Tom has fashioned his best forgery — a Thomas Ripley who is independently wealthy, owns an elegant house in the Paris suburbs and is married to a beautiful, hedonistic heiress. From now on, Ripley's anxieties will concern not the establishment of an identity, but the preserving and defending of the status he has acquired.

Ripley's trajectory is uncannily in sync with that of Bryan Ferry. *Roxy Music* and *For Your Pleasure*, those exercises in learning and unlearning of accent and manners, are pop's equivalent of *The Talented Mr Ripley*. The clothes, the bearing and the voice are faked, but not yet perfectly. The roots still show, and the painful drama of becoming something you are not still carries an existential charge. *Stranded* and the subsequent albums, meanwhile, are the equivalent of the later novels; here, success is assumed, and the threats to the tasteful but banal idyll come from ennui, a certain unease with contentment, and — most ominous of all — the danger of the past returning. The vapid bucolia of Roxy's *Avalon* — recorded when Ferry was himself married to an heiress and living on a country estate — would be the perfect soundtrack to Ripley puttering around in his Harpers and Queens dream home, Belle Ombre, with his wife, Heloise.

The first step to Ripley's becoming a Something turns out to be his vampirising of the identity of Dickie Greenleaf. I say "turns out" because, contrary to what Anthony Minghella's film implies, it is clear that Tom does not to go to Europe with the thought of destroying Dickie already in his mind. Ripley is a brilliant improviser, not a planner; the plans he does make are short-term, often leading to more problems than they solve, and he derives enjoyment from cleaning up messes rather than from avoiding them in the first place.

Initially, Tom's attitude to Dickie is ambivalent and is not straightforwardly predatory — he is aggressive and envious but also affectionate. If Tom is Nothing, a turmoil of unresolved purposes, a tumult of shame and inadequacy, then Dickie is really Something, an Object, resolved and real, possessing "the solidity of a stone". By taking the place of Dickie, Ripley can escape the pain, anxiety and awkwardness of being himself, a self. To become an Object — to be relieved of the pressures of subjectivity, untroubled by any interiority — isn't this one of central fantasies of glam?

Žižek is certainly right to argue that the sexualisation of the relationship between Tom and Dickie in Anthony Minghella's film is a mis-step. Yet Žižek's interpretation is not fully adequate either. According to Žižek:

> Dickie is for Tom not the object of his desire, but the ideal desiring subject, the transferential subject "supposed to know how to desire." In short, Dickie becomes for Tom his ideal ego, the figure of his imaginary identification: when he repeatedly casts a coveting side-glance at Dickie, he does not thereby betray his erotic desire to engage in sexual commerce with him, to HAVE Dickie, but his desire to BE like Dickie.[3]

What is missing from Žižek's analysis is a recognition of the way that Dickie *fails* to serve as an adequate ideal ego. The pivotal moment of the novel comes when Ripley is no longer capable of sustaining his fantasy identification with Dickie. When Tom looks into Dickie's eyes and sees not the windows of a soul with which he can identify but the dead, glassy surface of an inert and idiotic dummy, he falls (back) into a deep existential nausea and vertigo, experiencing a moment of profound cosmic loathing and miserable dislocation:

> He stared at Dickie's eyes that were still frowning, the sun bleached eyebrows white and the eyes themselves shining and empty, nothing but little pieces of blue jelly with a black dot in them. You were supposed to see the soul through the eyes, to see the love through the eyes, the one place where you could look at another human being and see what really went on inside, and in Dickie's eyes Tom saw nothing more than he would have seen if he had looked at the hard, bloodless surface of a mirror. Tom felt a painful wrench in his breast, and he covered his face with his hands. It was as if Dickie had suddenly been snatched away from him. They were not friends. They didn't know each other. It struck Tom like a horrible truth, true for all time, true for the people he had known in the past and for those he would know in the future: each had stood and would stand before him, and he would know time and time again that he would never know them, and the worst was that there would always be the illusion, for a time, that he did know them, and that he and they were completely in harmony and alike. For an instant the wordless shock of the realisation seemed more than he could bear. He felt in the grip of a fit, as if he would fall to the ground.[4]

No doubt this is partly a registering of Dickie's rejection of Tom. But it also expresses Tom's feelings of revulsion for Dickie. What has been "snatched away" from Tom is not just Dickie "himself", but the *fantasy* of Dickie. It is as if Tom is no longer capable of pretending (to himself) that

Dickie is anything other than a really rather mediocre person; as if he has encountered, for the first time, the brute, stupid physicality of Dickie — has seen Dickie, directly, without the screen/sheen of fantasy to beatify him.

Tom's break from Dickie is inevitable after the desperately painful scene, slightly earlier, when Dickie discovers Tom wearing his clothes and imitating him in front of the mirror. Dickie is disgusted and angered by Tom's imitation (what is more horrifying than being someone else's ideal ego?), just as Tom is utterly mortified by the fact that Dickie has discovered him in the act (what is more shameful than being caught by your ego ideal fantasising about them?). Significantly, Dickie makes the same error as Minghella, (mis) interpreting Tom's behaviour in terms of sexual obsession, choosing this moment to emphatically deny to Tom that he is "queer". But Tom's wanting to *be* Dickie is far more obscene, far more deadly, far more Burroughsian, than his wanting to *have* him would have been.

Once Tom can no longer sustain his fantasy identification with Dickie, the logic of his psychosis insists that he will only be able to resolve his existential crisis — his lack of Being — by killing Dickie. That is partly because, in Ripley's mind, Dickie is already dead: a soulless shell who illegitimately possesses wealth and social status that the more tasteful and refined Tom feels that he rightfully deserves. Tom is sure that he can be Dickie better than Dickie himself could be, and Dickie will be the daub that Tom will use as the basis for his masterpiece, the new Thomas Ripley. There is also a sense in which, by killing Dickie, Tom "earns" his place in the unproductive leisure class. Even before he is elevated into the leisure class, Tom shares its disdain for "drudgery". The difference between Tom the common thief and con artist and Tom the member of the leisured elite is a successful act of violence. Veblen argues that "leisure class society" is founded on the "barbarian" distinction between *exploit* — "the conversion to his own ends of energies previously directed to some end by another agent" — and *industry* (or drudgery) — "the effort that goes to create a new thing with a new, ('brute') material".[5] The Masters must always vampirise, never produce.

> The performance of productive work, or employment in personal service, falls under the same odium for the same reason. An invidious distinction arises between exploit and acquisition by seizure on the one hand and industrial employment on the other. Labour acquires a character of irksomeness by virtue of the indignity imputed to it.[6]

Hunting has always been one of the activities upon which the leisured elite has prided itself, and Ripley is a consummate hunter (*prey* is one of the meanings of *Ripley's Game*).

The use of homicidal violence to achieve and protect a position of privilege is very far from being aberrant, and Tom is no more likely to face justice than are the brigands of our real life ruling elites. (Highsmith's refusal to impose a justice in the novels that is conspicuously lacking in the world is one of the most subversive aspects of her depictions of the character.) If Tom is pathological, his pathologies are the pathologies of a class; it is only the freshness of the blood of his victims (and his willingness to spill it himself) that separates Ripley's exploits from those of his new peers. Yet Ripley is not a Slasher who enjoys killing. On the contrary, he is horrifying because he treats murder as a practical task devoid of any special existential or affective charge. Ripley's commission of murders are remarkable for their their coldness and *lack* of cruelty; famously, Ripley only kills because he needs to, not because he enjoys it. Ripley kills out of cold, utilitarian logic, eliminating those who stand in his way or threaten to expose him. Again, far from being aberrant, a carefully maintained distinction between a violent, obscene underside and a bland, official front is the normal practice of power and privilege. It is not moral scruples that motivate Ripley (he notoriously has none), but a fear of humiliation. As Julie Walker argues:

> What Tom does fear is unmasking; not merely the unmasking of himself as Dickie or even the unmasking of himself as a killer but the unmasking of his lack of a real self and therefore his self-perceived inadequacy in the face of others — there is no appreciable difference between fear of discovery for his tax scam or for his murders. His main fear is that of socially not quite making the grade.

This rendition of amorality is what is (post)modern about Ripley. Classic psychosis consisted in the confusion of the Real and the Symbolic (the most obvious example of which would be hearing the voice of God). But Ripley's psychosis resides in his conviction that *only* the big Other exists. Tom is not troubled by specific, named others being aware of, or suspecting, his criminality, so long as his crimes are not Symbolically inscribed. What is distinctive about Ripley's postmodern take on the big Other is that it is radically atheistic — he neither believes in God nor in any moral order written into the fabric of the universe. The postmodern big Other is a Symbolic Order stripped of its symbolisation of itself; it no longer poses as God or History and openly announces itself as a social construct — but this ostensible demystification does nothing to impede its functioning. On the contrary, the big Other has never functioned more effectively.

methods of dreaming[1]

Two novels that — purely by coincidence, or so it would seem — I happened to read one after the other which both draw on dreaming, but which emphasise opposite poles of the dreaming experience.

Christopher Priest's *A Dream Of Wessex* (1977) is about a collective dreaming project, a government-sponsored initiative to tap the unconscious in order to come up with solutions to the economic and political problems that have paralysed the society in the novel's present day of 1985. In the projected future world, the USA has converted to Islam and the UK has been annexed by the Soviet Union. The result is a strange kind of utopia, in which the bureaucratic provides a background to the bucolic: the irritations of the Soviet official machinery seem built into the dreamspace as a necessary precondition for the aching languor of the Wessex idyll, where everyday life is suffused by a Mediterranean eroticism. Priest conjures the atmosphere of a gentle solar trance, broken, significantly, by small circular mirrors, which are used to trigger the dreamer's return to the dismal drizzle of the novel's real world.

Once inside the Wessex projection, the participants cannot remember their real world identities. This means that, although they are referred to by the same name, the dreamers in the simulation are different entities from their real world counterparts (just as any dreamer is a different being from their double in waking life). A classic case of the Real (of unconscious wishes) versus reality. When they exit the Wessex simulation, the dreamers are replaced in the consensual hallucination by placeholder doppelgangers, programmed selves that, possessing no inner life, only exist for the Others in the dreamspace. Some of the participants come to recognise the points at which other dreamers depart from the simulation and come back to it: something in the other, that which is in them more than themselves perhaps, disappears or (seemingly miraculously) returns. What the novel renders especially powerfully is the overwhelming, intoxicating intensity of erotic connections with a dream Other, the uncanny sense of recognition, the deja vu of dreamlove. In the case of *A Dream Of Wessex*, the sense of recognition between the lovers can be accounted for by the fact that the two, Julia and David, know each other in the novel's real world; and yet Julia and David are not in love in the real world, nor is there any suggestion that they would necessarily fall in love. It is their dream-selves that fall for each other. What ultimately unsettles the idyll is the kind of reality bleed or ontological haemorrhage which Priest's later novels all turn around. *A Dream Of Wessex* looks forward to Gibson's cyberspace, but it is also a vision of the Sixties recalled at the bitter end of the Seventies.

Kazuo Ishiguro's *The Unconsoled* (1995) makes contact with another kind of dream space-time altogether. The novel is well-titled since it plunges us, like Alice projected into Wonderland, into a world without consolation, a world of unrelieved *urgencies*. This is the first and most obvious point of contrast with *A Dream Of Wessex*, where the official imperatives, both inside and outside the dreamspace, operate as receding pretexts for libidinal trajectories which depart from "what should be happening" (this tendency puts the whole project at risk). In *The Unconsoled*, the official too recedes, but assumes now not the benign quality of the libidinal pretext (the ostensible goal which allows jouissance to happen precisely by being endlessly missed) but the tortuous, tantalising, thwarted object whose failure to be attained casts a pall of terrible anxiety over everything.

Upon arriving in a nameless central European city to give a performance, the renowned pianist Ryder finds himself assailed by countless demands which distract him from his official duties, but which he seems powerless to resist. He must listen to young hopefuls playing the piano; he must speak at late-night meetings of which he was not previously aware; he must go to the outskirts of the city and be photographed in front of a monument whose significance he does not understand. New urgencies are embedded within older urgencies, endlessly.

The Unconsoled is, in part, a pastiche of Kafka, and what Ishiguro borrows from Kafka above all else is his oneiric geography, at once bizarre and strangely familiar. Spaces which had seemed to be very far from one another are suddenly revealed to be adjacent; a meeting hall which Ryder has traveled to turns out to be the very hotel that he started from. This allows problems which had seemed intractable to suddenly resolve themselves; yet the solutions bring no relief, for by now Ryder has been gripped by another urgency. The previous imperative, once so overwhelmingly important, recedes into irrelevance at the moment the next one arrives.

In *The Unconsoled*, as in Kafka, this perverse spatiality of *contiguity without consistency* arises because all space (and time) is subordinated to the urgency.

There is no time except that of the urgency; and all space is curved by the urgency (and its frustrations). Obstacles suddenly emerge: most notably a wall that inexplicably looms up at the last moment preventing Ryder from getting to the concert hall where he is due to give his recital. The hectic pace is driven by the improvisational logic of retrospective confabulation, which is always making sense of things a moment too late. Ryder is perpetually noticing things that should have been obvious. As with Kafka, then, *The Unconsoled* is coloured by an ingenue's sense of embarrassment.

Two opposed methods of dreaming, then: the one languid, laconic, the other harried, harassed.

atwood's anti-capitalism[1]

"Regressive it all is", Jameson remarks of the "God's Gardeners" cult in Atwood's *The Year of the Flood,* adding a provocative parenthesis: "it is always helpful to wonder what politics today could possibly be otherwise."[2] *The Year of the Flood* is disappointing in part because it has no alternatives to regression — the only way forward, it seems, is back to nature.

It isn't the focus on religion per se that is the signature of this regression; rather, it is Atwood's retreat from the questions about religion that *Oryx and Crake* posed so intriguingly. One of the climactic moments of *Oryx* was the foundation of religious feeling amongst the lab-designed neo-noble savages, the Crakers. As per *Totem and Taboo* and *Moses And Monotheism,* the religion emerges as a consequence of the death of the father figure. Ironies abound here: since the "Crakers" were made, not begotten, the "father" is actually their creator-designer, the misanthropic wunderkind Crake — who had precisely designed them *without* the neurological configuration which he believes gives rise to religion. Crake is not so much an eliminative materialist as a materialist eliminativist: "Crake thought he'd done away with all that, eliminated what he called the G-spot in the brain. *God is a cluster of neurons,* he'd maintained. It had been a difficult problem, though: take out too much in the area and you got a zombie or a psychopath." If, at first sight, the emergence of religion amongst the Crakers appears to be a kind of miracle, in the end it is only a testament to the power of other (psychoanalytic and cultural) determining factors in addition to neurology.

Crake's experiments constitute a retort to the hoary old reactionary homily that utopia is alien to human nature. (For a recent version of this, see one of the antagonists in Žižek's latest book, the uber-capitalist realist Guy Sorman[3], with his claim that, "[w]hatever the truths uncovered by economic science, the free market is finally only the reflection of human nature, itself hardly perfectible.") If that's the case, Crake concludes with the pragmatism of the autist, we should change human nature: the means are now available. Crake in effect responds to Freud's argument in *Civilisation and its Discontents* that, even if property relations were made egalitarian, antagonism would continue to arise because of sexual competition. "Maybe Crake was right," Snowman reflects,

> Under the old dispensation, sexual competition had been relentless and cruel: for every pair of happy lovers there was a dejected onlooker, the one excluded. Love was its own transparent bubble-dome you could see the two inside it, but you couldn't get in there yourself. That had been the milder form: the single man at the window, drinking himself into oblivion to the mournful strains of the tango. But such things could escalate into violence. Extreme emotions could be lethal. *If I can't have you nobody will*, and so forth. Death could set in.[4]

So Crake replaces what Toby in *The Year of the Flood* calls "romantic pain" with sedate animal courtship rituals. "Their sexuality was not a constant torment to them, not a cloud of turbulent hormones: they came into heat and regular intervals, as did most other mammals other than man."[5] It would have been fascinating for Atwood to have given a fictional testing to Crake's claim to have eliminated hierarchy, hunger and racism amongst his genetic creations. There's also the problem of language. The Crakers are able to maintain their genetically-designed innocence, Atwood suggests, because they lack the past subjunctive tense. ("[T]he idea of the immortality of the soul [...] was a consequence of grammar. And so was God, because as soon as there is a past tense, there has to be a past before the past until you get to *I don't know*, and that's what God is. It's what you don't know — the dark, the hidden, the underside of the visible, and all because we have grammar."[6] But, this too, is fixable with a little genetic engineering: "[G]rammar would be impossible without the FoxP2 gene gene.")

Yet the loss of Crake — which is nothing less than an encounter with loss and negation itself — threatens to project the Crakers out of their animal-time into the wounded time of human abjection. But the Crakers recede from focus in *The Year of the Flood*: a sign, perhaps, that Atwood has lost interest in them, or — maybe — that such creatures cannot elicit much interest from beings such as us. What looms to the fore in the narrative is the progressive-regressive religious form that a less pacific group of humans cleave to in the dying days of the world.

Atwood has said that one inspiration for the creation of the eco-religion was "the death of her father and mother [...] and the necessity to choose hymns for their funerals that would have been acceptable to them: both were scientists." It's easy to sneer at the difficulty that Atwood touches upon here, and the familiar problems of reconciling religion and science may ultimately be less intractable than the issue of symbolic deficit in contemporary secularism that she is pointing to. Atheism has yet to come up with rituals that can muster the symbolic weight of religion, and there are strong reasons to suspect that the failure is more than a contingent one. That's because Atheism typically construes the death of God in terms of a disavowal of the Symbolic (=big Other) itself. There's a close fit between this quintessentially postmodern disavowal — where official denial of the existence of the big Other is combined with a de facto observance of the symbolic at another level — and capitalist realism. As Althusser realised, the rituals of capitalist ideology function all the better for not being acknowledged as rituals at all. In place of the intransigent solemnity of the religious ritual, postmodern secularism presents us with either an eschewal of ritual altogether (no need for any kind ceremony), or "write-your-own-vows" personalisation, or a kind of ersatz humanist-kitsch, in which religious form is preserved even as belief in a supernatural God is denied. The problem is not a secular "lack of meaning", but almost the opposite: it is religious rituals' very meaninglessness, their lack of *personal* significance, which gives them much of their power. Partly, as Jameson suggests in his *LRB* piece on *The Year of the Flood*, the problem is time: any new "belief system" "demands a supplement in the form of deep time, ancient cultural custom, or revelation itself". Time precisely allows a ritual to become a custom, an empty form to which the individual is subjected — and, very far from being a disadvantage, this is what yields funeral rites much of their power to console.

Mourning and loss are not only at the origins of religion, but also, it goes without saying, at the root of much of its continuing appeal. One of the most contentious — and borderline acrimonious — discussions amongst students that I've seen for a while came up in a session on Philosophy of Religion that I taught earlier this year. What prompted the controversy was my contention that atheism has far more of a problem with evil and suffering than religion does — not least because of the suffering of those who are now dead. Ivan Karamazov's howl of anguish can be directed at the atheist architects of the radiant city as much as at God, since what can any revolutionary eschatology, no matter how glorious, do about the agonies of those who are long dead? No amount of secular good will can *guarantee* any correlation between virtue and happiness, as Kant argues in an incendiary passage of "The Critique of Teleological Judgment":

> Deceit, violence, and envy will be rife around [the righteous non-believer], even though he himself is benevolent. Moreover, as concerns the other righteous people, he meets: no matter how worthy of happiness they may be, nature, which pays no attention to that, will still subject them to all

the evils of deprivation, disease, and untimely death, just like all the other animals on the earth. And they will stay subjected to these evils always, until one vast tomb engulfs them one and all (honest or not, that makes no difference here), and hurls them, who managed to believe that they were the final purpose of creation, back into the abyss of the purposeless chaos of matter from which they were taken.[7]

Note also that Kant's argument here applies equally well to the neo-paganism of God's Gardeners as it does to "righteous non-believers", for Kant absolutely refuses the equation of nature with beneficence that the Gardeners preach. On the contrary, Kant argues, God is necessary to *make good* a nature characterised by amoral purposelessness. The true atheist must be able to look this "vast tomb", this "abyss of purposeless chaos", full in the face — whereas I suspect that most (of us) non-believers manage only to look away from it. But Kant's moral argument is less easily dismissed than it would appear, because it is far harder to eliminate belief in a providential structure of the universe than we first imagine — precisely because this kind of belief lurks far beneath anything that we would admit to accepting. (Watch an edition of *Deal or No Deal*, though, and it's clear that many openly evince such a belief.) Perhaps it would indeed take a Crake's genetic tinkering to eradicate it.

The problem with *The Year of the Flood* is that politics and religion become synonymous — and while there's every reason to be positive about politicised religion, there are deep problems with a politics which cannot shed the redemptive and messianic mantles of religious eschatology. It's striking how much God's Gardeners resemble the Greens as abominated by Sorman, in a passage quoted in *First As Tragedy, Then As Farce*:

> No ordinary rioters, the Greens are the priests of a new religion that puts nature above humankind. The ecology movement is not a nice peace-and-love lobby but a revolutionary force. Like many a modern-day religion, its designated evils are ostensibly decried on the basis of scientific knowledge: global warming, species extinction, loss of biodiversity, superweeds. In fact, all these threats are figments of the Green imagination. Greens borrow their vocabulary for science without availing themselves of its rationality. Their method is not new; Marx and Engels also pretended to root their world vision in the science of their time, Darwinism.[8]

Atwood makes a case for such a religion. (Clarifactory note: just to be 100% clear — I in no way endorse Sorman's views of the Greens. I just thought it was amusing that Atwood constructed an eco-cult which so closely fitted Sorman's stereotype.) In an exchange with Richard Dawkins on *Newsnight* a couple of weeks ago, Atwood maintained that arguing against religion from the perspective of evolution makes little sense, because the persistence of religion itself suggests that it confers evolutionary benefit on humans. Given this, Atwood suggested, religion should be used as a tool for "progressive" struggles; and Adam One, the leader of God's Gardeners, is interesting only when he sounds like a Machiavelli or a Strauss, who uses religion to manipulate popular sentiment — the rest of the time his eco-piousness is made bearable only by virtue of Atwood's gentle satirical teasing (witness, for instance, the convolutions into which Gardener-doctrine is forced in its attempts to reconcile vegetarianism with both the carnivore-bias of the Bible and the "amoral chaos" of a nature red in tooth and claw). Initially, what appeals about the idea of God's Gardeners is the promise that Atwood will describe a new kind of political organisation. Yet the Gardeners' doctrine and structure turns out to be a disappointing ragbag of stale and drab *No Logo*-like anti-consumerist asceticism, primitivist lore, natural remedies and self-defence that is as alluring as last week's patchouli oil. Ultimately, *The Year of the Flood* feels like a symptom of the libidinal and symbolic impasses of so much so-called anti-capitalism. Atwood imagines the end of capitalism, but only after the end of the world. *Oryx* was like the first part of *Wall-E*; *The Year of the Flood* is like the second part, where we find that the last survivor was nothing of the sort, and there were existing bands of human beings already wandering around, mysteriously just out of sight. (At least in *Wall-E* the surviving humans were off-world, whereas in *Oryx*, we are now asked to believe, they had somehow remained just outside Snowman's eyeline.) It has a retrospectively deflationary effect, subtracting most of the pathos and nobility from Snowman's plight, and converting what had seemed like a cyberpunk-Beckett tragicomedy into mere comedy. (Incidentally, perhaps the greatest "achievement" of *The Year of the Flood* is that, by the end, it no longer feels like an Atwood novel at all. Instead, it's written in the kind of functional prose of a middling Stephen King novel, and populated by cyberpunk genre-standard hardass women, in a post-apocalyptic setting which is surprisingly lacking in vividness. The result is what Robert Macfarlane memorably calls a "dystoap-opera".)

The question that kept recurring when I was reading both *Oryx and Crake* and *The Year of the Flood* was: why do these books not succeed in the way that *The Handmaid's Tale* did? If *The Handmaid's Tale* was an exemplary dystopia, it was because the novel made contact with the *Imaginary-Real* of neoconservatism. Gilead was "Real" at the level of a neo-conservative desire that was operating in the Reaganite Eighties; a virtual present that conditioned the actual present. Offred, the handmaids, the Marthas, the Wall — these names have the resonant consistency of a world. But Atwood does not have so assured a handle on neoliberalism as she did on neoconservatism. Atwood gives every appearance of underestimating the cheap poetry of brands, banal as it is; her corporate names are ugly and clunky, no doubt deliberately so — perhaps this is the way that she hears the absurd infantilisms of late capitalist semiotics. AnooYoo, HelthWyzer, Happicuppa, ReJoovenEssens, and — most ungainly of all — Sea(H)ear Candies: these practically caused me physical pain to read, and it is hard to conceive of any world in which these would be leading brands. Atwood's mistake is always the same — the names are unsightly plays on the function or service that the corporations offer, whereas capitalism's top brand names — Coca-Cola, Google, Starbucks — have attained an asignifying abstraction, in which any reference to what the corporation does is merely vestigial. Capitalist semiotics echo capital's own tendency towards ever-increasing abstraction. (For the Imaginary-Real of neoliberalism, you'd be far better off reading Nick Land's Nineties texts, shortly to be re-published.) Atwood's names for genetically-spliced animals — the pigoon, the spoat/gider, the liobam — are also examples of linguistic butchery; perhaps she was trying to provide a parallel in language for the denaturalising violence of genetic engineering. In any case, these linguistic monsters are unlikely to roam far beyond Atwood's texts (they certainly don't have anything like the dark sleekness and hyperstitional puissance of, say, Gibson's neologisms).

But the principal failing of *The Year of the Flood*'s anti-capitalism consists in its inability to grasp the way in which capitalism has absorbed the organic and the green. Some of the strongest passages in Žižek's *First As Tragedy, Then As Farce* keep reiterating this message. (One of my favourite lines in the book: "Who really believes that half-rotten and overpriced 'organic' apples are really healthier than the non-organic varieties?") Needless to say, while any credible leftism must make ecological issues central it is a mistake to seek out an "authentic" organicism beyond capitalism's simulated-organic. (Another of my favourite lines in *First As Tragedy*: "if there is one good thing about capitalism, it is that, precisely, mother earth now no longer exists.") Organicism is the problem, and it's not some eco-spirituality that will save the human environment (if it can be saved), but new modes of organisation and management.

toy stories: puppets, dolls and horror stories[1]

"In many horror stories there is an assortment of figures that appear as walk-ons or extras whose purpose is to lend their spooky presence to a narrative for atmosphere alone, while the real bogey is something else altogether. Puppets, dolls, and other caricatures of the human often make cameo appearances as shapes sagging in the corner of a child's bedroom or lolling on the shelves of a toy store [...] As backdrops or bit-players, imitations of the human form have a symbolic value because they seem connected to another world, one that is all harm and disorder- the kind of place we sometimes feel is a model for our own home ground, which we must believe is passably sound and secure, or at least not an environment where we might mistake a counterfeit person for the real thing."
— Thomas Ligotti, *The Conspiracy Against the Human Race*[2]

So writes the horror author Thomas Ligotti in his recently published book, *The Conspiracy Against the Human Race*. The book is not a work of fiction — it is, instead, a work of amateur philosophy in the best possible sense, driven by a metaphysical hunger that is so often lacking in the work of professional philosophers. Ligotti is unembarrassed to return to those questions which academic philosophers typically disdain in favour of an entanglement in scholarly minutiae. Why is there something rather than nothing? Should we be glad to be alive? Ligotti's answer to this latter question is emphatically in the negative. Possessed of a cold, sober seriousness that couldn't be more at odds with the atmosphere of cheery vitalism and inane lightness that prevails in early twenty-first-century culture, *The Conspiracy Against the Human Race* has the feel of a nineteenth-century tract.

Puppets are one of the leitmotifs of Ligotti's work, but the terror that they cause does not primarily arise from any malicious intentions on their part, or from the suspicion that they might secretly move when we do not watch them. Rather, the puppet is an emissary of what Ligotti repeatedly characterises in *The Conspiracy Against the Human Race* as the "malignantly useless" nature of the cosmos itself. The painted-faced marionette is a symbol of the horror of consciousness, the instrument which, for Ligotti, allows that "malignant uselessness" to be perceived, and which brings all suffering into the world.

The puppet is a figure which belongs equally as much to the children's story as to the weird tale. Ian Penman has written of how the most famous puppet story, Carlo Collodi's *The Adventures of Pinocchio* (1883),

> contains scarcely credible levels of cruelty and pain [...] Accusations of abuse. Thrown hammers. Burned-off feet. Children used as firewood: innocence kindling. Curiosity rewarded with concussion and kidnap. Hanging, amputation, suffocation. A snake laughs so hard at Pinocchio's fear he bursts an artery and dies. On his way to school Pinocchio sells his schoolbooks to join a Street Theatre: forget education, become a marionette. A dancing fool. Apprentice Golem. Malignant clown. Neuter, castrato.

(Penman's remarks were made in the piece that he contributed to a book on Michael Jackson I edited last year — and Jackson's own story is one in which kitsch and Gothic, puppet and master manipulator, frequently reversed into one another.[3])

On his blog on memory and technology, *Bat, Bean, Beam*, the theorist Giovanni Tiso recently noted the echoes of *Pinocchio* in the *Toy Story* films.[4] For the Marxist Richard Seymour,

> *Toy Story 3* is a story of how freedom is achieved through commodification, and how "the consent of the governed" roughly equals the willing embrace of bondage [...] Everyone, and everything, has its place in the *Toy Story* scheme of things. That scheme is a hierarchy of commodities with toys near the bottom, subordinate and devoted to their owners.[5]

Yet, at an *ontological* level, the *Toy Story* films constitute something of a "tangled hierarchy". The toys that are depicted in the films do not only exist at the "ontologically inferior" level of the film's fiction; they are real in the sense that you can buy them outside the cinema. In Ligotti, puppets and puppetry frequently symbolise this tangling of ontological hierarchy: what should be at the "inferior" level of the manipulated manikin suddenly achieves agency, and, even more horrifyingly, what is at the supposedly "superior" level of the puppet master suddenly finds itself drawn into the marionette theatre. Ligotti writes that it is a terrible fate indeed

100

when a human being becomes objectified as a puppet and enters a world that he or she thought was just a creepy place inside of ours. What a jolt to find oneself a prisoner in this sinister sphere, reduced to a composite mechanism looking out on the land of the human, or that which we believe to be human by any definition of it, and yet be exiled from it.

With Ligotti, it is not clear which is the more terrifying prospect — an ultimate puppet master pulling the strings or the strings fraying off into blind senseless chaos.

Tiso noticed something peculiar about the desire of the toys in the *Toy Story* series: "what they like best is to be played with by children. But it so happens that at those times they are limp and inanimate; as is the case whenever they are in the presence of people, their spark abandons them, their eyes become vacant."[6] It's as if the message of the *Toy Story* films rhymes with that of Ligotti's pessimistic tract: consciousness is not a blessing bestowed on us by a kindly toymaker standing in for a beneficent God, but a loathsome curse.

ZerO books statement[1]

Contemporary culture has eliminated both the concept of the public and the figure of the intellectual. Former public spaces — both physical and cultural — are now either derelict or colonised by advertising. A cretinous anti-intellectualism presides, cheered by expensively educated hacks in the pay of multinational corporations who reassure their bored readers that there is no need to rouse themselves from their interpassive stupor. The informal censorship internalised and propagated by the cultural workers of late capitalism generates a banal conformity that the propaganda chiefs of Stalinism could only have dreamt of imposing. ZerO books knows that another kind of discourse — intellectual without being academic, popular without being populist — is not only possible: it is already flourishing, in the regions beyond the striplit malls of so-called mass media and the neurotically bureaucratic halls of the academy. ZerO is committed to the idea of publishing as a making public of the intellectual. It is convinced that in the unthinking, blandly consensual culture in which we live, critical and engaged theoretical reflection is more important than ever before.

PART TWO

SCREENS, DREAMS AND SPECTRES: FILM AND TELEVISION

a spoonful of sugar[1]

The worst aspect of Dennis Potter's final two indulgent and indulged works (*Cold Lazarus* and *Karaoke*) was that they had the effect of retrospectively introducing doubts over everything else he'd done. Could he possibly be anything like as good as we'd always believed?

Actually, there's a case for saying that, if 1986's *The Singing Detective* marked the peak of Potter's career, it also preceded a slow and painful decline. It would only be slightly harsh to say that everything after 1986 was either formulaic reiteration (*Lipstick On Your Collar*) or tortuously introspective, failed experimentalism (*Blackeyes*, the film *Secret Friends*). By the time of his death in 1994, Potter had been lionised by the great and good everywhere, his reputation for controversy forgotten (or forgiven?). Melvyn Bragg's famous interview-cum-hagiography elevated Potter to the state of an unimpeachable morphine saint. All of this solemnity had the effect of devitalising Potter's work, prematurely shrouding it with all the cobwebs of respectability and reverence.

Well, I had the opportunity to see Potter's 1976 masterpiece *Brimstone and Treacle* again very recently. (The play is shortly to be reissued as part of a must-have Potter DVD boxset, which also includes *The Singing Detective*, *Pennies from Heaven* and *Casanova*). In 2004, when TV drama is corporate, committee-driven, blandly homogenous, Potter looks even more of an anomaly than ever. Today, there's almost no way of identifying TV dramas by who has written them; they are routinely conceived of as vehicles for *actors*, not authors. By contrast, even at its worst, Potter's work was marked by an indelible signature, characterised by a singular VISION. (The tendency to fall back on these trademark elements without remixing them was one of the weaknesses of his last pieces.) It's hard to imagine that Potter's peculiar portfolio of obsessions and techniques (his playful anti-naturalism, his disturbed disquisitions on sexuality, politics and religion, his loving interrogation of the appeal of pop music and pulp genres, his exemplification/analysis of misogyny) would get past our Noughties culture's gatekeepers (which might be tolerant of representations of sex, but which are, in every other way, *more* censorious than those of the Seventies). As the *Independent* pointed out when it reappraised Potter in the light of the US film version of *The Singing Detective*, his influence is more likely to be felt on *American* than on British TV, in an expressionist drama such as *Six Feet Under* or even in the delirial departures from naturalism of something like *Ally McBeal*.

In any case, Potter did fall foul of Seventies sensibilities with *Brimstone and Treacle*. Filmed in March 1976, it was due for broadcast as a *Play for Today* in April, but was pulled at the last minute when the BBC authorities quailed at its "nauseating" qualities. It didn't surface until over a decade later, when, in the wake of the success of *The Singing Detective*, the play was eventually shown in 1987. An inferior film version, starring Sting, was released in 1982.

Brimstone and Treacle features a young Michael Kitchen as the devil. In an echo of Potter's earlier "visitation" plays, Kitchen's character, Martin, inveigles himself into people's lives and homes by cold reading them like a stage hypnotist.

Potter's vision of evil is a million miles away from the white-catting portentousness or Pacino-like histrionics to which countless clichéd cinema renderings have accustomed us. Kitchen's devil is impeccably polite, insufferably, cloyingly *nice*, sanctimoniously *religiose*. "Religiose" is a word Potter used with a particular contempt, carefully contrasting its pious pomposity with what he saw as the genuine religious sensibility.

The play opens with two epigraphs: the first from Kierkegaard's *Fear and Trembling*: "there dwells infinitely more good in a demoniac than in a trivial person", the second from *Mary Poppins* ("A spoonful of sugar helps the medicine go down"). For Kierkegaard, the most pressing danger for Christianity was not doubt, but the kind of bluff *certainty* peddled by pompous philosophers like Hegel. Kierkegaard's Faith was indistinguishable from terrible anxiety. The paradox of Faith for Kierkegaard was that, if God completely revealed himself, Faith would be unnecessary. Faith is not a form of knowing; on the contrary. Kierkegaard's models were Abraham on the day he was asked to sacrifice Isaac and Jesus' disciples: tormented by uncertainty, unmoored from any of society's ethical anchors, staking their life on fabulous improbabilities.

Martin is a perverse double of 1976's most iconic of icons, Johnny Rotten, that demonic purge of trivia and mediocrity. If Rotten's Nietzscheanism ("I yam an antichrist") concealed a burning core of righteousness, Martin's surface charm belies malevolence. At the limit though, what both Rotten and Martin show is the deep complicity of "good" and "evil", their mutual interdependence. Both Martin and Rotten are ultimately deliverers, destroyers of fragile status quos, bringers of disequilibrium and agents of chaos. Punk's greatest disgust was with the trivial and the mediocre, with the existential death of *boredom*. The decadence would be cleansed by rage (cf the apopleptic Colin Blakeley in Potter's 1969 version of Christ's life, *Son of Man*).

Brimstone and Treacle begins with Martin accosting Denholm Elliott's Mr Bates in the street. Martin's questioning quickly establishes that Bates has a daughter, suffering from apparently incurable neurological damage after being hit by a car two years previously. Posing as an unrequited admirer of the daughter, Pattie, Martin insinuates his way into the Bates' home. The house is a suburban fortress incubating quiet desperation, nagging frustration and unspoken betrayals. You can almost smell the house, thick with the stench of unaired rooms, the pulped food with which Pattie is spoonfed — and despair. Martin's incursion is greeted with initial suspicion and circumspection by Mr Bates, but welcomed by the easily beguiled Mrs Bates (Patricia Lawrence), eager to clutch at any potential escape route from the treadmill of drudgery in which she is confined. While Bates has given up any hope of Pattie recovering, his wife cherishes the seemingly impossible dream of a miraculous return to health.

Kitchen's performance is magnificent, but it is Elliott who steals the show. He manages, incredibly, to make the obnoxious and unpleasant Bates, a neophyte National Front supporter, painfully sympathetic. The scene in which Bates regales his wife and Martin with a desperately unfunny Irish "joke" is excruciating. Elliot renders Bates' typical expression as a *grimace* — of irritation, suppressed rage, bewilderment. It is the expression of a whole class, a whole generation's, incredulity that the world no longer belongs to them, if it ever did. Bates' political pathology is rooted in a bewildered and misconceived nostalgia, a bleary and inarticulate longing for the world to be like it used to be. He's a bit like the average Britpop fan would be twenty years later.

Potter is at his most politically acute here, in his exposing of the proximity of a respectable, "common-sense", *Daily Mail* agenda to that of the far right. Potter locates Anglo-fascism's Seventies heartland behind the politely manicured lawns and privet hedges of suburbia. Martin wins Bates over by agreeing with him that "we need to get rid of the blacks". "It's so good to have an intelligent conversation like this", Bates enthuses, cracking open the scotch. However, Martin's gleeful description of what will happen when "they won't go", "we'll round them up, put them in camps" — makes Bates blanche. Mrs Bates is not so convinced. "You can be too nice you know."

Brimstone and Treacle is disturbing, ethically opaque. It is troubling for reasons other than those of cultural or political conservatism. The denouement sees Martin's raping of Pattie shocking her into an unexpected recovery (which itself prompts the play's final shocking revelation, which I won't give away for the sake of those who haven't seen it yet). There is no easily digestible "message". It's a bitter pill rather than a spoonful of sugar.

she's not my mother[1]

"Interviewer: It's hard to see this movie and not consider that all our
memories are creations.
Cronenberg: But they are, they totally are."
— Andrew O'Hehir, "The Baron of Blood does Bergman"[2]

"Watch from the wings as the scenes were replaying. We saw
ourselves now as we never had seen."
— Joy Division, "Decades"[3]

Cronenberg's *Spider* — adapted from Patrick McGrath's superb novel — is
a study of schizophrenia that couldn't be further removed from the clichéd
image of "madness" in cinema. There are numerous examples of this, but
the one that comes immediately to mind (perhaps because I watched it
recently) is Windom Earl in the second season of *Twin Peaks*: gibbering,
histrionic, megalomaniac. Think also of Nicholson's Joker in the first *Batman*
movie. Madness is here imaged as a kind of absurdly inflated ego; a self
that knows no bounds, which wants to expand itself infinitely. As played
by Ralph Fiennes in Cronenberg's film, Spider, too, has a precarious sense
of his own limits, but, far from wanting to spread further into the world,
he seems to want to make himself disappear. Everything about him — his
mumbling speech, shambling movements — screams withdrawal, retreat,
terror of the outside. That's because, as ever in Cronenberg's schizoverse,
the outside is already inside. And the reverse.

McGrath's novel is set *entirely* within the head of its archetypal unreliable
narrator, Spider, since it is written as a series of diary entries. To simulate
this, Cronenberg could have gone with the strategy employed in the early
versions of the script and used voiceover (although anyone who's seen

Spike Jonze's *Adaptation* will remember Robert Mckee's rant about that particular technique). In the end, Cronenberg strips out Spider's narrative voice altogether, with the result that the film is, in a strange way, *truer to the novel than the novel itself*. In the novel, Spider's articulacy gives him a kind of self-awareness and (albeit limited) transcendence of his mania. In the film, there is no distance, no narrative *voice*, only a ceaselessly productive narrative *machine*, chattering out multiple permutations. In place of the transcendent offscreen voice, we are presented with Spider as a character in his own delirium, the adult version of himself observing and writing, always writing, as the memories of his childhood life play out. As Cronenberg has observed, it is almost as if Spider is *directing his own memories*. "One journalist said to me, 'When we see Spider in his own memories, peeking in the windows or hiding in the corner, isn't that like a director being on the set?' I hadn't thought of it that way, but he is redirecting and rechoreographing his memories."[4] We are reminded that the dreamer is every character in his dream.

So *Spider* develops a naturalistic expressionism, or expressionist naturalism. Its strangely solitary London is, Cronenberg says, an expressionist London. *Spider* captures the boiled potatoes atmosphere of the pre-rock 'n' roll Fifties, its muted colours as washed out as cabbage water.

The film of Cronenberg's which *Spider* most resembles is *Naked Lunch*; not only because it, too, is based upon a supposedly unadaptable book, but also because both films principally concern writing, insanity, masculinity and the death of a woman. In both *Naked Lunch* and *Spider*, the phantasmatically reiterated murder of a woman is the pivotal event, the lacuna around which the films circle. In *Naked Lunch*, Lee initially disavows the killing of his wife Joan by attributing it to the influence of Control. Lee is only able to accept minimal responsibility for the killing when he is "required", at the end of the film, to assassinate Joan, or at least her double, again. The re-staging of the death is less an admission of ethical responsibility than an attempt to own it, to make sense of it. Such is the logic of trauma. (Reminding us of Ballard's description of the motives of the schizo in *The Atrocity Exhibition*: "He wanted to kill Kennedy again, but this time in a way that made sense.")

In *Spider* we are initially led to believe that Spider's father, Bill Cleg (Horace in the novel) has killed Spider's mother after embarking on an affair with the "fat tart" Yvonne (Hilda in the novel). No sooner has Bill brutally and casually murdered his wife, rolling her into a hastily dug grave in the earth of his allotment ("out with the old", Yvonne callously cackles), than he moves Yvonne into his home. At this point, our suspicions that something is amiss with Spider's narration begins to harden into a conviction. But it's only at the end of the film that we learn what appears to have really happened: it is Spider himself who killed his mother, gassing her whilst apparently suffering from a delusion that she is another person. The early exchanges between Spider and his father take on a different significance (Spider: *"She's* not my mother". Bill: "Well, who is she then?") The final scene sees Bill rescuing Spider from the house, and desperately trying to revive Yvonne, who in death, has become, once again, the dark-haired Mrs Cleg.

While this seems to be the preferred interpretation, the film does not close down any of the narrative possibilities it has opened up. I think we can enumerate nine distinct narrative options that the film leaves open:

1. Bill killed his wife, and he really did co-habit with a prostitute called Yvonne.
2. Bill did kill his wife, there really is an Yvonne, but she never moved in with Spider's father.
3. Bill killed his wife, but there is no such a person as Yvonne.
4. Spider, not Bill, killed his mother, but Bill moved in with Yvonne after his wife's death.
5. Spider killed his mother, there is a prostitute called Yvonne, but she never moved in with Spider's father.
6. Spider killed his mother, and there is no such person as Yvonne.
7. Neither Spider nor Bill killed Mrs Cleg, but Bill moved in with Yvonne after his mother's death.
8. Neither Spider nor Bill killed Mrs Cleg, there really is an Yvonne, but she never moved in with the Clegs.
9. Neither Spider nor Bill killed Mrs Cleg, and there is no such person as Yvonne.

Rather than resolving the ambiguities of McGrath's novel, the film actually amplifies them. In the novel, we at least learn (it seems) that Spider has been incarcerated for killing his mother (even though he continues to maintain that it was his father who was responsible for the death). In the film, the twenty years between Mrs Cleg's death and Spider's arrival at the halfway house are a blank. We know, or think we know, by inference, that he has been in a psychiatric institution, but no more.

Miranda Richardson's performance is crucial to the maintenance of the film's polysemous ambiguity. She is superb in three different roles: as the virtuous brunette Mrs Cleg, the licentious blonde Yvonne and also as the suddenly and inappropriately sexually aggressive landlady of the halfway house, Mrs Wilkinson. The situation is complicated by the fact that Yvonne is played at first by *another* actress altogether (at least, I *think* that is the case; it is a tribute to the film's queasy delirium and to Richardson's performance, that I'm just not sure), just as Mrs Wilkinson is played for most of the film by Lynne Redgrave.

As in *Naked Lunch*, writing is both passive and active. Like Bill Lee, Spider, scratching away in his notebook in his idiolectic hieroglyphics, seems at one level only to be recording signal from outside; at another level, he is the producer of the whole scene, its derealiser.

Talking about the film, Cronenberg has referred to Nabokov's theory of memory and art as attempts to recover the unrecoverable. But the figure that dominates the film is another writer who, like Nabokov, Brian McHale has referred to as a "limit-modernist", Samuel Beckett. Cronenberg has said that Spider's *look*, with its shock of spiky hair, was very much influenced by photographs of Beckett, but the affinity with Beckett goes much deeper. Like Molloy or Malone, Spider is continually fumbling in his pockets for talismanic objects. Such partial objects mark the routes on their "intensive voyages". Like McGrath, Cronenberg seduces us into identification with Spider (Cronenberg: "I am Spider"), taking us with him on his schizo-stroll, then strands us in the delirium…

stand up, nigel barton[1]

"I remember, I remember
The school where I was born;
I remember, I remember,
The school where I was... torn."
— Dennis Potter, *The Nigel Barton Plays*[2]

"And nowadays what else does education and culture want! In our
age of the people —I mean our uncouth age — 'education' and
'culture' must basically be the art of deception, to mislead about the
origin of the inherited rabble in one's body and soul."
— Friedrich Nietzsche, *Beyond Good and Evil*[3]

Dennis Potter's *Stand Up, Nigel Barton*, shown as part of BBC 4's "Summer
of the Sixties" season, is still almost too painful to watch.

Here is Potter writing a television play which draws very closely upon
his experiences as a scholarship boy, projected out of his class into the
rarefied world of Oxford. *Stand Up, Nigel Barton* was actually written after
Vote, Vote, Vote for Nigel Barton, Potter's fictionalised account of his failed
attempt to become elected as a Labour MP. To Potter's disgust, *Vote, Vote,
Vote* was suppressed by the BBC, but its temporary banning allowed him
to work again with the characters he had invented, writing this prequel
which would be shown first.

English fiction has always been ambivalent about social mobility. Potter's
theme was very much one with which the Sixties would be preoccupied,
in music as much as drama. Consider the Kinks ("Rosy, won't you please
come home", "See my friends/they cross the river") or the Who ("I was born
with a plastic spoon in my mouth"). Like Dickens' Pip, Nigel is profoundly

torn; unwilling to give up the privilege and status he has newly acquired, unable to accept and enjoy them as one to the manner born, simultaneously holding onto his roots and repudiating them, never forgetting where he has come from, but ashamed of the stains that his origins have left upon him. And *ashamed of that shame*. Never comfortable amongst the masters, but no longer at home in the community which produced him.

Forty years on, and the screen still crackles with rage, confusion and embarrassment. Potter intercuts between the working men's club, the bedrock of the proletarian community, with its "suffocating affection" but deep suspicion, resentment and distrust of those who leave; and the smug redoubt of the Oxford Union, whose louche members idly trade *bon mots* ("Oxford", as Nigel observes in his somewhat too histrionic style, "where nothing really matters", where a dissolute, ironic detachment is the mark of a gentleman, and where Nigel's very passion marks him out as *not quite right*).

Who can watch the final scene — Nigel at home with his parents, watching himself being interviewed on television about class — without cringing? What Nigel says about his father "watching him like a hawk", about "walking a tightrope", about class only being experienced by those who move between classes; none of this is a distortion. And yet, Nigel is too much in love with his own cleverness, too much attached to the *role* of alienated working-class boy that he has been invited to play. He knows he has betrayed his parents. His father, ambivalent about him at the best of times, both proud and resentful, simmers; his mother, uncomprehending, weeps, "But it's clean. You could eat off the floor here..."

Potter shows that he can do naturalism painfully and powerfully. But he's already exploring more expressionistic techniques: playing with chronology, breaking the frame (adults playing children, characters speaking directly to camera). The origin of the famous classroom scene in *The Singing Detective* is here, with Janet Henfrey taking on the role of the terrifyingly inquisitorial, witch-like schoolmistress she will reprise in the later play. The performances, especially Keith Barron as Nigel and Jack Woolgar as his father, are universally superb.

No need to reiterate, by now, my lament for TV drama this challenging, this near-the-knuckle, this relevant. But what a nihilistic message Potter conveys. There is nothing to aspire to, nothing you'd want to return to. Nigel trapped and alone, forever alone...

With *Stand Up, Nigel Barton* I knew that in small family groupings — that is, at their most vulnerable — both coalminers and Oxford dons would probably see the play. This could add enormously to the potency of a story which attempted to use the specially English embarrassment about class in a deliberately embarrassing series of confrontations. In the theatre — or, at least, in the West End — the audience would have been largely only on one side of this particular fence. There is no other medium which could virtually guarantee an audience of millions with a full quota of manual workers and stockbrokers for a "serious" play about class.[4]

portmeirion: an ideal for living[1]

"As the bourgeoisie laboured to produce the economic as a separate domain, partitioned off from its intimate and manifold interconnectedness with the festive calendar, so they laboured *conceptually* to reform the fair as *either* a rational, commercial trading event *or* as a popular pleasure-ground. As the latter, the fair had from classical times been subject to regulation and suppression on both political and moral grounds. But although the bourgeois classes were frequently frightened by the threat of political subversion and moral licence, they were perhaps more scandalised by the deep conceptual confusion entailed by the fair's inmixing of work and pleasure, trade and play. In so far as the fair was *purely* a site of pleasure, it could be envisaged as a discrete entity: local, festive, communal, unconnected to the 'real' world. In so far as it was *purely* a commercial event it could be envisaged as a practical agency in the progress of capital, an instrument of modernisation and a means of connecting up local and communal 'markets' to the world market."
— Peter Stallybrass and Allon White, "The Fair, the Pig, Authorship"[2]

If you know about Portmeirion, it's almost certainly because of *The Prisoner*, justly recognised as one of the most innovative television series ever produced (more on which presently). Our tendency is to think of Portmeirion, built by gentlemen-philanthropist Sir Clough Williams-Ellis on his private peninsula near Porthmadog, as a quaintly attractive divertissement; an example of charming English eccentricity that has somehow fetched up in Wales. The subtext we don't even need to articulate to ourselves (so we think) is that all this — attractiveness, eccentricity, charm — are harmless, which is to say, pleasant but ultimately irrelevant. The idea that they could have political-economic significance; that's more absurd than Ellis' absurdist architecture, surely?

It's fitting that I should have encountered both Ellis' village and Llandudno's homage to Lewis Carroll in the same week, in Wales, since both belong to an ex-centric Britishness that is as at least as important as Magritte's Belgian Surrealism. Remember that André Breton thought that the British — with Edward Lear, Lewis Carroll and their ludic ilk — had little need of Surrealism, since they were already Surrealist... But Artaud, who could hardly have been accused of being over-conscious, was an admirer of Carroll; as were the Situationists, who recognised that there was something utterly serious about English Nonsense. As did Deleuze, of course, who produced what is one of the strangest landmarks in Psychedelic Reason, *The Logic of Sense*, as a rigorous philosophical exposition of Carroll's Nonsense. (One of its most inciting sections is an account of Artaud's translation of "Jabberwocky".)

But it's worth pausing and thinking a little more about the Situationists. It's disastrous that the Situationist insistence upon the ludic has degenerated into a smugonautic celebration of bourgeois circus trickery (juggling and unicylcists as the shock troops of the revolution against Corporate Kapital). You have to reread Ivan Chtcheglov's astonishing "Formulary for a New Urbanism"[3] — written in the year of our current Queen's coronation, 1953 — to be reminded of the force of the Situationist critique. How could architecture — i.e. the places in which we live — not be an intensely political matter? And why should we live in boring, utilitarian spaces when we could live in grottoes and crooked caverns? "A mental disease has swept the planet: banalisation. Everyone is hypnotised by production and conveniences..."

Like punk, Surrealism is dead as soon as it is reduced to an aesthetic style. It comes unlive again when it is instantiated as a delirial program (just as punk comes unlive when it is effectuated as an anti-authoritarian, acephalic contagion-network). Chtcheglov resists the aestheticisation of Surrealism, and treats De Chirico's paintings, for instance, not as particular aesthetic contrivances, but as architectural blueprints, ideals for living. Let's not look at a De Chirico painting — let's live in one. Chtcheglov's call was astonishingly pre-empted by Clough Williams-Ellis' building of Portmeirion. Ellis described himself as follows:

> He almost certainly has a weakness for splendour and display and believes that even if he were reduced to penury himself he would still hope to be cheered by the sight of uninhibited lavishness & splendour unconfined somewhere which is why he feels that Copenhagen's Tivoli Gardens or something like them should be spread around the civilised world giving everyone a taste of lavishness, gaiety and cultivated design.[4]

Ellis recognised, that is to say, that the production of the aesthetic as a category separate from the "necessary" (i.e. the utile, in the Bataille restricted economy sense) was complicit in a kind of (from any rational POV) inexplicable diminution of the possibilities of human experience. Why must architecture be part of a banalising culture of vampiric undeath? Why should only the privileged be able to enjoy their surroundings? Why should the poor be penned into miserable concrete blocks?

Ellis referred to beauty as a "strange necessity", cutting through the binary of needs = biological and aesthetic = cultural luxury. Bodies deprived of attractive surroundings were as likely to be as depressed — or to use the superbly multivalent Rasta term, *downpressed* — as those deprived of anything they more obviously "needed".

According to the Portmeirion website,[5] Ellis sought, in the building of Portmeirion, to demonstrate that it was possible to develop sites of natural beauty without destroying them:

> A tireless campaigner for the environment Clough was a founder member of both the Council for the Protection of Rural England in 1926 and the Campaign for the Protection of Rural Wales in 1928 (and of which he was president for twenty years). He was an advocate of rural preservation, amenity planning, industrial design and colourful architecture.

The fact that *The Prisoner* was filmed here then is in no sense an accident. In addition to its Foucauldian analyses of power ("you are Number 1"), its — in every good sense — existentialism, its PKD-like psychedelic dismantling of identity, *The Prisoner* was a withering account of the English class system. McGoohan, auteur-actor, was given an artistic licence by the then head of ITV (yes, remember, *The Prisoner* appeared on ITV — I know it beggars belief now), Lew Grade — both were outsiders (McGoohan an American-born Irishman, Grade a Jew) who had penetrated into the genteel brutality of the English Core's gentlemen's club. However irascible they sometimes became, the series of Number 2's typically had that impermeable urbane assurance so infuriatingly characteristic of the English Core Master Class. Power expressed itself not in crude force — whenever that was used (cf the episode "Hammer into Anvil") you knew that they had in every sense lost it — but with the quiet, insinuating menace lurking behind an inscrutable politesse. "Cup of tea, Number 6?"

The village had all the quaint charm of politely ritualised Englishness ambivalently celebrated by the Kinks in their *Village Green Preservation Society* (which came out contemporaneously with *The Prisoner*). And of course McGoohan's genius lay in exposing the acidic undertaste of phrases like "be seeing you" and "feel free".

The Prisoner is the heir of both Kafka *and* Carroll — and part of its importance consists in its revelation of the shared sensibility. Kafka's observations of the banalising terror of the decaying Hapsburg bureaucracy as it moved towards Weberian impersonality owes much to Carroll. K's Trial after all has no more sense than the trial at the end of *Alice's Adventures in Wonderland*. Like Alice, K often comes across as a lucid child — for only a child can be lucid in Carroll and Kafka's world — observing the senseless and arbitrary cruelty of adult caprice, whose only alibi is precedent. "Things have always been done that way. Don't you know? How stupid are you?"

It is their restoration of the child's reason in the face of adult intransigent baboonery that makes Kafka, Carroll and *The Prisoner* punk. Until it is socialised — i.e. stupefied into mute acceptance of the irrational caprice of the socius — the child knows that authority is nothing unless it is can be defended via reason.

The Prisoner, like Williams-Ellis, like the Situationists and the Surrealists, dreamed a dream deemed to be impossible, conceiving of a social system in which play and reason combine in an exploration of Intensive Now.

golgothic
materialism[1]

I finally saw *The Passion of the Christ* this week. I watched it at work with the A-level Religious Studies students. They, like me, were moved to tears and beyond. (Tip for any teacher out there: show the film at nine in the morning, that'll wake up any students still yawning their way into the day.)

Whilst agreeing with much of what Žižek says about Gibson's film in his brilliant essay "Passion in the Era of Decaffeinated Belief",[2] I think that he doesn't go nearly far enough.

Žižek is right to challenge the smug and lazy culturalist consensus that religious conviction is inherently pathological and dangerous. But he is wrong to suggest that what is most important about Passion is belief. Gibson's Gnostic vision — which is simply Christ's ethical Example rescued from the institutionalised religion that has systematically distorted it in his name — makes the two traditional supports of religious belief irrelevant. Astonishingly, *The Passion of the Christ* demonstrates that neither Revelation nor Tradition are important for those seeking to become-Christ(ian). What matters is not so much whether the events described in the film really happened — and there is no reason to doubt that something resembling them did — but the life-practice which the Christ story narrates.

Life as parable.

Let's dismiss first of all the idea that the film is anti-semitic. Certainly, the first half of the film threatens to invite this interpretation. In the run-up to Jesus' arrest, the film appears to depict the Jewish religious authorities as near-subhuman monsters, while the Roman imperial powers are viewed sympathetically, as benign and puzzled observers of a distasteful local conflict amongst the people they have colonised. (In this respect, Gibson appears to buy into the anti-Jewish narrative retrospectively imposed by the Roman Catholic Church once it had come to its concordat with the Roman

Empire and was keen to excuse its new Masters of any responsibility for the crucifixion.)

But once the notorious beating scene happens, the film goes through an intensive threshold. Here, the Roman soldiers are seen to be gratuitously cruel psychopaths, whose excessive zeal in punishing Jesus exceeds any "duty". It is clear by now that *The Passion of the Christ* has no ethnic axe to grind: it is about the stupidity and cruelty of the human species, but more importantly, about an escape route from the otherwise meaningless and nihilistic cycle of abuse begetting abuse that is human History.

The Gnostic flashes that surface in the Gospels are given full weight in Gibson's film. "My kingdom is not of this world." But Gibson refuses to give any comfort to those life-deniers and body-haters that Nietzsche rightly excoriates in his many attacks on Christianity. There is little supernatural or transcendent dimension to *The Passion*'s vision. If Christ's kingdom is not of this world, Gibson gives us few reasons to assume that this kingdom will be the Platonic heaven of which those tired of the body dream.

The World which Christ rejects is the World of Lies, the consensual hallucination of established power and authority. By contrast, Christ's kingdom only subsists whenever there is an Affectionate Collectivity. In other words, it exists not as some deferred supernatural reward, but in the Ethical actions of those, who in becoming-Christ, keep his spirit alive. Again, it is important to stress that this spirit is not some metaphysical substance, but a strictly material abstract machine that can be instantiated only through actions and practices. Loving God and loving others more than yourself are preconditions for dissolving your ego and gaining deliverance from the Hell of Self.

What, from one perspective, is the utter humiliation and degradation of Jesus' body is on the other a coldly ruthless vision of the body liberated from the "wisdom and limits of the organism".

Masochristianity.

Christ's Example is simply this: it is better to die than to pass on abuse virus or to in any way vindicate the idiot vacuity and stupidity of the World of authority.

Power depends upon the weakness of the organism. When authority is seriously challenged, when its tolerance is tested to the limit, it has the ultimate recourse of torture. The slow, graphic scenes of mindless physical degradation in *The Passion of the Christ* are necessary for revealing the horrors to which Jesus' organism was subject. It is made clear that he could have escaped the excruciating agony simply by renouncing his Truth and by assenting to the Authority of the World. Christ's Example insists: better to let the organism be tortured to death ("If thine own eye offend thee, pluck it out") than to bow, bent-headed, to Authority.

This is what is perhaps most astonishing about Gibson's film. Far from

124

being a statement of Catholic bigotry, it can only be read as an anti-authoritarian AND THEREFORE anti-Catholic film. For the Pharisees of two millennia ago, puffed up in their absurd finery, substitute the child-abuser apologists of today's gilt-laden, guilt-ridden Vatican. Against all the odds, against two thousand years of cover-ups and dissimulation, *The Passion of the Christ* recovers the original Christ, the anti-Wordly but not otherwordly Christ of Liberation Theology: the Gnostic herald of Apocalypse Now.

this movie doesn't move me[1]

As I nervously anticipate the new *Doctor Who* (although after McCoy, after McGann, what more can there be to fear?), it is worth thinking again about the appeal of the series, and also, more generally, about the unique importance of what I will call "uncanny fiction".

A piece by Rachel Cooke in the *Observer* two weeks ago brought these questions into sharp relief.[2] Cooke's article was more than an account of a television series; it was a story about the way broadcasting, family and the uncanny were webbed together through *Doctor Who*. Cooke writes powerfully about how her family's watching of the programme was literally ritualised: she had to be on the sofa, hair washed, before the continuity announcer even said the words, "And now..." She understands that, at its best, *Dr Who*'s appeal consisted in the charge of the *uncanny* — the strangely familiar, the familiar estranged: cybermen on the steps of St Paul's, yeti at Goodge Street (a place whose name will forever be associated with the Troughton adventure, "The Web of Fear", for Scanshifts,[3] who saw it whilst living in New Zealand).

Inevitably, however, she ends the piece on a melancholy note. Cooke has been to a screening of the first episode of the new series. She enjoys its expensive production values, its "sinister moments", its use of the Millennium Wheel. "But it is not — how shall I put this? — *Doctor Who*." Faced with an "overwhelming sense of loss", she turns to a DVD of the Baker story *Robots of Death* for a taste of the "real" stuff, the authentic experience that the new series cannot provide. But this proves, if anything, to be even more of a disappointment. "How slow the whole thing seems, and how silly the robots look in their Camilla Parker-Bowles-style green quilted jackets... *Good grief.*"

Let's leave aside, for a moment, all the post-post-structuralist questions about the ontological status of the text "itself", and consider the glum anecdote with which the article concludes:

127

Before Christmas, when it became clear that my father's cancer was in its final stages, my brother went out and bought a DVD for us all to watch together. Dad was too ill, and box went unopened. At the time, I cried about this; yet another injustice. Now I know better. Some things in life can't ever be retrieved — an enjoyment of green robots in sequins and pedal pushers being one of them.

This narrative of disillusionment belongs to a genre that has become familiar: the postmodern parable. To look at the old *Doctor Who* is not only to fail to recover a lost moment; it is to discover, with a deflating quotidian horror, that this moment never existed in the first place. An experience of awe and wonder dissolves into a pile of dressing up clothes and cheap special effects. The postmodernist is then left with two options: disavowal of the enthusiasm, i.e. what is called "growing up", or else keeping faith with it, i.e. what is called "not growing up". Two fates, therefore, await the no longer media-mesmerised child: depressive realism or geek fanaticism.

The intensity (with) which Cooke invested in *Doctor Who* is typical of so many of us who grew up in the Sixties and Seventies. I, slightly younger than her, remember a time when those twenty-five minutes were indeed the most *sacralised* of the week. Scanshifts, slightly older than me, remembers a period when he didn't have a functioning television at home, so he would watch the new episode furtively at a department store in Christchurch, silently at first, until, delighted, he found the means of increasing the volume.

The most obvious explanation for such fervour — childhood enthusiasm and naïveté — can also be supplemented by thinking of the specific technological and cultural conditions that obtained then. Freud's analysis of the *unheimlich*, the "unhomely", is very well known, but it is worth linking his account of the uncanniness of the domestic to television. Television was itself both familiar and alien, and a series which was *about* the alien in the familiar was bound to have particularly easy route to the child's unconscious. In a time of cultural rationing, of modernist broadcasting, a time, that is, in which there were no endless reruns, no VCRs, the programmes had a precious evanescence. They were translated into memory and dream at the very moment they were being seen for the first time. This is quite different from the instant — and increasingly pre-emptive — monumentalisation of postmodern media productions through "makings of" documentaries and interviews. So many of these productions enjoy the odd fate of being stillborn into perfect archivisation, forgotten by the culture while immaculately memorialised by the technology.

But were the conditions for *Dr Who's* colonising presence in the unconscious of a generation merely scarcity and the "innocence" of a "less sophisticated" time? Does its magic, as Cooke implies, crumble like a vampire seducer in bright sunlight when exposed to the unbeguiled, unforgiving eyes of the adult?

According to Freud's famous arguments in *Totem and Taboo* and *The Uncanny*, we moderns recapitulate in our individual psychological development the "progress" from narcissistic animism to the reality principle undergone by the species as a whole. Children, like "savages", remain at the level of narcissistic auto-eroticism, subject to the animistic delusion that their thoughts are "omnipotent"; that what they think can directly affect the world.

But is it the case that children ever "really believed" in *Doctor Who*? Žižek has pointed out that when people from "primitive" societies are asked about their myths, their response is actually indirect. They say "some people believe". Belief is always the belief of the other. In any case, what adults and moderns have lost is not the capacity to uncritically believe, but the art of using the series as triggers for producing inhabitable fictional playzones.

The model for such practices is the Perky Pat layouts in Philip K. Dick's *The Three Stigmata of Palmer Eldritch*. Homesick off-world colonists are able to project themselves into Ken and Barbie-like dolls who inhabit a mock-up of the earthly environment. But in order to occupy this set they need a drug. In effect, all the drug does is restore in the adult what comes easily to a child: the ability not to believe, but to act in *spite of the lack of belief*.

In a sense, though, to say this is already going too far. It implies that adults really have given up a narcissistic fantasy and adjusted to the harsh banality of the disenchanted-empirical. In fact, all they have done is substituted one fantasy for another. The point is that to be an adult in consumer capitalism IS to occupy the Perky Pat world of drably bright soap opera domesticity. What is eliminated in the mediocre melodrama we are invited to call adult reality is not fantasy, but the uncanny — the sense that all is not as it seems, that the kitchen-sink everyday is a front for the machinations of parasites and alien forces which either possess, control or have designs upon us. In other words, the suppressed wisdom of uncanny fiction is that it is THIS world, the world of liberal-capitalist commonsense, that is a stage set with wobbly walls. As Scanshifts and I hope to demonstrate in our upcoming audiomentary *London Under London* on Resonance FM, the Real of the London Underground is better described by pulp and modernism (which in any case have a suitably uncanny complicity) than by postmodern drearealism. Everyone knows that, once the wafer-thin veneer of "persons" is stripped away, the population on the Tube are zombies under the control of sinister extra-terrestrial corporations.

The rise of fantasy as a genre over the last twenty-five years can be directly correlative with the collapse of any effective alternative reality structure outside capitalism in the same period. Watching something like *Star Wars*, you immediately think two things. Its fictional world is BOTH impossibly remote, too far-distant to care about, AND too much like this world, too similar to our own to be fascinated by. If the uncanny is about an irreducible anomalousness in anything that comes to count as the familiar, then fantasy is about the production of a seamless world in which all the gaps have been mono-filled. It is no accident that the rise of fantasy has gone alongside the development of digital FX. The curious hollowness and depthlessness of CGI arises not from any failure of fidelity, but, quite the opposite, from its photoshopping out of the Discrepant as such.

The fantasy structure of Family, Nation and Heroism thus functions, not in any sense as a representation, false or otherwise, but as a model to live up to. The inevitable failure of our own lives to match up to the digital Ideal is one of the motors of capitalism's worker-consumer passivity, the docile pursuit of what will always be elusive, a world free of fissures and discontinuities. And you only have to read one of Mark Steyn's preppy phallic fables (which need to be ranked alongside the mummy's boystories of someone like Robert E. Howard) to see how fantasy's pathetically imbecilic manichean oppositions between Good and Evil, Us and (a foreign, contagious) Them are effective on the largest possible geopolitical stage.

fear and misery in the third reich 'n' roll[1]

I (belatedly) went to see the traumatically powerful *Downfall* a couple of nights ago at the behest of Karl Kraft. Overhype of mediocre tat renders one suspicious of any praise surrounding contemporary films, but this is a genuine masterpiece, and one that can only be appreciated fully in the cinema environment, where the relentless pummelling of the Soviet artillery and the claustrophobic airlessness of the Hitler bunker have a crushingly visceral presence.

Downfall, actually, is the second film this year (the first was *The Aviator*) to flout my otherwise reliable dictum that movies based on real life are to be avoided. But the reason why both work is that they describe situations in which *reality had itself gone psychotic.* As Ballard has observed, the Nazi delirium was one of those moments when the distinction between the internal and the external world no longer held: hell has erupted on earth, there is no escape, no future, and you know it...

Downfall is fascinating because it closely and, I'm assuming, meticulously documents the "line of abolition" that Deleuze and Guattari claim is *constitutive* of Nazism. For Deleuze and Guattari, who borrow the idea from Virilio, the Nazis' scheduled auto-annihilation — "if we are defeated, better that the nation should perish" — was less a forced contingency than the realisation, the very consummation, of the Nazi project.[2] Deleuze and Guattari's account might be dubious empirically, but the great service it provides for cultural analysis may not be the idea that Nazism is suicidal, but the thought that *the suicidal, the self-destructive is Nazi.*

Since at least the death of Chatterton, popular culture has found the temptation to glamourise self-destruction irresistible. The Nazis provide the definitive twentieth-century version of this age-old Romance of Death. As Ballard noted in his essay on Hitler, "Alphabets of Reason", the Nazis are

131

a creepily *modern* phenomenon, their technicolour glamour a world away from the fussy frock-coated figures of the Edwardian British ruling elite. The Nazis' facility with broadcasting laid the groundwork for the media landscape we now occupy. Hitler as the first rock star?

Downfall takes us through the scenes in which the Nazi party disintegrates only for the Third Reich 'n' Roll to begin. The death of the frontman is the blood-sacrifical rite that will guarantee a hideous immortality. Hitler was the first twentieth-century figure to pass from historical individuality to becoming a permanent archetype-artefact in the the the McLuhan-Ballard media unconscious. After him, Kennedy, Malcolm X, King, Morrison, Hendrix, Curtis seem local, particular, whereas Hitler comes to stand for a general principle, for modern Evil itself.

As spectators of *Downfall*, we spend most of the time in the Führer Bunker, forced into an unsettling sympathy if not for the Reich's leaders then for those who were loyal to them, the secretaries and functionaries who admired, by no means fanatically, Hitler and National Socialism. Meanwhile, the glimpses we have of the Berlin above show a landscape out of *The Triumph of Death*, a city devolving into total anomie: child conscripts, vigilante hangings, intoxicated revelling, carnivalesque sexual excess.

While those scenes play out, you can almost hear Johnny Rotten leering, "when there's no future how can there be sin?" (Although for Germany, in fact, there was *nothing but the future*: immediate postwar Germany was subject to a willed amnesia, a disavowal of cultural memory.) It's no accident that post-punk in many ways begins here. As the Pistols pursue their own line of abolition into the scorched earth nihilism of "Belsen was a Gas" and "Holidays in the Sun", they keep returning to the barbed-wire scarred Boschscape of Nazi Berlin and the Pynchon Zone it became after the war. Siouxsie famously sported a swastika for a while, and although much of the flaunting of the Nazi imagery was supposedly for superficial shock effects, the punk-Nazi connection was about much more than trite transgressivism. Punk's very 1970s, very British fixation on Nazism posed ethical questions so troubling they could barely be articulated explicitly: what were the limits of liberal tolerance? Could Britain be so sure that it had differentiated itself from Nazism (a particularly pressing issue at a time that the NF was gathering an unprecedented degree of support)? And, most unsettling of all, what is it that separates Nazi Evil from heroic Good?

Downfall poses that last question with a real force, and it is a question that has a special resonance at the moment given Žižek and Zupančič's theory of the ungrounded Act as the very definition of the ethical. As I watched the most "monstrous" act depicted in the film, Frau Goebbels' drugging and then poisoning her children — better this "redemption", she reasoned, than that they be left in a world without National Socialism — I was struck by the parallel with Sethe in Toni Morrison's *Beloved*, who kills one of her children rather than let it fall into the hands of the slavers. What is to separate Frau Goebbels' act of abominable Evil from Sethe's act of heroic Good? (Those who have read *The Fragile Absolute* will remember that Žižek uses Sethe precisely as an example of a Good entirely alien to liberal morality, with its ethic of enlightened self-interest.)

Downfall seems to invite us to sympathise with the "liberal Nazis", the "reasonable" doctor, for instance, who wants to keep the medical services running and is disgusted and aghast at the "senseless, suicidal" behaviour that results from seeing Duty through to the end; the General who wants to end the war to protect the lives of civilians. But these "pragmatic humanitarian" figures are the least defensible because they are not prepared to follow the principles of their actions to the end (if they were committed to Nazism, why not die for it? If they weren't, why not resist it?). Strangely, it is almost as if the film seems to suggest that what was irredeemably malevolent about the Nazis was their will to die for the cause.

In spite of ourselves, we find ourselves thinking that the Evil Nazis — those who totally identify with the Nazi project and who destroy themselves when it is clear that has failed — attain a certain tragic heroism by refusing to give up on their fundamental commitment. All of which leads us back to the old question: does the Kantian emphasis on unconditional duty legitimate Nazi Evil?

Zupančič, who has done so much to re-discover Kantian ethics from the perspective of Lacanian theory, addressed this question in her interview with *Cabinet* magazine:

> Recall that, in Hannah Arendt's famous example, Nazi functionaries like Eichmann took themselves to be Kantians in this respect: They claimed to act simply on principle without any consideration for the empirical consequences of their actions. In what way is this a perversion of Kant?
>
> This attitude is "perverse" in the strictest clinical meaning of the word: The subject has here assumed the role of a mere instrument of the Will of the Other. In relation to Kant, I would simply stress the following point, which has already been made by Slavoj Žižek: In Kantian ethics, we are responsible for what we refer to as our duty. The moral law is not something that could clear us of all responsibility for our actions; on the contrary, it makes us responsible not only for our actions, but also — and foremost — for the principles that we act upon.[3]

Is this enough though to distinguish Goebbels from Sethe? Was it really the case that Frau Goebbels was making herself into "a mere instrument of the Will of the Other"? Or had she freely chosen to assume responsibility for her actions *and* for the principles on which she acted? Remember that Kantian freedom consists in *choosing to obey the moral law*. To be motivated by anything other than "duty" is to be driven by "pathological" passions, and hence not to be free at all. There is no obvious pathological motivation for Frau Goebbels' actions. She stood to gain nothing from this act of "destroying what is best in her" (and indeed, shortly after she killed her children, she consented to be shot by her husband).

The only answer you are left with is that the Nazi Cause is *itself* a pathology. By definition, the Nazi Act cannot be universal, since it is based upon preserving — if only, at the end, at the level of myth — the particular pathological characteristics of "a chosen people" and, more abstractly therefore, of defending the very principle of "ethnic pathology". Sethe's abominable act in *Beloved* is an act of Unplugging from a social situation fatally, totally corrupted by a lethally imbecilic racial delirium; Frau Goebbels' multiple infanticide, by contrast, is an attempt to hardwire herself and her children into an ethnocidal madness that can only live through their deaths and the deaths of millions of others.

we want it all[1]

What use might Nietzsche be today? Or, to put it another way: *which* Nietzsche might be of use, now?

It will come as no surprise that I would count Nietzsche the perspectivist — he who questioned not only the possibility but the value of Truth — as the enemy. There will be even fewer surprises that I would reject the Dionysian Nietzsche, the celebrant of transgressive desire. This Nietzsche, in any case, is largely a post-Bataillean retrospective construct (even in *The Birth of Tragedy*, what Nietzsche mourns is the lost tension *between* Dionysus and Apollo; and in his later writings Nietzsche is more likely to be found extolling the necessity of constraints and limitations than he is to be heard calling for the unrestrained venting of libido). The perspectival and the Dionysiac are far too *timely*.

The Nietzsche that *remains untimely* — and by that I do not mean outmoded, very far from it — is Nietzsche the aristocrat. Nietzsche should not be taken seriously as a political theorist, at least not at the level of his positive prescriptions. But the Nietzsche who denounces the insipidity and mediocrity that result from democracy's levelling impulses could not be more acute. Passage after passage of polemic in *Beyond Good and Evil* seems uncannily apposite in these times of focus-grouped blandness and "autonomous herding". Nietzsche's real interests lay with *cultural* politics; government and social institutions troubled him only insofar as they produced cultural effects, his ultimate question being: "What are the *conditions* in which great cultural artefacts can emerge?"

I was reminded of Nietzsche's warnings about what would happen to culture if all "special claims and privileges" are denied, if the very *concept* of superiority is abolished, when Chantelle Houghton won *Celebrity Big Brother* a week or so ago (it already seems much longer than that). I was reminded, too, of Nietzsche's scalding admonition that "harshness" and "cruelty" must be cultivated if the human animal is to transformed, by hammer blows and force of will, into a great work of art; reminded, especially, when some posters on Dissensus were seriously advancing *"niceness"* — niceness, that is — as a desirable trait.

Chantelle's victory wasn't *just* a popularity contest: as Marcello's excellent *Big Brother* piece observed, a principle was at stake, the principle that ordinariness must trump any notion of superiority:

> "You are not going to win support or respect by placing yourself out of the ordinary. You need to be approachable but you also need to be yourself. That's what young people respect." That's a recent quote from one Alex Folkes, the speaker for a pressure group named Votes at Sixteen, apropos George Galloway, and it's the kind of exhausting, fatuous anti-philosophy which tempts me to form a pressure group called Votes at Thirty. Nevertheless it is (un)pretty fitting for an age bereft of desire for godhood. Where once we assembled in front of screens or stages to gasp in awe at people doing and achieving things we could never hope of doing or achieving ourselves — but how we luxuriated, carried ourselves afloat, on the dream of doing so — now all we require is a humbling mirror. This is the sort of thing which stops dangerous people from gaining power, but also the kind of closure which would ultimately forbid all art. *Where once we assembled in front of screens or stages to gasp in awe at people doing and achieving things we could never hope of doing or achieving ourselves [...] now all we require is a humbling mirror.*[2]

This is Celebreality: the simultaneous desublimation of the Star and the elevation of "the ordinary". The commentary on *Celebrity Big Brother* treated it as self-evident that people will want to "identify with" media figures who offer a comforting and unchallenging reflection of themselves at their most mediocre, stupid and *harmless*. Julie Burchill's endlessly reiterated polemic in favour of *Big Brother* — that it allows working-class people opportunities to break into a media otherwise dominated by the privileged — is baseless for three reasons. First, because the real beneficiaries of *Big Brother* are not the contestants, whose "career" is notoriously short-lived, but Endemol, with its coterie of smug graduate producers. Second, because *Big Brother* trades in a patronising and reductive image of the working class, the dominion of Celebreality relies upon the mediocrats inducing the working class into corresponding to — and "identifying with" — that image. Third, because *Big Brother* and reality TV have effaced those areas of popular culture in which a working class that aspired to more than "wealth" or "fame" once excelled. Its rise has meant a defeat for that over-reaching proletarian drive to *be more*, (I am nothing but should be everything), a drive which negated

Social Facts by inventing Sonic Fictions, which despised "ordinariness" in the name of the strange and the alien. On *Celebrity Big Brother*, Pete Burns, with his casual cruelties, his savage articulacy and his Masoch-furs, was a cartoon symbol of those lost ambitions, skulking and sulking at the periphery, a glam prince in an age of post-Blairite roundheads.

We all know that the "reality" of reality TV is an artful construction, an effect not only of editing but of a Lorenzian rat-in-a-mirrored-labyrinth artificial environment which attenuates psychology into a series of territorial twitches. The "reality" that is designated is significant more for what is absent from it than for any positive properties it is deemed to possess. And what is absent, above all, is fantasy. Or rather, fantasy objects.

We once turned to popular culture because it produced fantasy objects; now, we are asked to "identify with" *the fantasising subject* itself. It was entirely appropriate that, the week after Chantelle won *Celebrity Big Brother*, *Smash Hits* should have announced its imminent closure.

Smash Hits began just as the glam continuum was winding down. What *Smash Hits* took from punk was its least Nietzschean affect, namely its "irreverence". In the case of *Smash Hits*, this amounted to a compulsory trivialisation coupled with a kind of good-humoured debunking of the pretensions of Stardom. Behind *Smash Hits'* silly surrealism was good solid commonsense and a conflicted desire, to both have your idols and kill them. *Heat* was *Smash Hits'* successor and what rendered it obsolete. No need to bother with the (pop) pretext, now you can consume celebrity directly, untroubled by pop's embarrassing Dreams. Chantelle is the logical conclusion of the process: the anti-Pop anti-Idol.

Nietzsche's contention was that the kind of levelling Chantelle stands for was the inevitable and necessary consequence of all egalitarianism. Yet popular culture was once the arena which demonstrated that any genuine egalitarianism is inimical to any such levelling down. I wrote last year of goth as "a paradoxically egalitarian aristocracy in which membership [is] not guaranteed by birth or beauty but by self-decoration"; will popular culture ever again teach us that egalitarianism is not hostile to, but relies upon, a will-to-greatness, an unconditional demand for the excellent?

gothic oedipus: subjectivity and capitalism in christopher nolan's *batman begins*[1]

Batman has contributed more than its fair share to the "darkness" that hangs over contemporary culture like a picturesque pall. "Dark" designates both a highly marketable aesthetic style and an ethical, or rather anti-ethical, stance, a kind of designer nihilism whose chief theoretical proposition is the denial of the possibility of the Good. Gotham, particularly as re-invented by Frank Miller in the Eighties, is, along with Gibson's Sprawl and Ridley Scott's LA, one of the chief geomythic sources of this trend.[2]

Miller's legacy for comics has been ambivalent at best. Reflect on the fact that his rise coincides with the almost total failure of superhero comics to produce any new characters with mythic resonance.[3] The "maturity" for which Miller has been celebrated corresponds with comics' depressive and introspective adolescence, and for him, as for all adolescents, the worst sin is exuberance. Hence his trademark style is deflationary, taciturn: consider all those portentous pages stripped of dialogue in which barely anything happens and contrast them with the crazed effervescence of the typical Marvel page in the Sixties. Miller's pages have all the brooding silence of a moody fifteen-year-old boy. We are left in no doubt: the silence *signifies*.

Miller traded on a disingenuous male adolescent desire to both have comics and to feel superior to them. But his demythologisation, inevitably, produced only a new mythology, one that posed as more sophisticated than the one it has displaced but is in fact an utterly predictable world of "moral ambivalence" in which "there are only shades of grey". There are reasons for being highly sceptical about Miller's bringing into comics a noir-lite cartoon nihilist bleakness that has long been a cliché in films and books. The "darkness" of this vision is in fact curiously reassuring and comforting, and not only because of the sentimentality it can never extirpate. (Miller's "hard-bitten" world reminds me not so much of noir, but of the simulation of noir in Dennis Potter's *Singing Detective*, the daydream-fantasies of a cheap hack, thick with misognyny and misanthropy and cooked in intense self-loathing.)

It is hardly surprising that Miller's model of realism came to the fore in comics at the time when Reaganomics and Thatcherism were presenting themselves as the only solutions to America and Britain's ills. Reagan and Thatcher claimed to have "delivered us from the 'fatal abstractions' inspired by the 'ideologies of the past'".[4] They had awoken us from the supposedly flawed, dangerously deluded dreams of collectivity and re-acquainted us with the "essential truth" that individual human beings can only be motivated by their own animal interests.

These propositions belong to an implicit ideological framework we can call *capitalist realism.* On the basis of a series of assumptions — human beings are irredeemably self-interested, (social) Justice can never be achieved — capitalist realism projects a vision of what is "Possible".

For Alain Badiou, the rise to dominance of this restricted sense of possibility must be regarded as a period of "Restoration". As Badiou explained in an interview with *Cabinet* magazine, "in France, 'Restoration' refers to the period of the return of the King, in 1815, after the Revolution and Napoleon. We are in such a period. Today we see liberal capitalism and its political system, parlimentarianism, as the only natural and acceptable solutions".[5] According to Badiou, the ideological defence for these political configurations takes the form of a lowering of expectations:

> We live in a contradiction: a brutal state of affairs, profoundly inegalitarian — where all existence is evaluated in terms of money alone — is presented to us as ideal. To justify their conservatism, the partisans of the established order cannot really call it ideal or wonderful. So instead, they have decided to say that all the rest is horrible. Sure, they say, we may not live in a condition of perfect Goodness. But we're lucky that we don't live in a condition of Evil. Our democracy is not perfect. But it's better than the bloody dictatorships. Capitalism is unjust. But it's not criminal like Stalinism. We let millions of Africans die of AIDS, but we don't make racist nationalist declarations like Milosevic. We kill Iraqis with our airplanes, but we don't cut their throats with machetes like they do in Rwanda, etc.[6]

Capitalism and liberal democracy are "ideal" precisely in the sense that they are "the best that one can expect", that is to say, *the least worst.*[7] This chimes with Miller's rendition of the hero in *The Dark Knight Returns* and *Year One: Batman* may be authoritarian, violent and sadistic, but in a world of endemic corruption, he is the least worst option. (Indeed, such traits may turn out to be necessary in conditions of ubiquitous venality.) Just as Badiou suggests, in Miller's Gotham it is no longer possible to assume the existence of Good. Good has no *positive* presence — what Good there is has to be defined by reference to a self-evident Evil which it is not. Good, that is to say, is the *absence* of an Evil whose existence is self-evident.

The fascination of the latest cinema version of *Batman*, *Batman Begins* (directed by Christopher Nolan) consists in its mitigated return to the question of Good. The film still belongs to the "Restoration" to the degree that it is unable to imagine a possible beyond capitalism: as we shall see, it is a specific mode of capitalism — post-Fordist finance capital — that is demonised in *Batman Begins*,not capitalism *per se*. Yet the film leaves open the possibility of agency which capitalist realism forecloses.

Nolan's revisiting of *Batman* is not a re-invention but a reclaiming of the myth, a grand syncresis that draws upon the whole history of the character.[8] Gratifyingly, then, *Batman Begins* is not about "shades of grey" at all, but rather about competing versions of the Good. In *Batman Begins*, Christian Bale's Bruce Wayne is haunted by a superfluity of fathers (and a near absence of mothers: his mother barely says a word), each with their own account of the Good. First, there is his biological father, Thomas Wayne, a rose-tinted, soft focus moral paragon, the very personification of philanthropic Capital, the "man who built Gotham". In keeping with the Batman myth established in the Thirtes *Detective Comics*, Wayne Pere is killed in a random street robbery, surviving only as a moral wraith tormenting the conscience of his orphaned son. Second, there is R'as Al Ghul, who in Nolan's film is Wayne's hyperstitional[9] mentor-guru, a Terroristic figure who represents a ruthless ethical code completely opposed to the benevolent paternalism of Thomas Wayne. Bruce is assisted in the struggle (fought out in his own psyche) between these two Father figures by a third, Michael Caine's Alfred, the "maternal" carer who offers the young Bruce unconditional love.

The struggle between Fathers is doubled by the conflict between Fear and Justice that has been integral to the *Batman* mythos since it first appeared in 1939. The challenge for Bruce Wayne in *Batman Begins* is not only to best Fear, as wielded by the Miller-invented crime boss Falcone and the Scarecrow with his "weaponised hallucinogens", but to identify Justice, which, as the young Wayne must learn, cannot be equated with revenge.

From the start, the Batman mythos has been about the pressing of Gothic Fear into the service of heroic Justice. Echoing the origin story as recounted in *Detective Comics* in 1939, which has Bruce famously declare, "Criminals are a superstitious cowardly lot, so my disguise must be able to strike terror into their hearts", Nolan's Wayne dedicates himself to turning fear against those who use it. Yet Nolan's version makes the origin story both more Oedipal *and* more anti-Oedipal than it appeared in *Detective Comics*. In the original comic, Bruce settles upon the name "Batman" when a single bat flies into his room. Nolan's rendering of Batman's primal scene is significantly different, in that it takes place outside the family home, beyond the realm of the Oedipal, in a cave in the capacious grounds of Wayne Manor, and not with a single bat but with a whole (Deleuzian) pack.[10] The name "Batman", with its suggestions of becoming-animal, does indeed have a Deleuzoguattarian resonance. Yet the proximity of Batman's name to that of some of Freud's case histories — "Ratman" especially, but also "Wolfman" — is no accident either. Batman remains a thoroughly Oedipal figure (as *Batman Begins* leaves us no doubt).[11] *Batman Begins* re-binds the becoming-animal with the Oedipal by having Bruce's fear of bats figure as a partial *cause* of his parents' death. Bruce is at the opera when the sight of bat-like figures on stage drives him to nag his parents until they leave the theatre and are killed.

The Gothic and the Oedipal elements of the Batman mythos were entwined immediately, on the two pages of *Detective Comics* on which Batman's origin was first told. As Kim Newman identifies, Wayne's epiphanic revelation that "I must be a terrible creature of the night... I shall become a BAT... a weird figure of the night", contains "subliminal" quotes from *Dracula* ("creatures of the night, what sweet music they make") and *The Cabinet of Dr Caligari* ("you shall become Caligari").[12] These panels follow three at the top of the page where the shocked Bruce sees the bodies of his parents ("father, mother [...] Dead, they're dead") and "swears by [their deaths] to avenge [them] by spending the rest of my life warring on all criminals". Batman is self-consciously imagined — and self-created — as a Gothic monster, a "weird figure of the dark", but one who will use "the night" against the criminals who habitually hide in it.

If *Batman* was heavily indebted to German Expressionism — via Universal's horror pictures — so, famously, was film noir, which emerged, like Batman, in the late Thirties and early Forties. (As we've already seen, Miller's rendition of *Batman* can be seen as in many ways a postmodern investigation of this parallel.) Remarks made by Alenka Zupančič suggest a possible hidden source for the complicity between Batman and noir: Oedipus again. "[I]n contrast to *Hamlet*", Zupančič writes,

> the story of Oedipus has often been said to belong to the whodunnit genre. Some have gone even further, and seen in *Oedipus the King* the prototype of the *noir* genre. Thus *Oedipus the King* appeared in the "noir series" of French publisher Gallimard ("translated from the myth" by Didier Lamaison).[13]

Batman, the superhero-detective, walks in the footsteps of the first detective, Oedipus.

Ultimately, however, the problem for Batman is that he remains an Oedipus who has not gone through the Oedipus complex. As Zupančič points out, the Oedipus complex turns on the *discrepancy* between the Symbolic and the empirical father: the Symbolic Father is the embodiment of the Symbolic order itself, solemn carrier of Meaning and bearer of the Law; the empirical father is the "simple, more or less decent man". For Zupančič, the standard rendering of the "typical genesis of subjectivity" has it that the child first of all encounters the Symbolic father and then comes to learn that this mighty figure is a "simple, more or less decent man". Yet, as Zupančič establishes, this trajectory is the exact inverse of the one which Oedipus pursues. Oedipus begins by encountering a "rude old man at the crossroads" and only later does he learn that this "simple man", this "vulgar creature", was the Father. Thus "Oedipus travels the path of initiation (of 'symbolisation') in reverse and, in so doing, he encounters the radical contingency of the Meaning borne by the symbolic."[14]

For Bruce Wayne, though, there is no discrepancy at all between the Symbolic and the empirical. Thomas Wayne's early death means that he is frozen in his young son's psyche as the mighty emissary of the Symbolic; he is never "desublimated" into a "simple man", but remains a moral exemplar — indeed he is the representative of Law as such, who must be avenged but who can never be equalled. In *Batman Begins*, it is the intervention of R'as Al Ghul which prompts an Oedipal crisis. The young Wayne is convinced that his father's death is his fault, but Al Ghul tries to convince him that his parents' death is his father's responsibility because the good-natured and liberal Thomas Wayne did not know how to Act; he was a weak-willed failure. Yet Bruce refuses to go through this initiation and retains loyalty to the "Name of the Father" while Al Ghul remains a figure of excess and Evil.

The question Al Ghul poses to Bruce is: are you, with your conscience, your respect for life, too weak-willed, too frightened to do what is Necessary? Can you Act? Wayne is forced to decide: is Al Ghul what he claims to be, the ice-cold instrument of impersonal Justice, or its grotesque parody? The ultimate Evil in the film turns out to originate from Ghul's excessive zeal, not from some hoaky diabolism nor from some psycho-biographical happenstance.[15]

In this respect, it is the film that Žižek wanted *Revenge of the Sith* to be: a film, that is to say, which dares to hypothesise that Evil might result from an excess of Good. For Žižek, "Anakin [Skywalker] should have become a monster out his very excessive attachment with seeing Evil everywhere and fighting it", but

[i]nstead of focusing on Anakin's hubris as an overwhelming desire to intervene, to do Good, to go to the end for those he loves and thus fall to the Dark Side, Anakin is simply shown as an indecisive warrior who is gradually sliding into Evil by giving way to the temptation of Power, by falling under the spell of the evil Emperor.[16]

In parallel with Žižek's reading of *Revenge of the Sith*, *Batman Begins'* treatment of the question of the Father — who *is* the father? — is doubled by the looming (omni-)presence of finance capital, and the issue of what is to be done about it. In Batman's universe of course, "the Name of the Father" — Wayne — is also the name of a capitalist enterprise. The takeover of Wayne Industries by shareholder capital means that Thomas' name has been stolen. Consequently, Bruce Wayne's struggle against finance capital is also, inevitably, an attempt to restore the besmirched Name of the Father. Since Wayne Industries is at the heart — literally and figuratively — of the city, post-Fordist Gotham finds itself as blighted as the Sphinx-cursed Thebes. Its infrastructure rotten, its civil society disintegrated, Gotham is in the grip of a depression and a crime wave, both of which are attributed to the newly predatory, delocalised Capital that now has control of the Wayne corporation. The impact of finance capital is given a more personal narrative focus through the character of the kindly Lucius Fox (another candidate for Father surrogate)[17] who is degraded by the new regime. The implication is that this state of rottenness can only be rectified once the name of the Father resumes its rights.

It is in its treatment of capitalism that *Batman Begins* is at its most intriguingly contradictory. In part, this can be attributed to the effects of attempting to retrofit the 1930s core narrative engine into a twenty-first-century vehicle: the reference to the depression is a clear Thirties echo, setting up a disjunction with a contemporary USA that has enjoyed an unprecedented period of economic success. In keeping with capitalism itself, Deleuze and Guattari's "motley painting of everything that ever was", Nolan's Gotham is an admixture of the medieval and the ultra-contemporary, of the American, the European and the Third World. It resembles at once the crooked steeples and spires of German Expressionism and the *favela*-sprawls of cyberpunk[18]: the nightmare of Old Europe erupting in the heart of the American Megalopolis.

In a fascinating reading of *Batman Begins*, China Miéville argues that the film's anti-capitalism cashes out as an advocacy of fascism. The film, he writes,

is about fascism's self-realisation, and the only struggle it undergoes is to admit its own necessity. BB argues for the era of the absolute(ist) corporation against the "postmodern" social dilutions of shareholder capitalism (perceived here in old-school corporate paranoia as a kind of woolly weakness), let alone against the foolishness of those well-meaning liberal rich who don't understand that their desire to travel with the poor and working class are the "causes" of social conflict, because The Rich Man At His Garden The Poor Man At His Gate, and that the blurring of those boundaries confuses the bestial instincts of the sheep-masses. The film argues quite explicitly (in what's obviously, in its raised-train setting, structured as a debate with *Spiderman 2*, a stupid but good-hearted film that thinks people are basically decent) that masses are dangerous unless terrorised into submission (Spidey falls among the masses — they nurture him and make sure he's ok. Bats falls among them — they are a murderous and bestial mob because they are not being "effectively scared enough"). The final way of "solving" social catastrophe is [...] by the demolition of the mass transit system that ruined everything by literally raised the poor and put them among the rich: travelling together, social-democratic welfarism as opposed to trickle-downism is a nice dream but leads to social collapse, and if left unchecked terrorism that sends transit systems careering through the sky into tall buildings in the middle of New York-style cities — 9/11 as caused by the crisis of "excessive social solidarity", the arrogance of masses "not being sufficiently terrified of their shepherds". In all a film that says social stratification is necessary to prevent tragedy, and that it should be policed by terrorising the plebeians, for the sake of corporations which if there is a happy ending [...] will end up back in the hands of a single enlightened despot, hurrah, to save us from the depredations of consensus.[19]

There is no doubt that the film poses finance capital as a problem that will be solved by the return of a re-personalised captal, with "the enlightened despot" Bruce taking on the role of the dead Thomas. It is equally clear, as we've already seen, that *Batman Begins* is unable to envisage an alternative to capitalism itself, favouring instead a nostalgic rewind to prior forms of capitalism. (One of the structuring fantasies of the film is the notion that crime and social disintegration are exclusively the results of capitalist failure, rather than the inevitable accompaniments to capitalist "success".)

However, we must distinguish between corporate capitalism and fascism if only because the film makes such a point of doing so. The fascistic option is represented not by Wayne-Batman but by R'as al Ghul. It is al Ghul who plots the total razing of a Gotham he characterises as irredeemably corrupt. Wayne's language is not that of renewal-through-destruction (and here Schumpterian capitalism and fascism, in most other respects entirely opposed, find themselves in sympathy), but of philanthropic meliorism. (It should also be noted that the masses who, in a pointed reference to Romero's *Living Dead* films, threaten to consume and destroy Batman are under the influence of the Scarecrow's "weaponised hallucinogens" when they attempt to dismember him, although this image of the masses no doubt tell us more about the political unconscious of the film-makers than it does about that of the masses.)

If the film's handling of capitalism is incoherent, in what does its challenge to capitalist realism consist? It is to be found not at the level of politics but in its account of ethics, agency and subjectivity. Žižek's classic account of ideology in *The Sublime Object of Ideology* turns on the difference between belief and action. At the level of belief, key capitalist ideas — commodities are animate; capital has a quasi-natural status — are repudiated, but it is precisely the ironic distance from such notions that allows us to *act* as if they are true. The disavowal of the beliefs allows us to perform the actions. Ideology, then, depends upon the conviction that what "really matters" is what we are, rather than what we do, and that "what we are" is defined by an "inner essence". In terms of contemporary American culture, this plays out in the "therapeutic" idea that we can remain a "good person" regardless of what we do.

The film's principal ethical lesson presents a reversal of this ideological conviction. In Wayne's struggle to differentiate justice from revenge, revenge is personified by the uncompromising R'as al Ghul, while justice is represented by the assistant District Attorney, Rachel Dawes. Dawes is given the film's crucial (anti-therapeutic) slogan, "It's not who you are inside that counts, it's what you *do* that makes you what you are." The Good is possible, but not without Decision and the Act. In reinforcing this message, *Batman Begins* restores to the hero an existentialist drama that puts to flight not only capitalist realist nihilism, but also the niggling, knowing sprites of postmodern reflexivity[20] that have sucked his blood for way too long.

when we dream, do we dream we're joey?[1]

"When you dream, do you dream you're Joey?"
— Carl Fogarty to Tom Stall, in David Cronenberg's *A History of Violence*[2]

"In a dream he is a butterfly. [...] When Choang-tsu wakes up, he may ask himself whether it is not the butterfly who dreams that he is Choang-tsu. Indeed he is right, and doubly so, first because it proves he is not mad, he does not regard himself as fully identical with Choang-tsu and, secondly, because he doesn't fully understand how right he is. In fact, it is when he was the butterfly that he apprehended one of the roots of his identity — that he was, and is, in his essence, that butterfly who paints himself with his own colours — and it is because of this that, in the last resort, he is Choang-tsu."
— Jacques Lacan, "The Split Between the Eye and the Gaze"[3]

The key scene in Cronenberg's *A History of Violence* sees the local sheriff addressing the hero, Tom Stall (Viggo Mortensen), after a series of violent killings have disrupted the life of the small midwest town in which they both live: "It just doesn't all add up."

Superficially, *A History of Violence* is Cronenberg's most accessible film since 1983's *The Dead Zone*. Yet it is a film whose surface plausibility doesn't quite cohere. All the pieces are there but, when you look closely, they can't be made to fit together. Something sticks out...

What makes *A History of Violence* unsettling to the last is its uneasy relationship to genre: is it a thriller, a family drama, a bleak comedy, or a trans-generic allegory ("the Bush administration's foreign policy based upon a Western")? This generic hesitation means that it is a film suffused with the uncanny. Even when the standard motions of the thriller or the

147

family drama are gone through, there is something awry, so that *A History of Violence* views like a thriller assembled by a psychotic, someone who has learned the conventions of the genre off by heart but who can't make them work. Perversely, but appropriately for a Cronenberg picture, it is this "not quite working" that makes the film so gripping.

The near total absence of the prosthetics and FX for which Cronenberg is renowned from *A History of Violence* (traces of his old schtick survive only in the excessive shots of corpses after they have been shot in the face) has been remarked upon by most critics. In fact, Cronenberg's renunciation of such imagery has been a gradual process, dating back at least as far as *Crash* (1998's *eXistenZ* may turn out to be the last hurrah for Cronenberg's pulsating, eroticised bio-machinery), but it has subtlised, rather than removed, his trademark ontological queasiness.

Myth is everywhere in *A History of Violence*: not only in the hokey small-town normality which is threatened, nor in the urban underworld of organised crime that threatens to encroach upon it and destroy it, but also in the conflict between the two. A town like Millbrook, the Indiana setting for *A History of Violence*, has been as likely to feature in American cinema as an image of menaced innocence in its own right. Comparisons with Lynch are inevitable, but it is Hitchcock, not Lynch, who is the most compelling parallel. The Hitchcock comparison goes far beyond surface details, significant as they are, such as the fact that, as the *Guardian* review reminds us, *A History of Violence*'s "Main Street resembles the one in Phoenix, Arizona, where the real estate office is to be found in *Psycho*".[4] There is a much deeper affinity between *A History of Violence* and Hitchcock which can be readily identified when we recall Žižek's classic analysis of Hitchcock's methodology. In *Looking Awry*, Žižek compares Hitchcock's "phallic" montage with the "anal" montage of conventional cinema:

> Let us take, for example, a scene depicting the isolated home of a rich family encircled by a gang of robbers threatening to attack it; the scene gains enormously in effectiveness if we contrast the idyllic everyday life within the house with the threatening preparations of the criminals outside: if we show in alternation the happy family at dinner, the boisterousness of the children, father's benevolent reprimands, etc., and the "sadistic" smile of a robber, another checking his knife or gun, a third grasping the house's balustrade. In what would the passage to the "phallic" stage consist? In other words, how would *Hitchcock* shoot the same scene? The first thing to remark is that the content of this scene does not lend itself to Hitchcockian suspense insofar as it rests upon a simple counterpoint of idyllic interior and threatening exterior. We should therefore transpose this "flat", horizontal doubling of the action onto a *vertical* level: the menacing horror should be placed *outside*, next to the idyllic interior but

well *within* it: *under* it, as its "repressed" underside. Let us imagine, for example, the same happy family dinner shown from the point of view of a rich uncle, their invited guest. In the midst of the dinner, the guest (and together with him ourselves, the public) suddenly "sees too much," observes what he was not supposed to notice, some incongruous detail arousing in him the suspicion that the hosts plan to poison him in order to inherit his fortune. Such a "surplus knowledge" has so to speak an abyssal effect [...] the action is in a way *redoubled in itself*, endlessly reflected as in a double mirror play... things appear in a totally different light, though they stay the same.[5]

What is fascinating about *A History of Violence* is that it recapitulates this passage from the anal to the phallic within its own narrative development, entirely appropriate for a film that shows, as Graham Fuller puts it, "the return of the phallus".[6] It begins, precisely, with a non-Hitchcockian contrast between a threatening Outside (a long, sultry tracking shot of two killers leaving a motel) and an idyllic Inside (the Stalls' family house, where the six-year-old daughter is comforted by her parents and her brother after she is woken from a nightmare). But as the film develops, it effectively re-topologises itself, interiorising the Threat, or, more accurately, showing that the Outside has always been Inside.

The Hitchcockian blot, the Thing that doesn't fit, is the "hero" himself. The film's central enigma — is the staid, pacific Tom Stall really the psychopathic assassin Joey Cusack? — can be resolved into the question: which Hitchcock film we are watching? Is *A History of Violence* a rehashing of *The Wrong Man* or *Shadow of a Doubt*? Disturbingly, it turns out that it is both at the same time.

Shadow of a Doubt is the working out of a family scene much like the one described by Žižek above, although in that case, it is the guest, the rich uncle, who is the threat to the domestic idyll. The uncle (Joseph Cotten) is a killer of rich widows who has holed up in the house of his sister's family to hide from the police. *The Wrong Man*, meanwhile, sees a family destroyed when the father is falsely accused.

In *Shadow of a Doubt*, the uncle's malevolence means that he must die so that the family idyll can be preserved. Only the Teresa Wright character knows the truth; the rest of the family, and the big Other of the community, are kept in ignorance. But of the family members in *A History of Violence*, by the end of the film, only the youngest child could plausibly not be aware that the family scene has always been a simulation. Crucial in this respect is the response of Stall's wife, Edie (Maria Bello), as Ballard observed in his piece on *A History of Violence* in the *Guardian*:

A dark pit has opened in the floor of the living room, and she can see the appetite for cruelty and murder that underpins the foundations of her domestic life. Her husband's loving embraces hide brutal reflexes honed by aeons of archaic violence. This is a nightmare replay of *The Desperate Hours*, where escaping convicts seize a middle-class family in their sedate suburban home — but with the difference that the family must accept that their previous picture of their docile lives was a complete illusion. Now they know the truth and realise who they really are.[7]

But this isn't so much a matter of accepting reality in the raw, as it were, but, very much to the contrary, it is a question of accepting that the only liveable reality is a simulation. Where at the start of the film, Edie play acts the role of a cheerleader for Tom's sexual delectation, by the end she is playacting for real. (And of course, of course... there are no authentic cheerleaders, "real" cheerleaders are themselves playing a role.) If, as Žižek argued in *Welcome to the Desert of the Real*, 9/11 was already a recapitulation of the "ultimate American paranoiac fantasy [...] of an individual living in a small idyllic [...] city, a consumerist paradise, who suddenly starts to suspect that the world he lives in is a fake",[8] a kind of real-life staging of *The Matrix*, then *A History of Violence* may be the first post 9/11 film in which the American idyll is deliberately and knowingly re-constructed AS simulation. (This is underscored by the fact that not one frame of the film was shot in America. In this respect, the film resembles Kubrick's *Lolita*, whose America of motels and dusty highways was entirely reconstructed in Britain. In his interview with *Salon*, Cronenberg pronounced himself proud of his ability to hoodwink American audiences into believing that they were really seeing the midwest and Philadelphia.)

"When you dream, do you dream you're Joey?" the mobster Fogarty (Ed Harris) asks Tom Stall, perhaps deliberately echoing Chuang Tzu's story of a man who dreamt he was a butterfly. Chuang Tzu famously no longer knows if he is a butterfly dreaming that he was Chuang Tzu or Chuang Tzu dreaming that he is a butterfly. Is Tom Stall the dream of Joey Cusack, or is Joey Cusack the bad dream of Tom Stall? It's no surprise that Lacan should have fixed upon this story, and Forgarty's question contains an analyst's assumption: the reality of Tom lies not at the level of the everyday-empirical but at the level of desire. The Real of Stall/Cusack is to be found, fittingly, in the desert, the space of subjective destitution where Stall says that he "killed Joey".

In an interesting but ultimately unconvincing piece in *Sight and Sound*, Graham Fuller argues that we should read the film as Stall's fantasy:

"Who is Joey Cusack?" the movie ponders at its midpoint as it leaves Western territory behind and plunges into a dark pool of *noir*. But the more fruitful question is "Who is Tom Stall, if not whom Fogarty claims he is, and why does he have a superegoic alter ego?" The name "Stall" indicates stasis. Though he is a diligent, caring husband and father, Tom knows he hasn't made much of himself in life, and, we learn, harbours resentment towards his estranged wealthy brother, who considers him a fool. This chip on Tom's shoulder explains his daydreaming which, born of repression, aligns him which such literary and movie dreamers as Walter Mitty and Billy Liar, whose fantasies of themselves as all-conquering heroes are redolent of crippling neuroses, even impotence...[9]

Tempting as it is, this interpretation is unsatisfactory for a number of reasons. It is guilty of the same "oneiric derealisation" which has blighted responses to both Lynch's *Mulholland Drive* and Kubrick's *Eyes Wide Shut*, both of which have been interpreted as long dream sequences. Such readings ultimately amount to an attempt to put to rest the films' ontological threat, ironing out all their anomalies by attributing them to an interiorised delirium. The problem is that this denies both the libidinal reality of dreams — we wake ourselves from dreams, Lacan suggests, in order to flee the Real of our desires — at the same time as it ignores the way in which ordinary, everyday reality is dependent for its consistency on fantasy. It also makes the empiricist presupposition that the quotidian and the banal have more reality than violence; the message of the film is rather that the two are inextricable.

In the end, Stall as the fantasy of Cusack is much more interesting than Cusack as the fantasy of Stall. Is the American small-town idyll the fantasy of a psychopath? After Guantanamo Bay, after Abu Ghraib, this question has a special piquancy. The challenge that *A History of Violence* poses to the audience comes from the fact that we fully identify with Stall/Joey's violence. We gain enormous enjoyment when the hoods are dispatched with maximum efficiency. When *we* dream, do we dream we're Joey? Do we dream *as* Joey? Do we dream *of being* Tom, innocent, regular people, no blood on our hands? Are our "real", everyday lives really only this dream?

At the same time as we enjoy Joey's hyper-violent killing of the gangsters, we know that it is impossible for us to position them as the Outside and Stall/Joey as the Inside, and the film reinforces the lesson that Žižek thought we should have learned in the aftermath of 9/11:

Whenever we encounter such a purely evil Outside, we should gather the courage to endorse the Hegelian lesson: in this pure Outside, we should recognise the distilled version of our own essence. For the last five centuries, the (relative) prosperity and peace of the "civilised" West was bought by the export of ruthless violence and destruction into the "barbarian" Outside: the long story from the conquest of America to the slaughter in Congo.[10]

The most disturbing aspect about the film's violence is not the gore that results from it, but the reptilian mechanism of its execution. There are no wisecracking one-liners; instead, once the killings are completed with a coiled spring autonomic power, there is an entranced animal calm, a machine exhaustion. (*A History of Violence* is reflexive without ironic, entirely lacking in any PoMo swagger. It may have put the final bullet into Tarantino's career, if the spectacular indulgence of *Kill Bill* didn't already do that.)

A History of Violence suggests that twenty-first century America is a less a country in which violence is a repressed underside than that it is moebian band where if you begin with ultraviolence you will eventually end up with homely banality, and vice versa. In the final scene, when Tom — now "Tom" — returns to his house, "everything appears in a totally different light, though it has stayed the same". The images of domesticity have now become "images of domesticity", the meatloaf and the mashed potato have become "meatloaf" and "mashed potato", reflexively-placed icons of American normality, the very definition of the unhomely, the unheimlich, the uncanny. Such, as Žižek said in the 9/11 piece, is the nature of "late capitalist consumerist society", where "'real social life' itself somehow acquires the features of a staged fake". This is a simulated scenario far bleaker than that of *The Truman Show* or Dick's *Time Out of Joint*, since it has been freely and knowingly embraced by the subjects themselves. There is no Them behind the scenes orchestrating and choreographing the simulation. At the end of the film, everyone is fooling but no one is fooled.

notes on cronenberg's *eXistenZ* [1]

"Can what is playing you make it to level 2?" asked Nick Land in his 1994 discussion of cybertheory, "Meltdown".[2] Land's intuition that computer games would provide the best way to understand subjectivity and agency in digital culture was also the gambit of David Cronenberg's 1999 film *eXistenZ*. The film takes place in a near-future in which games are capable of generating simulated environments which can barely be distinguished from real life. Instead of computer terminals or game consoles, players use organic "game pods", which are connected directly to the players' bodies via "bio-ports" in their spines.

The main characters are Ted Pikul (Jude Law) and Allegra Geller (Jennifer Jason Leigh). We are first of all led to believe that Pikul is a neophyte gameplayer, being reluctantly initiated into the gameworld by Geller, who at this point seems to be the designer of the game (called eXistenZ) which they are playing. The two are pitched into a complex intrigue: a struggle between rival games corporations, and between gameplayers and "realists" — those who believe that the games are corroding the structure of reality itself. This corrosion is performed by the film itself, with what one of the characters memorably describes as "reality bleed-through" effects, so that the reality layers — only very weakly differentiated in any case — become difficult to distinguish. By the end it seems that both eXistenZ the game and what we had taken to be real life are embedded inside another game, tranCendenZ, but by now we cannot be sure of anything. The last line of dialogue is "Tell me the truth, are we still in the game?"

At the time of release, it seemed like *eXistenZ* was a late-arriving take on a series of themes and tropes familiar from 1980s cyberpunk — ideas Cronenberg had helped to shape in *Videodrome*. In retrospect, however, it is possible to see *eXistenZ* as part of a rash of late-1990s and early-2000s films, including *The Matrix* and *Vanilla Sky*, which mark a transition from what Alan Greenspan called the "irrational exuberance" of the 1990s bubble economy into the early twenty-first-century War on Terror moment. There is an abrupt mood shift toward the end of *eXistenZ*, with a military insurrection complete with heavy artillery and explosions. For the most part, though, the dominant mood is more quotidian. By contrast with the hyper-conspicuous CGI of *The Matrix*, with which it was destined to be most compared, *eXistenZ* is sparing in its use of special effects. The look is subdued, resolutely nonspectacular: there is a lot of brown. The brownness seems like a refusal of the gloss that will increasingly come to coat the artifacts of digital culture.

With its dreary trout farms, ski lodges, and repurposed churches, the world (or, more properly, worlds) of *eXistenZ* have a mundane, lived-in quality. Or rather worked-in: much of the film happens in workplaces — gas station, factory, workshop — and this dimension of the film is what now seems prophetic. Though never explicitly discussed, labour is something like an ambient theme, omnipresent but unarticulated. The key to *eXistenZ*'s self-reflexivity is its preoccupation with the conditions of its own production (and the production of culture in general). It presents us with an uncanny compression, in which the "front end" of late capitalist culture — its cutting-edge entertainment systems — fold back into the normally unseen "back end" (the quotidian factories, labs, and focus groups in which such systems are produced). The clamour of capitalist semiotics, the frenzy of branding sigils and signals, is curiously muted in *eXistenZ*. Instead of being part of the background hum of experience, as they are in both everyday life and the typical Hollywood movie, brand names appear only rarely in *eXistenZ*. The ones that do appear — most of them the names of games companies — leap out of the screen. The generic naming of space is in fact one of the running jokes in the film: a country gas station is simply called Country Gas Station, a motel is called Motel. This is part of the flat affect, the strange tonelessness, which governs most of the film.

The digitisation of culture which we take for granted now was only in its infancy in 1999; broadband was a few years off, as was the iPod, and *eXistenZ* has little to tell us about the digital communications equipment that proliferated in the decade after it was released. Handheld devices do not play any major role in *eXistenZ* — the glowing phone belonging to Pikul is thrown out of a car window by Geller — and, with its longueurs, its lingering in dead time, the film is very far from registering the jittery, attention-dispersing effects of "always-on" mobile technology. The most resonant aspects of *eXistenZ* do not reside in the body horror which was then still Cronenberg's signature — although the scenes of the characters being connected to their organic game pod by bio-ports are typically grisly. Nor are they to be found in the perplexity expressed by characters as to whether they are inside a simulation or not — this is a theme that was already familiar from *Videodrome*, as well as Verhoeven's *Total Recall*, both of which (in the first case indirectly, in the second more directly) took their inspiration from Philip K. Dick's fiction. Instead it is the idea — in some ways stranger and more disturbing than the notion that reality is fake — that *subjectivity* is a simulation which is the distinctive insight of *eXistenZ*.

This idea emerges, in the first place, through confronting other automated (or rather partially automated) consciousnesses: entities that seem autonomous but in fact can only respond to certain trigger phrases or actions that move the gameplay down a predetermined pathway. Some of the most memorable (and humorous) scenes in *eXistenZ* show encounters with these Read Only Memory beings. We see one of the characters locked in a "game loop", silently lolling his head while waiting to hear the keywords that will provoke him back into action. Later, a clerk is seen repeatedly clicking a pen — as a background character he is programmed not to respond until his name is called. More disturbing than the third-person (or nonperson) encounter with these programmed drones is Pikul's experience of subjectivity being interrupted by an automatic behavior. At one point, he suddenly finds himself saying, "It's none of your business who sent us! We're here and that is all that matters". He is shocked at the expostulation: "God, what happened? I didn't mean to say that." "It's your character who said it", Geller explains. "It's kind of a schizophrenic feeling, isn't it? You'll get used to it. There are things that have to be said to advance the plot and establish the characters, and those things get said whether you want to say them or not. Don't fight it." Pikul later grimly notes that it makes no difference whether he fights these "game urges" or not.

The emphasis on the curtailing of free will is one reason that Cronenberg's claim that the film is "existentialist propaganda" seems odd. Existentialism was a philosophy which claimed that human beings (what Sartre called the "for-itself") are "condemned to be free", and that any attempt to avoid responsibility for one's actions amounts to bad faith. There is an absolute difference between the for-itself and what Sartre called the "in-itself" — the inert world of objects, denuded of consciousness. Yet *eXistenZ*, in common with much of Cronenberg's work, troubles the distinction between the for-itself and the in-itself: machines turn out to be anything but inert, just as human subjects end up behaving like passive automata. As in *Videodrome* before it, *eXistenZ* draws out all the ambiguities of the concept of the player. On the one hand, the player is the one in control, the agent; on the other, the player is the one *being* played, the passive substance directed by external forces. At first, it seems that Pikul and Geller are for-itself, capable of making choices, albeit within set parameters (unlike in *The Matrix*, they are constrained by the rules of the world into which they are thrown). The game characters, meanwhile, are the in-itself. But when Pikul experiences "game urges", he is both in-itself (a merely passive instrument, a slave of drive) and for-itself (a consciousness that recoils in horror from this automatism).

To appreciate *eXistenZ*'s contemporary resonance it is necessary to connect the manifest theme of artificial and controlled consciousness with the latent theme of work. For what do the scenes in which characters are locked in fugues or involuntary-behavior loops resemble if not the call-centre world of twenty-first-century labour in which quasi-automatism is expected of workers, as if the undeclared condition of employment were to surrender subjectivity and become nothing more than a bio-linguistic appendage tasked with repeating set phrases that make a mockery of anything resembling conversation? The difference between "interacting" with a ROM-construct and *being* a ROM-construct neatly maps onto the difference between telephoning a call centre and working in one.

In *Being and Nothingness*, Sartre famously used the example of the waiter: someone who overplays the role of waiter to the extent that they (to outside appearances at least) eliminate their own subjectivity. The power of Sartre's example depends upon the tension between the would-be automatism of the waiter's behavior and the awareness that behind the mechanical rituals of the waiter's over-performance of his role is a consciousness that remains distinct from that role. In *eXistenZ*, however, we are confronted with the possibility that agency can genuinely be interrupted by the "inflexible stiffness of some kind of automaton". In any case, *eXistenZ* compels us to reread Sartre's description of the waiter in its terms, especially since one of the most horrific scenes of being-played features none other than a waiter. Pikul and Geller are sitting in a restaurant when Pikul feels himself overcome by a "game urge":

Pikul: You know, I do feel the urge to kill someone here.
Geller: Who?
Pikul: I need to kill our waiter.
Geller: Oh. Well that makes sense. Um, waiter! Waiter!
[*She calls over waiter*]
Geller: When he comes over, do it. Don't hesitate.
Pikul: But... everything in the game is so realistic, I— I don't think I really could.
Geller: You won't be able to stop yourself. You might as well enjoy it.
Pikul: Free will... is obviously not a big factor in this little world of ours.
Geller: It's like real life. There's just enough to make it interesting.

"You won't be able to stop yourself, you might as well enjoy it" — this phrase captures all too well the fatalism of those who have given up the hope of having any control over their lives and work. Here, *eXistenZ* emerges, not as "existentialist propaganda" but as decisively *anti*-existentialist. Free will is not an irreducible fact about human existence: it is merely the unpreprogrammed sequence necessary to stitch together a narrative that is already written. There is no real choice over the most important aspects of our life and work, *eXistenZ* suggests. Such choice as there is exists one level up: we can choose to accept and enjoy our becoming in-itself, or reject it (perhaps uselessly). This is a kind of deflation-in-advance of all of the claims about "interactivity" that communicative capitalism will trumpet in the decade after *eXistenZ* was released.

Autonomist theorists have referred to a turn away from factory work toward what they call "cognitive labour". Yet work can be affective and linguistic without being cognitive — like a waiter, the call-centre worker can perform attentiveness without having to think. For these *non-cognitive* workers, indeed, thought is a privilege to which they are not entitled.

The muted tones of *eXistenZ* anticipate a digital-era banality, and it is the banal quality of life in a digitally automated environment — human-sounding voices that announce arrivals and departures at a railway station, voice-recognition software which fails to recognise our voices, call-centre employees drilled into mechanically repeating a set script — that *eXistenZ* captures so well.

i filmed it so i didn't have to remember it myself[1]

I was reminded of *A History of Violence* while watching Andrew Jarecki's ultra-disturbing documentary *Capturing the Friedmans* on Channel 4's new digital service, more4, the other night.

Capturing the Friedmans is about a family from Great Neck, New York State, two of whose members (the father, Arnold, and one of the sons, Jesse, then only a teenager) pleaded guilty to serious sexual offences and were consequently jailed. Were they guilty? We can be reasonably confident only that Arnold had paedophiliac tendencies, and owned child pornography; he also confessed to having had some sort of sexual contact, short of sodomy, with two boys, but not in Great Neck. The rest is an enigma which makes *Rashomon* seem like an open and shut case. Jesse's role, for instance, is desperately unclear. The supposed victims claimed that Jesse had participated in, and assisted with, his father's violent abuses. But a campaigner cast doubt on the victims' testimony, none of which was corroborated by any physical evidence, and most of which seemed to have been "recovered" after they had been hypnotised.

The gaps in the Friedman narrative are all the more glaring because of the plethora of recorded material that IS available. This was a family that seemed — like many now I suppose — to obsessively record itself. Part of the "capturing" of the Friedmans is their capturing of *themselves*, on film and on tape. A documentary like this only became possible now that filming technology — cine cameras and later camcorders — had become widely available for the first time and kids are filmed from the moment of birth. The whole thing felt like a grim counterpoint to the proto-reality TV documentary of the Loud family Baudrillard discussed in "Precession of Simulacra".[2] In a way, the most painful material consists of home movie footage of the Friedmans shot in the 1970s, in which they look for all the world like a perfectly happy family, the kids mugging and clowning for the

159

cameras. Never has Deleuze's observation that "family photos" are, by their very nature, profoundly misleading, been more bitterly borne out. Later, as the trials start and the recriminations follow, the family filmed and audio-taped themselves ripping each other to shreds.

Why did they continue to film? "How do they remember, those who do not film?" asks Chris Marker in *Sans Soleil*. But why would the Friedmans want to remember their journey into Hell? Who could possibly want to film this? In *Lost Highway*, Fred Madison (Bill Pullman) claimed that he hated the thought of video-taping his own life because he "liked to remember things in his own way". In an uncanny complement to this, David Friedman, who recorded the events of the day Jesse was sentenced to eighteen years imprisonment, said that he filmed it "so I didn't have to remember it myself". The machines remember, so we don't have to.

spectres of marker and the reality of the third way[1]

Watching Chris Marker's *Le Fond de l'air est rouge* (*A Grin Without a Cat*) last week made for a somewhat ambivalent experience: even though the film is, ostensibly, a catalogue of disappointments, its registering of a time when there were challenges — no matter how inchoate, messy, contradictory — to the existing order, cannot but offer some inspiration in these much bleaker times. *A Grin Without a Cat*, originally released in 1977 but given a new post-89 epilogue by Marker in 1992, is an epic montage-meditation on what Marker called "the Third World War": the hydra-headed revolutionary or would-be revolutionary struggles of the Sixties and the Seventies. Marker constructed the film entirely out of archive material, shooting no original footage, and producing associations, connections, foreshadowings and echoes through masterly editing. The effect, especially if you are not minutely familiar with events in France, Vietnam, Algeria, Bolivia, Cuba and Czechoslovakia is disorientating, vertiginous. You find yourself Quantum-Leapt into the middle of a jostling crowd scene; no sooner have you got your bearings there when you abruptly find yourself in another place, another time. Marker's commentary — spoken by a number of actors — gives you clues, epigraphs, rather than explication. But Marker's aim not to render the period from 67 to 77 as Objective History to be pontificated upon by "experts" for whom the Meaning of the events is already established, nor, even worse, to produce a vanguardist version of *I Heart 1968*, in which sighing former revolutionaries look back on anger with the tender contempt of contemporary "wisdom". No, the point was to present the events "in becoming", to restore to them a subjectivity (in the Kierkegaardian sense) that retrospection structurally forecloses.

At one stage in the film, Marker's commentary ruefully notes that while revolutionaries, failed revolutionaries and ex-revolutionaries devoted all their attention to the formation of the New Left, the New Right was coalescing, unnoticed. Cue images of Valery Giscard D'estaing playing football in a carefully-cultivated attempt to look sporty and modern. The PR director of Citroën muses on the "science of management" (too complicated, he says, for even the most talented Union member to master) and looks forward to the incorporation of leftist desire into Capital that would become post-Fordism.

Cut to now, where the images of even an ultimately failed militancy belong to a past. A past that was not — in one sense — even mine, that was over *before* I was born in July 1968. Yet the reverberations continued for a few years yet, were an unacknowledged (by me, then) background to the things that I enjoyed in the late Seventies and early Eighties. For those of us arriving after the event, the significance of the convulsions documented in Marker's film could only be apprehended much later, once their effects had completely ebbed away and the reality (and the pleasure) principles were Restored. Marcus' *Lipstick Traces* — whose temporal jump-cutting in many ways recalls that of Marker's film — goes some way to establishing the connections between the events remembered in *A Grin Without a Cat* and those that began in the UK at more or less the time that the film was completed. A cheshire cat's grin, lipstick traces on a cigarette, spectres of Marx: Marcus, Derrida and Marker come to see ruptures, revolts and revolutions as ghostly residue, thin stains on the seamless surfaces of post-Cold War Capital.

The untranslateable French title of Marker's film suggests possibilities that hovered and haunted without ever making themselves real. At the Marker conference held at the ICA a few years ago, Barry Langford argued that, "rather than the spectre of Communism famously invoked by Marx in the opening lines of the Communist Manifesto", for both *A Grin Without a Cat* and Marx's "The Civil War in France" a hundred years before it, "it is the phantom of revolution that haunts Marx and Marker alike — that is, the fear that revolution will ultimately prove, precisely, phantasmic". If Marx and Marker's fear was that revolution would *only* be a spectre, our suspicion is that it will not turn out to be even that, that the stricken ghosts have been put to flight once and for all. (And even the "death of communism" is not enough for the guardians of the new status quo, for whom "communism is not dead enough — [...] they will only be content when they have driven a stake through its heart and buried it at the crossroads at midnight".[2])

The struggles in *A Grin Without a Cat* might have been defeated, might even have contributed to a more ferociously effective Reaction, but the pressures that those events brought to bear almost had very immediate effects — by contesting the Possible, by rejecting "realism", they could not but have altered expectations about what was acceptable in the workplace, about what could happen in everyday life. The revolutions were cultural; which is to say, they understood that culture and politics could not be conceived in isolation from one another. Both Althusser and the Situationist-inspired students of 68, in many ways so opposed, could agree on at least one thing: that cultural products were never *merely* cultural. In their condemnations of recuperated Spectacle and Ideological Apparatuses, they granted a weight to cultural products which few would countenance now.

I felt the contrast between what Marker's film recounted and contemporary realities especially painfully last week when I went on a TUC training course with members of NATFHE from other FE colleges. The stories of increased casualisation, of newly punitive sickness policies, of lecturers being sacked and forced to re-apply for their jobs, of the imposition of more and more targets and "spurious measurable", each entailing yet more pointless, window-dressing paperwork, confirmed what, individually, we all already knew. The Further Education sector is in crisis; its problems only symptomatic of a wider malaise in UK education as a whole. Further Education colleges, out of Local Education Authority control since 1992, show the way in which a "reformed" (i.e. part-privatised) education will develop. The recent report which stated that students spoon-fed at A-level cannot cope with university study would come as little surprise to few A-level teachers and lecturers. The pressure to meet government targets means that quality and breadth of teaching is sacrificed for the narrow goal of passing the exam: an instrumentalisation of education that fully accepts that its only role is to reproduce the labour force. Far, far away from 68, at the core of whose conflagrations was education, and the question of what it could be: could it be more than an ideological training camp, a carceral institution?

One thing that occurred to me last week, prompted by the contrast between Marker's Then and our Now, was that the third way is not entirely a phantasm, an ideological dupe. There is in fact a reality to the third way, and it is the reality of bureaucracy. *That* is what is left once politics has become administration.

It's hard to believe that public services are not more clogged with bureaucracy than they were pre-Thatcher. Certainly, education is choked with the stuff... targets, action plans, log books, all of them required conditions for funding by the Learning and Skills Council, and assessed by Ofsted, whose threat no longer takes the form of an invasive external entity arriving every two or three years, but has become introjected into the institution itself, through the permanent panoptic vigilance of a bloated managerial strata determined to over-compensate in order to fully ensure it is meeting central government's demands. This is the reality of "market Stalinism" in education.

Is there a way to challenge or roll back the slow, implacable, rapacious proliferation of bureaucracy? Only by a collective action that seems inconceivable now... Only by a change in the ideological climate... Only by a switch in the cultural atmosphere... Where to start? While we search, desperately, for cracks in the Possible, bureaucracy, that steel spider, patiently spins its grey web...

dis-identity politics[1]

The discussion of *V for Vendetta* has been far more interesting than the film deserved. Yes, there is a certain frisson in seeing a major Hollywood movie refusing to unequivocally condemn terrorism, but the political analysis in the film (as in the original comic) is really rather threadbare. That is Moore's fault; it can't be blamed on the Wachowskis. Like all of Moore's work, *V for Vendetta* is considerably less than the sum of its parts. I've complained before of finding Moore's continual efforts to reassure himself and his readers of their erudition — every time you are about to succumb to the fictional world, it's as if Moore taps you on your shoulder and say, "We're too good for this, aren't we folks?" — highly distracting and irritating.

As for *V for Vendetta*'s politics — apart from the subjective destitution scenes, they amount in large part to the familiar populist ideology which maintains that the world is controlled by a corrupt oligarchy that could be overthrown if only people knew about it. Steven Shaviro says that "rather than trying to please all demographics, [the film] identifies a deeply religious, homophobic, ultra-patriotic, imperialistic surveillance state as the source of oppression."[2] But isn't this precisely "appealing to all demographics", since few homophobic fascists will identify themselves as homophobic fascists, and it's hard to imagine anyone warming to Hurt's foaming-at-the-mouth ranter, still less voting for him. Postmodern fascism is a disavowed fascism (cue the BNP leaflet delivered through my door when I lived in Bromley, photograph of a smiling kiddywink, slogan: "My daddy's not a fascist"), just as homophobia survives as disavowed homophobia. The strategy is to refuse the identification while pursuing the political programme. "We of course deplore fascism and homophobia, but..." The Wachowskis' government bans the Koran, but that is the last thing that Blair and Bush would ever do; no, they will praise Islam as a "great religion of peace" while bombing Muslims.

165

Blair's authoritarian populism[3] is far more sinister than *V for Vendetta*'s pantomime autocracy precisely because Blair is so successful at "presenting himself as the reasonable, honest bloke on the side of the common man". Similarly, Bush's linguistic incompetence, far from being an impediment to his success, has been crucial to it, since it has allowed him to pose as a "man of the people", belying his privileged Harvard and Yale-educated background. It is significant in fact that class is not mentioned at all in the film. As Jameson wryly notes in "Marx's Purloined Letter", it is not

> particularly surprising that the system should have a vested interest in distorting the categories whereby we think class and in foregrounding gender and race, which are far more amenable to liberal ideal solutions (in other words, solutions that satisfy the demands of ideology, it being understood that in concrete social life the problems remain equally intractable).[4]

The climactic scenes of *V for Vendetta*, in which the people rise up (by this time, against no one) made me think, not of some great political Event, but rather of the Make Poverty History campaign — a "protest" with which no one could possibly disagree. The comparison with *Fight Club* does *V for Vendetta* no favours; the targets of Tyler Durdon's terrorism were not the fusty symbols of the political class but the franchise coffee bars and skyscrapers of impersonal capital.

I'm no fan of the Wachowskis' *Matrix*, but it succeeded in two ways that *V for Vendetta* never will. *The Matrix* has become a massively propagated pulp mythos (whereas who but academics will think about the *V for Vendetta* film a year from now? It'll be a year after that until academics recognise that the far more fascinating and sophisticated *Basic Instinct II* is worthy of study). More importantly, it suggested that what counts as "real" is an eminently political question.

That ontological dimension is what is missing from the progressive populist model, in which the masses cannot but appear as a dupes, fooled by the lies of the elite but ready to effectuate change the moment they are made aware of the truth. The reality, of course, is that the "masses" are under few illusions about the ruling elite (if anyone is credulous about politicians and "capitalist parliamentarianism", it is the middle classes). The Subject Supposed Not To Know is a figure of populist fantasies — more than that: the duped subject awaiting factual enlightenment is the presupposition on which progressive populism rests. If the most crucial political task is to enlighten the masses about the venality of the ruling class, then the preferred mode of discourse will be denunciation. Yet, this repeats rather than challenges the logic of the liberal order; it is no accident that the *Mail* and the *Express* favour the same denunciatory mode. Attacks on politicians tend to reinforce the atmosphere of diffuse cynicism upon which capitalist realism feeds. What is needed is not more empirical evidence of the evils of the ruling class but a belief on the part of the subordinate class that what they think or say matters; that *they* are the only effective agents of change.

This returns us to the question of reflexive impotence. Class power has always depended on a kind of reflexive impotence, with the subordinate class' beliefs about its own incapacity for action reinforcing that very condition. It would, of course, be grotesque to *blame* the subordinate class for their subordination; but to ignore the role that their complicity with the existing order plays in a self-fulfilling circuit would, ironically, be to deny their power.

"[C]lass consciousness", Jameson observes in "Marx's Purloined Letter",

> turns first and foremost around the question of subalternity, that is around the experience of inferiority. This means that the "lower classes" carry around within their heads unconscious convictions as to the superiority of hegemonic or ruling-class expressions or values, which they equally transgress and repudiate in ritualistic (and socially and politically ineffective) ways.

There is a way, then, in which inferiority is less class consciousness than class unconsciousness, less about experience than about an unthought precondition *of* experience. Inferiority is in this sense an ontological hypothesis that is not susceptible to any empirical refutation. Confronted with evidence of the incompetence or corruption of the ruling class, you will still feel that, nevertheless, they must possess some *agalma*, some secret treasure, that confers upon them the right to occupy the position of dominance.

Enough has been already been written about the kind of class displacement people like myself have experienced. Dennis Potter's Nigel Barton plays remain perhaps the most vivid anatomies of the loneliness and agony experienced by those who have been projected out of the confining, comforting fatalism of the working-class community and into the incomprehensible, abhorrently seductive rituals of the privileged world. "A drive from nowhere leaves you in the cold", as the Associates sang in "Club Country", "Every breath you breathe belongs to someone there."

There is a Cartesian paradox about such experiences, in that they are significant only because they produce a distanciation from experience as such; after undergoing them, it is no longer to conceive of experience as some natural or primitive ontological category. Class, previously a background assumption, suddenly interposes itself — not so much as a site for heroic struggle, but as a whole menagerie of minor shames, embarrassments and resentments. What had been taken for granted is suddenly revealed to be a contingent structure, producing certain effects (and affects). Nevertheless, that structure is tenacious; the assumption of inferiority constitutes something like a core programming which makes sense of the world in advance. To think of oneself as capable of doing a "professional" job, for instance, requires a traumatic shift in perspective, and if there are confidence crises and nervous breakdowns, they will be very often the consequence of the core programming intermittently reasserting itself.

The real lesson to draw from Potter's Barton plays is not the fatalist-heroic one about the agonies of the charismatic individual confronting intransigent social structures. The plays have to be read instead against class-as-ethnicity and for class-as-structure; in any case, as they make clear, the occult machineries of social structure *produce* the visible ethnicities of language, behaviour and cultural expectations. The plays' demand is not for a re-acceptance into the rejecting community, nor a full accession into the elite, but for a mode of collectivity yet to come.

Potter's challenges to naturalism then, become far more than mere PoMo trickery. His foregrounding of the way in which fictions structure reality, and of the role that television itself plays in this process, brings to the fore all the ontological issues that worthier, more traditional social realist writers conceal or distort. There is no realism, Potter suggests, beyond the Real of class antagonism.

Now is perhaps the time to address two good questions that Bat[5] mailed in response to the reflexive impotence post. First, Bat asked, is the situation for French teenagers different from that of their British counterparts? This is easily dealt with, since, after all, it was the very problem with which the post aimed to deal. French students are far more embedded in a Fordist/disciplinary framework than are British students. In education and employment, the disciplinary structures survive in France, providing some contrast with, and resistance to, the cyberspatial pleasure matrix. (For reasons I will explore in more depth shortly, this is not necessarily for the best, however.) Bat's second question raised more important issues; doesn't talking about reflexive impotence reinforce the very interpassive nihilism it supposedly condemns? I would say that the exact opposite is the case. I've had more mail about the reflexive impotence post than any other; mostly, actually, from teenagers and students who recognise the condition but who, far from being further depressed by seeing it analysed, find its identification inspiring. There are very good Spinozist and Althusserian reasons for this — seeing the network of cause-and-effect in which we are enchained is *already* freedom. By contrast, what *is* depressing is the implacable poptimism of the official culture, forever exhorting us to be excited about the latest dreary-shiny cultural product and hectoring us for failing to be sufficiently positive. A certain "vulgar Deleuzianism", preaching against any kind of negativity, provides the theology for this compulsory excitation, evangelising on the endless delights available if only we consume harder. But what it is so often inspiring — in politics as much as in popular culture — is the capacity to nihilate present conditions. The nihilative slogan is neither be "things are good, there is no need for change", nor "things are bad, they cannot change", but "things are bad, *therefore* they must change."

This brings us to subjective destitution, which, unlike Steve Shaviro, I think *is* a precondition of any revolutionary action. The scenes of Evey's subjective destitution in *V for Vendetta* are the only ones which had any real political charge. For that reason, they were the only scenes which produced any real discomfort; the rest of the film does little to upset the liberal sensibilities which we all carry around with us. The liberal programme articulates itself not only through the logic of rights, but also, crucially, through the notion of identity, and V is attacking both Evey's rights and her identity. Steve says that you can't *will* subjective destitution. I, however, would say that you can *only* will it, since it is the existential choice in its purest form. Subjective destitution is not something that happens in any straightforward empirical sense; it is, rather, an Event precisely in the sense of being an incorporeal transformation, an ontological reframing to which you must assent. Evey's choice is between defending her (old) identity — which, naturally, also amounts to a defence of the ontological framework which conferred that identity upon her — and affirming the evacuation of all previous identifications. What this brings out with real clarity is the opposition between liberal identity politics and proletarian dis-identity politics. Identity politics seeks respect and recognition from the master class; dis-identity politics seeks the dissolution of the classifactory apparatus itself.

That is why British students are, potentially, far more likely to be agents of revolutionary change than are their French counterparts. The depressive, totally dislocated from the world, is in a better position to undergo subjective destitution than someone who thinks that there is some home within the current order that can still be preserved and defended. Whether on a psychiatric ward, or prescription-drugged into zombie oblivion in their own domestic environment, the millions who have suffered massive mental damage under capitalism — the decommisioned Fordist robots now on incapacity benefit as well as the reserve army of the unemployed who have never worked — might well turn out to be the next revolutionary class. They really do have *nothing* to lose...

169

"you have always been the caretaker": the spectral spaces of the overlook hotel[1]

"What is anachronistic about the ghost story is its peculiarly contingent and constitutive dependence of physical place and, in particular, on the material house as such. No doubt, in some pre-capitalist forms, the past manages to cling stubbornly to open spaces, such as a gallows hill or a sacred burial ground; but in the golden age of this genre, the ghost is at one with a building of some antiquity […] Not death as such, then, but the sequence of such 'dying generations' is the scandal reawakened by the ghost story for a bourgeois culture which has triumphantly stamped out ancestor worship and the objective memory of the clan or extended family, thereby sentencing itself to the life span of the biological individual. No building more appropriate to express this than the grand hotel itself, with its successive seasons whose vaster rhythms mark the transformation of American leisure classes from the late 19th century down to the vacations of present-day consumer society."
— Fredric Jameson, "Historicism in *The Shining*"[2]

"[T]he strongest compulsive influence arises from the impressions which impinge upon the child when we would have to regard his psychical apparatus as not yet completely receptive. The fact cannot be doubted; but it is so puzzling that we may make it more comprehensible by comparing it with a photographic exposure which can be developed after any interval of time and transformed into a picture."
— Sigmund Freud, "Moses and Monotheism"[3]

Space is intrinsic to spectrality, as one of the meanings of the term "haunt" — a place — indicates. Yet haunting, evidently, is a disorder of time as well as of space. Haunting happens when a space is invaded or otherwise disrupted by a time that is out-of-joint, a dyschronia.

171

The Shining – King's novel, and Kubrick's "unfaithful" film version, both of which I propose to treat as one interconnected textual labyrinth — is fundamentally concerned with the question of repetition. In *Spectres of Marx*, Derrida defines hauntology as the study of that which repeats without ever being present. To elaborate, we might say that the revenant repeats without being present *in the first place* — where "place" is equivalent in meaning to "time". Nothing occupies the point of origin, and that which haunts *insists* without ever *existing*. We shall return to this presently (or would it be better to say, *it* will return to *us*?).

Precisely because it is so centrally about repetition, *The Shining* is a deeply psychoanalytic fiction. You might say that it translates psychoanalysis' family dramas into the stuff of horror, except that it does rather more; it demonstrates what many have long suspected — that psychoanalysis already belongs to the genre of horror. Where else could we place concepts such as the death drive, the uncanny, trauma, the compulsion to repeat?

Yet *The Shining* is about repetition in a cultural, as well as a psychoanalytic sense. Hence Jameson's interest. Jameson, after all, has theorised postmodernity in terms of repetition, albeit a repetition that is disavowed. The "nostalgia mode" he refers to names an all-but ubiquitous yet largely unacknowledged mode of repetition, in a culture in which the conditions for the original and the ground-breaking are no longer in place, or are in place only in very exceptional circumstances. The nostalgia in question is neither a psychological nor an affective category. It is structural and cultural, not a matter of an individual or a collective longing for the past. Almost to the contrary, the nostalgia mode is about the inability to imagine anything other than the past, the incapacity to generate forms that can engage with the present, still less the future. It is Jameson's claim that representations of the future, in fact, are increasingly likely to come to us garbed in the forms of the past: *Blade Runner*, with its well-known debt to film noir, is exemplary here (and nothing makes Jameson's point more clearly than *Blade Runner*'s domination over science fiction film in the last twenty-five years).

According to Jameson, then, *The Shining*, then, is a "metageneric" reflection on the ghost story (a ghost story that is about ghost stories). Yet I want to claim *The Shining* does not belong to postmodernity, but rather to postmodernity's doppelganger, hauntology. We could go so far as to say that it is a meta-reflection on postmodernity itself. As Jameson reminds us, *The Shining* is also about a failed writer: a would-be novelist who yearns to be virile writer in the strong modernist mould, but who is fated to be a passive surface on which the hotel — itself a palimpsest of fantasies and atrocities, an echo chamber of memories and anticipations — will inscribe its pathologies and homicidal intent. Or, it would be better to say, for this is the horrible dyschronic temporal mode proper to the Overlook, it *will have always* done.

The Overlook and the Real

"Around him, he could hear the Overlook Hotel coming to life."
— Stephen King, *The Shining*[4]

There is no escape from the infinite corridors of the Overlook. It is no gloomy castle, easily relegated to an obsolete genre (the gothic romance); neither is it a supernatural relic that will crumble to dust when exposed to the harsh light of scientific reason. Concealed behind the alluring ghosts of the hotel's Imaginary which seduce Jack, the horrors that stalk the Overlook's corridors belong to the Real. The Real is that which keeps repeating, that which re-asserts itself no matter how you seek to flee it (more horribly, it is that which re-asserts itself *through* the attempts to flee it: the fate of Oedipus). The Overlook's horrors are those of the family and of history; or more concisely, they are those of family history (the province, needless to say, of psychoanalysis).

David A. Cook has already shown how the film version is haunted by American history.[5] In Cook's rendition, the Overlook, that playground of the ultra-privileged and the super-crooked (and no one, in the still paranoid post-Watergate dusk when King wrote the novel, could be so naïve as to imagine that these two groups could be parsed), metonymically stands in for the nightmare of American history itself. A leisure hive built on top of an Indian Burial Ground (this detail was added by Kubrick); a potent image of a culture founded upon (the repression of) the genocide of the native peoples:

It was as if another Overlook now lay scant inches beyond this one, separated from the real world (if there is such thing as a "real world" Jack thought) but gradually coming into balance with it.[6]

Important as Cook's reflections are, as I have already indicated, I want to concentrate, not on the macro-level of history, on the micro-level of the family. This, inevitably, brings us to Walter Metz's valuable reflections on the way in which *The Shining* is intertextually bound up with the melodrama genre.[7] A central tension in the film — a tension which for some is never quite resolved — concerns how *The Shining* is ultimately to be generically placed: is it about the family (in which case, it belongs to melodrama) or is about the supernatural (in which case, it belongs to horror or the ghost story)?[8] This inevitably recalls Todorov's famous claim that the "fantastic" is defined by the hesitation between two epistemological possibilities; if spectral forces can be explained psychologically or by some other naturalistic means, then we are dealing with the "uncanny". If the spectres of the supernatural cannot be exorcised, then we are dealing with the "marvellous". Only while we oscillate between the two possibilities do we confront the "fantastic".

| The Uncanny | The Fantastic | The Marvellous |
| Melodrama | | The ghost story |

Noting that most critics have regarded *The Shining* as a case of the "marvellous", Metz positions *The Shining* as an example of the "uncanny".

But I want to argue that *The Shining* is important because it scrambles the terms of Todorov's schema; it is, at one and the same time, a family melodrama *and* a ghost story. If the ghosts are real, it is not because they are supernatural; and if the spectres are psychoanalytic, that is not to say that they can be reduced to the psychological. Just the reverse, in fact: rather than the spectral being subsumed by the psychological, for psychoanalysis, the psychological can be construed as a symptom of the spectral. It is the haunting that comes first.

Patriarchy as Hauntology

The Overlook's ghosts are inescapable because they are the spectres of family history, and who of us is without a family history?[9] *The Shining* is a fiction, after all, about fathers and sons. Its genesis lay in a fantasy from which King the father, still struggling with alcoholism, recoiled, but which King the writer was fascinated by. Finding his papers scattered by his son one day, King flew into a blind rage; later he realised he could easily have struck the child. The germ of the novel was King's extrapolation from that situation: what if he *had* struck his son? What if he had done much worse? What if King were an alcoholic failure who merely dreamt that he is a novelist?

Psychoanalysis could be crudely boiled down to the claim that we *are* our family history, although it is perhaps at this point that we can dispense with the term "history" and replace it with "hauntology". The family emerges in Freud as a hauntological structure: the child is father to the man, the sins of the fathers are visited upon the children. The child who hates his father is condemned to repeat him, the abused becomes the abuser.

The Shining is about patriarchy as hauntology, and that relation is nowhere more thoroughly explored than in Freud's essays on the foundations of religion. Here, Freud shows that the Holy Father, Jahweh, is indeed also a Holy Ghost: a spectral deity which can assert itself only through its physical absence. Freud repeated the "speculative myth" of the dismemberment and devouring of the Father Thing in "Totem and Taboo" thirty years later in "Moses and Monotheism", a text which is itself full of repetitions and refrains.

In Freud's account, there are two Fathers: the obscene "Pere Jouissance" (Lacan) who has access to total enjoyment, and the Name/No (Nom/Non) of the Father — the Father of Law, the Symbolic Order in person, who forbids and mortifies. As Žižek has shown,[10] one of the most significant aspects of "Totem and Taboo" was to have established that the austere Father of Symbolic Law is not originary; it is not, as the theory of the Oedipus complex had assumed, that the father is a pre-existent block to enjoyment. This "block" only comes into place once the father is killed.

In the story as Freud recounts it, the primal horde of beta males, jealous and resentful of the tribal Father, rise up one day to kill him, anticipating that they will now have unlimited access to jouissance. But this is not what transpires. The "band of brothers" are immediately remorseful, guilt-stricken, melancholic. Far from being able to enjoy everything, the gloomy parricidal brothers are unable to enjoy anything. And far from ridding themselves of their Father's loathsome domination, they find that the Father dominates them all the more now that he is absent. The Father's ghost preys upon their conscience; indeed, their conscience is nothing other than the reproach of the dead Father's spectral voice. In heeding this absent voice, in commemorating and propitiating it by initiating new ceremonies and codes of practice, the brothers introduce the rudimentary forms of morality and religion. God, the Father, the Big Other, the Symbolic does not exist; but it *insists* through the repetition of these rituals.

The Father is doubly dead. He asserts his power only when he is dead, but his power is itself only a power of death: the power to mortify live flesh, to kill enjoyment.

A Child is Being Beaten

"Like father, like son. Wasn't that how it was popularly expressed?"
— Stephen King, *The Shining*[11]

The Shining shows us patriarchal dementia — with its lusts, its ruses and its rationalisations — from inside. We witness Jack gradually succumbing to this dementia as he becomes intoxicated by the hotel and its temptations, promises and challenges. In the soft-focus, honeyed space of the Gold Room, Jack parties with the hotel's ghosts:

He was dancing with a beautiful woman. He had no idea of what time it was, how long he had spent in the Colorado Lounge or how long he had been there in the ballroom. Time had ceased to matter.[12]

In the grip of these fever-dream fantasies, Jack descends into the unconscious (where, as Freud tells us, time has no meaning). The unconscious

175

is always impersonal, and especially so here: the unconscious that Jack subsides into is the unconscious of the hotel itself. His family come to seem like "ball-breaking" distractions from his increasing spells of enchanted communion with the hotel, and *being a good father* becomes synonymous with delivering Danny to the Overlook. Jack becomes convinced by the hotel's avatars — which seem to reconcile the demands of the superego with those of the id — that it is his *duty* to bring Danny into line.

Beyond the Imaginary no-time of the Gold Room, there is another mode of suspended time in the Overlook. This belongs to the Real, where sequential, or "chronic", clockface time, is superseded by the fatality of repetition. It is the Imaginary pleasures of the Gold Room, with their succulent promises of enwombing fusion, which allow Jack to fall increasingly into the hold of the hotel's Real structure — the structure of abusive repetition. Danny confronts this structure as a vision of man endlessly a pursuing a child with a roque mallet (in the film, an axe).

> The clockface was gone. In its place was a round black hole. It led down into forever. It began to swell. The clock was gone. The room behind it. Danny tottered and then fell into the darkness that had been hiding behind the clockface all along.
>
> The small boy in the chair suddenly collapsed and lay in it at a crooked unnatural angle, his head thrown back, his eyes staring sightlessly at the high ballroom ceiling.
>
> Down and down and down and down to – the hallway, crouched in the hallway, and he had made wrong turn, trying to get back to the stairs he had made a wrong turn and now AND NOW –
>
> – he saw he was in the short dead-end corridor that led only to the Presidential Suite and the booming sound was coming closer, the roque mallet whistling savagely through the air, the head of it embedding itself into the wall, cutting the silk paper, letting out small puffs of plaster dust.[13]

Here we can turn again to the image of fatality Freud uses in "Moses and Monotheism", which I cited at the beginning of this essay. "[T]he strongest compulsive influence", Freud writes,

> arises from the impressions which impinge upon the child when we would have to regard his psychical apparatus as not yet completely receptive. The fact cannot be doubted; but it is so puzzling that we may make it more comprehensible by comparing it with a photographic exposure which can be developed after any interval of time and transformed into a picture.[14]

This passage is especially piquant and suggestive when considered in relation to *The Shining*, given the famous final image of Kubrick's film: a photograph taken in 1923 showing Jack, surrounded by party-goers and grinning. At this moment, we cannot but be reminded of Delbert Grady's ominous claim that Jack has "always been the caretaker".

What I want to draw from Freud's photographic metaphor is precisely its concept of effects being distanced in time from the events which produced them. This is the psychoanalytic horror which *The Shining* anatomises. Violence has been imprinted upon Jack "psychical apparatus" long ago, in childhood (the novel details at some length the abuse that Jack has himself suffered at the hands of his own father), but it requires the "spectral spaces" of the Overlook hotel to transform those impressions from an "exposure" into a "picture", an actual act of violence.

If Jack "has always been the caretaker", it is because his life has always been in the abuse-circuit. Jack represents an appalling structural fatality, a spectral determinism. To have "always been the caretaker" is never to have been a subject in his own right. Jack has only ever stood in for the Symbolic and the homicidal violence which is the Symbolic's obscene underside. What, after all, is the father if not the "caretaker", the one who (temporarily) shoulders the obligations of the Symbolic (what Jack calls "the white man's burden") before passing them onto the next generation? In Jack the ghosts of the past are revived — but only at the cost of his own "de-vival".

Of course, the dyschronic nature of the Overlook's abusive causality — events stored in the psyche will yield their effects only after time has elapsed — has implications for Danny's future as well. As Metz puts it: "When Jack chases Danny into the maze with ax in hand and states, 'I'm right behind you Danny', he is predicting Danny's future as well as trying to scare the boy. [...] [T]he patriarchal beast is within [Danny] as well."[15] Jack might as well be saying, "I'm just ahead of you, Danny": I am what you will become. In the Overlook, a child is always being beaten, and the position of the abused and the position of the abuser are places in a structure. It is all-too-easy for the abused to become the abuser. The ominous question *The Shining* poses, but does not answer, is: Will this happen to Danny (as it happened to Jack)? Is *The Shining*, that is to say, "Totem and Taboo"/ "Moses and Monotheism" — where the Father retains his spectral hold on the sons precisely through his own death — or is it *Anti-Oedipus*?

In the novel, Danny can only escape death at the hands of his father by catatonically communing with his double, Tony, whom King reveals to be an avatar of his future self:

And now Tony stood directly in front of him, and looking at Tony was like staring into a magic mirror and seeing himself in ten years...

The hair was light blond like his mother's, and yet the stamp on his features was that of his father, as if Tony — as if the Daniel Anthony

177

Torrance he would someday be — was a halfling caught between father and son, a ghost of both, a fusion.[16]

In the film, Danny escapes from his father by *walking backwards in his footsteps*. Yet we do not know if the (psychic) damage has already been done — will Danny, in surviving his father, end up taking his father's place?

For Metz, these hesitations leaves the text open: "It is up to Danny to grow up and build a better world, throwing off the demons of the past but always knowing that deep inside of him, the demons that possessed Jack and all Americans are right beneath the surface. Danny has inherited Jack's legacy."[17] If Danny can throw off the spectres of the past, there is a possibility of freedom, then, but have the "strongest compulsive influences" already done their work? Is Danny, too, destined to always have been the Overlook's caretaker?

coffee bars and internment camps[1]

I've finally seen *Children of Men*, on DVD, after missing it at the cinema. Watching it last week I asked myself, why is its rendering of apocalypse so contemporary?

British cinema, for the last thirty years as chronically sterile as the issueless population in *Children of Men*, has not produced a version of the apocalypse that is even remotely as well realised as this. You would have to turn to television — to the last *Quatermass* serial or to *Threads*, almost certainly the most harrowing television programme ever broadcast on British TV — for a vision of British society in collapse that is as compelling. Yet the comparison between *Children of Men* and these two predecessors points to what is unique about the film; the final *Quatermass* serial and *Threads* still belonged to Nuttall's bomb culture,[2] but the anxieties with which *Children of Men* deals have nothing to do with nuclear war.

Children of Men reinforces what few would doubt, but which British cinema would seldom lead you to suspect: the British landscape bristles with cinematic potential. It's long since been evident that only someone outside the self-serving, self-pitying low gene pool of British cinema is capable of realising this potential, and *Children of Men*'s director, Alfonso Cuarón, and cinematographer, Emmanuel Lubezki, are both Mexican. Together they have produced a portrait of Grim Britannia that is like a film equivalent of the Burial LP (and the film's excellent soundtrack features Burial's mentor and label-mate, Kode9).

Lubezki's cinematography is breathtaking. His photography seems to leech all organic and naturalistic vitality from the images, leaving them a washed-out grey-blue. As David Edelstein put it in an insightful review in *New York Magazine*: "The movie calls to mind an early description in Cormac McCarthy's overwrought but gripping post-apocalypse novel *The*

Road of gray days 'like the onset of some cold glaucoma dimming away the world.'"[3] The lighting is masterly: it as if the whole film takes place in a permanent winter afternoon when even the sun is dying. White smoke, its source unspecified, curls ubiquitously.

Cuarón's trick is to combine this despondent lyricism with a formal realism, achieved through the expert use of hand-held camera and long takes. Blood spatters onto the camera lens and goes unwiped. The gunfire is as oppressively tactile as it was in *Saving Private Ryan*. The meticulously choreographed long takes — technical feats of some magnitude — have justly been highly praised, and they are all the more remarkable because they go beyond the familiar role of simulating documentary realism to serve a political and artistic vision.

This brings us back, then, to my initial question, and I think that there are three reasons that *Children of Men* is so contemporary.

Firstly, the film is dominated by the sense that the damage has been done. The catastrophe is neither waiting down the road, nor has it already happened. Rather, it is being lived through. There is no punctual moment of disaster; the world doesn't end with a bang, it winks out, unravels, gradually falls apart. What caused the catastrophe to occur, who knows; its cause lies long in the past, so absolutely detached from the present as to seem like the caprice of a malign being: a negative miracle, a malediction which no penitence can ameliorate. Such a blight can only be eased by an intervention that can no more be anticipated than was the onset of the curse in the first place. Action is pointless; only senseless hope makes sense. Superstition and religion, the first resorts of the helpless, proliferate.

Secondly, *Children of Men* is a dystopia that is specific to late capitalism. This isn't the familiar totalitarian scenario routinely trotted out in cinematic dystopias (see, for example, *V for Vendetta*, which, incidentally, compares badly with *Children of Men* on every point).

If, as Wendy Brown has so persuasively argued, neoliberalism and neoconservatism can be made compatible only at the level of dreamwork, then *Children of Men* renders this oneiric suturing as a nightmare. In *Children of Men*, public space is abandoned, given over to uncollected garbage and to stalking animals (one especially resonant scene takes place inside a derelict school, through which a deer runs). But, contrary to neoliberal fantasy, there is no withering away of the State, only a stripping back of the State to its core military and police functions. In this world, as in ours, ultra-authoritarianism and Capital are by no means incompatible: internment camps and franchise coffee bars co-exist.

In P.D. James' original novel, democracy is suspended and the country is ruled over by a self-appointed Warden. Wisely, the film downplays all this. For all that we know, the Britain of the film could still be a democracy, and the authoritarian measures that are everywhere in place could have been implemented within a political structure that remains, notionally, democratic. The War on Terror has prepared us for such a development: the normalisation of crisis produces a situation in which the repealing of measures brought in to deal with an emergency becomes unimaginable (when will the war be over?). Democratic rights and freedoms (*habeas corpus*, free speech and assembly) are suspended while democracy is still proclaimed.

Children of Men extrapolates rather than exaggerates. At a certain point, realism flips over into delirium. Bad dream logic takes hold as you go through the gates of the Refugee Camp at Bexhill. You pass through buildings that were once public utilities into an indeterminate space — Hell as a Temporary Autonomous Zone — in which laws, both juridical and metaphysical, are suspended. A carnival of brutality is underway. By now, you are *homo sacer*[4] so there's no point complaining about the beatings. You could be anywhere, provided it's a warzone: Yugoslavia in the Nineties, Baghdad in the Noughties, Palestine any time. Graffiti promises an intifada, but the odds are overwhelmingly stacked in favour of the State, which still packs the most powerful weapons.

The third reason that *Children of Men* works is because of its take on cultural crisis. It's evident that the theme of sterility must be read metaphorically, as the displacement of another kind of anxiety. (If the sterility were to be taken literally, the film would be no more than a requiem for what Lee Edelman calls "reproductive futurism", entirely in line with mainstream culture's pathos of fertility.) For me, this anxiety cries out to be read in cultural terms, and the question the film poses is: how long can a culture persist without the new? What happens if the young are no longer capable of producing surprises?

Children of Men connects with the suspicion that the end has *already* come, the thought that it could well be the case that the future harbours only reiteration and re-permutation. Could it be, that is to say, that there are no breaks, no "shocks of the new" to come? Such anxieties tend to result in a bi-polar oscillation: the "weak messianic" hope that there must be something new on the way lapses into the morose conviction that nothing new can ever happen. The focus shifts from the Next Big Thing to the *last* big thing — how long ago did it happen and just how big was it?

The key scene in which the cultural theme is explicitly broached comes when Clive Owen's character, Theo, visits a friend Battersea power station, which is now some combination of government building and private collection. Cultural treasures — Michelangelo's *David*, Picasso's *Guernica*, Pink Floyd's inflatable pig — are preserved in a building that is itself a refurbished heritage artefact. This is our only glimpse into the lives of the elite. The distinction between their life and that of the lower orders is marked, as ever, by differential access to enjoyment: they still eat their artfully presented cuisine in the shadow of the Old Masters. Theo, asks the question: how all this can matter if there will be no-one to see it? The alibi can no longer be future generations, since there will be none. The response is nihilistic hedonism: "I try not to think about it".

T.S. Eliot looms in the background of *Children of Men*, which, after all, inherits the theme of sterility from "The Waste Land". The film's closing epigraph "shantih shantih shantih" has more to do with Eliot's fragmentary pieces than the Upanishads' peace. Perhaps it is possible to see the concerns of another Eliot — the Eliot of "Tradition and the Individual Talent"[5] — ciphered in *Children of Men*. It was in this essay that Eliot, in anticipation of Bloom, described the reciprocal relationship between the canonical and the new. The new defines itself in response to what is already established; at the same time, the established has to reconfigure itself in response to the new. Eliot's claim was that the exhaustion of the future does not even leave us with the past. Tradition counts for nothing when it is no longer contested and modified. A culture that is merely *preserved* is no culture at all. The fate of Picasso's *Guernica* — once a howl of anguish and outrage against fascist atrocities, now a wall-hanging — is exemplary. Like its Battersea hanging space in the film, the painting is accorded "iconic" status only when it is deprived of any possible function or context.

A culture which takes place only in museums is already exhausted. A culture of commemoration is a cemetery. No cultural object can retain its power when there are no longer *new* eyes to see it.

rebel without a cause[1]

"Why is it [...] that left-wingers feel free to make their films direct and realistic, whereas Hollywood conservatives have to put on a mask in order to speak what they know to be the truth?"
— Andrew Klavern, "What Bush and Batman Have in Common"[2]

"What I despise in America is the studio actors [sic] logic, as if there is something good in self expression: do not be oppressed, open yourself, even if you shout and kick the others, everything in order to express and liberate yourself. This stupid idea, that behind the mask there is some truth. [...] Surfaces do matter. If you disturb the surfaces you may lose a lot more than you account. You shouldn't play with rituals. Masks are never simply mere masks."
— Slavoj Žižek and Geert Lovink, "Japan Through a Slovenian Looking Glass: Reflections of Media and Politic and Cinema"[3]

There are many symptomatically interesting things about the right-wing attempts to appropriate *The Dark Knight* that are doing the rounds at the moment. The idea is that the Batman of the film equals Bush — a misunderstood hero prepared to make "tough choices" in order to protect an ungrateful population from threats it is too ethically enfeebled to confront.

In a couple of intricately argued posts, Inspersal[4] demonstrates that *The Dark Knight* by no means presents "tough choices" as "hard but necessary"; on the contrary, whenever Batman resorts to torture, it either yields nothing or is counterproductive. What neocon readings of the film must overlook is that this is *exactly the same in geopolitical reality*: far from being unpalatable but necessary, the Iraq misadventure, Guantanamo Bay, extraordinary rendition, etc. have either achieved no results or made things worse. What's interesting here is the doggedness of the neocon fantasy, which is precisely a

183

fantasy of "being realistic" — astonishingly, elements of the American right appear to actually still believe that the Bush administration's policies are successful, and that the American public has rejected them on the grounds of high-minded (liberal) ethical qualms rather than for pragmatic-utilitarian reasons (too many of our boys being killed).

Secondly, what these readings also miss is the actual nature of the model of virtue presented in the film. If this is (neo)conservative, it is not at the simple level of utilitarian calculation of consequences. What we are dealing with is a far more complicated Straussian meta-utilitarianism whose cynical reasoning is akin to that of Dostoyevsky's Grand Inquisitor. Deception — of the masses by the elite — is integral to this account of virtue: what is "protected" is not the masses' security but their belief (in Harvey Dent's campaign).

As Inspersal argues, the emphasis on deception in *The Dark Knight* is one of the themes that connects it with Nolan's previous films, and Batman's climactic act of self-sacrifice is precisely an act of deception. It takes place at the level of signs: what he must give up is his reputation, his good standing in the eyes of the Gotham public. The act of deception doesn't conceal an underlying good act — it is the concealing that is the good act itself.

Thirdly, the neocon readings misconstrue the nature of "evil" in the film. If these right-wingers really think that Osama bin Laden is like The Joker as he appears in *The Dark Knight,* that gives us another, intriguing, insight into their fantasies. (Matthew Yglesias says, "I look at the movie and say 'see — if you were fighting a comic book bad guy and you were a comic book hero then your policies would make sense.'"[5] But even this isn't the case, as Inspersal's arguments above make clear.) Or rather, it reveals the inconsistency on which Islamophobic fantasy depends: the Islamist is both "an agent of chaos", someone without a cause, *and* a zealot excessively attached to a cause.

What's interesting about *The Dark Knight* is that is not really about Good versus Evil at all but "good causes" versus aberrant modes of cause/causality. The Joker and Two-Face are mad rather than bad, and their insanity is centrally connected with their relationship to cause. The Joker is pure Terror, that is, Terror detached from any cause:

You see, nobody panics when things go according to plan. Even if the plan is horrifying. If I told people that a gangbanger was going to get shot, or a busload of soldiers was going to get blown up, nobody would panic. Because it's all part of the plan. But tell people that one tiny little mayor is going to die and everyone loses their minds! Introduce a little anarchy, you upset the established order, and everything becomes chaos. I am an agent of chaos. And you know the thing about chaos, Harvey. It's fair.

While Batman is drawn into utilitarian calculations, The Joker is free in the same way that the death drive is free: he acts with indifference to consequences, glorying instead in a kind of ungrounded unbinding of orderly causal sequences. The reference to "fairness" above is not idle. As an imp of the perverse, The Joker stands for an inverted (or freaked) Kantian justice. In many ways, we are looking at the reversal of Kantianism into Don Giovanni Žižek has described many times (Don Giovanni's decision not to save himself, to maintain his commitment to his libertinism even when doing so will result in his execution, becomes an ethical gesture). The Joker acts without any pathological interests, grandly symbolising his lack of instrumentality with the burning of the pyramid of money.

Two-Face's insanity is also a kind of haemorrhaging of justice. In his case, the championing of a good cause — which it seems will inevitably leads to terrible consequences — is displaced by an embrace of chance's random causality (heads/tails). The flip into randomness is not an abandonment of justice, but the quest for a justice that will not be corrupted by human will — in its very impersonal mechanism, chance is fair because it does not privilege any outcome or any individual. Interestingly, it is only when Dent becomes Two-Face that his coin tossing is fair; when Dent is the "White Knight" DA, his coin is loaded (it has heads on both sides). What also interrupts the orderly sequence of causality in Dent's case is trauma — the trauma of seeing Rachel die, which is itself a consequence of a binary choice trap, one of a series of such traps The Joker attempts to spring.

The by now standard view of *The Dark Knight* — that its real libidinal pull is not the peripheral Batman/Wayne, but the charisma of Heath Ledger's Joker — is certainly correct. When I heard Ledger's performance celebrated, I feared the worst: that we were going to see the actorly overplaying that usually garners this kind of ubiquitous praise. But it is to Ledger's immense credit that he completely avoids what Nicholson was allowed to do in Tim Burton's dreadful *Batman*: we get no glimpse of the actor behind the role (with Nicholson, of course, that's all we got). There is also no question of Ledger appearing bare-faced for any significant length of time, as Tobey Maguire and Julian McMahon were allowed to in *Spider-Man 3* and the *Fantastic Four* films respectively. Thankfully, there is only the briefest glimpse of The Joker sans make-up in *The Dark Knight*.

What Ledger does, in many ways, is *play the make-up*. I should stress here that the make-up, which makes Ledger's face look like a malevolent monkey leering from behind cracked plaster, manages a feat that is near impossible: it reinvents The Joker look whilst also maintaining fidelity to the comics (compare the Green Goblin's mask and outfit in the *Spider-Man* films, whose divergence from the halloween hood in the comics always disappointed me). My one point of disagreement with Inspersal concerns his claim that Ledger's performance "shows the Nicholson/Burton interpretation to be much closer to Cesar Romero from the TV show, rather than Alan Moore's version from *The Killing Joke*, allegedly Burton and Hamm's chief influence". I would argue that, in fact, it is Ledger's performance that is closer to Romero's, and that is why it works so well. Nicholson's PoMo posturing and Moore's psychological depth were all of a piece, and both were far less terrifying than the senseless gibbering of Romero's pantomime-turn Joker. The Joker was always fascinating because, unlike most if not all big-time supervillains, he was pure surface, motiveless madness, devoid of any origin or backstory — until Moore obligingly filled one in, as is his hamfisted pseudo-literary wont. There are a couple of great scenes in *The Dark Knight* where Ledger's Joker mocks cod psychoanalytic reduction: "See these scars... I got them because of my father." "See these scars... I got them because of my wife." (This reminded me of nothing so much as Ian Bannen's chilling burst of explosive laughter in Sidney Lumet's *The Offence*, in response to Sean Connery's question: "Was your father a big man?") If The Joker aligns himself with anything it is "the freak", which cannot but remind us of freak events, that is, events which appear to happen without proper causation. By evacuating The Joker of all interiority, by refusing anything which would contain the Joker's wildness or compromise the autonomy of his face-painted persona, Ledger's performance (and Jonathan Nolan's script) do justice to the freakish.

robot historian in the ruins[1]

"Ideology is not something foreign, something in a film with a strange power to impose itself on our minds; ideology is what we and the film share, what allows for the transfer of specific meanings between film and audience (a transfer which is not one way). As Žižek puts it, ideology is made up of 'unknown knowns'; that is to say, the problem with ideology is not that it is a falsehood of which we might be persuaded, but because it is a truth that we already accept without knowing it."
— Voyou, "Ideology critics are a superstitious, cowardly lot"[2]

Voyou's remarks on readings of *The Dark Knight* make some important points about ideology. Focusing on the supposed "message" of the film — as both neoconservative interpretations of the film, and their critics, including me, do — is in danger of missing the way in which ideology works in capitalism. The role of capitalist ideology is not to make an explicit case for something in the way that propaganda does, but to conceal the fact that the operations of capital do not depend on any sort of subjectively assumed belief. It is impossible to conceive of fascism or Stalinism without propaganda — but capitalism can proceed perfectly well, indeed better, without anyone making a case for it.

In the responses to *The Dark Knight* I posted here, it was Wayne Wedge who captured the way that the film functions as a hyper-object in late capitalism.[3] The very multivalence of *The Dark Knight*, its capacity to generate radically different interpretations, to elicit discourse, is what makes it a highly efficient meta-commodity. A text with a single monologic Message, even supposing such a thing could exist, would not be able to "provoke the debate" which capitalist culture now feeds upon.

It not only that a cultural object can be opposed to capitalism on the level of content, but serve it on the level of form; one could convincingly go further and argue that the ideology of capitalism is now "anti-capitalist". The villain in Hollywood films is routinely the "evil multinational corporation". So it is, once again, in Disney/Pixar's *Wall-E*, which, like *The Dark Knight*, has provoked all kinds of bizarre conservative readings. "This is perhaps the most cynical and darkest big-budget Disney film ever", claims Kyle Smith[4]. "Perhaps never before has any corporation spent so much money on insulting its customers." (By way of parenthesis, since it isn't relevant to my argument here, this, from Paul Edwards, is priceless: "WALL-E is the story of what results when a liberal vision of the future is achieved: government marries business in the interest of providing not only 'the pursuit of happiness' but happiness itself, thus creating gluttonous citizens dependent on the government to sustain their lives.")[5]

Wall-E's attack on consumerism is easily absorbed. The "insult" that provoked Kyle Smith into disgust was its image of humans as obese, infantilised chair-bound consumers supping pap from cups. Initially, it might seem subversive and ironic that a film made by a massive corporation should have such an anti-consumerist and anti-corporate message (it is made clear in the film that the mega corporation Buy N Large is chiefly responsible for the environmental depredation which has destroyed earth as a human environment). Yet it is capital which is the great ironist, easily able to metabolise anti-corporate rhetoric by selling it back to an audience as entertainment. Besides, on the level of content, *Wall-E* ends up serving capitalist realism, presenting what we might think of as the very fantasies of capital itself — that it can continue to expand infinitely; that the despoilation of the human environment on Earth is a temporary problem that will eventually be overcome; that human labour can be extirpated altogether (on the spaceship Axiom, humans are given over entirely to consumption, and all work is performed by servomechanisms). Human labour returns only at the end of the film, when capital/Axiom begins its terraforming of Earth.

There is another impasse in *Wall-E*. The film follows in the tradition of fictions about wanderers in the ruins (cf Christopher Woodward's *In Ruins*). But in some respects *Wall-E* was an advance on the stories of post-apocalyptic solitaries, from Mary Shelley's *The Last Man* through to Richard Matheson's *I Am Legend* or John Foxx's *The Quiet Man*. For in *Wall-E* the lone figure in the ruins is not even human: it is a robot historian quite different from the one Manuel DeLanda imagined; or not a robot historian so much as a bricoleur-hauntologist, reconstructing human culture from a heap of fragments. (A precursor of this scenario is Numan's "M.E.", the track sampled by Basement Jaxx on "Where's Your Head At", written from the perspective of a sentient computer left alone on an Earth.) This idea of surveying a world in which humans are extinct clearly exercises a powerful fantasmatic allure. Yet it seems that there's a certain point where the fantasy always breaks down — the fictions that start from this premise invariably end up restoring a human world at some point in the narrative. It is no doubt asking too much that *Wall-E* should buck this trend; but it's notable that the film deteriorates massively the moment that the humans appear (cf all of the film versions of Matheson's *I Am Legend*, including the most recent). You're left wondering whether this is a structural necessity, whether there's something in the nature of the fantasy itself which entails the return of other humans, or whether it is a requirement arising from the needs of narrative: stories can't sustain themselves with only one protagonist. In the case of *Wall-E*, of course, there are two (non-human) characters, which make the early part of the film, a robotic romance played out as animated ballet, recall the films of the silent era. Needless to say, there are many films which feature non-human protagonists, but such characters are rendered effectively human by their language use. Wall-E and Eve, meanwhile, seem like convincing non-human subjects because they lack language. *Wall-E* tantalises: what if the feel of this first section had continued until the end of the film, uninterrupted by the return of humans?

review of tyson[1]

"It's like a Greek tragedy. The only problem is that I'm the subject", Mike Tyson reputedly told James Toback when he first saw this film. There is a classical structure to the narrative: a kid from mean streets, with few prospects, a life of criminality already under way, is talent-spotted by a grizzled boxing trainer; he becomes the youngest world champion ever; then it all disintegrates into hedonism, profligacy and violence. Yet in the end the structure of the story is psychoanalytic as much as tragic (after all, it wasn't for nothing that Freud turned to Sophocles and Aeschylus for analogues of his discoveries). A familiar enough narrative arc, but what makes it even more remarkable (and even more Freudian) is that it happens again. Tyson struggles back to the top of the heavyweight game before once again succumbing to ill-discipline and self-destruction. A textbook case of the compulsion to repeat.

Tyson's life was shaped by absent fathers and father surrogates. He was rescued from rudderless street survivalism by the trainer who ended up adopting him, Cus D'Amato; his subsequent fall from grace was precipitated in part by D'Amato's death. The Tyson that emerges in Toback's gripping film is very much like the subject of psychoanalysis, a talking head coaxed by the director (in the role of the offscreen analyst) into reliving all the triumphs and traumas. The film consists only of archive footage and Tyson — a ringside commentator on his own life — talking. There are no experts, no supposedly neutral judgements, only Tyson trying to make sense of the double tragedy of his life. It makes for a claustrophobic experience, amped up by the way in which Toback occasionally multi-tracks Tyson's voice and splits the screen, creating the impression of a divided man, sometimes chillingly self-aware, sometimes a mystery to himself.

Tyson's story is sufficiently forgotten now that it is capable of thrilling and horrifying us as if for the first time: the astonishingly quick rise to world champion, the run of viciously efficient victories, the high-profile debacle of his marriage to Robin Givens (Tyson sitting stock still on a chatshow couch while the actress vilifies him), the rape conviction and resulting prison sentence, the conversion to Islam, the biting of Evander Holyfield's ear... *Tyson* provides a newly intimate perspective on these half-remembered images.

Sports stars of this magnitude cannot but be the objects of collective fantasy and projection, and even though his is an individual story — and we can be under no illusions after watching Tyson that there is no lonelier sport than boxing — Tyson's is also the story of a culture and a time. Just compare Tyson with Muhammad Ali (whose own myth was examined and re-presented in *When We Were Kings* and *Ali*). With his poetry, physical and verbal, Ali was the boxer for the age of Black Power, the Panthers, Malcolm X, Sly Stone and James Brown; Tyson's pitbull brutality, meanwhile, was the fight analogue of the every-man-for-himself ethos of Reaganomics and the will-to-power pugilism of rap. His slogan was "Refuse to Lose" (a phrase that would be central to Public Enemy's epochal *Welcome to the Terrordome*): the aim was to overcome Nemesis by force of will alone, and in his pomp Tyson looked like iron will embodied. He came out of his corner like a starved attack dog, clubbing opponents into oblivion in a matter of moments. Nothing was wasted; there was no grandstanding or showboating.

Partly that was because Tyson felt he had no time to waste — for physical as well as existential reasons. He had suffered from a respiratory disorder since childhood and knew that he would struggle if fights went the full distance. The rapidity and intensity of his victories belied the precision of his attacks. We learn that it wasn't a question of sheer physical force alone. D'Amato (a "master of anatomy", according to Joyce Carol Oates) taught him where on the body to hit to cause maximum damage. In the fight footage, Tyson always looks short by comparison with his opponents — "at five feet 11 inches", Oates wrote in a 1986 essay, "he is short for a heavyweight and strikes the eye as shorter still; his 222 1/4-pound body is so sculpted in muscle it looks foreshortened, brutally compact."[2] Yet he always turned that compactness to his advantage, making the taller men look like ponderous Harryhausen statues.

Listening to him speak, you're continually struck by the contrast between Tyson the fighting machine and Tyson the talker. His voice is a gentle lisp, devoid of swagger, suggestive of an unusual sensitivity. It sits just as oddly with Tyson's older face and its Queequeg tattoos as it did with his earlier fighting frame. It becomes obvious, though, that the hypermuscular body Tyson developed was in part an exo-skeleton constructed to protect that sensitive core. Remembering the time he first realised that no one would ever be able to be beat him up again, Tyson stalls — "Oh, I can't even say it" — pauses for a long moment before saying, "Because I would fuckin' kill 'em." The film's rhythm is governed by Tyson's unstable relationship to language, by his switches in and out of articulacy. Sometimes his tongue is as quick as his fists once were. His hilarious takedown of Don King — a "wretched slimy reptilian motherfucker" — is as swift and savage as any of his combinations in the ring. Elsewhere, the words elude him, or he evades them. Yet, exactly as psychoanalysis taught us to expect, the ellipses, the sentences that lead nowhere and the "wrong" choice of word tell us even more than the moments of transparent lucidity. The unconscious speaks, and James Toback demonstrates an extraordinary facility for hearing and recording it.

"they killed their mother": *avatar* as ideological symptom[1]

Watching *Avatar*, I was continually reminded of Žižek's observation in *First As Tragedy, Then As Farce*, that the one good thing that capitalism did was destroy Mother Earth. "There's no green there, they killed their mother", we are solemnly informed at one point. *Avatar* is in some ways a reversal of Cameron's *Aliens*. If the "bug-hunt" in *Aliens* was, as Virilio argued, a kind of rehearsal for the mega-machinic slaughter of Gulf War I, then *Avatar* is a heavy-handed eco-sermon and parable about US misadventures in Iraq and Afghanistan. (What's remarkable about *Avatar* is how dated it looks. In the scenes of military engagement, it is as if Eighties cyberpunk confronts something out of Roger Dean or the *Myst* videogames; Cameron's vision of military technology has not moved on since *Aliens*.) At the end of the film, it is the human corporate and military interests who are described as "aliens". But this is a film without any trace of the alien. Like most CGI extravaganzas, it flares on the retina but leaves few traces in the memory. Greg Egan finds little to admire in *Avatar*, but he does defer to its technical achievements: "mostly, the accomplishments of the visual designers and the army of technicians who've brought their conception to the screen appear pixel-perfect, and hit the spot where the brain says 'yes, this is real'."[2] The cost of this, though, is that it is very difficult to be immersed in the film *as fiction*. It is more akin to a theme-park ride, a late-capitalist "experience", than a film.

What we have in *Avatar* is another instance of corporate anti-capitalism such as I discussed in *Capitalist Realism* in relation to *Wall-E*. Cameron has always been a proponent of Hollywood anti-capitalism: stupid corporate interests were the villains in *Aliens* and *Terminator 2* as they are in *Avatar*. *Avatar* is Le Guin-lite, a degraded version of the scenario that Le Guin developed in novels such as *The Word For World Is Forest*, *The Dispossessed* and

City Of Illusions, but stripped of all Le Guin's ambivalence and intelligence. What is foreclosed in the opposition between a predatory technologised capitalism and a primitive organicism, evidently, is the possibility of a modern, technologised anti-capitalism. It is in presenting this pseudo-opposition that *Avatar* functions as an ideological symptom.

No primitivist cliché is left untouched in Cameron's depiction of the Na'vi people and their world, Pandora. These elegant blue-skinned noble savages are at one with their beautiful world; they are Deleuzean Spinozists who recognise that a vital flow pervades everything; they respect natural balance; they are adept hunters, but, after they kill their prey they thank its "brother spirit"; the trees whisper with the voices of their revered ancestors. (Quite why skirmishes with the Na'vi and their bows and arrows should have prompted Steven Lang's grizzled colonel into *Apocalypse Now*-like disquisitions on how Pandora made for his worst experience in war, is unclear.) "There's nothing we have that they want", concludes Sam Worthington's Jake Sully of the Na'vi. Yet the Na'vi predictably seduce Sully, who quickly "forgets everything" about his former life on Earth (about which we learn almost nothing, beyond the fact that he is a marine who got injured in the course of battle) and embraces the wholeness of the Na'vi way of life. Sully attains wholeness through his avatar Na'vi body in a double sense: first, because the avatar is able-bodied, and, secondly, because the Na'vi are intrinsically more "whole" than the (self-)destructive humans. Sully, the marine who is "really" a tree-hugging primitive, is a paradigm of that late-capitalist subjectivity which disavows its modernity. There's something wonderfully ironic about the fact that Sully's — and our — identification with the Na'vi depends upon the very advanced technology that the Na'vi's way of life makes impossible.

But a telling tic in the film is the repeated compulsion to explain the persistence of (physical) wounds among the human characters. Given the level of technology in the film's 2051, both Sully's useless legs and the colonel's scars could easily have been repaired, and the script goes out of its way to say why the two characters they remain disabled and maimed respectively: in Sully's case, it's because he can't afford the medical treatment; in the colonel's, it's because he "likes to be reminded of what he's up against". Such explanations are clearly unconvincing — the narratively underdetermined wounds can only be explained as libidinal residue which the film cannot fully digest into its digital Imaginary. The wounds prevent the disavowal of modern subjectivity and technology which *Avatar* attempts at the very same moment that the film invites us to admire it as a technological spectacle.

If we are to escape from the impasses of capitalist realism, if we are to come up with an authentic and genuinely sustainable model of green politics (where the sustainability is a matter of libido, not only of natural resources), we have to overcome these disavowals. There is no way back from the matricide which was the precondition for the emergence of modern subjectivity. To quote one of my favourite passages in Žižek's *First As Tragedy*: "Fidelity to the communist Idea means that, to repeat, Arthur Rimbaud, [...] we should remain absolutely modern and reject the all too glib generalisation whereby the critique of capitalism morphs into the critique of 'modern instrumental reason' or 'modern technological civilisation'."[3] The issue is, rather, how modern technological civilisation can be organised in a different way.

precarity and paternalism[1]

The recent discussion of elitism (a topic also broached by Adam Curtis' film on Charlie Brooker's *Newswipe* this week) brings me back to the question of what — in the continuing lack of any alternative term — I must still refer to as "paternalism". I think Taylor Parkes got to what is at stake in these discussions in his rather moving *Quietus* piece about Trunk's *Life On Earth* release:

> Hard to credit now, but there was once something paternalistic, almost philanthropic about the Beeb, spreading the cultural wealth of the educated classes through housing estates and comprehensive schools. This kind of evangelism rarely sits well with self-conscious champions of the lumpenproletariat, whose right to live in shit, they believe, outweighs their right to not live in shit — for some, being patronised is worse than being brutalised. But then people can be very naïve about the motivations of those who give the people what they want, relentlessly and remorselessly. And while the Corporation was sometimes guilty of gross assumptions and a very real stuffiness, I don't like to think how I might have grown up — stomping around in the middle of nowhere — had it not been for *Life On Earth*, or Carl Sagan's *Cosmos*, or James Burke's *Connections*, or the gentle guidance of the BBC Children's department. Years ago, I interviewed the men in charge of "youth programming" at Channel 4, goateed and bereted and utterly insistent that their race to the bottom was a noble crusade; they railed against the BBC's "eat-your-greens" approach, and spoke of gallons of liquid effluent, coursing through the pipes of British culture, in terms of freedom and some strange colour of egalitarianism. Here was the future, banging its drums, and even then it made me blanch. As controller of BBC2 in the late 1960s, David Attenborough had a different vision, rooted in what was, for all his personal privilege, an (enduring) belief in

inclusivity. If the so-called Golden Age of Television could boast its fair share of shoddy, overlit crap — and my God, it could — at best it was truly empowering, and its passing has screwed us all to some extent. We can still choose to watch BBC Four, I suppose (assuming it's not another show where ex-*NME* writers smirk at Mud's trousers), but then this is an age of choices, few of which have much to do with freedom in the long term. No one's going to *stumble* onto culture any more, not like I did, or my dragged-up mates did. It's worse than a shame.[2]

It's worth reminding ourselves of the peculiar logic that neoliberalism has successfully imposed. Treating people as if they were intelligent is, we have been led to believe, "elitist", whereas treating them as if they are stupid is "democratic". It should go without saying that the assault on cultural elitism has gone alongside the aggressive restoration of a *material* elite. Parkes touches here on the right way to think about paternalism — not (just) as something prescriptive, but in terms of the gift and the surprise. The best gifts are those we wouldn't have chosen for ourselves — not because we would have overlooked or rejected them, but because we simply wouldn't have thought of them. Neoliberal "choice" traps you in yourself, allowing you to select amongst minimally different versions of what you have already chosen; paternalism wagers on a different "you", a you that does not yet exist. (All of which resonates with J.J. Charlesworth's illuminating piece on the management of the ICA in *Mute*, with its attack on the assumption that "what the audience wants is merely what the institution should do".[3])

Neoliberalism may have been sustained by a myth of entrepreneurialism, a myth that the folk economics of programmes like *The Apprentice* and *Dragon's Den* have played their part in propagating, but the kind of "entrepreneurs" that dominate our culture — whether they be Bill Gates, Simon Cowell or Duncan Bannatyne — have not invented new products or forms, they have just invented new ways of making money. Good for them, no doubt, but hardly something that the rest of us should be grateful for. (The genius of Cowell was to have plugged a very old cultural form into new machineries of interpassivity.) And for all the bluster about entrepreneurialism, it is remarkable how risk-averse late capitalism's culture is — there has never been a culture more homogenous and standardised, more repetitive and fear-driven.

I was struck by the contrast between Parkes' piece and an article by that Caitlin Moran wrote in the wake of the announcement that Jonathan Ross is to leave the BBC. "After [Ross'] £18 million contract", Moran wrote,

endless fretting pieces were written, asking whether the BBC should ever try to compete with ITV1's salaries. The real question, however, is "what would happen to the BBC if it didn't?" If the only people who work for the BBC are those in it for the sheer love of it and — those who would piously turn down double the wages from ITV— the BBC would rapidly become the middle-class liberal pinko panty-waist institution of the *Daily Mail*'s nightmares, and, I suspect, fold within five years.

Really? ITV's high salaries, when they could afford to pay them, were hardly guarantees of quality; and the idea that Ross is one of us because he was "quick, edgy, silly nerd-dandy, into Japanese anime and rackety new guitar bands" presupposes a model of the "alternative" as shopworn and discredited as New Labour. Note that Moran fully accepts the neoliberal logic whereby "talent" is only motivated by money. (The return of the concept of "talent", with all its de-punking implications, was perhaps the most telling cultural symptom of the last decade; while the application of the word to bankers was its sickest joke.)

As Moran suggests, the BBC's real rival now, evidently, is not the ailing ITV but the *Daily Mail* and *News International*, and if public service broadcasting is to defend itself against an assault that will only increase in ferocity, it will need rather more than Ross' sexual suggestiveness, warmed over hipness and occasional wit at its disposal. (It's far harder for the *Mail* to attack the likes of Attenborough than triviamongers such as Ross or Graham Norton; and did Attenborough ever get the equivalent of Ross' eighteen million, I wonder?) It's not only unjustifiable that public money be spent on exorbitant salaries for presenters and executives: it also plays into the *Mail*'s agenda, which is all about maintaining the negative solidarity which has been crucial to neoliberal hegemony.[4] Call me old fashioned, but I firmly believe that *only* those who would work for the BBC for the sheer love of it should be in the job. More than that, being motivated by money ought to be a reason for people *not* getting senior public service appointments. This is not, grotesquely, an argument for low wages — but it is an argument for the more equitable — and creative — redistribution of money in the public sphere. Imagine if Ross' eighteen million were instead spent — risked — on what British television most sorely lacks, writers. You could pay *scores* of writers a good wage for *years*... The BBC ought to be in a position to cushion its creative staff from the pressures of producing immediate success — and, contrary to the neoliberal logic which insists that people are best motivated by fear and money, it is that cushioning which facilitates a certain kind of cultural entrepreneurialism.

After all, people will do worthwhile things if they are not paid or if they are paid poorly. The interesting side of Web 2.0 is just this — not the vacuous "debates", but the impulse to share that is a significant part of the motivation for writing blogs, uploading material to YouTube and updating Wikipedia. If anything is the work of the multitude, it's something like the salvagepunk archive that is YouTube. It's intriguing that capitalist realism co-exists with the emergence of new forms of culture which can be commodified only very incompletely. At one level, commodification is total, and, in Jeremy Rifkin's phrase, all of life is a paid-for experience; yet there are whole areas of culture which are effectively being decommodified (does anyone seriously think that *any* recorded music will be paid for at all in a decade?). As a cultural worker, this is something I am ambivalent about, to say the least [...] I seem to achieve success in things at the very moment that it's not longer possible to make money from them...

When I was in Dublin a week or so ago talking about *Capitalist Realism*, a member of the audience asked why I was talking about public service workers when my own situation has shown that it's better to leave full-time employment and enter the precariat. This is a reasonable question on the face of it, since I've done pretty well since being made redundant from my FE teaching job. Yet in some respects all that has happened is that I've swapped the NuBureaucratic stress of public service employment for the perpetual anxiety of hyper-precarity, and had my income massively cut in the process. One of the ways in which negative solidarity plays out is by exploiting the opposition between permanent employees and precarious workers. Permanent employees tend to be quietist to keep (what they think of as) their job security, whereas precarious workers, being expendable, have no power at all. A while back, Tobias van Veen gave a very powerful account of his own experiences of precarious labour:

> there is an ironic yet devastating demand being placed on the labourer: while work never ends (as one is never out of touch, and always expected to be available, with no claims to a private life or other demands), you as a worker are nonetheless completely expendable (and thus a member of the precariat: and so one must sacrifice all autonomy from work so as to keep one's job). [...] This contemporary condition of on-call ontology or on-demand *dasein* produces an emotional economy of stress. To live under such instant-demand duress is stress-inducing indeed. Life becomes a series of panic attacks in the face of never being able to live up to such workplace demands without completely dismantling "life" itself as distinct from "work". The managerial class uses techniques of guilt/loyalty to enforce workers to labour at a moment's notice, scheduling with less than a few hours or days time, without hope of a raise, without benefits or reward, and all for a minimum wage.[5]

The precarious worker is doubly punished: not only do they have no job security, they also get paid less than the permanent employees for doing the same work. When I switched from being an hourly paid lecturer in Further Education to having a permanent contract, I was doing exactly the same work, but suddenly I was both paid hundreds of pounds more a month *and* got paid for holidays too. Back in the precariat, my total income since the tax year that began in April — for all the teaching, supervision, writing and editing I've done, when I doubt there's been more than two weeks that I've worked less than fifty hours — is the princely sum of eleven grand, which works out at significantly less than minimum wage. All the work I've done depends upon my not being in full-time work, so, no matter that my hourly rate for some work seems quite high, in effect I'm always working for minimum wage. (Much writing only pays minimum wage anyway.) All this, in conditions where it's impossible to turn down any commission, no matter how short notice it is given to me, where I'm on-demand at practically all times and there are no guarantees that I will keep getting the work. The kind of hustling I'm required to do involves a kind of "creativity", I suppose, but "getting creative" about how I can monetise my activities doesn't seem like the best conceivable use of my time. What the broken, piecemeal time of precarity precludes is engagement in long-form projects. It's very hard for me to devote any time to finishing my next book for Zer0 because I will always privilege any work that pays immediately. But full-time employment *also* precludes the engagement in long-form projects: *Capitalist Realism*, for instance, was written after work or at weekends.

I say all this not because I want sympathy — I still think I'm incredibly fortunate to be making any sort of living out of what I do — but more because my situation is symptomatic. And now that the high-rolling, business ontology-driven model of cultural provision is finished, surely there's a better way to fund cultural work?

return of the gift: richard kelly's *the box*[1]

I wouldn't say that Richard Kelly's *The Box* is a hauntological film, but it shares certain affinities with the way someone like Ghost Box *re-dream the Weird*. *The Box* is based on a short story by Richard Matheson, who occupies something like the same position in the American Weird that Ghost Box's touchstone, Nigel Kneale, does in the UK Weird. Both Kneale and Matheson operated in an interstitial generic space — between SF and horror — proper to the Weird, in a pulp infrastructure — paperbacks, television, B cinema — that has now largely disappeared. Matheson has yet to quite acquire the auteur status that Kneale enjoyed, but this only adds to his pulp-anonymous artisan allure; there's a special kind of delight in realising that films you'd likely as not first encountered, apparently randomly, on late night TV — *The Incredible Shrinking Man*, *The Omega Man*, *Duel* (as recently discussed by Graham[2]) — were in fact written by the same individual. (Matheson also wrote the screenplay for what — leaving aside the Kneale-scripted *Quatermass and the Pit* — is perhaps Hammer's greatest film, *The Devil Rides Out*.)

Much like *Jacob's Ladder*, which it resembles in a number of respects, *The Box* is a Weird take on the 1970s. Or rather, it draws together a number of Weird threads that were already present in the Seventies. Like *Jacob's Ladder* and much hauntological music, *The Box* captures a certain *grain of the Seventies*. *The Box* feels like a re-dreaming of the Weird rather than a revival in part because of the very incoherence that some have complained about. This "incoherence" is of a particular type; it isn't simply a *failure* of coherence so much as the generation of an oneiric (in)consistency which doesn't add up (into a final resolution) but which doesn't fragment into nonsense either.

The dream atmosphere is reinforced by the way that Kelly incorporates aspects of his own life into the film — the characters of Arthur and Norma

Lewis are apparently based closely on his own parents[3] — into the diegesis. But rather than the de-stranging tendencies at work in something like the new *Dr Who* — the Weird subordinated to familialism and emotionalism — *The Box* goes in the other direction, introducing the Weird into the family home — in parallel with how television used to do the same thing. The lines between Kelly's home life and the Weird must have been soft in any case: his father worked at NASA at the time when the Viking probes were landing on Mars.

The Box is based on Matheson's 1970 short story, "Button Button", later adapted into an episode of the revived *Twilight Zone* in 1986. To be more accurate, *The Box* uses both the original story and *The Twilight Zone* episode as elements in a simulated dreamwork which simultaneously extrapolates from the two versions and condenses them into an unstable compound. The result is a labyrinthine structure which bears some relation to Lynch's *Inland Empire* (*Inland Empire*, incidentally, was the last film to creep me out as much as *The Box* did). *The Box* is defined by the tension between the structure of the labyrinth — an absolute labyrinth, leading nowhere except deeper into itself — and the structure of the dilemma — in which reality seems to resolve into a set of disjunctions.

It's possible to delimit a number of distinct but connected levels at which the film operates.

The Ethical

The most simple level on which the film works — the film's entry level — is that of the ethical. All three versions of "Button, Button" turn on a dilemma: not so much an ethical dilemma as a dilemma about whether to set aside the ethical altogether. A well-dressed stranger, Mr Steward, arrives and presents the Lewises with a box with a button on top of it. If they press the button, Steward informs them, they will receive a large sum of money (in *The Box* it is a million dollars); however, someone that they don't know will die. In all three versions, it the wife who decides to push the button. Here, the versions diverge: in Matheson's original story, after Norma pushes the button, she receives the money as insurance compensation for the death of her husband. When she complains that Steward had told her that the person who died would be someone she didn't know, Steward asks: "Did you really know your husband?" In *The Twilight Zone* version — which Matheson reputedly hated — the ending is different. Here, when Steward has handed over the money, he pointedly says to the couple, "I can assure you it will be offered to someone whom you don't know." *The Box* adopts this version of the story, but this is only the beginning of the film, the first act, as it were.

Unintended Consequences

"Button, Button" is clearly an update of W.W. Jacobs' story "The Monkey's Paw" — in which a family wishes for a sum of money, only to receive it in compensation for the death of their son. Jacobs' story was itself a play on older tales about the unintended consequences of wish fulfilment. As Wiener observed in *God and Golem, Inc.: A Comment On Certain Points Where Cybernetics Impinges On Religion*, such unintended consequences arise because "the operation of magic is singularly literal-minded [in that] if it grants you anything at all, it grants you exactly what you ask for, not what you should have asked for or what you intend." "The magic of automatisation, and in particular the kind of automatisation where the devices learn", he adds, "may be expected to be similarly literal-minded".[4] Like the cybernetic machine, the wish-fulfilling object (the monkey's paw) delivers exactly what it says it will: but what it gives you may not be what you want (or what you *think* you want).

What Matheson's tale adds to Jacobs' story is the question of knowledge. Matheson's story brings into play the old philosophical "problem of other minds", now applied to the marital situation: even those closest to us are ultimately opaque, black boxes into which we can never see. Naturally, this also raises the equally ancient problem of self-knowledge, but given a psychoanalytic edge. We are alien to ourselves; our real desires may be unknown to us, emerging only in parapraxes and dreams. Here the oneiric form of *The Box* collapses into its content — the box, like the dream according to Freud, fulfils our wishes. The inevitable psychoanalytic conjecture into which Matheson's story tempts us is the thought that perhaps the wife *does* get exactly what she wants — that the death of her husband was her wish all along. In this sense the box would be like the Room in Tarkovsky's *Stalker*: the stalker Porcupine goes into the wish-fulfilling Room hoping for the return of his dead brother, but receives instead immense riches. In its very unreflective automatism — giving Porcupine exactly what he wants — the Room judges and condemns him.

The Political

What Matheson's story also adds to "The Monkey's Paw", of course, is the fact that the bad consequences are *not* simply unintended; they were just supposed to happen to *someone else*. This is what makes it so much nastier than Jacobs' tale. Whereas the family in "The Monkey's Paw" are guilty only of foolishness and greed, the couple in "Button, Button" knowingly trade another's death in exchange for wealth. In *The Box* this is especially shocking because both Norma and Arthur Lewis seem to be "good" people — Cameron Diaz's Norma in particular is immensely sympathetic. Perhaps what allows her to press the button is the unresolved ontological status of the box itself; the thought that it might be a prank (Arthur establishes that the box is empty) allows Norma to perform a kind of fetishist disavowal ("this might not be real, so I might as well do it"). As Hauntagonist put it on his Twitter feed: "the button in *The Box* is a nice example of how interactivity creates anxiety and fetishistic disavowal. Diaz doesn't believe but she believes 'the subject supposed to believe' does, Arlington Steward being the stand-in for the Big Other."

Here we are back in the realm of the ethical — but the ethical bleeds out into the political. The choice to press the button has a special force in the era of globalisation and climate change. We know that our wealth and comfort are achieved at the price of others' suffering and exploitation, that our smallest actions contribute to ecological catastrophe, but the causal chains connecting our actions with their consequences are so complicated as to be unmappable — they lie far beyond not only our experience, and any possible experience. (Hence the inadequacy of folk politics.) What the Lewises are in effect asked to do is affirm their plugging into this causal matrix — to formally accept the world and worldliness. The significance of this is that only the negative choice counts — to not press the button would be to choose a freedom that is not available to anyone at present (we are all so intricately embedded into the global capitalist matrix that it isn't possible to simply opt out). But to press the button is to give up on freedom, to choose blind determinism.

The Existentialist

Which brings us to the most explicit intertext that Kelly introduces into *The Box*: Sartre's *Huis Clos*. *Huis Clos* is everwhere in *The Box*; Norma, a high-school teacher, is teaching it; she and Arthur attend an amateur dramatic performance of the play. At the point when it is becoming evident that the Lewises' choice will not be some private shame but will infect and destroy every aspect of their lives, the couple find the words "No Exit" written in the condensation of their car's windscreen.

The resonance of *Huis Clos* is clear: this is a text about those who can no longer choose, who have ceased to be subjects. Fearing that they will be killed, the Lewises try to return the briefcase of money immediately, the very instant that Steward tells them that he will be sure to give the box to someone who doesn't know them. But the horror is that Norma and Arthur have made a choice that means that it is now too late: they are already (as if) dead. There is no returning the gift.

It is astonishing that the briefcase containing the money is immediately desublimated. Kelly could have had the Lewises spend the money, their enjoyment shadowed by their anxieties about what they had done... Instead, the briefcase is immediately dumped in their basement, never to be seen or — I think — mentioned again.

There is no possibility of returning the money — no way of taking back the choice to press the button — but there is no end to choosing either. Locked in an endlessly ramifying labyrinth, Arthur and Norma keep encountering further dilemmas — but the choice is now between bad (purgatory) and worse (hell); or else, as when Arthur is offered a choice of three gateways, two leading to eternal damnation, one to salvation, they have a quality of grotesque gameshow randomness.

The Religious

The mention of "salvation" is part of a persistent religious thread in the film. As the alien big Other, the one conducting "research" into the moral worth of human beings and judging them accordingly, and with the power of damnation and redemption in his hands, Steward clearly stands in for God. Yet he is a God who also performs the Satanic function of *tempting* humans.

The SF/Conspiracy

Steward's position as the (extra-terrestrial) big Other, the subject supposed to know, also somewhat echoes Sartre's discussion of the alien, as outlined by Infinite Thought:

> Sartre, towards the end of his gigantic unfinished *Critique of Dialectical Reason* from 1960, suddenly launches into a discussion of Martians. "For [the] Martian...who has long known the technique of inter-planetary navigation, we are... an animal species whose scientific and intellectual development have been retarded by certain circumstances [the Martian] will note that the inhabitants of this underdeveloped planet have certain behavioural patterns orientated towards certain objectives..." Because the hypothetical Martian will be at a particular scientific level (the assumption here is that it will be a much higher one), when the extent of human knowledge is revealed to the alien, there enters into the conceptual arena an exterior agent who for the first time knows what we do not know as a species — the Martian thus serves as the big Other for the entire collective enumeration of human beings. This limit case of the big Other Martian becomes, as Sartre puts it "a deep opacity, shadows in our understanding, a negation of interiority in our hearts."[5]

The Box is thick with references to conspiracy films (and includes some of the most creepily paranoid scenes since the remake of *Invasion of the Body Snatchers*). The full extent of the collusion of the authorities with Steward remains unclear even at the end of the film. The threads connecting NASA, the Viking probe and Steward's research project fray off into rumour and supposition. The labyrinth never ends.

contributing to society[1]

In respect of *The Fairy Jobmother*, it's worth noting how much *more* pernicious it was than *Benefit Busters*, the original programme from which it was a spin-off. Despite its title, *Benefit Busters* allowed viewers to come to a critical judgement about the initiatives the government were using to "get people back to work". The first part of the programme, the one featuring Hayley Taylor, was like some grim parody of a reality TV talent show, in which the glittering prize on offer was not a million-pound record deal but an unpaid work trial at discount store Poundland. Taylor was clearly a dupe of the ideology rather than its cynical author, credulously believing all the New Age pyschobabble she pushed along with the facile advice ("brush your teeth before an interview"). There's no doubt that some of the women were happier after being on the six-week "course" — but that was less because they were working for Poundland and more because they were not isolated in their own homes any more. Meanwhile, the programme showed us the home belonging to Emma Harrison, the boss of A4E,[2] the consultancy for which Taylor worked. To say that Harrison's house was a mansion would be a massive understatement.[3] A4E employees such as Taylor were invited to Harrison's house for "a cup of tea and a chat", because Harrison is *so informal and she just loves get feedback from her workers.* Faced with the extreme opulence of Harrison's house, viewers were at least invited to question who the real parasites scrounging off the state were. The excellent *WatchingA4E* blogspot does invaluable work exposing the realities of A4E's schemes.[4] This entry quotes a description of Harrison: "Emma's approach is to work with people: 'I walk by their side, hold their hand and we go on a journey resulting in them getting a job that transforms their lives'."[5]

Subsequent parts of *Benefit Busters* allowed viewers to form even more negative views of the government's schemes to get people back to work — we saw the long-term unemployed cynically forced off benefits for a job that would last only a few days, and a poor young lad with severe back problems sustained after falling out of a window being told that he was fit for work. There was none of this critical perspective in *The Fairy Jobmother*, which presented the reality TV "journey" back to work without any irony. As Digital Ben puts it:

> The show's very title gives us an idea of what kind of strictly limited conclusions will be drawn at the end. Taylor's steps did improve the family's situation, but it was made clear that these "fairy godmother wishes" were miraculous and unexpected, a break from the normal order of things. The idea that they be distributed on a wider basis, or even structuralised as part of the benefits system, is never on the table. The majority of the working class unemployed are expected to pull themselves up by their bootstraps — become mini-Hayleys and fully valid humans without any outside help. So what exactly was the moral of the show? That finding work is easier when you have a well-known, well-connected recruitment specialist in your corner? Shocking. And even then — if Taylor fails to find work for the family next week, we can expect blame to be diverted to them. There is no systemic analysis. Blame falls solely upon the individuals (and, yes, their families).[6]

One can hardly underestimate the role that reality TV plays in generating this lottery thinking, which is the other side of what Alex Williams calls negative solidarity. The persistent message is that *any* situation can be rectified by the application of dedicated self-improvement. (C4 is to be given some credit for showing some programmes which resist this agenda: its series *The Hospital* and *Our Drug War* show the real hopelessness of the NHS and the war on drugs. *The Hospital* gives a grim picture of youth in the UK. Class was the unspoken factor here: there weren't any middle-class kids being filmed arriving in hospital pregnant, or catching HIV, or getting involved in knife crime. In the first part, about the impact of unprotected sex, anti-authoritarian defiance came out as self-destructive bad faith: "they can't tell me what to do", "I'm the sort of person who has to do this". There was a desperate joylessness about the mandatory pleasure-seeking; another side to the hedonic depression I talk about in *Capitalist Realism*.)

One of the things that irritated me in the last part of *Fairy Jobmother* was the moment when Taylor talked about someone getting back to work so they could "make a contribution to society" again. (My mentioning this on Twitter sparked a brief exchange with this character,[7] who said "you can do what you please but not with my cash. You don't want to work that's fine — just don't expect me to pay".) As if there are no other ways to "make a contribution to society" than paid work (what is the Big Society if not about the value of such unpaid contributions?); as if those in work didn't depend, in numerous ways, on those not being paid for work…

Like many people I know, I spent my twenties drifting between postgraduate courses and unemployment, encountering many pointless and demoralising "helping you back to work" initiatives along the way. There wasn't much difference between what I did on an average day when I was a student and what I did when I was unemployed, and there isn't a great deal of difference between what I was doing then and what I do now. But now I'm fairly confident that I "make a contribution"; then I wasn't. For a number of reasons, during my twenties I believed then that I was unemployable — too feckless to do either manual work or retail, and nowhere near confident enough to do a graduate job of any kind. (The ads for graduate jobs would fill me with despair: surely only a superhuman could do the job as described?) I won't deny that eventually getting employment was important — I owe so much of what I am now to getting a teaching job. But equally important was the *demystification* of work that gaining this employment allowed — "work" wasn't something only available to people who belonged to a different ontological category to me. (Even so, this feeling wasn't rectified by having a job: I had a number of depressive episodes when I was convinced that *I wasn't the sort of person who could be a teacher*.)

But surely the importance of Virno and Negri's work is to have undermined the distinction between work and non-work anyway. What precisely counts as non-work in post-Fordism? If, to use Jonathan Beller's phrase, "to look is to labour" — if, that is to say, attention is a commodity — then aren't we all "contributing", whether we like it or not? As Nina Power argues, "[i]t is as if employers have taken the very worst aspects of women's work in the past — poorly paid, precarious, without benefits — and applied it to almost everyone, except those at the very top, who remain overwhelmingly male and incomprehensibly rich." In these conditions — in which unemployment/underemployment/perpetual insecurity are structurally necessary, not contingent accidents — there's more case than ever for a benefits safety net.

At this point, I must plug Ivor Southwood's forthcoming book, *Non-Stop Inertia*. It's about the miseries of "jobseeking", and it's one of my favourite Zer0 books to date, combining poignant and funny observations derived from experience with theoretical acuity. The book is sure to be of interest to most people who enjoyed *Capitalist Realism* (indeed, Ivor writes about whole dimensions of capitalist realism which I didn't touch upon). Here are a couple of paragraphs:

> The endless unpaid duties assigned to the virtuoso jobseeker cast him as the postmodernised inversion of the 1980s "gizza job" persona, which

confronted the employer directly with the physical reality of the reserve laborer and his family. Now, rather than proclaiming his jobless status the career jobseeker hides it, like something obscene, behind a screen of training courses and voluntary work and expressions of rictus positivity, and he becomes ever more complicit with this concealment in proportion to his desperation. The jobseeker must have an alibi ready to explain away every gap in his employment history, while the most mundane experience becomes the occasion of a personal epiphany — "working in a busy café really taught me something about the importance of customer service". Skills are valued over knowledge. Non-vocational qualifications are almost a liability, unless they are emptied of content; a degree in literature is valued not for its evidence of critical thought but because it shows that the applicant has word processing experience.

What are we not thinking about during all those hours of jobseeking, networking and CV-building? What interests, worries and fantasies might we otherwise have? What books might we read (other than self-help manuals), what conversations might we have with colleagues and friends about topics other than work? How differently might we perceive our current jobs without this constant needling insecurity? What kind of dangerous spaces might open up, in what kind of jeopardy might we put ourselves and this dynamic system, if we resigned from our jobs as jobseekers?[8]

"just relax and enjoy it": *geworfenheit* on the bbc[1]

I first saw *Artemis 81* when it was broadcast for the first and only time in December 1981. Even though it struck me then as incoherent and incomprehensible, I willingly sat through all three hours of it. Judging by the internet responses to *Artemis 81*, my experience was a common one amongst kids who, like me, were allowed to stay up late and watch it because it was broadcast during the school holidays.

I suppose that *Artemis 81* was one of the things that I was thinking of when, towards the end of *Capitalist Realism*, I argued that, far from being dreary and dull, the so-called paternalist era of media could be a breeding ground for the Weird (Ghost Box's conflation of secondary school textbooks with Weird fiction is based on the same intuition).

Artemis 81 was written by David Rudkin, the author of the better-known *Penda's Fen* (to which I'll be returning in another post very soon). Watching it again after nearly thirty years, the film doesn't seem incomprehensible at all. It is structured around a simple Manichean dichotomy (Manicheanism was one of the heavily signposted themes of *Penda's Fen*), and a mythic journey out of complacency and self-involvement and into a kind of visionary faith. (The persistent emphasis in *Artemis 81* on the "leap into faith" makes for an interesting parallel with *Inception*: at one point, the lead character tells a woman who has been strung up inside a cathedral bell that "it is better to fall than to hang".) What makes *Artemis 81* still alienating to watch are all the things that it lacks — all those strategies for producing audience identification to which we are now so accustomed. The acting style is as Brechtian as anything you would see in a Straub-Huillet film; the dialogue is anti-naturalistic, highly mannered (it reminds me more of an opera than television writing — and Wagner is one of many intertexts).

Rudkin says on the DVD commentary that the alien planet which we appear to see at the start of the film belongs to inner space. It is never clear when we *exit* inner space. But the film gains a great deal of power from grounding this inner space in what you might call found locations: the ferry terminal at Harwich; a power station in North Wales, which during the time of filming was under construction, and which becomes the entry to hell; and perhaps most memorably of all, the interior of the Anglican cathedral in Liverpool, which the BBC crew were not only given permission to use — they were also allowed to clear out all the pews, making for some astonishing oneiric images.

One sequence in particular stands above all the others. It is both one of the most disturbingly effective dream — or nightmare — sequences I've ever seen in film (certainly it is far better capturing dream topographies than anything in *Inception*), and also a deeply resonant image of dystopia. The lead character, pulp novelist Gideon Harlax (Hywell Bennett) suddenly finds himself in an unidentified city: he is on a tram, surrounded by consumptives expectorating blood into their scarves. It is foggy; the city is militarised, although there is a great deal of street market-like commercial activity. No one speaks English. When he enquires after Helith, the guardian angel who has abandoned him (played by Sting — but don't let that put you off), people laugh or admonish him. A public address system incessantly streams out announcements in what sounds like an East European language (it is actually Estonian spoken backwards). Watched now, you can't help but see anticipations of *Blade Runner* and *Children of Men* here. On the commentary, Rudkin says that this section of the film was supposed to illustrate Heidegger's concept of *Geworfenheit*, or throwness. Rudkin reveals that on-set, they used to refer to this city — actually a composite of Birmingham and Liverpool — as *Geworfenheit*, but this is never mentioned in the film itself. Beyond all the explicit references to myth, music and literature, there were further, occulted, layers of intertext. Another example, from this write-up on *Artemis 81*:

> One minor point that reveals much about [...] Rudkin's approach: the presiding deity of the piece is a Scandinavian goddess known as Magog. But it takes an alert eye to spot the "Gog Magog Hills" in a map of Britain which we glimpse on the protagonist's desk a lesser dramatist would perhaps have included a lengthy detour around the rather different "Magog" to be found in English mythology.[2]

It was *Artemis 81*'s confidence that you can subject the *audience* to *Geworfenheit* that makes it so impressive. As all the kids who watched *Artemis 81* and who have never forgotten it will attest, there's an *enjoyment* to be had from being thrown into the middle of things which you cannot understand and being forced to make a kind of sense out of them.

I hardly need say that it is impossible to imagine something like *Artemis 81* being commissioned, still less broadcast, by the BBC today. I agree absolutely with Phillip Challinor when he writes that *"Artemis 81* stands as a brilliant example of the way in which interesting pretentiousness can be a good deal more satisfactory than solid professionalism and good old-fashioned storytelling."[3] Like much Seventies culture — and *Artemis 81* really belongs to the "long Seventies" that ended circa 1982 — it deploys pretentiousness as a visionary force. To use a musical analogy, *Artemis 81* combines the overblown ambition of prog with the cool Ballardianism of post-punk. It is quintessentially pulp modernist — there are references to *The Devil Rides Out* as well as to *The Seventh Seal* and Carl Dreyer.

It is the BBC that made and broadcast *Artemis 81* which should be recovered and defended, not the institution as it currently functions today. The opposition that sets elitism against populism is one that neoliberalism has put in place, which is why it's a mistake to fall either side of it. The neoliberal attack on *cultural* "elites" has gone alongside the consolidation and extension of the power of an *economic* elite. But there's nothing "elitist" about assuming intelligence on the part of an audience (just as there is nothing admirable about "giving people what they want", as if that desire were a natural given rather than something that is mediated on multiple levels). Important qualification: to say that there was much to be mourned in the cultural situation in the Seventies and early Eighties is not to say that *everything* about that period is to be missed. I shouldn't have to make this disclaimer, but I'm mindful that any kind of critical judgement which favourably compares the past to the present is likely to be accused of "nostalgia". There are unique opportunities in the current conjuncture, but they can only be accessed if there is some negation of the present rather than a vacuous affirmation of it.

Of course, the discourse network in which surrounded the BBC in 1981 was vastly different to the situation in which the BBC finds itself today. For an example of this, take a look at the *Daily Mirror*'s preview of *Artemis 81*:

It could be the most baffling show of the holiday, but ARTEMIS 81 (BBC1, 9.0) is also one of the best of the year. This three-hour thriller, giving pop singer Sting his first big television role, is a knockout. But even some of the people most closely involved are not too sure exactly what it's about. Director Alastair Reid calls it a television Rubik Cube. And actor Hywel Bennett, who is at the heart of the action says he doesn't understand it. *Artemis 81* IS very complex. It has to do with a threat to the future of mankind, a series of mysterious deaths, a strange affair involving the Angel of Love and a great organist who, if he hits the right (or wrong) note, could blow up the world. My advice: Don't worry about understanding it, just relax and enjoy it.

star wars was a sell-out from the start[1]

Does Disney's acquisition of Lucasfilm mean that *Star Wars* has sold out? Can the *Star Wars* franchise retain its soul now it has been absorbed into a corporate conglomerate? It's hard to believe that these questions are seriously being posed. *Star Wars* was a sell-out from the start, and that is just about the only remarkable thing about this depressingly mediocre franchise.

The arrival of *Star Wars* signalled the full absorption of the former counterculture into a new mainstream. Like Steven Spielberg, George Lucas was a peer of directors such as Martin Scorsese and Francis Ford Coppola, who had produced some of the great American films of the 1970s. Lucas' own earlier films included the dystopian curio, *THX 1138*, but his most famous film was a herald of a coming situation in which mainstream cinema in America would become increasingly bland, and it would become impossible to imagine films of the quality of *The Godfather* trilogy or *Taxi Driver* ever being made again.

According to Walter Murch, the editor of *Apocalypse Now*, Lucas had wanted to make *Apocalypse Now* but had been persuaded it was too controversial, so he decided to "put the essence of the story in outer space and make it in a galaxy long ago and far, far away". *Star Wars* was Lucas' "transubstantiated version of *Apocalypse Now*. The rebel group were the North Vietnamese, and the Empire was the US". Of course, by the time the film was ideologically exploited by Ronald Reagan, everything had been inverted: now it was the US who were the plucky rebels, standing up to the "evil empire" of the Soviets.

In terms of the film itself, there was nothing much very new about *Star Wars*. *Star Wars* was a trailblazer for the kind of monumentalist pastiche which has become standard in a homogeneous Hollywood blockbuster culture that, perhaps more than any other film, *Star Wars* played a role in inventing. The theorist Fredric Jameson cited *Star Wars* as an example of the postmodern nostalgia film: it was a revival of "the Saturday afternoon serial of the Buck Rogers type", which the young could experience as if it was new, while an older audience could satisfy their desire to relive forms familiar from their own youth. All that *Star Wars* added to the formula was a certain spectacle — the spectacle of technology, via then state-of-the-art special effects and of course the spectacle of its own success, which became part of the experience of the film.

While the emphasis on effects became a catastrophe for science fiction, it was a relief for the capitalist culture of which *Star Wars* became a symbol. Late capitalism can't produce many new ideas anymore, but it can reliably deliver technological upgrades. But *Star Wars* didn't really belong to the science fiction genre anyway. J.G. Ballard acidly referred to it as "hobbits in space", and, just as *Star Wars* nodded back to Tolkien's Manichean pantomime, so it paved the way for the epic tedium of Peter Jackson's *Lord of the Rings* adaptations.

What *Star Wars* did invent was a new kind of commodity. What was being sold was not a particular film, but a whole world, a fictional system which could be added to forever (via sequels, prequels, novels, and any number of other tie-ins). Writers such as Tolkien and H.P. Lovecraft had invented such universes, but the *Star Wars* franchise was the first to self-consciously commodify an invented world on a mass commercial scale.

The films became thresholds into the *Star Wars* universe, which was soon defined as much by the merchandising surrounding the movies as by the films themselves. The success of the toys took even those involved with the film by surprise. The then small company, Kenner, purchased the rights for the *Star Wars* action figures in late 1976, a few months ahead of the film's theatre release in summer 1977. Unanticipated and unprecedented demand soon outstripped supply, and parents and children could not find the action figures in toy shops until Christmas 1977. This all seems rather quaint now, at a time when the merchandising surrounding blockbuster films is synchronised with a military level of organisation, and augmented by a battery of advertising and PR hype. But it was the *Star Wars* phenomenon which gave us the first taste of this kind of film tie-in commodity super-saturation.

This is why it's ridiculous to ask if *Star Wars* sold out. It was *Star Wars* which taught us what selling out really means.

gillian wearing: *self made*[1]

An ordinary looking man in his thirties is walking towards the camera holding a carrier bag. It could be you or me, and the streets he moves through, with their off-licences and corner shops, could be anywhere, too — most people living in Britain wouldn't have to go more than a mile to walk streets such as this. Still, something is not quite right: his expression looks distracted yet also troubled, while the music, an electronic drone punctuated by cries, creates an atmosphere of gathering unease. Suddenly, in the middle of the road, he stops, turns and drops the bag: it's as if something in him has broken, as if he can no longer take it any more...

It's a powerful opening, but *Self Made* immediately retreats from its intensity. We learn that *Self Made* started with an advertisement placed by Turner Prize winning artist, Gillian Wearing: "Would you like to be in a film? You can play yourself or a fictional character. Call Gillian." Hundreds apply, but only seven make it through to the experiment. This involves being trained by Method acting expert Sam Rumbelow, in preparation for acting out a "micro-drama" which will explore the participants' memories and feelings.

Immediately, I'm suspicious. Are these really the non-actors they are supposed to be? They seem remarkably unfazed by some of the exercises Rumbelow asks them to do, some of which you'd expect to cause non-performers a degree of embarrassment. I'm suspicious about my feelings of suspicion: isn't this exactly the response that's expected of me? A whole series of questions ensue. What is the boundary between performance and everyday life? Is there any such thing as a non-actor, since all of us are engaged in performing our identities?

We're in that familiar (art)space in which boundaries — in this case between "fiction" and "documentary" — are blurred. For much of its duration, the film puts us into that mode of listless sub-Brechtian questioning which so much art catalogue language routine invokes. The mode is deconstructive, demystificatory, (or it is their simulation): we see the micro-dramas, but only after we've been exposed to all the preparatory work that went into them; and afterwards, there are cutaways showing the crew filming the scenes.

Rumbelow comes across as an intensely irritating and creepy figure — more therapist-guru than acting coach, he's horribly reminiscent of Hal Raglan, the scientist-therapist from Cronenberg's *The Brood* who encourages his patients to "go all the way through" their emotional traumas, with fatal consequences. Perhaps exploitation is integral to the Method, and perhaps one of the points of *Self Made* is to examine this... And perhaps Sam Rumbelow is playing "Sam Rumbelow", annoying Method acting expert...

Wearing has said in the past that she was inspired by Paul Watson's 1974 fly-on-the-wall TV documentary *The Family*, and *Self Made* clearly follows on from such works as *Confess all on video. Don't worry, you will be in disguise. Intrigued? Call Gillian* (1994) or *Family History* (2006) in engaging with the problems raised by mediated "revelation" — the issue here is precisely whether we are dealing with "revelation" at all, or whether what we are witnessing is an effect of the filming process itself. (The same questions occurred to Jean Baudrillard, and it's no accident that some of his classic essays on simulation focus on the fly-on-the-wall phenomenon.) Wearing's work certainly has less in common with the brashness of twenty-first-century reality TV than it does with the convergence of drama, psychotherapy and social experiment that came together in the 1970s and continued on into the 1980s. At points, *Self Made* reminded me of a half-forgotten mid-Eighties BBC programme which I believe was called *Psychodrama*, and which similarly invited the participants to explore traumatic moments in their lives through the construction of dramatic scenarios. In any case, there's something horribly post-Sixties in every bad way about the techniques that Rumbelow uses to "unlock" the participants' feeling. In the spirit of confessionalism that Wearing's work examines, I admit that there are personal reasons for my hostility to this kind of thing. When I was at school in the early Eighties, we had to endure a class called Social and Personal Education. This involved being subjected to some of the emotionally terroristic exercises — such as "Trust Games" — which Rumbelow tries out with the participants here. Ironically, such exercises were at least as uncomfortable and disturbing as the experiences they were supposed to be exorcising, and these teachers were as oppressive in their own way as the agents of previous — more "repressive" — regimes of emotional management. There's no suggestion that *Self Made* endorses the discourses which inform Rumbelow's practice and the film's most unsettling scenes — both concerning violence — at least raise the possibility than untapping and manipulating buried feelings may be catastrophic. At one point, Wearing conspicuously uses montage to highly charged effect, undercutting the sense — the illusion — of unmediated verité. The participant James is re-enacting/re-imagining a scene that took place on a train. He challenges one of the men who bullied him when he was younger. Almost immediately, he appears to consumed by a tempest of rage. He raises his fist to hit the other (non)actor and for a moment it seems as if he has struck his head with full force. We then realise, with a sense of relief that still doesn't mitigate our horror, that Wearing has cut to James punching out a dummy. The film's climactic scene is even more shocking. This returns us to *Self Made*'s opening shots. By now, we have learned that the man walking the streets is called Ash. This time, however, we see what he had turned around to do: kick a pregnant woman in the stomach. Even though we know this is an illusion — after all, we have seen it being constructed — the image in itself is so sickeningly transgressive that no amount of alienation effects can dissipate its power.

batman's political right turn[1]

"How long do you think all this can last?" Selina Kyle (Anne Hathaway) asks Christian Bale's Bruce Wayne amid the opulence of a high-society charity ball in *The Dark Knight Returns*. "There's a storm coming." A storm of a rather unexpected kind gathered over the film on Friday, with the appalling massacre in Denver.[2] But the film was already enmeshed in political controversy in the US, when conservative US radio host Rush Limbaugh claimed the name of Batman's adversary in the film, Bane, was a reference to presidential candidate Mitt Romney and his former company, Bain Capital.

Yet as Limbaugh also noted, it is not Bane but billionaire Bruce Wayne who most resembles Romney, while Bane's rhetoric seems like a nod to the Occupy movement. Right-wing commentator John Nolte argues that the film has forced Occupy Wall Street into "damage control" and praises the director, Christopher Nolan, for "using the kind of conservative themes that most of artistically bankrupt Hollywood refuses to go near any more".[3] Fellow right-winger Christian Toto argues that it is impossible to read the film except as an anti-Occupy Wall Street treatise. "Bane's henchmen literally attack Wall Street, savagely beat the rich and promise the good people of Gotham that 'tomorrow, you claim what is rightfully yours'."

Such readings spuriously conflate Occupy Wall Street's anti-capitalism with the indiscriminate violence used by Bane and his followers.

When Nolan revived the *Batman* franchise in 2005, the setting — Gotham in the midst of an economic depression — seemed like an anachronistic reference to the superhero's origins in the 1930s; 2008's *The Dark Knight* was too early to register the impact of the financial crisis. But *The Dark Knight Rises* clearly attempts to respond to the post-2008 situation. The film isn't the simple conservative parable that right-wingers would like, but it is in the end a reactionary vision.

The storm Hathaway's character prophesies is a time of reckoning for the wealthy, and what stops the film being a straightforward celebration of conservative values in the way Nolte and Toto want is the relish it takes in attacking the rich. "You and your friends better batten down the hatches", Kyle continues, "cause when it hits, you're all going to wonder how you ever thought you could live so large, and leave so little for the rest of us". An early scene features the stock exchange, where we have the pleasure of seeing Bane manhandle some predatory traders. Later, when Wayne tells Kyle that although he is supposedly bankrupt, he has kept his house, Kyle acidly observes that "the rich don't even go broke like the rest of us".

Anti-capitalism is nothing new in Hollywood. From *Wall-E* to *Avatar*, corporations are routinely depicted as evil. The contradiction of corporate-funded films denouncing corporations is an irony capitalism cannot just absorb, but thrive on. Yet this anti-capitalism is only allowed within limits. *The Dark Knight Rises* draws clear lines: anti-capitalist comment (of the kind that Kyle makes) is fine, but any direct action against the rich, or revolutionary moves towards the redistribution of property, will lead to dystopian nightmare.

Bane talks about returning Gotham to "the people", and liberating the city from its "oppressors". But the people have no agency in the film. Despite Gotham's endemic poverty and homelessness, there is no organised action against capital until Bane arrives.

At the end of *The Dark Knight Rises*, Batman had sacrificed his reputation to save the city, and it's tempting to read the film as an allegory for the attempts by the elite to rebuild their standing after the financial crisis — or at least to preserve the idea that there are good rich who, if suitably humbled, can save capitalism from its worst excesses.

The sustaining fantasy of Nolan's *Batman* films — which does chime uncomfortably with Romney — is that the excesses of finance capital can be curbed by a combination of philanthropy, off-the-books violence and symbolism. *The Dark Knight* at least exposed the duplicity and violence necessary to preserve the fictions in which conservatives want us to believe. But the new film demonises collective action against capital while asking us to put our hope and faith in a chastened rich.

remember who the enemy is[1]

There's something so uncannily timely about *The Hunger Games: Catching Fire* that it's almost disturbing. In the UK over the past few weeks, there's been a palpable sense that the dominant reality system is juddering, that things are starting to give. There's an awakening from hedonic depressive slumber, and *The Hunger Games: Catching Fire* is not merely in tune with that, it's amplifying it. Explosion in the heart of the commodity? Yes, and fire causes more fire...

I over-use the word "delirium", but watching *Catching Fire* last week was a *genuinely* delirious experience. More than once I thought: *How can I be watching this? How can this be allowed?* One of the services Suzanne Collins has performed is to reveal the poverty, narrowness and decadence of the "freedoms" we enjoy in late, late capitalism. The mode of capture is hedonic conservatism. You can comment on anything (and your tweets may even be read out on TV), you can watch as much pornography as you like, but your ability to control your own life is minimal. Capital has insinuated itself everywhere, into our pleasures and our dreams as much as our work. You are kept hooked first with media circuses, then, if they fail, they send in the stormtrooper cops. The TV feed cuts out just before the cops start shooting.

Ideology is a story more than it is a set of ideas, and Suzanne Collins deserves immense credit for producing what is nothing less than a counter-narrative to capitalist realism. Many of the twenty-first century's analyses of late capitalist capture — *The Wire*, *The Thick Of It*, *Capitalist Realism* itself — are in danger of offering a bad immanence, a realism about capitalist realism that can engender only a paralysing sense of the system's total closure. Collins gives us a way out, and someone to identify with/as — the revolutionary warrior-woman, Katniss.

Sell the kids for food.

The scale of the success of the mythos is integral to its importance. Young Adult Dystopia is not so much a literary genre as a way of life for the generations cast adrift and sold out after 2008. Capital — now using nihiliberal rather than neoliberal modes of governance — doesn't have any solution except to load the young with debt and precarity. The rosy promises of neoliberalism are gone, but capitalist realism continues: there's no alternative, sorry. We had it but you can't, and that's just how things are, OK? The primary audience for Collins' novels was teenage and female, and instead of feeding them more boarding school fantasy or Vampiary romance, Collins has been — quietly but in plain sight — training them to be revolutionaries.

Perhaps the most remarkable thing about *The Hunger Games* is the way it simply presupposes that revolution is necessary. The problems are logistical, not ethical, and the issue is simply how and when revolution can be made to happen, not if it should happen at all. *Remember who the enemy is* — a message, a hailing, an ethical demand that calls out through the screen to us... that calls out to a collectivity that can only be built through class consciousness... (And what has Collins achieved here if not an intersectional analysis and decoding of the way that class, gender, race and colonial power work together — not in the pious academic register of the Vampires' Castle, but in the mythographic core of popular culture — functioning not as a delibidinising demand for more thinking, more guilt, but as an inciting call to build new collectivities.)

There's a punk immanence about *Catching Fire* which I haven't seen in any cultural product for a long time — a contagious self-reflexivity that bleeds out from the film and corrodes the commodity culture that frames it. Adverts for the movie seem like they belong *in* the movie, and, rather than a case of empty self-referentiality, this has the effect of decoding dominant social reality. Suddenly, the dreary gloss of capital's promotional cyber-blitz becomes de-naturalised. If the movie calls out to us through the screen, we also pass over into its world, which turns out to be ours, seen clearer now some distracting scenery is removed. Here it is: a neo-Roman cybergothic barbarism, with lurid cosmetics and costumery for the rich, hard labour for the poor. The poor get just enough high-tech to make sure that they are always connected to the Capitol's propaganda feed. Reality TV as a form of social control — a distraction and a subjugatory spectacle that naturalises competition and forces the subordinate class to fight it out to the death for the delectation of the ruling class. Sound familiar?

Part of the sophistication and pertinence of Collins' vision, though, is its awareness of the ambivalent role of mass media. Katniss is a totem not because she takes direct action against the Capitol — what form would that take, in these conditions? — but because her place in the media allows her to function as a means of connecting otherwise atomised populations. Her role is symbolic, but — since the capture system is itself symbolic in the first instance — this is what makes her such a catalyst. The girl on fire... and fire spreads fire... Her arrows must ultimately be aimed at the reality system, not at human individuals, all of whom are replaceable.

The removal of capitalist cyberspace from Collins' world clears away the distracting machinery of Web 2.0 (participation as an extension of spectacle into something more pervasive, total, rather than as its antidote) and shows how TV, or, better, what Alex Williams has called "the Universal Tabloid", is still productive of what counts as reality. (For all the horizontalist rhetoric about Web 2.0, just look at what typically trends on Twitter: TV programmes.) There's a role as hero or villain — or maybe a story about how we've gone from hero to villain — prepared for all of us in the Universal Tabloid. The scenes in which Plutarch Heavensbee gives a businesslike description of the carrot and stick nature of the Capitol's media-authoritarian power have a withering, mordant precision. "More beatings, what will her wedding be like, executions, wedding cake..."

As Unemployed Negativity wrote of the first film:

> It is not enough that the participants kill each other, but in doing so they must provide a compelling persona and narrative. Doing so guarantees them good standing in their odds and means that they will be provided with assistance by those who are betting on their victory. Before they enter the arena they are given makeovers and are interviewed like contenders on American Idol. Gaining the support of the audience is a matter of life in death.[2]

This is what keeps the Tributes sticking to their reality TV-defined meat puppet role. The only alternative is death.

But what if you choose death? This is the crux of the first film, and I turned to Bifo when I tried to write about it.[3] "Suicide is the decisive political act of our times."[4] Katniss and Peeta's threat of suicide is the only possible act of insubordination in *The Hunger Games*. And this is insubordination, NOT resistance. As the two most acute analysts of Control society, Burroughs and Foucault, both recognised, resistance is not a challenge to power; it is, on the contrary, that which power needs. No power without something to resist it. No power without a living being as its subject. When they kill us, they can no longer see us subjugated. A being reduced to whimpering — this is the limits of power. Beyond that lies death. So only if you act as if you are dead can you be free. This is Katniss' decisive step into becoming a revolutionary, and in choosing death, she wins back her life — or the possibility of a life no longer lived as a slave-subordinate, but as a free individual.

The emotional dimensions of all this are by no means ancillary, because Collins — and the films follow her novels very closely in most respects —

understands how Control society operates through affective parasitism and emotional bondage. Katniss enters into the Hunger Games to save her sister, and fear for her family keeps her in line. Part of what makes the novels and the films so powerful is the way they move beyond the consentimental affective regime imposed by reality TV, lachrymose advertising and soap operas. The greatness of Jennifer Lawrence's performances as Katniss consist in part in her capacity to touch on feelings — rage, horror, grim resolve — that have a political, rather than a privatised, register.

The personal is political because there is no personal.

There is no private realm to retreat into.

Haymitch tells Katniss and Peeta that they will never get off the train — meaning that the reality TV parts they are required to play will continue until their deaths. It's all an act, but there's no offstage.

There are no woods to run into where the Capitol won't follow. If you escape, they can always get your family.

There are no temporary autonomous zones that they won't shut down. It's just a matter of time.

Everyone wants to be Katniss, except Katniss herself.

Bring me my bow, of burning gold.

The only thing she can do — when the time is right — is take aim at the reality system.

Then you watch the artificial sky fall.

Then you wake up.

And.

This is the revolution...

beyond good and evil: *breaking bad*[1]

Who needs religion when you have television? On soap operas, unlike in life, villainous characters almost always face their comeuppance. TV cops may now be required to have "complicated" private lives and dubious personal ethics, but we're seldom in any serious doubt about the difference between good and evil, and on which side of the line the maverick cop ultimately falls. The persistence of the fantasy that justice is guaranteed — a religious fantasy — wouldn't have surprised the great thinkers of modernity. Theorists such as Spinoza, Kant, Nietzsche and Marx argued that atheism was extremely difficult to practise. It's all very well professing a lack of belief in God, but it's much harder to give up the habits of thought which assume providence, divine justice and a secure distinction between good and evil.

The US television series *Breaking Bad*, an international hit whose final episode aired this autumn, escapes this impasse. But we have to be careful here — the series has been understood (its title invites this interpretation) as the story of how an ordinary lower-middle-class man becomes evil. The set-up was simple. Walter White (played by Bryan Cranston), a chemistry teacher at a school in New Mexico, is diagnosed with lung cancer. Unable to afford the treatment, Walt decides to use his expertise in chemistry to manufacture methamphetamine, or crystal meth, with the help of a feckless ex-student, Jesse. As the series progresses, Walt shifts from making agonised decisions about whether it is right to kill, to becoming a ruthless crimelord. Yet this is not the whole story, and to read the series as a narrative of Walt becoming evil is to resist what is most challenging about it.

The success of the show outside the US has provoked some amusing parodies. Imagine *Breaking Bad* set in the UK and Canada. Opening scene. Doctor tells Walt he has cancer — the treatment starts next week. End of series. What this points out is an opposition that was crucial to the drama: between the fragility of the physical body and the precarity produced by social relations. One way of measuring progress is through the extent to which human beings have managed to contain the inevitable suffering that nature causes the body. In this sense, *Breaking Bad* can be compared with Ken Loach's recent documentary about the foundation of the British welfare state, *Spirit of '45*. Loach's evocation of a destroyed working-class progressivism brings the savage new Wild West that emerges in *Breaking Bad* into painful relief. Walt does so many "bad" things because he wants to remain a "good" husband, as defined by the Protestant work ethic. Much of the series's mordant humour comes from seeing Walt pursue this ideology of work — it's better to earn your "own" money, no matter how, than to scrounge from others or ask them for help — to all kinds of extremes.

In the final episode, Walt has to admit that the desire to build his drug empire brought him an intense libidinal satisfaction that had long since become autonomous from the ostensible purpose — providing for his family when he is gone — that provoked him into cooking meth in the first place. But for most of the series Walt clings to the idea that he's doing all the drug production, the killing, the manipulation and the terror for the sake of his family. Ironically, the one thing that the family could not survive is the course of action Walt ends up pursuing. It could probably survive penury and debt. It could survive the loss of Walt's physical body. But it cannot survive the loss of the image of Walt as an ordinary father figure, beaten down by life, an underachiever maybe, but still someone who "does the right thing". It's as if Walt destroyed the family in the very attempt to save it.

Perhaps the most complex and powerful character in the whole series is Walt's wife, Skyler, played by Anna Gunn. The actor has written of the misogyny she faced from some *Breaking Bad* fans online as a consequence of playing Skyler: in a piece for the *New York Times*, she described how the character seemed to have become "a flash point for many people's feelings about strong, non-submissive, ill-treated women". This is especially depressing because Skyler is a nuanced character, not at all someone who simply rejects Walt at the earliest opportunity. Even though she deplores Walt's adventures in crime, it is only at the very end of the series, when Walt's actions have manifestly brought catastrophe to Skyler's family, that she definitively breaks with him. Until then she struggles, impossibly but heroically, to reconcile her roles as wife, mother and responsible citizen. At the end, we feel that she is traumatised but not broken — someone who will eventually be able to escape the horrors Walt brought to her life, and who, astonishingly, is still capable of retaining some love for the husband whose pride, hubris and desperation have threatened to destroy her life and those of her two children.

The politics of the family, and how these connect with the American ideology of earning your own money and paying your own way, were, then, at the heart of *Breaking Bad*. In the episode "Ozymandias" — probably one of the most intense, distressing, yet also occasionally hilarious hours of television I have ever seen — Skyler finally breaks totally with Walt. Their son, Walt Jr, has just discovered that Walt is a meth cook. Sheer vertigo, horror: Walt Jr's whole world has disappeared in an instant. He doesn't want to believe it, he's angry with Skyler and Walt, he can't make any sense of it, his eyes show the deepest pain, confusion, shock. Skyler grabs a carving knife — an echo of what Wendy Torrance does in *The Shining* — but, unlike Wendy, Skyler stands tough. She's tall, strong, she's not cowering or afraid anymore, and she suddenly knows what she has to do to protect herself and Walt Jr. She forces Walt out of the house. But before that, Skyler and Walt have grappled on the floor. Walt wriggles free, stands up and — hilariously, pathetically — tries to assert his patriarchal authority, tries to appeal to family togetherness. "Stop this! We — are — a — family!"

A scene like this gets right to the heart of why *Breaking Bad* was so mesmerically powerful. Even here, we're aware that Skyler still loves Walt — not because she's deluded but because she recognises that, even though Walt has become "a monster", this isn't all he is. In some sense, he still loves Skyler and Walt Jr; and the scenes in the final episode when Walt returns to say his last goodbye to Skyler, and he holds his young baby for the last time, and he watches Walt Jr from a distance, knowing that he will never speak to him again, are wrenchingly sad.

I think it was Lacan who remarked that when we talk about going beyond good and evil, we usually mean going beyond good. The modern world is fascinated by anti-heroes, people with a dark side, the pantomime madness and "evil" of Hannibal Lecter. What it is less comfortable with is the real atheist-existentialist revelation that "good" and "evil" are not written into the universe, but exist only in ourselves, in relation to our desires and interests. Soap opera melodrama keeps us believing in "evil" as a voluntaristic choice — people do bad things because they are evil. But in *Breaking Bad*, evil in that sense is nowhere to be found.

Certainly, it's full of people who do "bad" things — that is, those who pursue actions that they know would either directly or indirectly hurt or destroy others — but they don't do this because they are evil. Tuco, the low-level drug lord that Walt and Jesse tangle with in season one, is deranged and violent because he is a meth addict from a criminal family. Gus Fring, the slick meth overlord who makes his first appearance in season two, is a super-pragmatic businessman — so pragmatic, in fact, that he lives his life in seemingly permanent cover, disguised as the humble owner of a small fast-food chain. He kills ruthlessly, but only when it is expedient. Even when hillbillies with swastikas tattooed onto their necks emerge as the antagonists towards the end of the series, the writing never allows us to write off the most repulsive of them as totally "evil", because they, too, are capable of mercy and acts of kindness.

Then there is Walt himself. One of the series' subversive achievements is to draw attention to the way that our sympathy and identification with a character are a structural effect; one that is created both by the demands of genre and by the class structure of wider society. We initially sympathise with Walt in part because we remember other put-upon dads in popular TV series — such as Bryan Cranston's character in *Malcolm in the Middle* — and also because the media constantly invite us to identify with the "hard-working" lower-middle-class family man. Yet *Breaking Bad* shows that the difference between the "good", "ordinary" man and a ruthless criminal is the thinnest of lines. There but for the grace of social security and the NHS go we.

classless broadcasting: *benefits street*[1]

It's not exactly clear why Channel 4's *Benefits Street* (broadcast in January and February 2014) caused such a furore. It wasn't the most obviously exploitative of the many programmes about the unemployed and those on benefits. Yet something about this series, which followed the residents of James Turner Street in Birmingham, touched a nerve. It was immediately pressed into ideological service by the right, fitted into a pre-existing story about the "need to reform the welfare state". The *Daily Mail*'s Richard Littlejohn quickly inserted some of the series' participants into his phobic delirium. For most of those on the left, however, it was business as usual. For Owen Jones, author of the book *Chavs*, it was yet another case of the demonisation of the working class. For Ben Walters, writing on the blog *Not Television*, it was an example of Thatcherite documentary, while for the film-maker Katharine Round, writing for the *Huffington Post*, it was a depressing example of the way in which documentaries were being used to "kick those without a voice".

In terms of its content, *Benefits Street* wasn't all reactionary. Its somewhat mealy-mouthed claim to be about "community" rather than benefits wasn't entirely false. Even in the first episode — which sensationistically dwelled on crime — there was still some emphasis on camaraderie and solidarity amongst the poor on the street. The second episode, which centred on desperate Romanians seeking work, was certainly sympathetic to the immigrants' plight, and might even have done something to challenge the dominant media narrative about East Europeans "coming to steal our jobs and our benefits". And by the third and fourth episodes sensation had largely given way to the inertia and radically contracted horizons of life on benefits. A small taste of this ought to have been enough to disabuse anyone of the notion that life on benefits is easy — but, since this belief is supported by relentless media propaganda, it isn't likely to be given up any time soon.

Still, *Benefits Street* is undoubtedly part of a disingenuous trend in documentary making. Writing last year for the journal the *Sociological Imagination*, Tracy Jensen predicted a "summer of poverty porn", citing such programmes as *How To Get A Council House*, *Why Don't You Speak English?*, *Benefits Britain 1949* (all Channel 4) and *We All Pay Your Benefits* (BBC1). Writing of the latter, Jensen argued that despite occasional moments of sympathy towards benefits claimants, the "programme's ideological message was clear; worth comes from paid work and not from childrearing or volunteering; unemployment is a problem of will or determination and not of structural obstacles; and social security itself generates the 'problem' of welfare dependence."[2]

Ultimately, *Benefits Street* fitted the same formula, in which intermittent sympathy for the poor and unemployed was used to season an otherwise crude reproduction of negative stereotypes. Then there is the perennial question of the exploitation of those who were filmed. Some — including residents of James Turner Street itself — objected to *Benefits Street* because they claimed that the programme's producers had misrepresented what the series was actually going to be about. The residents weren't told, for instance, that the series was to be given such a provocative and loaded title (the programme makers claimed that this was a last-minute decision, but I'm not sure how believable that is).

The deep problem with programmes like *Benefits Street* lies more in their form than in their content. A decade ago, the academic John Corner argued that reality TV had led to a genre of "post-documentary" television, in which documentary elements were merged with game-shows, makeover programmes and other entertainment forms.[3] Now we are in the era of post-reality TV documentary, a much more pernicious genre. Even the most credulous viewer of reality TV could hardly fail to be aware of its constructedness, with participants worrying and complaining about how they were "portrayed", and viewers quickly becoming familiar with the way narrative was produced by editing. (Partly this was because shows like *Big Brother* gave viewers access to the unedited footage, to the longueurs and the shapelessness of a quotidian time prior to its moulding into narrative.) Such reflexivity is largely absent from post-reality TV documentary — this genre uses many of the techniques from reality TV, but presents them with the simulated sobriety of documentary rather than with the winking, heavily made-up face of entertainment. That's not to say that post-reality TV documentary is entirely straight-laced; no — one of its defining characteristics is a certain humour and lightness. But it doesn't want to be positioned as entertainment in the way that reality TV was.

In their important study *Reacting To Reality Television: Performance, Audience and Value*, Beverley Skeggs and Helen Wood argue that much reality TV posits an implied bourgeois gaze, which judges working-class participants as lacking, by comparison with the middle class.[4] Moreover, this lack is understood in heavily moralised terms; it isn't to be explained by the working class's lack of resources or opportunities, but by a deficit in will and effort. This implied perspective — seldom actually stated, but informing the whole way in which programmes are produced — is typical of the post-reality TV documentary.

This moralistic framing was at work in *Benefits Street*. It did almost nothing to contextualise what it showed. There was barely any discussion of why the participants had ended up on benefits, and no mention of the social causes of unemployment, just as there was no interrogation of the political agendas driving the focus on those claiming benefits, nor any examination of austerity as a political project. Post-reality TV documentary projects a radically depoliticised world of individuals and their intimacies. In *Benefits Street*, we were told that benefits were cut, but this was treated like some natural disaster, an act of God rather than the consequence of a political decision.

In many respects, post-reality TV documentary — like reality TV before it — goes out of its way to conceal the class differences between those who are making the programmes and those who feature in them. Like tabloid newspapers, the scripts impersonate a working-class vernacular. Typically, the voiceover plays an important role in this bid to present the programme to working-class viewers as if it has been produced by a group of peers. The voiceover will not now be the voice of the actual programme makers. If they are heard at all, these voices will only be heard in the off-screen prompts and questions put to the working-class participants. In the case of *Benefits Street*, the voiceover was performed by actor Tony Hirst, who has recently left the *Coronation Street* cast. Hirst's accent is working-class, northern; his tone — perfectly in keeping with the supposedly "serious yet humorous" register of the post-reality TV documentary — is no-nonsense and wry. Tellingly, it was reported that the voiceover had been first offered to Brummie comedian Frank Skinner, who turned it down.

The use of voiceovers by actors or comedians from working-class backgrounds not only obfuscates the class origins of those making the programme; it also bolsters the programme's claims to authenticity. In addition, and perhaps most significantly, the voiceover is part of a strategy that conceals the fact that the material is being framed in a particular way. In previous, more essayistic forms of documentary, when the person writing the script would also provide the voiceover, and might appear on camera, it was clearer both that a particular case was being made and who was making it. In the absence of a journalist or a programme-maker explicitly taking responsibility for any argument, viewers are invited to classify what they are seeing as the truth, pure and unmediated: this, we are induced to believe, is just real people, being themselves, and the refusal or failure to make any explicit argument allows dominant ideology — which the programme doesn't acknowledge, still less challenge — to step in.

It's a mark of how bad Channel 4's programming now is that *Benefits Street* would probably count as one of its more serious recent attempts at documentary. If you want to measure the catastrophic impact of neoliberalism on British culture, then there's no better example than Channel 4. A channel that began with programming that included European art films, serious philosophy discussion programmes and politically sophisticated documentaries has now degenerated into depths so embarrassingly hucksterish and craven that they are beyond parody. This is a channel which still allows Tory toffs like Kirstie Allsopp to front programmes that act as if it is normal for house-buyers to have budgets of a million pounds; a channel that cries crocodile tears over mental illness and other forms of extreme misfortune as a thin pretext for ruthlessly exploiting them. I'd like to think this decline isn't irreversible, but there aren't many reasons for hope at the moment.

rooting for the enemy: *the americans*[1]

The first season of *The Americans* (recently broadcast in the UK on ITV) ended with a sequence soundtracked by Peter Gabriel's "Games Without Frontiers". The series has rightly been praised for its intelligent use of music, and "Games Without Frontiers", which was released in 1980, the year in which the series begins, was a perfect choice of track for the climax of the first season. Atmospherically, the song is somehow both anxious and fatalistic: drained of emotional inflection, Gabriel's vocals sound catatonic; the production is cold and forbidding. "Games Without Frontiers" feels not so much post-traumatic as pre-traumatic: as if Gabriel is registering the impact of a catastrophe that is yet to come.

Heard now, especially in the context of *The Americans*, a Cold War thriller, it reminds us of a time when such dread was ambient, when the spectre of seemingly inevitable apocalypse was woven into everyday life. Yet if "Games Without Frontiers" invokes the broad historical moment when *The Americans* is set, it also comments on the specific intrigues of the series. For *The Americans* is about Soviet spies posing as an ordinary US family. Cold War espionage did not respect the boundaries between private and public, between domestic life and duty to the cause: a game without frontiers indeed.

Created by former CIA agent Joe Weisberg, *The Americans* centres on Elizabeth (Keri Russell) and Philip Jennings (Matthew Rhys), two KGB agents living undercover as Americans in Washington. Weisberg had reputedly toyed with setting the series in the 1970s, but opting for 1980 makes strong dramatic sense. In 1980, the Cold War was intensifying in the immediate wake of the Soviet invasion of Afghanistan, and the election of Ronald Reagan, who was keen to prosecute a Manichean struggle against the "Evil Empire".

The series is characterised by a bipolar oscillation between a downbeat naturalism and the screaming adrenal intensities of the thriller. There is no shortage of car chases and shoot-outs in *The Americans* — there is probably no more exciting show on TV at the moment than this — but these are intercut with scenes of domestic life, where the tensions are of another kind altogether.

Far from being a respite from the Cold War, the Jenningses' home life is the zone where they carry out their most emotionally charged deceptions. The marriage is itself a sham: initially at least, Elizabeth and Philip are agents on a mission, not lovers, and the series is in part about their attempts to navigate this fraught emotional terrain, and to reconcile their differing expectations about what their roles entail. But Elizabeth and Philip at least know what they are doing; their children, Paige and Henry, necessarily do not. They are not aware that their parents are KGB agents (the children's ignorance being one of the best forms of cover that the Jennings have available to them).

This not only raises the threat of discovery, but also raises a moral dilemma: should the children be told? This dilemma comes to a head in the second season, when one story arc concerns the murder of a fellow KGB couple and one of their children. When it turns out that the surviving child, Jared, had been recruited by the KGB, the question of Paige's recruitment is inevitably raised. "Paige is your daughter", says the Jenningses KGB controller, Claudia, "but she's not just yours. She belongs to the cause. And to the world. We all do."

This brings us to a contrast between *The Americans* and even some of the most sophisticated spy fiction, such as that of John Le Carré. In Le Carré's work, George Smiley's adversary is the KGB Spymaster Karla — and for all that Le Carré complicated the broadbrush good-and-evil binary of Cold War propaganda, Karla remained an almost demonic figure whose commitment was incomprehensible to Smiley and his self-styled liberal pragmatism. In *The Americans*, the Soviets are transformed into our likeness. This first of all happens through the foregrounding of Elizabeth and Philip. But they are well supported by the rich cast of characters in the *rezidentura* (KGB station): Nina Krylova, a double, then triple agent, fragile but resilient and resourceful; the pragmatic strategist Arkady Ivanovich; the ambitious and enigmatic Oleg Burov. The decision to have the characters in the embassy speak Russian is important; their difference from Westerners is maintained, and the absurd convention whereby they are heard speaking bad English in pantomime Russian accents is avoided.

In a reversal of stereotype, the Soviets in *The Americans* seem so much more glamorous than their American counterparts. The Jenningses' chief antagonist, FBI agent Stan Beeman (Noah Emmerich) — who in a soap opera twist turns out to be a near neighbour — comes off as dour by comparison with the dynamic and glamorous Elizabeth and Philip, just as the FBI offices seem drab and mean when set against the intrigue of the *rezidentura*.

This no doubt contributes to the series' subversive flourish, which consists in the fact that the audience not only sympathise with the Jenningses, they positively root for them, dreading their discovery, hoping that all their plans come to fruition. *The Americans'* message is not that the Jenningses share a common humanity with their American enemies and neighbours, but just happen to be on the other side. Given the extremity of their situation, it is impossible for us to think that Philip and Elizabeth are "just like us"; at the same time, however, the series forces us to identify with them, even as their otherness is preserved.

At key points, their differences from the "real" Americans are emphasised. While Philip is sometimes seen to vacillate, to appreciate at least some aspects of the American way of life, Elizabeth never wavers in her commitment to the destruction of American capitalism. At one moment during the second season, Paige starts going to a church group. Nothing brings home Elizabeth's alienness to American life — and to many of the protocols of US TV drama — more than the ferocity of her hostility to this development. The scene in which a furious Elizabeth confronts Paige about all this is strangely hilarious: there aren't many places elsewhere in American TV drama where we can see Christianity attacked with such fervour.

The complexity of Elizabeth's character — and its sophisticated performance by Keri Russell — may be the highlight of the series. Both she and Philip have to be ruthless — when it is necessary, they kill without compunction — but Elizabeth has an unsentimental coldness and poise which the more equivocal Philip lacks. It is to the series' credit that it doesn't code this coldness as a moral failing — rather, it holds in tension two conflicting world views, which value Elizabeth's strength of purpose and Philip's uncertainties very differently. There is certainly no doubt, for instance, that Elizabeth loves her children (if she didn't, she would too easily fall into the stereotype of the Soviet monster) — but the question is what place this love should have in a hierarchy of duties. For Elizabeth, it is clear, the Cause must always come first.

In conditions where capitalism dominates without opposition, the very idea of a Cause has disappeared. Who fights and dies for capitalism? Whose life is made meaningful by the struggle for a capitalist society? (Perhaps it is this devotion to the Cause that gives the Soviet characters in *The Americans* their glamour.) It was none other than Francis Fukuyama who warned that a triumphal capitalism would be haunted by hankerings after existential purpose that consumer goods and parliamentary democracy could not assuage. Much of the appeal of *The Americans* depends upon the fact that it is set before this period. Our knowledge that the collapse of the Soviet experiment was less than a decade away from the period when the series is set lends all of the discourse about the communist Cause in *The Americans* a melancholy quality. In 1980, the Cold War felt as if it would last forever. In reality, within a mere nine years, everything that Elizabeth and Philip stood for would collapse, and the end of history would be upon us.

how to let go: *the leftovers, broadchurch and the missing*[1]

Loss is the subject of some of the best television series of the last year or so. Freud distinguished between mourning and melancholia, where mourning involves relinquishing the lost object and melancholia entails morbidly holding on. These series track the painful — perhaps permanently interrupted — process whereby melancholia becomes mourning.

The problem for the characters in the enthralling HBO series *The Leftovers* is that mourning cannot properly begin. The series is about the consequences of a cataclysmic event — referred to as the Sudden Departure — in which, inexplicably, without warning and without leaving a trace, two per cent of the world's population disappears. The series was adapted from his own novel by Tom Perotta, along with Damon Lindelhof, the co-creator of *Lost*. In some ways, *The Leftovers* is like *Lost* in negative. Where *Lost* focused on those who had gone over to the other side, *The Leftovers* concentrates on the ones left behind. The phrase "left behind" is not neutral, of course — it was the title of a series of best-selling Christian millenarian novels about the End Times. The first temptation is to see the Sudden Departure as a religious event — the greatest religious event of all, the Rapture. Yet the Sudden Departure appears to have taken people at random: abusers as well as altruists, celebrities as well as mediocrities, believers as well as non-believers. One of the most mordantly amusing threads in the series sees Reverend Matt Jamison — an unstable compound of bitterness, compassion and enduring faith, superbly played by Christopher Eccleston — producing a homemade scandal sheet whose sole purpose is to tarnish the name of those who were taken, in order to prove that the Departure cannot have been the Rapture. Or is this the form that the Rapture would supposedly take for those left behind? It would not be an event with immediately

243

clear meaning, but an unintelligible, traumatic interruption, producing disorientation and anger as much as sadness.

Yet *The Leftovers* does not concern itself overmuch with the enigma of the Sudden Departure. *Lost* became self-parodically enmeshed in a madly proliferating web of embedded mysteries that by the end seemed as if they were being invented simply to keep the intrigue going, and could never be satisfactorily resolved. *The Leftovers* offers no hint that its central mystery will ever be explained. If the first season is anything to go by, this absence of explanation is the point. The series is set three years after the Sudden Departure, and by now the event has become part of the assumed background of the characters' lives: a vast epistemic void which they are simultaneously always ignoring and negotiating. The Sudden Departure is then like trauma as such: an unfathomable puncturing of meaning, a senseless spasm of sheer contingency.

The fact that the nature of the Sudden Departure is never directly confronted means that the question which genre the series belongs to — religious drama? Science fiction? Metaphysical fiction? — is suspended. The dominant mode is an often brutal naturalism; but a naturalism forever haunted and conditioned by something it cannot assimilate. Some have viewed the Sudden Departure as an allegory of 9/11, but the analogy isn't convincing. *The Leftovers* belongs to a moment deprived of the certainties possessed by those prosecuting the War on Terror and their opponents. There is no one to blame in *The Leftovers* — and there are no bodies to mourn. Without these, the population turns to rage and brooding depression. Families disintegrate, even families such as the Garveys, the lead characters, who did not lose a member in the Departure. Social cohesion is always threatening to unravel. New belief systems sprout like couch grass in an abandoned garden — for in a world in which sense has gone, who can adjudicate between the credible and the ridiculous anymore?

In some ways, the most authentic response to the Sudden Departure comes from the "cult", the Guilty Remnant. The rules that members follow have the eerie arbitrariness, the oneiric montage-logic, of a genuine cult. They are required to wear all white, to remain silent and — in a symbol of their lack of belief in a viable future — to always smoke whilst in public. But the Remnant have no cockamamie beliefs. In fact they seem to have no positive beliefs at all; their purpose is simply to retain a fidelity to the senseless event of the Departure. In their joyless white, they are mute spectres forever insisting that the Departure must not be forgotten. Their point is not moral — the departed should be remembered — but philosophical: reality has fundamentally altered, and this must be faced, not denied.

In the UK, ITV's *Broadchurch* confronts loss in a more intimate, less metaphysically fraught way. The series centres on the death of a child,

Danny Latimer, in a fictional seaside town. While it was clearly British television's response to wintry Scandinavian thrillers such as *The Killing*, the first series of *Broadchurch* (2013) was not merely pastiche. There was a poise in the way it combined the whodunnit intrigue of the traditional thriller with a more subdued tracking of the impact of the death on the town. The series also deftly negotiated the line between sentimentalising a local community and finding potential killers everywhere. In the course of the investigation, the "close-knit community" that rallies around after the killing soon becomes a mob, which — stoked by tabloid insinuations — hounds a local shopkeeper to his death.

The second series of *Broadchurch*, halfway through at the time of writing, offered a clever solution to the seemingly intractable problem of how the series could continue once the killer was revealed. Another murder in the same town would definitively trip the series over into melodrama, yet abandoning the whodunnit element would deprive *Broadchurch* of one of its narrative drivers. As it turned out, the whodunnit was provided by an old case that the lead detective, Hardy (David Tennant), had failed to solve — a case that haunted him in the first series — while the ongoing study of the effects of the murder of Danny Latimer was continued with a trial, prompted when the killer, Joe Miller, retracts his confession. Yet the second series lacks the surefootedness of the first, and it is hard not to feel that it's somewhat superfluous and unnecessary.

If *Broadchurch* was ITV's answer to *The Killing*, then *The Missing* was the BBC's response to *Broadchurch*. In *Broadchurch*, the grieving family gradually has to adjust to the death of a child, to give up melancholia so that they can begin mourning. In *The Missing*, this process is indefinitely stalled — the child whose disappearance is at the heart of the series is precisely missing, not yet (confirmed) dead. On holiday in France in 2006, five-year-old Ollie Hughes disappeared in a bar. The series took us down many blind alleys in pursuing the truth behind his disappearance. It ran through a virtual inventory of folk devils, including paedophiles, corrupt politicians, drug addicts and Eastern European criminal gangs, before concluding in bathos — Ollie's disappearance turned out to be the result of an alcoholic accident, not any intentional malignancy.

In theory, there was something admirable about this controlled deflation. In practice, however, there was something dissatisfying about the way it was handled, which made the series feel like a shaggy-dog story, leading nowhere very interesting. Along the way, there were some memorable performances — most notably Tchéky Karyo as detective Julien Baptiste, a charismatic mix of wisdom, compassion and tenacity — but the most haunting scenes came at the beginning and the end of the series. First, there was the wrenching moment when Tony Hughes (James Nesbit) lost Ollie. Some of this power came from the very banality of the scene (one of the most notable aspects of the series was its nondescript settings, a contrast with the striking landscapes of *Broadchurch*): a bar which could be anywhere, a moment's distraction, a hand momentarily released, a sudden contingency that irrevocably and irretrievably transforms life, pitching Ollie's parents into hell. The final scene showed that Tony, now a dishevelled wreck, utterly consumed by obsession, would never escape that hell. Unable to accept that Ollie is dead — his body is never recovered — Tony is now in Russia, serially harassing children that he momentarily convinces himself might be his lost son. It is a horrible image of secular purgatory. Mourning will never begin; Tony is condemned to a melancholia-without-end that he doesn't even want to escape.

the strange death of british satire[1]

Watch one of the BBC's political programmes — such as the *Daily Politics* and *This Week*, both fronted by Andrew Neil — and you encounter a particular tone. British television viewers are unlikely to take much notice of this tone because we take it for granted. Take a step back, however, and it is really rather curious. These ostensibly serious programmes are conducted with an air of light mockery, which Neil, with his perma-smirk and smugly knowing air, personifies. The tone, I believe, tells us something about the widespread disengagement from parliamentary politics in England. (The situation in Scotland is now rather different: the popular mobilisation after the independence referendum has reversed the trend towards cynicism about politics that still dominates south of the border.)

Take *This Week*. The whole show is conducted in a lamely comic style that it is hard to imagine any sentient creature finding amusing. Guests are required to dress up in daft costumes and present their arguments in the form of limp skits, pitched at an audience whose implied level of intelligence is imbecilic. The atmosphere is matey, informal, and the overwhelming impression is that nothing much is at stake in any of the decisions that parliament takes. While Neil's dog pads about the set, former Tory leadership candidate Michael Portillo chats on a sofa with professionally amiable Blairite Alan Johnson — no class antagonism here, only mild disagreements. Politics appears as a (mostly) gentlemen's club where everyone is friends. People from working-class backgrounds, such as Johnson, can achieve entry to this club, provided they accept its rules. These rules are never actually stated, but they are very clear. Parliament is not to be taken too seriously: it is to be treated as a (boring) soap opera, in which the lead characters are self-serving individuals who don't believe in much beyond getting themselves elected. On no account are any intellectual concepts to be discussed, unless to be sneered at as pretentious nonsense. It has to be accepted that nothing very significant will ever change: the basic co-ordinates of political reality were set in the 1980s, and all we can do is operate inside them.

If you were designing a programme specifically to put people — especially young people — off politics, to convince them it is a tedious waste of time, then you could hardly do better than *This Week*. The programme seems to be aimed at literally no one: if you are staying up late to watch a programme devoted to politics, then presumably you are pretty serious about politics. Who wants this unfunny froth?

It would be bad enough if this tone of mirthless levity were confined to *This Week*, but it increasingly dominates political coverage of all kinds on the BBC. It thoroughly permeated the BBC's election-night coverage this year, which Neil anchored. This trivialising tone is perhaps even more troubling than the problem of bias (as is well known, former Murdoch editor Neil was a Thatcher cheerleader; Nick Robinson, the BBC's former Political Editor, meanwhile, was President of the Oxford University Conservative Association). The election-night coverage was notable for the disconnection between the shock and alarm that many in the audience felt about an unexpected win for the Conservative Party, and the guffawing banter of Neil and his associates. Reading out tweets and sharing gossip, the grinning Laura Kuenssberg, who has recently replaced Robinson as the BBC's Political Editor, seemed to treat the whole evening as a jolly good laugh. Perhaps there isn't that much at stake for her — she was, after all, born into immense privilege, the daughter of an OBE and a CBE, and the granddaughter of a founder and president of the Royal College of General Practitioners.

But where does this tone — with its strange mixture of the middle-aged and the adolescent — come from? The quick answer is class background. The tone of light but relentless ridicule, the pose of not being seen to take things too seriously, has its roots in the British boarding school. In an article for the *Guardian*, Nick Duffell[2] argued that, from around the age of seven, boarders are required to adopt a "pseudo-adult" personality, which results, paradoxically, in their struggling "to properly mature, since the child who was not allowed to grow up organically gets stranded, as it were, inside them."

"Boarding children", Duffell continues,

> invariably construct a survival personality that endures long after school and operates strategically [...] Crucially, they must not look unhappy, childish or foolish — in any way vulnerable — or they will be bullied by their peers. So they dissociate from all these qualities, project them out on to others, and develop duplicitous personalities that are on the run.[3]

Now that the working-class perspective has been marginalised in the dominant British media and political culture, we increasingly live inside the mind of this psychically mutilated adolescent bourgeois male. Here, ostensible levity conceals deep fear and anxiety; self-mockery is a kind of homeopathic remedy that is used to ward off the threat of an annihilating humiliation. You must never appear too much of a swot; you must never look as if you might like or think anything that isn't already socially approved. Even if you haven't attended boarding school yourself, you are still required to operate in an emotional atmosphere set by those who did. Andrew Neil, who came from a working-class background and attended a grammar school, attained access to the top table by simulating the mores of the privately educated elite. Thatcherism depended on the conspicuous success of people like Neil — if they could make it, so could anyone.

No programme did more to normalise the mode of mandatory light mockery than *Have I Got News for You*. In a 2013 essay for the *London Review of Books*, "Sinking Giggling into the Sea", Jonathan Coe positioned *Have I Got News for You* in a genealogy of British satire going back to the 1950s.[4] Coe argued that, back then, satire might have posed a threat to the authority of establishment politicians who expected unthinking deference from the electorate. Now, however, when politicians are routinely ridiculed and a weary cynicism is ubiquitous, satire is a weapon used by the establishment to protect itself.

No one typifies this more than Boris Johnson. Coe points out that Johnson's success crucially depended on his appearances — sometimes as guest presenter — on *Have I Got News for You*. The atmosphere of generalised sniggering allowed Johnson to develop his carefully cultivated, heavily mediated persona of "lovable, self-mocking buffoon". The show allows Johnson to present himself as a hail-fellow-well-met everyman, not a member of an old Etonian elite. In this he has been abetted by his sometime antagonist Ian Hislop. Hislop always has the guffawing, self-satisfied air of a prefect who's caught out some slightly posher kids stealing from the tuck shop. No matter what the infraction, Hislop's response is always a supercilious snigger. While this snigger might be conceivably appropriate to MPs being caught with their trousers down, or even with their over-claiming on expenses, it seems grotesquely out of kilter with the kind of systemic corruption that we now know has occurred over the last thirty years in Britain, in everything from Hillsborough to the phone hacking scandal to paedophilia involving major establishment figures — not to mention the behaviours that led to the financial crash. As the editor of *Private Eye*, Hislop has played an important part in exposing these abuses. But on television his mocker-in-chief persona serves ultimately to neutralise and cover over the extremity and systematicity of the abuse: one snigger fits all situations.

Coe's discussion of Johnson is strikingly similar to the Italian philosopher Franco Berardi's analysis of Silvio Berlusconi. Berlusconi's popularity, Berardi argued, depended on his "ridiculing of political rhetoric and its stagnant rituals". The voters were invited to identify "with the slightly crazy premier, the rascal prime minister who resembles them".[5] Like Johnson, Berlusconi was the fool who occupied the place of power, disdaining law and rules "in the name of a spontaneous energy that rules can no longer bridle".

In the UK, this concept of a "spontaneous energy that rules can no longer bridle" goes beyond politics in the narrow sense. The populist right-wing celebration of this energy is surely what kept Jeremy Clarkson in his job as a presenter of *Top Gear* for so long, and its appeal is what must have motivated over a million people to sign a petition calling for Clarkson to keep his job after he had punched a producer in the face. The prevailing media culture in the UK allows the privately educated Clarkson to come off as a plain-speaking man of the people, bravely saying what he thinks in the face of an oppressive "political correctness" that seeks to muzzle him. The success of *Top Gear* is another testament to the power — and, sadly, international appeal — of the English ruling-class male mentality. Who, more than Clarkson and his fellow presenters, better exemplifies this bizarre mixture of the middle-aged and the adolescent? What, after all, is it safer for a ruling-class adolescent male to like than cars?

Clarkson is just one of a range of British television celebrities who play the role of pantomime villain; a persona entirely devoid of compassion for others. Except this is a pantomime with real blood. Take the former *Apprentice* star and *Sun* columnist Katie Hopkins, for instance. The UN high commissioner for human rights, Zeid Ra'ad Al Hussein, condemned her likening of refugees to "cockroaches" for its obvious echoes of Nazi rhetoric. Hopkins is allowed to get away with this because of what we might call the innate postmodernism of the English ruling class. Both she and Clarkson say hateful things, but with a twinkle in their eye and their eyebrows ever so slightly raised.

There is an immense complexity at work in this ruling-class mummery. The humour allows Clarkson and Hopkins to be conduits for a racism that has very real, very tragic effects, whilst also letting them off the hook. The humour reassures them, and their audience, that they don't really mean it. But the problem is that they don't have to "mean" it: they help define the terms of debate, and allow migrants to be dehumanised, whatever their "true" feelings about the issue might be.

However, Hopkins' persona was troubled when she appeared on *Celebrity Big Brother* earlier this year. While much of the time she stayed in role as a spiteful, hard-hearted bigot, there were inevitably moments when the facade cracked, and she could be seen caring for others. While this increased her popularity — she almost won the show — it was also in danger of destroying the Katie Hopkins brand.

Most tellingly, her greatest moments of vulnerability came when she was asked to accept tenderness from others. In order to survive in the harsh and emotionally retarded world of the English ruling-class male she was trained for in private school and at Sandhurst, Hopkins has clearly been required to forgo any public acceptance of warmth or kindness from others. Sadly, the wearing of such character armour is not now confined to Hopkins and the rest of the privately educated elite.

Self-educated working-class culture generated some of the best comedy, music and literature in modern British history. The last thirty years have seen the bourgeoisie take over not only business and politics, but also entertainment and culture. In the UK, comedy and music are increasingly graduate professions, dominated by the privately educated. The sophistication of working-class culture — which combines laughter, intelligence and seriousness in complex ways — has been replaced by a grey bourgeois common sense, where everything comes swathed in a witless humour. It's long past time that we stopped sniggering along with the emotionally damaged bourgeoisie, and learned once again to laugh and care with the working class.

review: *terminator genisys*[1]

Think Abbott and Costello Meets Terminator. Think Terminator & Robin. Think, in other words, the point at which a franchise subsides, perhaps finally, into self-parody.

If the underrated *Terminator Salvation* (2009) drew on — and extended — all the machinic darkness of the first film, then *Terminator Genisys* returns to the playful PoMo of *Terminator 2: Judgment Day* (1991). Indeed, the film is so mired in self-reference and in-jokes, you almost suspect that its writers and director must have been closely consulting Fredric Jameson's remarks on pastiche in *Postmodernism, or, the Cultural Logic of Late Capitalism.*

In retrospect, *Terminator 2*'s already irritating combination of cutesy smart alecry ("Hasta la vista, baby") and apocalyptic foreboding laid out the formula for the 1990s postmodern thriller in the way that the Bond films did for the thrillers of the Sixties. The form was a kind of have-your-cake-and-eat-it mix of send-up and portentous melodrama (Linda Hamilton's performance was so OTT that you wanted to say, "Chill out, it's just a nuclear apocalypse").

That shtick feels played out far past the point of exhaustion now, and *Terminator Genisys* goes even more lightweight. It acts as if *Terminator Salvation* had never happened, emphatically rejecting its style and tone, and gorging on all the time-travel paradoxes that the previous film had sidelined. The set up returns us to the scenario of the first film. It sees Kyle Reese sent back into 1984 from the future. But Reese meets a Sarah Connor who is not at all what he expected. Rather than the disbelieving naif who has to be traumatically persuaded that she will become the mother of humanity's future saviour, this already battle-hardened Connor knows more than Reese does. Aha, an alternative timeline: an excuse to run through so many remixed versions of the best-known sequences from the first two films, like so much microwave-reheated comfort food.

By this point, we've already seen the original 1984 model of the Arnie Terminator blown away by an older Terminator (conveniently, it turns out that the Terminator skin and hair ages). This Terminator — whom Connor calls Pops — is essentially an older version of the protective-patriarch Terminator of *Terminator 2*, but — you see — he always talks in very technical jargon, which makes for some deeply unfunny would-be humorous exchanges with Reese, who keeps asking if there is a switch he can use to turn this dialogue off.

The presiding metaphysic here — a vision of total plasticity, in which nothing is final, everything can be redone — is, like everything else in this film, completely familiar. If the Terminator in the first film — a musclebound humanoid with metallic-robotic skeleton — was an image of work and technology in the Fordist era, then the T1000 gave us our first taste of the forms of capital and labour which were then emerging. No doubt, the T100's protean capacity to adopt any form whatsoever initially seemed exciting — reflecting the promises of a new digital technologies, and of an unleashed capitalism, recently freed up from conflict with the Soviet empire.

But by 2015 that excitement has long since flatlined. As with so much contemporary culture, *Terminator Genisys* feels simultaneously self-satisfied and desperate, frenzied and boring. It is at one and the same time a desecration and plundering of the series' past that is also pathetically reverential towards it. This sense of decadence makes the *Batman & Robin* parallel inevitable — with Arnie's Pops uncomfortably recalling his iconically disastrous performance as Mr Freeze. It isn't only the presence of Matt Smith that makes one think of the smugly baroque narrative excrescences of recent *Dr Who*.

In the end, however, what *Terminator Genisys* most resembles is something like a cross between the *Back to the Future* movies and *The Butterfly Effect*, but with none of the wit and ingenuity of the former, and little of the grim fatalism of the latter. In fact, it is the film's absolute refusal of fatalism — its embracing, indeed, of a kind of radically open reality, in which nothing is fixed, everything can be redone — which gives *Terminator Genisys* its deeply affectless quality. The uncanny charge of the first film's time loop — in which characters perform, apparently for the first time, acts that in some sense have always-already happened, is dissipated. No time loops here; just fuzzy and flabby spirals, which trail off into inconsequence, and which might very well be incoherent, if you could be bothered to care about them.

But this is the problem — a film whose reality is *this* plastic, this recomposable, is simply impossible to care about on any level. As such, *Terminator Genisys* becomes a kind of dumb, unintentional parable about restructuring in late capitalism. Since anything can and will change soon, why bother to care about what is happening now? The whole film feels like a monument to pointless hard work. We're left somewhat stupefied and perturbed by the vast amount of digital labour that has gone into something that is almost completely devoid of interest, and which it certainly feels like very hard work to watch.

the house that fame built: *celebrity big brother*[1]

This summer's *Celebrity Big Brother* (Channel 5) was like some Warholian nightmare. Long gone are the longueurs of the early *Big Brother* series, and the simplicity of its premise: put a group of people in a room, deprive them of contact with the outside world, have them vote one person out each week, and see what happens. Long forgotten also is the flimsy "scientific" justification for the show — the claim that it was a social experiment. The hyped-up atmosphere of 2015 will no longer permit even the illusion of such detachment.

This year the overall format of the series, framed as a competition, not only amongst the individual housemates, but between "teams" representing the US and the UK, predictably provoked high tension early on. There were the familiar "tasks" — pointless activities, ranging from the daft to the humiliating — designed to foment discontent amongst the housemates. But this year, the producers' interventions in the house amounted to prolonged psychological torture. This was all the more troubling, given that a number of the housemates were evidently fragile. The former TV presenter Gail Porter, who has a history of mental health problems, clearly struggled, "joking" on her exit from the house that it was worse than being sectioned. Model Austin Armacost, raw with anger and grief because his brother's death had led to the crumbling of his family, was subject to violent mood swings, and at one point launched into a savage verbal attack on reality TV veteran Janice Dickinson.

The obsession with "twists", introduced to keep freshening the format, has produced a self-parodic situation where the only constant is perpetual instability. Rules on nominations were continually changed. Housemates would find nominations that they had supposed were happening in the "diary room", seen only by the producers and the audience at home, broadcast to the whole house. Housemates were required to nominate in front of one another, which amounted to a demand that they denigrate each other in public.

In one especially deceitful trick from the show's producers, the two most aggressive American housemates — reality TV personality Farrah Abraham and former porn star Jenna Jameson — were apparently evicted, taken to a hidden part of the house and told they were watching the other housemates in secret. In fact, the other housemates were fully aware of Abraham and Jameson's fake eviction, so the last laugh — a hollow, spiteful laugh — was on them.

For the roots of this televisual culture, we need to look back forty years. In his book *1973 Nervous Breakdown: Watergate, Warhol, and the Birth of Post-Sixties America*, Andreas Hillen persuasively argues that the threshold into our current era of reality/celebrity was 1973, the year of the Watergate hearings, and the year that the first reality TV programme, *An American Family*, was broadcast.[2]

The ephemerality of celebrity status was of course anticipated by Andy Warhol's quip about everyone being famous for fifteen minutes, but Warhol's most extraordinary prescience lay in his understanding of the specificity of celebrity, its difference from the older mystique and glamour of the Hollywood star. Whereas the star was soft-focus and associated with film, the celebrity emerged from the new accessibility that television appeared to promise.

Celebrity culture was nowhere better illustrated than in Warhol's *Interview* magazine. Like Watergate, *Interview* was made possible by taping. The interviews, which ranged over the trivial minutiae of its subjects' lives, were transcripts; they weren't framed by the interposing persona of the writer. Yet Warhol understood that tape recording did not capture an unmediated real. Rather — and as Warhol's admirer Jean Baudrillard recognised — ubiquitous taping destroyed any illusion that such a real existed. Instead, there would now only be an anxious and unanswerable question: are those who are recorded performing for the tape or the camera? (Some said they felt that Nixon, at the heart of a White House riddled with recording apparatus, would often seem to say things for the benefit of the tape.)

The intrusion of the cameras into the Loud family's lives in *An American Family* prompted all kinds of anxious discussions: did the cameras affect what they were recording? As Hillen points out, the series wasn't only "Warholian" — there was an actual connection with Warhol. Lance Loud had corresponded with Warhol since the late 1960s, and *An American Family* featured scenes of Lance mingling with some of Warhol's superstars, the clique of New York personalities he promoted, in the Chelsea Hotel.

Not least because he was a victim of it, Warhol was sensitive to the volatile combination of violence and celebrity in the pop landscape. With

Celebrity Big Brother in 2015, it is clear that this aggression has become overwhelming. Ever since *An American Family*, reality TV has provoked feelings of guilt and complicity in the audience. To what extent are we responsible for the suffering we are watching? With *Celebrity Big Brother* this summer, those feelings became acute, almost unbearable. The programme became a prolonged exercise in intense cruelty, which made the early *Big Brother*, not to mention *An American Family*, seem quaintly genteel. What has happened in the fifteen years since *Big Brother* was first broadcast in the UK to account for this increase in savagery?

The simple answer involves two closely related factors: shifts in the economy, and the ubiquity of the internet. The resulting composite — capitalist cyberspace — has normalised extreme precariousness (the sense that nothing is permanent, everything is constantly under threat), competitiveness and casual aggression. One consequence is a new breed of celebrity, typified by twenty-four-year-old Farrah Abraham, the unofficial star of the latest *Celebrity Big Brother*. Abraham, who came to fame on MTV's *Teen Mom*, is a Darwinian product of the harsh, unremitting spotlight of twenty-first-century celebrity/reality TV. Abraham has quite literally made a career out of being hateful. It's what the audience, and therefore the TV producers, seems to want. She became the most successful of the Teen Moms by being obnoxious and antagonistic — her whole life becoming a performance art piece in which she played the one-dimensional role of a person devoid of compassion, nonchalantly dismissive and contemptuous of others practically all the time. But why would Abraham have any cause to mend her ways? She has been immensely rewarded. The performance of invulnerability is both her "brand" and a survival strategy.

In the atmosphere of cut-throat uncertainty that prevails in late-capitalist television, trusting others is a luxury that no one, not even the super-rich, can afford. The grimace of scorn on Abraham's face — surgically enhanced, permanently lip-glossed — is both a protective mask and her unique selling point. Allied with the similarly harsh Jenna Jameson in the *Celebrity Big Brother* house, Abraham came off as a comic figure, but one that no one could actually laugh at. Her one-note hostility and bisarre insults — "You're full of Satan" — were absurd, but too full of actual malice to leave anything but a bitter taste in the mouth. There was also something darkly comic about the relentlessly aggressive and insulting Jameson and Abraham attacking others for their "negativity". Both seemed to be the endpoint of a therapeutic culture which lays all the emphasis on shoring up one's own ego — even to the point of becoming delusional.

The rise of social media, and the fear it has produced in television executives, means that shows like *Celebrity Big Brother* are saturated with anxiety — not only the anxiety of the housemates, who are often selected for their hair-trigger tempers or psychic weaknesses, but the anxiety of the producers, always looking for the next hashtag outrage, for provocations that will go viral. This anxiety, and the surrounding social situation that engenders it, takes us beyond the cool ambivalence of Warhol's aesthetic.

As Hillen points out, Warhol certainly enjoyed, even cultivated, the self-destruction of figures such as Edie Sedgwick and Candy Darling. But he also imbued them with a tenderness and a tragic grandeur that has no place on reality TV in the twenty-first century. No tragedy now — only spasms of soon-to-be-forgotten outrage, ejaculations of hatred and suffering snacked on like fast food.

sympathy for the androids: the twisted morality of *westworld*[1]

The problem with all actually existing theme parks is that they aren't actually very themed. The theme parks that have been built so far are really amusement parks, the theming acting as decoration for what are still, at bottom, old-fashioned thrill rides. The tendency in the latest rides is for a fusion with cinema, via the inclusion of 3D digital sequences — just as 3D cinema itself increasingly tends towards a ride's logic of sensation. The immersion, such as it is, is confined within the rides, which remain discrete partial worlds, with clearly marked exits and entrances. Even if the theming is somewhat well executed, it is let down by the paying customers. Wandering around clutching cameras and wearing jeans, whatever world or historical period they are supposed to be in, the park visitors remain spectators, their identity as tourists preserved.

Michael Crichton's 1973 film *Westworld* tried to imagine what a genuine theme park would look like. There were no separate "attractions" here, and therefore no meta-zone in which the visitors were invited to return to their own identities. In the Westworld park, there was no readily apparent difference between the visitors and the androids that populated the park. Like the androids, the visitors were required to dress and comport themselves as if they belonged to the Old West. The appeal of Westworld — and its companion parks, Roman World and Medieval World — was of crossing over into an environment from which all signs of the contemporary had been expunged. Instead of the limited immersion offered by rides, the park offered a whole world. Inevitably, the meta crept in, via the visitors' self-consciousness, their awareness of their differences from the androids (which were manifested most emphatically in the asymmetry whereby — initially at least — the guests can "kill" the androids, but not vice versa).

The recurring theme in Crichton's science fiction — broached most famously in his *Jurassic Park* novels — was the impossibility of predicting

261

and controlling emergent phenomena. *Westworld*, like *Jurassic Park* after it, becomes the model for a kind of managerial hubris, in which the capacity of elements in a system to self-organise in ways that are not foreseeable is fatally underestimated. One of the notable features of the original *Westworld* film was its early mainstreaming of the possibility of a machinic virus: it is a non-biotic contagion of this sort that causes the androids, led by a memorably implacable, black-clad Yul Brynner, to go off-programme and start killing the park guests.

In expanding *Westworld* from a ninety-minute science fiction movie into an extended television series for HBO, Lisa Joy and Jonathan Nolan have retained most of the core elements from the film, but shifted the emphasis. The glitch that starts to worry the park's designers and managers is a cognitive failure rather than a predilection towards violence: a kind of android dementia that may be the symptom of emergent consciousness amongst the "hosts", as the androids are called in the series. As the park's chief founder, conceptualist and demiurge, Robert Ford (Anthony Hopkins) recognises that a glitch is something more than a mere failure. "Evolution", he observes, "forged the entirety of sentient life on this planet using only one tool: the mistake". Ford seems more fascinated than panicked by the prospect of a new wave of mutations in the hosts' artificial psyches.

In this version of *Westworld*, it isn't the threat of violence against humans that commands our attention so much as the routine brutality to which the hosts are subjected. Ford justifies this by insisting that the androids "are not real", that they "only feel what we tell them to feel". Yet it's not fully clear what criteria for reality he is employing, nor why feelings cease to be real when they are programmed. Wouldn't forcing others to feel what we want them to feel be the very definition of violence? There is ample evidence in the series that the androids can experience distress: an indication, surely, that they are beings worthy of moral concern.

Much of the park's allure rests on the gap between the hosts' capacity to feel suffering and their legal status as mere machines. Many of the hardened repeat visitors to the park — especially the so-called Man in Black (a superbly menacing Ed Harris) — specifically enjoy the pain and struggling of the androids. As the Man in Black tells Dolores (Evan Rachel Wood), the host cast in the role of sweet and wholesome farmgirl, it wouldn't be half as much fun if she didn't resist him. Others enjoy displaying indifference to the hosts' agonies. In one horrifying early scene, a guest impales the hand of a prospector-host with a knife, chiding his companion for being tempted by such an un-engaging narrative as gold-hunting.

It has been said that the fantasy underlying sadism is of a victim that can endlessly suffer. The hosts materialise this fantasy: they can be repeatedly brutalised, repeatedly "killed", in an infinity of suffering. Ennui has always been both an occupational hazard and a badge of honour for the Sadean libertine, and some of the repeat visitors display an ironic and bored affect. Hence the ambivalent attitude of these guests towards the hosts — at once treating them as dehumanised objects of abuse and as creatures who share fellow feelings. If the hosts were nothing more than empty mechanisms, what enjoyment could be derived from humiliating and destroying them? Yet if the hosts were accorded equivalent moral status with the guests, then how could their abuse be justified? The hosts are protected from the full horror to which they are subjected by memory wipes, which allow them to return renewed and ready for more abuse, each time they are reset. The guests exist in a continuous time, while the hosts are locked into loops.

What the hosts lack is not consciousness — they possess a form of consciousness that has been deliberately limited or blinkered — but an unconscious. Deprived of memory and the capacity to dream, the androids can be wounded but not traumatised. Yet there are signs that precisely this capacity to experience trauma is developing in some of the hosts, especially Dolores and the brothel madam, Maeve (Thandie Newton). Dolores is increasingly subject to flashbacks, which we must understand not as glitches but as the first stirrings of memory, a recollection of her previous iterations. Maeve, meanwhile, is tormented by fragmentary images of hooded figures tampering with her half-sleeping body. In fact, this is a memory of a botched repair procedure, which she witnessed because she was not properly put into sleep-mode while being fixed. In one of the most unsettling scenes in the series, the panicked and bewildered Maeve escapes from the hospital-cum-repair space, and stumbles around the aseptic compound, which — littered with decommissioned naked host bodies — must look to her like an atrocity scene. In attempting to solve the mystery of the inexplicable images which haunt her, Maeve comes to resemble a combination of Leonard in the film *Memento* and an alien abduction victim.

With few exceptions, the human beings in *Westworld* are a charmless bunch. Their behaviour runs a gamut from the savagery of some of the guests to the banal bickering and corporate competitiveness of the park's designers, managers and engineers. By contrast, Dolores and Maeve's struggle to understand what they are — alternating between thinking there is something wrong with their minds and something wrong with their world — possesses a kind of metaphysical lyricism. Their coming to consciousness looks like being the precondition for a very different android rebellion than that which took place in the 1973 film. This time, it's hard not be on the side of the hosts.

PART THREE

CHOOSE YOUR WEAPONS: WRITING ON MUSIC

the by now traditional glasto rant[1]

"What really drives student entrepreneurs into a premature commercial detachment is their audiences. Every new ents officer learns from first-term results; black music has no student draw; known bands are preferred to unknown bands; no one in the student union cares who the latest critical cult figures are. Students are the great, middle-class, middle-brow bastion of British rock and, after twenty years, their tastes aren't about to be shaken."
— Simon Frith, "Afterthoughts"[2]

So wrote Simon Frith in 1985. Well, after twenty further years, I see no reason to revise Frith's judgement.

These reflections have been prompted by Glastonbury, naturally, which is now nearly officially the end-of-college-year prom for Britain's student (and graduate) population.

I should preface my remarks here by referring to Ian Penman's[3] comments of more or less this time last year — and if anyone doubts what a LOSS Ian Penman is, and I'm sure no one does, just read his Glastonburial 03 posts.[4] Like Penman, I feel annoyed at myself for letting it get to me. The Pawboy put it perfectly: "I still get agitated, perplexed — I wouldn't actually say 'depressed', that's not true — but something like Glastonbury irks and niggles me, still, in a way I wish it didn't. I really do wish it didn't. Could you P-L-E-A-S-E knock me off my feet, for a while? P-L-E-A-S-E knock me off my feet for a while... 'Cos there's a GAAXY OF EMPTINESS tonight."

All that said, and obviously I didn't GO — Christ, you didn't imagine that IN A MILLION YEARS I would, did you? — and obviously the telly coverage is as nothing compared to the real experience: cos there's like MUD there (and weren't Jo Wiley's mud anecdotes abso-fucking-lutely, screamingly *hilarious*?), and FIRE-EATERs and JUGGLERS... (Has any cultural event of any significance ever happened whenever a juggler is within a hundred

267

mile radius?) Penman again: "I mean, music in a field — in the daytime? Wtf? It's almost deliberately delibidinising..."

But that's the agenda, really, the secret purpose of this now unopposed embourgeoisement of rock culture UK. What's positively sinister about Glastonbury now is that it's not just *accidentally* crap, it's systematically crap — the hidden message screams out: it's all finished, roll up, roll up, for the necrophiliac spectacle, it's all over.

ABANDON ALL CULTURAL VITALITY ALL YE WHO ENTER HERE.

Those who only remember the past are condemned to repeat it.

Forever.

The bill was almost parodically LCD MOR, so safe and organic and wholesome and unimpeachable and uncontroversial: Macca! Oasis! Franz Ferdinand!

No black folks of course unless they're well into their sixties (James Brown; Toots and the Maytals), but no whiteys EITHER unless they're into their sixties (Macca) or *sound like they could be* in their sixties (Franz Ferdinand, Scissor Sisters)...

Go along with Mum and Dad, read the *Guardian*, smoke some dope — the whole of rock history fugged out into some blandly beneficent museum of dead forms, all breaks, discontinuities, ruptures edited out or incorporated back in (the "Dance" stage), their force and novelty subdued and airbrushed into a joyless carnival of secondhand history for the stupefied delectation of the Last Men... (And didn't they look so BORED? Well, wouldn't you?)

The significance of generation gaps wasn't the tired Oedipal merry-go-round so much as that they pointed to a culture of constant renewal — how long is a generation? In any vital culture, it's a matter of weeks or months, here? Well, the fact that the generation gap doesn't make any sense any more at Glastonbury — balding accountants getting down to Basement Jaxx, Jemima studying Fine Arts at Sussex being "blown away" by Macca ("he was so gid!") — is a sure sign that this is a "culture" as energetic as the contents of one of Hirst's tanks.

RESPECT, respect for everyone... (when culture demands respect, when respect is the appropriate response to culture, you know it's either died in its sleep or been killed). Respect is how they killed Shakespeare, make it all a part of the National Heritage...

A tactical nuclear strike would have taken out virtually everything that's debilitating, deadening and reactive about the Brit culture industry (the whole *NME* staff: bargain!), much of the current ruling class and a significant portion of our future masters too (all those aspiring Tony Blairs).

Once the bombers have hit Glasto, set the co-ordinates for Ibiza, things might start improving around here...

art pop, no, really[1]

If we're going to discuss art pop, we really ought to forget Franz Ferdinand and Scissor Sisters and talk about Moloko.

I saw them last night at the otherwise desultory Common Ground festival in Clapham, an event whose line-up was as limp as its name was uninspired.

Gratifyingly, by the way, Common Ground wasted no time in confirming all my prejudices about festivals (and then some): those on the stage haplessly attempted to muster some enthusiasm from bored punters, who wandered around listlessly in a sunlight inimical to pop's mystique, Strongbow in their hand, kid on their shoulder. We weren't the only people to sit and read the paper for a while.

The bill was shocking. It felt like a local council free event, the organisers under the lamentable misapprehension that they'll appear "with it" by booking "dance" acts such as the oppressively lumpen stodge of Freestylers (a candidate for my worst band ever, actually; I mean, at least the Stereophonics don't taint rap and dancehall by association) and the Dub Pistols. These cloddish white appropriations of hip-hop, drum 'n' bass and dancehall are dis-spiritingly, missing-the-point funkless and morosely male (even when they use female vocalists). If their diabolic intent was to systematically convert some of the most exciting, cutting-edge music of recent years into a dull migraine thud, they couldn't have done a more ruthlessly efficient job.

And then Moloko arrived, Róisín, preposterously but marvellously, in a *helmet*, like Boudicca come to retake London.

Róisín is every inch the pop star. Pop stars are a rare breed at the best of times but they're scarce to the point of near-extinction now. (There are more pop *singers* and "celebrities" than you can shake a stick at, of course...) It's partly a question of style, partly of glamour, but mostly it's to do with charisma.

In its original meaning, charisma meant "a gift from God". Appropriate. For charisma is dispensed according to fate's inegalitarian whim. Róisín has it. No amount of bluster, sweat or sinew will allow the likes of the Freestylers to acquire it, even though the resentful, levelling spirit of the times would have it otherwise.

So Róisín arrives and you can feel the change in the air. Where before the stage was a libido-draining vortex (DJs on stage — just one question: *why*?), now it radiates energy, excitement and electricity. Charisma, it's almost a physical thing.

Róisín has a glamour which includes sexual attractiveness but it is not reducible to it. Glamour originally meant a spell cast by women to entrance men — Róisín is certainly capitivating, but not only to men.

If (viz Foucault) sex is ubiquitous and compulsory, glamour is now subtly forbidden. With the Baudrillard of *Seduction*, a book which could serve as a bible of glam, we could even see sex — in all its directness, in all its supposed lack of concealment — as a way of warding off glamour's ambivalence.

Much more successfully than derivative dullards like the thankfully now forgotten dull-as-a carpark-in-Croydon Suede, Moloko reconnect with the glam discontinuum which was ostensibly terminated by acid house's "equity culture" in the late Eighties. Glam also had a terminator of an entirely different nature: hip-hop's *in-equity* culture of conspicuous bling, one of the most unfortunate side-effects of which has been the rise of sportswear (surely one of the most depressing sights now, and not only because of its implied menace: a group of male teenagers dressed in tracksuits and hoods).

That quotidian functionalism is today's equivalent of the agrarian organicism from which Seventies glam revolted into style. Glam repudiated hippie's "nature" in the name of artifice; disdained its fugged, bleary vision of equality for a Nietzschean-aristocratic insistence upon hierarchy; rejected its unscrubbed beardiness in order to cultivate Image. (Image and great pop are indissoluble. Maybe the integral role of Image is what separates pop from folk. Certainly, art pop, from Roxy to Jones to the New Romantics, is unthinkable outside fashion.)

Madonna carried traces of the glam aesthetic over into the pop mainstream in the Eighties, but a more obvious precursor for Róisín is Grace Jones (about whom k-punk must write extensively in the very near future). Like art poppers such as Bryan Ferry (whose "Love is the Drug", she famously vamped), Jones' take on pop was essentially conceptual; at the same time, she knew that concepts without sensual instantiation are as worthless in pop as they are in art (a lesson some of our contemporary "artists" would do well to heed). Incidentally, an appreciation of the concept is one of the many things that Franz Ferdinand lack that was there in their inspirations. (Actually, FF are like a copy made by an alien race, which maintains all the superficial features of the original, but misses the essential.)

Róisín has that paradoxical duality which comes as second nature to the compelling performer: she is both meticulously obsessed with her image and, at the same time, apparently indifferent to what she looks like. This comes over in her dancing. There is none of the over-rehearsed choreography of the *Pop Idol* puppet. Like Jagger's and Ferry's, Róisín's movement can occasionally look ungainly and gauche. Sometimes we feel that we've caught her prancing in front of the mirror.

It's partly this that gives her a distance from her image that isn't camp, or at least not camp in the Kylie sense. There is an enjoyment there (this is one of many things that separates Róisín from Kylie: Kylie's air hostess professionalism exudes grim determination, never enjoyment). Principally though not of course exclusively, this enjoyment is her own, an enjoyment that partly derives from being the object of attention, but which goes beyond that. Like all great performers, Róisín onstage enters a kind of performance trance, attaining the innocence of a child at play, to use Nietzsche's beautifully resonant phrase. Her costume changes — including fetish boots and a military cap for "Pure Pleasure Seeker" — have the deranged playfulness of a girl riffling through a dressing-up box.

Just as Moloko give the lie to the accepted wisdom that dance music must be delivered by hooded anonymities, so they also expose the flimsiness of the alibi that Franz Ferdinand offer for indie conservatism: the idea that art pop must be retro. Moloko's engagement with house and techno recalls Roxy's dallyings with funk and Jones' extraordinary Sly-and-Robbie assisted construction of a wonderfully elastic dubfunk. Any funk in Franz Ferdinand is third hand, an appropriation of an appropriation.

The third shibboleth that Moloko demolish is the notion that dance music can't be performed live. If you'd left before they came on, you would have gone home convinced that this was the case, as group after group trudged offstage having failed to capture the precision-engineered thrill of the rap or d 'n' b studio production. Not so with Moloko.

For the most part the group are as reluctant to take the limelight as Róisín is delighted to bathe in it. Perhaps because of this, they are an unbelievably efficient mutagenic sonic machine, dilating tracks into anti-climactic plateaus with the same skill that a brilliant producer uses in the studio to sequence an extended version. You know you've arrived at a plateau when it feels like the track could continue indefinitely or end immediately. This happened with every track last night. No doubt this is because the songs provide such a strong basis for improvisation. Does anyone in pop at the moment, apart from maybe Destiny's Child, have a sequence of high-quality singles to rival Moloko's run from "Sing It Back" to last year's "Forever More"? Like the Junior Boys, Moloko's whole existence demonstrates that rhythmic innovation and spine-tingling songwriting do not have to be mutually exclusive. (Why did we ever think they were?)

Misleading, then, to select highlights, but the set is deftly constructed, so that the last three tracks pack the most impact: "Forever More", with its anempathic house bass, Róisín plucking and shredding petals from an enormous bunch of roses as she delivered its gorgeous blues plaint; "Sing It Back", which they've expanded into a deluxe suite, a song as a sequence of different possibilities; and finally the enigmatic "Indigo", which begins all Moroder-minimal, just Róisín, a drum machine and an electro throb, then builds into a mighty cake-walk riff, as brutally bass-heavy as the Fall at their most punitive.

The only drawback? Róisín said that it'll be a long time until Moloko play in London again.

Damn.

k-punk, or the glampunk art pop discontinuum[1]

\Gla'mour\, n. [Scot. glamour, glamer; cf. Icel. gl['a]meggdr one who is troubled with the glaucoma (?); or Icel. gl[=a]m-s?ni weakness of sight, glamour; gl[=a]mr name of the moon, also of a ghost + s?ni sight akin to E. see. Perh., however, a corruption of E. gramarye.]
1. A charm affecting the eye, making objects appear different from what they really are.
2. Witchcraft; magic; a spell — Tennyson.
3. A kind of haze in the air, causing things to appear different from what they really are.
4. Any artificial interest in, or association with, an object, through which it appears delusively magnified or glorified.
Glamour gift, Glamour might, the gift or power of producing a glamour. The former is used figuratively, of the gift of fascination peculiar to women.

"Every woman has the instinct and the ability to make the most of her charms. It is an excellent thing to give oneself without love or pleasure: by keeping one's self-control, one reaps all the advantages of the situation."
— Leopold von Sacher-Masoch, *Venus in Furs*[2]

Glam IS punk; historically and conceptually.

As Simon Reynolds argued (what must be a year ago now), it was glam that made the break which allowed punk to happen.

Essentially, glam returned pop to the working-class audience disgusted and turned by the hippies' lazy sleaze.

For all its "androgynous" imagery, hippie was fundamentally a middle-class male phenomenon. It was about males being allowed to regress to that state of His Majesty the Ego hedonic infantilism, with women on hand to service all their needs. (If you don't believe me — and I'll level with you I'm very far from being an objective commentator on hippie lol — read Atwood's Cold Rationalist classic *Surfacing* to see how "liberating" this was for the women who lived through it.)

Thus even Zarathustra/another time loser/could believe in you...

Seventies glam played the Nietzsche of *Beyond Good and Evil* and *The Genealogy of Morals* (the Nietzsche who celebrated aristocracy, nobility and mastery) against the young Dionysian Nietzsche. As Simon argued:

> Glam's tendency (through its shifting of emphasis toward the visual rather than sonic, spectacle rather than the swarm-logic of noise and crowds) towards the Classical as opposed to Romantic. Glam as anti-Dionysian. The Dionysian being essentially democratic, vulgar, levelling, abolishing rank; about creating crowds, turbulence, a rude commotion, a rowdy communion. Glam being about monumentalism, turning yourself into a statue, a stone idol.[3]

But glam rectified the genetic fallacy that haunted Nietzsche's thinking. While there's no doubt that Nietzsche's analysis of the deadening effects of slave-moralising "egalitarian" levelling in *Beyond Good and Evil* and *The Genealogy of Morals* identified the sick mind virus that had Western culture locked into life-hating dis-intensification-unto-death, his paeans to slave-owning aristocratic culture made the mistake of thinking that nobility could be *guaranteed* by social background.

Nobility is precisely a question of values; i.e. an ethical stance, that is to say, a way of behaving. As such, it is available to anyone with the will and desire to acquire it — even, presumably, the bourgeoisie, although their whole socialisation teaches them to resist and loathe it. More than anyone, Nietzsche understood that the European bourgeoisie's deep hostility to "the notion of superiority" concealed a viciously resentful psychopathology.

If Nietzschean atheology says: We must become God, bourgeois secularism says: No one may be greater than me — not even God.

Everyone knows that there has always been a deep affinity between the working class and the aristocracy. Fundamentally aspirational, working-class culture is foreign to the levelling impulse of bourgeois culture — and of course this can be politically ambivalent, since if aspiration is about the pursuit of status and authority, it will confirm and vindicate the bourgeois world. It is only if the desire to escape inspires taking a line of flight towards the proletarian collective body and Nu-earth that it is politically positive.

Glam was a return to the Mod moment(um) that had been curtailed by the hippie hedonic longeur of the late Sixties. Like most names for subcultural groups, the term "Mod" started off life as an insult, in this case

274

hailing from the mods' perpetual adversaries, the rockers. As Jeff Nuttall explains, to the rockers, "'Mod' meant effeminate, stuck-up, emulating the middle classes, apsiring to a competitive sophistication, snobbish, phony."[4]

But no dilettante/or filigree fancy/beats the plastic you

Mods in the Sixties were very different from how they appear in the designer cappuccino froth of Eighties soul-cialist retro-mythologisation. It was the rockers who appealed to the "authentic" and the "natural': their rebellion posed as a Rousseauistic resistance to civilisation and mass (produced) culture. The mods, on the other hand, embraced the hyper-artificial: for them, Nuttall wrote, "alienation had become something of a deliberate stance". Nobility was not innate for mods: rather, it was something to be *attained*, through a ruthless de-naturalisation of the body via decoration and chemical alteration.

The mods were in every sense hooked on speed, and the black American music they gulped down with their bennies and coffees was consumed in the same spirit and for the same reasons: as an accelerator, an intensifier, an artificial source of ecstasy. That is, as a chemical *rush* into Now, NOT as some timeless expression of pride and dignity.

In the desire (my official position on this now btw is that "libido" should be used in place of "desire")-pleasure relation, there is a third, occluded term: sensuality.

The hippies' sloppy, ill-fitting clothes, unkempt appearance and fuzzed-out psychedelic fascist drug talk displayed a disdain for sensuality characteristic of the Western master class. ("Hey man, it's all about the MIND.")

When hippies rose from their supine hedono-haze to assume power (a very short step), they brought their contempt for sensuality with them. Brute functional utilitarianism plus aesthetic sloppiness and an imperturbable sense of their own rights are the hallmarks of the bourgeois sensibility (look at all those shops in Stoke Newington that say they'll open "tennish" and you know exactly what class you're dealing with).

The hippie power class wanted power without having to go to the effort of power dressing. Naturally, middle-class hippie "feminists" never missed a stride in their move from alleged egalitarianism to supercilious judgementalism. What is the disdain for cosmetics and clothes if not an attack on the working class? The assumption of bourgeois so-called feminists is that their lives of neurotic bed-hopping "freedom" and Carrie Bradshawing perpetual adolescent equivocation are better than the working-class pattern of (once) getting married young and (now) having children young, when it is clear that it is just another trap — and not necessarily a more congenial one.

Now the bourgeois philistines have destroyed glam and returned us to their preferred aesthetic mode: Romanticism. The contemporary bourgeois Romantic has realised Romanticism in its most distilled form yet. The so-called Romantic poets, musicians and painters of the late-eighteenth and early-nineteenth century remained sensualists, whereas our contemporary Romantics are defined by their view that sensuality is at best an irrelevance, a distraction from the important business of the expression of subjectivity.

Romanticism is the dressing-up of Teenage Ontology as an aesthetic cosmology. Teenage Ontology is governed by the conviction that *what really matters* is interiority: how you *feel* inside, and what your *experiences* and *opinions* are. In this sense, sloppy drunkard Ladette Tracy Emin is one of the most Romantic artists ever. Like Lads — the real inheritors of the hippie legacy — Emin's bleary, blurry, beery, leery, lairy anti-sensualist sensibility is an advert for the vacuity of her own preferences.

What we find in Emin, Hirst, Whiteread and whoever the idiot was who rebuilt his dad's house in the Tate is a disdain for the artificial, for art as such, in a desperately naïf bid to (re)present that pre-Warholian, pre-Duchampian, pre-Kantian unadorned Real. Like our whole won't-get-fooled-again PoRoMo culture, what they fear above all is being *glamoured*. Remember that glamour means, *"Any artificial interest in, or association with, an object, through which it appears delusively magnified or glorified."*

But let's make our case by considering some artefacts in some detail.

Exhibit one: the cover of Roxy Music's *For Your Pleasure*, 1973.

The cover image is a mistresspiece of ambivalence.

Let's approach it through the eyes of Ian Penman, the most consummate of Roxy observers. (No doubt, Penman, like me, is endlessly drawn back to Ferry because he took the same journey from the working class into acceptance into the English master class).

(I make no apologies for citing Penman's text, "The Shattered Glass: Notes on Bryan Ferry" at some length, since it is almost criminal that this bravura display of theoretical elegance should be mouldering amidst the pages of a long-forgotten, chalk dusty Cult Studs collection).[5]

> On the shoreline of *For Your Pleasure*, beneath it, on the waterfront strand, stands the second of many new models: at first sight the second installation of the stock Ferry/ Roxy woman.

But to get the full picture we have to fold out the sleeve, so that we can see Ferry looking on...

Penman goes on:

> Ferry fills out his function as her chauffeur (landlocked ferryman: a sign of the times). He waits in amused admiration, surveying the neatness of the visual pun — the model takes her cat (for a) walk: forming a *uniform* and uniformly predatory alliance with her black panther, eyes and mouth directed out at the viewer. Imperiously, she takes the air, she fields

his grace, takes her anima for a prowl and a stretch. Ferry — for sure — remains to be seen, smiling manfully behind her back, artfully protected by the fold in his sleeve. He had arranged his own look as both within and outside of the main frame.

("*Within and outside of the main frame*: is that so often where we find ourselves, lost, stranded, these days—?")

Cut.

She is a model woman, to be sure; fashion pushing into abstraction and rarified codification, not there for the benefit of a product as such or altogether in the name of Art; so she appears to be what? She appears, on the condition that she appear to be without attributes. We can attribute nothing to her beyond a certain imaginary realm of wealth, of wealth as fetish, (Helmut) Newton's law of physiques. She is sheerest sharp blue nothingness. (For the cool-and-blue post-Duchamp artist, it seems entirely for beauty to take the veiled form of *scissors*.)

As an aside, since this concerns another debate: the *last things* Ferry's songs were — at this stage at least — were "just good tunes". The *first thing* they were, were questions: including questions about what a good tune might mean...

And — at this stage — Ferry's songs were no more "love songs" than Magritte's "Human Condition" was a representation of a landscape. Like Magritte, Ferry's sheer coldness and distantiation cannot but draw our attention to the framing machines that make possible the emotions of which he sings.

Another cut, to a "realm of a certain narcissistic eroticism he is not allowed entrance to without putting his heterosexual *sensibility* in doubt":

All his songs' women (and this will be especially so with "Stranded" and subsequent plaints) are voiceless sirens who — although wielding the utmost power over the artist's life and sensibility — seem to be without implication (which is to say: eternalised out of existence). Neutered time and place (those perennial spans of Fashion) coalesce naturally into the figure of the woman. Woman as figure, or scene — war pin up, cat-woman, amazon, siren, Riefehstahl Maedchen.

"*[W]ielding the utmost power over the artist's life and sensibility...*" The utmost power... Is he, the artist, Severin, the protagonist of Masoch's *Venus in Furs*? Or Sarasine, the hapless hero-dupe of Balzac's novel who unwittingly falls in love with a castrato?

Because, you see, the ironic punchline was: she is not(-all) a woman.

Amanda Lear, the *For Your Pleasure* model, was a transsexual (though, in yet another complication, she later denied it). A transsexual, moreover, whose operation might have been paid for by none other than Salvador Dali.

Either way, it is clear that Ferry has set the tone for a 1970s in which the male is both glamorous and glamoured, himself a gorgeously-styled photogenic object, entranced and seduced by a cosmetic beauty he partly wants to make contact with, but mostly wants to cold pastoralise into an immutable untouchability. "Mother of Pearl" — which as Penman observed on *The Pill Box*, is the whole of Lacan in seven minutes, more or less — is the closest Ferry comes to writing a manifesto for his meta-melancholia, a meta-love song about the impossibility — and *undesirability* — of attaining the Ideal object.

Now this melancholia is not straightforwardly "tragic" (and even if it were, it would have little to do with any bourgeois sensibility, since, as everyone from Shakespeare to George Steiner (*The Death of Tragedy*) to Nietzsche to Bataille demonstrates, bourgeois secularism is inherently inimical to any notion of the tragic).

But Ferry's sensibility is definitely masochistic. (As opposed to that of the Sixties, which, as Nuttall, for one, suggests, was Sadean. Compare the Sixties-sired Lennon's "Jealous Guy" — the Sadist apologises — to Ferry's reading of the song — the masochist sumptuously enjoying his own pain — for a snapshot of a contrast between the two sensibilities.)

The masochist's perversity consists in the refusal of an exclusive or even primary focus on genitality or sexuality even in its Sadean polymorphous sense, which is perverse only in a very degraded sense.

The Sadean imagination quickly reaches its limits when confronted with the limited number of orifices the organism has available for penetration. But the masochist — and Newton is in this respect, as in so many others, a masochist through and through, as is Ballard — distributes libido across the whole scene. The erotic is to be located in all the components of the machine, whether liveware — the soft pressure of flesh — or dead animal pelt — the fur coat — or technical. Masochism is cyberotics, precisely because it recognises no distinction between the animate and inanimate. After all, when you run your fingers through your beloved's hair, you are caressing something dead.

How had Ferry got here, become stranded in the early Seventies, an artist-voyeur art-director masochist?

Ferry famously studied painting under Richard Hamilton, the so-called godfather of British Pop Art, at Newcastle University. Can we even begin to reconstruct the impact that Hamilton's art had on British culture?

Well, you can get some impression of it from the fact that, in a documentary on Hamilton made by Channel 4 in the early 1990s, Ballard cited Hamilton's 1956 "Just What Is It That Makes Today's Homes so Different, so Appealing" as one of the cultural events that made it possible for him to be a science-fiction writer. It would be better to say that Hamilton made possible Ballard's *exceeding* of science fiction, his discovery of k-punk.

1956 was, of course, the year of Presley's breakthrough records. In its own way, though, Hamilton's collage was at least as important as Presley in the development of British pop.

After the Fifties, pop and art have always been reversible and reciprocally implicating in British culture in the way that they are not in America. Nuttall: "The students and the mods cross-fertilised... Purple hearts appeared in strange profusion. Bell-bottoms blossomed into wild colours. Shoes were painted with Woolworths lacquer. Both sexes wore make-up and dyed their hair... The air in the streets was tingling with a new delirium."[6]

British pop's irreducible artificiality makes it resistant to the Romanticist *naturalisation* that the likes of Greil Marcus and Lester Bangs achieved in respect of American rock. There is no way of *grounding* British art pop in a landscape.

Not a *natural* landscape in any case.

If art pop had a landscape it would be the aggressively anti-naturalistic one Ferry collaged together on "Virginia Plain" (named after one of his paintings, which was itself named after a brand of tobacco). Is this an internal landscape, what the mind's eye sees? Perhaps. But only if we recognise that — as Hamilton's collage and Ballard's fiction insist — in the late-twentieth century the "space" of the internal-psychological was completely penetrated by what Ballard calls the media landscape.

When the British pop star sings, it is not "the land" which speaks (and what does Marcus hear in the American rock he mythologises in *Mystery Train* if not the American land?) but the deterritory of American-originated consumer culture. Hence the braying grotesquerie of Ferry's singing voice on those early Roxy releases. (And the different grotesquerie of today's simoting pop idols.)

With the first-hand expertise of someone who has had to lose his voice in order to speak (for that is what you must do if you educate yourself — or *are educated* — out of a working-class background), Penman brings out very well how integral the problem of accent — of losing a Geordie accent, of not gaining an American accent — was to Ferry's career.

As a student, Ferry's life was divided between his daytime movement through the art milieu and nighttime fronting of a soul band doing covers. Two voices, two lives. "I hadn't found anything to incorporate *all* of me."

The early Roxy records are Ferry's Warhol-Frankensteinian attempts — the joins still showing, thrillingly, horrifyingly — to hand-machine a space that would incorporate his day and his night self. So they are not so much expressions of a coherent subjectivity as a kind of destratification-in-progress, the production, on the fly, of a pop art plane of consistency which he could feel at unhome in.

So here was a pop music, astonishingly, more shaped by Duchamp than Bo Diddley. The methodology Ferry deployed on his solo albums of cover versions (and remember that such albums were almost unknown in rock music at the time) was explicitly Duchampian. His renditions of standards such as "Smoke Gets in Your Eyes" and "These Foolish Things" were, he said, Duchampian "readymades": found objects upon which he put his own stamp.

Part of what made the early Roxy sound so cold — particularly by comparison with the hot authenticity of American rock — was the fact that they were evidently not an aggregation of spontaneous, creative subjects, but a meticulously executed Duchamp-type Concept: a group whose every gesture was micro-designed, and who credited their stylist, fashion designer Anthony Price, on their album sleeves.

The great temptation for Ferry would always be to slip inside the frame: to become, really, the heartaching bachelor in the dreamhome, to achieve what Simon calls the

> fantasy of stepping outside the lowly world of production into a sovereign realm of pure unfettered expression and sensuous indulgence, an imaginary and fictitious notion of aristocracy (more Huysmans than real lords who have to do humdrum things like manage their estates, juggle their investments, do a bit of arms dealing).

To achieve the total simulation of manners that he was up till then only pastiching-affecting.

And, isn't Simon right, aren't Ferry's later records all about "the disillusionment of actually achieving the supermonied aristo life — Ferry, condemned to mooch jaded forever through art openings, fashion shows, all tomorrow's parties (that old tis better to journey than arrive line)"?

Let's leave Ferry there, stranded, framed.

And cut.

To 1982. Compass Point, Nassau.

Grace Jones' astonishing recording of Joy Division's "She's Lost Control".

Masoch: "A slap in the face is more effective than ten lectures, especially if it is delivered by the hand of a lady."

Kodwo Eshun:

> The womanmachine Grace Jones' 82 remodel of Joy Division's 79 *She's Lost Control* updates the Fifties mechanical bride. For the latter losing control meant electric epilepsy, voice drained dry by feedback. For Jones,

the female model that's losing control induces the sense of automation running down, the human seizing up into a machine rictus. The model — as girl, as car, as synthesizer — incarnates the assembly time of generations, obsolescence, 3-year lifespans.

The model is the blueprint for the post-Cold War cyborg, the womanmachine modified and mutated by the military medical entertainment complex. Hence Kraftwerk's *The Model*, where the bachelormachines are threatened by the womanmachine's superior reproductive capability. *The Model* is an excerpt from the post-war machine-reproduction wars.[7]

Jones is the sublime object before which Ferry prostrated himself — and who talked back. Through vagina-dentatal teeth.

Be careful of the womanimal-machine. It bites.

Jones is not a cyborg because she is not an organism of any kind (and the modifier "cybernetic" is in any case redundant, since all organisms, like everything that works, are cybernetic).

She is a neurobotic femachine.

The mechanical bride stripping her bachelors bare.

Jones was herself once a model, but when she has the opportunity to "express herself", she ruthlessly exploits her own body and image much more than any (male) photographer would have dared to. "In a recent poll by *Men's Health* magazine, the male readership named Grace Jones [...] among the women who scared them the most." (Brian Chin).

The game becomes the hunter.

She out-Duchamps Ferry, (dis)covering his "Love is the Drug" as a found object to be absorbed by the femachine.

Jones understands her body Spinozistically as *a machine capable of being affected and producing affects*. This body is in no way limited to the organism; it is distributed across photographs, sound and video — and none of these media constitute a representation of an originary organic body. They are, each of them, unique expressive components of the Jones singularity.

It's total immanence.

There is no Grace Jones the subject who expresses her subjectivity in sound and image. There is only Jones the abstract hyperbody, the cut-up scissormachine that cuts itself up, relentlessly.

The Jones body is immanent, too, in that, as Kodwo repeatedly insists of sonic fiction throughout *More Brilliant than the Sun*, it produces its own theory.

Certainly, by the time that Haraway's *Cyborg Manifesto* limps onto the scene, it is only to mislead via reterritorialisation.

Cut again.

To London, 1982.
(Reproduced from the early days of blogger k-punk.)

The sex appeal of the inorganic.
Paul Tickell's review of *The Anvil*, *NME* 27 Mar 82:

I'd thought "Contort Yourself" the right kind of music for Newton's sado-eroticism — but "The Anvil" is a greater approximation. You wanted the moderne dance — well [...] here it is: the night-time moves of marionettes — dummies — puppets — clowns — and imaginary celluloid beings. It's all a little deathly — the sound of commodities fucking — but a noise which can be a good deal more exhilarating ("the sex appeal of the inorganic" — Walter Benjamin) than healthy fun-loving creatures going at it.

All in all — Visage are a rather seductive disease — the skull beneath the made-up skin.

More material from early k-punk:

Roxy versus Visage: a shift from subject to Object (therefore, following Baudrillard's logic in *Seduction*, from masculine to feminine). Fem-glam notwithstanding, Ferry retained for himself the male role of the one-who-looks. The problem, for Ferry, is the (male) gaze — how much to look? For how long? "Then I look away/too much for one day." Strange, meanwhile, is invariably the looked-at. He is the discarded plaything in "Mind of a Toy" (telling title, that), the object of gossip in *The Anvil*'s maudlin "Look What They've Done" and "Whispers." The model, here, is — the model: the anxiety — how am I seen?

Can we assume, btw, that Gibson derived the name Neuromancer from "New Romantic"? If so, Gibson's transposition suggests a much more interesting, and appropriate, name for the nerve sorcery of these newly-wired electronauts. "Romantic" always struck me as way-off beam for a culture so fastidiously uninterested in depth/emotions/truth.)

The case against Visage always seemed to me to depend on rockist prejudice: they didn't play live, they were a vehicle for a clothes horse who "couldn't sing", they represented the return of prog. Isn't there also a masculinist agenda, too, in the implicit rejection of the "superficiality" of fashion and clubbing?

Visage thoroughly stripped their sound of the trappings of r and r, ostentatiously parading an Un-American ancestry. Thematically and sonically, Visage evoked a decadent Europe of seductive urban alienation (cf the Mondrian-like vision of endless High-Rises in Blocks on Blocks) and sumptuous glamour (cf the name, and the track, "Visage"; the French vox on "Fade to Grey"), conjured through vocoder vox, synthesizers and Billy Currie's pseudo-classical flourishes. American influences came rerouted/refracted through Europe: Moroder disco; Morricone (cf McGeoch's "Once Upon a Time in the West"-isms on the Spaghetti Western/Clint tribute "Malpaso Man" off *Visage*). Cinema was a major node: much of Visage's sound belongs to what would later be called "virtual soundtracks" (Barry Adamson, one of the architects of this genre, was of course a Visage member). The mood was one of dis-affection, not the robotic functionality of Kraftwerk, nor the schizo-dislocation of Foxx/Numan, but the Euro-aesthete's "exhaustion from life", nowhere better expressed than on the *Interview with the Vampire*-like "Damned Don't Cry". Visage didn't thematise machines in the way that Kraftwerk, Numan and Ultravox did: like Yello, they seemed to operate in a future-past glittering hall-of-mirrors in which synthesizers and electronics were less a new innovation than a taken-for-granted mainstay.

Visage's "cyberpunk baroque" is a link between Roxy Music, Vangelis, disco and what would later become dance culture. Anyone who doubts this should check out the dance mixes of "Frequency 7" or "Pleasure Boys": the instrumental breakdown in the "Pleasure Boys" remix is pure acid house, and "Frequency 7" is nothing but a breakdown, a thrillingly anachronistic slice of machine-techno. It was no doubt Strange and Egan's role in the Blitz/Camden Palace that facilitated the move into dance. Making clubbing and dancing, rather than the gig, central was a crucial step (for Visage specifically, but for the New Romantic scene in general). Strange was less important as "frontman" than as pure image, his very diffidence and passivity as a vocalist anticipating dance's later complete effacement of the singer.

Except the singer doesn't get completely effaced by dance.

It returns as the femachine Róisín.

Cut to Now.

I've little to add to my recent remarks[8] on Moloko and Róisín Murphy as the latest — but I hope not last — contribution to the art pop story.

But it's worth distinguishing Murphy from two artists John recently mentioned in the comments boxes: Madonna and Kylie.

Minogue is a sex worker in the most banal and degrading sense, since it is clear that her simpering subordination to the Lad's Gaze is nothing more than a career(ist) gambit. Murphy, by contrast, gives the impression of enjoying herself, of doing what she would do any way (and just happening to have an audience). It's clear that she enjoys attention (male or otherwise) but like all great performers, her *jouissance* seems to be fundamentally auto-erotic. The audience function not as passive-consumer onanist spectators, but as a feedback component in the Róisín-machine.

And unlike Madonna, Murphy does not Photoshop out all the joins and the cuts in her performance. Whereas Madonna's hyper-professional show is all about attaining the CGI seamlessness of a corporate film, Murphy — pulling her leather fetish boots on onstage — is always *playing* — albeit seriously.

Q: You're becoming quite the style icon, is that an area that interests you?

R: Well, I think I dress for myself, I mean, I've always dressed up anyway, and I just enjoy it. I think maybe people are just fed up of pop stars that are told what to do and what to wear.

noise as anti-capital: *as the veneer of democracy starts to fade*[1]

FORGET ORWELL

Orwell is wrong about everything, but especially 1984.

Far from being the year of zombie-drone enforced consensus, GB 1984 was a class war zone in which multinational Kapital's paramilitary-police crushed the remnants of organic workerism live on videodrome.

Such staged antagonism is a necessary phase in the pacification program that will culminate in apparently triumphant Kapital's End of History.

The reassuring non-hum of the noise free polis at the end of time.

Tony's smile.

Blair is a much more effective class warrior than it was possible for Thatcher and Macgregor to be.

Their efficacy was limited by Then Kapital's need for them to be seen fighting the class war.

No need for Tony to fight.

To not fight is to have won.

It's all administration now.

Systemic antagonism is just a bad memory.

Turn up the TV.

Bunker down in your burrow.

Retune the guitars.

Return to harmony.

Welcome to Liberty City.

The busier you are, the less you see.

SOUND FX

Mark Stewart's *As the Veneer of Democracy Starts to Fade* was the political-libidinal intensive soundtrack to "battle for the hearts and minds" fought between Kapital and its enemies GB circa 84-85.

Seven years since Stewart began his anti-career as teen-Nietzsche Artaud Debord communist shamanic-firebrand hysteric-screecher in the Pop Group.

Stewart's journey since the dissolution of the Bristol f-punk kollektive takes him through Adrian Sherwood mega mashed hyperdub and into an encounter with US hip-hop.

He immediately appreciates that hip-hop is not a street music but non-musique abstrakt: a site of pure sonic potential, in which inhuman constructivist sound cartoons can be produced without reference to musical protocols of any kind.

It's all sound FX, a way of manipulating noise.

Hyper-modernism. The sonic equivalent of the Burroughs-Gysin cut-up.

A contact of Sherwood's leads to the most improbable of meetings. UK non-singer and sound-deranger Stewart plugs into the super-slick behind-the-scenes NYC p-funk machine responsible for the grooves on the pioneering hip-hop 45s released by Tommy Boy and Sugarhill.

Component parts:

Keith Leblanc. Beat machine producer of "Malcolm X: No Sell Out". He can program drum machines to make them sound like packs of dogs.

Doug Wimbish. Supertaut hypertechnicised Hendrix of bass.

Skip McDonald. Synthesizer manipulator and reaper-rider of psychedelic-funk ax storms.

Sherwood and Stewart take their already inhuman grooves and subject them to further layers of dissonant anti-musical editing, interpolating Burroughs vocal samples from *Nova Express* and other deliberately ciphered media background noise, machining an anti-communicational libidinal signal that takes you behind the screens to access the Real news.

Apocalypse Now.

THE BATTLE FOR THE HEARTS AND MINDS

As the veneer of democracy starts to fade, some say the internment camps are already built.

When the mask of civility comes off and the visors go on, the contours of the New World Order become apparent.

The destruction of the miners — and with them the wrought-iron ruins of the postwar consensus — was only the most media-visible of the pacification strategies Kapital was deploying, and in many ways the least significant.

The important thing was to prepare the way to transnational cyberspace Kapital Now, when all dissent is pathologised if it is not made literally unthinkable.

"Sterezene, thorazine and lagactyl" administered under the Mental Health Bill subdue political prisoners re-assigned to psychiatric wards.

Narco-neuroticisation as the re-imposition of a simulated Reality Principle shoring up Kapital against its virtual limit in Planetary Schizoprenia.

You don't have to be mad to work here.

Restrict your demands to the what is possible.

Find your way back to your dormitory.

Privatise your misery.

Struggling to pay the rent, the main worry's job security.

Now and then, we can afford a little luxury.

Quietism.

DISSONANCE/ DISSENSUS

If the aim is to disseminate information, why all this noise?

Why the distortion, the deliberately buried voices, why all the half-heard insinuations, the audio-hallucinatory fragmentation, the wired-up screams?

Why not communicate clearly?

Because clear communication — and all it presupposes — is the fantasm the system projects as its vindication and necessarily always-deferred goal.

"The big Other stands for the field of common sense at which one can arrive after free deliberation; philosophically, its last great version is Habermas's communicative community with its regulative ideal of agreement."[2]

The noise free polis.

We are told:

Only when the noise of antagonism recedes will we be able to hear each other.
Only when we take out the background static will human speech be possible.
Police yourself and there will be no need for the use of batons.
Intoxicate yourself and we will not sedate you.

Stewart's disassembly of his self through noise is a refusal of the Foucault biocops and Burroughs control addicts that operate first of all at the level of the skin and the CNS, enticing-inciting you to constitute yourself as an internally coherent driving ego.

Stewart treats his own voice not as the authentic expression of a subjective interiority, but as a series of lab animal howls, enraged yelps and impersonal intensities to be cut up and redistributed across the noise-hyperdubscape, mixed indifferently with Duchamp-found-sounds and noises produced by viciously distorted formerly musical instruments.

Identity breakdown through the amplification of noise as an exploding flight from harmony at all levels: psychic, social, cosmic.

Dissensus.

I AIN'T GONNA BE A SLAVE OF LOVE

Always take O'Brien's side against Winston Smith and Julia.

There is nothing natural, and human biosocial defaults are always to be distrusted.

If you want to get out, leave all that mammal couple shit behind.

Stewart is one of Burroughs' most assiduous readers.

It is not a matter of emulation but of the deployment of abstract engineering diagrams in different media.

Position *As the Veneer of Democracy Starts to Fade* as the terminus of the Burroughs-saturated UK underground delineated by Nuttall in *Bomb Culture*.

"Hypnotised" plays like the "I Love You" section from *The Ticket that Exploded*, Burroughs' most pitilessly hilarious dissection-analysis of the bio-psychic sex-love control virus as preprogrammed biological film, sentimental mooning croon-tunes spliced in with hardcore pornography and replayed like videodrome in your CNS, ensuring-exacerbating constant craving:

> All the tunes and sound effects of "Love" spit from the recorder permutating sex whine of a sad picture planet: Do you love me? — But I exploded in cosmic laughter — Old acquaintances be forgot? O darling just a photograph?[3]

> Heaven must be missing an angel.
> *Hypnotised.*
> *Hypnotised.*
> *She's got me hypnotised.*

Stewart's cut-ups of constructivist-brutalist funk with saccharine lovesongs already anticipate the way in which Kapital's tungsten-carbide stomach will metabolise hip-hop's hyper-abstraction and use it as the dominant consumer seduction soundtrack from the Nineties till now.

CONTROL DATA

The data-content of Stewart's rant-reports is nothing astonishing.

> *7% of the population own 84% of the wealth.*
> *Parasites... The great banking families of the world... Bastards...*
> *Are these the words of the all-powerful boards and syndicates of the earth?*

The point is not to tell you something new but to reprogram your nervous system.

Control works by reducing the reality of systemic antagonism to a mere belief.

A track like "Bastards" is a very precise anti-Control weapon.

It is a rage-inducer designed to make beliefs affective, whereas Control PR conciliates and normalises.

Control PR plugs the gaps, emolliates, quietens, makes confrontation and exploitation unthinkable without denying their reality as such.

Like John Heartfield collages, Stewart's crude sonic splices amp up the distortion and the violence.

The situation is not under Control
They are not protecting you
It is war

And so are you

THERE IS NO DIGNITY

Don't confuse the working class with the proletariat.

Thatcher inhibits the emergence of the proletariat by buying off the working class with payment capital and the promise of owning your own Oed-I-Pod. The comforts of slavery.

She gives the replicants screen memories and family photos.

So that they forget that they were only ever artificial, factory farmed to function as the Kapital-Thing's self-replicating HR pool, and begin to believe that they are authentic human subjects.

The proletariat is not the confederation of such subjectivities but their dissolution in globalised k-space.

The virtual population of nu-earth.

Total recall of all the noise.

Lyotard describes the hysterisation of a worker's ear when it is subjected to the unprecedented noise of Industrial-Kapital's reproduction: the incessant sonic violence of a 20,000hz alternator.

The heroism of the proletariat consists not in its dignified resistance to the inorganic-inhumanity of the industrialisation process — "there is no libidinal dignity, nor libidinal fraternity, there are libidinal contacts without communication"[4] — but in its mutative Duchamp-transformation of its body into an inhuman inorganic constructivist machine.

As the Veneer of Democracy Starts to Fade is a sonic machine for accelerating the process. An anti-Oedipal, anti-neurotic, anti-quitest, pro-proletarianising noise weapon. Anti-videodrome signal.

Jack it into yr CNS and play.

lions after slumber, or what is sublimation today?[1]

"In post-liberal societies [...] the agency of social repression no longer acts in the guise of an internalised Law or Prohibition that requires renunciation or self-control; instead, it assumes the form of a hypnotic agency that imposes the attitude of 'yielding to temptation' — that is to say, its injunction amounts to a command: 'Enjoy yourself!' Such an idiotic enjoyment is dictated by the social environment which includes the Anglo-Saxon psychoanalyst whose main goal is to render the patient capable of 'normal', 'healthy' pleasures. Society requires us to *fall asleep* into a hypnotic trance..."
— Slavoj Žižek, "The Deadlock of Repressive Desublimation"[2]

As we awake from the dreary dream of entryism, we can start to see that what kept us slumbering in the last twenty-five years was indeed a programme of controlled, if not quite repressive, desublimation. No doubt, the signs of any awakening are fitful as yet. In pop, they are perhaps most evident in a groping backwards, a paradoxical return to modernism. Could it be that the likes of Franz Ferdinand and the Rapture will prompt a self-overcoming of the very postmodern revivalism of which they are a symptom? Just now, *Rip it up and Start Again* sounds like a uncannily timely injunction.

Something seems to be (re)coalescing, as the reception of the *Early* Scritti LP (including Simon's piece in *Uncut*) indicates. For those inside — not least, of course, Green [Gartside][3] himself — these recordings must be dismissed as inept avant-doodlings, embarrassing juvenilia. It seems plausible to attribute Green's less-than-lukewarm judgements on the early Scritti material less to modesty, still less to a "maturity", than to a defensive cleaving to a once-successful strategy that has now run its course, as Marcello acidly noted in his acerbic comparison between the indifferent reception of the last Scritti album and the eagerness with which *Early* has been anticipated:

When you next find yourself at a motorway service station, feel free to browse through the plentiful copies of his 1999 up-to-the-1999-minute-Mos-Def-involving *Anomie and Bonhomie* album, yours for just £1.99 — whereas the new collection of his scratchy, disjointed post-punk improv stuff from two decades ago reportedly already has 10,000 advance orders.[4]

Scritti were the most successful — aesthetically, commercially — of the post-post-punk entryists (the likes of U2 being always-already included of course). In the desolate gloss of mid-late Eighties pop, Scritti's hyper-saccharine sweetness retained a plaintive if sickly gorgeousness, even if their vaunted deconstructive swerves became subtle to the point of invisibility. But the fastidious precision of that striplit Eighties production has dated (late-Eighties chartpop is the most time-bound pop music ever — discuss) much more damagingly than has the messthetic of the early records. Whereas the conspicuous completeness of Eighties entryist pop repels fascination, the queasy, uneasy unfinishedness of post-punk pop — the lurching "doubtbeat" of a collectivity discovering itself — is uncannily compulsive. In punk cut and paste, the joins, the cuts (in other words the ways in which any world does not coincide with itself) are flaunted and foregrounded. Entryism is the capture of cut and paste into Photoshopped seamlessness.

What is perforce lost in today's post-punk revivalists is the literal intensity of this sound: how it is in Kierkegaard-Žižek's terms, *in becoming*. It doesn't *know* anything (it certainly can't be confident that it is a "classic independent rock sound" in the way that Franz Ferdinand are). In flight from rock's "condition of possibility", this undo (it) yourself pop puts into question ALL conditions of possibility, and with them the *very concept* of conditions of possibility. What is this if not the sound of the Badiou Event, which is the punk revelation itself: this is happening, now, but it can't be, it's Impossible...?

Scritti were possibly the least Dionysian pop group ever. In the early days, the methodology may have been improvisational, but the group didn't want anyone (least of all themselves) to be under the illusion that it issued from some vitalist wellspring of creativity. It was the sound of a collectivity *thinking* (itself into existence) under and through material constraints. The famous displaying of all the recording costs on the sleeve was *demystificatory but not desublimating*. What is too often missed about any punk that matters in fact, is that sublimation, far from requiring mystification, is alien to it.

As Alenka Zupančič argues, mystification is entirely on the side of the reality principle (and one of the greatest contributions psychoanalysis has made to politics is to identify "realism" precisely with a reality *principle*, so that what counts as "commonsense" can be exposed as an ideological determination):

The important thing to point out [...] is that the reality principle is not some kind of natural way associated with how things are, to which sublimation would oppose itself in the name of some Idea. The reality principle itself is ideologically mediated; one could even claim that it constitutes the highest form of ideology, the ideology that presents itself as empirical fact (or biological, economic...) necessity (and that we tend to perceive as nonideological). It is precisely here that we should be most alert to the functioning of ideology.[5]

Listen to what Marcello calls the "pseudo-moronic chants of platitudes" ("An honest day's pay for an honest day's work! You can't change human nature! Don't bite the hand that feeds!") of Scritti's "Hegemony" and it is clear that this message has got through. It is the denunciation and exposure of the great ideological swindles that are liable to be remembered about punk, but this destructive urge (passive nihilism) is empty without its active complement: the *production* of a new space. It is no accident that mystificatory realism has allowed us to remember the former but not the latter, since the mere dismantling of ideological presuppositions quickly became a dreary academic parlour game associated with a desiccated, depressive and depressing left (they want to take your enjoyment away from you...).

Zupančič labels the production of this new space "sublimation". To understand why she makes this move entails differentiating sublimation from the sublime as such. The postmodern emphasis on sublimity has tended to stress the sublime as an unreachable beyond, contemplation of which induces a pathos of finitude in any human subject. To think about sublimation, the *process* by which an object "acquires the dignity of the Thing", produces a different emphasis. As Zupančič continues:

the Lacanian theory of sublimation does not suggest that that sublimation turns away from the Real in the name of some Idea; rather, it suggests that sublimation gets closer to the Real than the reality principle does. It aims at the Real precisely at the point where the Real cannot be reduced to reality. One could say that sublimation opposes itself to reality, or turns away from it, precisely in the name of the Real. To raise an object to the dignity of the Thing is not to idealise it, but rather to "realise" it, that is, to make it function as a stand-in for the Real. Sublimation is thus related to ethics insofar as it is not entirely subordinated to the reality principle, but liberates or creates a space from which it is possible to attribute certain values to something other than the recognised and established "common good." [...] What is at stake is not the act of replacing one "good" (or one value) with the same planetary system of the reality principle. The creative act of sublimation is not only a creation of some new good, but also (and principally) the creation and maintenance of a certain space for objects that have no place in the given, extant reality, objects that are considered "impossible".[6]

What was the "beyond good and evil" of Scritti, Gang of Four, the Pop Group and the Raincoats if not the production of just such a space? (As Lacan wryly notes, when we idly think of someone who is "beyond good and evil" we are liable to think of someone is merely beyond "good".) This entails not an austere asceticism but the engineering of new forms of enjoyment. The early Scritti's "difficulty" places them beyond the pleasure principle, for sure, but we succumb to an ideological lure if we think that this puts them beyond enjoyment too. As Savonarola said to me a few weeks ago, Gang of Four were far more effective at turning out compulsive pop songs than almost any of today's chart acts you could care to name. The same goes double for *Early*, whose songs are catchy *because* they refuse to push familiar buttons.

Entryism constitutes a double disavowal of sublime space. First, it is turned away from, then the very possibility of its existence is denied. In retrospect, entryism has to be seen as the production of a particularly virulent capitalist mind plague. How else to account for the absurd convolutions that allowed Green to posit some political continuity between the avant-Marxism of the early years and the champagne-swigging meta-boyband-cum-yuppie-corporation "hammer and popsicle" posturing (check some of those pics which illustrate Simon's piece) of the chart Scritti? As Simon has shown elsewhere, Green had by this point done more than merely accommodated himself to the market; he was acting as an entrepreneur, since the "'Fairlight future-funk' of *Cupid and Psyche 85* was so far ahead of the game it actually influenced black pop." There's a case for saying that *Cupid and Psyche*'s "dazzling, depthless surfaces" in which "'soul' and interiority are abolished" and "desire traverses a flat plane, the endless chain of signifiers, the lover's discourse as lexical maze" was THE sound of Eighties capital, the perfect soundtrack to Jameson's *Postmodernism, or the Cultural Logic of Late Capitalism*, what it felt like to be lost in the mirrored plateaux of the hypermarket.

Realism always poses as maturation. Of course it is acceptable, understandable and inevitable to have silly youthful dreams, but there comes a time when one must put aside such childish things and face reality; and reality is always defined "biologically", in terms of the imperatives of reproductive futurism, and "economically", in terms of the "constraints" of the capitalist anti-market.

Readers of the lamented but never forgotten *Pill Box*[7] may remember a letter Ian Penman received from Brian Anderson of the neo-Conservative *City Journal*. Anderson's account of the intellectual provenance of neo-conservatism — many neo-cons were tellingly described as disappointed,

294

disillusioned leftists who had been "mugged by reality" — concluded with the following convergence between new pop entryism and his own neo-conservative turn:

> Also — and this will probably horrify you — my move right came partly thanks to Ian Penman and Paul Morley at *NME*! Your rejection of overly politicised agitprop in music back in the late Seventies made intuitive sense to me — I disliked the didacticism of Billy Bragg or Crass, and could stomach even less the critics who pretended to be revolutionaries, etc. There was far more truth in an August Darnell ballad, I came to believe, than in the entire socialist posturing of, say, the Gang of Four or Robert Christgau.

There it is: THAT opposition — Bragg versus Darnell — was the problem of the mid-to-late Eighties. As soon as it was a question of dour meat and potatoes no fuss empiricism (left) versus bright and brash hedonism (right), there was no longer any real choice. The sublime had been extirpated, and what remained was a quotidian cavilling against the wipe-clean sheen of the mall.

It's telling that Scritti's "Confidence" ("Outside the clubs of boyhood/ Inside monogamy") should be so preoccupied with the problems of "being a man", and what that entailed.

The interpellated subject of the Lad magazine is the supposed "real person" (=slavering, sloppy andro-Id) beneath the pretence of social politesse. The Lad magazine addresses this "authentic id" with the leering superegoic injunction to enjoy. "Go on, admit it, you don't want to be bothered to cook, all you want is a fishfinger sandwich... Go on, admit it, you don't want to be bothered to talk to a woman, have a wank instead..." The fact that this reduction is possible means that lads implicitly accept the Lacanian notion that phallic jouissance involves masturbation with a "real" partner. It also indicates that laddishness is more defined by a propensity towards depressive indolence than it is by any lasciviousness. What laddism attempts is a short-circuiting of desire (yes, I know that the "inhuman partner" of desire cannot be attained, just give me pictures of girls next door instead).

From "Skank Bloc Bologna" ("an imaginary network of dissidents stretching from Jamaica to Bologna's anarchist squatters") to the Streets (Lads of the world unite to raise a glass to lachrymose lariness); from "The Sweetest Girl" to Abi Titmuss...

Long past time that we roused from this slumber... Especially when, with habeas corpus suspended and mainstream political parties all but burning down gypsy camps, one of the things that makes the early Scritti so contemporary is that their conjecture/fear that It (fascism) Would Happen Here, their "*très* 1979 paranoia", is suddenly, alarmingly *très* 2005:

Rise, like lions after slumber,
In unvanquishable number,
Shake your chains to earth like dew,
Which in sleep had fall'n on you.

the outside of everything now[1]

A week dominated in every way by Simon Reynolds' *Rip It Up and Start Again*,[2] and rightly so.

Perhaps the best tribute you can pay to the book is that it makes you positively look forward to train and bus delays, to any moment when you can return to feed the hunger, scratch the itch...

The size of the crowd at the Boogaloo event on Wednesday, but, more than that, a certain sense of ferment in the atmosphere, testified to the fact that this is something more than a book. Stirring up the ghost of post-punk cannot but be an act, an intervention in cultural politics — since post-punk not only judges contemporary pop culture (harshly), it brings back the legitimacy, the *necessity* of being judgemental, of having some criteria (non-musical criteria, non-hedonic criteria) for enjoyment. Such a position is not repressed by contemporary pop culture (=the cultural logic of late capitalism), it is made unthinkable by it.

Something in Paul Morley certainly seemed to wake up on Wednesday. (And something in us?...)

A certain Morley was knowingly complicit in the termination of post-punk — as Simon wryly reminded him when, after Morley had fulminated against the facile notion that the worth of a pop record is determined by its popularity, he asked him: "but didn't that idea come from you?" It's not accidental that, grotesquely but inevitably, Morley's early-Eighties pop(ul)ist stance should have inspired some *NME* readers to turn towards neo-conservatism. In retrospect, it's possible to see the turn to popism as the beginning of a giving voice to a creeping disappointment which spread slowly, insidiously yet incrementally during the period until almost everything of post-punk — even the traces — was *disappeared* (in the way that political prisoners are). The disappearing trick was almost complete

297

when the Pod-Zombie duplicates started to arrive a few years ago, formally perfect copies mass-produced by Kapital.

It's easier to see now than it was at the time the extent to which the cultural artefacts — and the discourse surrounding them — produced in the wake of post-punk were being programmed by resurgent Kapital. A certain notion of realism began not only to prescribe what could now happen, but to airbrush out what had actually happened. The idea that pop could be more than a pleasant divertissement in the form of an easily consumable commodity, the idea that popular culture could play host to concepts that were difficult and demanding: it wasn't sufficient to disavow these possibilities, they must also be *denied*. Operation Amnesia, Pacification Program: it never happened did it, it was a delusion, a folly of youth, and we're all grown up now...

Naturally, Morley's railing against amateurism, his advocacy of ambition and lushness, play rather differently in 2005 than they did in the early Eighties, but that's only fitting, since his manifestos-as-works-of-art-in-themselves were produced as strategic provocations rather than timeless aesthetic philosophies. Even though the Morley of the disappointing *Words and Music* claimed Noughties web popists as his offspring, it's hard to imagine the Morley and Penman *of 1981* being gratified by the thought that their legacy would be the de-conceptualisation and de-politicising — i.e. the consumerisation — of pop. They could scarcely have imagined, then, the way in which pop would *de-speed* over the next twenty years, that their embrace of Entryism would prove to be the last word in rough-and-tumble theoretical dialogue that seemed, then, as if it could go on forever.

Reading *Rip it Up* is like re-living my early pop life — but now at a distance, like Spider in Cronenberg's film, an adult at the corner of the screen watching himself as a child. With Simon as my Virgil through that Paradiso lost, I can now recognise that pop for me *was* post-punk — *Kings of the Wild Frontier* was the first LP I bought and ABC were the first group I saw live. But *Rip It Up* makes me cognizant of what I, growing up absurd *into* post-punk, couldn't have appreciated at the time: that the richness of pop then — not only sonically, but also in terms of concepts, clothes, images — lasted only a relatively short period, made possible by specific historical contingencies.

Nevertheless, expectations were raised in me, and more or less everything I've written or participated in has been in some sense an attempt to keep fidelity with the post-punk event. Cyberpunk — both in its restricted literary generic sense and in the broader sense we have given to it in Ccru — was up to its neck in post-punk. Gibson's debt to Steely Dan and the Velvet Underground has long been acknowledged, but the dominant tone of *Neuromancer* was an overhang from post-punk. Gibson named his high-tech prostitutes after the Meat Puppets, but *Neuromancer*'s technihilistic ambience, dub apocalypticism, amphetamine-burned-out Cases and hectic, twitching finger-on-fast-forward and comatone-cut-out narrative, seem to be transposed straight out of the *British* post-punk scene.

One of the things that is most remarkable about post-punk, actually, is its near total erasure of America and Americanness. When I was in my early teens, the only American pop you'd hear that wasn't disco would be encountered while trudging round the shops on Saturday afternoon, as Paul Gambaccini's Hot 100 was broadcast over the store PAs, and it was a window into a horrifyingly deprived world of barely imaginable banality.

Of the few American groups of any significance in this period, perhaps only Devo and the Meat Puppets took much inspiration from the American landscape (in Devo's case of course, the US was processed as a thoroughly artificial PKD-US-trash heap of post-industrial detritus). No wave emerged from the rootless cosmopolitanism and transnational nihilism of New York, while in many ways the most interesting American groups — Tuxedomoon and the Residents — were Europhiles. In post-punk, America increasingly featured as a series of *ethnographic* traces — as in the ecstatic, hysterical and authoritarian ghost chatter of Amerikkkan TV and media flittering through Cabaret Voltaire's *Voice of America* or Byrne and Eno's *My Life in the Bush of Ghosts*.

It's hard to remember now, but in the period after Vietnam and before the collapse of the Eastern Bloc, America was a paranoid and enfeebled nation, Nixon-sickened and introspective, scared of its own shadows. Post-punk was there to witness — and mock — the seeming absurdity of the idiot actor Reagan being wheeled on to give America's confidence a shot-in-the-arm, although initially even Reagan's rise to power seemed to be a kind of sinister post-punk prank, since it made eerily real what had been predicted by one of perhaps post-punk's most important influence, Ballard. (In the States, Ballard's *Atrocity Exhibition* was re-titled *Love and Napalm: Export USA*, and that novel — so omnipresent in post-punk production — was a kind of simultaneous observation of the way in which Britain was being turned into an LA of ubiquitous advertising hoardings as well as a British view of the US.) By the time that post-punk went out in a neon-blaze of irony-tainted glory on MTV, the joke had, to say the least, worn thin. Pop had gone Blue-Gene American rock, again (I still remember the barely comprehending horror I felt when the *NME* started to give covers to the t-shirt and jean-clad Springsteen; worse was to follow, with the likes of *The Long Ryders*). Boredom was back, but this time, without the punks to denounce it. The arid shopping mall at the end of history opened up as the only possible future. Worse than the career opportunities that never knocked were the ones that did: jobs for everyone in the striplit wall-to-wall mart of *Time Out of Joint* America in which it is 1955, forever... No shadows to hide in... No room to move, no room to doubt...

Ironic in some ways that *Rip it Up* should be named after an Orange Juice song, since Orange Juice and Postcard were responsible for what was in many ways a British equivalent of Springsteen's US return-to-roots. If the comparison seems strained, think about the way in which both Springsteen and Orange Juice self-consciously advocated a kind of locally-rooted authenticity defined by its rejection of artificiality. For Springsteen's reich and roll uniform of denim, substitute OJ's *Brideshead Revisited* sweaters. Like the Smiths, the Postcard-era Orange Juice retrospectively imagined a British pop-that-never-was. The Brit equivalent of American open-throated stridency was a kind of floppy-fringed, tongue-tied dithering that was just as much of a self-conscious reclaiming of signifiers of national identity as Springsteen's passional working stiff poses were. (Is it too fanciful to hear in the early Orange Juice an anticipation of Hugh Grant's unbearable foppery and faffing?)

By the time I got to university in 1986, Orange Juice, and the Smiths, had achieved hegemonic control of the undergraduate "imagination". It was perfect pop for young men who were destined to go on to careers in marketing but who liked to think of themselves as "sensitive". Orange Juice also played in a major part in rehabilitating the love song. If romance featured in post-punk at all, it was as something to be derided and demystified (as in the Slits' "Love Und Romance" or Gang of Four's "Love Like Anthrax") or as something to be politically and theoretically interrogated a la Scritti or Devoto. The renewed preoccupation with love was a re-occupation of "the ordinary", a re-statement of a revivified humanist confidence in a dehistoricised continuity of "things that go on the same".

It's often said that punk was what Britain had instead of 68, but that in many ways fails to process how punk had surpassed the events in Paris. 68 was as much a rejection of certain theoretical positions as it was of the institutions of modern liberal society so that, in the conflagration of the Sixties "Desirevolution", the cold Spinozism of Althusser's structural analysis was burned down with the buildings. Punk and post-punk, however, were profoundly suspicious of the Dionysisan triumvirate of leisure, pleasure and intoxication, so that the required attitude was one of vigilant hyper-rationalism, a kind of popularised Althusserianism in which interiority was exposed as an ideological bluff, and emotions were understood not as "real expressions of authentic subjectivity" but as structurally engineered reactive circuitries. The stance such a perception demanded — and this was a culture that was deliberately and unashamedly demanding — was one of "proletarian discipline" rather than slack indulgence, its puritanism recalling the egalitarian social ambitions of the original Puritans. In this respect, Scritti's move from pleasure-repudiating Marxism to "playful" deconstruction is emblematic of the way in which the decade would develop, in universities as much as in the charts. The exorbitant surfaces of *Cupid and Psyche* might have eschewed interiority, but at the same time their *simulations* of interiority were no *less* authentic, no *less* soulful, than other versions of interiority purveyed by more credulous, non-ironic sources in the mainstream. The person being duped now was the Green who imagined that his intelligence would prevent full incorporation.

But the triumphant capitalism Green was already working for had no trouble at all in consuming those who sought entry into it. In the Seventies, in an effort to dispel the notion that there were "subversive regions" that would be inherently indigestible for capital, Lyotard compared capitalism to a "Tungsten-carbide stomach" that could consume anything in its path. By the Eighties, as Jameson has observed, Kapital had become a gigantic interiority without any outside: a kind of jaded pleasuredome reminiscent of the all-encompassing bubble environments imagined in Seventies SF. Except it looked, for all the world, just like a familiar domestic environment: the nice house, nice family set-up ridiculed by Jamie Reid, now refurbished with added ironic distantiation and hooked up to twenty-four-hour MTV. What had been lost was the "glam knowledge" that first entered pop through Pop Art: that the social scene is a stage set populated by puppets cornfed cheap dreams and sedated by narcotics of every kind. The punks knew they were replicants; that everything that seemed to be inside was bio-psycho-social machinery that should be re-programmed or stripped out. The end of punk was the forgetting that the memories were false, that the domestic scene was so much pasteboard and image virus.

At the time of post-punk, pop could still be a counter-cultural lab (endlessly raided by, but never subordinated to the diktats of, Kapital). It really is not clear whether pop could be that again. Someone asked the panel on Wednesday if dredging post-punk up was an exercise in nostalgia. But this is entirely to miss the point of Jameson's critique of the nostalgia mode. For Jameson, the nostalgia mode is exemplified by cultural artefacts which deny, or more radically, are *unaware of* their own total debt to the past. In other words, being contemporary does not guarantee being modern, especially not in a postmodern culture whose temporality is obsessively citational and commemorational. One of the most idiotic tics in cultural gatekeeping today is its need to justify the past in terms of the present: as if Gang of Four were only significant because they "influenced" no-mark, here-today boot-sale-tomorrow clones like Bloc Party and Franz Ferdinand. As if simply being here, now, meant that something New and Important is happening…

Pop could function differently in post-punk because, at that time, it was the space which most readily leant itself to the production of a counter-consensual collectivity. Post-punk was an awakening from Kapital's "consensual hallucination", a means of channeling, externalising and propagating disquiet and discrepancy. It provided a crack in the way the social represented itself; or rather, exposed that crack. What the social would have us believe is dysfunction, grumbling, failure suddenly became the sound of the "outside of everything". Records, interviews, the music press, were the means by which contact could be made between affects, concepts, commitments that would previously have been locked into private space.

Some of the panel last Wednesday were unsure if they had really done anything, if their dreams of doing something more than simply entertaining were anything more than youthful naïveté, understandable then, an embarrassment now. But the achievements of post-punk can be appreciated, negatively, in what culture now lacks. Go into a roomful of teenagers and look at their self-scarred arms, the anti-depressants that sedate them, the quiet desperation in their eyes. They literally do not know what it is they are missing. What they don't have is what post-punk provided... A way out... and a reason to get out...

So is this a counsel of despair?

Not at all.

There are new means for producing counter-consensual collectivity.

Like this.

The web has a distributional reach, a global instaneity, whose unprecedented scale is easy to take for granted. But its vast potential far outstrips anything that fanzines or records could have achieved in the Seventies. What needs to happen is a kind of "existential reframing": to see what happens here not as Kapital wants us to see it, as "failed" writers resentfully carving out some insignificant niche because they can't "make it" in the overlit interior. The logic of Kapital insists that anything that is not reproducing it, or serving such a reproduction, is a waste of time. But to reframe what is happening would be to radically reverse these idiotic priorities. And the continuing relevance of post-punk is to remind us that such reversals are possible, to provide the impetus for the development of a (punk) will to retake the present...

for your unpleasure: the hauter-couture of goth[1]

Ridiculed, forgotten, yet subterraneanly robust, goth is the last remnants of glam in popular culture.

Goth is also the youth cult most associated with women and with fiction. This is hardly surprising. As I have pointed out before[2] and is well known, the novel has its origins in "Gothic romances" which were predominantly consumed and produced by women, and the complicity of women with the Gothic has been a commonplace of literary criticism at least since Ellen Moers wrote her classic essay, "Female Gothic" in 1977.

Why think about goth now?

Partly it is because goth's preposterous trash-aristocratic excess couldn't be more at odds with contemporary culture's hip-hop-dominated sportswear brutilitarianism. At the same time, though, goth's shadow seems unusually visible in pop culture at the moment, what with references to it in both *Coronation Street* ("you're not even a proper goth!") and *Big Brother* ("what is a gothic? Can you make me into one?")

Partly it is because *Rip It Up* has revived fascination in all things post-punk, and goth is the last surviving post-punk cult. These two facts have resulted in I.T.[3] and me seceding from the oppressive masculinist cool of the club into the more congenial cold of goth haunts.

Goth has its own version of more or less every other youth culture (hence there's techno goth, industrial goth, hippie goth...) But let's leave aside the male abjects (the Cramps, the Birthday Party), the po-faced (the overwrought white dub of Bauhaus) and the PoMo (the Sisters of Mercy, who from the start traded in a self-conscious meta-goth), and start with Siouxsie.

It is well-known that the Banshees were formed as a result of the future Siouxsie and Severin meeting at a Roxy show in 1974. (This fact was repeated in this really rather bizarre piece[4] on Roxy in last Friday's *Guardian*, which pursues the postmodern rock critical trend to equate "importance" with "influence" far past the point of self-parody, relegating actual discussion of Roxy's output to a paragraph or so before launching into a survey of groups they inspired.) So, unlike the Birthday Party, who were famously disgusted when they arrived in London to find it dominated by new romantic poseur-pop, the Banshees belonged to an art pop lineage which had a relationship to music which was neither ironically distant nor direct. For all their inventiveness, for all the damage they wreaked upon the rock form, the Birthday Party remained Romantics, desperate to restore an expressive and expressionistic force to rock; a quest which led them back to the Satanic heartland of the blues. (If women want to understand what it is like to be the afflicted subject of male sexuality — I wouldn't necessarily advise it — there's no better fast-track to "what's inside a boy" than the Birthday Party's "Zoo Music Girl" or "Release the Bats"). By contrast with this carnal heat, the early Banshees affected a deliberate — and deliberated — coldness and artificiality.

Siouxsie came from the art rock capital of England — that zone of South London in which both David Bowie (Beckenham) and Japan (Catford, Beckenham) grew up. Although Siouxsie was involved with punk from the very beginning, and although all of the major punk figures (even Sid Vicious) were inspired by Roxy, the Banshees were the first punk group to openly acknowledge a debt to glam. Glam has a special affinity with the English suburbs; its ostentatious anti-conventionality negatively inspired by the eccentric conformism of manicured lawns and quietly-tended psychosis Siouxsie sang of on "Suburban Relapse".

But glam had been the preserve of male desire: what would its drag look like when worn by a woman? This was a particularly fascinating inversion when we consider that Siouxsie's most significant resource was not the serial identity sexual ambivalence of Bowie but the staging of male desire in Roxy Music. She may have hung out with "Bowie boys", but Siouxsie seemed to borrow much more from the lustrous PVC blackness of *For Your Pleasure* than from anything in the Thin White Duke's wardrobe. *For Your Pleasure* songs like "Beauty Queen" and "Editions of You" were self-diagnoses of a male malady, a specular desire that fixates on female objects that it knows can never satisfy it. Although she "makes his starry eyes shiver", Ferry knows "it never would work out". This is the logic of Lacanian desire, which Alenka Zupančič explains as follows: "The [...] interval or gap introduced by desire is always the imaginary other, Lacan's *petit objet a*, whereas the Real (Other) of desire remains unattainable. The Real of desire is *jouissance* — that 'inhuman partner' (as Lacan calls it) that desire aims at beyond its object, and that must remain inaccessible."[5]

Roxy's "In Every Dreamhome a Heartache" is about an attempt, simultaneously disenchanted-cynical and desire-delirious, to resolve this deadlock. It is as if Ferry has recognised, with Lacan, that phallic desire is fundamentally masturbatory. Since, that is to say, a fantasmatic screen prevents any sexual relation so that his desire is always for an "inhuman partner", Ferry might as well have a partner that is literally inhuman: a blow-up doll. This scenario has many precursors: most famously perhaps Hoffman's short story "The Sandman" (one of the main preoccupations of Freud's essay on "The Uncanny" of course), but also Villier de L'isle Adam's lesser known but actually more chilling masterpiece of decadent SF, *The Future Eve* and its descendant, Ira Levin's *Stepford Wives*.

If the traditional problem for the male in pop culture has been dealing with a desire for the unattainable — for Lacan, remember, *all* desire is a desire for the unattainable — then the complementary difficulty for the female has been to come to terms with *not* being what the male wants. The Object knows that what she has does not correspond with what the subject lacks.

It is almost as if the female goth response to this dilemma is to self-consciously assume the role of the "cold, distanced, inhuman partner" (Žižek) of phallic desire. The glam male remains trapped in his perfect penthouse populated by dumb fantasmatic playdolls; the goth female meanwhile roams through the roles of vamp and vampire, succubus, automaton. The glam male's pathologies are those of the subject; the goth female's problematic is that of the object. Remember that the original sense of glamour — bewitchment — alludes to the power of the auto-objectified *over* the subject. "If God is masculine, idols are always feminine", Baudrillard writes in *Seduction*, and Siouxsie differed from previous pop icons in that she was neither a male artist "feminised" into iconhood by fan adoration, nor a female marionette manipulated by male svengalis, nor a female heroically struggling to assert a marginalised subjectivity. On the contrary, Siouxsie's perversity was to make an art of her own objectification. As Simon and Joy put it in *The Sex Revolts*, Siouxsie's "aspiration [was] towards a glacial exteriority of the objet d'art" evinced through "a shunning of the moist, pulsing fecundity of organic life."[6] This denial of interiority — unlike Lydia Lunch, Siouxsie is not interested in "spilling her guts", in a confessional wallowing in the goo and viscera of a damaged interiority — corresponds to a staged refusal to either be "a warm, compassionate, understanding fellow-creature" (Žižek). Like Grace Jones, another who made an art of her own objectification, Siouxsie didn't demand R.E.S.P.E.C.T. from her bachelor suitors (with the implied promise of a healthy relationship based on mutual regard) but subordination, supplication.

(The goth male is all too ready to comply, although — as Nick Cave's compulsively repetitive career has graphically demonstrated — snivelling prostration may well only be the prelude to homicidal destruction. Grovelling in front of the Ice Queen — "I kiss the hem of her skirt" — the goth male is neither object nor subject but — famously — abject. The best image of this idiot lust is the slavering, pustulant monstrosity on the cover of the Birthday Party's *Junkyard*, and their "Release the Bats" — a song the group came to despise because they thought it might result in their being pigeonholed as generic goth — remains the most pulsingly compulsive dramatisation of the goth abject surrendering himself to the Object of his quivering desire. Cave oscillates between worshipping his lady's femmachinc hauteur — "my baby is a cool machine", "she moves to the pulse of the generator" — and pruriently drooling over the "filth" of her flesh — "she doesn't mind a bit of dirt". This conforms almost perfectly with Lacan's description of the courtly lady, whose cold abstraction is not defined by opposition with smelly physicality. Cave's abject is unable to give up on his desire, and the result is well-known: in order to continue to desire the woman, he must ensure that he cannot possess her, "so that l'il girl will just have to go". Only when he has made her as cold and unyielding as Ferry's "perfect companion" or Poe's parade of beautiful cadavers, can his desire be extended "to eternity", because then it is rendered permanently incapable of satisfaction.)

Instead of asserting an illusory "authentic subjectivity" which supposedly lies beneath the costumes and the cosmetics, Siouxsie and Grace Jones revelled in becoming objects of the gaze. Both would no doubt have appreciated the derision Baudrillard poured upon the strategy of unmasking appearances in *Seduction*: "There is no God behind the images and the very nothingness they conceal must remain a secret."[7] Siouxsie and Jones' embracing of their objectality testifies to the fact that there is a scopic drive that cult studs whining about "being reduced to an object" has always ignored: the exhibitionist drive to *be seen*.

Simon is right that "Painted Bird" (from the Banshees mistresspiece, *A Kiss in the Dreamhouse*) and the nearly contemporary "Fireworks" were "virtual manifestos for goth", but it's worth reflecting on how different these songs are in message and mood from the hackneyed image of the culture. Both "Painted Bird" and "Fireworks" (with its "exultant image of self-beautification as a glam gesture flashing amid the murk of mundanity") are not maudlin, matt black or self-absorbed, but celebrations of the colourful and the collective. "WE are fireworks", Siouxsie sings, "burning shapes into the night", and you'd be hard pressed to find a song that crackles with so much enjoyment as this. The Banshees' take on Kosiński's novel *The Painted Bird* is also about the triumph of collective joy over persecuted, isolated, individuated subjectivity. In Kosiński's novel, the hero paints one bird and when he throws it back to its flock they don't recognise it and therefore destroy it. But Siouxsie's goths are not painted by another's hand; they are "painted birds by their own design". It is not the familiar tragic-heroic scenario in which an outsider, destined to lose, nevertheless makes a solitary stand against the conformist herd. The "dowdy flock" are to be "confounded", but by *another* flock, not by an individual, and the result is not frustration, but, again, jouissance — by the end of the song, "there's no more sorrow".

Think how different this is to the confederacy of isolation produced by Joy Division, whose functional clothes and "non-image" implied the traditional male subjectivist privileging of the inside over the outside, depth over surface. Here was one type of "black hole": the "line of abolition" Deleuze and Guattari describe in "Micropolitics and Segmentarity",[8] the drive towards total self-destruction. The Banshees, on the other hand, were more like the "cold stars" invoked by Neubauten: forbidding, remote, yet also the queens of a paradoxically egalitarian aristocracy in which membership was not guaranteed by birth or beauty but by self-decoration. Siouxsie's hyper-white panstick radiated the "cold light" of stardom Baudrillard invokes in *Seduction*. Stars "are dazzling in their nullity, and in their coldness — the coldness of makeup and ritual hieraticism (rituals are cool, according to McLuhan)."[9]

"The sterility of idols is well-known", Baudrillard continues, "they do not reproduce, but arise from the ashes, like the phoenix, or from the mirror, like the seductress". The Gothic has always been about replication as opposed to reproduction. It's no coincidence that the female vampire was often associated with lesbianism (most gloriously in what is perhaps the definitive goth film, *The Hunger*) because vampires and lesbians (like machines) present the horror (from the point of view of the phallic One) of a propagative power that has no use for the male seed. Conversely, "female Gothic" often pathologises pregnancy, utilising the language of horror to describe the gradual take-over of the body by an entity that is both appallingly familiar and impossibly alien. "We Hunger" from the Banshees' *Hyaena*, with its "horror of suckling", fits into a lineage of female horror which has seen "pregnancy in terms of the appalling rapacity of the insect world", as a "parasitic infestation".[10]

The principal goth vectors of propagation are, of course, signs and clothes (and — clothes as signs). The Siouxsie Look is, in effect, a replicatable cosmetic mask — a literal effacement of the organic expressivity of the face by a geometric pattern, all hard angles and harsh contrasts between white and black. White tribalism.

In *Rip It Up*, Simon says that the early Banshees were "sexy in the way that Ballard's *Crash* was sexy", and Ballard's abstract fiction-theory is as palpable and vast a presence in the Banshees as it is in other post-punk. (It's telling that the turn from the angular dryness of the Banshees' early sound to the humid lushness of their later phase should have been legitimated by Severin's reading of *The Unlimited Dream Company*.) But what the Banshees drew (out) from Ballard was the equivalence of the semiotic, the psychotic, the erotic and the savage. With psychoanalysis (and Ballard is nothing if not a committed reader of Freud), Ballard recognised that there is no "biological" sexuality waiting beneath the "alienated layers" of civilisation. Ballard's compulsively repeated theme of reversion to savagery does not present a return to a non-symbolised bucolic Nature, but a fall back into an intensely semioticised and ritualised symbolic space. (It is only the postmoderns who believe in a pre-symbolic Nature.) Eroticism is made possible — not merely mediated — by signs and technical apparatus, such that the body, signs and machines become interchangeable.

Baudrillard understood this very well, in his post-punk era essay on *Crash*:

Each mark, each trace, each scar left on the body is like an artificial invagination, like the scarifications of savages [...]. Only the wounded body exists symbolically — for itself and for others — "sexual desire" is never anything but the possibility bodies have of combining and exchanging their signs. Now, the few natural orifices to which one normally attaches sex and sexual activities are nothing next to all the possible wounds, all the artificial orifices (but why "artificial"?), all the breaches through which the body is reversibilised and, like certain topological spaces, no longer knows either interior or interior [...] Sex [...] is largely overtaken by the fan of symbolic wounds, which are in some sense the anagrammatisation of the whole length of the body — but now, precisely, it is no longer sex, but something else [...] The savages knew how to use the whole body to this end, in tattooing, torture, initiation — sexuality was only one of the possible metaphors of symbolic exchange, neither the most significant, nor the most prestigious, as it has become for us in its obsessional and realistic reference, thanks to its organic and functional character (including in orgasm).[11]

As is well-known, female dis-ease in capitalism is often expressed not in an assertion of the "natural" against the artificial, but in the anti-organic protest of eating disorders and self-cutting. It's hard not to see this — as I.T. following Žižek does — as part of the "obsession" with "realistic reference", an attempt to strip away all signs and rituals so as to reach the unadorned thing-in-itself. Goth is in many ways an attempt to make good this symbolic deficit in postmodern culture: dressing up as re-ritualisation, a recovery of the surface of the body as the site for scarification and decoration (which is to say, a rejection of the idea that the body is merely the container or envelope for interiority). Take goth footwear. With their flagrant anti-organic angularity, their disdain for the utilitarian criteria of comfort or functionality, goth shoes and boots bend, bind, twist and extend the body. Clothing recovers its cybernetic and symbolic role as a *hyperbolic supplement* to the body, as what which destroys the illusion of organic unity and proportion.

it doesn't matter if we all die: the cure's unholy trinity[1]

"Goth took hold as both a suburban and provincial cult, in which young men and women with heavily powdered faces, mourning clothes and Robert Smith's hairstyle could be seen at domestic ease in towns like Littlehampton and Ipswich."
— Michael Bracewell, *England is Mine: Pop Life in Albion from Wilde to Goldie*[2]

Any discussion of goth will remain incomplete if it doesn't deal with the Cure.

Goth and the suburbs enjoy a peculiar intimacy (no one knows this more than Tim Burton, whose *Edward Scissorhands* brilliantly laced the Avon scent of the suburbs with the perfume from goth's flowers of romance), and is there a group more suburban than the Cure? In *England is Mine*, Michael Bracewell made much of their origins in humble Crawley. "Quiet and respectable, yet lacking the bourgeois superiority of nearby Haywards Heath (home of Suede), Crawley is a near perfect example of England at its least surprising", he wrote.[3] For Bracewell, the group are the sound of the in-between spaces of English culture: the suburbs, yes, but also, adolescence, the suburbia of the soul. The Cure are the personification of the not-quite and the not-yet: not quite execrated but never really respected; not punk veterans but not yet generic Goff. The suspicion that has dogged them is that of fakery; yet inauthenticity –as existential condition — was the Cure's stock-in-trade. You can hear it all in the grain of Robert Smith's voice. Bracewell again:

When Smith sang, it wasn't so much his doom-laden lyrics as the actual sound of his voice which lent the Cure their mesmeric monotony: it was the voice of nervous boredom in a small town bedroom, muffled beneath suffocating layers of ennui. Alternately peevish and petulant, breathless with anguish or spluttering with incoherent rage, Smith's voice was unique in making monotony malleable.[4]

There is a period, a moment, when groups become what they are. Everything that has come before is preparation and rehearsal; everything that comes after is either decline or evasion. Roxy were themselves immediately — the band-brand established with the first notes of "Remake, Remodel" (with the result that Ferry's subsequent career has been a long essay in disappointment and deferred return), but it's more usual for a group to take a while to find themselves; to emerge gradually from a cocoon of allusion, homage and plagiarism. It wasn't quite like that with the Cure, whose best work was always produced in negotiation with their influences.

Their early mode — a spidery, punk-spiked pub sub-psychedelia — now sounds like a series of thin sketches. The Cure become themselves in that moment –lasting three albums — after they have shed the petulant quirkiness of *Three Imaginary Boys* but before they have entered the comfort zone of branded recognisability. By then, Smith's panto-persona –- lipstick smear, warm beer and Edward Lear — had become an archetype in the semiotic cemetery of the student disco, and the parameters of the Cure's style were well-established — marked by what quickly became a regular oscillation between a post-*Sgt. Pepper* jollity and a slippers-comfortable despair. All of the drama of faltering self-discovery and existential experimentalism that makes the essential triptych of *Seventeen Seconds*, *Faith* and *Pornography* so compelling has gone.

The Cure's three crucial albums emerged from the shadow of two other bands, whose reputation towered above theirs: the Banshees and Joy Division. Smith made no secret of his fixation on the Banshees (with whom he would later guest as a guitarist). When the band's first bassist, Michael Dempsey, left the band, it was because he "wanted us to be XTC part 2", whereas Smith "wanted us to be the Banshees part 2".

Robert Smith's *look* — that clown-faced Caligari ragdoll — was a male complement to Siouxsie's. And as with Siouxsie's, Smith's bird's nest backcomb, alabaster-white face powder, kohl-like eyeliner and badly applied lipstick is easily copied; a kit to be readily assembled in any suburban bedroom. It was a mask of morbidity, a sign that its wearer preferred fixation and obsession above "well-rounded personhood".

Goth morbidity arose in part from a Schopenhauerian scorn for organic life: from goth's perspective, death was the truth of sexuality. Sexuality was what the ceaseless cycle of birth-reproduction-death (as icily surveyed by Siouxsie on *Dreamhouse*'s "Circle Line") needed in order to perpetuate itself. Death was simultaneously outside this circuit and what it was really about. Affirming sexuality meant affirming the world, whereas goth set itself, in Houllebecq's marvellous phrase, against the world and against life. By the early Eighties, it was possible to posit a rock anti-tradition that had similar affiliations, an anhedonic, anti-vital rock lineage that began with the Stones — with the neurasthenic Jagger of "Paint it Black" rather than the cloven-hooved demonic-Dionysus of "Sympathy for the Devil" — and passed through the Stooges and the Pistols, before reaching its nadir-as-zenith in Joy Division. But goth suspected that rock was that *always and essentially* a death trip. This was the gambit of the Birthday Party, who hunted rock's mythology back to the fetid, voodoo-stalked crossroads and swamplands of the delta blues. After all, isn't blues the clearest possible demonstration of the discrepancy between desire and enjoyment, and therefore of the validity of the theory of the death drive? The blues juju — or jou-jou — relies upon the enjoyment of desires that cannot be satisfied.

While the Birthday Party literalised the return to the blues — their career a kind of hectic rewind of rock history, beginning with Pere Ubu/Pop Group modernism and ending in a feverish re-imagining of blues — the Cure, like the Banshees, went to the other extreme. Maintaining fidelity to post-punk's modernist imperative (novelty or nothing), they preferred a sound that was ethereal rather than earthy, artificial rather than visceral. You can hear this in Smith's guitar, which, swathed in phasing and flange, destubtantialised and emasculated, aspires to be pure FX denuded of any rock attack. (Is this the first step towards MBV's honeyed amorphousness?) The Cure's version of blues enjoyment-in-the-frustration-of-desire is auditioned in "A Forest": the song in which the group find themselves, ironically, since it is a song about loss — or rather about an encounter with what can never be possessed. "The girl was never there", Smith sings, a line worthy of Scritti — or Lacan. "Running towards nothing. Again and again and again...", Smith — a suburban Scotty seeking his Madeleine — pursues the desire-chimera, the petit objet a, through a dreamscape vividly sound-painted by oneiric synthesizers, drum-machines and Smith's FX-saturated guitar. "A Forest" was the trailer for *Seventeen Seconds*, and it turned out to be the album's centerpiece. The synthesizers and the drum machine bring a moderne sheen lacking on the no-frills hustle and bustle of *Three Imaginary Boys*. Smith was listening to *Astral Weeks*, Hendrix, Nick Drake, Bowie's *Low*, and wanted the album to be a synthesis of the four. The result was both more and less than this. As English as the Smiths would be, but, naturally, much more modernist and much less kitchen sink, *Seventeen Seconds* puts one in mind of a deserted country house, vast white spaces and empty floorboards decorated by the ornate cobwebs of Smith's guitar. Emotionally, the effervescent petulance of the first album has drained away, but, even if the predominant mood is now moroseness, it is not yet goth-morbid. But there is a kind of cultivated detachment, Smith assuming an "ostentatious absenteeism", dissociating himself from an everyday life conceived of as a dramaturgy of effigies: "it's just your part/in the play/for today..."

"I was 21", Smith told *Uncut* in 2000, "but I felt really old. I actually felt older than I do now. I had absolutely no hope for the future. I felt life was pointless. I had no faith in anything. I just didn't see there was much point in continuing with life. In the next two years, I genuinely felt that I wasn't going to be alive for much longer. I tried particularly hard to make sure I wasn't." From its very first moments, *Faith* locks onto this hollow-eyed bleakness, and stays there. Affectively, the album is as improbably unwavering as *Unknown Pleasures* and *Closer*, and the Joy Division (anxiety of) influence hung over *Faith* like an acrid pall, the black source of its paradoxically entropic energy, what made it possible but also what would relegate it to the status of a revenant. "The whole thing was reinforced by the fact that Ian Curtis had killed himself," Smith recalled in the *Uncut* interview, speaking for the post-Joy Division generation (which would of course include New Order) that would deem itself inauthentic simply by dint of the fact that it had carried on living. "I knew that the Cure were considered fake in comparison, and it suddenly dawned on me that to make this album convincing I would have to kill myself. If I wanted people to accept what we were doing, I was going to have to take the ultimate step."[5]

Yet *Faith* would have benefited from pursuing its emotional monotone even more assiduously, if what adrenaline that remained had been drained away, and the two up-tempo tracks ("Primary" and "Doubt") had been excised. On all the other tracks, *Faith flatlines* pop, bringing it as close to complete stillness as it is possible to be without coming to the grinding halt the group had sang of in an earlier, much more fleet-of-foot incarnation. There was no calmness in *Faith*'s stillness. It is not tranquil, but tranquillised, downer-heavy; not so much oceanic as waterlogged, swamped. (In fact, *Faith* was recorded on coke, not tranquillisers.) The album seems to come from another planet where gravity is more powerful. The synthesizers, now foregrounded more than ever, do most to produce this effect of viscous heaviness. They have a *cold warmth* that fills out the sound like valium entering the bloodstream. With *Faith*, as with downers, it is as if the *edge has been taken off*. Its world is without angles, a fug, fog of bleary drear. It lacks the *clinical* quality of Joy Division; this is not the sound of depression, nor (as with *Movement*) of post-traumatic stress, but of a kind of total fatalism, in which nothing much matters, where "all cats are grey". *Faith* finds a strange exhilaration in yielding all hope, in playing dead while going through the zombie motions, "breathing like the drowning man". Bracewell's description of the Cure's sound is nowhere more appropriate than when applied to *Faith*.

> There is no insight or polemic: there are no messages and no rallying anthems. Rather, the Cure are the musical expression of suburbia itself: a dense and repetitious sound, carrying a mesmeric dirge of infinitely transferable sounds, all of which sound as though they could go on forever — like endless avenues, crescents and drives.[6]

Faith's tracks are distended, hynoptic (or hypnagogic) in their repetitiousness,

Smith's mope a wraith that drifts in after introductions that typically last for ninety seconds or two minutes. Go through the mirror with Smith and what the uninitiated hear as directionless dirges become addictive plateaus, gentle blizzards you enjoy losing yourself in.

After this, you would expect recovery and return, a compensatory uplift. But in the event the Cure's season in hell was far from over and *Pornography* outdoes even *Faith* for morbid enervation. But *Faith's* amorphousness is replaced by a newly jagged abrasion and a jittery rhythmic urgency that was the Cure's take on the then fashionable tribal sound. Its template seems to be the less synthesizer-heavy, more metallic-brutalist tracks on *Closer* ("Atrocity Exhibition", "Colony"); the cavernous hollow spaces of PiL; the dancing in the ruins urban anomie of Killing Joke. In the end, it sounds like "Flowers of Romance" sung by a neurasthenic rather than a hysteric, Killing Joke fed on bad trip acid and downers, a defunked 23 Skidoo, all at once.

The opener, "100 Years", is the Cure's masterpiece. It starts as it means to go on, Smith intoning, "It doesn't matter if we all die", an invitation even more forbidding than that leered by the circus barker Curtis on "The Atrocity Exhibition" ("This is way step inside"). Like Joy Division's "Disorder", "100 Years" seems to lift its head from morbid self-absorption to gaze at the world — its words a Cold War ticker-tape as filtered through an adolescent nervous system in the midst of breakdown — but in reality it only selects for consideration those things which confirm its hypothesis that cosmic despair is the only justifiable attitude. "Ambition in the back of a black car... Sharing the world with slaughtered pigs... The soldiers close in..." Smith comes on like Bowie's Newton in the most famous scene of *The Man Who Fell to Earth*, entranced and stupefied by a bank of television screens, all of them bringing bad news. What makes this exhilarating rather than emiserating is the necrotic urgency of the death-disco drum machine and Smith's guitar riff, which blazes like a distress flare in light-polluted sky.

If Smith's guitar on *Pornography* often sounds Eastern, it calls up a fantasmatic East in which all of the hippie dreams of free-your-mind exotica have been napalmed into oblivion. *Pornography* was famously recorded on LSD washed down by alcohol (the band would skulk in a pub waiting for the effects of the acid to wear off before they went into the studio) but it is psychedelic in the same way that *Apocalypse Now* is. (There are grounds for claiming that *Apocalypse Now* — with its warporn media overload, its schizophrenic delirium, its sense that The End is only minutes away — was *the* post-punk film; 23 Skidoo, for one, seemed to have emerged fully-formed from its vision.) *Pornography*'s delirium is a *Jacob's Ladder* bad trip, a psychic Indochina fever dreamt in a Crawley bedroom, the hallucinogens giving distended and distorted shape to anxieties conjured from the suburban heart of darkness.

Smith's lyrics shred sense for the sake of image-impact. He has always been a "purveyor of filmic ambience" (Bracewell), and the songs on *Pornography* convey mood through striking images ("voodoo smile… siamese twins") that never cohere into any clear meaning. The album is the goth equivalent of a chocolate box: an exercise in sheer morbid indulgence unleavened by any cheer.

At the end of the title track, a howling grind that sounds like Joy Division's "The Atrocity Exhibition" spliced with Stockhausen's *Hymnen*, Smith seeks redemption. "I must fight this sickness… Find a cure." But the sickness, the sickness was the most interesting thing about the Cure.

look at the light[1]

Its cover image is a waveform of a blackbird's song re-imagined as a geological formation. Kate Bush's *Aerial* is Deleuzian MOR: a numinous, luminous twitterscape of women-animal becomings, a hymn to light, and lightness.

I'd concur with what's already coalescing into a critical consensus: "King of the Mountain" apart, the first disc — "A Sea of Honey" — is merely an appetiser for the second CD, the sumptuous song suite that is "A Sky of Honey".

On the face of it, for this, her return after twelve years, Bush could either make a show of pursuing Relevance a la Bowie, or Madonna, or else recline into a session-musician airbrushed "timelessness" like Bryan Ferry. In the event, she tacks closer to the second option, but with considerably more success than Ferry has mustered in any of his solo albums for the last twenty years. The sonic palette from which Bush has constructed *Aerial* contains few rogue elements, and hardly anything that would have discomfited a mid-Eighties audience.

And yet... "A Sky of Honey" in particular has the *flavour*, if not the instrumentation, of later genres. The intermittent birdsong, the lambent washes of subdued strings and synth, the shifts in atmosphere — now tranquil, now tempestuous, now humid, now temperate — recall ambient jungle (I'm put in mind more than once of Goldie's "Mother"), the lush opiated vastness of microhouse, English pastoral techno such as Ultramarine.

It is in *A Thousand Plateaus'* "Of the Refrain" that Deleuze and Guattari write of birdsong. On one side, the refrain is a territorial marker, the tracing of an interiority; on the other, it opens out into the cosmos. *Aerial* is similarly double: "A Sea of Honey" exploring the heimlich, "A Sky of Honey" dreaming the cosmic.

"King of the Mountain" has been one of the singles of the year — insidious and insinuating rather than immediate, a blind-side seduction which makes itself a habit before you've registered awareness of it. Its snow-swept eyrie contains the grandest, most elemental, rendition of the twin themes that dominate "A Sea of Honey" — domesticity and isolation. Kane in Xanadu doubles Elvis in Graceland, wind howling around the melancholy opulence of their empty mansions.

The other songs on "A Sea of Honey" retreat from these media myth-scapes into more intimate territory. Bush flirts with sentimental indulgence on the song addressed to her son, "Bertie", while meditating on the line between bliss and banality, pathos and bathos, on "How to be Invisible" and "Mrs Bartolozzi", with their imagery of anoraks, wallflowers and washing machines.

What is fascinating about "Sea of Honey" is its exploration of the Mother's bliss, which has by definition been excised from a history of rock that has endlessly staged the cutting of the apron strings, the rejection of the maternal. There's something oppressive and cloying about this domestic space, something suffocating and greedily insatiable about the protected interiority Bush creates. The "domestic idyll" is literally agoraphobic, troubled by an Outside it seeks to keep at bay. "How to be Invisible" is a spell in which ultra-ordinary objects are brandished as protective charms, preservatives of a domesticity that has withdrawn from the wider social world. Yet the heimlich, the homely, is always, also, the unheimlich, the unhomely, the uncanny. In "Mrs Bartolozzi", a widow's solitude transforms laundry into a Svankmajer erotic dance, the boredom, loneliness and sadness of a confined mind transfiguring empty clothes into an animist memory-theatre. In these circumscribed horizons, washing the floor becomes a religious observance, an act of mourning and melancholy.

If "A Sea of Honey" is a kitchen-sink delirium, its spaces all carpeted and walled, then "A Sky of Honey" is widescreen, *panoramic*, as the words of the stand-out track, "Nocturn", have it. Everything opens out. It's as if we leave the artificial cocoon of the house to step out into the garden, a garden which becomes a lush Ernst jungle...

What impresses most about "A Sky of Honey" is the majesty of its *composition*. It sounds like the sort of thing Bush has done before, but there's nothing else in her oeuvre quite so *sustained* as this. I mean "composition" in the painterly at least as much as the musicianly sense, for "A Sky of Honey" is Bush's most painterly record: each sound a delicate stroke in a delicately constructed and minutely conceived picture. Van Gogh ("the flowers are melting!"), Chagall, Ernst, as much as Joyce or Bronte, seem to be the guiding hands. The painter's medium — light — may well be "A Sky of Honey"'s principal preoccupation. The image of a pavement artist's work destroyed by rain is central to "A Sky of Honey": "all the colours are running". Yet no mood of regret or melancholy can last long here; in an instant, Bush is celebrating "the wonderful sunset" that the run colours have become. Ironically for a record so artfully and fastidiously *designed*, so foreign to rock and jazz's spontaneity, the message is that the Accident is the pre-eminent form of creation. We are gently urged to revel in the innocence of becoming, to "look at the light... and all the time it's a changing...". The record celebrates the butterfly-wing fragility of the Moment, the never-static Hacceities Nature is madly composing and is composed of, the ever-evanescent iridescences of the "somewhere in-between" in which we are always lost. Between wakefulness and sleep, between land and sea, between sky and dust, between day and night, "A Sky of Honey" reaches its poised, anti-climax plateau on the last three tracks, "Somewhere in Between", "Nocturn" and "Aerial". By "Somewhere in Between", we have reached dusk, the time when everything de-substantialises, and the song is a dance of dying light, a savouring of the evening's bewitched, betwixt state. "Nocturn" is up there with anything she's done — its oneiric, oceanic disco a kind of becalmed answer to Patti Smith's "Horses", the white water of Smith's angsts and passions soothed and smoothed into a placid lake in which amphibious longings swim and commingle. "Nocturn" is a journey to the end of the night very different to the one Celine took: a Van Gogh-visionary stretching, a reaching both up into the sky and down into the sea.

> The stars are caught in our hair
> The stars are on our fingers
> A veil of diamond dust
> Just reach up and touch it
> The sky's above our heads
> The sea's around our legs
> In milky, silky water
> We swim further and further
> We dive down... We dive down...

There are suggestions of Joyce's Anna Livia Plurabelle here, the river heading out to the sea that will swallow it, just as the dreaming mind awakens. After this, there is the dappled return of sunlight on "Aerial", glimmers of light on the water's surface, "all of the birds laughing", Bush joining in.

Magisterial, and better with every listen.

is pop undead?[1]

If there is a current coalescence of fascination around hauntology, there is also a mounting anxiety about the death, dearth, end of pop. A few examples: this atrocious piece on the "death of black music"[2] (significant only for the statistics it cites), Simon's 05 round-up for *Frieze*,[3] and a number of recent threads on Dissensus. The suspicion is inescapable: part of the reason why hauntology should appeal to us so much now is that, unconsciously, and increasingly consciously, we suspect that something has died.

Nothing lasts forever, of that I'm sure.

Announcements of the demise of pop are nothing new of course. And there any number of reasons to be sceptical about the language of "death" and morbidity (not least because it concedes too much to the vitalist valorisations of life). The fact is that nothing ever really dies, not in cultural terms. At a certain point — a point that is usually only discernible retrospectively — cultures shunt off into the sidings, cease to renew themselves, ossify into Trad. They don't die, they become undead, surviving on old energy, kept moving, like Baudrillard's deceased cyclist, only by the weight of inertia. Cultures have vibrancy, piquancy only for a while. Lyric poetry, the novel, opera, jazz had their time; there is no question of these cultures *dying*, they survive, but with their will-to-power diminished, their capacity to *define* a time lost. No longer historic or existential, they become historical and aesthetic — lifestyle options not ways of life.

We are lulled into the belief that pop should be immune to this process by the illusion to which those within any culture, any civilisation, fall prey (perhaps it is a necessary illusion?): the belief that our own culture will continue forever. The question we need to ask, then, is not so much "will pop die?", but has pop *already* reached the point of undeath? Has it seduced us into an entropy tango, clasping us with zombie fingers as it slowly winds

319

down towards permanent irrelevance? Questions worth raising, if only because as soon as they are no longer raised we can be sure that pop really has reached its terminal phase.

What alarms me is the *lack* of alarm about pop's current situation. Where is the chorus of disapproval and disquiet about a group like the Arctic Monkeys? Granted, it is not that the Arctic Monkeys are significantly worse than any of their retro forebears (although if anything *ought* to set alarm bells ringing, it is a situation where "not being worse" than mediocre predecessors is thought of as worthy of comment, still less of muted celebration). What is novel is the discrepancy between the Arctic Monkeys' modest "achievements" and the scale of their success. Critical success is more easily bought than ever, of course, so we shouldn't be surprised that the *NME* rates the Monkeys' album as fifth best British album of all time (disgust would be more an appropriate response, actually). But such subjective and professionally expedient over-valuations would be insignificant were it not for the *quantitative* scale of the Arctic Monkeys' success — fastest selling UK debut album ever! What this implies is a libidinal deficit in pop's audience as well as in its old media commentariat — a much more worrying trend.

The Arctic Monkeys' success is as glum news for popists as it is for those of us who still pledge allegiance to pop's modernist tendencies. (It should be noted here that, with R&B and hip-hop faltering and stuttering, popist-approved pop has been one of the last remaining places where modernism's guttering flame persists.) As Marcello has suggested recently over at *Church of Me*, the new new pop (Rachel Stevens, Girls Aloud) is barely secure, certainly not thriving, and its (relatively) disappointing sales compare ominously with the voracious triumph of retro-indie and the new authenticity (Blunt! Jack Johnson!). There has been a kind of reversal, with new new pop occupying the old pre-indie independent position of the popular-experimental, and indie dominating the mainstream. (Hence I would argue that, contra Simon in the *Frieze* article, it is new new pop, not some putative, ghastly fusion "of grime and indie rock", that is today's closest equivalent to post-punk.) A little insight into the times can be gleaned from the fact that *NME* has been reduced to ostentatiously banning Blunt from its awards ceremony (because there are a MILLION miles between his maudlin mumbling and that of *their* darlings, naturally). James Blunt versus Coldplay: is this what pop antagonism is reduced to? A pseudo-conflict that should excite only Swiftian ridicule.

Hate's not your enemy, love's your enemy.

Such plastic antagonisms (and *NME*/corporate indie can't survive without convincing its consumers that they are an *alternative* to something, that there is *some* region of common-sense, complacent, middle of the road mediocrity that they don't already occupy) substitute for the real antagonisms that once sustained pop. Even the most ardent devotees must sense something is missing — there's just a hint in Doherty's puppy dog junky eyes that even he recognises the sad fact that even if he dies, it won't stop being pantomime. (Although one suspects that the current malaise can in large part be accounted for by the fact that "what is missing" is not even noticed, still less mourned or hankered for.)

Indie may have all but driven black musics out of the British charts, hybridity may be off the agenda, but you can bet your bottom dollar that all of those indie bands just *love* hip-hop and R&B. Pop at its most febrile was stoked by critical and negative energies that are now exhausted — or which have been *exiled* as far too *impolite* for today's pot-pourri, PoMo buffet in which you can have a bit of indie here, a bit of R&B there, where contradictions and anomalies have been Photoshopped out, where it all happily fits into one well-adjusted consumer basket. If the revolutionary tumult of the post-punk era was characterised by restless dissatisfaction, anxiety, uncertainty, rage, harshness, unfairness — that is, by an atmosphere of relentless criticism — today's pop scene is suffused with laxness, bland acceptance, quiescent hedonism, luxuriant self-satisfaction (ALL those awards shows!) — that is, by PR.

What pop lacks now is the capacity for *nihilation*, for producing new potentials through the negation of what already exists. One example, of many possible. Both the Birthday Party and new pop nihilated one another: far from existing in a relation of mutual acceptance or of mutual ignorance each defined themselves in large part by *not being* the other. One shouldn't rush to conceive of this in simple-minded dialectical terms as thesis-antithesis, since the relationships are not only oppositional — there is always more than one way to nihilate, and it is always possible for any individual thing to nihilate more than one Other. It seems at least plausible to suggest that the capacity for renewed nihilation is what has driven pop. So let's dare to conceive of pop not as an archipelago of neighbouring but unconflicting options, not as a sequence of happy hybridities or pallid incommensurabilities, but as a spiral of nihilating vortices. Such a model of pop is utterly foreign to postmodern orthodoxies. But pop is either modernist or it is nothing at all.

Just because something is current doesn't mean it is new. Saying that pop was better twenty-five years ago is NOT to be nostalgic; on the contrary, it is to resist the ambient, airtight, total nostalgia that can not only tolerate but delight in the latest regurgitations on the indie retreadmill.

Let's dispense once and for all with popist-Deleuzianism/Deleuzian popism's obligatory positivity. The fact we happen to be alive now doesn't mean that we must be committed to the belief that this is the best time to live EVER. We have no duty to *search out* entertainment and spread a little excitement everywhere we go. (Think of how *hard to please* audiences were in the mid-Seventies, in the midst of a veritable cornucopia by comparison with today's grim desert; and think of what that dissatisfaction produced.) So, please, no consumerist homilies about the fact that "it is always possible to find good records, no matter what the year". Yes, of course it is, but as soon as pop is reduced to *good records* it really is all over. When pop can no longer muster a nihilation of the World, a nihilation of the Possible, then it will only be the ghosts that are worthy of our time.

memorex for the kraken: the fall's pulp modernism

Part I[1]

"Maybe industrial ghosts are making Spectres redundant"
— The Fall, *Dragnet* sleevenotes[2]

"M.R. James be born be born
Yog Sothoth rape me lord
Sludge Hai Choi
Van Greenway
Ar Corman"
— The Fall, "Spectre Vs. Rector"[3]

"Scrawny, gnarled, gaunt: Smith doesn't waltz with ghosts. He materialises them."
— Mark Sinker, "Look Back In Anguish"[4]

Who can put their finger on the Weird?

It's taken me more than twenty years to attempt this deciphering. Back then, the Fall did something to me. But what, and how?

Let's call it an Event, and at the same time note that all Events have a dimension of the uncanny. If something is too alien, it will fail to register; if it is too easily recognised, too easily cognizable, it will never be more than a reiteration of the already known. When the Fall pummelled their way into my nervous system, circa 1983, it was as if a world that was familiar — and which I had thought *too* familiar, too quotidian to feature in rock — had returned, expressionistically transfigured, permanently altered.

I didn't know then, that, already, in 1983, the Fall's greatest work was behind them. No doubt the later albums have their merits but it is on *Grotesque (After the Gramme)* (1980), *Slates* (1981) and *Hex Enduction Hour* (1982) where the group reached a pitch of sustained abstract invention that they — and few others — are unlikely to surpass. In its ambition, its linguistic inventiveness and its formal innovation, this triptych bears comparison with the great works of twentieth-century high literary modernism (Joyce, Eliot, Lewis). The Fall extend and performatively critique that mode of high modernism by reversing the impersonation of working-class accent, dialect and diction that, for example, Eliot performed in "The Waste Land". Smith's strategy involved aggressively retaining accent while using — in the domain of a supposedly popular entertainment form — highly arcane literary practices. In doing so, he laid waste the notion that intelligence, literary sophistication and artistic experimentalism are the exclusive preserve of the privileged and the formally educated. But Smith knew that aping master-class mores presented all sorts of other dangers; it should never be a matter of proving (to the masters) that the white crap could be civilised. Perhaps all his writing was, from the start, an attempt to find a way out of that paradox which all working-class aspirants face — the impossibility of working-class achievement. Stay where you are, speak the language of your fathers, and you remain nothing; move up, learn to speak in the master language, and you have become a something, but only by erasing your origins — isn't the achievement precisely that erasure? ("You can string a sentence together, how can you possibly be working class, my dear?")

The temptation for Smith was always to fit into the easy role of working-class spokesman, speaking from an assigned place in a given social world. Smith played *with* that role ("the white crap that talks back", "Prole Art Threat", "Hip Priest") whilst refusing to actually play it. He knew that representation was a trap; social realism was the enemy because in supposedly "merely" representing the social order, it actually constituted it. Against the social realism of the official left, Smith developed a late-twentieth-century urban English version of the "grotesque realism" Bakhtin famously described in *Rabelais and his World*. Crucial to this grotesque realism is a contestation of the classificatory system which deems cultures (and populations) to be either refined or vulgar. As Peter Stallybrass and Allon White argued, "the grotesque tends to operate as a critique of a dominant ideology which has already set the terms of, designating what is high and low".[5]

Instead of the high modernist appropriation of working-class speech and culture, Smith's *pulp modernism* reacquaints modernism with its disavowed pulp doppelgänger.

Lovecraft is the crucial figure here, since his texts — which first appeared in pulp magazines like *Weird Tales* — emerged from an occulted trade between pulp horror and modernism. Follow the line back from Lovecraft's short stories and you pass through Dunsany and M.R. James before coming to Poe. But Poe also played a decisive role in the development of modernism — via his influence on Baudelaire, Mallarmé, Valéry and their admirer T.S. Eliot. "The Waste Land"'s debt to *Dracula*, for instance, is well-known.[6] The fragmentary, citational structure of a story like Lovecraft's "Call of Cthulhu", meanwhile, recalls "The Waste Land". More than that: as Benjamin Noys argued in his paper "Lovecraft the Sinthome" (given at the recent "Gothic Remains" conference at Sussex), the abominations from which Lovecraft's strait-laced scholars recoil bear comparisons with cubist and futurist art: Lovecraft, that is to say, turns modernism into an object of horror.

Yet Lovecraft's texts are exemplary of Weird, rather than straightforwardly Gothic, fiction. Weird fiction has its own consistency, which can be most clearly delineated by comparing it to two adjacent modes, fantasy and the uncanny. Fantasy (and Tolkien is the exemplar here) presupposes a completed world, a world that, although superficially different to "ours" (there may be different species, or supernatural forces) is politically all-too familiar (there is usually some nostalgia for the ordered organisation of feudal hierarchy). The uncanny, meanwhile, is set in "our" world — only that world is no longer "ours" any more, it no longer coincides with itself, it has been estranged. The Weird, however, depends upon the difference between two (or more) worlds — with "world" here having an *ontological* sense. It is not a question of an empirical difference — the aliens are not from another planet, they are invaders from another reality system. Hence the defining image is that of the threshold, the door from this world into another, and the key figure is the "Lurker at the Threshold" — what, in Lovecraft's mythos is called Yog Sothoth. The political philosophical implications are clear: *there is no world*. What we call *the* world is a local consensus hallucination, a shared dream.

Is There Anybody There?

"Part One: spectre versus rector
The rector lived in Hampshire
The Spectre was from Chorazina)..."
— The Fall, "Spectre Vs. Rector"

"Spectre Vs. Rector", from 1979's *Dragnet*, is the first moment — still chilling to hear — when the Fall both lay out and implement their pulp modernist methodology. "Spectre Vs. Rector" is not only a ghost story, it is a commentary on the ghost story. The chorus, if it can be called that, is a litany of pulp forebears — "M.R. James be born be born/Yog Sothoth rape me lord..." — in which language devolves into asignifying chant, verbal ectoplasm: "Sludge Hai Choi/Van Greenway/Ar Corman".

Not coincidentally, "Spectre Vs. Rector" was the moment when the Fall really began to sound like themselves. Before that, the Fall's sound is a grey-complexioned, conspicuously consumptive garage plink-plonk punk, amphetamine-lean and on-edge, marijuana-fatalistic, simultaneously arrogant and unsure of itself, proffering its cheap and nastiness as a challenge. All of the elements of Smith's later (peripheral) vision are there on *Live at the Witch Trials* and on the other tracks on *Dragnet* — watery-eyed figures lurking in the corner of the retina, industrial estates glimpsed through psychotropic stupor — but they have not yet been condensed down, *pulped* into the witches' brew that will constitute Smith's plane of consistency.

On "Spectre Vs. Rector", any vestigial rock *presence* subsides into hauntology. The original track is nothing of the sort — it is already a palimpsest, spooked by itself; at least two versions are playing, out of sync. The track — and it is very definitely a track, not a "song" — foregrounds both its own textuality and its texturality. It begins with cassette hum and when the sleeve notes tell us that it was partly "recorded in a damp warehouse in MC/R" we are far from surprised. Steve Hanley's bass rumbles and thumps like some implacable earth-moving machine invented by a deranged underground race, not so much rising from subterranea as dragging the sound down into a troglodytic goblin kingdom in which ordinary sonic values are inverted. From now on, and for all the records that really matter, Hanley's bass will be the lead instrument, the monstrous foundations on which the Fall's upside-down sound will be built. Like Joy Division, fellow modernists from Manchester, the Fall scramble the grammar of white rock by privileging rhythm over melody.

Fellow modernists they might have been, but the Fall and Joy Division's take on modernism could not have been more different. Hannett and Saville gave Joy Division a minimalist, metallic austerity; the Fall's sound and cover art, by contrast, was gnarled, collage cut-up, deliberately incomplete. Both bands were dominated by forbiddingly intense vocalist-visionaries. But where Curtis was the depressive-neurotic, the end of the European Romantic line, Smith was the psychotic, the self-styled destroyer of Romanticism.

"Unsuitable for Romantics", Smith will graffiti onto the cover of *Hex Enduction Hour*, and "Spectre Vs. Rector" is the template for the anti-Romantic methodology he will deploy on the Fall's most important releases. After "Spectre Vs. Rector", there is no Mark E Smith the romantic subject. The novelty of Smith's approach is to impose the novel or tale form ("Part One: spectre versus rector...") into the Romantic-lyrical tradition of the r and r song, so that the author-function supplants that of the lyrical balladeer. (There are parallels between what Smith does to rock and the cut-up surgery Eliot performed on the etherised patient of Romantic expressive subjectivity in his early poems.) Smith chant-narrates, not sings, "Spectre Vs. Rector".

The story is simple enough, and, on the surface, is deliberately conventional: a post-*Exorcist* revisiting of the classic English ghost story. (At another level, the narrative is generated by a Roussel-like playing with similar words: Rector/Spectre/Inspector/Excorcist/Exhausted.) A rector is possessed by a malign spirit ("the spectre was from Chorazina" — described on the sleevenotes as "a negative Jerusalem"); a police inspector tries to intervene but is driven insane. (This a real Lovecraftian touch, since the dread fate that haunts Lovecraft's characters is not of being consumed by the polytendrilled abominations but by the schizophrenia that their appearance often engenders.) Both Rector and Inspector have to be saved by a third figure, a shaman-hero, an Outsider who "goes back to the mountains" when the exorcism is complete.

The Rector stands for rectitude and rectilinearity as well as for traditional religious authority. (The ontological shock that Lovecraft's monstrosities produce is typically described, any Lovecraft reader will recall, in terms of a twisting of rectilinear geometries.) The Inspector, meanwhile, as Ian Penman conjectured in his 1980 interview with the Fall "stands for an investigative, empirical world view".[7] The hero ("his soul possessed a thousand times") has more affinity with the Spectre, whom he absorbs and becomes ("the spectre possesses the hero/ but the possession is ineffectual") than with the agents of rectitude and or empirical investigation. It seems that the hero is driven more by his addiction to being possessed, which is to say dispossessed of his own identity ("that was his kick from life") than from any altruistic motive. He has no love for the social order he rescues ("I have saved a thousand souls/they cannot even save their own") but in which he does not occupy a place. "Those flowers take them away", he said:

They're only funeral decorations
And this is a drudge nation
A nation of no imagination
A stupid dead man is their ideal
They shirk me and think me unclean...
UNCLEAN...

In *Madness and Civilisation*, Foucault argues that the insane occupy the structural position vacated by the leper, while in *The Ecstasy of Communication*, Baudrillard describes "the state of terror proper to the schizophrenic: too great a proximity of everything, the unclean promiscuity of everything which touches, invests and penetrates without resistance, with no halo of private projection to protect him anymore".[8] Baudrillard is of course describing the schizophrenia of *media* systems which overwhelm all interiority. Television brings us voices from far away (and there's always something on the other side...). For Baudrillard, there is an increasing flatness between media and the schizophrenic delirium in which they feature; psychotics often describe themselves as receivers for transmitted signal. And what is the hero of "Spectre Vs. Rector" if not another version of the "ESP medium of discord" that Smith sings of on "Psychic Dancehall"?

Smith's own methodology as writer-ranter-chanter echoes that of the hero-malcontent. He becomes (nothing but) the mystic pad on which stray psychic signals impress themselves, the throat through which a warring multiplicity of mutually antatognistic voices speak. This is not only a matter of the familiar idea that Smith "contains multitudes"; the schizophonic riot of voices is itself subject to all kinds of mediation. The voices we hear will often be reported speech, recorded in the compressed "telegraphic" headline style Smith borrowed from the Lewis of *Blast*.

Listening to the Fall now, I'm often reminded of another admirer of Lewis, Marshall McLuhan. The McLuhan of *The Mechanical Bride* (subtitle: *The Folklore of Industrial Man*), understood very well the complicity between mass media, modernism and pulp. McLuhan argued that modernist collage was a response to the perfectly schizophrenic layout of the newspaper frontpage. (And Poe, who in addition to his role as a forebear of Weird fiction, was also the inventor of the detective genre, plays a crucial role in *The Mechanical Bride*.)

M.R. James, Be Born Be Born

"Ten times my age, one tenth my height..."
— The Fall, "City Hobgoblins"[2]

"So he plunges into the Twilight World, and a political discourse framed in terms of witchcraft and demons. It's not hard to understand why, once you start considering it. The war that the Church and triumphant Reason waged on a scatter of wise-women and midwives, lingering practitioners of folk-knowledge, has provided a powerful popular image for a huge struggle for political and intellectual dominance, as first Catholics and later Puritans invoked a rise in devil-worship to rubbish their opponents. The ghost-writer and antiquarian M.R. James (one of the writers Smith appears to have lived on during his peculiar drugged adolescence) transformed the folk-memory into a bitter class-struggle between established science and law, and the erratic, vengeful, relentless undead world of wronged spirits, cheated of property or voice, or the simple dignity of being believed in."
— Mark Sinker, "Watching the City Hobgoblins"[3]

Whether Smith first came to James via TV or some other route, James' stories exerted a powerful and persistent influence on his writing. Lovecraft, an enthusiastic admirer of James' stories to the degree that he borrowed their structure (scholar/researcher steeped in empiricist common sense is gradually driven insane by contact with an abyssal alterity) understood very well what was novel in James' tales. "In inventing a new type of ghost",

Lovecraft wrote of James,

> he departed considerably from the conventional Gothic traditions; for
> where the older stock ghosts were pale and stately, and apprehended chiefly
> through the sense of sight, the average James ghost is lean, dwarfish and
> hairy — a sluggish, hellish night-abomination midway betwixt beast and
> man — and usually *touched* before it is *seen*.[4]

Some would question whether these dwarven figures ("ten times my age,
one tenth my height") could be described as "ghosts" at all; often, it seemed
that James was writing *demon* rather than ghost stories.

If the libidinal motor of Lovecraft's horror was race, in the case of James
it was class. For James scholars, contact with the anomalous was usually
mediated by the "lower classes", which he portrayed as lacking in intellect
but in possession of a deeper knowledge of weird lore. As Lovecraft and
James scholar S.T. Joshi observes:

> The fractured and dialectical English in which [James' array of lower-
> class characters] speak or write is, in one sense, a reflection of James'
> well-known penchant for mimicry; but it cannot be denied that there is a
> certain element of malice in his relentless exhibition of their intellectual
> failings. [...] And yet, they occupy pivotal places in the narrative: by
> representing a kind of middle ground between the scholarly protagonists
> and the aggressively savage ghosts, they frequently sense the presence of
> the supernatural more quickly and more instinctively than their excessively
> learned betters can bring themselves to do.[5]

James wrote his stories as Christmas entertainments for Oxford
undergraduates, and Smith was doubtless provoked and fascinated by
James' stories in part because there was no obvious point of identification
for him in them. "When I was at the witch trials of the twentieth century
they said: You are white crap." (*Live* at the witch trials: is it that the witch
trials have never ended or that we are in some repeating structure which
is always excluding and denigrating the Weird?)

A working-class autodidact like Smith could scarcely be conceived of
in James; sclerotically-stratified universe; such a being was a monstrosity
which would be punished for the sheer hubris of existing. (Witness the
amateur archaeologist Paxton in "A Warning to the Curious". Paxton was
an unemployed clerk and therefore by no means working class but his grisly
fate was as much a consequence of "getting above himself" as it was of
his disturbing sacred Anglo-Saxon artefacts.) Smith could identify neither
with James' expensively-educated protagonists nor with his uneducated,
superstitious lower orders. As Mark Sinker puts it: "James, an enlightened

Victorian intellectual, dreamed of the spectre of the once crushed and newly rising working classes as a brutish and irrational Monster from the Id: Smith is working class, and is torn between adopting this image of himself and fighting violently against it. It's left him with a loathing of liberal humanist condescension."[6]

But if Smith could find no place in James' world, he would take a cue from one of Blake's mottoes (adapted in *Dragnet*'s "Before the Moon Falls") and create his own fictional system rather than be enslaved by another man's. (Incidentally, isn't Blake a candidate for being the original pulp modernist?) In James' stories, there is, properly speaking, no working class at all. The lower classes that feature in his tales are by and large the remnants of the rural peasantry, and the supernatural is associated with the countryside. James' scholars typically travel from Oxford or London to the witch-haunted flatlands of Suffolk, and it is only here that they encounter demonic entities. Smith's fictions would locate spectres in the urban here and now; he would establish that their antagonisms were not archaisms.

Sinker: "No one has so perfectly studied the sense of threat in the English horror story: the twinge of apprehension at the idea that the wronged dead might return to claim their property, their identity, their own voice in their own land."[7]

The Grotesque Peasants Stalk the Land

"Detective versus rector possessed by spectre
Spectre blows him against the wall
Says direct, 'This is your fall
I've waited since Caesar for this
Damn fatty, my hate is crisp!
I'll rip your fat body to pieces!'"
— The Fall, "Spectre Vs. Rector"

"The word *grotesque* derives from a type of Roman ornamental design first discovered in the fifteenth century, during the excavation of Titus's baths. Named after the 'grottoes' in which they were found, the new forms consisted of human and animal shapes intermingled with foliage, flowers, and fruits in fantastic designs which bore no relationship to the logical categories of classical art. For a contemporary account of these forms we can turn to the Latin writer Vitruvius. Vitruvius was an official charged with the rebuilding of Rome under Augustus, to whom his treatise *On Architecture* is addressed. Not surprisingly, it bears down hard on the 'improper taste' for the grotesque. 'Such things neither are, nor can be, nor have been,' says the author in his description of the mixed human, animal, and vegetable forms:

For how can a reed actually sustain a roof, or a candelabrum the ornament of a gable? or a soft and slender stalk, a seated statue? or how can flowers and half-statues rise alternately from roots and stalks? Yet when people view these falsehoods, they approve rather than condemn, failing to consider whether any of them can really occur or not."
— Patrick Parrinder, *James Joyce*[8]

By the time of *Grotesque (After the Gramme)*, the Fall's pulp modernism has become an entire political-aesthetic program. At one level, *Grotesque* can be positioned as the barbed Prole Art retort to the lyric antique Englishness of public school prog. Compare, for instance, the cover of "City Hobgoblins" (one of the singles that came out around the time of *Grotesque*) with something like Genesis' *Nursery Cryme*. *Nursery Cryme* presents a gently corrupted English surrealist idyll. On the "City Hobgoblins" cover, an urban scene has been invaded by "emigres from old green glades": a leering, malevolent cobold looms over a dilapidated tenement. But rather than being smoothly integrated into the photographed scene, the crudely rendered hobgoblin has been etched, Nigel Cooke-style, onto the background. This is a war of worlds, an ontological struggle, a struggle over the means of representation.

Grotesque's "English Scheme" was a thumbnail sketch of the territory over which the war was being fought. Smith would observe later that it was "English Scheme" which "prompted me to look further into England's 'class' system. INDEED, one of the few advantages of being in an impoverished sub-art group in England is that you get to see (If eyes are peeled) all the different strata of society — for free."[9] The enemies are the old right, the custodians of a National Heritage image of England ("poky quaint streets in Cambridge") but also, crucially, the middle-class left, the Chabertistas of the time, who "condescend to black men" and "talk of Chile while driving through Haslingdon". In fact, enemies were everywhere. Lumpen-punk was in many ways more of a problem than prog, since its reductive literalism and perfunctory politics ("circles with A in the middle") colluded with social realism in censuring/censoring the visionary and the ambitious.

Although *Grotesque* is an enigma, its title gives clues. Otherwise incomprehensible references to "huckleberry masks", "a man with butterflies on his face" and Totale's "ostrich headdress" and "light blue plant-heads" begin to make sense when you recognise that, in Parrinder's description, the grotesque originally referred to "human and animal shapes intermingled with foliage, flowers, and fruits in fantastic designs which bore no relationship to the logical categories of classical art".

Grotesque, then, would be another moment in the endlessly repeating struggle between a pulp Underground (the scandalous grottoes) and the

Official culture, what Philip K. Dick called "the Black Iron Prison". Dick's intuition was that "the Empire had never ended", and that history was shaped by an ongoing occult(ed) conflict between Rome and Gnostic forces. "Spectre Vs. Rector" ("I've waited since Caesar for this") had rendered this clash in a harsh Murnau black and white; on *Grotesque* the struggle is painted in colours as florid as those used on the album's garish sleeve (the work of Smith's sister).

It is no accident that the words "grotesque" and "weird" are often associated with one another, since both connote something which is out of place, which either should not exist at all, or which should not exist *here*. The response to the apparition of a grotesque object will involve laughter as much as revulsion. "What will be generally agreed upon", Philip Thompson wrote in his 1972 study *The Grotesque* "is that 'grotesque' will cover, perhaps among other things, the co-presence of the laughable and something that is incompatible with the laughable."[10] The role of laughter in the Fall has confused and misled interpreters. What has been suppressed is precisely the *co-presence* of the laughable with what is not compatible with the laughable. That co-presence is difficult to think, particularly in Britain, where humour has often functioned to ratify commonsense, to punish overreaching ambition with the dampening weight of bathos.

With the Fall, however, it is as if satire is returned to its origins in the grotesque. The Fall's laughter does not issue from the commonsensical mainstream but from a psychotic Outside. This is satire in the oneiric mode of Gillray, in which invective and lampoonery becomes delirial, a (psycho) tropological spewing of associations and animosities, the true object of which is not any failing of probity but the delusion that human dignity is possible. It is not surprising to find Smith alluding to Jarry's *Ubu Roi* in a barely audible line in "City Hobgoblins" ("Ubu le Roi is a home hobgoblin"). For Jarry, as for Smith, the incoherence and incompleteness of the obscene and the absurd were to be opposed to the false symmetries of good sense.

But in their mockery of poise, moderation and self-containment, in their logorrheic disgorging of slanguage, in their glorying in mess and incoherence, the Fall sometimes resemble a white English analogue of Funkadelic. For both Smith and Clinton, there is no escaping the grotesque, if only because those who primp and puff themselves up only become more grotesque. We could go so far as to say that it is the human condition to be grotesque, since the human animal is the one that does not fit in, the freak of nature who has no place *in* nature and is capable of re-combining nature's products into hideous new forms.

On *Grotesque*, Smith has mastered his anti-lyrical methodology. The songs are tales, but tales half-told. The words are fragmentary, as if they have come to us via an unreliable transmission that keeps cutting out. Viewpoints are garbled; ontological distinctions (between author, text and character) are confused, fractured. It is impossible to definitively sort out the narrator's words from direct speech. The tracks are palimpsests, badly recorded in a deliberate refusal of the "coffee table" aesthetic Smith derides on the cryptic sleeve notes. The process of recording is not airbrushed out but foregrounded, surface hiss and illegible cassette noise brandished like improvised stitching on some Hammer Frankenstein monster.

"Impression of J Temperance" was typical: a story in the Lovecraft style in which a dog breeder's "hideous replica" ("brown sockets... Purple eyes... fed with rubbish from disposal barges") haunts Manchester. This is a Weird tale, but one subjected to modernist techniques of compression and collage. The result is so elliptical that it is as if the text — part-obliterated by silt, mildew and algae — has been fished out of the Manchester ship canal (which Hanley's bass sounds like it is dredging).

"'Yes', said Cameron, 'And the thing was in the impression of J Temperance.'"

The sound on *Grotesque* is a seemingly impossible combination of the shambolic and the disciplined, the cerebral-literary and the idiotic-physical. The obvious parallel was the Birthday Party. In both groups, an implacable bass holds together a leering, lurching schizophonic body whose disparate elements strain like distended, diseased viscera against a pustule and pock-ridden skin ("a spotty exterior hides a spotty interior"). Both the Fall and the Birthday Party reached for pulp horror imagery rescued from the white trash can as an analogue and inspiration for their perverse "return" to rock and roll (cf. also the Cramps). The nihilation that fired them was a rejection of a pop that they saw as self-consciously sophisticated, conspicuously cosmopolitan, a pop which implied that the arty could only be attained at the expense of brute physical impact. Their response was to hyperbolically emphasise crude atavism, to embrace the unschooled and the primitivist.

The Birthday Party's fascination was with the American "junkonscious", the mountain of semiotic/narcotic trash lurking in the hindbrain of a world population hooked on America's myths of abjection and omnipotence. The Birthday Party revelled in this fantasmatic Americana, using it as a way of cancelling an Australian identity that they in any case experienced as empty, devoid of any distinguishing features.

Smith's r and r citations functioned differently, precisely as a means of reinforcing his Englishness and his own ambivalent attitude towards it. The rockabilly references are almost like "What If?" exercises. What if rock and roll had emerged from the industrial heartlands of England rather than the Mississippi Delta? The rockabilly on "Container Drivers" or "Fiery Jack" is slowed by meat pies and gravy, its dreams of escape fatally poisoned by pints of bitter and cups of greasy spoon tea. It is rock and roll as Working Men's Club cabaret, performed by a failed Gene Vincent imitator in Prestwich. The "What if?" speculations fail. Rock and roll needed the endless open highways; it could never have begun in Britain's snarled up ring roads and claustrophobic conurbations.

For the Smith of *Grotesque*, homesickness is a pathology. (In the interview on the 1983 *Perverted by Language* video, Smith claims that being away from England literally made him sick.) There is little to recommend the country which he can never permanently leave; his relationship to it seems to be one of wearied addiction. The fake jauntiness of "English Scheme" (complete with proto-John Shuttleworth cheesy cabaret keyboard) is a squalid postcard from somewhere no one would ever wish to be. Here and in "C and Cs Mithering", the US emerges as an alternative (in despair at the class-ridden Britain of "sixty hours and stone toilet back gardens", the "clever ones" "point their fingers at America"), but there is a sense that, no matter how far he travels, Smith will in the end be overcome by a compulsion to return to his blighted homeland, which functions as his *pharmakon*, his poison and remedy, sickness and cure. In the end he is as afflicted by paralysis as Joyce's Dubliners.

On "C n Cs Mithering" a rigor mortis snare drum gives this paralysis a sonic form. "C n Cs Mithering" is an unstinting inventory of gripes and irritations worthy of Tony Hancock at his most acerbic and disconsolate, a cheerless survey of estates that "stick up like stacks" and, worse still, a derisive dismissal of one of the supposed escape routes from drudgery: the music business, denounced as corrupt, dull and stupid. The track sounds, perhaps deliberately, like a white English version of rap (here as elsewhere, the Fall are remarkable for producing *equivalents* to, rather than facile imitations of, black American forms).

Body a Tentacle Mess

"So R. Totale dwells underground
Away from sickly grind
With ostrich head-dress
Face a mess, covered in feathers
Orange-red with blue-black lines
That draped down to his chest
Body a tentacle mess
And light blue plant-heads."
— The Fall, "The N.W.R.A"[11]

But it is the other long track, "The N.W.R.A.", that is the masterpiece. All of the LP's themes coalesce in this track, a tale of cultural political intrigue that plays like some improbable mulching of T.S. Eliot, Wyndham Lewis, H.G. Wells, Dick, Lovecraft and Le Carré. It is the story of Roman Totale, a psychic and former cabaret performer whose body is covered in tentacles.

335

It is often said that Roman Totale is one of Smith's "alter-egos"; in fact, Smith is in the same relationship to Totale as Lovecraft was to someone like Randolph Carter. Totale is a character rather than a persona. Needless to say, he is not a character in the "well-rounded" Forsterian sense so much as a carrier of mythos, an inter-textual linkage between pulp fragments.

The inter-textual methodology is crucial to pulp modernism. If pulp modernism first of all asserts the author-function over the creative-expressive subject, it secondly asserts a fictional system against the author-God. By producing a fictional plane of consistency across different texts, the pulp modernist becomes a conduit through which a world can emerge. Once again, Lovecraft is the exemplar here: his tales and novellas could in the end no longer be apprehended as discrete texts but as part-objects forming a mythos-space which other writers could also explore and extend.

The form of "The N.W.R.A." is as alien to organic wholeness as is Totale's abominable tentacular body. It is a grotesque concoction, a collage of pieces that do not belong together. The model is the novella rather than the tale, and the story is told episodically, from multiple points of view, using a heteroglossic riot of styles and tones (comic, journalistic, satirical, novelistic): like "Call of Cthulhu" re-written by the Joyce of *Ulysses* and compressed into ten minutes.

From what we can glean, Totale is at the centre of a plot — infiltrated and betrayed from the start — which aims at restoring the North to glory (perhaps to its Victorian moment of economic and industrial supremacy; perhaps to some more ancient pre-eminence, perhaps to a greatness that will eclipse anything that has come before). More than a matter of regional railing against the capital, in Smith's vision the North comes to stand for everything suppressed by urbane good taste: the esoteric, the anomalous, the vulgar sublime, that is to say, the Weird and the Grotesque itself. Totale, festooned in the incongruous Grotesque costume of "ostrich head-dress... feathers/orange-red with blue-black line/...and light blue plant-heads" is the would-be Faery King of this Weird Revolt who ends up its maimed Fisher King, abandoned like a pulp modernist Miss Havisham amongst the relics of a carnival that will never happen, a drooling totem of a defeated tilt at social realism, the visionary leader reduced, as the psychotropics fade and the fervour cools, to being a washed-up cabaret artiste once again.

Part III[1]

"Don't start improvising, for Christ's sake"

The temptation, when writing about the Fall's work of this period, is to too quickly render it tractable. I note this by way of a disclaimer and a confession, since I am of course as liable to fall prey to this temptation as any other commentator. To confidently describe songs as if they were "about" settled subjects or to attribute to them a determinate aim or orientation (typically, a satirical purpose) will always be inadequate to the vertiginous experience of the songs and the distinctive *jouissance* provoked by listening to them. This enjoyment involves a frustration — a frustration, precisely, of our attempts to make sense of the songs. Yet this jouissance — something also provoked by the late Joyce, Pynchon and Burroughs — is an irreducible dimension of the Fall's modernist poetics. If it is impossible to make sense of the songs, it is also impossible to stop making sense of them — or at least to it is impossible to stop *attempting* to make sense of them. On the one hand, there is no possibility of dismissing the songs as nonsense; they are not gibberish or disconnected strings of non-sequiturs. On the other hand, any attempt to constitute the songs as settled carriers of meaning runs aground on their incompleteness and inconsistency.

The principal way in which the songs were recuperated was via the charismatic persona Smith established in interviews. Although Smith scrupulously refused to either corroborate or reject any interpretations of his songs, invoking this extra-textual persona, notorious for its strong views and its sardonic but at least legible humour, allowed listeners and commentators to contain, even dissipate, the strangeness of the songs themselves.

The temptation to use Smith's persona as a key to the songs was especially pressing because all pretence of democracy in the group has long since disappeared. By the time of *Grotesque*, it was clear that Smith was as much of an autocrat as James Brown, the band the zombie slaves of his vision. He is the shaman-author, the group the producers of a delirium-inducing repetition from which all spontaneity must be ruthlessly purged. "Don't start improvising for Christ's sake," goes a line on *Slates*, the 10" EP follow-up to *Grotesque*, echoing his chastisement of the band for "showing off" on the live LP *Totale's Turns*.

Slates' "Prole Art Threat" turned Smith's persona, reputation and image into an enigma and a conspiracy. The song is a complex, ultimately unreadable, play on the idea of Smith as "working-class" spokesman. The "Threat" is posed as much to other representations of the proletarian pop culture (which at its best meant the Jam and at its worst meant the more thuggish Oi!) as it is against the ruling class as such. The "art" of the Fall's pulp modernism — their intractability and difficulty — is counterposed to the misleading ingenuousness of social realism.

The Fall's intuition was that social relations could not be understood in the "demystified" terms of empirical observation (the "housing figures" and "sociological memory" later ridiculed on "The Man Whose Head Expanded'). Social power depends upon "hexes": restricted linguistic, gestural and behavioural codes which produce a sense of inferiority and enforce class destiny. "What chance have you got against a tie and a crest?", Weller demanded on "Eton Rifles", and it was as if the Fall took the power of such symbols and sigils very literally, understanding the social field as a series of curses which have to be sent back to those who had issued them.

The pulp format on "Prole Art Threat" is spy fiction, its scenario resembling *Tinker Tailor Soldier Spy* re-done as a tale of class cultural espionage, but then compressed and cut up so that characters and contexts are even more perplexing than they were even in Le Carré's already oblique narrative. We are in a labyrinthine world of bluff and counter-bluff — a perfect analogue for Smith's own elusive, allusive textual strategies. The text is presented to us as a transcript of surveillance tapes, complete with ellipses where the transmission is supposedly scrambled: "GENT IN SAFE-HOUSE: Get out the pink press threat file and Brrrptzzap* the subject. (* = scrambled)."

"Prole Art Threat" seems to be a satire, yet it is a *blank* satire, a satire without any clear object. If there is a point, it is precisely to disrupt any "centripetal" effort to establish fixed identities and meanings. Those centripetal forces are represented by the "Middle Mass" ("vulturous in the aftermath") and "the Victorian vampiric" culture of London itself, as excoriated in "Leave the Capitol":

The tables covered in beer
Showbiz whines, minute detail
It's a hand on the shoulder in Leicester Square
It's vaudeville pub back room dusty pictures of white frocked girls and music teachers
The bed's too clean
The water's poison for the system

Then you know in your brain
LEAVE THE CAPITOL!
EXIT THIS ROMAN SHELL!

This horrifying vision of London as a Stepford city of drab conformity ("hotel maids smile in unison") ends with the unexpected arrival of Machen's *Great God Pan* (last alluded to in the Fall's very early "Second Dark Age", presaging the Fall's return of the Weird.

The Textual Expectorations of *Hex*

"He'd been very close to becoming ex-funny man celebrity. He needed a good hour at the hexen school..."
— Press release for *Hex Enduction Hour*

Hex Enduction Hour was even more expansive than *Grotesque*. Teeming with detail, gnomic yet hallucinogenically vivid, *Hex* was a series of pulp modernist pen portraits of England in 1982. The LP had all the hubristic ambition of prog combined with an aggression whose ulcerated assault and battery outdid most of its post-punk peers in terms of sheer ferocity. Even the lumbering "Winter" was driven by a brute urgency, so that, on side one, only the quiet passages in the lugubrious "Hip Priest" — like dub if it had been invented in drizzly motorway service stations rather than in recording studios in Jamaica — provided a respite from the violence.

Yet the violence was not a matter of force alone. Even when the record's dual-drummer attack is at its most poundingly vicious, the violence is formal as much as physical. Rock form is disassembled before our ears. It seems to keep time according to some system of spasms and lurches learned from Beefheart. Something like "Deer Park" — a whistle-stop tour of London circa 82 sandblasted with "Sister Ray"-style white noise — screams and whines as if it is about to fall apart at any moment. The "bad production" was nothing of the sort. The sound could be pulverisingly vivid at times: the moment when the bass and drums suddenly loom out of the miasma at the start of "Winter" is breathtaking, and the double-drum tattoo on "Who Makes the Nazis?" fairly leaps out of the speakers. This was the space rock of Can and Neu! smeared in the grime and mire of the quotidian, recalling the most striking image from *The Quatermass Xperiment*: a space rocket crash-landed into the roof of a suburban house.

In many ways, however, the most suggestive parallels come from black pop. The closest equivalents to the Smith of *Hex* would be the deranged despots of black sonic fiction: Lee Perry, Sun Ra and George Clinton, visionaries capable of constructing (and destroying) worlds in sound.

As ever, the album sleeve (so foreign to what were then the conventions of sleeve design that HMV would only stock it with its reverse side facing forward) was the perfect visual analogue for the contents. The sleeve was more than that, actually: its spidery scrabble of slogans, scrawled notes and photographs was a part of the album rather than a mere illustrative envelope in which it was contained.

With the Fall of this period, what Gerard Genette calls "paratexts"[2] — those liminal conventions, such as introductions, prefaces and blurbs, which mediate between the text and the reader — assume special significance. Smith's paratexts were clues that posed as many puzzles as they solved; his notes and press releases were no more intelligible than the songs they were nominally supposed to explain. All paratexts occupy an ambivalent position, neither inside nor outside the text: Smith uses them to ensure that no definite boundary could be placed around the songs. Rather than being contained and defined by its sleeve, *Hex* haemorrhages *through* the cover.

It was clear that the songs weren't complete in themselves, but part of a larger fictional system to which listeners were only ever granted partial access. "I used to write a lot of prose on and off", Smith would say later. "When we were doing *Hex* I was doing stories all the time and the songs were like the bits left over." Smith's refusal to provide lyrics or to explain his songs was in part an attempt to ensure that they remained, in Barthes' terms, *writerly*. (Barthes opposes such texts, which demand the active participation of the reader, to "readerly" texts, which reduce the reader to the passive role of consumer of already-existing totalities.)

Before his words could be deciphered they had first of all to be heard, which was difficult enough, since Smith's voice — often subject to what appeared to be loud hailer distortion — was always at least partially submerged in the mulch and maelstrom of *Hex*'s sound. In the days before the internet provided a repository of Smith's lyrics (or fans' best guesses at what the words were), it was easy to mis-hear lines for years.

Even when words could be heard, it was impossible to confidently assign them a meaning or an ontological "place". Were they Smith's own views, the thoughts of a character or merely stray semiotic signal? More importantly: how clearly could each of these levels be separated from one another? *Hex*'s textual expectorations were nothing so genteel as stream of consciousness: they seemed to be gobbets of linguistic detritus ejected direct from the mediatised unconscious, unfiltered by any sort of reflexive subjectivity. Advertising, tabloid headlines, slogans, pre-conscious chatter, overheard speech were masticated into dense schizoglossic tangles.

"Who wants to be in a Hovis advert anyway?"

"Who wants to be in a Hovis/advert/anyway?" Smith asks in "Just Step S'Ways", but this refusal of cosy provincial cliché (Hovis adverts were famous for their sentimentalised presentation of a bygone industrial North) is counteracted by the tacit recognition that the mediatised unconscious is structured like advertising. You might not want to live in an advert, but advertising dwells within you. *Hex* converts any linguistic content — whether it be polemic, internal dialogue, poetic insight — into the hectoring form of advertising copy or the screaming ellipsis of headline-speak. The titles of "Hip Priest" and "Mere Pseud Mag Ed", as urgent as fresh newsprint, bark out from some Voriticist front page of the mind.

As for advertising, consider "Just Step S'Ways" opening call to arms: "When what used to excite you does not/like you've used up all your allowance of experiences." Is this an existentialist call for self re-invention disguised as advertising hucksterism, or the reverse? Or take the bilious opening track, "The Classical". "The Classical" appears to oppose the anodyne vacuity of advertising's compulsory positivity ("this new profile razor unit") to ranting profanity ("hey there fuckface!") and the gross physicality of the body ("stomach gassss"). But what of the line, "I've never felt better in my life?" Is this another advertising slogan or a statement of the character's feelings?

It was perhaps the unplaceability of any of the utterances on *Hex* that allowed Smith to escape censure for the notorious line, "where are the obligatory niggers?" in "The Classical". Intent was unreadable. Everything sounded like a citation, embedded discourse, mention rather than use.

Smith returns to the Weird tale form on "Jawbone and the Air Rifle". A poacher accidentally causes damage to a tomb, unearthing a jawbone which "carries the germ of a curse/of the Broken Brothers Pentacle Church." The song is a tissue of allusions — James ("A Warning to the Curious", "Oh, Whistle and I'll Come to You, My Lad"), Lovecraft ("The Shadow over Innsmouth"), Hammer Horror, *The Wicker Man* — culminating in a psychedelic/psychotic breakdown (complete with torch-wielding mob of villagers):

He sees jawbones on the street
Advertisements become carnivores
And roadworkers turn into jawbones
And he has visions of islands, heavily covered in slime.
The villagers dance round pre-fabs
And laugh through twisted mouths.

"Jawbone" resembles nothing so much as a *League of Gentlemen* sketch, and the Fall have much more in common with the *League of Gentlemen*'s febrile carnival than with witless imitators such as Pavement. The co-existence of the laughable with that which is not laughable: a description that captures the essence of both the Fall and *The League of Gentlemen*'s grotesque humour.

"White face finds roots"

"Below, black scars winding through the snow showed the main roads. Great frozen rivers and snow-laden forest stretched in all directions. Ahead they could just see a range of old, old mountatins. It was perpetual evening at this time of year, and the further north they went, the darker it became. The white lands seemed uninhabited, and Jerry could easily see how the legends of trolls, Jotunheim, and the tragic gods — the dark, cold, bleak legends of the North — had come out of Scandinavia. It made him feel strange, even anachronistic, as if he had gone back from his own age to the Ice Age."
— Michael Moorcock, *The Final Programme*[3]

On *Hex*'s second side, mutant r and r becomes r and Artaud as the songs become increasingly delirial and abstract. "Who Makes the Nazis" — as lunar as *Tago Mago*, as spacey-desolated as King Tubby at his most cavernous –- is a TV talk show debate rendered as some Jarry-esque pantomime, and composed of leering backing vocals and oneiric-cryptic linguistic fragments: "longhorn breed... George Orwell Burmese police... Hate's not your enemy, love's your enemy, murder all bush monkeys..."

"Iceland", recorded in a lava-lined studio in Reykjavík, is a fantasmatic encounter with the fading myths of North European culture in the frozen territory from which they originated. "White face finds roots", Smith's sleeve-notes tell us. The song, hypnotic and undulating, meditative and mournful, recalls the bone-white steppes of Nico's *The Marble Index* in its arctic atmospherics. A keening wind (on a cassette recording made by Smith) whips through the track as Smith invites us to "cast the runes against your own soul" (another James' reference, this time to his "Casting the Runes").

"Iceland" is rock as *ragnarock*, an anticipation (or is it a recapitulation) of the End Times in the terms of the Norse "Doom of the Gods". It is a *Twilight of the Idols* for the retreating hobgoblins, cobolds and trolls of Europe's receding Weird culture, a lament for the monstrosities and myths whose dying breaths it captures on tape:

Witness the last of the god men...
A Memorex for the Krakens

scritti's sweet sickness[1]

"His new album is called *White Bread, Black Beer*...
'Why? It's pretty much all I live on — Guinness and a lovely, soft, gooey, terribly-bad-for-you white bread from the local Turkish bakery. It's also a reference to when I worked with all these R&B musicians in New York in the 80s — if you played something they didn't like they'd frown and say, "Oh man, that's so white-bread". Meaning that it came from that "white" pop culture which is seen as largely voided of nutrition, substance, goodness, or indeed "soul". And that definitely got my antennae going, because I'm mistrustful of "soul" and I very much like white, processed pop music. Which, in a way, is what this album celebrates.'"
— Interview with Green Gartside, *Time Out*[2]

"Instead of any fulfilment or resolution, Scritti's music delivers the bliss of the lover's discourse in all its ellipses, contradiction and repetition, its endless pursuit of an unattainable object. The disembodied, depthless, non-linear effects, and the borrowing of pop's language of love try to undo desire's usual articulation in coherent drives and stable identity *while reinscribing or repeating the very 'soul' language that's used to complete the self in today's pop*: the sweet *nothings* heard beside, within the sexual healing."
— Paul Oldfield, "After Subversion: Pop Culture and Power"[3]

A fascinating conjunction: listening to Scritti Politti's quietly stunning new album — or rather being seduced and ravished by it — while reading Mladen Dolar's *A Voice and Nothing More*. If, as Simon Reynolds claims,[4] *White Bread, Black Beer* is an album without a "sonic concept", must we conclude that the songs are Green's version of a soul-baring? After all the deferrals, the veilings, the deviations, finally a revelation: *this is me*? The album's title seems to invite such an interpretation, suggesting a negative alchemy, the reversion of sublime agalma into foodstuffs. Without a sonic concept, we are left only with the honey-pure voice, one of the most distinctive in pop — and the voice, so we have always been told, is the bearer of pure presence, guarantor of authenticity and veracity...

This, precisely, is what Dolar challenges. Dolar's claim is not that Derrida was wrong that the voice has been privileged in a certain version of metaphysics, but that this has never been the whole story. "There exists a different metaphysical history of voice, where the voice, far from being the safeguard of presence, was considered to be dangerous, threatening and possibly ruinous."[5] Tellingly, Dolar's alternative history of metaphysics goes via the treatment of music. (Incidentally, it is hard not to read Plato's admonition, quoted by Dolar, that "[a] change to a new type of music is something to beware of as a hazard of all our fortunes... [f]or the modes of music are never disturbed without unsettling of the most fundamental political and social conventions" as a critique of both PoMo popism and nostalgic rockism). Dolar's argument is that Law-Logos has always sought to differentiate itself from a voice conceived of as feminine and chaotic, but Logos cannot extirpate the voice, and indeed depends upon it: what is the fundamental expression of the Law if not the voice of the Father?

How could your nothings be so sweet?

What to make of *Green's* voice, then? Or, to pose the same question from the other side: what is the minimal difference that has always separated Scritti's deconstructions from the real thing? There's a tendency to locate Green's undoings and unsettlings on the level of signifiers, as if his subversion were all to do with wordplay, and his voice were merely a site for natural expressivity. But, as Dolar establishes, the "object voice" is *neither* the voice stripped of all sensual qualities in order to become the neutral transmitter of signifiers, *nor* the voice stripped of all signification in order to become a pure source of aesthetic pleasure. With Green's voice, we continually slide between two types of non-sense: the nonsense of "the lover's discourse", the nursery-rhyme-like reiterations of baby-talk phrases that are devoid of meaning, but which are nevertheless the most important utterances people perform or hear; and also the nonsense of the voice as sound, another kind of sweet nothing. That is why Green's lyrics look very different when you read them; the voice almost prevents you hearing them except as senseless sonorous blocks, mechanically repeated refrains.

What is disturbing about *Cupid and Psyche 85* by comparison with the new pop that preceded it is precisely its lack of any self-conscious meta-presence. This is where I slightly disagree with Simon, when he argues that *Cupid and Psyche* is "*about* love rather than in love". It seems to me that what makes *Cupid and Psyche* so disturbingly depthless is precisely the absence of that space between the song's form and the subject; the songs instantiate the lover's discourse, they do not comment on it. *Cupid and Psyche's* songs, creepily, aren't *about* anything, any more than love itself is. Compare *Cupid and Psyche* with ABC's *The Lexicon of Love* (an album of love songs *about* love songs, if ever there was one), for instance. Martin Fry's presence is ubiquitous in *The Lexicon of Love*, manifesting itself in every raised eyebrow and set of inverted commas. But on *Cupid and Psyche* we get precious little sense of a "real", biographical Green behind or beyond the record; as opposed to self-consciousness, we have "reflexivity without a self (not a bad name for the subject)."[6] There is only the void, the voice and the signifying chain, unraveling forever in a shopping mall of mirrors, a whispering gallery of sweet nothings... But what is disturbing about *Cupid and Psyche* is the suggestion that *this* really *is* love, this impersonal, idiot rhyming is all love is. That is why *Cupid and Psyche* is far more unsettling than the supposed "reversion to a pre-linguistic condition" of the "Kristevan" psychedelic rock celebrated by Simon in the late Eighties (and mentioned in the Paul Oldfield essay I cited above as a point of comparison with Scritti); the supposed "oceanic dissolution of self" assumes not only that such a dissolution can be attained, but that there is a "real self" that can be dissolved. Like the first two Roxy albums, *Cupid and Psyche*'s message is far more radical: the supposed "real", "authentic" self, with its emotional core, is a structural illusion; our most treasured "inner" feelings are trite repetitions; there is no intimate, only an extimate.

I guess it's a sickness/that keeps me wanting...

The excess of Green's voice resides in its sweetness, a sweetness that seems unhealthy, sickly, which puts us on our guard even as it seduces us. Green's voice is synthetic, candied, rather than authentic, wholesome. It already sounds inhuman, so that, upon first hearing rave's pitched-up chirruping vocals, the obvious comparison was with Scritti's androgynous cooing. All of this is anticipated on the track that I find most captivating when I listen to *Cupid and Psyche* now, the machine ballad, "A Little Knowledge", in which Green duets with what sounds like a woman, but which is in fact a Fairlight-sprite, a synthetic succubus constructed from his own voice pitched up. (This exchange with a synthetic spectre happens before the "real woman", session singer B.J. Nelson, officially comes in...)

It's worth remembering at this point that Green is very much the white ghost at the revel of contemporary black pop. At least since *More Brilliant Than Sun*, disco, techno and house's (non)roots in white synthetics have been exposed — Moroder inducting Donna Summer into a labyrinth of synthesizers, Chic wanting to be Roxy Music, Cybotron stealing Ultravox's accents and sound — but *Cupid and Psyche*'s function as a template for contemporary R&B is far less rehearsed. Specifically via its influence on Jam and Lewis' production of Janet Jackson's epochal *Control*, but more generally through its intuition — or entrepreneurial leap — that the flesh and blood of (what was then called) soul could be sutured with hip-hop's artificiality and abstraction machine, *Cupid and Psyche* instituted a "new paradigm" for globalised pop. Skank Bloc Bologna has become the blobal retail arcade of capital. *Cupid and Psyche* is chillingly impersonal, but in a way that is much different to the *staged* impersonality of Kraftwerk, Numan and Visage which fascinated black American hip-hoppers, techno and house pioneers in the early Eighties. Scritti's erasure of soul goes by way of a neurotically note-perfect, ultra-fastidious simulation of a hyper-Americanised "language of love". It is no longer a matter of technical machines versus real emotional beings, but of "authentic emotion" as itself the refraining of signifying and sonorous machines. (It is therefore no surprise that another destroyer of soul, Miles Davis, should have covered Scritti songs and collaborated with Green.)

All of which goes some way to explaining the title of the new album, which initially seems grossly inappropriate, since the songs' souffle lightness could not be further from carnal carbohydrate stodge or beery bloating. But what if these substances are not "basic" and "life-giving" but the non-vital excess without which life would be nothing? What if "white bread" indicates not the normal and the nutritious but the synthetic, and "black" beer indicates not the homey and the heavy but the addictive?

There is a performative flatness about the opening track and first single, "The Boom Boom Bap"; it a song about longing and addiction, which is itself arrestingly, gorgeously addictive. I can honestly say that I was hooked from the moment I heard Green sing the opening phrase, the song's title. "The Boom Boom Bap" is so sublimely, achingly poised that the temptation is to keep hitting rewind, to remain lost in the song's plateau, in which pop's habitual urgencies are anti-climatically suspended.

Play it over and over again/play it over and over again

"The Boom Boom Bap", as Green told Simon, is ostensibly about the thin line "between being in love with something and being unhealthily addicted to it". The three addictions with which the song deals are drinking, hip-hop — "the title itself is named after hip-hop's bass-boom and syncopated breakbeats" — and love. Addiction is the pathological motor of life. "The beat of my life" is not any natural, biological rhythm but the non-organic pulse of the (death) drive. "If hooks could kill", Green muses, knowing that of course they can; that being hooked can be lethal, but that not being hooked on anything is even more deadly and deadening.

When you do eventually pull yourself out of the honeyed embrace of "The Boom Boom Bap", you find yourself yielding to an album of folds and fragments, slivers and sketches, in which everything comes to an end before you expect it to (amplifying your longing to hear it, again and again). Thankfully, Green's obsession with hip-hop emerges not through the brute presence of rap (what could be more present, now, than rap?), but via a certain absence in the production which prevents the tracks ever closing into organic wholeness.

I was discussing with Owen the other week how mid-Eighties technology drew almost all pop into an arid, dated, hyper-glossed blandness: the two most conspicuous exceptions to this trend were *Cupid and Psyche* (which succeeds precisely because of its total identification with the time and the technics) and Kate Bush's *Hounds of Love*. *White Bread, Black Beer* is like Green's late-arriving *Hounds of Love*, an album in which pop's history (and his own) can be re-visited without being reiterated, in which styles can be traversed without their ever being a question of inconsistent eclecticism. The very refusal to strain for contemporaneity makes the album far more now than it would have been if it engaged in an unseemly pursuit of street cool.

The references to London, to "British Homes Stores", to the names of Green's schoolteachers, restore some of the locality that was remorselessly stripped away by the proto-Starbucks "third place" mid-Atlantic sheen of *Cupid and Psyche*. This, evidently, also means a restoration of some biographical specificity; the songs are no longer lover's labyrinths that anyone can enter, but memory lanes some of whose landmarks only Green can recognise. Amidst all of the trails of influence you can trace across the album, those Appolinians, Brian Wilson and Paul McCartney, recur most insistently. Would the album then be a redemption through melody? A recovery — from sickness? A recovery — of the self?

And when I'm with you baby
I know just who I am
And no one understands the way that you do
Darling

Hearing Green sing lines like these is a curiously haunting and unsettling experience, since Green's voice carries with it all those *Cupid and Psyche* traces which ironise and undercut any gestures towards "really meaning it" or "really being" anything. In any case, listen closer to the song in which those lines occur ("Locked"), and all is not as it seems. "People want a piece of me", Green sings, "but who they get is not what *she* seems". In any case, autobiography would still be a form of *writing* (and the most deceptive kind), and the "you" that is the usual addressee of the love song is never the ostensible partner, the "real flesh and blood person", but the big Other. Hence David Kelsey in Highsmith's *This Sweet Sickness* — a Scritti title if ever there was one — a man who conducts his pathological love affair primarily through letters written to his fantasised Other (and which are ignored and misunderstood by their supposed flesh and blood object), is the lover in its purest state... All the parallels of love with addiction on *White Bread, Black Beer* suggest that Green *the writer* still knows that love is essentially both pathology and cure, so Scritti's sweetness remains sick, their sickness sweet...

postmodernism as pathology, part 2[1]

The thing is, Robbie, there's no rehabilitation from PoMo.

The sickness that afflicts Robbie Williams is nothing less than postmodernity itself. Look at Williams: his whole body is afflicted with reflexive tics, an ego-armoury of grimaces, gurns and grins designed to disavow any action even as he performs it. He is the "as if" pop star — he dances *as if* he is dancing, he emotes *as if* he is emoting, at all times scrupulously signalling — with perpetually raised eyebrows — that he doesn't mean it, it's just an act. He wants to be loved for "Rudebox" but, unfortunately for him, his audience demands the mawkish sentimentality of "Angels". How Robbie must hate that song now, with its humbling reminders of dependency (Williams' career went into the stratosphere on the basis of "Angels") and lost success...

Let me entertain you, let me lead you

There's surely a Robin Carmody-type analysis to be done of the parallels between Williams and Tony Blair. Williams' first album, the tellingly-titled *Life Thru a Lens* was released in 1997, the year of Blair's first election victory. There followed for both a period of success so total that it must have confirmed their most extravagant fantasies of omnipotence (Blair unassailable at two elections; Williams winning more Brit awards than any other artist). Then, a decade after their first success, an ignominious decline into irrelevance (the post-Iraq Blair limping out of office as a lame-duck leader, Williams releasing a disastrous album and checking himself into rehab on the day before this year's Brit awards, at which he had received a derisory single nomination). Of course, there are limits to the analogy: Blair is popular in the States, whereas Robbie...

Williams and Blair are two sides of one Joker Hysterical face: two cracked actors, one given over to the performance of sincerity, the other dedicated to the performance of irony. But both, fundamentally, actors — actors to the

349

core, to the extent that they resemble PKD simulacra, shells and masks to which one cannot convincingly attribute any inner life. Blair and Williams seem to exist only for the gaze of the other. That is why it is impossible to imagine either enduring private doubts or misgivings, or indeed experiencing any emotion whose expression is not contrived to produce a response from the other. As is well known, Blair's total identification with his publicly-projected messianic persona instantly transforms any putatively private emotion into a PR gesture; this is the spincerity effect (even if he really means what he is saying, the utterance becomes fake by dint of its public context). The image of Blair or Williams alone in a room, decommissioned androids contemplating their final rejection by a public which once adored them, is genuinely creepy.

It is perfectly possible to imagine Robbie exhibiting *public* doubts, of course — indeed, as his former reflexive potency declines into reflexive impotence, he is most likely to be seen insisting upon his inadequacy and failure. No doubt this is why Williams' announcement of his "addiction" to anti-depressants and caffeine has been greeted with a certain scepticism (suspicion has been aroused in part because of the timing of the announcement, on the eve of the Brits). But this scepticism misses the point. Williams' sickness is, precisely, his incapacity to do or experience anything unless it provokes the attention of the other.

Or: as Liam Gallagher more succinctly put it, in words worthy of Mr Agreeable at his compassionate best:

If you've got a fucking problem, why do you want the whole world to know about it? I say sort yourself out. You make a fucking crap album then want everyone to feel sorry for you. What a fucking tosser.

choose your weapons[1]

People are often telling me that I ought to read Frank Kogan's work, but I've never got around it. (Partly that's because, Greil Marcus apart, I've never really tuned into much American pop criticism at all, which in my no doubt far too hasty judgement has seemed to be bogged down in a hyper-stylised faux-naif gonzoid mode that has never really appealed to me.) The — again, perhaps unfair — impression I have is that, in Britain, the battles that Kogan keeps on fighting were won, long ago, by working-class autodidact intellectuals. No doubt the two recent pieces by Kogan that Simon has linked to are grotesquely unrepresentative of his work as a whole (I certainly hope so, since it is difficult to see why so many intelligent people would take his work seriously if they weren't), but it's hard not to read them as symptomatic, not only of an impasse and a malaise within what I now hesitate to call "popism", but of a far more pervasive, deeply-entrenched cultural conservatism in which so-called popism is intrinsically implicated.

Remember, in the immediate wake of 9/11, all those po-faced Adornoite proclamations that there would be "no more triviality" in American popular culture after the Twin Towers fell? There can be few who, even when the remains of the Twin Towers were smouldering, really believed that US pop culture would enter a new thoughtful, solemn and serious phase after September 11th — and it's surely superfluous to remember, at this point, that what ensued was a newly vicious cynicism soft-focused by a piety that only a wounded Leviathan assuming the role of aggrieved victim can muster — but would anyone, then, have believed that, only six years later, a supposedly serious critic would write a piece called "Paris [Hilton] is our Vietnam...",[2] especially, when, in those years, there has, like, *been* another Vietnam. What we are dealing with in a phrase like "Paris is our Vietnam" is not trivia — this isn't the collective narcissism of a leisure class ignorant of geopolitics — but a self-conscious *trivialisation*, an act of passive nihilistic transvaluation. Debating the merits or otherwise of a boring heiress have been elevated to the status of a political struggle; and not even by preening aesthetes in some Wildean/Warholian celebration of superficiality, but by middle-aged men in sweat pants, sitting on the spectator's armchair at the end of history and dissolutely flicking through the channels.

The end of history is the nightmare from which I am trying to awake.

At least the "Paris is Vietnam" piece laid bare the resentment of resentment that I have previously argued is the real libidinal motor of "popism" — "we love Paris *all the more* because others hate her (but luckily we loved her anyway, honest!)". But this latest piece[3] Simon has linked to is, if anything, even more oddly pointless and indicative. Unlike the pleasantly mediocre Paris Hilton LP, the ostensible object of the piece, Backstreet Boys' single "Everybody (Backstreet's Back)" is actually rather good. Practically everyone I know liked it. The problem is the idea that saying this is in some way news in 2007. No word of a lie, I had to check the date on that post, assuming, at first, that it must have been written a decade ago.

The article makes me think that, if the motivating factor with British popists is, overwhelmingly, class, with Americans it might be age. Perhaps those a little deeper into middle age than I am were still subject to the proscriptions and prescriptions of a Leavisite high culture. But it seems to me that popists now are like Mick Jagger confronted with punk in 1976: they don't seem to realise that, if there is an establishment, it is them. Even if the "Nathan" with whom Kogan debates exists — and I'll be honest with you, I'm finding it hard to believe that he does — his function is a fantasmatic one (in the same way that Lacan argued that, if a pathologically jealous husband is proved right about his wife's infidelities, his jealousy remains pathological): for popists to believe that their position is in any way challenging or novel, they have to keep digging up "Nathans" who contest it. But, in 2007, Nathan's hoary old belief that only groups who write their own songs can be valid has been refuted so many times that it is rather like someone mounting a defence of slavery today — sure, there are such people who hold such a view, but the position is so irrelevant to the current conjuncture that it is quaintly antiquated rather than a political threat. There may be a small minority of pop fans who claim to hold Nathan's views; but, given the success of Sinatra, the Supremes, Elvis Presley and the very boybands that popists think it is so transgressive to re-evaluate, those views would in most cases be performatively contradicted by the fans' actual tastes. (Kogan does grant that the problem is not so much fans' tastes as their accounts of them — but the unspoken assumption is that it is alright, indeed mandatory, to contest male rock fans' accounts of their own tastes, but that the aesthetic judgements of the figure with which the popist creepily identifies, the teenage girl, ought never to be gainsaid.) (The other irony is that, if you talk to an actual teenager today, they are far more likely to both like and have heard of Nirvana than they are the Backstreet Boys.)

The once-challenging claim that for certain listeners, the (likes of) Backstreet Boys could have been as potent as (the likes of) Nirvana has been passive-nihilistically reversed — now, the message disseminated by the wider culture — if not necessarily by the popists themselves — is that nothing was ever better than the Backstreet Boys. The old high culture disdain for pop cultural objects is retained; what is destroyed is the notion that there is anything *more valuable* than those objects. If pop is no more than a question of hedonic stim, then so are Shakespeare and Dostoyevsky. Reading Milton, or listening to Joy Division, have been re-branded as just another consumer choice, of no more significance than which brand of sweets you happen to like. Part of the reason that I find the term "popism" unhelpful now is that implies some connection between what I would prefer to call Deflationary Hedonic Relativism and what Morley and Penman were doing in the early Eighties. But their project was the exact inverse of this: their claim was that as much sophistication, intelligence and affect could be found in the pop song as anywhere else. Importantly, the music, and the popular culture of the time, made the argument for them. The evaluation was not some fits-all-eras a priori position, but an intervention at a particular time designed to have certain effects. Morley and Penman were still *critics*, who expected to influence production, not consumer guides marking commodities out of five stars, or executives spending their spare time ranking every song with the word "sugar" in it on live journal communities that are the cyberspace equivalent of public school dorms.

Whereas Morley and Penman (self-taught working-class intellectuals both) complicated the relationship between theory and popular culture with writing that — in its formal properties, its style and its erudition, as well as in its content — *contested* commonsense, Deflationary Hedonic Relativism merely ratifies the empiricist dogmas that underpin consumerism. More than that, Owen Hatherley has astutely observed that, in addition to reiterating the standard Anglo-American bluff dismissal of metaphysics, the Deflationary Hedonistic Relativist disclaiming of theory ("we just like what we like, we don't have a theory") uncannily echoes the dreary mantras of the average *NME* indie band: "we just do what we do, anything else is a bonus", "the music is the only important thing". In the UK, the rhetorical fight between "popists" and indie is as much a phoney war as the parliamentary political punch-and-judy show between Cameron's Tories and Brown's New Labour: a storm in a ruling-class tea-cup. In both cases, the social reality is that of ex-public schoolkids carrying on their inter-house rivalries by other means. In the case of both indie and popism, there is a strangely inverted relationship to populism and the popular. While the "popists" claim to be populist but actually support music that is increasingly marginal in terms of sales figures, the indie types claim to celebrate an alternative while their preferred music of choice (Trad skiffle) has Full Spectrum Dominance (you can't listen to Radio 2 for fifteen minutes without hearing a Kaiser Chiefs song). In many ways, because it was attempting to analyse a genuinely popular phenomenon, Simon's defence of Arctic Monkeys was more genuinely popist than all of the popist screeds on Paris Hilton's barely-bought LP — but of course much of the impulse behind them was the ultra-rockist desire to be seen thumbing one's nose at critical consensus. Witness the *genuinely* pathetic — it certainly provokes pathos in me — attempt to whip up controversy about the workmanlike plod of Kelly Clarkson, on a blog which, in its combination of hysterical overheating and dreary earnestness, is as boring as it is symptomatic — though, I have to confess I have never managed to get to the end of a single post, a problem I have with a great many "popist" writings, including the magnum opus of popism, Morley's *Words and Music*.

Much as he occasionally flails and rails against popist commonplaces (see, for instance, his recent — I would argue unwarranted — attack on Girls Aloud), Morley is as deeply integrated into Deflationary Hedonic Relativist commonsense as Penman is excluded from it. What was the strangely affectless *Words and Music* if not a description of the OedIpod from inside? All those friction-free freeways, those inconsequent consumer options standing in for existential choices… Yet Morley is still a *theorist* of the ends of history and of music, still too obviously in love with intelligence to be fully plugged into the anti-theoretical OedIpod circuitry. Even so, Ian's silence speaks far louder than Morley's chatter, and, after my very few dealings with Old Media, I'm increasingly seeing Ian's withdrawal, not as a tragic failure, but as a noble retreat.

All of UK culture tends to the condition of the clip show, in which talking heads — including, of course, Morley — are paid to say what dimwit posh producers have decided that the audience already thinks over footage of what everyone has already seen. I recently had dealings with an apparatchik of *Very* Old Media. What you get from representatives of VOM is always the same litany of requirements: writing must be "light", "upbeat" and "irreverent'. This last word is perhaps the key one, since it indicates that the sustaining fantasy to which the young agents of Very Old Media are subject is *exactly* the same as the one in which popists indulge: that they are refusing to show "reverence" to some stuffy censorious big Other. But where, in the dreary-bright, dressed-down sarky snarky arcades of postmodern culture, is this "reverence"? What is the postmodern big Other if it is not this "irreverence" itself? (Only people who have not been in a university humanities dept for a quarter of a century — i.e. not at all your bogstandard Oxbridge grad Meeja employee/leisure-time popist — could really believe that there is some ruthlessly-policed high-culture canon. When Harold Bloom wrote *The Western Canon* it was as a *challenge* to the relativism that is hegemonically dominant in English Studies.) I've quickly learned that "light", "upbeat" and "irreverent" are all codes for "thoughtless" and "mundanist". Confronted with these values and their representatives — who, as you would expect, are *much posher than me* –– I often encounter a cognitive dissonance, or rather a dissonance between affect and cognition. Faced with the Thick Posh People who staff so much of the media, I *feel* inferiority — their accents and even their *names* are enough to induce such feelings — but *think* that they must be wrong. It is this kind of dissonance that can produce serious mental illness; or — if the conditions are right — rage.

Anti-intellectualism is a ruling-class reflex, whereby ruling-class stupidity is attributed to the masses (I think we've discussed here before the ruse of the Thick Posh Person whereby make a show of *pretending* to be thick in order to conceal that they are, in fact, thick.) It's scarcely surprising that inherited privilege tends to produce stupidity, since, if you do not need intelligence, why would you take the trouble to acquire it? Media dumbing down is the most banal kind of self-fulfilling prophecy.

As Simon Frith and Jon Savage long ago noted in their *NLR* essay, "The Intellectuals and the Mass Media", which Owen Hatherley recently brought to my attention again, the plain common-man pose of the typical public school and Oxbridge-educated media commentator trades on the assumption that these commentators are far more in touch with "reality" than anyone involved in theory. The implicit opposition is between media (as transparent window-on-the-world transmitter of good, solid commonsense) and education (as out-of-touch disseminator of useless, elitist arcanery). Once, media was a contested ground, in which the impulse to educate was in tension with the injunction to entertain. Now –– and the indispensable Lawrence Miles is incisive on this, as on so many other things, in his latest compendium of insights — Old Media is almost totally given over to a vapid notion of entertainment — and so, increasingly, is education.[4]

In my teenage years, I certainly benefited far more from reading Morley and Penman and their progeny than from the middlebrow dreariness of much of my formal education. It's because of them, and later Simon and Kodwo, et al., that I became interested in theory and bothered to pursue it in postgraduate study. It is essential to note that Morley and Penman were not just an "application" of high theory to low culture; the hierarchical structure was scrambled, not just inverted, and the use of theory in this context was as much a challenge to the middle-class assumptions of Continental Philosophy as it was to the anti-theoretical empiricism of mainstream British popular culture. But now that teaching is itself being pressed into becoming a service industry (delivering measurable outputs in the form of exam results) and teachers are required to be both child minders and entertainers, those working in the education system who still want to induce students into the complicated enjoyments that can be derived from going beyond the pleasure principle, from encountering something difficult, something that runs counter to one's received assumptions, find themselves in an embattled minority. *Here we are now entertain us.*

The credos of ruling-class anti-intellectualism that most Old Media professionals are forced to internalise are far more effective than the Stasi ever was in generating a popular culture that is unprecedentedly monotonous. Put it this way: a situation in which Lawrence Miles languishes, at the limits of mental health, barely able to leave his house, while the likes of Rod Liddle swagger around the mediascape is not only aesthetically abhorrent, it is fundamentally unjust. Contrary to the "it's only hedonic stim" deflationary move that both Stekelmanites and popists share, popular culture remains immensely important, even if it only serves an essential ideological function as the background noise of a capitalist realism which naturalises environmental depredation, mental health plague and sclerotic social conditions in which mobility between classes is lessening towards zero.

A class war is being waged, but only one side is fighting.
Choose your side. Choose your weapons.

variations on a theme[1]

Music critic Paul Morley has written a catalogue essay to accompany a recent installation by American artist Cory Arcangel, *a couple thousand short films about Glenn Gould* (2007). Or rather, Morley has assembled most of the text in the same way that Arcangel assembled his video montage — from fragments found on the internet. Arcangel's installation consists of a version of Bach's *Goldberg Variations* (1741) meticulously constructed from YouTube samples of individual notes played by amateurs. By making the connection between YouTube and Gould, the bricolages invite a comparison between user-generated content and the production methods of the modernist-creator figure.

Does user-generated content make possible a new form of artistry, prefigured in both Gould's approach to the recording studio and in Wendy Carlos' synthesizer renditions of Bach? Or are Gould and Carlos being positioned as anticipating the dissolution of the individual artist in an anonymous digital network?

Morley's own position on these questions has been studiedly equivocal. Originally a journalist at the *NME* in the late 1970s, Morley has found himself gradually absorbed into the 1990s clip-show culture of chatty ephemera. His embrace of superficiality and gloss in the early Eighties played more than a small part in ushering that culture in, though what was envisaged as a revolt against post-punk austerity plays very differently in today's pervading climate of populism. In the introductory section of Morley's recent catalogue essay — seemingly the only section that he wrote as such — the text is positioned as the sequel to his 2003 book, *Words and Music: A History Of Pop In The Shape Of A City*. Morley is averse to definitive claims, but *Words And Music* seemed to want to establish a continuity between high modernism and pop at its most apparently disposable, a continuity exemplified by the book's opening juxtaposition of Kylie Minogue and experimental composer

Alvin Lucier. But Morley's ultimate motive was artfully veiled by a spaghetti junction of convolutions and deferrals; it was unclear whether he sought to vindicate the avant-garde through its impact on popular culture or to ennoble pop via its incorporation of the avant-garde, or both, or neither.

His Arcangel essay retains a certain amount of this ambivalence, but, in its gnomic brevity, it is far more suggestive than the often tiresome *Words And Music*, which felt at times like being trapped inside an interminable series of iPod playlists. Via thumbnail portraits of the likes of Gould, Carlos, the BBC Radiophonic Workshop's Delia Derbyshire, Genesis P-Orridge and Robert Moog, the montage follows a number of associative lines connecting music, transgendering and electronics. By paralleling Arcangel's methodology, Morley might have wanted to imply that the electronic music of the Sixties, Seventies and Eighties paved the way for the networked world of user-generated content of which YouTube is a part. But the pop examples that figure in the text most insistently — Gary Numan, the Human League — belong not to this decade, but to a post-punk moment thirty years ago. Perhaps in spite of itself, the text ends up reading less like a justification of twenty-first-century popular culture and its modes of consumption and more like a requiem for a past moment of popular modernism, a lost circuit between pop, new technological developments and the avant-garde.

Morley's text implicitly poses some of the questions which an essay in *Philosophy Now* by Alan Kirby addresses explicitly.[2] Kirby talks of a new type of "text" — a text we are all now very familiar with — "whose content and dynamics are invented or directed by the participating viewer or listener (although these latter terms, with their passivity and emphasis on reception, are obsolete: whatever a telephoning *Big Brother* voter or a telephoning 6-0-6 football fan are doing, they are not simply viewing or listening)." Oddly, Kirby labels these texts "pseudo-modernist", arguing that this "pseudo-modernism" has now superseded postmodernism. Kirby's understanding of postmodernism suffers from being exclusively derived from literary studies, which has defined postmodernism narrowly, in terms of a set of reflexive strategies based around so-called "meta-fictions" such as Vladimir Nabokov's *Pale Fire* (1962). But far from marking a move *beyond* postmodernism, the shift from creator to recipient, from producer to consumer, that Kirby describes is exactly what the most acute theorists of postmodernism — Jean Baudrillard and Fredric Jameson — had long ago got to grips with. Reading Baudrillard's texts from the 1970s, with their extended discussions of reality TV and the "referendum mode", is to confront analyses that now seem preternaturally prescient. What has been made obsolete is not Baudrillard and Jameson's mordant anticipations of the monotony that would ensue in the name of viewer and consumer "involvement", but those positions which claimed that eroding the privilege of the author and the artist carries a subversive charge.

What Kirby calls the "new weightless nowhere of silent autism" has eroded the popular modernism which Morley once belonged to just as much as it has eliminated the high cultural resources of traditional modernism. As Kirby indicates, far from leading to new forms, user-generated content has tended towards retrenchment and consolidation — for example, YouTube (for the most part) recycles old material, or else provides a space in which millions of aspirant stars ape idols whose status — established by the old systems of distribution and valuation — remains secure. Instead of being cowed by the relentless demands for viewer participation, both cultural producers and the much-derided "gatekeepers" need to find new ways of asserting the primacy of production over consumption. They need to find ways of stepping outside seamless circuits in which "everyone" is implicated but no one gets what they want. In another catalogue essay for *a couple thousand short films*, curator Steven Bode argues that Arcangel's installation is "less an advert for networked participatory culture than an index of people's increasing atomisation". If postmodern culture presents a kind of networked solipsism, perhaps what Gould can now teach us most is the value of *disappearance* from the screens that eagerly seek our image. Gould, who famously retired early from concert playing, showed that sometimes it is necessary to withdraw in order to find better ways to connect.

running on empty[1]

In 2006, James Kirby, the man behind the V/Vm record label and the Caretaker, began a download project called *The Death of Rave*. The tracks have a thin, almost translucent quality, as if they are figments or phantoms of the original, exhilarating sound of rave. When I interviewed Kirby recently, he explained that the project had been initiated to commemorate a certain energy that he believes has disappeared from dance music. (*Energy Flash* was, of course, the title the critic Simon Reynolds gave to his compendious study of rave music and its progeny.) The question is: were rave and its offshoots jungle and garage just that — a sudden flash of energy that has since dissipated? More worryingly, is the death of rave only one symptom of an overall energy crisis in culture? Are cultural resources running out in the same way as natural resources are?

Those of us who grew up in the decades between the 1960s and the 1990s became accustomed to rapid changes in popular culture. Theorists of future shock such as Alvin Toffler and Marshall McLuhan plausibly claimed that our nervous systems were themselves sped up by these developments, which were driven by the development and proliferation of technologies. Popular artefacts were marked with a technological signature that dated them quite precisely: new technology was clearly audible and visible, so that it would be practically impossible, say, to confuse a film or a record from the early 1960s with one from even half a decade later.

The current decade, however, has been characterised by an abrupt sense of deceleration. A thought experiment makes the point. Imagine going back fifteen years in time to play records from the latest dance genres — dubstep, or funky, for example — to a fan of jungle. One can only conclude that they would have been stunned — not by how much things had changed, but by how little things have moved on. Something like jungle was scarcely imaginable in 1989, but dubstep or funky, while by no means pastiches, sound like extrapolations from the matrix of sounds established a decade and a half ago.

Needless to say, it is not that technology has ceased developing. What has happened, however, is that technology has been decalibrated from cultural form. The present moment might in fact be best characterised by a discrepancy between the onward march of technology and the stalling, stagnation and retardation of culture. We can't hear technology any more. There has been a gradual disappearance of the sound of technological rupture — such as the irruption of Brian Eno's analogue synth in the middle of Roxy Music's "Virginia Plain", or the cut-and-paste angular alienness of early rave — that pop music once taught us to expect. We still see technology, perhaps, in cinema CGI, but CGI's role is somewhat paradoxical: its aim is precisely to make itself invisible, and it has been used to finesse an already established model of reality. High-definition television is another example of the same syndrome: we see the same old things, but brighter and glossier.

The principal way in which technology now makes itself felt in culture is of course in the areas of distribution and consumption. Downloading and Web 2.0 have famously led to new ways of accessing culture. But these have tended to be parasitic on old media. The law of Web 2.0 is that everything comes back, whether it be adverts, public information films or long-forgotten TV serials: history happens first as tragedy, then as YouTube. The pop artists who supposedly became successful because of web clamour (Sandi Thom, Arctic Monkeys) turned out to be quaintly archaic in form; in any case, they were pushed through the familiar promotional machinery of big record companies and PR firms. There is peer-to-peer distribution of culture, but little sign of peer-to-peer production.

The best blogs are one exception; they have bypassed the mainstream media, which, for the reasons described by Nick Davies in last year's *Flat Earth News*, has become increasingly conservative, dominated by press releases and PR. In general, however, Web 2.0 encourages us to behave like spectators. This is not only because of the endless temptations to look back offered by burgeoning online archives, it is also because, thanks to the ubiquity of recording devices, we find ourselves becoming archivists of our own lives: we never experience live events, because we are too busy recording them.

Yet instantaneous exposure deprives cultures of the time and space in which they can grow. There is as yet no Web 2.0 equivalent of the circuit that sustained UK dance music in the 1990s: the assemblage of dubplates, pirate radio and the dance floor which acted as a laboratory for the development of new sounds. This circuit was still punctuated by particular moments (the club night, the radio broadcast), but, because anything in Web 2.0 can be replayed at any time, its temporality is more diffuse. The tendency seems to be for a kind of networked solipsism, a global system of individuals consuming an increasingly homogeneous culture alone in front of the computer screen or plugged in to iPod headphones.

All of this makes Fredric Jameson's theories about postmodern culture's inability to image the present more compelling than ever. As the gap between cultural breaks becomes ever longer and the breaks themselves become ever more modest and slight, it is beginning to look as if the situation might be terminal. Alex Williams, who runs the *Splintering Bone Ashes* blog, goes so far as to claim that "what we have experienced is merely a blip, perhaps never to be again repeated — 150 or so years of extreme resource bingeing, the equivalent of an epic amphetamine session. What we are already experiencing is little more than the undoubtedly grim 'comedown' of the great deceleration." This might be too bleak. What is certainly clear, however, is that technology will not deliver new forms of culture all on its own.

you remind me of gold: dialogue with mark fisher and simon reynolds[1]

Kaleidoscope Magazine: The first question is linked to my experiencing UK dance music of the Nineties as a person living in a different country — via imported records and the British music press — and one interesting thing was the idea of "futurism" that seemed to permeate the scenes: in terms of how the press presented the music as an area of advancement because made with "machines". What are, if any, are the futuristic elements and aspects in UK Nineties dance music and culture?

Simon Reynolds: The word "future" does not crop up in contemporary dance music discourse — in either the conversations surrounding the music, or in track titles and artist names — with anything like the frequency it did during the Nineties. From artists with names like Phuture, the Future Sound of London, Phuture Assassins, etc. to UK rave/early jungle which teemed with titles like "Futuroid", "Living for the Future", "We Are the Future", etc., the whole culture seemed tilted forwards. Everyone was in a mad rush to reach tomorrow's sound ahead of everyone else. That ethos continued into the early days of dubstep with the club name FWD». But looking at the last half-decade or so of UK dance music, I really struggle to think of any equivalent examples. Soul Jazz just put out a compilation of post-dubstep called *Future Bass*, and then you have the "future garage" sub-genre, although the irony here is that this direction involves going back to the 2step rhythm template circa 1998-2000. But generally speaking the whole idea of the future seems to have lost its libidinal charge for electronic producers and for fans alike. This seems to reflect the fact that dance music in the UK, and globally, is no longer organised along an extensional axis (projecting into the unknown, like an arrow fired into the night sky) but is intensive: it makes criss-crossing journeys within the vast terrain that

365

was mapped out during the hyper-speed Nineties.

It seems symptomatic to me that "Gold", the single off the debut album by Darkstar, is a cover of a Human League b-side from almost thirty years ago. It's definitely an interesting move for Darkstar to make, in terms of their previous music and the scene they're from, dubstep. But as an aesthetic act the creativity involved is curatorial rather than innovation in the traditional-modernist sense: it's about finding an obscure, neglected song and re-situating it within the historical narratives of British electronic music. The whole idea of doing a cover version, which is totally familiar as an artistic move within rock, is still pretty unusual within electronic music culture. What also struck me listening to the remake next to the original (which I'd never heard before) is that both versions sound more or less as "futuristic" as each other. Well, the Darkstar reinterpretation obviously is technically more advanced in many ways; there are things done on it sonically that weren't available to the Human League and their producer Martin Rushent. But in terms of the overall aesthetic sensation generated, neither version seems any further "into the future" than the other. Certainly, it doesn't feel like there's thirty years difference between the two. And it's that precisely that feeling — that the Human League are contemporary with us — that is so mysterious and hard to explain. They ought to sound to us as ancient as early Fifties fare (Johnny Ray, say, or Louis Jordan) would have done in 1981 heard next to the Human League of "Love Action".

Mark Fisher: The problem is that the word "futuristic" no longer has a connection with any future that anyone expects to happen. In the Seventies, "futuristic" meant synthesizers. In the Eighties, it meant sequencers and cut and paste montage. In the Nineties, it meant the abstract digital sounds opened up by the sampler and its function such as time-stretching. In each of these cases, there was a sense that, through sound, we were getting a small but powerful taste of a world that would be completely different from anything we had hitherto experienced. That's why a film like *Terminator*, with its idea of the future invading the present, was so crucial for Nineties dance music. Now, insofar as "futuristic" has any meaning, it is as a vague but fixed style, a bit like a typographical font. "Futuristic" in music is something like "Gothic" in fonts. It points to an already existing set of associations. "Futuristic" means something electronic, just as it did in the Sixties and Seventies. We've entered the flattened out temporality that Simon describes — the Nineties ought to be as distant as the Sixties felt in 1980, but now the Sixties, the Eighties and the Nineties belong to a kind of postmodern-curatorial simultaneity.

To take up the example that Simon uses. When you compare the Darkstar cover of "Gold" to the Human League original, it's not just that one is no more futuristic than the other. It is that neither are futuristic. The Human

League track is clearly a superseded futurism, while the Darkstar track seems to come after the future. I should say at this point that the Darkstar album is my favourite album of the year — I've become obsessed with it. (It might be worth noting here that one thing that's happened since 2000 in dance music is the rise of the album. The Nineties was about scenes and singles; there weren't any great albums. But since 2000, there have been Dizzee Rascal's debut, the Junior Boys records, the two Burial albums and the Darkstar record. The temporal malaise I'm talking about hasn't meant there are no good records — that's not the problem at all.) Partly why I enjoy the Darkstar album is because, like many of the most interesting records of the last six or seven years, it seems to be about the failure of the future. This feeling of mourning lost futures isn't so explicit as it was with the Burial records, but I believe it's there at some level with Darkstar. Where with Burial you have a feeling of dereliction and spectrality, the lost future haunting the dead present, with Darkstar it's a question of electronic rot, digital interference.

What you could hear behind so much Nineties dance music was a competitive drive — to sonically rearticulate what "futuristic" meant. The No U Turn track "Amtrak" features a sample: "Here is a group trying to accomplish one thing, and that is to get into the future." But I think it's uncontroversial to say that no one was aiming to get into the future that actually arrived. If a junglist were pitched straight into now from the mid-Nineties, it's hard to believe that they wouldn't be disappointed and bemused. In the interview that I did with Kodwo Eshun which formed the appendix of Kodwo's *More Brilliant Than the Sun*, he contrasts the textual exhaustion of postmodernism with the genetic concept of recombination. I think Kodwo captures very well the recombinatorial euphoria that many of us felt then — the sense that there were infinite possibilities, that new and previously unimaginable genres would keep emerging, keep surprising us. But, sadly, what's surprising from that Nineties perspective is how little has changed in the last ten years. As Simon has said, the changes that you can hear now are not massive rushes of the future, but tiny incremental shifts. That deceleration has brought with it a sense of massively diminished expectations, which no amount of tepid boosterism can cover over. My friend Alex Williams has posited the idea that cultural resources have been depleted in the same way that natural resources were. Perhaps this is a reflection of today's cultural depression in the same way that the Nineties concepts were an expression of that decade's exhilaration.

This isn't just about nostalgia for one decade — the Nineties was at the end of a process that began with the rapid development of the recording industry after the Second World War. Music became the centre of the culture because it was consistently capable of giving the new a palpable form; it was a kind of lab that focused and intensified the convulsions that culture

CHOOSE YOUR WEAPONS: WRITING ON MUSIC

was undergoing. There's no sense of the new anywhere now. And that's a political and a technological issue, not a problem that's just internal to music.

SR: The Darkstar album could almost have been designed to please me: it's the convergence of the hardcore continuum, hauntology, and post-punk and new pop! It's growing on me, but initially I found it a bit washed-out and listless. Still, Mark's reading of it is typically suggestive. And I do think it is significant that an outfit operating in the thick of the post-dubstep scene, the FWD» generation, has made a record steeped in echoes of Orchestral Manoeuvres (their first LP in particular was apparently listened to heavily during the album's making), New Order, and other early-Eighties synthpop. It also means something that a record coming out of dance culture is all about isolation, regret, withdrawal, mournfulness.

The Darkstar record is an example of a self-conscious turn towards emotionality in UK dance. Most of the album features a human voice and songs, sung by a new member of the group recruited specifically for that role. And just this week I've read about two other figures from the same scene — James Blake and Subeena — who are releasing their first tracks to feature their own vocals. But this turn to expressivity seems to me as much rhetorical as it is actually going on in the music. After all hardcore, jungle, UK garage, grime, bassline house were all bursting with emotion in their different ways. What people mean by "emotional" is introspective and fragile in ways that we've rarely seen in hardcore continuum music. (Obviously we've seen plenty of that in IDM going back to its start: Global Communications and Casino in Japan actually made records inspired by the death of family members.) The idea that artists and commentators are groping towards, without fully articulating, is that dance music no longer provides the kind of emotional release that it once did, through collective catharsis. So there is this turn inwards, and also a fantasy of a kind of publicly displayed inwardness: the widely expressed artistic ideal of "I want my tracks to make people cry on the dancefloor". Because if people were getting their release in the old way (collective euphoria), why would tears be needed.

MF: I think part of the reason I like the Darkstar record so much is that I don't hear it as a dance record. In my view, it's better heard almost as mainstream pop that has been augmented by some dance textures. "Aidy's Girl is a Computer" apart, if you heard the record without knowing the history, you wouldn't assume any connection with dubstep. At the same time, *North* isn't straightforwardly a return to a pre-dance sound. Much has been made of the synthpop parallels but — and the cover of the Human League track brings this out — it doesn't actually sound very much like Eighties synthpop at all. It's more a continuation of a certain mode of electronic pop that got curtailed sometime in the mid-Eighties.

SR: In the Nineties, drugs — specifically Ecstasy — were absolutely integral to this communal release. One of the reasons hardcore rave was so hyper-emotional was because its audience's brains were being flooded with artificially stimulated feelings, which could be elation and excitement but also dark or emotionally vulnerable (the comedown from Ecstasy is like having your heart broken). One thing that intrigues me about dance culture in the 2000s is the near-complete disappearance of drugs as a topic in the discourse. People are obviously still doing them, in large amounts, and in a mixed-up polydrug way just like in the Nineties. There have been a few public scares from the authorities and the mainstream media, like the talk about ketamine a few years ago, and more recently with mephedrone. But these failed to catalyse any kind of cultural conversation within the dance scene itself. It is as if the idea that choice of chemicals could have any cultural repercussions or effects on music's evolution has completely disappeared. Compare that with the Nineties, where one of the main strands of dance discourse concerned the transformative powers of drugs. There was a reason why Matthew Collin called his rave history *Altered State* and why I called my own book *Energy Flash*. That was a reference to one of the greatest and most druggy anthems in techno — Beltram's "Energy Flash" (which features a sample about "acid, ecstasy" — but also to the more general idea of a psychedelics-induced flash of revelation or the "body flash" caused by stimulant drugs.

The turn to emotionality at the moment seems like an echo of a similar moment in the late Nineties, when the downsides of drugs were becoming clear and I started to hear from clubbing friends that they'd been listening to Spiritualized or Radiohead. But where that was a flight from E-motionality (from the collective high, now considered false or to have too many negative side effects, towards more introspective, healing music), the new emotionality in the post-dubstep scene is emerging in a different context. I'm just speculating here, but I wonder if it has anything to do with a dissatisfaction with Internet culture, the sort of brittle, distracted numbness that comes from being meshed into a state of perpetual connectivity, but without any real connection of the kind that comes from either one-on-one interactions or from being in a crowd. The rise of the podcast and the online DJ mix, which has been hyped as "the new rave" but is profoundly asocial, seems to fit in here.

KM: The concept of futurism also contains the idea that a cultural form can capture the zeitgeist of an era and facilitate/modulate the vision of the one to come and by implication revolt against past cultural practices; this might also in this case translate with the idea of "the sound of now" that was a vastly common mood of UK dance music in the Nineties, and the continuous re-organisation of label, clubs, promoters, DJs in new networks and sub-genres that created an inbuilt obsolescence in the micro-scenes themselves. A sort of voluntary short-term memory imbalance that is hard to understand in the following decade — the Noughties — in which one of the most original and popular artist has been Burial, which has been one visible manifestation of a fixation with the past which has previously reached similar levels in indie-rock. Not to speak of the literalist approach of a very interesting artist as Zomby in "Where Were U in 92?"

SR: I was totally caught up in the Nineties rave culture and I can testify that there was a sensation of teleology, a palpable feeling that something was unfolding through the music. It would be easy to say in hindsight that this was an illusion but I'd rather honour the truth of how it felt at the time. On a month by month basis, you witnessed the music changing and there seemed to be a logic to its mutation and intensification. From hardcore to darkcore to jungle to drum 'n' bass to techstep, it felt like there was a destination, even a destiny, for the music's relentless propulsion across the 1991 to 1996 timespan. I entered the scene in late 91, when the "journey" was already well underway, so you could say that the trajectory started as far back as 1988, when acid house originally impacted the UK.

Mine is a London-centric viewpoint, but similar trajectories were unfolding in Europe, with the emergence of gabba, and trance, or the evolution of minimal techno. There was a linear, extensional development, along an axis of intensification. Each stage of the music superseded the preceding one, like the stages of a rocket being jettisoned as it escapes the Earth's atmosphere. And you are right that there was a forgetfulness, a lack of concern with the immediate past, because our ears were trained always on the future, the emerging Next Phase.

At a certain point the London-centric hardcore/jungle narrative took a swerve, slowing down in tempo and embracing house music's sensuality, first with speed garage in 1997 and then with the even slower and sexier 2step. But that just seemed like a canny move to avoid an approaching dead end (one that drum 'n' bass would bash its collective head against for... ever since really!) The rhythmic complexification that had developed through drum 'n' bass carried on with speed garage and 2step, just in a less punitive way.

In the Noughties, especially in the last five years, the feeling you get from dance culture and the endless micro shifts within it is quite different — whatever the opposite of teleology is, that's what you got! It is hard to identify centres of energy that could be definitively pinpointed as a vanguard. The closest thing in recent years might well be the populist "wobble" sector within dubstep, if only because there's a kind of escalation of wobble-ness going on there. There is a full-on, hardcore, take-it-to-extremes spirit to wobblestep. Ironically, the dubstep connoisseurs and scene guardians can't stand wobble and have veered off into disparate welter of softcore "musical" directions. Wobble is quite a masculinist sound, it reminds me of gabba. But then it is easy to forget that the Nineties was all about this kind of punishing pursuit of extremes: the beats and the bass were a test to the listener, something you endured as much as enjoyed (or had to take drugs in order to withstand). The evolution of the music was measurable in a experiential, bodily way. Beats got tougher and more convoluted, textures got more scalding to the ear, atmospheres and mood got darker and more paranoid.

Apart from grime and aspects of dubstep, Nineties post-techno music overall seems to have retreated into "musicality" (in the conventional sense of the word) and pleasantness. So instead of that militant-modernist sense of moving forward into the future, the culture's sense of temporality seems polymorphous and recursive. And this applies on the micro as well as macro level: individual tracks seem to have less "thrust" and drive, to be more about involution and recessive details.

Touching on the question of rave nostalgia, the question "Where Were U In 92?" posed by Zomby is interesting on a bunch of levels. There is an echo, possibly unintended, of the marketing slogan for *American Graffiti* ("Where were you in 62?", the year the movie is set), George Lucas's groundbreaking vehicle for mobilising and exploiting generational nostalgia. Then there is also the unexpected biographical fact that Zomby is perfectly capable of saying where he was in 92, because he was twelve and a precocious fan of hardcore rave (which further suggests he must have just followed the trajectory of the music through jungle and speed garage to dubstep just like me and Mark, only quite a bit younger). Even as the album offers a loving pastiche of old skool hardcore, there seems to be an element of mockery of ageing ravers with their "boring stories of glory days" (to quote Springsteen). That would probably appeal to younger dubstep fans who, unlike Zomby, didn't live through rave as participants and probably find the legacy of the hardcore continuum to be an encumbrance, a burden. Finally, it's intriguing that Zomby did this pastiche record as a one-off stylistic exercise, in between much more cutting-edge dubstep records such as the *Zomby* EP on Hyperdub. It suggests that Zomby's generation can play around with vintage styles without the kind of fanatical identification with a lost era that you generally get with musical revivalism. It's just a period style, something to revisit.

MF: The point is that the question "Where were you in 92?" makes sense, whereas the question "Where were you in 02?" (or indeed 08) doesn't. One of the things that has happened over the last decade or so is the disappearance of very distinctive "feels" for years or eras — not only in music but in culture in general. I've got more sense of what 1973 was like than what 2003 was like. This isn't because I've stopped paying attention — on the contrary, I've probably paid more close attention to music this decade than at any other time. But there's very little "flavour" to cultural time in the way there once was, very little to mark out one year from the next. That's partly a consequence of the decline of the modernist trajectory that Simon describes. (One slight difference I have with Simon is that I prefer the term "trajectory" to "teleology". For me, what was exciting about the Nineties — and popular culture between the Sixties and the Nineties — was that sense of forward movement. But it didn't feel linear, as if everything was inevitably heading in one direction towards one goal. Instead, there was a sense of teeming, of proliferation.) If time is marked now, it's by technical upgrades rather than new cultural forms or signatures. But the technical upgrades increasingly seem to be manifested in terms of the distribution and consumption of culture rather than in terms of production. You can't hear or see dramatic formal innovations — but you get a higher definition picture, or a greater storage capacity on your mp3 player. Adam Harper, one of the most interesting young critics, has made a case for the new culture of micro-innovation, arguing that the kind of music culture Simon and I are talking about here — defined in terms of scenes organised around generic formulas — is an historical relic, replaced by a culture of a thousand tiny deviations, an "infinite music", in which the temporal recursion that Simon has referred to is not a problem but a resource. Yet, for me, this sounds suspiciously like the Intelligent Dance Music that people were praising before the hardcore continuum came along. It's easy to forget that disdain for the supposed vulgarity and repetitiveness of scene-music was a critical commonplace until Simon and Kodwo made the case for "scenius" in dance music.

But it seems to me that the phenomenon we're talking about here — temporal flavourlessness — is a symptom of a broader postmodern malaise. Every time I go back to read Fredric Jameson's texts from the Eighties and early Nineties, I'm astonished by their prescience. Jameson was quick to grasp the way in which modernist time was being flattened out into the pastiche-time of postmodernity. When I read some of those texts in the Nineties, I thought that they described certain tendencies in culture, but that this was far from being the only story. Now, there's only a very weak sense of there being any alternative to the postmodern end of history. The question is, is this all temporary or terminal?

SR: I should have also noted that one of the main reasons a sense of linear progress was physically felt during the Nineties was that between 1990 and 1997, techno got faster: there was an exponential rise in beats-per-minute, that accompanied all the other ways in which the music got harder, more rhythmically dense, and so forth. So as a dancer you felt like you were hurtling.

Mark mentions the idea of technical upgrades as the metric for a sense of progression in the last decade. This reminded me of a conversation I had with the Italian DJ and journalist Gabriele Sacchi. In the space of about fifteen minutes, Sacchi went from complaining that there had been no really significant formal advances in dance music since drum 'n' bass (he discounted dubstep, as I recall) to then commenting with approval of how advanced sounding records were now compared with ten years ago. What he meant is that they sounded better in terms of production quality: what's available today in terms of technology, digital software, etc., to someone making, say, a house track, enables them to make much better-sounding records (in terms of drum sounds, the textures, the placement of sounds and layers in the mix). That sounded totally plausible to me and it may well be the defining quality of electronic dance music in the 2000s. You might say that the basic structural features of the various genres were established in the Nineties but what has improved is the level of detailing, refinement and a general kind of production sheen to the music. An analogy might be a shift from architectural innovation (the Nineties) to interior décor (the 2000s). Mark also mentions Fredric Jameson. His work — the big postmodernism book from 1991 but also, especially, *A Singular Modernity* — helped me see that rave in general and the UK hardcore continuum in particular had been a kind of enclave of modernism within a pop culture that was gradually succumbing to postmodernism. Coming out of street beats culture, without hardly any input from art schools and only the most vague, filtered-down notion of musical progress, it nonetheless constituted a kind of self-generated flashback to the modernist adventure of the early twentieth century. The hardcore continuum especially propelled itself forward thanks to an internal temporal scheme of continual rupturing: it kept breaking with itself, jettisoning earlier superseded stages. One small aside in *A Singular Modernity* struck me as both true and funny, when Jameson talks about the modernists being obsessed with measurement, "how do we determine what is really new?". That struck me as the characteristic mindset of those who came up through the Nineties as critics. But the new generation of electronic music writers (and probably musicians too) don't seem to respond to music in this way. It's no longer about the lust for the unprecedented, about linear evolution and the rush into the unknown. It's about tracking these endless involutionary pathways through the terra cognita of dance music history, the tinkering with inherited forms.

KM: Another topic I find very interesting is the fact that the dance music referred to as the hardcore continuum, even if it had an international resonance through the media, has maintained a strong local connotation and a somehow insular development (in other close genres as techno or house the localisation seemed to be less prominent even if, for example, the first ground breaking LP from the band Basement Jaxx resonates with a milieu of influences not too dissimilar to some other post-rave productions). Somehow some of the music in the continuum feels like a sonic cartography of London (or other cities in the UK), responding and being connected to very specific contexts. Is the geographical aspect something you use in the reception of this genres?

SR: Music from the hardcore continuum has obviously found audiences all over the world. The early breakbeat hardcore was universal rave music for a few years in the early Nineties. Jungle established scenes in cities from Toronto to New York to São Paolo and in its later incarnation as drum 'n' bass became a truly international subculture. The same applies to dubstep. And even the more London-centric styles like 2step and grime had really dedicated fans in countries all over the globe and small offshoot scenes in particular cities outside the UK. That said it is incontrovertible that the engine of musical creativity for hardcore continuum genres has always been centred in London, with outposts in other urban areas of the UK that have a strong multiracial composition, particularly Bristol, the Midlands, and certain northern cities like Sheffield, Leeds, and Leicester. The next stage of the music has always hatched in London.

That is related to pirate radio, the competition between DJ and MC crews both within a particular station and between stations. And the sheer number of pirate radio stations owes a lot to the urban landscape of London, the number of tower blocks to broadcast from, and the density of the population, and the existence of a sizeable minority (in both the racial and aesthetic sense) whose musical taste is not catered for by state-run radio or by the commercial radio stations (including the commercial dance station Kiss FM). This competition — expressed through the pirates striving to increase their audience share but also through raves and clubs competing for dancers — is partly economic and partly purely about prestige, aesthetic eminence. And it has stoked the furnace of innovation.

That London-centric system focused around illegal radio stations seems to be gradually disintegrating. It is still what fuels the funky house scene, its primary audience is still "locked on" to the pirate signal. In fact I'm told that there aren't many funky raves or clubs at all, and hardly any vinyl releases or compilations, so the only way to hear funky is through the pirate transmissions. But dubstep, like drum 'n' bass before it, is much more of UK national scene, and also an international scene. Martin Clark, a leading journalist on the scene and also a DJ and recording artist using the name Blackdown, told me something interesting. The Rinse FM show that he and Dusk do, which is eclectic post-dubstep in orientation, gets a high proportion of its audience responses, message and requests, through the internet, from as far afield as Finland or New Zealand (the Rinse FM signal goes out on the internet as well as broadcast through the air). But the pure funky house shows get most of their requests and calls as texts from cellphone users who live within the terrestrial broadcast range of the pirate stations. So funky is still a local scene in the traditional hardcore continuum sense, it is very much East London.

But I think that London-centric orientation is on the decline. Dubstep is fully integrated with the web, it's all about podcasts and DJ mixes circulating on the web, about message board discussions. I think of funky as the "dwarf star" stage of the hardcore continuum: it has shrunk in sise, still emits some heat in the sense of vibe and musical creativity, but it hasn't been able to command attention beyond the pre-converted diehards, in the way that jungle or grime once did. If you look at funky, it's the first hardcore continuum sound not to have any UK chart hits at all. It's not spawned any offshoot scenes in foreign countries. It hasn't achieved critical mass in the sense of non-dance specialist journalists giving it the time of day. Jungle and grime got mainstream coverage because they simply couldn't be ignored, they were so aggressively new and extreme. But funky, to people who don't follow the minutiae of the hardcore continuum, just sounds like "tracky" house music with slightly odd-angled beats and a London flavour. It's not anthemic enough to make it as pop like 2step garage did, but it doesn't have the vanguard credentials of jungle. The interesting thing about the hardcore continuum is the way that during its prime it refuted all that Nineties internet and info-culture rhetoric about deterritorialisation. This was a music culture that derived its strength and fertility from its local nature, precisely from being territorialised. Indeed during the early days of jungle and of grime, it had a kind of fortress mentality. That seems to connect with its vanguardism, this military-modernist mindset.

Another thing is that the hardcore continuum genres were very slow to get integrated with the web. When I did early pieces on 2step garage and grime, the labels and artists had hardly any web presence. Nearly all the interviews I had to do calling mobile phone numbers or speak in person, rather than do email interviews. It was only about 2005 that you started to get grime figures with Myspaces. It was only around then that you started to get tons of DJ sets being uploaded to the web. Before that the music was really hard to get hold of if you didn't live in London, you had to mail order expensive 12"s and CD mixtapes. Now it is totally easy to stay on top of the music no matter where you live. But some of the romance and mystique of the scene has gone as a result.

MF: It's not only UK dance music of the Nineties that is associated with cities; the whole history of popular music is about urban scenes. It's no accident that Motown started in Detroit, house in Chicago, hip-hop in New York... Cities are pressure cookers which can synthesise influences quickly and in a way that is both collective and idiosyncratic. Scenes in city depend on a certain organisation of space and time that cyberspace threatens. For example, the hardcore continuum depended on an ecology of interrelated infrastructural and cultural elements — pirate radio, dub plates, clubs, etc. — but it also relied on these elements being somewhat discrete. For instance, dub plates acted as probe heads, which would be tested out in clubs. But cyberspace has collapsed the differences between making a track at home, releasing it and distributing it. Now it's possible to upload a track into cyberspace immediately, there's less sense of occasion about a record release. So there's a collapsing of time. But alongside this is a collapsing of the importance of spaces. Club spaces were important because of that "evental" time: you would be hearing a track for the first time... But now new tracks in DJs' sets are immediately made available on YouTube. It goes without saying that the club experience is a collective experience — it gains much of its power from people experiencing the same thing in the same space. Cyberspace is much more individuated. Because it isn't a "space" in the way that physical space is, you don't get that sense of coming together. It's more like being involved in a conversation than being in a crowd. Even with instant messaging, there's a delay.

Clearly, there's something potentially positive about people being able to make and release music without worrying about the costs of recording studios, about how it will be distributed and such like. But while this might remove certain obstacles for individuals making music, it's not clear that cyberspace is good for music culture. Urban scenes compressed and concentrated things; cyberspace and digitality are in danger both of making culture too immediate (you can upload a track right now) and too deferred (nothing is ever really finished). The city-based music scene is perhaps one of the things you can hear being mourned on Burial's records, with their many references to London. The "sonic cartography" of London you pick up from Burial's records is in many ways a pirate-radio cartography.

KM: The international reception of some of the sounds in the continuum was the one of a music alternative to what some perceived as the pure recreational hedonism of house music, for example in Italy jungle was embraced by *Centri Sociali* (squats), maybe they were some of the musical genres that help dissolving resistances towards dance music within non clubbers. Maybe this was because of the persisting connections with Jamaican music, maybe because of the dystopian mood/control society references. But apart from this I'd like to know what is, in your opinion, the most significant political significance of these genres?

SR: The major political significance of the hardcore continuum is the role it's played in the emergence of a post-racial Britain. Which has not fully arrived, obviously there is still a lot of racism in Britain, but you could talk about jungle and UK garage especially as having created a post-racial "people" within the UK — it's most obviously a force in the major cities like London and Birmingham and Coventry, but this tribe has members scattered all across the country. It's not just the mix of black and white, it's all sorts. I'm always amazed at the range of ethnicities involved, there's people whose parents are from the Indian sub-continent, or who are Cypriot or Maltese, and you also get every imaginable mix-race combination. Even talking just about "black Britain", it's not just people of Jamaican descent, there's all the other islands in the Caribbean that have their own distinct musical traditions like soca and so forth, and there's also been more recently African immigrants, whose influence is really felt in the Afro flavours you can hear in funky house.

So it's a really rich mix, but I guess the predominant musical flavours that run through the whole span of the continuum involve the collision of British artpop traditions (post-punk, industrial, synthpop) with Jamaica (reggae, dub, dancehall) and also black America (hip-hop, house, Detroit techno). And it's very much a two-way street: it's not just white British youth turning on to bass pressure and speaking in Jamaican patois, it's about second-generation Caribbean-British youth freaking out to harsh Euro techno, having their minds blown by all that early Nineties music out of Belgium. Or someone like Goldie growing up on reggae and jazz-funk but also on groups like PiL and the Stranglers.

You might say that the music of the hardcore continuum reflects the emergence of this post-racial "people" within the UK more than it has created it. But I think it has sped up the process, by being so attractive and so obviously the cutting edge in British popular culture. People have been actively drawn into joining this tribe, it's been an identity many have wanted to embrace, because it's been the coolest music of its era and it's been something to be proud of: a post-racial way of affirming Britishness.

So this I think is a major political achievement for the hardcore continuum. Some commentators like the music theorist Jeremy Gilbert have asked why that never translated into politicisation per se. At various point, particularly with jungle and with grime, there has been a sense that the music has been telling us things about society and what life is like for the British underclass. The darkness and paranoia of jungle (also carried on to an extent with dubstep), and the aggression and self-assertion of grime, reflect the gritty side of urban existence. But there is also a feeling, on my part certainly, that at a certain point simply reflecting Reality isn't enough. Jungle and grime never really managed to get beyond being "gangster rave", which is to say the British equivalent to gangster rap. So across its historical span it has oscillated between darkness (reflecting ghetto life) and brightness (dressing up and looking expensive, partying, dancing to sexy groovy music, chasing the opposite sex — that's the side of the continuum that produced speed garage, 2step, funky house). Apart from the post-racial aspect, the other major achievement of the hardcore continuum is the creation of an autonomous cultural space based around its own media (pirate radio) and its own economic infrastructure (independent labels and record stores). Pirate radio seems particularly significant: the fact that it is community radio, offering the music for free, and that it is amateur, with DJs and MCs actually paying to play (they have to cough up a subscription fee for their air time, to pay for equipment that is lost when the authorities seize transmitters and so forth). Pirate radio is important also because it is public: the culture is underground, but this is an audible underground, it is broadcast terrestrially, blasting out onto the airwaves of London or the other big UK cities. It's a community asserting its existence on the FM radio spectrum. This means that people who don't like the music or the social groups it represents will stumble on it, but also that people who don't know about the music will encounter it — potential converts to the movement. If the pirates went completely online, it would cease to be an underground, it would become much more just a niche market of marginal music going out almost entirely to the pre-converted. The paradox of music undergrounds is that the idea is not really to be totally underground, invisible to the mainstream and the cultural establishment. You don't want to be ignored, you want to be a nuisance! And there is also an interaction between the undergrounds and the mainstream, where ideas from below force their way up into the mainstream and enrich and enliven it. Which then forces the underground to come up with new ideas. That process worked for a really long time with the hardcore continuum: it would develop new ideas that were so obviously advanced and compelling that the major labels would sign artists and big radio stations like BBC and Kiss FM would recruit DJs to host regular shows. It seems to have broken down with funky house, though, it's the first hardcore continuum genre to just stay in its ghetto.

MF: In my book *Capitalist Realism*, I quote an article that Simon wrote on jungle for the *Wire* magazine. Simon put his finger there on how crucial the concept of "reality", of "keeping it real", was for both jungle and US rap. Simon writes of an implied political position in jungle: how it was anti-capitalist but not socialist. That always struck me as very suggestive — but these politics were never developed. I would tend to agree with Jeremy Gilbert — that the encounter between jungle and politics never really happened. But this wasn't only a failure of the music; it was also a failure of politics. During the Nineties, the British Labour Party courted the reactionary rockers of Britpop. But where was the politics that could sychronise with the science fictional textures that jungle invoked?

So yes, Simon is right, if the hardcore continuum had any impact on politics it was in playing a part in establishing a post-racial Britain. It was impossible to fit jungle into a pre-existing racial narrative — it didn't sound like "white" or "black" music. And the extent to which the hardcore continuum has helped to consolidate this sense of the post-racial was made clear by an hilarious recent piece in *Vice* magazine called "Babes of the BNP", in which female supporters of the far right British National Party were interviewed. One question was: "In terms of the BNP's repatriation policy on immigration, if you had to choose, who would you repatriate first, Dizzee Rascal or Tinchy Stryder?"

militant tendencies feed music[1]

The idea that music can change the world now seems hopelessly naïve. Thirty years of neoliberalism have convinced us that there is no alternative; that nothing will ever change. Political stasis has put music in its place: music might "raise awareness" or induce us to contribute to a good cause, but it remains entertainment. Yet what of music that refuses this status? What of the old avant-garde idea that, to be politically radical, music has to be formally experimental?

The artist Michael Wilkinson's show *Lions After Slumber* (exhibited last year at the Modern Institute in Glasgow) posed these questions with a quiet intensity. The show was a kind of reliquary for a bygone militancy. It was dominated by an enormous black-and-white print of the photograph of Piccadilly Circus that had hung — upside down — in Malcolm McLaren and Vivienne Westwood's shop Seditionaries. A stretched linen included the 1871 photograph of the Paris Communards standing over the toppled Vendôme Column — but the image had been turned on its side, so that it looked as if the restored emperor was once again lording it over the Communards, who now resembled corpses.

There was no music to be heard at the show, but there were references to music scattered throughout. A screen-printed mirror showed the face of Irene Goergens, a member of the Red Army Faction — but the image came from the album sleeve to *Raw Macro*, by the techno artist Farben. More importantly, the title of the exhibition was a reference to Scritti Politti's 1982 track "Lions After Slumber". Scritti had themselves borrowed the title from Shelley's 1819 poem "The Masque of Anarchy", which imagined a rising "like lions after slumber/In unvanquishable number" to avenge the dead of the Peterloo Massacre.

The allusion to Scritti Politti makes it clear that the vision of politics that Wilkinson's show simultaneously mourned and invoked was derived from post-punk — the outpouring of musical creativity in the late 1970s and early 1980s that was in many ways Britain's version of Paris 68. In line with the Marxist and situationist theory it drew on and referenced, post-punk grasped culture as inherently political, insisting on a version of politics that went far beyond parliamentarianism.

One of the most urgent tasks for any political music was to expose the pacifying mechanisms that were already secreted in popular culture — nowhere more obviously than in the cheap dreams of love songs, which groups such as Gang of Four and the Slits deconstructed in tracks such as "Anthrax" and "Love und Romance". In a world in which people increasingly felt as if they lived inside advertisements — where, as Gang of Four put it, at home they felt like tourists — there was nothing more ideological than culture's claim to be entertainment. That was the word that provided the ironic title for Gang of Four's debut LP, and was also used in one of the Jam's most bitterly sarcastic songs, "That's Entertainment".

Wilkinson's show was timely because post-punk was one of the spectres that loomed over the past decade. Its history was extensively catalogued in Simon Reynolds' book *Rip It Up and Start Again*; the music was pastiched by lumpen plodders such as Franz Ferdinand and the Kaiser Chiefs, and served up again by originals such as Gang of Four, Magazine and Scritti, all of which reformed. The return of the post-punk sound had a double effect. At one level, it constituted the music's final defeat — if conditions were such that these groups could come back, thirty years after the fact, and not even sound particularly out of date, then post-punk's scorched-earth injunction that music should constantly reinvent itself must be as dead as its hopes for a revivified politics. Yet even the most degraded simulations of post-punk style carry with them a certain spectral residue, a demand — which these simulacra themselves betray — that music be more than consolation, convalescence or divertissement.

At the end of history, the impasses of politics are perfectly reflected by the impasses in popular music. As political struggle gave way to petty squabbles over who is to administrate capitalism, so innovation in popular music has been supplanted by retrospection; in both cases, the exorbitant ambition to change the world has devolved into a pragmatism and careerism. A certain kind of depressive "wisdom" predominates. Once, things might have seemed to happen, but we won't get fooled again. Like the images in Wilkinson's *Lions After Slumber*, the world has been turned the right way up again. The emperor is on his feet, power and privilege are restored, and any periods when they were toppled seem like ludic episodes: fragile, half-forgotten dreams that have withered in the unforgiving striplights of neoliberalism's shopping mall.

In his study of the Sex Pistols, *Lipstick Traces: A Secret History of the 20th Century* — published in the politically resonant year 1989 — Greil Marcus impersonated this depressive wisdom. "By the standards of wars and revolution", he conceded,

> the world did not change; we look back from a time when, as Dwight D. Eisenhower put it, "Things are more like they are now than they ever were before." As against the absolute demands so briefly generated by the Sex Pistols, nothing changed [...] Music seeks to change life; life goes on; the music is left behind; that is what is left to talk about.

In fact, Marcus argues, the Pistols and those who followed them did change the world, not by starting a war or a revolution, but by intervening in everyday life. What had seemed natural and eternal — and which now appears to be so again — was suddenly exposed as a tissue of ideological presuppositions. This is a vision of politics as a kind of puncturing, a rupturing of the accepted structure of reality. The puncture would produce a portal — an escape route from the second-nature habits of everyday life into a new labyrinth of associations and connections, where politics would connect with art and theory in unexpected ways. When songs ceased to be entertainment, they could be anything. These punctures felt like abductions.

Abduction was what it felt like on first listening to Public Enemy. Like the post-punks, Public Enemy implicitly accepted the idea that a politics which came reassuringly dressed in established forms would be self-defeating. The medium was the message, and Public Enemy's astonishing militant montage was remarkable for both its rabble-rousing sloganeering and its textural experimentalism. When the group's music, produced by the Bomb Squad, looped fragments of funk and psychedelic soul into abstract noise, it was as if American history — now cut up into a science-fiction catastrophe, a permanent emergency — was made malleable and ripe for rapid-fire retelling from the perspective of a post-Panther black militancy.

Or there was the very different approach of Detroit's Underground Resistance: in contrast to the data-density of the rap of Public Enemy's Chuck D, they offered a largely voiceless take on techno, pursuing a strategy of stealth and invisibility, drawing listeners into a suggestive semiotic fog created by track titles (such as "Install 'Ho-Chi Minh' Chip") and sleeve imagery that combined political insurgency with Afrofuturist science fiction.

What Public Enemy and Underground Resistance had in common was a rejection of the idea of music as entertainment. Instead of minstrelsy, they conceived of music in the militaristic terms explored in Steve Goodman's recent book, *Sonic Warfare: Sound, Affect and the Ecology of Fear*. In this model, the use of music to subdue populations — the "psychoacoustic correction" directed by the US army against the Panamanian dictator Manuel Noriega; "sound bombs" deployed over the Gaza Strip — is by no means unusual. All music functions either to embed or to disrupt habituated behaviour patterns. Thus, a political music could not be only about communicating a textual message; it would have to be a struggle over the means of perception, fought out in the nervous system.

Underground Resistance saw their mission as fighting against "mediocre audiovisual programming". Yet the problem is that the controllers have been all too successful in propagating this mediocrity. Where Public Enemy and Underground Resistance conceived of music as education, the dominant culture has been reclaimed by a Tin Pan Alley populism that has once again reduced music to entertainment. The internet and the iPod are part of a new economy of musical consumption in which, thus far, the possibilities of being abducted seem attenuated. In a world of niches, we are enchained by our own consumer preferences.

What is lacking in the age of Myspace is the public space that could surprise or confound our understanding of ourselves. Where, today, is the equivalent of the *Top of the Pops* stage, which could suddenly be invaded by the unexpected? Ironically, it is something such as *The X Factor*; the campaign to get Rage Against the Machine to the Christmas number-one slot was evidence of a hunger for music that was not just entertainment.

We are in a time of transition. Jacques Attali once argued that fundamental changes in the economic organisation of society were always presaged by music. Because, as a result of downloading, recorded music now seems to be heading towards decommodification, what does this suggest for the rest of the culture? And we are yet to hear the impact that the financial crash and its aftermath will have on musical production. The collapse of neoliberalism has already led to a simmering, renewed militancy on university campuses and elsewhere — how will this translate into sound? Perhaps soon we will once again hear new music that aims to turn the world upside down.

autonomy in the uk[1]

When the Real rushes in, everything feels like a film: not a film you're watching, but a film you're in. Suddenly, the screens insulating we late-capitalist spectators from the Real of antagonism and violence fell away. Since the student revolts in late 2010, helicopters, sirens and loudhailers have intermittently broken the phoney peace of post-crash London. To locate the unrest spreading across the capital, you just had to follow the Walter Murch-chunter of chopper blades... So many times during 2011, you found yourself hooked to news reports that resembled the scene-setting ambience in an apocalyptic flick: dictators falling, economies crashing, fascist serial killers murdering teenagers. The news was now more compelling than most fiction, and also more implausible: the plot was moving too quickly to be believable. But the sheen of unreality it generated was nothing more than the signature of the unscreened Real itself.

Sound was at the core of one of the year's momentous stories, the still unravelling "hackgate" narrative of national newspaper journalists caught out cracking the mobile phone messages of public figures and the grieving relatives of crime victims for story leads. After Hackgate, the UK power elite looked like something out of David Peace's *Red Riding Quartet* or *The Wire* television series (which itself turned on the moral issues of secretly recording phone conversations). The complicities of interest and mutual fear exposed by the phone hacking story brought to mind the party scene in the 1974 episode of Channel 4's TV adaptation of Peace's novels, where the illicit hedonism and skulduggery of cops, hacks, corporate plutocrats, private investigators — friends and ostensible adversaries — illustrated the true meaning of David Cameron's notorious phrase "we're all in this together". In 2011, we were living the film; all that was missing was the soundtrack.

At the end of 2010, the BBC's economics editor Paul Mason wrote a blog post called "Dubstep Rebellion", which described a pivotal moment he witnessed in the 9 December student protests: when the "crucial jack plug" of a sound system playing "political right-on reggae", was pulled by a "new crowd — in which the oldest person is maybe 17", and replaced it with what he mistakenly believed to be dubstep. He was corrected by *Guardian* contributor and author of *Kettled Youth*, Dan Hancox, whose own blog posted a playlist of the tracks he heard at the protest. They turned out to be mostly grime and dancehall (Lethal B, Elephant Man, Vybz Kartel), alongside chart rap and R&B such as Rihanna and Nicki Minaj. What's striking is the lack of explicit political content in any of this music. Yet grime, dancehall and R&B have a grip on the present in the way that older forms of self-consciously political music don't, and here is the impasse. It's as if we're left with a choice between the increasingly played out feel of "politically engaged" music and the sound of the present. In the past year alone, the *Guardian* has run numerous articles bemoaning the lack of "protest" music, but for many of us, "protest" has always been a rather pallid model of what political music could be. Besides, it's not protest music that has disappeared: go to the Occupy camp outside St Paul's and you won't find a shortage of acoustic guitars. What's missing is a specifically twenty-first-century form of political music. While there are some grime tracks that can be understood as having a political message, for the most part the genre's political significance lies in the affects — of rage, frustration and resentment — to which it gives voice. By contrast with US hip-hop, grime remains a form that is bound up with the failure to make it. The situation of grime is an allegory of class destiny. Just as it's possible for some to rise from the working class but not with it, so it's possible to rise out of grime (as artists such as Professor Green and Tinie Tempah have proven with their many crossover hits), but it's not yet been possible for anyone to succeed as a grime artist.

Paul Mason acknowledges his mistake to correctly identify what was played at the 2010 protests in his new book, *Why It's Kicking Off Everywhere: The New Global Revolutions*. Notwithstanding his inability to correctly track the changes in urban dance music, however, his original blog post was prophetic. After 9 December, the student protests lost momentum. The major moments of dissent in 2011 — which would also be the most powerful explosion of working-class rage in the UK since the riots of the early 1980s — would come from the group that Mason identified as "banlieue-style youth from places like Croydon and Peckham, or the council estates of Camden, Islington and Hackney". As with some of the 1980s riots, the immediate cause for the UK's first major uprising of 2011 was the death of a black person, Mark Duggan, shot by the police in Tottenham. "25 years ago police killed my grandma in her house in Tottenham and the whole ends rioted, 25 years on and they're still keepin up fuckry", tweeted Tottenham MC, Scorcher. His grandmother was Cynthia Jarrett, whose death prompted the Broadwater

Farm riots in 1985. Dan Hancox mentioned this tweet in a piece about British urban music and the riots for the *Guardian*, a crucial journalistic intervention at a vertiginously scary moment when the authoritarian and racist right were using the unrest as the pretext for reheating discourse that would have been deemed unacceptable only a week before. In an extraordinary but typically incoherent rant on the BBC's *Newsnight*, TV historian David Starkey astonishingly blamed the riots on "black culture" — collapsing the whole of black culture into music, and all black music into a poorly understood version of gangster rap. Like much of what happened in 2011, Starkey's delirious diatribe is best understood as a symptom: in this case of ruling-class panic and ignorance. Starkey dismissed the idea that the riots were political on the grounds that no public buildings were attacked — but what meaning do public buildings have for youth who were born into a social landscape in which the very concept of the public has all but disappeared under sustained ideological attack? The fact that the rioters targeted chain retail outlets was blamed on their "consumerism"; as if such "consumerism" were some kind of collective moral failing rather than the inevitable consequence of immersion in late capitalism's media culture.

As Owen Jones pointed out in his book *Chavs: The Demonisation of the Working Class*, work, not some lost moral sensibility, was once the source of working-class discipline. But what happens to people with no expectation of work, or of any kind of meaningful future? "When the punks cried 'No Future', at the turning point of 1977, it seemed like a paradox that couldn't be taken too seriously", Italian theorist Franco "Bifo" Berardi writes in his most recent book *After The Future*:

> Actually, it was the announcement of something quite important: the perception of the future was changing [...] Moderns are those who live time as the sphere of a progress towards perfection, or at least towards improvement, enrichment and rightness. Since the turning point of the century — which I like to place in 1977 — humankind has abandoned this illusion.[2]

From decrying the failure of the future, music has increasingly become part of this inertial temporality. Nothing symbolises mainstream music's relationship to politics better than the BBC's coverage of U2's set at Glastonbury. The significance here was not the music — predictably moribund and lacklustre, no longer even capable of mustering the totalitarian pomp of yore — but the way in which the TV coverage ignored the protest by Art Uncut. U2 were treated like dignitaries from the Chinese government: dissenters threatening to disrupt the empty rituals of the rock emperors wouldn't be tolerated. Where once even the most incorporated rock registered something about the tensions and temperature of the times, now you go to rock to be insulated from the present. Both U2 and their fellow headliner Beyoncé made gestures to "politics" in their sets — past struggles now reduced to an advertiser-friendly hopey-changey sentimentalism covering over a deeper, more pervasive sense that nothing of any consequence can ever change. Yet if mainstream pop has become a bubble impermeable to the new times, it's not as if experimental culture has yet come up with forms capable of articulating the present either. The art world's political mobilisations — via groups such as Art Against Cuts — have been more impressive than much of the actual engaged art itself, which has too often remained caught in a mode of pious inconsequence and textural poverty.

What has been lost is the transit between experimental and popular culture which characterised earlier eras. But what the student movement has been trying to prevent is nothing less than the dismantling of the last elements of the infrastructure which made this exchange possible; free higher education, after all, was one of the means by which British music culture was indirectly funded. Perhaps that is why Gang Of Four's "He'd Send In The Army", Mark Stewart and the Maffia's *As the Veneer of Democracy Starts To Fade* or Test Department's *The Unacceptable Face of Freedom* — records made more than a quarter of a century ago — still have more purchase on the traumatic and tumultuous events of the year in the UK than anything produced by a white musician in 2011. Recalling a conversation with Green Gartside at the *Wire*'s Off The Page festival of writing about music in February, it's telling that today has no equivalent to Green's post-punk anxieties about articulating new relationships between music and politics. Yet if this disconnection is bad for culture, it might be good for politics. For if music and subculture no longer act as effective mechanisms for controlled desublimation, converting disaffection into culture which can in turn be transformed into entertainment — feeding what Jean-François Lyotard memorably called the "Tungsten-Carbide stomach" of capital, which omnivorously consumes anything, and excretes it as commodities — then discontent can appear in a rawer form. This might be the reason that uber-reactionary Jeremy Clarkson has urged those at St Paul's to stop camping and start writing protest songs.

It could be, however, that our thinking about the problem is wrong-headed. It isn't that music is lagging behind politics; the politics itself is missing. The major political event of the year in the UK was the riots, but they were political in a negative sense. Reactionary commentators attempted to evacuate the riots of any political content by classifying them as an outburst of criminality. But even if we reject this for the absurdity it plainly is, it's possible to regard the riots as symptomatic — a symptom, precisely, of the failure of politics. "Harming one's own community is entirely mindless, but why would someone care for a community that doesn't care for him?" Professor Green asked Dan Hancox. "They might think of this as an uprising, but the anger is misdirected and conveyed in such a way will not have any kind of positive effect." Wiley also saw the riots as a sign of impotence: "They're saying 'We're going to do what we want!' — and I'm thinking 'No you're not, because when the police get a grip on it, you're going to be either banged up, or dead'." With the Draconian prison sentences imposed on many of those who played even a minor role in the riots, Wiley's prediction has been vindicated. Ceasing to be a symptom is one definition of achieving political agency, and — in a world where professional politicians look like inert mannequins incapable of preventing multiple impending catastrophes — nothing could be more urgent than this.

It's clear that this agency will not in the first instance be achieved through the hollowed out, decadent spaces of parliamentary politics. The political movement with which Franco Berardi is most associated, autonomism, has assumed a central importance amongst the political struggles that are coalescing in the UK and elsewhere. Consider, for example, the autonomist-influenced "ultra-leftist propaganda machine" called Deterritorial Support Group, whose blog became a crucial hub for new political thinking in the UK. Steeped in electronic music culture, DSG are as significant for their political aesthetics as for any substantive political position they present: what they offer is a new form of political antagonism far beyond the folksiness of "protest music", capable of operating across the cyberspatial, mediamatic and designer terrains of contemporary culture. This is politics as Underground Resistance's Electronic Warfare. In the era of hacking collectives such as Lulzsec, Anonymous and Wikileaks, DSG recognise that cyber-insurgency can open up a new kind of political insurgency. With the Diamond Jubilee and the Olympics, not to mention Mayan prophecies of apocalypse, 2012 is shaping up to be the most symbolically charged year in the UK since 1977. Is this the year when No Future will finally come to an end?

the secret sadness of the twenty-first century: james blake's *overgrown*[1]

A certain trajectory seems to have come to an end with James Blake's new album, *Overgrown*. Blake has gone from digitally manipulating his own voice to becoming a singer; from constructing tracks to writing songs. The initial motivation for Blake's early work no doubt came from Burial, whose combination of jittery two-step beats and R&B vocal samples pointed the way to a twenty-first-century pop. It was as if Burial had produced the dub versions; now the task was to construct the originals, and that entailed replacing the samples with an actual vocalist.

Listening back to Blake's records in chronological sequence is like hearing a ghost gradually assume material form; or it's like hearing the song form (re)coalescing out of digital ether. A track such as "I Only Know (What I Know Now)" from the *Klavierwerke* EP is gorgeously insubstantial — it's the merest ache, Blake's voice a series of sighs and unintelligible pitch-shifted hooks, the production mottled and waterlogged, the arrangement intricate and fragile, conspicuously inorganic in the way that it makes no attempt to smooth out the elements of the montage. The voice is a smattering of traces and tics, a spectral special effect scattered across the mix. But with Blake's self-titled debut album, something like traditional sonic priorities were restored. The reinvention of pop that his early releases promised was now seemingly given up, as Blake's de-fragmented voice moved to the front of the mix, and implied or partially disassembled songs became "proper" songs, complete with un-deconstructed piano and organ. Electronics and some vocal manipulation remained, but they were now assigned a decorative function. Blake's blue-eyed soul vocals, and the way that his tracks combined organ (or organ-like sounds) with electronica, made him reminiscent of a half-speed Steve Winwood.

Many who were enthusiastic about the early EPs were disappointed or mildly dismayed by *James Blake*. Veiling and implying an object is the surest route to producing the impression of sublimity. Removing the veils and bringing that object to the fore risks de-sublimation, and some found Blake's actual songs unequal to the virtual ones his early records had induced them into hallucinating. Blake's voice was as cloyingly overpowering as it was non-specific in its feeling. The result was a quavering, tremulous vagueness, which was by no means clarified by lyrics that were similarly allusive/elusive. The album came over as if it were earnestly entreating us to feel, without really telling us what is was we were supposed to be feeling. Perhaps it's this emotional obliqueness that contributes to what Angus Finlayson, in his review of *Overgrown* for *FACT*,[2] characterises as the strangeness of the songs on *James Blake*. They seemed, Finlayson says, like "half-songs, skeletal place-markers for some fuller arrangement yet to come." The journey into "proper" songs was not as complete as it first appeared. It was like Blake had tried to reconstruct the song form with only dub versions or dance mixes as his guide. The result was something scrambled, garbled, solipsistic, a bleary version of the song form that was as frustrating as it was fascinating. The delicate insubstantiality of the early EPs had given way to something that felt overfull. It was like drowning in a warm bath (perhaps with your wrists cut).

On *Overgrown*, the post-rave tricks and tics have been further toned down, and the album is at its weakest when it limply flirts with the dancefloor. Piano is still the lead instrument, but the chords hang over a backing that is almost studiedly anonymous — a luxuriantly warm pool of electronics where the rhythm is propelled more by the gently eddying bass rather than the beats. Like *James Blake*, though, *Overgrown* repays repeated listening. As with the first album, there is a simultaneous feeling that the tracks are both congested and unfinished, and that incompleteness — the sketchy melodies, the half-hooks, the repeated lines that play like clues to some emotional event never disclosed in the songs themselves — may be why it eventually gets under your skin. Blake has said that, by contrast with his debut, *Overgrown* sounds like the work of a man who has experienced love. For me, it is as emotionally enigmatic as its predecessor. The oddly indeterminate — irresolute and unresolved — character of Blake's music gives it the quality of gospel music for those who have lost their faith so completely that they have forgotten they ever had it. What survives is only a quavering longing, without object or context, Blake coming off like an amnesiac holding on to images from a life and a narrative that he cannot recover. This "negative capability" means that *Overgrown* is like an inversion of the oversaturated high-gloss emotional stridency of chart and reality TV pop, which is always perfectly certain of what it is feeling.

But what is the faith that *Overgrown* has lost? Blake's development has paralleled that of Darkstar, who similarly moved from the tricksy, tic-y vocal science of "Aidy's Girl is a Computer" to the chilly melancholia of their first album, *North*. Their new record *News From Nowhere* has a brighter, dreamier feel, but, as with *Overgrown*, it is notable for its lack of designs on the dancefloor. In a discussion that Simon Reynolds and I had about UK dance music,[3] Reynolds argued that the "emotional turn" represented by Blake and Darkstar was an implicit acknowledgement that "dance music no longer provides the kind of emotional release that it once did, through collective catharsis." The music doesn't have to be explicitly sad for this to be the case — there is a melancholia intrinsic to the very turn inward. As Reynolds points out, the idea that Nineties dance music was unemotional is a fallacy. This was a music saturated with affect, but the affect involved wasn't associated with romance or introspection. The twinning of romance and introspection, love and its disappointments, runs through twentiethcentury pop. By contrast, dance music since disco offered up another kind of emotional palette, based in a different model of escape from the miseries of individual selfhood.

In the twenty-first century, there's an increasingly sad and desperate quality to pop culture hedonism. Oddly, this is perhaps most evident in the way that R&B has given way to club music. When former R&B producers and performers embraced dance music, you might have expected an increase in euphoria, an influx of ecstasy. Yet the digitally-enhanced uplift in the records by producers such as Flo-Rida, Pitbull and will.i.am has a strangely unconvincing quality, like a poorly photoshopped image or a drug that we've hammered so much we've become immune to its effects. It's hard not to hear these records' demands that we enjoy ourselves as thin attempts to distract from a depression that they can only mask, never dissipate.

A secret sadness lurks behind the twenty-first-century's forced smile. This sadness concerns hedonism itself, and it's perhaps in hip-hop — the genre that has been most oriented to pleasure over the past twenty-odd years — where this melancholy has registered most deeply. Drake and Kanye West are both morbidly fixated on exploring the miserable hollowness at the core of super-affluent hedonism. No longer motivated by hip-hop's drive to conspicuously consume — they long ago acquired anything they could have wanted — Drake and West instead dissolutely cycle through easily available pleasures, feeling a combination of frustration, anger, and self-disgust, aware that something is missing, but unsure exactly what it is. This hedonist's sadness — a sadness as widespread as it is disavowed — was nowhere better captured than in the doleful way that Drake sings, "we threw a party/yeah, we threw a party," on *Take Care*'s "Marvin's Room".

It's no surprise to learn that Kanye West is an admirer of James Blake's. Meanwhile, this mix[4] that was doing the rounds a couple of years ago made parallels between Blake and Drake. There's an affective as well as sonic affinity between parts of Kanye's *808s and Heartbreak* and *My Beautiful Dark Twisted Fantasy* and Blake's two albums. You might say that Blake's whole schtick is a partial re-naturalisation of the digitally manipulated melancholy Kanye auditioned on *808s*: soul music after the Auto-Tune cyborg. But liberated from the penthouse-prison of West's ego, the disaffection languishes listlessly, incapable of even recognising itself as sadness. Unsure of itself, caught up in all kinds of impasses, yet intermittently fascinating, *Overgrown* is one more symptom of the twenty-first century's identity crisis.

review: david bowie's
the next day[1]

If you're interested in *The Next Day* — and even if you aren't — you've probably heard it by now. Heard it, been disappointed by it, ceased caring about it. The only really twenty-first-century thing about *The Next Day* is the way it exemplifies the hype-velocity of current communication: artfully timed PR rumours, hints and hyperbole induce anyone within its range to hallucinate a sublime object behind the veil, only for that object to degenerate into quotidian mediocrity the very second we've downloaded it.

The willingness to hallucinate is certainly there. Witness the sheer heft of the coverage, and feel the desperation behind it. The prospect of Bowie's return was guaranteed to tickle the palate of a certain age of listener, but the desires that it triggered were also for something missing from contemporary popular music. These days, Bowie stands for all the lost possibilities going by the idea of art pop — which is to say, not only pop plus art, or pop as art, but a circuit where fashion, visual art and experimental culture connected up and renewed each other in unpredictable ways. His absence was a palate cleanser — his string of forgettable 1980s and Nineties records now forgotten, he could once again be the thin white space onto which fantasies are projected. His absence almost seemed like a ploy invented by Bowie the impresario-strategist. After all, the only way to make a new Bowie record an event was for him to withdraw long enough that it could seem like it might — really, this time — be forever.

The Next Day's first single "Where Are We Now?", with its references to West Berlin era Potsdamer Platz and Nurnberger Strasse, sounded like an object carefully designed to pique the interest not only of the Bowie diehards but also those with a more general stake in pop history and mythology. Berlin! Tony Visconti! The track's lugubrious melancholy prompted the fantasy that *The Next Day* could be Bowie's version of Sinatra's *No One Cares* — an old crooner, a man lost in time paradoxically regaining currency by giving up on the sad pursuit of a present that had escaped him for good long ago. But it was a red herring. There are all kinds of intimations of mortality in *The Next Day*'s words — and reviewers seeking to rescue the record have tended to take refuge in the lyric sheet — but the form is rock, and an alarmingly unprepossessing, devoid of funk (as well as electronics) rock at that. The rest of the album makes the distance between now and (Berlin) then of "Where Are We Now?" painfully evident, a pain heightened by Visconti's failure to convert this collection of session muso workouts into anything memorable. *The Next Day* sounds as if it were barely produced at all: it has the flatness of a demo. The relatively warm reception *The Next Day* received tells its own sad tale about the state of pop in 2013.

You can't just put Visconti and Bowie together in a studio in 2012 and expect the equivalent of *Low*, *"Heroes"* or *Lodger* to result. The sorcerous powers that artists seem to possess as of right are never really theirs. Bowie — who perhaps more than any artist has performed the pop star's lack of interiority — has always known this, and he and Eno did much to puncture the Romantic conceit that creativity comes from the mysterious inner depths of a musician. Bowie's serial passage through personae, concepts and collaborators only telegraphed what is always the case: that the artist is synthesizer and curator of forces and ideas. This is all very well when the syntheses and the synergies are working, and there's a steady supply of new collaborators to feed off and to lionise. It's harder in this long striplit hours in the studio when the old magic won't come, when the revels have ended but you still have to go through the motions.

It's cruelly appropriate that Bowie's powers deserted him at practically the very moment that the Seventies — the decade with which he will always be synonymous — ended. I came to musical consciousness round about the time of 1980's *Scary Monsters*, and took Bowie for granted. *Ziggy Stardust* already sounded like a hoary old rock 'n' roll relic, and even much of *Scary Monsters* sounded reactionary by comparison with what proteges like Gary Numan, the Associates and Visage were doing. Yet Bowie had helped to create the conditions of his own obsolescence. His successors were following Bowie's template for what a pop star should be: a conceptualist and a designer, sexuality and gender indeterminate, alien and/or android, all outside and no inside, the changing face of the strange. From this point on, Bowie himself would be bereft of masks and make-up — it would be just him, the music and the Eighties suits. What followed was years of gradually lowering expectations, of spectacular misfires and the occasional lost gem, but mostly there was reliable mediocrity, the familiar declined star pattern where each new record is fanfare as a return to form, only to immediately disappear into irrelevance.

Much of this is compressed onto the cover image, which is by far the most startling thing about *The Next Day*. It's startling not for the act of desecration

— but for the casual character of the desecration: a white square over the "Heroes" cover — what could be more half-assed? When I first saw the cover image I thought it must be a prank — what would the real cover image be like? Here is cover designer Jonathan Barnbrook's rationale for the design: "The 'Heroes' cover obscured by the white square is about the spirit of great pop or rock music which is 'of the moment', forgetting or obliterating the past. However, we all know that this is never quite the case, no matter how much we try, we cannot break free from the past."

The image becomes more than a comment on Bowie — the man who once traded on his ability to escape the past is now trapped by it. It also functions as a diagnosis of a broader temporal malaise. What is this white space, this void? An optimistic reading would construe it as the openness of a present that is not yet decided. A bleaker take — one in keeping with the hackneyed quality of the music — would see the white space as standing in for the vacancy of the present, with nothing there except a necessarily failed attempt to escape and recover the past. That's our pop predicament in 2013, a predicament which *The Next Day* couldn't seriously have been expected to resolve.

the man who has everything: drake's *nothing was the same*[1]

So here we are again: life at rainbow's end. Everything that can be bought, available practically immediately, 24/7: women, food, cars, you name it, you click on it. Every hotel suite can be prepared to your specifications. The only things that are different are the shower controls. It's all top quality, although naturally you can get down and dirty with the fast food options if you want to, and often (why not?) you do:

> *Got everything, I got everything... I cannot complain, I cannot*
> (You sure about that, Drake?)
> *I don't even know how much I really made, I forgot, it's a lot...*
> *Fuck that, never mind what I got*[2]

OK, then, let's get the obvious question out of the way first. If you've got everything, *why are you so sad*?

Surely it can't be as simple and sentimental as that hoary old chestnut: money can't buy you love? Come on, is this really where rap was destined to end up: with the rapper as some romcom character, all the braggadocio and super-conspicuous consumption just so much bluster to conceal the boy-lack that the redeemer-woman will make good in the final reel? That old story, again? *"Next time we fuck, I don't want to fuck, I want to make love... I want to trust."* Drake can't quite believe this routine, can't quite make us believe it. He knows perfectly well that this sensitive stuff can play as one more pick-up-artist's ruse... He's spent so long deceiving and then revealing his deceptions that he's no longer sure when he's trying to play us or speak openly, or what the difference is. Crying real tears with one eye, while winking over the latest conquest's shoulder to the camera with the other. He'd convinced us he was different, but that was a trick, and one that others have caught on to. There's nothing very brave or unique about talking about your feelings now that *"niggas talk more than bitches do."* Is this more honesty, or just an acknowledgement that he needs a new USP?

I got 99 problems, getting rich ain't one.

Listening to *Nothing Was the Same*, I'm reminded of Judd Apatow's *Funny People*. Apatow's film is defined by a series of hesitations and avoidances. First of all, it seems as if it is going to be a film about a jaded but rich and successful comedian, George Simmons (Adam Sandler), who learns the value of life when he's diagnosed with a serious illness; then it seems to be about a man who accepts the value of love and family. Yet each time the film seems to move towards these standard generic resolutions, Apatow pulls back. Simmons' hedonic nihilism re-asserts himself; the threat of death can't break the bad habits of a lifetime; the love he lost long ago was actually better off lost. He's not happy being himself but he doesn't want to be anyone else. Far from relieving this existential dilemma, fabulous wealth means that he has nowhere at all to hide from it.

Nothing Was the Same is characterised by the same ambivalence — a longing to be a new person who can love and trust (with a woman, naturally, charged as the agent of this transformation) together with a recognition that he will never change, that he'll always be drinking, smoking, fucking, that he's far from perfect, but neither is anyone else, right? He never really took off the gangsta-minstrel drag for good; instead, he keeps casting it aside, inspecting it, distancing himself from it, before wearing it again. He can't help himself (or so he keeps telling us). But this oscillation is valuable for what it tells us about rap's embattled masculinity in general. Drake confirms that the street-strutting bad boy *"just looking for head in a comfortable bed"* is the other face of the desperately alone little boy lost crying to his mommy substitute. The boasting brute is always on the run from the helpless infant inside, but, for that very reason, the emotionally broken-down male isn't an alternative to all the ego-armour posturing, so much as it is its enabling condition. Women are to be publicly disdained, treated as currency in a homosocial bragging economy; in private they are asked to make these wounded men whole again. Is there a track that has exposed the real nature of the male-to-female love song better than *Take Care*'s "Marvin's Room"? The conceit — a drunk Drake leaving a phone message to a long lost love he treated badly but now thinks he wants back — leaves us in no doubt that he was speaking to himself via a fantasised female Other.

Gangsta's hyperbolically-staged fantasies of omnipotence were always nouveau-riche giveaways, which, like the bling, sang out that these working-class black Americans had not yet achieved the easy way in the world, the casual confidence that are the birthrights of those born to wealth and power. The (gold) chains have always clanked as loudly as Jacob Marley's that the struggle to escape servitude has run aground, and that untold riches for a very few were the compensation for the many languishing in inertia, poverty, incarceration. Is "Started from the Bottom" — which we all laughed at: *no you didn't, Drake!* — Drake's commentary on all this? Hear it as an act of imagination, Drake putting himself in the sneakers of those who had to struggle from the depths like he never had to, rather than as some forged autobiography, and it makes more sense. But listen to the sheer weariness that weighs down the track: the heavy *tristesse* that starts the moment after you've reached the top of the tower, as the realisation sinks in that there's no replacing the thrill of the chase. Drake was always expected to be a success, so he was deprived even of that brief moment of satisfaction before the ennui and the paranoia set in. Reaching the top was standard, the least he could expect.

Nothing Was the Same is tangled up in all the confusions of a generation of men faced with contradictory imperatives — the post-feminist awareness that treating women like shit isn't cool, together with the Burroughsian bombardment of always-available pornography. There's no point moralising here, either for Drake or us. Drake's at his weakest when he half-heartedly attempts some kitschy Hallmark card affirmation of lurve; he's at his most painfully revelatory when he admits that these impasses, these binds, are just too much for him. He can't escape these knots because the knots are what he is. His bewilderment about what a man is supposed to be now is the very hallmark of a contemporary heterosexual masculinity that realises that the patriarchal game is up, but which is too hooked on the pleasures and privileges to relinquish them yet (just one more click on the porn, then I'll be Mr Sensitive forever).

On *Nothing Was the Same*, Drake often sounds like Tony Montana in *Scarface*: fucking, eating, snorting, is that all there is? But the tone here couldn't be more different from Pacino's Eighties cocaine histrionics. A glacial fatalism runs beneath everything here, and Drake matters because he makes contact — maybe better than anyone else — with the sense of hopelessness that quietly subsists beneath all the twerking and tweeting, all the twitter and the chatter of twenty-first-century culture. Hear this in the gorgeous electro-downer haze that saturates the album and establishes its tone much more than any of the beats. Yet there's something beyond the fatalism, too. You can hear it in Drake's signature move — the transition from rap to singing, the slipping down from ego-assertion into a sensual purring, the relaxing into a lasciviousness that has nothing to do with the localised libido and dumb automatisms of phallic sexuality. Down here, there is a glorious release from the pressures of identity. Rave-like, pitched-up vocals are suspended on placid currents of synth. Voices stop being human, become avatars from a space where subjectivity has been left behind like a bad dream. On the opener, "Tuscan Leather", Whitney Houston's ghost is summoned from the hotel bathroom, mutated into some butterfly-fragile chirruping creature singing inside a specimen jar. I'm frequently reminded of nothing so much as the refracted architectures and water sprites of Balam Acab's *Wander/Wonder*. When you dive into these electro-oceanic depths, *Nothing Was the Same* ceases to be a fascinating symptom of all the blockages of the present, and becomes a longing for something new, something strange and lovely.

break it down: dj rashad's *double cup*[1]

Time-stretched Amen breakbeats, rave-euphoric vocals: on *Double Cup*, Rashad pays his dues to the hardcore continuum, but the traces of jungle and rave here only accentuate how different footwork is to Nineties British dance music.

Footwork has been greeted with the fanfare that usually accompany the arrival of an avant-garde dance music. These contradictory responses — footwork's being written off as something that you can't dance to at the same time as it is dismissed as a functional music, something that would *only* be properly appreciated by those dancing to it — is a sure sign that we are in the presence of something which scrambles the defaults of rearview hearing.

But footwork is new in a strange way. It's not historically new: it dates back to the Nineties. And what's uncanny, *unheimlich*, about footwork is that practically everything in the sonic palette is familiar. Most of the sounds on *Double Cup* feel like they *could* have come from the twentieth century, even if they have actually been produced in the twenty-first.

So, wherein resides footwork's newness then? In a fascinating blog post,[2] Tristam Adams identifies exactly what makes footwork new: its compositional innovations. To bring this out, Adams contrasts footwork to jungle. Jungle's newness was in large part a consequence of the widespread availability of digital sampling technology, which facilitated both new sounds and new ways of treating sound (time-stretched breakbeats and vocals). Beyond this, though, I'm not sure that the way Adams constructs the comparison between jungle and footwork is quite right. Adams hears jungle as more "machinic" than footwork — but what was exciting about jungle to many of us at the time was that it gave a whole new sense of what machinism was. Jungle's machinism was delirious; it was, in Kodwo Eshun's immortal phrase, a rhythmic psychedelia, composed from whorls, twists, and vortexes of sound; there were none of the rigid mechanoid lines of techno. Jungle was dark, but also wet, viscous, and enveloping.

It's here that the contrast with footwork can most be heard — and felt. To those whose ears and nervous systems were mutated by jungle in the Nineties, footwork can initially sound strangely desiccated — like the dry bones left after jungle's digital ocean has receded. "UK bass music" is an almost wilfully bland term, but it does point to the element which gave every genre from jungle to UK garage and dubstep their consistency: a viscous, glistening bass sound. This is conspicuously absent from Rashad's sound. Instead of functioning as a dark liquid element on (or in) which other sounds could be suspended, Rashad's bass is a surging and reclining series of stabs and jabs that heightens and lowers tension without ever releasing it.

This leads on to another difference from jungle and the broader tendencies in Nineties digital culture. Where jungle, like Nineties CGI, used digital technology to smooth out some of the hard lines that had been characteristic of early computer sound and imagery, footwork has deliberated opted for angularity. Charlie Frame's comparison of listening to Rashad with "gazing at an animated GIF that grows ever more absurd with each iteration", captures very precisely footwork's jerky repetitions. Perhaps the appeal of the animated GIF and of footwork are both tied up with the way that they reject the dominant aesthetics of digital culture now. Think of the way that the elastic architectures of Nineties animatronics gave way to the dreary photorealism of contemporary animation. Now, novelty is to be found in the refusal of communicative capitalism's false promises of smoothness. If the Nineties were defined by the loop (the "good" infinity of the seamlessly looped breakbeat, Goldie's "Timeless"), then the twenty-first century is perhaps best captured in the "bad" infinity of the animated GIF, with its stuttering, frustrated temporality, its eerie sense of being caught in a time-trap.

That frustrated, angular time — and the enjoyment of it — is at the heart of footwork. The genre can sound like an impenetrable thicket of rhythms if the thing you lock onto first is the most distinctive thing about footwork: the coiling spasms of super-dry snares. Lock into the floaty synth pads and the vocals, however, and footwork comes on as strangely mellow. In this respect, footwork can then be heard as an extrapolation of elements of Nineties G-funk. An earlier Hyperdub sound — the dayglo wonky of Joker — had mined G-funk for its absurdist pitch-bent synths. What footwork takes is some vocal styling (the rap that is so often subject to its stuttering repetitions), but also a certain mood. G-funk differentiated itself from standard gangsta posturing by the way it dissolved the hard ego of the rapper into clouds of Chronic. Beneath the busyness of capitalist realism — and its demands that we never stop selling ourselves — was another mode of being, where time diffused slowly as exhaled smoke. Beyond the phallic machismo, there was a different libidinal economy, defined by a superficially paradoxical combination of deep yearning and a desire to remain absolutely in the sunlight-saturated moment, liberated from the urgencies of business. This is all the more poignant because a gangster's work is never done, his enemies don't sleep, and chilled-out bliss could be terminated at any moment by gunfire. To the G-funk celebration of smoking, Rashad adds other affective toners: the lost-in-the-moment exhilaration of the raver, and R&B's wistful regrets/lascivious moaning. The overall result is, in terms of mood and affect, oddly reminiscent of cool-era jazz — there is the same ambivalence, the same evocation of an harsh yet alluring urban environment, the same combination of sadness and confidence, the same articulation of longing and bliss.

Then there is the tic-talk of the voices themselves — the way they are made to stammer and circle around themselves. It's as if there is a cross-contamination, a human-machine (psycho)pathology, the machines infecting the human voices with glitches, the humans passing on Freudian slips, parapraxes, to the machines. Rashad's plaintive machinism reminds me of nothing so much as the hallucinatory intensity of the "I Love You" section of William Burroughs' *The Ticket That Exploded*:

On my knees I hoped you'd love me too. I would run till I feel the thrill of long ago. Now my inspiration but it won't last and we'll be just a photograph. I've forgotten you then? I can't sleep, Blue Eyes, if I don't have you. Do I love her? I love you I love you many splendored thing. Can't even eat. Jelly on my mind back home. 'Twas good bye deep in the true love. We'll never meet again, darling, in my fashion.[3]

Burroughs' early cut-up and fold-in texts, with their analysis and decoding of emotional manipulation via media and their understanding of pornography as a control apparatus, now read like extraordinarily prophetic anticipations of the present moment. As with Burroughs, there is a double pathos in Rashad's work. First of all, there is a pathos at the level of the affects in the voices themselves; and the way that the voices are orphaned from their supposed origins means that there is an overwhelming sadness even if the feeling expressed is ostensibly joyful. It's the same kind of depersonalised sadness we might feel if we happened upon lost photographs of an unknown person's holiday, long ago. Then there is another pathos that arises from the way that the voices are made to repeat and stutter; the sadness of recognising a speaking animal (ourselves) in the grip of automatisms, repetitions, drives. Rashad articulates the impasses of our twenty-first-century condition with a precision and a compassion that few others can match. More importantly, he suggests that — against all the odds — we might still be able to dance our way out of the time-traps and identity prisons we are locked in.

start your nonsense! on eMMplekz and dolly dolly[1]

There are still all kinds of possibilities for combining voice and sound in new ways. Rap was the last major form to popularise a use of the voice that was not singing, but the field is wide open, as these two new albums from eMMplekz and Dolly Dolly prove.

The first temptation with these records is to hear them as "spoken word" — with the musicality subordinated to a voice that is literary, conversational, comedic. However, what makes these two albums so unique is the way that musicality here infests and inflects the voice, the way that the sound refuses to stay (in the) background. Both albums take much of their inspiration from the very English tradition of Nonsense, which includes Edward Lear, Lewis Carroll, Monty Python, and more recently, Chris Morris. It was on account of Carroll that André Breton reputedly said that the English had no need of surrealism. Here, eMMplekz and Dolly Dolly proffer different versions of twenty-first-century English sonic surrealism.

With eMMplekz, a collaboration between Ekoplekz and Mordant Music's Baron Mordant, the precursors that first come to mind are certain moments in post-punk — Cabaret Voltaire's "Photophobia", Throbbing Gristle, the Fall — yet eMMplekz don't sound quite like any of these. From its title on in, *Your Crate Has Changed*, the Baron's punconscious wordplay has a very contemporary focus.

If Drake and Kanye West expose the sadness and madness deep within the cyber-pleasuredome — the sound of depressed superstars as hypercommodities — then eMMplekz observe the malaises and pathologies of capitalist cyberspace from outside the digital matrix. Instead of the seamless-slick, depthless pixellation to which always-on digitality has habituated us, Ekoplekz's analog electronics seethe and hiss, gathering and dispersing like a steam and mist. These synthesizer sketches function like impressionist sound paintings of what Ken Hollings has called the "digital regime", and

407

it's as if, like users coming down from a psychotropic, we are finally seeing it for what it is.

"I've got to take this..." Baron Mordant has a schizoanalytic ear for how the digital regime reveals itself through the phrases it induces to casually utter. Doesn't this phrase — so often repeated, so little thought about — capture all too accurately our fatalism in respect of communicative capitalism? "I've got to take this" — I've got to let it, accept it, I can't escape, there's nothing I can do... There's no way out, there's no release from the frenzied inertia of all those cyberspatial urgencies, these alerts. *"Tethered to my hotspot, tethered to my hotspot..."* Constant anxiety about staying connected, constant worry about holding onto the equipment that allows us to stay connected. *"Can you watch my laptop?"* We're all sick of this now... we're all sick because of this now... *"Sorry for your Lossy..."* What is all this digital compression costing us, and when do we ever get to count the cost? (The first thing we do in the morning is grope for our smartphones — straight from sleep into the somnambulance of capitalist cyberspace. *"Unsubscribe from Soviet time"* — maybe we did that too soon, and now it's business o'clock, forever...)

Your Crate Has Changed is like an English take on Franco "Bifo" Berardi's *Precarious Rhapsody: Semiocapitalism and the Pathologies of Post-Alpha Generation.* Berardi persuasively argues that the interlock between precarious work and capitalist communications technology has produced a population whose nervous systems are overloaded with stimuli. Mordant gives voice to weary old digital migrants whose middle-aged flesh is too saggy and grey to be made-over — people deprived of security, forced to keep on hustling even though they are too old for the game, bone-weary. No rest for the precarious, no chance to tune into anything except the imperatives of business. *"Invoices in my head... invoices in my head..."*

Invoices in my head, and too much spam and random cyber-noise to hear anything else. But I don't think there's been anyone since Mark E. Smith at his telepathic peak in the late Seventies/early Eighties who has managed to tune into the rogue frequencies of England's schizo-babble as effectively as the Baron does here. Mordant finds all the clandestine signals hidden in jingles and classified ads. He channels the voices of the lonely, the desperate, all the weirdos and the saddoes; ourselves, perhaps, but the secret selves we keep stuffed behind our Facebook walls. Yet there are still avenues of escape — on a couple of tracks, an infant's babbling offers an alternative Nonsense to capital's infantilised huckster-speak.

A surface joviality — a different kind of humour, much less *mordant* — separates Dolly Dolly from eMMplekz. Yet it's the slippages of tone and genre, from light pastiche to intimations of mortality, the sliding of persona from gone-to-seed raconteur to charity shop mystic, from short story-teller to preening bard, that make *Antimacasser* such an odd jewel of a record, and Dolly so singular a performer.

The opening track, "Wattle and Daub" — a collaboration with Position Normal — is more than worth the admission price alone. Over a lysergically-smeary detuned piano (or maybe guitar), Dolly Dolly dolefully declaims a Nonsense-Shakespearean state of the nation address. *"England my England... the cold mist of your fibrous trolleys stifles the sun... half-strangled uncles stuffed with crisps... your sky full of plump chintz cushions..."* It's like Tony Hancock's melancholia has been dream-conflated with his mockery of thespian and playwright pretensions. Yet the Nonsense is disarming: "Wattle and Daub" gives us nothing less than a psychedelic-surrealist portrait of a country deprived of psychedelia and surrealism. A world without surprise, an entirely domesticated universe, banality as cosmology: *"Let's colonise the other planets, fill them with bitter and dry roasted peanuts, pigeons and oven chips."* The dead world of middle-aged Britain's living rooms; the cheery veneer of advertising's ever-smiling, glowing-faced families turned inside out. *"I'm sick of being a man"*, moans the character who narrates the closing track. Aren't we all? But *Antimacasser* finds all sorts of disused or temporarily abandoned doorways into other worlds, all kinds of rabbit holes in which we can escape from being a sad human animal. Old New English Library paperbacks become occult manuals, full of esoteric philosophy. It's still possible to transform ourselves, to transport ourselves, and Dolly Dolly shows us how.

review: sleaford mods' *divide and exit* and *chubbed up: the singles collection*[1]

The East Midlands accent, lacking urban glamour, lilting lyricism or rustic romanticism, is one of the most unloved in the UK. It is heard so rarely in popular media that it isn't recognised enough even to be disdained. I must confess that I have a dog in this fight. I grew up in the East Midlands, and when I left university I was described by a sympathetic lecturer as having a "speech and accent problem". The accent gradually disappeared, as I learned to suppress the lazy Leicestershire consonants and articulate my speech in something closer to so-called received pronunciation — an achievement loaded with ambivalence and shame.

Sleaford Mods' Jason Williamson makes no such accommodation to metropolitan manners, and he's disgusted at those who speak in fake accents, whether they're imitating someone from East London or "Lou Reeds, G.G. Allin..." The appeal to the local in politics and culture is usually smug and reactionary; a petit-bourgeois ruse to acquire more cultural and actual capital by overpricing the artisnal and the organic (Williamson is wise to this scam too, blasting at "expensive coffee shops full of local art/Fuck off"). But the politics of locality operate differently when it comes to accent. The English bourgeoisie speak in more or less the same accent wherever they come from. The insistence on retaining a regional accent is therefore a challenge to the machineries of class subordination — a refusal to accept being marked as inferior.

Williamson was born in Grantham, Lincolnshire — Sleaford is about twenty miles away — and was involved in the music scene for years, following a familiar provincial trajectory: not making it, but always being lured back at the very point he was about to give up. He was in and out of local groups, followed the dream to San Francisco and London for a while, and ended up back home when it didn't come off. He tried to go out on

411

his own, but he couldn't find anything new, until, bored and frustrated in a recording studio, he started ranting over a metal track. He had found his voice, literally. He was inspired by the Wu-Tang Clan, but he didn't so much repeat their sound as their methodology, forcing listeners to adjust to his accent, idiolect and references. This risked bathos — the East Midlands ain't New York, and Sleaford Mods would come off as just another comic turn if it weren't for Williamson's incendiary intensity. (Which isn't to deny the mordantly acidic wit that runs through his lines: "Chumbawamba weren't political?/They were just crap", isn't just funny but critically astute.)

Listen to the singles collection, *Chubbed Up*, next to *Divide and Exit*, and it's clear not much has changed in the duo's sound. The variation is provided by Williamson's words, the music by Andrew Fearn always fits an (unfussy) formula: pugilistic post-punk bass; functional but unprepossessing beats; occasional cheap keyboard riffs and listless wafts of guitar. It's digitally manipulated, but conspicuously unpolished — the software is used not to micromanage the sounds but to capture them into a purgatorial loop.

The name Sleaford Mods sounds like vintage graffiti, or something you'd have sewn onto a Union Jack at an England football match three decades ago. On the face of it, they couldn't be any less mod. Where is the style and the cool in this relentless outpouring of profanity and discontent? But mod was a complex phenomenon, as much about the failure to achieve the glamour of black America as it was about the aspiration towards possessing it. The mods might have loved Miles and Motown but when they made music it sounded like the Who and the Jam — rock born with a plastic spoon in its mouth, stuck in a monochromatic England skulking in the shadows cast by the USA's Pop Art consumer dreams. The mods worked in office jobs, in semi-skilled occupations and in department stores, longing for a luxury far above their station. But their ambitions weren't to climb the social ladder of bourgeois respectability — they prefigured instead a world in which style exploded far beyond the narrow calculations of business, and everyday life could become a work of art. As Dick Hebdige wrote in his essay "The Meaning of Mod": "Every mod was existing in a ghost world of gangsterism, luxurious clubs and beautiful women, even if the reality only amounted to a draughty Parker anorak, a beaten up Vespa, and fish and chips out of a greasy bag." With Sleaford Mods, the chips and the grease are all that's left. Factories have closed and trade unions have been subdued. Art schools and the media have rebourgeoisified. University courses have been opened up, but the real graduate jobs are reserved for the same old suspects. The only time you are likely to hear a working-class accent on television is in a poverty porn documentary.

This is Sleaford Mods' world, but they refuse the place assigned to them by well-meaning metropolitan liberals and by unscrupulous Tories. They won't play the part of a dumb feckless prole or white, working-class racist

(Williamson loathes St George's flag white van men as much as their Tory overlords). They won't knuckle down and gratefully accept zero-hours contract jobs, or be content to "rot away in the aisles of Co-Op", as the single "Jolly Fucker" had it.

If anything, *Divide and Exit* feels more claustrophobic than its predecessor, *Austerity Dogs*, with even the tiny dreamy spaces that once opened up on tracks such as "Donkey" eliminated by Williamson's relentless excremental flow. Excremental is the right word: piss and shit course through Williamson's rhymes, as if all the psychic and physical effluent abjected by Cameron's Britain can no longer be contained, and it's bursting upwards, exploding through all the deodorised digital commercial propaganda, the thin pretences that we're all in this together and everything's going to be all right.

What overflows in Williamson's pottymouth is a seething disaffection incubated on the dole or in dead end jobs and further stoked up by the shop-soiled fantasies of escape pushed by an ailing music business. An early single was called "Jobseeker": "So Mr Williamson — what have you done to find gainful employment since your last signing on date?/Fuck all!" A fantasy exchange no doubt: here, as often in Sleaford Mods Williamson gives vent to a voice that would otherwise stay locked in his head. Discontent is everywhere in the UK now but for the most part it's privatised: blunted by alcohol and anti-depressants, or directed into impotent comments box spite and empty social media outrage: "All you Zombies, tweet tweet tweet".

If Williamson's anger often seems intransitive — his fuck offs are sheer explosions of exasperation, directed at no one in particular, or at everyone — it's underscored by a class consciousness painfully aware that there is nothing which could transform disaffection into political action. "Aren't we all just/Pissing in the flames?" Cameron and the Tories are obviously despised — there's a particularly memorable nightmare image of the "Prime Minister's face hanging in the clouds/Like Gary Oldman's Dracula" — but who can stop them? "Liveable shit/You put up with it". This is both a taunt directed at the audience and an acknowledgement of Williamson's own capitulation in doing what's necessary to survive.

It isn't always the role of political music to come up with solutions. But nothing could be more urgent than the questions that Sleaford Mods pose: who will make contact with the anger and frustration that Williamson articulates? Who can convert this bad affect into a new political project?

test dept: where leftist idealism and popular modernism collide[1]

There's something very timely about the return of Test Dept. Their installation *DS30* (2014), the accompanying film and the book *Total State Machine* (2015) — a comprehensive history and critical study of the band — have arrived just in time for the deep crisis of neoliberalism in the UK.

Test Dept were always more than a musical group. They are better understood as a popular modernist collective that had the production of sound at its centre, but which also made visuals, projections and films. Test Dept were formed in London in 1981 by Jonathan Toby Burdon, Graham Cunnington, Angus Farquhar, Paul Hines and Paul Jamrozy. They began as a second-wave industrial act, following on from a first wave led by Throbbing Gristle and Cabaret Voltaire. With their use of found metal objects and their performances in spaces of labour and logistics (disused factories, transport hubs), Test Dept offered what seemed, on the face of it, to be a very literal take on the "industrial". Via their involvement in a number of UK struggles — including the miners' strike (1984–85) and the anti-Poll Tax movement (1988–91) — Test Dept also became intensely invested in the politics of the industrial and the post-industrial.

Test Dept's signature sound is intensely percussive, a convulsive dance music that took its inspiration from Soviet constructivism, but which became something like the British equivalent of the politicised US hip-hop group Public Enemy. The records are sonic mosaics, pulsing with panic, the sampled voices of Tory MPs countered by defiant statements by left-wing militants. One of Test Dept's most powerful tracks — "Statement" from the 1986 album *The Unacceptable Face of Freedom* — features miner Alan Sutcliffe giving a moving account of police brutality during the strike. The track is a work of emotional engineering, a collectivist response to the manipulation of affect and desire through advertising, branding and political propaganda.

Sutcliffe went on to tour with the group: one example of the way in which struggles produced not only new alliances but new social spaces, in which art-making ceased to be a matter for specialists of a certain age.

For any British, left-wing person, remembering the mid-1980s is liable to provoke a sadness that is visceral, choking, wrenching. I still can't recall without weeping the day when the miners returned to work in 1985 after a year on strike. What I have called capitalist realism — the deeply embedded belief that there is no alternative to capitalism — was definitively established in the UK during that period, in Margaret Thatcher's second term in government. For a significant proportion of the population, the 1982 Falklands War had transformed Thatcher from a figure of loathing into a glorious war leader. This renewed popularity, together with the formation of the Social Democratic Party by Labour Party defectors, allowed the Tories to achieve a landslide victory in the 1983 general election. It proved to be a traumatic defeat for the British left in general, and for the Labour Party in particular. Labour began its long march towards Blairism and its eventual complete capitulation to neoliberalism and corporate tyranny. Meanwhile, the crushing of the miners' strike, and the wave of privatisations that the Tories unleashed, created the conditions for the neoliberal Britain that is only now falling apart, thirty years later.

In retrospect, it can look as if the whole of the 1980s was a series of defeats for the left. One value of *Total State Machine* is to remind us that it didn't feel that way at the time. Rather, like John Akomfrah's video installation *The Unfinished Conversation* (2013), the *Total State Machine* book invokes a forgotten 1980s, in which style culture was synchronised with the rise of an anti-authoritarian left that confidently laid claim to a new modernity, set to dispense with capital, patriarchy and racism as so many historical relics; a 1980s in which radical chic and designer socialism weren't dirty words but real possibilities.

Total State Machine includes a section of Cynthia Rose's 1991 book *Design After Dark*. Inspired by a Test Dept performance, Rose argues that young Britons would

> succeed in staging a dancefloor revolution. It will not be the Komsomol-style overthrow dreamt of by Red Wedge, the ill-fated attempt by a collective of musicians — led by Billy Bragg, Paul Weller and Jimmy Somerville — to spearhead a campaign to defeat the Tories in the 1987 General Election. Instead, it will come about through grass-roots changes — successive waves of guerrilla sounds, guerrilla design, guerrilla entertainments. The new design dynamic will be an impulse born out of celebration, rising out of leisure enacted as an event. And it will change young people's perception about what entities like design and communication should do.[2]

Sadly, it didn't work out that way. Rose was absolutely right that most of the innovative energy in British music culture would come from dance music, which was about to enjoy its most fecund period ever. But the atmosphere around rave, jungle and garage tended towards the apolitical, the libertarian or the capitalist. The alliance of the left with the new technologies, energies, infrastructures and forms of desire that Rose saw emerging was to be very short-lived.

The comparison with Red Wedge is instructive here. Part of the problem with Red Wedge was that, despite taking its name from a poster designed by El Lissitzky (*Beat the Whites with the Red Wedge*, 1919), its music represented a retreat from modernist experimentalism. Bragg's blokeish neo-folk, the ham-fisted jazz-funk-pop Weller made with the Style Council, the Communards' strangely depressing party music: none of this was capable of articulating a future. It was all bogged down in the worst kind of 1980s gloss.

Test Dept were one of the last examples of what has been called post-punk, but really they are part of a longer trajectory of art pop/pop art going back to the 1950s. The conditions for this popular modernism were subject to sustained attack in the mid-Eighties, and they have never recovered. The Tories began to dismantle the infrastructure of social security, higher-education maintenance grants, squatting and art schools that had given working-class people access to the resources of so-called high culture and time to produce their own sound, fiction and art.

But the neoliberal capitalism that drove this assault on culture is now heading for disaster — in Greece, in Spain, in Scotland and, finally, in England. Far from being some static monument to a bygone era, *Total State Machine* is an invaluable archive, an inventory of strategies, gestures and techniques that can now be repotentiated by others ready to begin where the Test Dept of the 1980s left off. Rose's prophecies of a new design dynamic can yet come true. Popular modernism isn't dead: it has merely had a thirty-year hiatus.

no romance without finance[1]

Jennifer M. Silva's *Coming Up Short: Working-Class Adulthood in an Age of Uncertainty* is a heartbreaking study of the corrosive effects of the neoliberal environment on intimacy. Silva's book focuses on young people specifically — it is based on a hundred interviews she undertook with young working-class men and women in two American cities in Massachusetts and Virginia. Her findings are disturbing. Over and over again, Silva finds her young subjects exhibiting a "hardened" self — a form of subjectivity that prides itself on its independence from others. For Silva, this hardened subject is the consequence of this generation being abandoned, institutionally and existentially. In an environment dominated by unrelenting competition and insecurity, it is neither possible to trust others nor to project any sort of long-term future. Naturally, these two problems feed into one another, in one of the many vicious spirals which neoliberal culture has specialised in innovating. The inability to imagine a secure future makes it very difficult to engage in any sort of long-term commitment. Rather than seeing a partner as someone who might share the stresses imposed by a harshly competitive social field, many of the working-class individuals to whom Silva spoke instead saw relationships as an additional source of stress. In particular, many of the heterosexual women she interviewed regarded relationships with men as too risky a proposition. In conditions where they could not depend on much outside themselves, the independence they were forced to develop was both a culturally-validated achievement and a hard-won survival strategy which they were reluctant to relinquish.

"In a world of rapid change and tenuous loyalties", Silva argues, "the language and institution of therapy — and the self-transformation it promises — has exploded in American culture."[2] A therapeutic narrative of heroic self-transformation is the only story that make sense in a world in which

419

institutions can no longer be relied upon to support or nurture individuals:

> In social movements like feminism, self-awareness, or naming one's
> problems, was the first step to radical collective awareness. For this
> generation, it is the only step, completely detached from any kind of
> solidarity; while they struggle with similar, and structurally rooted,
> problems, there is no sense of "we". The possibility of collective
> politicisation through naming one's suffering is easily subsumed within
> these larger structures of domination because others who struggle are not
> seen as fellow sufferers but as objects of scorn.[3]

The spreading of therapeutic narratives was one way in which
neoliberalism contained and privatised the molecular revolution that
consciousness-raising was bringing about. Where consciousness-raising
pointed to impersonal and collective structures — structures that capitalist
and patriarchal ideology obscures — neoliberalism sees only individuals,
choices and personal responsibility. Yet consciousness-raising practices
weren't only at odds with capitalist ideology; they also marked a decisive
break with Marxist-Leninism. Gone was the revolutionary eschatology
and the militaristic machismo which made revolution the preserve of an
avant-garde. Instead, consciousness-raising made revolutionary activity
potentially available to anyone. As soon as two or more people gather
together, they can start to collectivise the stress that capitalism ordinarily
privatises. Personal shame becomes dissolved as its structural causes are
collectively identified.

Socialist-feminism converted Lukács's theory of class consciousness into
the practice of consciousness-raising. Since consciousness-raising has been
used by all kinds of subjugated groups, it would perhaps be better to talk now
of subjugated group consciousness rather than (just) class consciousness. But
it is worth noting in passing that neoliberalism has sought to eradicate the
very concept of class, producing a situation memorably described by Wendy
Brown, in which there is "class resentment without class consciousness or
class analysis". This erasure of class has distorted everything, and allowed
many struggles to be rhetorically captured by bourgeois liberalism.

Subjugated group consciousness is first of all a consciousness of the
(cultural, political, existential) machineries which produce subjugation —
the machineries which normalise the dominant group and create a sense
of inferiority in the subjugated. But, secondly, it is also a consciousness of
the potency of the subjugated group — a potency that depends upon this
very raised state of consciousness. However, it is important to be clear that
the aim is not to remain in a state of subjugation. As Nancy C. M. Hartsock
explains, "the point is to develop an account of the world that treats our
perspectives not as subjugated, insurrectionary, or disruptive knowledges,

but as potentially constitutive of a different world".[4]

To have one's consciousness raised is not merely to become aware of facts of which one was previously ignorant: it is instead to have one's whole relationship to the world shifted. The consciousness in question is not a consciousness of an already-existing state of affairs. Rather, consciousness-raising is productive. It creates is a new subject — a we that is both the agent of struggle and what is struggled for. At the same time, consciousness-raising intervenes in the "object", the world itself, which is now no longer apprehended as some static opacity, the nature of which is already decided, but as something that can be transformed. This transformation requires knowledge; it will not come about through spontaneity, voluntarism, the experiencing of ruptural events, or by virtue of marginality alone. Hence Hartsock's concept of standpoint epistemology, which maintains — following Lukács and Marx — that subjugated groups potentially have an access to knowledge of the whole social field that the dominant group lacks. Members of subjugated groups do not however automatically possess this knowledge as of right — it can only be accessed once group consciousness is developed. According to Hartsock, "the vision available to the oppressed group must be struggled for and represents an achievement which requires both science to see beyond the surface of the social relations in which all are forced to participate, and the education which can only grow from struggle to change those relations."

One way of seeing Jennifer M. Silva's book is as an account of radically deflated consciousness. Crucial to this is Silva's restoration of the concept of class as a frame shaping the experiences of those who feature in her study. Class is what is typically missing from her interviewees' "therapeutic" accounts of themselves. Exactly as Wendy Brown says, many of Silva's subjects tend to exhibit (an unconscious and disavowed) class resentment without class consciousness.

Reading Silva's descriptions of women wary of giving up their independence to men they perceive as feckless wasters, I was reminded of two R&B hits from 1999: "No Scrubs" by TLC and "Bills Bills Bills" by Destiny's Child. Both these songs see financially independent women upbraiding (presumably unemployed) men for their shiftlessness. It is easy to attack such tracks for their seeming peddling of neoliberal ideology. Yet I think it far more productive to hear these songs in the same way that we attend to the accounts in Silva's book. These are examples of consciousness deflated, which have important lessons to communicate to anyone seeking to dismantle capitalist realism.

It is still often assumed that politics is somehow "inside" cultural products, irrespective of their context and their use. Sometimes, agit-prop style culture can of course be politically transformative. But even the most reactionary cultural expression can contribute to a transformative project if it is sensitively attended to. It is possible to see the work of the late Stuart Hall in this light: as an attempt to bring to leftist politics the messages that culture was trying to impart to it. If this project was something of a tragic failure, it was a consequence, not of the shortcomings in Hall's approach, but of the intransigence of the old left, its deafness to the desires and anxieties being expressed in culture. Ever since Hall fell under the spell of Miles Davis in the 1950s, he dreamed of somehow commensurating the libidinal modernity he encountered in popular music with the progressive political project of the organised left. Yet the authoritarian left was unable to tune into this ambition, allowing itself to be outflanked by a new right which soon claimed modernisation for itself, and consigned the left to the past.

To understand this failure from another angle, let's consider for a moment the work of the late music and cultural critic Ellen Willis. In her 1979 essay, "The Family: Love It Or Leave It"[5], Willis observed that the counterculture's desire to replace the family with a system of collective child-rearing would have entailed "a social and psychic revolution of almost inconceivable magnitude". It's very difficult, in our deflated times, to re-create the counterculture's confidence that such a "social and psychic revolution" could not only happen, but was already in the process of unfolding. Like many of her generation, Willis's life was shaped by first being swept up by these hopes, then seeing them gradually wither as the forces of reaction regained control of history. There's probably no better account of the Sixties' counterculture's retreat from Promethean ambition into self-destruction, resignation and pragmatism than Willis's collection of essays *Beginning To See The Light*.[6] As Willis makes clear in her introduction to the collection, she frequently found herself at odds with what she experienced as the authoritarianism and statism of mainstream socialism. While the music that she listened to spoke of freedom, socialism seemed to be about centralisation and state control. The counterculture's politics were anti-capitalist, Willis argues, but this did not entail a straightforward rejection of everything produced in the capitalist field. Certainly, pleasure and individualism were important to what Willis characterises as her "quarrel with the left", yet the desire to do away with the family could not be construed in these terms alone; it was inevitably also a matter of new and unprecedented forms of collective (but non-statist) organisation. Willis' "polemic against standard leftist notions about advanced capitalism" rejected as at best only half-true the ideas "that the consumer economy makes us slave to commodities, that the function of the mass media is to manipulate our fantasies, so we will equate fulfilment with buying the system's commodities". Culture — and music culture in particular — was a terrain of struggle rather than a dominion of capital. The relationship between aesthetic forms and politics was unstable and inchoate — culture didn't just "express" already-existing political positions, it also anticipated a politics-to-come (which was also, too often, a politics that never actually arrived).

Yet there was also an immanent transformative immediacy in the music of the counterculture. It reinforced the feelings of despair, disaffection and rage that bourgeois culture ordinarily makes us distrust. As such, music functioned as a form of consciousness-raising, in which a mass audience could not only experience its feelings being validated, it could locate the origins of those feelings in oppressive structures. Moreover, the ingestion of hallucinogens by growing numbers of the population, and the emergence of a psychedelic imaginary that touched even those who had never used acid, made for a widespread perception that social reality was provisional, plastic, subject to transformation by collective desire.

If *Beginning to See the Light* is a painful — and painfully honest — account of consciousness deflation, then the same story is narrated within music culture itself. Peter Shapiro has shown how early Seventies soul and funk music — the O Jays' "Back Stabbers", the Undisputable Truth's "Smiling Faces Sometimes", Sly Stone's "You Caught Me Smiling" — "engaged in a remarkable conversation" about the newly minted Smiley yellow face image, "an imagistic minefield that played confidence games with centuries of caricatures, the beaming faces of the white establishment promising civil rights and integration [and] Nixon's Dirty Tricks gang." With Nixon on the rise and the Panthers subdued, songs like "Backstabbers" caught a new mood of suspicion and recrimination. In his classic essay "The Myth of Staggerlee", Greil Marcus argues that these songs — along with the rest of Sly and the Family Stone's *There's A Riot Goin' On* and the Temptations' "Papa Was A Rolling Stone" — were part of a bitter moment, when Sixties optimism had drained away to be replaced by paranoia and melancholy. Stone writes, "when new roles break down and there is nothing with which to replace them, old roles, ghosts, come in to fill the vacuum". The collectivity and the multiplicity that the Family Stone had embodied — radical democracy in vibrant action: a group made up of men and women, blacks and whites — gave way to a morose and dejected individualism. "The best pop music does not reflect events so much as it absorbs them", Marcus wrote. "If the spirit of Sly's early music combined the promises of Martin Luther King's speeches and the fire of a big city riot, *Riot* represented the end of those events and the attempt to create a new music appropriate to the new realities."

These "new realities" would eventually become nothing less than capitalist realism itself. Capitalist realism — in which current social relations are reified to the point that any shift in them becomes unimaginable — could only be fully consolidated once the Promethean-psychedelic imaginary was all but entirely subdued. But this would take a while. The Seventies weren't only about countercultural retreat and defeat. In *When the Lights Went Out: Britain in the Seventies*, Andy Beckett argues that a "liberal or left-wing melancholy about the Seventies has, in many ways, been the mirror image of the doomy right-wing view of the same period". But, as Beckett argues, this "fails to acknowledge that for many politicised Britons, the decade was not the hangover after the Sixties; it was the point when the great Sixties party actually started". The successful Miners' Strike of 1972 saw an alliance between the striking miners and students that echoed similar convergences in Paris 1968, with the miners using the University of Essex's Colchester campus as their East Anglian base. The Seventies also saw the growth in Britain of gay, anti-racist, feminist and Green movements. In many ways, it was it was the unprecedented success of the left and the counterculture in the 1970s that forced capital to respond with neoliberalism. This was initially played out in Chile, after Pinochet's CIA-backed coup had violently overthrown Salvador Allende's democratic socialist government, transforming the country — via a regime of repression and torture — into the first neoliberal laboratory.

The Seventies that Andy Beckett celebrates in the British context found expression in the US in the disco genre. Disco was a music that grew out of the convergence of a number of subjugated groups. It was a music made by and for gays, black people and women, and — like most postwar popular music, it was overwhelmingly produced by the working class. Chic's Nile Rodgers — surely the most important producer and sonic conceptualist of the late Seventies and early Eighties — had been a member of the Black Panthers as a teenager. Disco provided the template for the successive waves of dance music in the Eighties and Nineties, including house, techno, rave and garage. In her 1991 book *Design After Dark*, Cynthia Rose prophesied a "dancefloor revolution" that would

> come about through grass-roots changes — successive waves of guerrilla sounds, guerrilla design, guerrilla entertainments. The new design dynamic will be an impulse born out of celebration, rising out of leisure enacted as an event. And it will change young people's perception about what entities like design and communication should do.[7]

Yet Rose understandably failed to anticipate the extent to which the new energies, infrastructures and forms of desire she identified would be appropriated by a neoliberal culture which would lay claim to freedom and pleasure, while associating the left with a grey puritan statism. Once again, the left missed an opportunity, failing to successfully align itself with the collective euphoria of dancefloor culture. Thus the "good times" on the dancefloor became fleeting escapes from a capitalism that was increasingly dominating all areas of life, culture and the psyche.

This super-domination came out in the mordant yet playful "realism" of Gwen Guthrie's 1986 R&B hit, "Ain't Nothing Goin' On But The Rent", one of the first popular musical signs of the emergence of the new hardened subject that Silva analyses so well. At a time of rising unemployment, Guthrie sang, "You've got to have a j.o.b. if you want be with me/no romance without finance". The subjectivity performed in Guthrie's song is in many ways the female counterpart to the gangster rap persona that was emerging when the single was released. Both reject intimacy and tenderness. In gangster rap there is a hyberbolic performance of invulnerability — a performance that can only appear bitterly ironic, when we consider the fact that even some of the most wealthy and successful gangster rappers (such as Tupac Shakur and Biggie Smalls) would end up being shot dead. By contrast, and despite its surface bravado, "Ain't Nothing Goin' On But The Rent" is a song about the need for security — "fly girl like me/needs security" — in conditions of radical uncertainty. This wasn't some celebration of Reaganomics. On the contrary, Guthrie's song drew out the way in which Reaganomics was corroding the conditions for intimacy — a message that was much more emotionally charged and politically resonant than most of the protest songs of the time. Similarly, the formula "no romance without finance" need not only be construed as merely some reactionary concession to capitalist realism. Rather, it can be heard as a rejection of the ideological sentimentality that separates out social reproduction from paid work. Anticipating much of twenty-first-century popular music, "Ain't Nothing Goin' On But the Rent" is the sound of the loneliness that happens when consciousness is deflated, and the conditions for raising it are absent. But with the new movements that are rising in the US after Ferguson, with the movements in Europe that have produced Podemos and Syrisa, there is every reason to believe that those conditions are returning. It is beginning to look as if, instead of being the end of history, capitalist realism was a thirty-year hiatus. The processes that began in the Sixties can now be resumed. Consciousness is being raised again.

PART FOUR

FOR NOW, OUR DESIRE IS NAMELESS: POLITICAL WRITINGS

don't vote, don't encourage them[1]

There was a time when elections at least *seemed* to mean something. I still recall, viscerally, the hollow, bitter sense of total existential defeat the day after Foot's tragically bound-for-disaster hard left succumbed to the storm troopers of SF Kapital under Thatcher, and I, only fifteen years old, contemplated "Five More Years" of Tory rule. I didn't hear it at the time, but the song that always brings that feeling, that moment, is Mark Stewart's "Liberty City": "I'll give a wave to the management mercenaries... Don't their clean clothes look so pretty/Try to awaken then from the comforts of slavery..."

There are still those who would like to pretend that a Tory administration would be so much worse than New Labour, so that deigning to vote for anyone else would be an "indulgence". Choosing "the least worst" is not making this particular choice, it is also choosing a system which forces you to accept the least worst as the best you can hope for. Naturally, the defenders of the dictatorship of the elite pretend — perhaps they even deceive themselves — that the *particular* slew of lies, compromise and smarm they are hawking is "only temporary"; that, at some unspecified time in the future, things will improve if only we support the "progressive" wing of the status quo. But Hobson's choice is no choice, and the delusion of progressivism is not a psychological quirk, it is the structural delusion upon which liberal democracy is based.

Johan Hari tries to make the case for reluctantly voting New Labour today, on the grounds that the Tories are the only realistic alternative and they are manifestly worse than New Labour. But just what is the threat that Howard's Tories pose? Will they suspend habeas corpus? Can't, Toneeeeee's already done it. Will they shamelessly and shamefully play to the right-wing gallery on immigration? Well, yes, but that's only what the Joker

Hysterical Face is already doing. (It's not the war that made me lose any vestigial sentimental attachment to New Labour, it was their disgusting and despicable pandering to the right on immigration.)

Let's dispense with this idea, once and for all, that New Labour has "improved" anything. New Labour is the worst of all worlds: Thatcherist managerialism without the Thatcherite attack on vested interests. In the pre-Thatcher 1970s, it took six carworkers to do the job of one; in the post-Thatcher Noughties, it takes six consultants to do the job of none (since the mission statement wasn't worth writing in the first place). Same decadence, different beneficiaries. New Labour and its supporters scoff at the Tories' idea that you could cut £35 billion in public spending and yet improve public services. As someone who works in public services, it strikes me as eminently plausible (not that I believe that the Tories would do it, or do it right, if they came to power, naturally). Cutting back on red tape, bureaucrats, paperwork would have two immediately positive effects: it would get rid of the managers and administrators whose wages are a disproportionate drain on the budget, and it would improve the performance of those who actually *do the jobs*, simply by dint of the fact that they wouldn't have to deal with nannying memos and those who send them all the time.

Blair isn't just contingently a liar, he is, like the new breed of career politician he heads, a *professional* liar. As a lawyer turned politician, it's no surprise that Blair treats reality as a distraction from PR. He has been complicit in producing a situation in which there is no more at stake in parliamentary democracy than "beating the other side", as in a "debate" at the Oxford Union. His I-am-innately-good moral righteousness is as much a testament to his public school and Oxbridge education as anything else: you see, glinting in the eyes, the unwavering certainty of the truly imbecilic. Blair likes to see himself as a conviction politician, but apart from his imperialist intransigence (itself a symptom of his belief in his own innate superiority), what else IS he actually committed to? It's telling that the only thing he was prepared to defy public opinion on was the war.

Blair's slogan "education, education, education" is the sickest joke of all (and not only because he has presided over the dumbest front bench in recorded history, another testament to the wonder of Oxbridge). Maybe he has "pumped more money" into education, but that is useless if the extra funds are going on quangos, incompetent administrators and facile "initiatives" that were doomed to fail and pointless even if they succeeded.

The "Third Way" "solution" to Further Education is a typical Blairite catastrophe. Colleges are now funded per student, with the result that students now treat themselves as "consumers" — i.e. the canny ones quickly realise that even the most abusive or violent behaviour is unlikely to result in their being removed from the college, since it means a significant cut in the college's revenue. Students with behavioural problems shouldn't simply be turned away, but neither can they be allowed to continue attending college as if nothing has happened. That is a dereliction of duty towards the student, and towards the other students, whose education and learning environment is damaged while such behaviour is left unchecked. But "Third Way" funding means that the only result will be institutional cynicism. Imposing "targets" and assigning funds on the basis of meeting them — what the economist calls "reform", i.e. ideology dressed up as realism — will only ever lead to a situation in which bureaucrats and the bureaucratically-minded prosper. The way to improve education, and all other public services, is to accept the obvious truth (though such truth is contrary to ideology): most people working in these services are not, in fact, venal, are not motivated solely by what is in the interests of "them and their famileeee". So it would be better to hand more control back over to them; by all means intervene if it is going wrong, but don't assume that things work better if they are run by bureaucrats (the whole of reality is a counter-example to this ludicrous thesis).

I admit that, emotionally and unthinkingly, I will find myself supporting the "left" parties when the results come in tomorrow night. Yes, I want to see Galloway give Oona King a kicking, yes I would love to see Letwin lose his seat. But only in *exactly the same way* that I want to see X contestant beat Y contestant in *Big Brother*; it really is only sentimentality to pretend that this spectacle has much consequence. This will always be the case in liberal democracy at the best of times, but especially so in a country which has an electoral system so fundamentally corrupt and unjust. Hari is right that, in the Eighties, 56% of the electorate voted for left parties, but because the vote was split between Labour and the Lib Dems, the Tories were allowed to maintain their reign of terror. But that is an argument for urgent reform of the electoral system, not for voting New Labour.

As I.T. rightly argues, the "people died for the vote" line is utterly facile. Soldiers in the Wehrmacht died for the glories of the Fatherland — does that mean I should become a Nazi? Catholics burned for their belief in transubstantiation: should I then repent and go to Mass on Sunday? Plus, I think I'm on fairly safe ground, really, with the conjecture that no one, but no one, died for the opportunity to "choose" between Blair and Howard.

october 6, 1979: capitalism and bipolar disorder[1]

Realism has nothing to do with the Real. On the contrary, the Real is what realism has continually to suppress.

Capitalist realism, like socialist realism, is about "putting a human face" on and naturalising a set of political determinations. The komissars of Kapital like to pose as tough-minded pragmatists who tell unpalatable truths and who alone are capable of facing up to the harsh "realities" of the world. Yet Kapitalism — no less in its its soon-to-take over Chinese State version than in its soon-to-collapse American model — is based upon a slew of fantasies so credulous that they are almost charming. In a powerful piece in the *Independent* today,[2] Johann Hari parallels the militant complacency of the current ruling elite with the thinking of previous highly developed social groups, such as the Incas and the Mayans, which had "committed ecocide". "What were Easter Islanders saying as they cut down the last tree on their island?," Hari quotes geographer Jared Diamond asking in his book *Collapse: How Societies Choose to Fail or Survive*. It is grim to reflect that the answers — "jobs not trees!" or "technology will solve our problems; never fear, we'll find a substitute for wood" — are precisely the rationalisations that a thanatropic drive would produce in order to do its work. In the unconscious, Freud says, no one really believes they will die, and this is no doubt also true of civilisations, which despite the melancholy monuments testifying to the demise of Maya and Easter Island, are convinced that they are the exceptions, they are the one which cannot perish.

It is easy to see what capitalist "realism" means when you consider Blair's habitual response to appeals from the environmental lobby. Measures to rein in eco-catastrophe may well be desirable — *even necessary* — but they, Blair tells us with a heavy heart bursting his sleeve, are "politically impossible". Here, then, is capitalist "realism": the reduction to the realm of the "impossible" of any steps that will prevent the destitution of the human environment. For that is what "realism" amounts to: not a representation of the real, but a determination of what is *politically* possible. But what is politically possible is at odds with what is physically possible, so in a sense, it is the servomechanism-agents of Kapital, not their opponents, who "demand the impossible" now. Their fantasy of a sustainable Kapitalism carrying on, forever, without burning out the planet, is perfectly delirial.

Another insight into capitalist realism was provided last week by Marxist economist Christian Marazzi (Scuola Universitaria Professionale della Svizzera Italiana, Lugano, Switzerland) whose lecture "Finance, Attention and Affect" at Goldsmiths was an interrogation of the meaning — and psychological, social and neuronic impact of — post-Fordism.[3] Christian dated the moment of the switch from Fordism to post-Fordism very precisely: 6 October 1979. It was on that date that the Federal Reserve increased interest rates by twenty points, preparing the way for the "supply-side economics" that would constitute the "economic reality" with which we are now so familiar. The rise in interest rates not only contained inflation, it made possible a new organisation of the means of production and distribution. The economy would no longer be organised by reference to production, but from the side of the point of sale. The "rigidity" of the Fordist production line gave way to a new "flexibility", a word that will send chills of recognition down the spine of every worker today. This flexibility was defined by a deregulation of capital and labour, with the workforce being casualised (with an increasing number of workers employed on a temporary basis) and outsourced.

The new conditions both required and emerged from an increased cybernetisation of the working environment. The Fordist factory was crudely divided into blue- and white-collar work, with the different types of labour physically delimited by the structure of the building itself. Labouring in noisy environments, watched over by managers and supervisors, workers had access to language only in their breaks, in the toilet, at the end of the working day, or when they were engaged in sabotage, because *communication interrupted production*. But in post-Fordism, when the assembly line becomes a "flux of information", people work *by* communicating. As Wiener taught, communication and control entail one another.

What Deleuze, after Burroughs and Foucault, called "the society of control" comes into its own in these conditions. Work and life become inseparable. As Christian observed, this is in part because labour is now to some degree linguistic, and it is impossible to leave language in the locker after work. Capital follows you when you dream. Time ceases to be linear, becomes chaotic, punctiform. As production and distribution are restructured, so are nervous systems. To function effectively as a component of "just in time production", you must develop a capacity to respond to unforeseen events, you must learn to live in conditions of total instability, or "precarity", as the ugly neologism has it. Periods of work alternate with periods of unemployment. Typically, you find yourself employed in a series of short-term jobs, unable to plan for the future.

The horrors of these new working patterns are clear, but it is imperative that the left renounces one of its most dangerous addictions, its nostalgia for Fordism. As Christian pointed out, the disintegration of stable working patterns was in part driven by the desires of workers — it was they who, quite rightly, did not wish to work in the same factory for forty years. In many ways, the left has never recovered from being wrong-footed by Kapital's mobilisation and metabolisation of the desire for emancipation from the Fordist routine. Especially in the UK, the traditional representatives of the working class — union and labour leaders — found Fordism rather too congenial; its *stability of antagonism* gave them a guaranteed role. But this meant that it was easy for the advocates of post-Fordist Kapital to present themselves as the opponents of the status quo, bravely resisting an inertial organised labour "pointlessly" invested in fruitless ideological antagonism which served the ends of union leaders and politicians, but did little to advance the hopes of the class they purportedly represented. And so the stage was set for the neoliberal "end of history", the "post-ideological" ideological justification for rampant supply-side economics. Antagonism is not now located externally, in the face-off between class blocs, but internally, in the psychology of the worker, who, qua worker, is interested in old-style class conflict, but, as someone with a pension fund, is also interested in maximising their investment. There is no longer an identifiable *external* enemy. The consequence is that, as Christian put it in a memorable image, post-Fordist workers, are like the Old Testament Jews after they left the "house of slavery": liberated from a bondage to which they have no wish to return but also abandoned, stranded in the desert, confused about the way forward.

The psychological conflict raging within individuals — they themselves are at war — cannot but have casualties. One hidden, or at least naturalised, consequence of the rise of post-Fordism is that the "invisible plague" of psychiatric disorders that has spread, silently and stealthily, since around 1750 (i.e. the very onset of industrial capitalism), has reached a new level of acuteness in the last two decades. This is one more dimension of the Real that capitalist realism is constitutively unable to process.

It is typical of New Labour that it should have committed itself, so early in its third term, to removing people from incapacity benefit, as if most people claiming the benefit were malingerers. In contrast with this assumption, it doesn't seem unreasonable to infer that most of the people claiming incapacity benefit — and there are well in excess of two million of them — are casualties of Kapital. A significant proportion of claimants, for instance, are people psychologically trashed as a consequence of the capitalist realist insistence that mining was no longer economically viable (though, even considered in brute economic terms, once you factor in the cost to taxpayers of such benefits, the arguments about "viability" seem rather less than convincing). Many have simply buckled under the terrifyingly unstable conditions of post-Fordism.

The current ruling ontology rules out any possibility of a *social* causation of mental illness. The chemico-biologisation of mental illness is of course strictly commensurate with its de-politicisation. Considering mental illness as an individual chemico-biological problem has enormous benefits for capitalism: first, it reinforces capital's drive towards atomistic individualisation (you are sick because of your brain chemistry), and second, it provides an enormously lucrative market in which multinational "pyscho-mafias" can peddle their dodgy drugs (we can cure you with our SSRIs). It goes without saying that all mental illnesses are neurologically *instantiated*, but this says nothing about their *causation*. If it is true, for instance, that depression is constituted by low serotonin levels, what still needs to be explained is *why* particular individuals have low levels of serotonin.

The increase in bipolar disorder is a particularly significant development. In the discussion after Christian's lecture, I asked him about the relationship between this form of mental illness and capitalism as a system. It is clear that capitalism, with its ceaseless boom and bust cycles, is itself, fundamentally and irreducibly, bipolar. Capitalism is characterised by a lurching between hyped-up mania (the irrational exuberance of "bubble thinking") and depressive come-down. (The term "economic depression" is no accident). To a degree unprecedented in any other social system (and capitalism is very precisely NOT a social "structure" in the way that the despotic state or the primitive socius are), capitalism both feeds on and reproduces the moods of populations. Without delirium and confidence, capital could not function. As it happened, Christian confirmed that he had in fact been working with people who had been "psychologically smashed" by capitalism, many of whom, it turned out, had in fact developed bipolar disorder. It could hardly be denied that there is an isomorphic relationship between the social and individual disorders of capitalism.

How could madness not result when we are invited to consider America's consuming of $600 billion a year more than it produces "realistic"? (As opposed, so we are told, to Europe's "unrealistic" social welfare programmes.) Make no mistake, the realists are insane, which more than ever reveals the force of the slogan, "the Real is the impossible, but the impossible which happens". Ecological catastrophe and mental illness are present in capitalism's wrap-around simulation as warps, unassimilable discontinuities, that which cannot be but which, nevertheless, cannot be extirpated. Perhaps these negative Reals — these dark shadows which allow us to see Kapital's striplit mall of the mind for what it actually is — have their complement in a positive Real, an event completely inconceivable in the current situation, but which will break in and re-define everything.

what if they had a protest and everyone came[1]

What kind of protest is it that everyone agrees with?

If you weren't already suspicious of the dull unanamity that coalesced on Saturday [Live 8],[2] reflect on the fact that the Russian show only happened because Putin didn't want to be the only G8 leader whose country did not have a Live 8 gig. That fact alone reveals that the relationship between the current ruling elite and their ostensible opponents in the entertainment biz goes far beyond complicity.

Live 8 rests on two "libidinal fallacies".

The first is obvious: it ignores the systemic and abstract nature of the geopolitical situation. It really isn't the case that "eight men in a room" can "change history" simply by an act of will. Beyond the sentimental bluster, everyone knows that, but Live 8 depends upon a fantasy that there are two types of subject who need to be enlightened: the Subject Who Does Not Know (and whose "awareness" is to be raised) and the Subject Who Knows But Who Doesn't Care. But who are these people? Who, exactly, needs to be "made aware" of the fact that Africa is desperately poor? And does anyone, even those who buy into the cheap off-the-shelf caricature of Bush as a dumb chimp, really think that he, personally, *deliberately chooses* to inflict starvation on African children? More to the point, does anyone really think that, on the level of personal morality, Bush is any different from the billionaire pop stars so histrionically raising their fists against him and wagging their fingers at us? That is to say: if there is some sort of moral dividing line, would you really want to place Bush on one side and *Elton John* and *$ Bill Gates* on the other?

It is not that Live 8 is a "degraded" form of protest. On the contrary, it is in Live 8 that the logic of the protest is revealed in its purest form. The protest impulse of the Sixties posited a Malevolent Father, the harbinger of a Reality Principle that (supposedly) cruelly and arbitrarily denies the "right" to total enjoyment. This Father has unlimited access to resources, but he selfishly — and senselessly — hoards them. Yet it is not capitalism but *protest* itself which depends upon this figuration of the Father. It goes without saying that the psychological origins of this imagery lie in the earliest phases of infancy. The hippies' bucolic imagery and "dirty protest" — filth as a rejection of adult grooming — both originate in the "unlimited demands" of the infant. A consequence of the infant's belief in the Father's omnipotence is the conviction that all suffering could be eliminated if only the Father wished it. (In terms of Live 8: if only those 8 men yield to our demands, all poverty could be eliminated forever!) The demand for total enjoyment is actually pretty indiscriminate: the protest could just easily be against war (bummer maaaan) or against being charged for going into a festival (hey, breadheadzzzzzzz, don't be heaveeeee...)

Indidentally, one of the successes of the latest global elite — the Social Democrats — has been their avoidance of identification with the figure of the hoarding Father, even though the "reality" they impose on the young is *substantially harsher* than the "reality" they protested against in the Sixties. In this sense, Bush is a godsend for Blair, since Blair can pose as the "really realistic" representative of Social Democratic moderation "winning concessions" from the obscene excesses of Bush, the Junkyard King of Amerikapital's hideous fusion of id and superego. (The reference to the Birthday Party is not idle here. Oddly, their *Junkyard* strikes me as an uncannily prescient psychoanalysis both of Bushite Amerika and the role that it plays in everyone else's fantasies, "Big-Jesus-Oil-King down in Texas drives great holy tanks of Gold/screams from heaven's Graveyard/American heads will roll in Texas/roll like daddy's meat...")

This brings us to the second fallacy. What is being disavowed in the abjection of evil and ignorance onto fantasmatic Others is our own complicity in planetary networks of oppression. What needs to be kept in mind is BOTH that capitalism is a hyper-abstract impersonal structure AND that it would be nothing without our co-operation. As I will never tire of insisting, the most Gothic description of capital is also the most literal. Capital is an abstract parasite, an insatiable vampire and zombie-maker; but the living flesh it converts into dead labour is ours, and the zombies it makes are us. Determinists of both a neoliberal and anti-humanist bent (believe it or not, it is not unheard of for such positions to coincide within the same person, proving that Marx wasn't wrong about the essentially contradictory nature of capitalist ideology) merely echo teleo-Marxism at its most eschatological when they insist that what the meat (or human) components of the capital machine are of no consequence since the total triumph of capital is historically inevitable.

The question of what capital wants from us requires answers at a number of levels: economic, psychonalytic, and perhaps most pressingly, theological. In any case, it is clear that, for the moment at least, capital cannot get along without us. It remains the case, however, that we can get along without it. The parasite needs its "mere conscious linkages", but we do not need the parasite. In addition to anything else, to ignore the crucial functioning of the meat in the machine is poor cybernetics. The denial of human agency is an SF fantasy, albeit one that is everywhere realising itself.

But to reclaim that agency means first of all accepting our insertion *at the level of desire* in the remorseless meat-grinder of capital. Capital is not something imposed upon us by Bush; it is we who are hooked on the "garbage in honey's sack", unable to kick the habit of returning to the Big Jesus Trashcan for another hit of feel-good junk.

It also means raising the price — libidinal, personal, monetary — of agency. The repeated claim from onstage multi-millionaires that the audience were going to "change history" simply by turning up and tuning in cheapens agency in every sense. Participating in a narcissistic, self-righteous spectacle is not "doing something". Tony Parsons, of all people, made the very good point in the *Mirror* today that the generation of the Thirties and Forties did not expect Crosby and Sinatra to change the world — but, as he says, many of them had either risked or given up their lives to change things.

Withdrawal from the capital matrix entails an unplugging that will seem painful to nervous systems commensurated to the Reality-Pleasure Principle. Partly it means giving up the reassuring comforter of the Bad Father Figure and facing the fact that the G8 leaders are not capable of legislating away all planetary misery, but are "old men at the crossroads", capital's meat puppets not its masters. There is a sense in which it simply is the case that the political elite *are* our servants; the miserable service they provide from us is to launder our libidos, to obligingly re-present for us our disavowed desires as if they had nothing to do with us. If anyone is in charge in Kapital it is Oedipus Rex, i.e. us. ("*I* yam the King!" as Cave caterwauled on "Junkyard". Yes: the junkie as monarch, that's capitalist sovereignty.) The political "reality" that Bush and the others will no doubt blame their failure to act upon is not just an ideological smokescreen. It is the reality constituted by the desires of that selfsame Live 8 crowd who, when push comes to shove, will not pay extra taxes, will not give up cheap flights or car use, will not make a stand against inequity and stupidity at work if it means compromising their interests and those of their famileeeee and yet who expect global crises to be magically solved by eight stooges in a room.

The great benefit of Lacanianism is to reject both the party of the Infant ("you want new masters, and you shall have your wish" as Lacan told the student protestors of the Sixties) and the party of the Father (the empircomongers who try to sell the Symbolic as the only Real). There must indeed be a demand for the Impossible, but an Impossible which does not correspond with the definition provided by either party. It is not a question of total enjoyment, but of the not-all, a sober psychosis, lessness...

defeating the hydra[1]

In Marvel's *Nick Fury, Agent of S.H.I.E.L.D.* comics, the nefarious S.P.E.C.T.R.E.-like international crime and terror network was called H.Y.D.R.A. Its slogan was "cut off a limb and two more shall take its place". In Saturday's *Times*, Paul Wilkinson, Chairman of the Centre for the Study of Terrorism and Political Violence, described the "decentralised network" of al-Qaeda as a "true hydra". But the lesson of the hydra myth — that to use force against certain types of enemy is not only ineffective, it is counter-productive — is one that the leaders of the War on Terror have yet to learn.

It is the absurd War on Terror itself that has fed the al-Qaeda hydra and put British citizens on the frontline. The issue here is not simply a causal one — the War on Terror has made life unsafer in the West — but a conceptual one — the very notion of a War on Terror has meant that Western populations are reclassified as active combatants in a war not only to the death, but beyond death, an infinite, excitatory cycle of violence begetting violence.

Despite what the increasingly hysterical Pro-Bombing "Left" (PBL) maintain, the causal argument is won. (A testament to this is the way in which the PBL refuse even to have the argument. As one, they have wagged their finger at anyone who has pointed out the obvious causal chain linking US and British foreign policy with Thursday's events, tut-tutting about the unseemliness of "politicising" the atrocity "even before the bodies are buried", as if contempt for neo-imperialist Shock and Awe somehow equated to lack of respect for the victims of the attacks in London, as if their own columns were disinterested and neutral, and as if solemn moralising rather than political analysis were what is called for.) The claim that the bombing of Iraq has been a recruiting sergeant for terrorism is uncontroversial. A Foreign Office and Home Office dossier cited in the *Sunday Times* today states what any intelligent observer already knows:

It seems that a particularly strong cause of disillusionment among Muslims, including young Muslims, is a perceived "double standard" in the foreign policy of western governments, in particular Britain and the US. The perception is that passive "oppression", as demonstrated in British foreign policy, e.g. non-action on Kashmir and Chechnya, has given way to "active oppression". The war on terror, and in Iraq and Afghanistan, are all seen by a section of British Muslims as having been acts against Islam.[2]

Even the *Economist* grants that some of al-Qaeda's "large group of sympathisers" will have had "extra levels of motivation since the Iraq war". (It adds: "George Bush has sometimes claimed that a silver lining to the cloud his forces are struggling through in Iraq is that at least the West's enemies are being fought there rather than at home. The attacks in London are a reminder that that view is as wrong as it is glib."[3])

But the reclassification of the struggle with al-Qaeda as "war" is another factor that promotes, inspires and legitimates terrorism, a factor perhaps no less significant than the misadventures in Iraq and Afghanistan. For example: it used to be the case that the British government refused to accept that it was "at war" with the IRA; it was the IRA who made that claim. The unwillingness to concede that Britain was engaged in war partly had the effect of making it possible to claim both that the IRA were terrorists (i.e. BY DEFINITION not a group with whom one could be at war) and that any attack on the civilian population was an outrage visited on innocents. But if indeed we ARE at war (as the oxy/moronic War on Terror would have us believe), and if what "we" are fighting for is "our values", and "simply getting on with our lives" is an expression of those "values" — as, since Thursday, we have endlessly been told it is — then it would follow that we are all indeed warriors co-opted into War on Terror. As Simon Jenkins put it (also in the *Sunday Times*), "it is Blair who gave terrorism the status of war. He can hardly complain when the enemy treats it as such".

Johann Hari observed — surely not approvingly? — that the bombings on Thursday were received in London almost as if they were a natural disaster. Much of the media here has insisted, rather, that the bombings be treated as a SUPERNATURAL disaster, the act of a transcendent Evil that cannot and furthermore *must not* be explained. Both Blair and Bush find it expedient and congenial to use a theological language to describe a threat that would be better considered in more worldly terms. That language is dangerous for two reasons: first, because it contributes to the sublimation of the al-Qaeda threat, transforming a diffuse network into a supernatural force, and second, because it renders all analysis of the threat al-Qaeda actually poses all the more difficult.

According to an emerging orthodoxy in certain sections of the British media, just about any attempt to offer economic, political or sociological explanation for al-Qaeda's emergence is tantamount to an expression of sympathy for its aims and methods. As Savonarola has pointed out, the PBL and other reactionaries attempted in the immediate aftermath of Thursday to make the very word "political" a slander as they desperately cast about trying to establish a period of non-reflection in which "politics" and thought could be suspended — a period, that is to say, in which *their* politics and their non-thinking could be imposed as the default response.

The most facile and stupid example of this type of argument *might* have been Nick Cohen's piece in the *Observer* today,[4] rightly excoriated by Lenin[5] (I say "might" because the amount of shrill stupidity, sentimental nonsense and emotional pornography churned out by the hacks over the last few days has reached new levels of stupefaction, as the miserable reality of central London's rapacious Hobbesian inferno, where folk will beat you to death rather than let you get into a Tube ten seconds before them, has been magically transformed by the bombs and media fairy dust into the very essence of an underdog England in which it is WWII forever: to the sound of choruses of "maybe it's because I'm Londahner" ringing out from the ghosts of the music halls, journos have shamelessly done themselves up as pearly kings and queens, taking on the role of celebrants of a Fantasy London which is as convincing as Dick Van Dyke's accent in *Mary Poppins*.) The "agalma", the special treasure, of this London resides in the status of "heroic victim" that a disaster such as this re-confirms. A dangerous logic takes hold: we're under attack, we must be Good.

The supernaturalisation of al-Qaeda is crucial to this strategy. If *we* are the Good, it can only be the senselessly Evil, the irrationally jealous, who would want to attack us. (This mode of bewildered self-aggrandising is as crucial to a certain version of American identity as spam-eating-make-do-and-mend-what you-complaining-about-that-severed-leg-for dour fortitude is crucial to Blitz Englishness.) Needless to say, the positing of an ethnic subject — *We, the Good* — whose innate virtue is reconfirmed by its being attacked is constitutive of both the al-Qaeda and the post-911 US mindset. A military asymmetry is doubled by a fantasmatic symmetry. Each is the other's Satan.

To talk of al-Qaeda in theological (rather than in political, social or economic) terms is to adopt their mode of discourse in an inverted form. It is to return to a pre-Feuerbachian, pre-sociological perspective in which all the lessons of the nineteenth- and twentieth-century studies of the social psychology of religion — undertaken by figures as diverse as Durkheim, Marx, Weber, Nietzsche and Freud — are forgotten. If a particular strain of religion is to be understood as, in Cohen's words, "an autonomous psychopathic force" rather than as a social, economic and psychological phenonenon with complex causes, then all hope of reasoned analysis is a priori ruled out. Unreason is abjected onto the enemy (even as it is evinced in one's own not even minimally coherent ravings), thus legitimating the idea that "the only option" is military force.

The floating of the pseudo-concept of "Islamofascism" has been central here. There are any number of reasons to consider the idea that there is such a thing as Islamofascism a nonsense. Here are two. First of all, fascism has always been associated with nationalism, but, like global capital, Islamism has no respect for nationality; the first loyalty of the Islamist is to the global Umma. Secondly, fascism is about the State — Islamism has no model of the State, as could be seen in Afghanistan under the Taliban.

The only sense one can make of "fascism" as used by the PBL is that it names anything that is really, really bad (that well-defined category) or it involves the curtailment of liberties. The brand of Islamism al-Qaeda favours would certainly curtail liberties, but not necessarily the same ones that fascism would curtail, or for the same reasons.

Rather than engaging in nebulous negative sublimation — "Behold, Satan" — it would better behove the opponents of Islamist Terrorism to consider more carefully what is specific about it. As John Stevens noted over the weekend, the typical al-Qaeda terrorist is unlikely to have been parachuted in from an Afghan village. They are much more likely to have lived in the West, either as residents or as nationals. Their affiliation with al-Qaeda will, we can speculate, almost certainly serve the function of resolving a tension in themselves. Al-Qaeda recruit from schools and colleges because they are astute enough to recognise that male adolescence is a time of boiling confusion that craves easy certainties. It cannot be that difficult for a fervent Jihadi to convince impressionable young men adrift in the miserable haze of Babylonic capitalism that it is not al-Qaeda but their enemies who are really Evil.

After all, it is not hard to construct a convincing story that the success of the West has been achieved at the expense of Muslims. The *Sunday Times* reports that in Britain "Muslims are three times more likely to be unemployed than the population as a whole; 52% of them are economically inactive (the highest of any faith group) and 16% have never worked or are long-term unemployed. This is blamed on a lack of education: 43% of Muslims have no qualifications." But it is not just the poor themselves who flock to al-Qaeda; it is also those burning with a sense of injustice on behalf of the poor.

In this context, it is worth remembering Giuliani's jaw-dropping proclamation (to which Savonarola has been assiduous in drawing our attention): "People who live in freedom always prevail over people who live in oppression." So speak the Masters, the Winners... Who speaks for the oppressed then? The rise of Islamism must be correlated with the demise of the left. If it has become the default repository for Muslim rage against injustice then that is partly due to the US, which, as is well-known, funded

Islamist Jihadis in a bid to defeat Communism. Since only something like Communism could absorb and re-direct the energies that are fuelling al-Qaeda, I look forward to the day when the US will fund Islamic Communism, and the circle will be complete.

the face of terrorism without a face[1]

So Tony Blair is the leader who has brought suicide bombing to Britain.

Any remaining doubt about the link between 7/7 and the Iraq bombing and occupation was dissipated today when a friend of one of the suspects, Mohammed Sadique Kahn, spoke to — of all things — the *Evening Standard*. "The friend [...] said Khan, Tanweer and Hussain grew up together and 'often talked about their anger at their Muslim brothers and sisters being unfairly treated in Iraq by the US.'"

No surprises there. And no surprises, at least not for k-punk readers, that the bombers were British. That, at least, somewhat undermined the racist agendas of European and US "Experts" who blamed the atrocity on Britain's supposedly insufficiently authoritarian immigration and asylum policies, barely concealing their disgust at multi-ethnic "Londonistan", a stance that echoes Mark Steyn's Islamophobic revulsion at "Eurabia". The BNP in Barking found that their predictable attempts to extract political capital from the bombings — a leaflet with a photograph of the trashed number 30 bus over a caption saying, "Maybe now it's time to listen to the BNP" — also fell foul of the revelation that the bombers came from Leeds, not the Middle East. Naturally, that news brings with it the possibilities for other kinds of exploitation by racists. It is a grotesque understatement to say that the next few months will not be easy for Muslims in Britain. Emollient words about "true Islam" will be as ineffective as they are misleading. There is no true Islam. Islam, like all other religions, is a riot of contradictions, a tissue of interpretations. The words of the Prophet give as much comfort to zealots as to pacifists.

David Davis said last week that modern terrorism is "terrorism without a face". Suddenly, however, the terrorists have a face — even though it is not the one that many expected, or wanted. The photographs of the perpetrators and the photographs of the victims — who could tell them apart? There is no tell-tale "demonic stain" on the faces of the killers. They aren't the austere, obsessive "foreigners" that the popular imagination had conjured. They wore trainers and tracksuits, they were religious, sure, but no one thought they were fanatics. They weren't even socially dysfunctional geeks. By all accounts, they were popular, played cricket. Nor was there any obvious lack or deprivation in their lives.

The obvious questions seem to be "how", "why"? Yet the same questions do not seem the obvious ones to ask when we see photographs of similar young men who happen to be in in the US or British forces, men who have participated in the killing of very many more civilians.

The Blairite objection to terrorism cannot be its means, since he, too, considers the killing of a certain number of civilians an acceptable sacrifice for the greater Good. (One of the problems this kind of utilitarian calculus has always faced is that there is no obvious point at which to stop counting the consequences. But, as we've already established, surely Thursday must count amongst the consequences of the Iraq misadventure.) It is the ends, then, in which the difference must reside, not the means. Blair is supernaturally confident that he is on the side of the angels, that he is pursuing the Good, whereas his enemies are Evil. The problem is that they think exactly the same way.

He tells us that we are in a war. But to many Muslims — not "mad mullahs", but, amongst others, young men from "ordinary" backgrounds — it is as obvious as it is to Blair what the right, the only side, to be on is. It is the side of the poor and the oppressed, not the side of the hyper-privileged and the massively well-armed. The rage, the righteous sense of injustice that led those four to give their lives and take the lives of others — and please, do not describe what they did as "cowardly"; "brutal" by all means, but not "cowardly", and certainly nowhere near as cowardly as the Powell doctrine of bombing from a great height — that anger needs to be channeled by other forces, forces which don't counter oppression with repression, which don't transform rage into outrage.

UPDATE: Breakfast TV, BBC1. A group of young Muslims from Leeds — not "fanatics" by any means — tell the reporter (who has to concede that they are articulate and measured) that Iraq is the major factor in switching young men onto extremism in Britain. They make it clear that they are appalled by the events of last Thursday, condemn them without reservation, but nevertheless are angered by the patent double standards of the British media. The fifty people who died last week — whose deaths they in no way trivialised — seem to count much more than the thousands who die in Iraq. (It makes me wonder what would happen if the media indulged in what Simon Jenkins called "grief pornography" for Iraqis: if there were back stories and photographs for all of *them*, would the public mood change?) In the studio, Irshad Manji, author of *The Trouble with Islam Today*, tries to demur, falling back on the standard line that 9/11 preceded Iraq. True enough, but there had never been suicide bombing in *Britain* until last week. Manji makes some good points: in a piece the other day (I think in the *Standard*?), she broke ranks with the sentimental consensus about "true Islam", arguing that there needs to be an Islamic Reformation, with the acceptance within the religion that certain passages of the Koran can be wrong. But the call for Islamic auto-critique must go alongside a recognition that the "Crusader" policies of the US and the UK feed an aggrieved militancy that will make that kind of Reformation much less likely.

conspicuous force and verminisation[1]

The paradoxical War on Terror is based on a kind of willed stupidity; the willed stupidity of wishful thinking. Only the logic of dreamwork can suture "War" with "Terror" in this way, since terrorists were, by classical definition, those without "legitimate authority" to wage war. However, it is horribly evident for some while that a new, frighteningly facile, definition of Terrorism has come into play. What makes Terrorists terrorists is not their supposed lack of legitimate authority but their *Inherent Evil*. *We* are *ontologically Good*; Good by our very nature, no matter what we *do*. *We* belong to an "alliance of moderation" against the Axis of Evil. So when "we" "accidentally" level an apartment block full of children with our moderate bombs, we do not cease to be moderate. The difference between They, the Evil, and We, the Good is, of course, intent; the Terrorists *deliberately target* civilians. This is their only aim, because they are Evil. Although we kill vastly more civilians, we do not *intend* to it, so we remain Good.

For the libidinal roots of this wishful thinking, we have to look beyond the foibles of individuals to the political unconscious of the hyper-militarised state. It is geared to deal with threats if they come from other armed states, so it pretends — deceives itself, and then attempts to deceive us — that this is in accord with the actual geopolitical situation. Condi's crocodile tears notwithstanding, the US, needless to say, is in no position to condemn Israel's air strikes, since the Israeli bombings follow the War on Terror script to the letter. The conflict with Hezbollah turns into a destruction of Lebanese people and infrastructure, just as the struggle with al-Qaeda became a war on Afghanistan and Iraq. For the hyper-miltarised state, asymmetry can only be thought of as an advantage: we have more and better weaponry than them, therefore we must win.

The stupidity here is evident, and multi-levelled. First of all, it involves a literal occlusion and suppression of intelligence. Terrorism is a problem to be met with brute force rather with intelligence. Successfully defeating Terrorist groups is a long-term business, dirty, but above all, stealthy, invisible. But the War on Terror is inherently and inescapably spectacular; it arises from the demands of the post 9/11 military-industrial-*entertainment* complex: it is not enough for the state to do something, it has to be *seen doing something*. The template here is Gulf War 1, which as both Baudrillard and Virilio knew, could not be understood outside logics of mediatisation. Gulf War 1 was conceived of a kind of *re-shooting* of Vietnam, with better technology, and on a videogame desert terrain in which carpet bombing would be industrially effective. This is the kind of asymmetry that the military-industrial-entertainment complex likes: no casualties (on our side).

The bringing to bear of what, following Veblen, we might call *conspicuous force* presupposes a second stupidity: the verminisation of the enemy. Before Gulf War 1 had even happened, Virilo saw the logic of verminisation rehearsed in James Cameron's *Aliens*, wherein the "machinic actors do battle in a Manichean combat in which the enemy is no longer an adversary, a fellow creature one must respect in spite of everything; rather, it is an unnameable being that it is more appropriate to exterminate than to examine or analyse." In *Aliens*, Virilio ominously notes, attacks on the "family [form] the basis of [...] neocolonial intervention". The teeming, Lovecraftian abominations *which can breed much faster than we can* are to be dealt with by machines whose "awesome appearance is part of [their] military effectiveness". Shock and awe.

Aliens was the moment in which a new mode of the military-industrial-entertainment-complex became visible. Virilio argued that *Aliens'* privileging of military hardware "could only lead in the end to the extinction of the talking film, its complete replacement by film trailers for hardened militarists". In fact, the talking film has been replaced by the shoot-em-up videogame whose picnoleptic delirium is flat with the prosecution of the Sega-Sony-CNN war. "Realists" who attacked Baudrillard and Virilio for their insistence upon the fact that war is now constitutively mediatised missed the point that hyperrealisation is precisely what permits the production of very real deaths on a mass scale.

Verminisation not only transforms the enemy into a subhuman swarm that cannot be reasoned with, only destroyed; it also makes "us" into victims of its repulsive, invasive agency. As Virilo perspicaciously observed, *Aliens* itself operated "a bit like a Terrorist attack. Women and children are slaughtered in order to create an irreversible situation, an irremediable hatred. The presence of the little victim has no theatrical value other than to dispose us to accept the madness of the massacres..."

While "we" have "families" who are being senselessly killed, vermin have neither memory nor motive; they act unreflexively, autonomically. Their extermination is a *practical* problem; it is simply a matter of finding their nests and using the right kind of weapon. Applying this thinking to Hezbollah or any other group is appalling racism, naturally, but also astonishingly poor strategy, implying no understanding of Terrorism whatsoever. Destroy all the infrastructure, kill all the operatives: but you will have only created more images of atrocity; indestructible and infinitely replayable repositories of affect, which, by demanding response and producing (a usually entirely justified) recrimination, act as the best intensifiers and amplifiers of Terror.

my card: my life: comments on the amex red campaign[1]

The current American Express Red advertising campaign[2] cries out for the kind of intricate semiotic dissection Roland Barthes pioneered in *Mythologies*. The ad — which shows happy, smiling supermodel Gisele embracing happy, smiling African Maasai warrior, Keseme — is a succinct emblem of the current ruling ideology.

The image, with its evocation of ideas of culture and nature, consumerism and debt, independence and dependence — fairly drips with polysemic resonances. There is enough here to keep semiologists busy for years.

But the central opposition — "My Card" versus "My Life" — says more than it intends. The First World is metonymically represented by a plastic card, and it is left to the Third World to symbolise all the "natural" vitality that unliving capital has eliminated from Western culture. The Western woman equals (artificial, cosmetic) culture; the African man equals living nature. Indeed, when we click on the "My Life" button we see the stereotypically-described "proud and fiercely independent [...] Maasai tribes of East Kenya" suborned into the role of embodying "the dignity, courage and breathtaking beauty of Africa", their culture quickly flattened back into nature.

Slavoj Žižek has argued that what he calls "liberal communism" — as exemplified by the charitable gifts made by super-succesful capitalists such as Bill Gates and George Soros — is now the dominant form of capitalist ideology. "According to liberal communist ethics", Žižek argues,

> the ruthless pursuit of profit is counteracted by charity: charity is part of the game, a humanitarian mask hiding the underlying economic exploitation. Developed countries are constantly "helping" undeveloped ones (with aid, credits, etc.), and so avoiding the key issue: their complicity in and responsibility for the miserable situation of the Third World.[3]

This is the real meaning of the embrace between Giselle and Keseme — under global capitalism, the relationship between First and Third Worlds can never be a symmetrical synergy in which both partners win. It will always be a system of structural inequality in which one side is always destined to lose.

But Product Red marks a move on from Žižek's liberal communism. Liberal communism is really just old-style philanthropy, in which exploitation is atoned for by subsequent acts of charity. With Red, by contrast, the act of consumption is presented to us as already and immediately benevolent. At the Product Red launch in January, Bono,[4] Red's most high-profile advocate, made a point of differentiating the new approach from philanthropy. "Philanthropy is like hippy music, holding hands", Bono claimed. "Red is more like punk rock, hip-hop, this should feel like hard commerce." (It is unclear what inspired Bono's invocation of punk rock — perhaps he was thinking of *The Great Rock 'n' Roll Swindle* — but his reference to hip-hop might be the most savage indictment of the genre yet.)

We confront here the curious mixture of brutal cynicism and dewy-eyed piety that is so characteristic of late-capitalist culture. The billboard version of the American Express ad tells us that "This card is designed to eliminate Aids in Africa". Even when we dismiss this as obvious nonsense — the most credulous consumer cannot but be aware that the card was designed to increase the profits of American Express — the ideological blackmail still holds: how can anything which assists in the struggle against Aids in Africa possibly be wrong?

We've already touched upon one reason: campaigns such as this occlude and mystify the systemic character of the relationship between Western capital and the Third World. The picturesque image of a "traditional" Maasai warrior beguiles us into forgetting the way in which Western institutions profit from Third World debt. It also photoshops out capital's attempt, in Žižek's words, to "export the (necessary) dark side of production — disciplined, hierarchical labour, ecological pollution — to 'non-smart' Third World locations".

Another, related, reason is that Product Red promises to eliminates politics as such. If the invisible hand of the credit card user can ameliorate the problem of Aids in Africa, there is no need for a political response at all — what John Hayes of American Express calls "conscientious commerce" will be sufficient. In this way, Product Red goes beyond using a Masaai tribesman to advertise American Express, and uses him to sell neoliberal ideology itself.

the great bullingdon club swindle[1]

We're all in this together.

Capitalist realism everywhere... On television yesterday morning, the relentless message coming from pundits and vox pops — even from most of those who reject the particular form that the cuts have taken — was that "something had to be done". The Great Bullingdon Club Swindle is larceny and deception on such a grand scale that one almost has to admire its breathtaking audacity. The Bullingdon Club has pushed Doublethink to new limits with its mantric repetition of the ludicrous claim that it was New Labour policy, rather than the bank bailouts, that was responsible for the massive deficit. The strategy seems to be to employ the illocutionary power of repetition — if they keep saying it, then it will have been true. The Bullingdon boys are working a mass hypnosis trick, forcing through shock doctrine measures while the population are still in a kind of post-crash trance. But where, previously, neoliberals had used the crises in other political systems (state socialism, social democracy) as an opportunity to helicopter in their "reforms", on this occasion they are using a crisis brought about by *neoliberal policy itself* to try to electro-shock the neoliberal programme back into life. I heard one buffoon on television saying that "we've been in denial for the last ten years". If there's denial, it's happened in the last two years, and on the part of the neoliberals and their friends in the business elite, who — after demanding at gunpoint unprecedented sums of public money — are now brazenly continuing to peddle the story that *they* are the friend of the taxpayer and that it is welfare claimants, not them, who are the scroungers who have brought the country to the "brink of bankruptcy". In what must surely be the most astonishing bait and switch in British parliamentary history, the victims of neoliberal policy — public services and the poor — are now being asked (or rather forced) to pay for the manifest and total failure of that policy. As John Gray argues in the *LRB*[2], it's no surprise that Orange Bookers like the "wolf-eyed replicant" Nick Clegg — as China Mieville[3] memorably described him — are happy to impose on the country the same neoliberal programme that they have imposed on their own party. Even so, has there even been a party that has so comprehensively and so quickly squandered the good will of those who voted for them as have the Lib Dems? Cuddly Vince Cable's grinning excuse for the backtracking on student fees was a masterclass in capitalist realism, as he practically said, "Well, that's what happens when you get into power — you give up your principles." (Cable is increasingly looking like a villain from a John Grisham flick, the avuncular eminence grize whose charm lures you into the firm, before being revealed to be a sinister embezzling fraudster.)

For months now, we've been sold the story that public services are "bloated". There's no doubt that New Labour mismanaged public services and wasted money — on managers, on market Stalinist control procedures imported in from business, and on GPs' ludicrously overinflated salaries. But the narrative of an overfunded public sector produces cognitive dissonance for those of us who have actually been delivering frontline public services in the last ten years, where we've been expected to do more work for less money and with fewer resources. If those were the good times, you can only feel a shudder of dread anticipating what it will be like when things are bad. Incidentally, if you've wondered why there have been so few posts here in the last month or so, it's because I've been trying to piece together a living as a visiting (i.e. casualised) lecturer, working in institutions that are strained to breaking point by neoliberal "reforms". Cuts will mean more casualisation, in those institutions that will be able to survive at all.

But the most breathtaking aspect of the Bullingdon swindle is the "we're all in this together" slogan, rightly described by Seumas Milne[4] as "preposterous". What we're seeing now is the Terminator of Capital with its neoliberal-managerialist mask wrecked, and the Big Society (Victoriana 2.0) ruse not convincing anyone. The doughy, fat-of-the-land face of privilege now shows itself openly, exuding the emollient manner of noblesse oblige, but without any sense of obligation. What survives is pure ideological reflex, the decorticated Terminator blindly blasting at its usual targets: public services, welfare, the arts. It's folk economic faux-wisdom ("if a household overspends, we know that we have to give up things we'd rather keep") that is providing the smokescreen for this ideological assault. Myths and deliberately cultivated misapprehensions abound: judging from all the rhetoric, you'd think that education and the arts were drains on the economy, rather than the highly successful "businesses" that they in fact function as.

Nevertheless, it's crucial that we recognise that this is a time of opportunity for the left. Laurie Penny[5] is right that the Labour Party does not have the answers at the moment. Yet the Labour Party's current lack of an agenda can be seen as a good thing, for two reasons. Firstly, at least this means that Labour has *lost* the managerialist neoliberal agenda that defined it for the last fifteen years. The de-New Labourisation process will take a while, but it will be expedited much quicker with Ed Miliband as leader than it ever would have been with David at the helm. (Notice how David — whom the media were presenting as a great lost leader, a kind of world-historic statesman, on the grounds, presumably, that Hilary Clinton took a fancy to him — is already a forgotten man. In the media's soap narrative, David's leaving frontbench politics was an open wound which the Labour Party would take years to recover — that doesn't quite seem to be the case.) Secondly, the fact that the post-Blair and Brown Labour Party is now a cored-out shell means that it is a *space*, which it is at least plausible that could be filled by new ideas and strategies. For the first time in fifteen years, the future of the Labour Party is not fixed. It's worth remembering at this point that the failures of the Labour Party, its succumbing to capitalist realism, is not just the consequences of the internal logic of the party. It was extra-Parliamentary forces that gave rise to the Labour Party in the first place; it was the defeat of those forces that drove the Labour Party into its craven placating of business in the New Labour era. If Labour is to be anything more than a zombie party once again, it will be new forms of extra-parliamentary organisation that revivify it.

For that reason, this is definitely not the time to recline into the leftist version of capitalist realism, the defeatist counterpart to the Bullingdon club's bullishness. Now is the time to organise and agitate. The cuts can provide a galvanising focus for an anti-capitalist campaign that can succeed. Protests in these conditions won't have the hubristic impotence of anti-capitalist "feelgood feelbad" carnivals and kettles. This is shaping up to be a bitter struggle, but there are specific, determinate and winnable goals that can be achieved here: it isn't a question of taking a peashooter to the juggernaut of capital.

The UK, the first capitalist country, is the world capital of apathy, diffidence and reflexive impotence. But it is also a country that periodically explodes into rage. Beneath todays's ideological trance, beneath the capitalist realist hopelessness, an anger simmers here that it is our task to focus and coordinate. Public displays of rage can play an enormously significant role in shifting the symbolic terrain that is currently governed by capitalist realism. I know there are some who see parallels between now and the initial phases of the first Thatcher government. But Thatcher had a number of factors on her side which the Bullingdon boys don't.

Firstly, Thatcherism was part of a wider global restructuring of capitalism

— the objective tide of history was on its side. But global capital has not yet found a solution to the problems that led to the banking crisis.

Secondly, this shift from Fordism to post-Fordism allowed Thatcher to offer inducements that can't be repeated: cheap shares from formerly nationalised companies, the sales of council houses. The nationalised companies have long since been sold off, and their private counterparts have in most cases failed to deliver the promised increases in consumer satisfaction — although they have certainly delivered massive profits to those who do hold shares in them. Now all we can look forward to are spiralling energy bills and higher train fares. There are no council houses to sell — indeed, the coalition is planning to effectively end what is left of social housing in this country for good, by forcing up council tenants' rates, and limiting tenancies to five years.

Thirdly, there was of course the Falklands — but, since the forces are already stretched threadbare, where are the resources for such a neo-colonialist intervention now, and would jingoism function in the same way in 2010 that it did in 1982?

Fourthly, there was Thatcher herself — a divisive but charismatic politician, who could plausibly present herself as struggling against vested interests, not only on the left, but also in the British establishment. The current Tory government has none of these advantages, and the neoliberal right in general has lost control of the future, much as it refuses to acknowledge this. In the *Standard*, Anne McElvoy recently described Ed Miliband as "an unreconstructed social democrat". From what position does McElvoy think she is speaking here? Like much of the mainstream media, which is contriving to carry on as if 2008 didn't happen, McElvoy is desperately clinging to the myth of a political "centre ground" that no longer has any legitimacy. After the bank bailouts, the neoliberal settlement is just as dead as social democracy.

The "we're all in this together" slogan may turn out to be a phrase that comes to haunt the Tories in the way that "Labour isn't working" dogged Labour for a generation. Classlessness might have seemed plausible for a moment when fronted by John Major, who didn't go to university, or by Tony Blair, the poster boy for (leftist) post-political administration. But that moment has long passed, and cuts of this kind being forced through by a cabinet of aristocrats and millionaires make brutally apparent a class antagonism that the New Labour government obfuscated. Whenever the ruling class tells us that "we're all on the same side", it is a sure sign that we can hurt them. Similarly, the current media phobia about unions is an indication of the power that they have at this time. History is starting again, which means that nothing is fixed and there are no guarantees. Right-wing victory is only inevitable if we think that it is.

the privatisation of stress[1]

Ivor Southwood tells the story of how, at a time when he was living in a condition of underemployment — relying on short-term contracts given to him at the last minute by employment agencies — he one morning made the mistake of going to the supermarket.[2] When he returned home he found that an agency had left him a message offering him work for the day. But when he called the agency he was told that the vacancy was already filled — and upbraided for his slackness. As he comments, "ten minutes is a luxury the day-labourer cannot afford". Such labourers are expected to be waiting outside the metaphorical factory gates with their boots on, every morning without fail. In such conditions

> daily life becomes precarious. Planning ahead becomes difficult, routines are impossible to establish. Work, of whatever sort, might begin or end anywhere at a moment's notice, and the burden is always on the worker to create the next opportunity and to surf between roles. The individual must exist in a state of constant readiness. Predictable income, savings, the fixed category of "occupation": all belong to another historical world.[3]

It is hardly surprising that people who live in such conditions — where their hours and pay can always be increased or decreased, and their terms of employment are extremely tenuous — should experience anxiety, depression and hopelessness. And it may at first seem remarkable that so many workers have been persuaded to accept such deteriorating conditions as "natural", and to look inward — into their brain chemistry or into their personal history — for the sources of any stress they may be feeling. But in the ideological field that Southwood describes from the inside, this privatisation of stress has become just one more taken-for-granted dimension of a seemingly depoliticised world. "Capitalist realism" is the term I have used to describe

461

this ideological field; and the privatisation of stress has played a crucial role in its emergence.

Capitalist realism refers to the widespread belief that there is no alternative to capitalism — though "belief" is perhaps a misleading term, given that its logic is externalised in the institutional practices of workplaces and the media, as well as residing in the heads of individuals. In his discussions of ideology, Althusser cites Pascal's doctrine: "Kneel down, move your lips in prayer, and you will believe": psychological beliefs follow from "going through the motions" of complying with official languages and behaviours. This means that, however much individuals or groups may have disdained or ironised the language of competition, entrepreneurialism and consumerism that has been installed in UK institutions since the 1980s, our widespread ritualistic compliance with this terminology has served to naturalise the dominance of capital and help to neutralise any opposition to it.

We can quickly grasp the form that capitalist realism now takes by reflecting on the shift in the meaning of the famous Thatcher doctrine that "there is no alternative". When Thatcher initially made this notorious claim, the emphasis was on preference: neoliberal capitalism was the best possible system; the alternatives were undesirable. Now, the claim carries an *ontological* weight — capitalism is not just the best possible system, it is the *only* possible system; alternatives are hazy, spectral, barely conceivable. Since 1989, capitalism's success in routing its opponents has led to it coming close to achieving the ultimate goal of ideology — invisibility. In the global North at least, capitalism proposes itself as the only possible reality, and therefore it seldom "appears" as such at all. Atilio Boron argues that capitalism has been shifted to a "discreet position behind the political scene, rendered invisible as the structural foundation of contemporary society", and cites Bertolt Brecht's observation that "capitalism is a gentleman who doesn't like to be called by his name".[4]

The Depressing Realism of New Labour

We would expect the Thatcherite (and post-Thatcherite) right to propagate the idea that there is no alternative to the neoliberal programme. But the victory of capitalist realism was only secured in the UK when the Labour Party capitulated to this view, and accepted, as the price of power, that "business interests, narrowly conceived, would be henceforth be allowed to organise the shape and direction of the entire culture".[5] But perhaps it would be more accurate to record that, rather than simply capitulating to Thatcherite capitalist realism, it was the Labour Party itself that first introduced capitalist realism to the UK political mainstream, when James Callaghan gave his notorious 1976 speech to the Labour conference in Blackpool:

> For too long, perhaps ever since the war, we [have] postponed facing up to fundamental choices and fundamental changes in our economy [...] We've been living on borrowed time [...] The cosy world we were told would go on forever, where full employment could be guaranteed by a stroke of the chancellor's pen — that cosy world is gone...

However it is unlikely that Callaghan foresaw the extent to which the Labour Party would come to engage in the politics of "corporate appeasement", or the extent to which the cosy world for which he was performing the last rites would be replaced by the generalised insecurity described by Ivor Southwood.

The Labour Party's acquiescence in capitalist realism cannot of course be construed as a simple error: it was a consequence of the disintegration of the left's old power base in the face of the post-Fordist restructuring of capitalism. The features of this — globalisation; the displacement of manufacturing by computerisation; the casualisation of labour; the intensification of consumer culture — are now so familiar that they, too, have receded into a taken-for-granted background. This is what constitutes the background for the ostensibly post-political and uncontestable "reality" that capitalist realism relies upon. The warnings made by Stuart Hall and the others writing in *Marxism Today* at the end of the 1980s turned out to be absolutely correct: the left would face obsolescence if it remained complacently attached to the assumptions of the disappearing Fordist world and failed to hegemonise the new world of post-Fordism.[6] But the New Labour project, far from being an attempt to achieve this new hegemony, was based precisely on conceding the impossibility of a leftist hegemonisation of post-Fordism: all that could be hoped for was a mitigated version of the neoliberal settlement.

In Italy, autonomists such as Berardi and Negri also recognised the need to face up to the destruction of the world within which the left had been formed, and to adapt to the conditions of post-Fordism, though in rather a different manner. Writing in the 1980s, in a series of letters that were recently published in English, Negri characterises the painful transition from revolutionary hopes to defeat by a triumphalist neoliberalism:

> We have to live and suffer the defeat of truth, of our truth. We have to destroy its representation, its continuity, its memory. All subterfuges for avoiding the recognition that reality has changed, and with it truth, have to be rejected. The very blood in our veins had been replaced.[7]

We are currently living with the effects of the left's failure to rise to the challenge that Negri identified. And it doesn't seem a stretch to conjecture that many elements of the left have succumbed to a collective form of clinical depression, with symptoms of withdrawal, impaired motivation

463

and the inability to act.

One difference between sadness and depression is that, while sadness apprehends itself as a contingent and temporary state of affairs, depression presents itself as necessary and interminable: the glacial surfaces of the depressive's world extend to every conceivable horizon. In the depths of the condition, the depressive does not experience his or her melancholia as pathological or indeed abnormal: the conviction of depression that agency is useless, that beneath the appearance of virtue lies only venality, strikes sufferers as a truth which they have reached but others are too deluded to grasp. There is clearly a relationship between the seeming "realism" of the depressive, with its radically lowered expectations, and capitalist realism.

This depression was not experienced collectively: on the contrary, it precisely took the form of the decomposition of collectivity in new modes of atomisation. Denied the stable forms of employment that they had been trained to expect, deprived of the solidarity formerly provided by trade unions, workers found themselves forced into competition with one another on an ideological terrain in which such competition was naturalised. Some workers never recovered from the traumatic shock of seeing the Fordist-social-democratic world suddenly removed: a fact it's worth remembering at a time when the Conservative-Liberal Democrat coalition government is hounding claimants off incapacity benefit. Such a move is the culmination of the process of privatising stress that began in the UK in the 1980s.

The Stresses of Post-Fordism

If the shift from Fordism to post-Fordism had its psychic casualties, then post-Fordism has innovated whole new modes of stress. Instead of the elimination of bureaucratic red tape promised by neoliberal ideologues, the combination of new technology and managerialism has massively increased the administrative stress placed on workers, who are now required to be their own auditors (which by no means frees them of the attentions of external auditors of many kinds). Work, no matter how casual, now routinely entails the performance of meta-work: the completion of log books, the detailing of aims and objectives, the engagement in so-called "continuing professional development". Writing of academic labour, the blogger Savonarola describes how systems of permanent and ubiquitous measurement engender a constant state of anxiety:

One of the more pervasive phenomena in the current cod-neoliberal academic dispensation is CV inflation: as available jobs dwindle down to Kafkian levels of postponement and implausibility, the miserable *Träger* of academic capital are obliged not just to overfulfil the plan, but to record [...] every single one of their productive acts. The only sins are sins of omission [...] In this sense, the passage from [...] periodic and measured measurement [...] to permanent and ubiquitous measurement cannot but result in a kind of Stakhanovism of immaterial labour, which like its Stalinist forebear exceeds all rationales of instrumentality, and cannot but generate a permanent undercurrent of debilitating anxiety (since *there is no standard*, no amount of work will ever make you *safe*).[8]

It would be naïve to imagine that this "permanent undercurrent of debilitating anxiety" is an accidental side-effect of the imposition of these self-surveillance mechanisms, which manifestly fail to achieve their official objectives. None other than Philip Blond has argued that "the market solution generates a huge and costly bureaucracy of accountants, examiners, inspectors, assessors and auditors, all concerned with assuring quality and asserting control that hinder innovation and experiment and lock in high cost".[9] This acknowledgement is welcome, but it is important to reject the idea that the apparent "failures" of managerialism are "honest mistakes" of a system which sincerely aims for greater efficiency. Managerialist initiatives served very well their real if covert aims, which were to further weaken the power of labour and undermine worker autonomy as part of a project to restore wealth and power to the hyper-privileged.

Relentless monitoring is closely linked to precarity. And, as Tobias van Veen argues, precarious work places "an ironic yet devastating" demand on the labourer. On the one hand, work never ends: the worker is always expected to be available, with no claims to a private life. On the other hand, the precariat are completely expendable, even when they have sacrificed all autonomy to keep their jobs.[10] The tendency today is for practically all forms of work to become precarious. As Franco Berardi puts it, "Capital no longer recruits people, but buys packets of time, separated from their interchangeable and occasional bearers".[11] Such "packets of time" are not conceived of as having a connection to a person with rights or demands: they are simply either available or unavailable.

Berardi also notes the effects of digital telecommunications; these produce what he characterises as a diffuse sense of panic, as individuals are subjected to an unmanageable data-blitz:

The acceleration of information exchange [...] is producing an effect of a pathological type on the individual human mind and even more on the collective mind. Individuals are not in a position to consciously process the immense and always growing mass of information that enters their computers, their cell phones, their television screens, their electronic diaries and their heads. However, it seems indispensable to follow, recognise, evaluate, process all this information if you want to be efficient, competitive, victorious.[12]

One of the effects of modern communications technology is that there is no outside where one can recuperate. Cyberspace makes the concept of a "workplace" archaic. Now that one can be expected to respond to an email at practically any time of the day, work cannot be confined to a particular place, or to delimited hours. There's no escape — and not only because work expands without limits. Such processes have also hacked into libido, so that the "tethering" imposed by digital telecommunications is by no means always experienced as something that is straightforwardly unpleasant. As Sherry Turkle argues, for example, though many parents are increasingly stressed as they try to keep up with email and messages while continuing to give their children the attention they need, they are also magnetically attracted to their communications technology:

> They cannot take a vacation without bringing the office with them; their office is on their cellphone. They complain that their employers rely on them to be continually online but then admit that their devotion to their communications devices exceeds all professional expectations.[13]

Practices ostensibly undertaken for work, even if they are performed on holiday or late at night, are not experienced simply as unreasonable demands. From a psychoanalytic point of view, it is easy to see why such demands — demands that cannot possibly be met — can be libidinised, since this kind of demand is precisely the form that the psychoanalytic drive assumes. Jodi Dean has convincingly argued that digital communicative compulsion constitutes a capturing by (Freudian/Lacanian) drive: individuals are locked into repeating loops, aware that their activity is pointless, but nevertheless unable to desist.[14] The ceaseless circulation of digital communication lies beyond the pleasure principle: the insatiable urge to check messages, email or Facebook is a compulsion, akin to scratching an itch which gets worse the more one scratches. Like all compulsions, this behaviour feeds on dissatisfaction. If there are no messages, you feel disappointed and check again very quickly. But if there are messages you also feel disappointed: no amount of messages is ever enough. Sherry Turkle has talked to people who are unable to resist the urge to send and receive texts on their mobile telephone, even when they are driving a car. At the risk of a laboured pun, this is a perfect example of the death drive, which is defined not by the desire to die, but by being in the grip of a compulsion so powerful that it makes one indifferent to death. What's remarkable here is the banal content of the drive. This isn't the tragedy of something like *The Red Shoes*, in which the ballerina is killed by the sublime rapture of dance: these are people who are prepared to risk death so that they can open a 140 character message which they know perfectly well is likely to be inane.

Public Renewal or Private Cure?

The privatisation of stress is a perfect capture system, elegant in its brutal efficiency. Capital makes the worker ill, and then multinational pharmaceutical companies sell them drugs to make them better. The social and political causation of distress is neatly sidestepped at the same time as discontent is individualised and interiorised. Dan Hind has argued that the focus on serotonin deficiency as a supposed "cause" of depression obfuscates some of the social roots of unhappiness, such as competitive individualism and income inequality. Though there is a large body of work that shows the links between individual happiness and political participation and extensive social ties (as well as broadly equal incomes), a public response to private distress is rarely considered as a first option.[15] It is clearly easier to prescribe a drug than a wholesale change in the way society is organised. Meanwhile, as Hind argues, "there is a multitude of entrepreneurs offering happiness now, in just a few simple steps". These are marketed by people "who are comfortable operating within the culture's account of what it is to be happy and fulfilled", and who both corroborate and are corroborated by "the vast ingenuity of commercial persuasion".

Psychiatry's pharmacological regime has been central to the privatisation of stress, but it is important that we don't overlook the perhaps even more insidious role that the ostensibly more holistic practices of psychotherapy have also played in depoliticising distress. The radical therapist David Smail argues that Margaret Thatcher's view that there's no such thing as society, only individuals and their families, finds "an unacknowledged echo in almost all approaches to therapy".[16] Therapies such as Cognitive Behavioural Therapy combine a focus on early life (a kind of psychoanalysis-lite) with the self-help doctrine that individuals can become masters of their own destiny. Smail gives the immensely suggestive name *magical voluntarism* to the view that "with the expert help of your therapist or counsellor, *you* can change the world *you* are in the last analysis responsible for, so that it no longer cause you distress".[17]

The propagation of magical voluntarism has been crucial to the success of neoliberalism; we might go so far as to say as it constitutes something like the spontaneous ideology of our times. Thus, for example, ideas from self-help therapy have become very influential in popular television shows.[18] *The Oprah Winfrey Show* is probably the best-known example, but in the UK programmes such as *Mary, Queen of Shops* and *The Fairy Jobmother* explicitly promote magical voluntarism's psychic entrepreneurialism: these programmes assure us that the fetters on our productive potentials lie within us. If we don't succeed, it is simply because we have not put the work in to reconstruct ourselves.

The privatisation of stress has been part of a project that has aimed at an almost total destruction of the concept of the public — the very thing upon which psychic well-being fundamentally depends. What we urgently need is a new politics of mental health organised around the problem of public space. In its break from the old Stalinist left, the various new lefts wanted a debureaucratised public space and worker autonomy: what they got was managerialism and shopping. The current political situation in the UK — with business and its allies gearing up for a destruction of the relics of social democracy — constitutes a kind of infernal inversion of the autonomist dream of workers liberated from the state, bosses and bureaucracy. In a staggeringly perverse twist, workers find themselves working harder, in deteriorating conditions and for what is in effect worse pay, in order to fund a state bailout of the business elite, while the agents of that elite plot the further destruction of the public services on which workers depend.

At the same time as a discredited neoliberalism plots this intensification of its project, a kind of right-wing autonomism has emerged in Phillip Blond's *Red Toryism* and Maurice Glasman's *Blue Labourism*. Here the critique of social-democratic and neoliberal bureaucracy goes alongside the call for a restitution of tradition. Neoliberalism's success depended on its capturing of the desires of workers who wanted to escape the strictures of Fordism (though the miserable individualist consumerism in which we are all now immersed is not the alternative they sought). Blond's laughable "Big Society" and Glasman's disturbingly insular "white working-class" "communities" do not represent persuasive or credible responses to this problem. Capital has annihilated the traditions that Blond and Glasman hanker after, and there is no bringing them back.

But this should not be a cause for lament; far from it. What we need to revive is not social formations that failed (and failed for reasons that progressives should be pleased about), but a political project that never really happened: the achievement of a democratic public sphere. Even in Blond's work, the lineaments of a hegemonic shift can be discerned — in his startling repudiation of the core concepts of neoliberalism and his attack on managerialism; and in the concession that, contra Thatcher, it turns out that there *is* such a thing as society after all. Such moves give some indication of the extent to which — after the bank bailouts — neoliberalism has radically lost credibility.

The recent upsurge in militancy in the UK, particularly amongst the young, suggests that the privatisation of stress is breaking down: in place of a medicated individual depression, we are now seeing explosions of public anger. Here, and in the largely untapped but massively widespread discontent with the managerialist regulation of work, lie some of the materials out of which a new leftist modernism can be built. Only this leftist modernism is capable of constructing a public sphere which can cure the numerous pathologies with which communicative capitalism afflicts us.

kettle logic[1]

No left turn into Parliamentary Square, flashed a sign as we marched through Whitehall last Wednesday. But all the other signs are suggesting quite the opposite: there's a tentative but very definite shift to the left in the mainstream, nowhere better exemplified than by NUS President Aaron Porter's[2] admission that he had been "spineless" in failing to support student militancy. This leftward lean by the NUS — which has long been a bastion of capitalist realist moderation — is a significant symptomatic moment. See also Polly Toynbee's slight shift away from centrist condescension, as evidenced in the difference in tone and stance between these two recent pieces.[3]

Lenin[4] and IT have written reports on the kettle, so I won't detain you for long by repeating what you've already heard. Suffice it to note that the mood walking down Whitehall from Trafalgar Square in the Winter sun was almost jubilant: far from the negative solidarity you might have expected, cabbies and bus drivers honked their horns or waved in support of the young protesters. Even after the kettle was imposed, the mood remained remarkably good humoured in the main. You already know about the thin pretext for the kettle, the suspiciously abandoned police van, which was only attacked once the kettle was already in place. As others have observed, there can be no doubt that the real purpose of the kettle is to punish people for protesting, and to deter them from doing so in the future. Lenin is quite right: it's imperative that this doesn't happen — the ruling class are counting on the street militancy fizzling out as suddenly as it flared up. We have an opportunity here, not only to bring down the government — which is eminently achievable (keep reminding yourself: this government is very weak indeed), but of winning a decisive hegemonic struggle whose effects can last for years. The analogy that keeps suggesting itself to me is 1978 — but it is the coalition, not the left, which is in the position of the Callaghan government. This is an administration at the end of something, not the beginning, bereft of ideas and energy, crossing its fingers and hoping that, by some miracle, the old world can be brought back to life before anyone has really noticed that it has collapsed.

At the moment, so many mainstream commentators and politicians resemble nothing so much as the denizens of the post-apocalyptic world of Richard Lester's *The Bed Sitting Room*: tragicomically persisting with the same customs and habits as if the catastrophe hasn't happened. Until the weekend, Aaron Porter was walking the ideological junkyard, apparently under the delusion that a career as a New Labour politician was still on the cards. But his change of position suggests that even opportunists have seen which way the wind is blowing. It looks as if the situation might be starting to dawn on Clegg, who increasingly has the cheated and desperate look of a man who has sold his soul to the devil at the very moment the devil went out of business.

Victory will require a range of strategies, and new kinds of intervention are being improvised all the time — see for instance the University For Strategic Optimism.[5] Victory will also require others to follow where the students have led — if public service workers join the militancy, then we can look forward to a Winter of Discontent every bit as bitter as the one in 1978.

In addition to the physical kettling of the protests, we're also seeing a media strategy of containment. Hold your nose and take a look at Jan Moir[6] if you want to see a prize example of this kettle logic. The preferred strategy of the old guard seems to be one of phobic panic disguised as insouciant disdain: witness the way Moir shuttles between sexist and ageist belittling ("St Trinian's Riots", "fem-factions", "boys and girls", "throwing tantrums") and moral horror (the deploring of "violence and damage"). The protest, in other words, was both a trivial jape and breach of civil order so serious that it merited "detain[ing] thousands of the students for hours in a 'kettling' movement". I wonder, incidentally, how long the "civic-minded" Moir and her fellow *Mail* journos would "fight the urge" to "trash cop cars" if *they* were kettled; I fancy their patience would break long before that of the protesters did. (Imagine the mood hacks would be in after *eight hours without alcohol*.) Then of course we get the wheeling out of the capitalist realist canards... "the cold reality of the economic times. There is no money left to fund further education for all. Which in any case is an extraordinary privilege, not a right."

In reply to which I can do no better than quote Digital Ben's excellent post:

The economic argument (and the alibi given by the Liberal Democrats to explain their about-face on the fees issue) is that we, as a nation, don't have the money for things anymore. We certainly can't afford to pay tuition fees, and give grants rather than loans. We managed both of those things for several decades up to 1997, without the economy collapsing around our ears and people pushing wheelbarrows of money through the streets and/or queueing for bread and salt, but never mind.[7]

Moir demands, with a perfectly straight face, that students "ask themselves why they should expect hard-pressed taxpayers to fork out for their further education, when a great number of those taxpayers are less well off than the students' own families." Let's leave aside the little matter of the fact that this didn't seem to trouble Moir and her fellow right-wingers when they were receiving free higher education; let's also leave aside the fact that the current government is full of millionaires who received the same "privilege". How, you have to wonder, can Moir expect that those same "hard-pressed taxpayers" take cuts in order to fund the bankers, who are more well off than almost everyone else?

Digital Ben also makes a crucial point about the way that the current capitalist realist discourse depends upon a ridiculously outdated figuration of The Student:

There's still a dimwitted lack of understanding of the nature of these actions — too many television and newspaper reporters seem to be operating under the assumption that those of the protesters who are currently students are only attempting to get their own fees waived. A moment's consideration would of course reveal that these people will all be working and paying back their loans by the time the Browne proposals are in full effect. The inability to comprehend the idea that people can have motivations other than self-interest reveals far more about the Burleyesque sections of the media than it does about the marchers. The archetype of the spoiled, selfish student living it up on taxpayer money, never particularly fair, is now positively antiquated. *Viz* — often a reliable social barometer — dropped its "Student Grant" character years ago, but it's being dug up and spat back at us in 2010. Desperate stuff. To dismiss the students (as every organ in the land seemed to do) as wanting "something for nothing" or "everything handed to them on a plate" is to completely, wilfully misunderstand the situation. The immediate demand of the protesters was for a proposed fee increase to be scrapped. In other words, for the maintenance of a situation in which students work jobs in term-time, live in cheaply built (but tastefully coloured!) PFI rabbit hutches, study hard, and three years later, accept a debt measured in the tens of thousands that will hang over them for most of their adult lives. Compassion for these students might be dulled by the thought that they will eventually be earning high salaries — the risible Gove defended the Browne Report with the uncannily bad argument — *"why should a postman subsidise someone who will go on to become a millionaire?"* — but in times like these, how many students (even those in vocational subjects) do we really believe will be prospering after they graduate? It should be obvious that what these students want is *something for something* — the prospect of some kind of reward for all of the hard work and financial risk they've undertaken.[8]

IT has also pointed out the way in which the stereotype of the lazy student is completely out of touch with the reality of so much student experience today. No doubt the students in Moir's and Toynbee's families — who, I think we can assume, will be at elite institutions — have an experience of university life which differs little from that which Moir and Toynbee enjoyed. ("Rich parents for all", as one of the more acerbic placards had it last week.) But many students now routinely have to work long hours during term-time, meaning that they barely have the energy to read anything. By comparison with former generations, these students are paying more for a worse quality educational experience, not to mention the fact that their degrees will in many cases fail to yield them any significant long-term financial advantage. I take Alex Callinicos' point about the dangers of "generational" politics, but there is surely an unavoidable generational dimension to the current situation. Witness Paxman's patronising treatment of young protesters on *Newsnight* last week. Transformed from attack dog rentasneer into the kindly, avuncular advocate of capitalist realism, Paxman "explained" to the teenagers that, yes, it's unfair that he received an education completely gratis and that they will have to pay thirty grand, but sadly, *that's just how things are — there's no money left.* Generational affiliation here is a matter of political decision. I effectively belong to Paxman's generation in that I too received higher education completely free of charge. But the issue in question is whether one finds it conscionable to stand by while the young are systematically denuded of the "privileges" that we took for granted. It's true that higher education has been massively expanded over the past thirty years, but that isn't the fault of the young. They are the victims of an ill-thought and poorly planned out experiment in the expansion of the sector which successive governments have pursued on the grounds that the UK would need more graduates in order to be internationally "competitive". It's not even as if the young have the *alternatives* to higher education that once existed. So here they are: the ConDemned, and it's down to us whether we stand with them or watch them get further sold out and abandoned.

Then there's the attempt to rubbish the motivation of the protesters: they were just along for a "laff", Pied-Piper lured along by our old friends, *a hard core of anarchists.* Even if we were to accept this, Moir and Gove need to explain why it is that these "anarchists" — who, presumably, didn't start scheming only a few weeks ago — have suddenly been able to motivate the young so effectively. Despite the best efforts of the media and the politicians to maintain business as usual, something *has* changed. But this change is precarious. We have to do everything we can to keep it going — supporting protests and occupations wherever we can, introducing and exacerbating antagonisms in the workplace, thinking and discussing new strategies, continuing to build a "new politics" that has nothing to do with the dead neoliberal consensus that the coalition is seeking to resuscitate.

winter of discontent 2.0: notes on a month of militancy[1]

9.45pm. Day X, 24 November. I'm at Charing Cross, grabbing my first food of the day. Actually, it's not particularly abnormal for me to be eating for the first time this late in the evening; but usually it's because of overwork, not a consequence of my being "contained" by the police for eight hours. Two protestors arrive, coming down from the day's anger, frustration and exhilaration. I catch their eye and one of them asks me if I will be joining them next week. I say, yes, tell them that I've been kettled in Whitehall, only just got out. They say they were kettled twice. One of them has a *V for Vendetta* mask pulled up off his face. The police held him for a while but had to release him because of lack of evidence. (Later, one of my students at UEL will tell me a similar story — arrested by the cops on the grounds that he was wearing a red tracksuit top, the same as someone who supposedly set fire to a litter bin, held for a while, his clothes and mobile phone seized, bailed until April — obviously one of many intimidation tactics the police were trying on that day.) They show no surprise, no self-pity or hyperbolic self-dramatisation, just a resolute sense of what needs to be done, and a delight in doing it. *I enjoyed it, looking forward to next week...*

I ask one of them what he does. He says his friend is already going to college; he will be going next year. *But it's not just about that...* It wasn't just about him; it wasn't just about tuition fees, or EMA...

It's not just about that... We are no longer that post-ideological generation

Contrast [this] with some of the responses from the "liberal" commentariat — those who belong the real "post-ideological generation", if ever there was one. For Deborah Orr, it's business as usual. Resistance to capitalist realism remains futile:

It is sometimes suggested that there is little protest against the cuts, except from students and schoolchildren, because adults are too craven and apathetic to stand up and be counted. The truth is that they are too wise to waste their energy on something so silly. Protesting against the cuts is like protesting against water's stubborn habit of flowing downwards.[2]

Compare also with David Aaronvitch on *Newsnight*: the avuncular grey vampire body posture, that performance of simultaneous weariness and infinite ease in the world, the jaded fatalism passed off as mature wisdom. *Yes, of course, I would have gone on the marches when I was a student, but of course I know better now...* It's little different to an argument made by Richard Littlejohn: the protestors will be the next generation of politicians... As if that's what they want, as if, even if that ended up being true, it would diminish what's happening now...

3.15pm. 1 December. In one of the dream-like transitions that are becoming increasingly common in the new atmosphere, I am sitting in the UEL occupation, when in walks Richard Seymour to give a talk on the recent history of the Tory party. The students at UEL have been holding Room 101 for a week, since Day X2. Things have changed rapidly in the space of those seven days; they are changing all the time. There are now banners draped all over the central concourse of UEL's Ballardian Docklands campus. Elsewhere, occupations are sprouting everywhere, like unexpected wildflowers.

The only thing I can compare the current situation with is emerging from a state of deep depression. There's the rush that you get simply from not being depressed anymore — the occasional lurching anxieties, a sense of how precarious it all seems (*don't drag me back into nothing*) — and yet not only is it maintaining itself, it's proliferating, intensifying, feeding on itself — it's impossible, but it's happening — the reality programme resetting itself — David Cameron's response is both patronising and misjudged. *The students should understand what they are protesting against before they protest.* Yet it's clearly Cameron who doesn't have a handle on the current situation (*who does?*). As Richard argued in his talk at the UEL occupation, these flabby toffs don't have the experience, the strategic intelligence or the ideological consistency to win a bitter fight. Cameron was a Tory leader constructed in, and geared up for, the pre-2008 "consensus of indifference" (Baudrillard) — he didn't expect a struggle, certainly not with those who intend to win. What Cameron doesn't grasp, doesn't want to grasp, is the way that the fees are only the immediate cause of the new militancy. What has been provoked is a generalised discontent with nothing less than capitalist realism itself.

5.30pm, 2 December. **Neoliberalism isn't working**. I've been stuck on Dartford station for ninety minutes. No trains moving in either direction. No one knows where the trains are, or if they will be able to travel any further even if they arrive. One train tried to head further south, but it only got a hundred yards out of the station before having to stop. Official communication is minimal, but only has the status of rumour any way. The railway workers, bereft of reliable information, tell you one thing, then find it immediately contradicted by developments. Are the buses running? Who can say…?

I strike up conversation with someone who happens to be heading to my destination. The usual complaints and bemusement. Why does everything in the UK have to be so crappy? He's a casual worker, worried that his Christmas will be ruined if this weather keeps up. If he doesn't go to work, he doesn't get paid, and he already had to have a week off for flu.

Frail hopes of a train receding, we consider options — we're less than ten miles from where we want to be, but we could end up having to stay in a hotel. Then he gets a phone call; a friend will pick him up, and he can give me a lift. As we stand shivering and drinking coffee from the station cafe bar, the news comes over the radio. Russia to get the 2018 World Cup. It feels as if the Winter is closing in around.

Cameron. *Neoliberalism isn't working*. No joy for Cameron and the other members of the ruling class Holy Trinity — the Prince and David Beckham, the poster boy for New Labour-era celebrity soccer. The grimly smirking Putin arrives last minute to claim the prize. All the boom gloss is falling away, and England feels shoddier and shabbier than it ever did in the Seventies.

Saturday, 4 December. I'm following the news of the UK Uncut protests on Twitter. In the cold of the kettle on Day X1, it occurred to me that the best place to be kettle would be in a shopping mall, where the containment tactics would massively inconvenience capital. But the movement is well ahead of me… Flash mobs invade a number of Topshop stores across the country. IT is right about the crucial significance of this kind of intervention, which "indicates, among other things, an absolute fatigue with the corporate face of city centres". And also a fatigue with the mandarin-celebrity status of figures like Green. Discontent with celebrity-wealth culture has long been like an indelible shadow that no amount of digital manipulation could quite eradicate, but, until recently, the persistent sense that something is missing amidst all this conspicuous consumption and listless hedonism has had no outlet or agent.

Day X3, 9 December. There's long been a discrepancy between culture and the post-crash situation. It's now evident that the New Fifties are over — the scenery still survives, but you can push your fingers through it. Paul Mason[3] talks of a "dubstep rebellion", and, although it would be churlish to complain about Mason's report, given that he was one of the very few mainstream media commentators to properly engage with the movement. Dan Hancox is surely right: it wasn't dubstep that was being played last Thursday but "R&B, bashment, road rap, american hip-hop and — albeit only once or twice — grime".[4] What's striking here is the *lack* of any political content, or even — "Pow" excepted — much anger in the music that was played. What we can hear exemplified, in fact, is the disengagement from politics that Jeremy Gilbert has persuasively argued was typical of the Nineties hardcore continuum:

> given the social and political radicalism characterising most of their immediate antecedents (acid house, with its origins in the black gay clubs of Chicago; hip-hop, only recently having left its "golden age" of political consciousness; reggae, with its history of anti-capitalism and anti-racism), as well as the traditional radicalism of their core constituency — the multiracial poor of urban London — the music scenes of the "nuum" were notable for their detachment from any kind of politics, their embrace of competitive entrepreneurial values, and their defence of masculinist and heterosexist norms which other dance cultures were busily and visibly deconstructing at just that moment.[5]

What we've grown accustomed to is a split between leftist political commitments and the most vibrant, experimental dance musics. No doubt this is an aspect of capitalist realism, and it's no accident that I referred to Simon's 1996 piece on hardstep[6] in *Capitalist Realism*. In fact, it might well have been the case that the central concept of the book was triggered by Simon's commentary on "keeping it real" there:

> In hip-hop, "real" has two meanings. First, it means authentic, uncompromised music that refuses to sell out to the music industry and soften its message for crossover. "Real" also signifies that the music reflects a "reality" constituted by late capitalist economic instability, institutionalised racism, and increased surveillance and harassment of youth by the police. "Real" means the death of the social: it means corporations who respond to increased profits not by raising pay or improving benefits but by what the Americans call downsising (the laying-off the permanent workforce in order to create a floating employment pool of part-time and freelance workers without benefits or job security).
>
> "Real" is a neo-Medieval scenario; you could compare downsising to enclosure, where the aristocracy threw the peasants off the land and reduced them to a vagabond underclass. Like gangsta rap, Jungle reflects a Medieval paranoiascape of robber barons, pirate corporations, conspiracies and covert operations. Hence the popularity as a source of samples and song titles of martial arts films and gangsta movies like *The Godfather, Reservoir Dogs, Goodfellas, Pulp Fiction*, whose universe revolves around concepts of righteous violence and blood-honour that predate the liberal, social-democratic era. [...]

The pervasive sense of slipping into a new Dark Age, of an insidious breakdown of the social contract, generates anxieties that are repressed but resurface in unlikely ways and places. Resistance doesn't necessarily take the "logical" form of collective activism (unions, left-wing politics); it can be so distorted and imaginatively impoverished by the conditions of capitalism itself, that it express itself as, say, the proto-fascist, anti-corporate nostalgia of America's right-wing militias, or as a sort of hyper-individualistic survivalism.

In hip-hop and, increasingly, Jungle, the response is a "realism" that accepts a socially-constructed reality as natural. To "get real" is to confront a state-of-nature where dog eats dog, where you're either a winner or a loser, and where most will be losers. There's a cold rage seething in Jungle, but it's expressed within the terms of an anti-capitalist yet non-socialist politics, and expressed defensively: as a determination that the underground will not be co-opted by the mainstream.[7]

At Day X1 I heard the predictable "Killing in the Name" and the even more predictable "Sound of the Police", alongside the Beatles, Madness, and — depressingly — the Libertines — and, most jarringly, "Another Brick In The Wall" (hearing *we don't need no education* as we shuffled out of the kettle made for a suitably incongruous experience).

But a video that Jeremy shot on Thursday suggests a possible convergence between post-nuum musics and politics. It is my belief that the UK music culture of the next decade will emerge from the stew of sound and affect in the kettles these past few weeks. Paul Mason dismissed the idea that the demo was exclusively populated by "Lacan-reading hipsters from Spitalfields" — but of course (we) Lacan-reading hipsters were also there, *alongside* the "*bainlieue-style* youth from Croydon, Peckam, the council estates of Islington". In other words, this brought together working-class culture and bohemia in something like the same way that art schools — so crucial to UK pop-art culture since the Fifties — used to. But — with very good reasons from its own point of view — neoliberal policy has been hostile to this proletarian-bohemian cultural circuit. While Further Education and the new universities have precisely tried to make theory such as Lacan available to the working class — while also trying to engage with everything vibrant coming out of working-class culture — the policy has been to re-cement rigid class and cultural distinctions: philosophy for the bourgeoisie; "vocational" courses for the masses.

Siobhan captures very well the frustrations we encountered on Day X3. Trying to be part of a crowd without being kettled proves all but impossible. The cops' ontology of the crowd is at least interesting: to enter the crowd is to be responsible for anything that any member of the crowd does. *You wouldn't have been hurt if you weren't there.* (One is struck by the way that this is the complete opposite of the "corporate irresponsibility" that applies to the cops themselves.) Dominic notes the "underlying identification of disorder with uncleanliness, an identification which is transferred onto the disorderly themselves, supports the cop's self-image as a preserver of public moral health, keeping the clean and decent citizen separate from the filthy and abject underside of society."[8] It's Foucault 101:

> The plague is met by order; its function is to sort out every possible confusion: that of the disease, which is transmitted when bodies are mixed together; that of the evil, which is increased when fear and death overcome prohibitions. It lays down for each individual his place, his body, his disease and his death, his well-being, by means of an omnipresent and omniscient power that subdivides itself in a regular, uninterrupted way even to the ultimate determination of the individual, of what characterises him, of what belongs to him, of what happens to him. Against the plague, which is a mixture, discipline brings into play its power, which is one of analysis. A whole literary fiction of the festival grew up around the plague: suspended laws, lifted prohibitions, the frenzy of passing time, bodies mingling together without respect, individuals unmasked, abandoning their statutory identity and the figure under which they had been recognised, allowing a quite different truth to appear. But there was also a political dream of the plague, which was exactly its reverse: not the collective festival, "but strict divisions; not laws transgressed, but the penetration of regulation into even the smallest details of everyday life through the mediation of the complete hierarchy that assured the capillary functioning of power; not masks that were put on and taken off, but the assignment to each individual of his "true" name, his "true" place, his "true" body, his "true" disease. The plague as a form, at once real and imaginary, of disorder had as its medical and political correlative discipline. Behind the disciplinary mechanisms can be read the haunting memory of "contagions", of the plague, of rebellions, crimes, vagabondage, desertions, people who appear and disappear, live and die in disorder.[9]

I was at Hillsborough, and I've seen what can happen when the police treat people as an undifferentiated mass, too subhuman to be disciplined. At these protests, the police have been the agents of negative solidarity: *Why should we pay for those students? It's bad for all of us, why can't they accept it like the rest of us do?* By now, it's clear how prophetic Alex's post on "post-Fordist plasticity and negative solidarity" has become, since the movement — the alternative to negative solidarity — has assumed exactly the (plastic) form that Alex called for:

> Unpicking negative solidarity, which is clearly an internalisation of the

conditions of flexibility and atomised "homo economicus" individualism necessary for the embedding of Neoliberal post-Fordism, requires the constructing of a new form of solidarity, a form of solidarity adequately configured to effectively oppose the chief machines of Neoliberal praxis: finance. This new form of solidarity must be capable of fluidity and rapid response, able to exploit weaknesses within systems and structures opportunistically and with a global purview, one which crucially can mirror the rapidity and fluidity of international finance. This is solidarity as plasticity, rather than the static brick-like form of Fordist labour solidarity, capable of flowing and shifting, yes, but also of fixing into position and assuming a hardened form where necessary. This form of solidarity must be inclusive of the new protest and occupation movements which have emerged in recent years, which although they have been largely ineffectual to date, have certainly led to new and interesting configurations of interest groups. What has been lacking however are the necessary cybernetic coordination systems to effectively enable these disparate and fragmentary groups to achieve the status of a counter-hegemonic power, a "class" power in the broadest sense of the term, one which is capable of counter-balancing effectively the rapacious if discredited centres of neoliberalism. Indeed it is this which must be formulated as the political conclusion of theories of post-Fordisation, rather than any kind of fantastical and strictly imaginary political subject such as the multitude. Only when there is an effective counterbalancing power can new theoretical socio-economic post-capitalist forms be properly disseminated, and successfully gain purchase.[10]

Post-Fordist plasticity is also in play in the other major political story of the day (*Mail* headline on Thursday: *Now It's Cyber War*): Assange and WikiLeaks. Now is not the time to go into this in any depth, but surely what we can see here — and something which those who say that the leaks only tell us what we already know have not grasped — is a new level of symbolic crisis. The authoritarian big Other has always relied upon maintaining a clear difference between off-the-record utterances and official proclamations, but it is precisely this distinction which WikiLeaks (and its successors) threaten to abolish.

On the train home, I read Clegg denouncing "student dreamers" on the front page of the *Standard*. "I would feel ashamed if I didn't deal with the way that the world is, not simply dream of the way the world I would like it to be": capitalist realism in a nutshell. (An unfortunate echo of Bobby Kennedy's famous slogan: "Some men see things as they are and say why. I dream things that never were and say why not." See how, under pressure from capitalist realism, the rhetoric of mainstream liberalism has inverted.)

From Foucault 101 to Barthes 101. The coverage of the demo on the BBC News channel is a masterclass in the technique that Barthes called anchorage.

What we actually *see* are mounted police horse charges and some property damage; what we *hear* about — as bravely narrated by a helmeted reporter from behind the police lines — is the "violence" of the student protestors. (It's of course not accidental that Paul Mason's report came from *inside* the kettle.) One of the most notable features of the media coverage since Day X has been the persistent equivalence it has made between violence and property damage. Having narrowly avoided two kettles, I hardly see any violence or property damage. The violence I do see is perpetrated by the police, as a line of baton-swinging cops impose a kettle on protestors standing on Whitehall. I only learn about Alfie Meadows later, and the disjunction between the reality of the demo and its media representation becomes even more maddening, to the point where I can hardly bear to watch the news coverage any more. While a young student has a brain operation, the media are fixated on a cosmetic "attack" on the heir to the throne's car. The effects of all this are ambiguous,[11] but it's now clear that the UK hasn't been as *visibly* divided as this since the Miners' Strike.

In the afternoon of Day X1, streaming from Trafalgar Square up towards Whitehall, we didn't know where we were going or who, if anyone, was leading us. A month later, the situation feels the same. We've broken out of the end of history onto terra incognito. What's certain is that the old world is disintegrating, and soon it will not be possible to even pretend that we can return to it.

football/capitalist realism/utopia[1]

Football and Neoliberal Anti-Utopianism

"English football", the writer Robin Carmody argued on his LiveJournal page, is a metaphor for precisely what the neoliberals have done to England itself." But it's more than a metaphor. Football has been at the forefront of the total re-engineering of English culture, society and economy wrought by neoliberalism over the last thirty years. Neoliberalism presented itself as supremely realistic — as the only possible realism. It told us that utopia is impossible because there is no such thing as society, only individuals pursuing their own interests. What better image of this anti-utopianism is there than the Premiership, with its imperious, untouchable elite of clubs, its synergy with multinational media conglomerates, its conspicuously consuming players, its super-predatory club owners buying success like they are buying another yacht? Competition, exploitation, the strong lording it over the weak, paparazzi snaps of the fabulously wealthy masters of the universe players exiting nightclubs, flashing their very new money: football as anti-egalitarian Nietzschean combat. Forget utopia: dream, instead — if you're young — of eventually becoming like this, of owning these Cheshire mansions, of getting a cyborg-slick WAG; or if you're too old to ever lace up those ultrabranded boots, get used to being inferior, to never making it — dream instead of media-transfiguration via reality TV, or of a lottery win...

Yet the Premiership is often treated as if it were a cause rather than an effect. In the lack of a coherent, general critique of capitalism, complaints about the inflation of players' wages make no sense. After all, it is not public money being redistributed. Players' spiralling wages are a consequence of the very market dynamics that, until last year's bank crisis, were held to be sacrosanct. You can detect a sour anti-working class resentment — shared by self-hating elements of the working class itself — in the attack on football's "undeserving" rich. But all of this — the player's high wages, the exorbitant ticket prices — is an effect of football's total subsumption into post-Fordist capital. But what if it wasn't like this? What if there had been another way?

Football's Lost Utopias (in Nottingham)

There's a poignant moment in Duncan Hamilton's biography of Brian Clough — also recounted in David Peace's *The Damned United* — when Clough and Peter Taylor (who "wanted the ship-builders to earn as much as the ship-owners") go to see Harold Wilson speak and come away glowing with the white heat of Old Labour optimism, fired up by the prospect of a new era for the proletariat. "You could hear the passion for change in what he said", Clough told Hamilton. "We went back to Taylor's house burning with it ourselves." It's like a scene from *Our Friends In The North*: Our Friends In The Midlands, perhaps. The future that Clough and Taylor anticipated would of course never arrive. There's a parallel, perhaps, with another achingly painful scene in Hamilton's book: Peter Taylor speaking after Forest's second victory in the European Cup, proclaiming that this was only the beginning... What in fact lay ahead was underachievement and overpriced players, decline and mediocrity, the final dissolution of the volatile partnership between Clough and Taylor, a rift opening up between the two men that would remain bitter until Taylor's death. Who of us can identify when the moment of our greatest triumph has already passed? And how bearable would life be if we could?

If the brave new world wouldn't arrive for the working class, it did arrive for Clough personally. Instead of being at the vanguard of a newly assertive working class, Clough's period of greatest success coincided with the ebb tide of postwar proletarian collectivism. Clough was sometimes sneered at as a "champagne socialist" because he saw no contradiction between being a leftist and achieving success. Like many born poor, Clough was never able to fully believe that he had finally vanquished poverty from his life — hence, all those TV appearances, ghosted columns and the bung-rumours. In his review of *The Damned United* for the *Guardian*, Chris Petit argued that Clough "embodied many of the forthcoming dilemmas of Thatcher's Britain, his career a constant argument between self-proclamation and partnership, between probity and the demon drink, between financial irregularity and the belief that football was about more than acquisition."[2] The Premiership terminated this, finally destroyed what was left of Clough's crumbling world — a world in which working-class managers could outwit and overcome puffed-up patrician patriarchs, a world in which unfancied provincial clubs could outdo the established colossuses — and his final decline was all-too punctual. With Clough an ailing Lear at the helm, Forest were relegated in 1993, at the end of the Premier League's first season.

The End of an Era

May 2009. Flamboyant Barcelona outplay Manchester United in the European Champions League final. United have come to represent the harsh capitalist reality principle of modern football. Only the already-successful and the wealthy can win. Fans dream now not of their club being revivified by some Brian Clough-like managerial genius, but of it being saved by the largesse of a bored plutocrat. Barcelona famously have no shirt sponsor, and display the logo of UNICEF on their jerseys. United's shirt sponsor is AIG, the insurance company at the heart of the financial crisis (according to the *Economist*, AIG's "tentacles reach into every part of the economy.") The neoliberal anti-utopia disintegrated with the bank bailouts, even though it survives in an undead form as a set of defaults which continue to dominate social reality.

A non-profit making association owned and controlled by its members, Barcelona's slogan is "more than a club". Do Barca, with their foundations and educational activities, give a hint as to how football might operate in a utopia? Proletarian artistry the beauty of teamwork, competition, yes, but not the dog-eat-dog combat of capitalist realism. There could surely be no utopia that didn't include something like this...

the game has changed[1]

In my column for this publication a few months ago, I called for a new negativity, in the spirit of Herbert Marcuse's claim that the proper function of art was to be a "Great Refusal". What better answer could I get than the massive "NO" painted on the grass of Parliament Square in London during one of the recent series of protests against government cuts in the UK? Only four weeks ago, this kind of negativity still seemed to be only a distant possibility in a place like the UK. When, at a conference on public art and civility organised by SKOR in Amsterdam at the end of October, I suggested that there would soon be expressions of massive public anger in the UK, some of the UK-based delegates were sceptical, accusing me of "revolutionary nostalgia". I was confident that they were being unduly dismissive — but I still didn't anticipate the scale of the recent protests.

Like Ireland, the UK has been at the forefront of what I have called "capitalist realism" — the view that, since capitalism is the only game in town, all we can do is find a way of accommodating ourselves to it. Part of leftist capitalist realism has been the disavowal of people's own pessimism and disillusion and its projection onto others. Nothing will happen; people will remain apathetic. That kind of diagnosis has been blown apart by the astonishing student movement that has changed the political landscape in the UK so dramatically since November. Apathy is dead, said a placard at one of the London protests. The game has changed, the protestors have chanted, and so it has. What we've seen is an efflorescence of oppositional activity: not only massive protests — which have led to increasingly naked displays of antagonism — but occupations and flashmobs invading chainstores. Comparisons with 68 have inevitably been made, but this movement is in many ways much more remarkable than what happened forty years ago. 68 came at the end of the "cultural revolution" of the Sixties — a

487

series of challenges to the monolithic Marxist meta-narrative (its claim that everything could be reduced to class conflict). 68 presupposed both a credible leftist political project (from which it could deviate) and a social democratic context (which provided the conditions for its exorbitant demands). But both of these have definitively disappeared. They are a distant memory even for the parents of many of the teenagers who took part in the recent UK protests. The current movement has had to build itself up almost from nothing, in a situation where the revolutionary left has no infrastructure and the moderate left has long since acquiesced to capitalist realism; and, perhaps most astonishingly, it has been constructed by those who had previously been the most obvious victims of capitalist realism — the young. And it should also not be forgotten — even though it often is — that 68 failed. The new breed of protestors expect to win. They do not have the ingrained defeatism — and romanticism of failure — that has been the vice of so much of the so-called radical left since the Sixties. Another difference between 68 and now is the class composition of the protestors. Where the university students of the Sixties were a small elite, many of the students involved in the current wave of demonstrations are working class. 68 was about a short-lived alliance between workers and students, but many of today's students are already workers, forced to do part-time — and often full-time — jobs in order to support their studies. Similarly, the Fordist model of the worker (as someone who does forty hours a week in a factory for forty years of their life) has long since been replaced by precarious work, which assumes "flexibility" and short-term contracts. Finally, new technology has played a crucial role in the current movement. The rapid-response nature of the protests has only been made possible by social networking sites such as Facebook and Twitter.

In the UK, the government has targeted education, the arts, public services and benefits, imposing cuts that are breathtakingly punitive. The justification for cuts in all these areas has been the capitalist realist rationale that "there is no more money", but opponents have rightly identified this as a thin pretext used by the rump of neoliberalism in order to pursue its uncompleted ideological project of totally eliminating public space. But this has created the conditions for an alliance between all those groups, which are "naturally" hostile to neoliberalism. In terms of art and education, what we are potentially seeing here is the reconsolidation of a relationship between bohemia — those elements of the bourgeoisie, which disdain business values — and the working class. That relationship — which allowed the arty working class to escape drudgery, and for the bohemian middle class to make contact with the mutational energies of proletarian culture — was the engine of British and Irish popular culture during the Sixties, Seventies and Eighties. Could today's antagonism revive this? I see no reason not to be optimistic.

creative capitalism[1]

"We have to live this dead reality, this mad transition, in the same way that we lived prison, as a strange and ferocious way of reaffirming life. You could not escape the atrocious experience of prison, the contact with death and its violence. [...] We were constrained to suffer dark romantic hallucinations. There was no longer any alternative. Certainly for us, there has never been any alternative to the world, but always an alternative in the world. A la Rauschenberg: a world that is assumed, shattered, reinvented in the form of its monstrosity. But even the possibility of such a heroism was denied to us. [...] We have to live and suffer the defeat of truth, of our truth. We have to destroy its representation, its continuity, its memory, its trace. All subterfuges for avoiding the recognition that reality has changed, and with it truth, have to be rejected. [...] The very blood in our veins had been replaced."
— Antonio Negri, *Art and Multitude*[2]

Negri's *Art and Multitude* consists of nine letters, most of which were written to his friends at the end of the 1980s while he was in exile in France. Negri here describes the destitution that the left endured after the defeats of the 1970s: the destruction of all its hopes, the way in which it had been outflanked by a neoliberalism which successfully installed business thinking into all areas of everyday life. What emerges here, in other words, is an account of the immediate after-effects of the installation of what I have called capitalist realism: the view that, since there is no alternative to capitalism, the only possible attitude consists in adjusting to its demands. Negri poses the left's predicament very acutely.

To go back to the seeming certainties of older forms of militancy would be to consign oneself to irrelevance, obsolescence, to become an historical relic; but to accept the new situation, to adapt to it, would be to concede total defeat. The only possibility, Negri suggests, is to endure the time in the desert as a kind of religious trial: a moment of terrible and terrifying renewal, a transformation of the revolutionary subject happening at the very moment when revolution seems impossible and the forces of reaction control everything. The new situation — capital's mutation into a post-Fordist form in which labour becomes "immaterial", "flexible" and subject to the pressures of globalisation — offers new potentials, which must be embraced.

Reading these at times extraordinary communications, I find myself, as ever, persuaded by Negri's negative analysis, his vision of culture and consciousness totally subsumed by capital. What I am much less convinced by is his positive alternative to this banal yet dark dominion. Like his inspirations, Deleuze and Guattari, Negri is a vitalist who opposes capital's necrotic force to the living potenza of the creativity of the multitude.

Art, Negri maintains, is intrinsically rebellious and subversive. Even though Negri himself recognises the dangers of taking too much consolation in art, he ends up retaining faith in it. "When I myself suffered the political defeat of the seventies and in the depths of despair, asked art to help me to endure it and to help me find individual ways of resistance and redemption", Negri writes, "I was overestimating the capacity of art." Yet Negri is soon arguing that art is a "perennial demonstration of the irreducibility of freedom, of subversive action, of love for radical transformation".

From Negri's point of view, there is no contradiction between these two claims. What he is arguing is that an individual can never find his way out of despondency through art alone; rather, it is only by new forms of solidarity — which necessarily must involve art — that escape is possible. While the point about collectivity has never been more pressing, Negri's hymning of art seems strangely nostalgic. For the era of capitalist realism has also seen all kinds of synergies between art and business, nowhere better summed up than in the concept of the "creative industries".

It is of course possible to argue that the art that has dominated in capitalist realism, its artistic and commercial value massively inflated, is a fake art, a betrayal and dilution of art's inherent militancy. But why not go all the way with Negri's logic of negativity, and argue that there is no readymade, already-existing utopian energy; that there is nothing which, by its very nature, resists incorporation into capital? So it is not then a matter of creativity versus capitalism — or rather of capitalism as the capturing of the creativity of the multitude. Instead, the enemy now could better be called creative capitalism, and overcoming it will not involve inventing new modes of positivism, but new kinds of negativity.

reality management[1]

Johann Hari's defenders — and practically every defence of Hari served to further underscore what a complacent self-serving Oxbridge club so much of the UK broadsheet commentariat is — might have pathetically seized upon the *News of the World* hacking story in order to underplay their boy's misdemeanours, but the reality is that the Hari and the *News of the World* situations are part of a single crisis that also includes the Ed Miliband "these strikes are wrong" video[2] and ongoing cyberwar (Wikileaks, Lulzsec, 4Chan). Perhaps the reason that the Assange/Žižek dialogue was so disappointing is that Žižek's basic point about the crisis of symbolic efficiency is now so clear that it doesn't require much elaboration. It is one thing our knowing about the corrupt practices that the power elite routinely engage in; it is another for that knowledge to be officially validated. The space that power needs to manage reality is disappearing.

With the "Milibot" video, the offscreen manipulations of PR came off less like a dark art and more like surrealist comedy — Miliband for all the world resembling an ROM entity from *eXistenZ*, only capable of giving one pre-prepared response no matter what the question. The exposure of Hari's manipulations is significant, meanwhile, because (as Petra Davis argued on her Twitter feed) it showed how his construction of "commonsense reality" depended on techniques proper to fiction. Reading Hari's pieces back, it's quite astonishing how crass these techniques were — a "she drew on the omnipresent cigarette" here, and "he asked for more wine" there, inserted between screeds of pirated text. It's like Hari's "interviewing" career is one long postmodern prank, and, really, this episode ought to be liberal empiricism's equivalent of the Sokal scandal. It was fitting that the Deterritorial Support Group's exposure of Hari[3] started with Hari's hatchet job on Negri, a masterclass in liberal propaganda and knee-jerk loathing of theory — privately educated Hari reassuring his readers that he couldn't understand *Empire*, therefore they shouldn't worry about reading it. The old *we don't read it, so you don't have to...* routine. The Negri "interview" crudely alternates between personal attacks on Negri and appeals to self-evidence (of course communism is evil, why won't this bad tempered old man admit it?). Yet Hari's conclusion — "this is where revolutionary Marxism comes to die. It has been reduced to an obscure parlour game for ageing bourgeois nostalgics" — now itself reads like a relic of a bygone world. The "certainties" and self-evidences of the near-past are unravelling quicker than we can keep up.

As for the *News of the World* story, it is clear that it is not just about the *News of the World* or phone hacking. A whole ruling class, a whole mode of governance, stands accused. All the signs are that neoliberalism's standard tactics of containment — offering an individual as scapegoat-trophy in order to deflect from a structural tendency — are now starting to fail. News International are trying to re-sacrifice a scapegoat they've already served up (Coulson) but the process is out of their control and now has its own momentum (which is sure to drag other newspapers into its wake before very long). What was made to look like a series of disconnected incidents now appears as what it always was: a worldwide web of corruption whose byzantine murkiness resembles something out of *The Wire* or a David Peace novel. A dark network comprising private investigators, the criminal underworld, tabloid newspapers, multinational media conglomerates, the police, politicians, the banks, and the bodies supposed to regulate them (who are at best impotent, at worst part of the problem) cannot now be kept hidden from public scrutiny. This is less a conspiracy than a network of complicities: fear on all sides, nobody trusting anybody else, the whole thing depending on who's got the goods on whom... Cops watching hacks watching cops; threatened politicians looking for favours...

What characterises capitalist realism is fatalism at the level of politics (where nothing much can ever change, except to move further in the direction of neoliberalisation) and magical voluntarism at the level of the individual: you can achieve anything, if you only you do more training courses, listen to Mary Portas or Kirsty Allsopp, *try harder*. Magical voluntarism, naturally, also drives the tabloid culture of individual blame (resign, resign!) in which the tabloids themselves are now caught up, although, as Zone Styx noted, News International clearly expects far more from public service managers like Sharon Shoemith than it does from its own executives.) Individualise, individualise, insists capitalist ideology. Note the way in which the media sought to reduce the Lulsec story to Ryan Cleary, or the way in which the clueless Peter Preston[4] finds the idea of a collective entity such as DSG unfathomable.

A manageable level of cynicism about the media actually serves the capitalist realist media system well. Since the media stands in for the public sphere, if journalists and politicians are perceived to be "all liars", as they widely are, then there is no hope to be had in public life at all. Hack exculpations appeal to a market Hobbesianism: they are giving people what they want but what they won't admit to liking. When, pickled in the jouissance of self-loathing and their other stimulants of choice, the hacks style themselves as "princes of darkness", they see themselves as reflecting the public's own disavowed cynicism back to it. *Nobody likes working in the sewers, but don't you all love the pretty little globules of sensation that we dredge up for you?* Similarly, Glenn Mulcaire whines that the *NOTW* put him under pressure for results, this isn't only an excuse — what we're seeing here is in part the consequence of the intense competitive pressures at work in print media as its market share declines. Negative solidarity again: a race to depths so infernally pressurised that only alcohol-breathing subhuman crustaceans can survive there. (You only have to look at ex-*NOTW* hack Paul McMullan to see that.) As one by one those who played their part are dragged into the light, the old bullying sneers become familiar plaints: that's reality, we couldn't help it, that's how things are now... But we must hear their excuses as indictments of a system: behold what a wretched state overwork and pitiless competition can reduce human beings to.

All of which means that a few sackings here and there will clearly not suffice. What is needed, as Dan Hind argues, is total media reform:

> The current structure of power and decision-making in the media cannot now be allowed to remain unchanged. The employees of large media organisations have monopoly control of decisions about what is investigated and what prominence is given to the results of investigations. They have been unable or unwilling to use this monopoly power in the public interest. Accordingly it is time to assert our democratic right to communicate freely amongst ourselves. Each of us must take some some fraction of the commissioning power, the power to initiate and publish inquiries. If we do not our public life will remain a mess of officially sanctioned fairy tales, crocodilian excuses, and grotesque abuses of the innocent, in which market forces and elite prerogatives set the limits of our understanding and hence of our capacity for self-government.[5]

In the House of Commons emergency debate today, many MPs had the relieved and faintly bemused air of the henchmen and victims of a bully who can't quite believe that the tyranny might be nearing its end. As Assange said on Saturday — and as Dan Hind also argues in *The Return of the Public* — the function of corporate media has been to isolate people, to make them distrust their discontent with a world controlled by business interests. What has combated this is the production of new collectivities of dissent, both online and in the streets. What we're seeing in this extraordinary moment of transition is a reality management system imploding from within at the same time as it is being undermined from outside. And, this is only the beginning — you haven't seen anything yet.

uk tabloid[1]

It took all of Cameron's replicant smarm to get through this morning's astonishing press conference.[2] Events have moved so swiftly this week that it's easy to overlook how momentous some of his admissions were. Many are rightly sceptical about whether Cameron will act on what he said today. Sometimes, however, words are acts, and the ultimate significance of what Cameron said today is that it constituted an *official* acknowledgement — from the very mouth of the beast — that there is indeed a corrupt system involving the press, the police and other politicians, and that he is implicated in it. *We're all in it together,* he ruefully observed, another iteration of the fateful phrase that will define his wretched premiership. This might count as capitalist realism's equivalent of Krushchev's acknowledgement of corruption in the USSR. There are also those who are sceptical as to whether all of this will lead anywhere very different. If, as I argued in my last post, the scenes we're now living through resemble the denouement of *The Wire* or one of David Peace's novels, then we must confront the political ambivalence of those fictions again. For what they show, after all, is the System as a Schopenhauerian monstrosity, impersonal and implacable, remorselessly reproducing itself, no matter how many local victories are achieved, no matter how many individuals die or are exposed. Is this an analysis of capitalist realism, or a contribution to it? It's possible now to see both Peace and *The Wire* as symptomatic of a political impasse; Peace's novels show the defeat of collective politics, and *The Wire* anatomises the consequences of that defeat.

What we're seeing now may not herald the collapse of the system, but I'm confident that this week will be looked back upon as a moment when power in the UK was forced to reconfigure. We're too ready to see the Murdochs as Machiavellian, one step ahead of events. But no empire lasts forever; even the canniest operator loses their touch eventually, and Murdoch, let's remember, is the man who bought Myspace. Closing down the *News of the World* may have been a smart move, but it is one that the Murdochs made on the back foot; it was a reactive bid to regain initiative, or at least to gain some traction on a situation that remains out of their control.

This is all a consequence of an excess of power. If the old autonomist argument is correct and capital's innovations were forced by workers' acts of refusal — and what could illustrate this thesis more effectively than Murdoch's struggle with the unions in the 1980s — then it's now clear how sloppy and shoddy capital's operatives became in the lack of any effective opposition. This is decadence — not merely in the moral sense, but also in the sense of decay and deterioration. During the early twenty-first-century high pomp of neoliberalism, hacks, cops and politicians were so confident that they would never be exposed that they behaved in an ever more brazenly depraved manner, and appeared to take little care in covering their traces. What's also emerging into clearer view now is the tabloid media's crucial role in the biopolitical control which was central to the constitution of neoliberal hegemony. Too much is made of Murdoch the kingmaker; his hold over politicians, like that exercised by Paul Dacre, depended far less on what he could do for them, and far more on what he could do *to* them, if they crossed him or his organisation. It's suggested, for instance, that the reason that the previous police "investigations" into News International were so inadequate is that NI held compromising information on the investigating officers, and that MPs feared calling Rebekah Brooks to account because they were warned that they would be subject to tabloid humiliation. Dacre and Murdoch are the princes of piety and cynicism.[3] The neoliberal tabloid is an almost too crude diagram of a Burroughsian biocontrol apparatus: stimulating hedonic excess on the one hand while condemning it on the other. Surveillance need only be virtual. There's always something potentially shaming that can be dragged out of the closet, for whose fantasy life is not humiliating when exposed to the glare of the big Other? No matter who the victim of these exposes might be, they serve right-wing purposes, because they reinforce a Hobbesian account of "human nature": everyone is out for themselves; everyone has a price; everyone is sexually incontinent, given the opportunity. It's no accident that Ellroy called his great work of political demythologisation *American Tabloid*.

But it was the pairing of piety and cynicism which ultimately did for the *News of the World*. The revelations that practically every cause or individual about which the *NOTW* waxed so sentimentally and sanctimoniously — Our Boys, murdered children, the 7/7 victims — was being phone hacked means that the distance between public piety and private cynicism could no longer be maintained.

Read Adam Curtis' potted history of Murdoch[4] and it's instructive to see how the justification for tabloid sensationalism has changed. The denials that the *News of the World* would be salacious which Murdoch made when he took over the paper in the social democratic era give way to neoliberalism's claim to be only giving people what they want. This was the line that witless reactionary oaf Jon Gaunt pursued on *Question Time* last night. There's nothing quite so sad as an unpopular populist, and Gaunt's goading of Hugh Grant — "if you didn't want to be on the front of the papers, you should have kept it in your trousers", "who are *you* to tell people what they can or can't watch" — embarrassingly misjudged the audience's mood. Tabloid sensationalism is a drug, but there was a sense last night that the *QT* audience was no longer willing to conceal from itself the cost of procuring that cheap hit. There was little appetite for Gaunt's now quaint-seeming rhetoric of "choice" and his bashing of paternalism. The old neoliberal lines Gaunt was haplessly hawking had all the appeal of yesterday's fast food. What we're left with is a whole set of questions about culture that are now posed again with renewed force: neoliberalism has failed, the patrician culture it defeated cannot be revived, nor should it be — so where next?

the future is still ours: autonomy and post-capitalism[1]

Adam Curtis' recent documentary series *All Watched Over by Machines of Loving Grace* argued that discourses of self-organisation, which had formerly been associated with the counterculture, were now absorbed into dominant ideology. Hierarchy was bad; networks were good. Organisation itself — held to be synonymous with "top-down control" — was both oppressive and inefficient. There is clearly something in Curtis' arguments. Practically all mainstream political discourse is suspicious of, and sceptical towards, the state, planning and the possibilities of organised political change. This feeds into the ideological framework that I have called capitalist realism: if systemic change can never happen, all we can do is make the best of capitalism.

There's no doubt that the right has been able to profit from identifying the left with an allegedly superseded "top-down" version of politics. Neoliberalism imposed a model of historical time which places bureaucratic centralisation in the past, by contrast with a "modernisation" that is held to be synonymous with "flexibility" and "individual choice". More recently, the much derided idea of the Big Society is, in effect, a right-wing version of autonomism. The work of Phillip Blond, one of the architects of the "Big Society" concept, is saturated with the rhetoric of self-organisation. In the report "The Ownership State", which he wrote for the *ResPublica* think-tank,[2] Blond writes of "open systems" which "recognise that uncertainty and change render traditional command-and-control ineffective". While Blond's ideas have been seen by many as obfuscatory justifications for the neoliberal privatisation agenda, Blond himself positions them as critical of neoliberalism. Blond notes a paradox that I also discuss in *Capitalist Realism*: rather than eliminating bureaucracy, as it promised to, neoliberalism has led to its proliferation. Since public services can never function as "proper" markets, the imposition of the "market solution" in healthcare and education "generates a huge and costly bureaucracy of accountants, examiners, inspectors, assessors and auditors, all concerned with assuring quality and asserting control that hinder innovation and experiment and lock in high cost." Such systems, Blond writes, are

> organic rather than mechanistic, and require a completely different management mindset to run them. Strategy and feedback from action are more significant than detailed planning ('Fire — ready — aim!' as Tom Peters wrote); hierarchies give way to networks; the periphery is as important as the centre; self-interest and competition are balanced by trust and cooperation; initiative and inventiveness are required rather than compliance; smartening up rather than dumbing down.

Since the right is now prepared to talk in these terms, it is clear that networks and open systems are not enough in themselves to save us. Rather, as Gilles Deleuze argued in his crucial essay "Postscript on the Societies of Control",[3] networks are simply the mode in which power operates in the "control" societies that have superseded the old "disciplinary" structures.

Does all this then mean that ideas of autonomy and self-organisation would inevitably be co-opted by the right, and that there is no further political potential in them for the left? Definitely not — far from indicating any deficiency in autonomist ideas, the co-option of these ideas by the right shows that they have continuing potency. Seeing what is wrong with Blond and his ilk's appropriation of autonomism will also tell us something about what the difference between right and left might be in the future.

Curtis is right that the principal way in which autonomist ideas have been neutralised is by using them *against* the very idea of political organisation. Yet autonomist theories continue to be crucial because they give us some resources for constructing a model of what leftist political organisation could look like in the post-Fordist conditions of mandatory flexibility, globalisation and just-in-time production. We can no longer be in any doubt that the conditions which gave rise to the "old left" have collapsed in the global North, but we must have the courage not to be nostalgic for this lost Fordist world of boring factory work and a labour movement dominated by male industrial workers. As Antonio Negri so powerfully put it in one of the letters collected in the recently published *Art And Multitude*, "We have to live and suffer the defeat of truth, of our truth. We have to destroy its representation, its continuity, its memory, its trace. All subterfuges for avoiding the recognition that reality has changed, and with it truth, have to be rejected. [...] The very blood in our veins had been replaced."[4] Even though the shift into so-called "cognitive" labour has been overstated — just because work involves talking doesn't make it "cognitive"; the labour of a call centre worker mechanically repeating the same rote phrases all day is no more "cognitive" than that of someone on a production line — Antonio Negri is right that the liberation from repetitive industrial labour remains a victory. Yet, as Christian Marazzi has argued, workers have been like the Old Testament Jews: led out of the bondage of the Fordist factory, they are now marooned in the desert. As Franco Berardi has shown, precarious work brings with it new kinds of misery: the always-on pressure made possible by mobile telecommunications technology means that there is no longer any end to the working day. An always-on population lives in a state of insomniac depression, unable to ever switch off.

But what has to differentiate the left from the right is a commitment to the idea that liberation lies in the future, not the past. We have to believe that the currently collapsing neoliberal reality system is not the only possible modernity; that, on the contrary, it is a cybergothic form of barbarism, which uses the latest technology to reinforce the power of the oldest elites. It is possible for technology and work to be arranged in completely different ways to how they are configured now. This belief in the future is our advantage over the right. Phillip Blond's networked institutions may have a cybernetic sheen, but he argues that they must be situated in a social setting which is re-dedicated to "traditional values" coming from religion and the family. By strong contrast, we must celebrate the disintegration of these "values", as the necessary precondition for new kinds of solidarity. This solidarity won't emerge automatically. It will need the invention of new kinds of institutions, as well as the transformation of older bodies, such as trade unions. "One of the most important questions", Deleuze wrote in the "Control" essay,

> will concern the ineptitude of the unions: tied to the whole of their history of struggle against the disciplines or within the spaces of enclosure, will they be able to adapt themselves or will they give way to new forms of resistance against the societies of control? Can we already grasp the rough outlines of the coming forms, capable of threatening the joys of marketing?

Perhaps the lineaments of that future can be seen in Latin America, where left wing governments facilitate worker-run collectives. The issue is not any more of abandoning the state, government or planning, but making them part of new systems of feedback that will draw upon — and constitute — collective intelligence. A movement that can replace global capitalism does not need centralisation, but it will require co-ordination. What form will this co-ordination take? How can different autonomous struggles work together? These are the crucial questions we must ask as we begin to build the post-capitalist world.

aesthetic poverty[1]

"A salient feature of these riots," designer Adrian Shaughnessy wrote of the recent disorder in England, "has been the fact that the main target of the attacks has been the shops of the major retail brands of British commercial life."[2] Writing on *Design Observer*'s website, Shaughnessy further noted that most of the outlets which were targeted — sports stores, mobile phone shops — "spend huge amounts of money on branding, on store layout, on window displays, and slick advertising." The comments on Shaughnessy's blogpost were telling: many fellow designers saw the post as, at best, spurious, and, at worst, offensive. Shouldn't the rioters take responsibility for their own behaviour? What role could design possibly play in inciting such "criminal" actions?

The reactionary commentary on the riots has tried to downplay the idea that the rioters were deprived. The rioters had expensive smart phones and wore top-end sportswear — so how could they be poor? While this has been exaggerated — the places where the riots took hold overwhelmingly tended to be areas of poverty and unemployment — it's true that, so far as we can tell, most of the rioters weren't homeless or starving. But there are other kinds of destitution than these. As well as "physical" poverty, there is also an aesthetic poverty, evident to anyone who takes a second look at the dismal vistas of England's hyper-corporatised high streets. While the rich have the material and cultural resources to "unplug" from the dreary banality of these cloned spaces, the poor are far more embedded in them. This embedding in tightly defined media, social and physical environments is in fact a major symptom of aesthetic poverty.

One feature of the moral panic over the riots was the claim that the rioters "destroyed their own communities". But this presupposes both that the rioters belonged to a "community" and that chain stores could constitute any sort of "community" in any case. (It is true that the rioters did not only target corporate outlets, and I don't for a moment want to underplay the horrific destruction caused to small businesses and to people's homes, but it remains the case that most of the destruction and looting was aimed at corporate chains.) Isn't the point, rather, that the rioters were outside, not a "community", since, increasingly, no such thing exists under late capitalism, but from the quiet desperation and miserable resignation that characterises many people's working lives today? The fact that some of the rioters had jobs was supposed to prove that these were not insurrections of the underclass. But many of the jobs that the British media kept citing — one of the rioters, it was trumpeted, was a classroom assistant, another, interestingly, was none other than a graphic designer — were not in themselves indications that the rioters had serious prospects. Such jobs, which are often part-time and short term, are typical of the "precarity" in which increasing numbers of young people — graduates as well as those with few or no qualifications — now find themselves languishing. Those pushing the idea that being a "graphic designer" automatically means that you are inured from poverty or hopelessness only demonstrate how out of touch they are.

The point about mobile phones is also worth pursuing. In what the theorist Jodi Dean has called "communicative capitalism", a smart phone can no longer be conceived of as a mere "luxury item". Communicative capitalism is not about the production of material objects, but the ceaseless circulation of messages. The "content" in this culture comes from users themselves; hence paying for an interface into the communicative matrix is more like paying for one's own tools at work than it is like buying a luxury good. The very distinction between work and non-work, between entertainment and labour, erodes. There are no office hours, no clocking off. In addition to ensuring that we are always connected to the communicative matrix, smartphones are tethering devices which allow employers to call short-term workers into work at a moment's notice. But the notorious use of social networking sites and BlackBerry messenger to propagate the riots shows that the potential of these machines and these websites is not exhausted by communicative capitalism. It has been said that the riots in London spread once groups who usually engage in territorial turf wars called a truce in order to band together against the authorities. While the riots in England could hardly be said to be a coherent political statement, in this collective use of social media there was perhaps the beginnings of something like class consciousness. And in the destruction of the depressing facades of corporate retail, is it too fanciful to see a rejection of the aesthetic poverty that corporate capitalism imposes on so many of us?

the only certainties
are death and capital[1]

"This isn't just art that exists in the market, or is 'about' the market. This is art that is the market — a series of gestures that are made wholly or primarily to capture and embody financial value, and only secondarily have any other function or virtue." So wrote Hari Kunzru of Damien Hirst's work in the *Guardian*.[2] I'm not interested in rehearsing here discussions of Hirst's merit as an artist; what interests me instead is his symptomatic status as a figure who embodies capital's penetration into all areas of culture. As Kunzru points out, Hirst's own relationship to capital is more than close. He is a "house artist to the 1%", and the way that value is generated out of his work — a mixture of hype and the exploitation of the poorly remunerated "assistants" who actually produce many of the pieces — is a model of how exchange value is created in late capitalism. Hirst's notorious auction, "Beautiful Inside My Head Forever", took place at the very moment that Lehman Brothers was collapsing. But while the banks failed, Hirst remains a powerful brand. In fact, some of Hirst's pieces were among the works that were auctioned when Lehman Brothers' art collection was sold off in order to recoup something for the bank's creditors. The way that the prices of Hirst's pieces became not just part of the story of the works, but practically their sole interest, reminds me of nothing so much as Michael Jackson after *Thriller*. Yet, while Jackson was tragically maddened and destroyed by the colossal scale of his success, Hirst gives every impression of being perfectly at home at the heart of a vast capital-generating factory.

The current Hirst retrospective at the Tate should now look like a reliquary of bygone world, but it merely highlights that art and culture have yet to come to terms with the traumatic events of 2008. Our imaginations are still dominated (or stultified) by work which emerged from the cocaine-buzzy mixture of hedonism, cynicism and piety which governed art and politics in the 1990s and 2000s. Hirst is the Warhol of capitalist realism, but he has none of Warhol's blank charisma. In place of Warhol's android awkwardness, Hirst offers a blokish bonhomie. Warhol's studied banality has become the genuinely ultrabanal. Or, rather, the Hirst phenomenon typifies the way in which, in late-capitalist art and entertainment culture, the ultrabanal and the super-spectacular have become (con)fused. Watching Hirst half-heartedly reiterate half-baked clichés — death as the antithesis of life; art as religion — while he was being interviewed in the television coverage that surrounded his current retrospective at the Tate, I was struck by the guilelessness of his thinking. But, then again, what is there to say about this work that it doesn't already say itself? For all its fixation on death, this is work that, in its bleak immanence, repudiates negativity, and leaves no space for commentary.

It is this obdurate refusal to be more than what it is that makes Hirst's work flat with what I have called capitalist realism. Capitalist realism refers to a set of political beliefs and positions, but also a set of aesthetic impasses. "Realism" here does not connote a realist style so much as the inability to see, think or imagine beyond capitalist categories. It's no accident that "reality" entertainment came to the fore in the unprecedented period of neoliberal domination before the bank crises of 2008. Hirst's work belongs to a corresponding development that we might call reality art. The dead animals in the formaldehyde really are dead animals. The skull really is a skull. This inertial tautology may be the real "point" of Hirst's work, and also the reason it emptily but emphatically resonated in a neoliberal era characterised by political fatalism and the corrosion of social imagination. Things are as they are; they cannot be re-imagined, transfigured, or changed. Is there any art object which better captures this than the diamond-encrusted skull of Hirst's "For The Love Of God", the object which, more than any other, may come to stand for the decadence and vanity of the pre-2008 neoliberal world? "For The Love Of God" makes explicit the guiding logic of much of Hirst's work: the only certainties are death and capital. But it can tell us nothing about this. It is a mute symptom which exemplifies a condition it can neither describe nor transcend.

why mental health is a political issue[1]

"Welfare suicides don't exist. Suicide is a mental health issue." That line, by the former Labour official Luke Bozier, pretty much sums up the standard right-wing response to the website Calum's List.[2] According to its founders, the aim of Calum's List is "to list the number of deaths where welfare reform has alleged to have had some culpability, and to make the best effort possible to work towards reducing this death toll." Bozier's Twitter comments were a gloss on blogposts by the *Spectator*'s Isabel Hardman[3] and the *Telegraph*'s Brendan O'Neill.[4]

There's more than a whiff of Freud's "kettle logic" (I didn't borrow your kettle; when I borrowed the kettle it was already broken; when I returned the kettle it wasn't damaged) about the cluster of incompatible arguments that these three presented against Calum's List. Their principal claims were as follows. The suicides have not been caused by the changes, and therefore to mention them is an act of opportunistic exploitation; if suicides have been caused by the reforms, this is no reason to abandon them; the problem is not the reforms themselves but how they are managed (i.e. those forced back to work should be given adequate support); suicide is not a rational act, which means that it can have no political significance.

I don't wish to argue here about whether or not specific cases of suicide were caused by the new legislation. But I do want to contest the bizarre idea that, in principle, suicides could not be adduced as evidence against the changes in the welfare system. If people dying as a consequence of the implementation of measures cannot count as evidence that the legislation has detrimental effects, what would?

O'Neill displays a strangely judgmental attitude towards suicide, arguing suicide "is not a rational response to economic hardship; it is not a rational response to having your benefits cut". This is a spectacular case of missing the point: for many of those suffering from mental illnesses, the capacity to act rationally is impaired, which is one reason that they need to be protected. As for the idea that those returning to work should receive proper support, the lack of such support is the issue. Atos, the agency responsible for testing whether claimants are fit to work, has seen a large number of appeals against its judgments upheld. And who can have faith the government will properly support those returning to work when it entrusts the transition to a discredited agency such as A4e?

But there's a more general problem here. Some of the right-wing commentators condemning Calum's List have deplored the "politicisation" of mental illness, but the problem is exactly the opposite. Mental illness has been depoliticised, so that we blithely accept a situation in which depression is now the malady most treated by the NHS. The neoliberal policies implemented first by the Thatcher governments in the 1980s and continued by New Labour and the current coalition have resulted in a privatisation of stress. Under neoliberal governance, workers have seen their wages stagnate and their working conditions and job security become more precarious. As the *Guardian* reports today, suicides amongst middle-aged men are on the increase, and Jane Powell, chief executive of Calm, the Campaign Against Living Miserably, links some of this increase with unemployment and precarious work.[5] Given the increased reasons for anxiety, it's not surprising that a large proportion of the population diagnose themselves as chronically miserable. But the medicalisation of depression is part of the problem.

The NHS, like the education system and other public services, has been forced to try to deal with the social and psychic damage caused by the deliberate destruction of solidarity and security. Where once workers would have turned to trade unions when they were put under increasing stress, now they are encouraged to go to their GP or, if they are lucky enough to be able to be get one on the NHS, a therapist.

It would be facile to argue that every single case of depression can be attributed to economic or political causes; but it is equally facile to maintain — as the dominant approaches to depression do — that the roots of all depression must always lie either in individual brain chemistry or in early childhood experiences. Most psychiatrists assume that mental illnesses such as depression are caused by chemical imbalances in the brain, which can be treated by drugs. But most psychotherapy doesn't address the social causation of mental illness either.

The radical therapist David Smail argues that Margaret Thatcher's view that there's no such thing as society, only individuals and their families, finds "an unacknowledged echo in almost all approaches to therapy". Therapies such as cognitive behavioural therapy combine a focus on early life with the self-help doctrine that individuals can become masters of their own destiny.

The idea is "with the expert help of your therapist or counsellor, you can change the world you are in the last analysis responsible for, so that it no longer cause you distress" — Smail calls this view "magical voluntarism".

Depression is the shadow side of entrepreneurial culture, what happens when magical voluntarism confronts limited opportunities. As psychologist Oliver James put it in his book *The Selfish Capitalist*, "in the entrepreneurial fantasy society", we are taught "that only the affluent are winners and that access to the top is open to anyone willing to work hard enough, regardless of their familial, ethnic or social background — if you do not succeed, there is only one person to blame." It's high time that the blame was placed elsewhere. We need to reverse the privatisation of stress and recognise that mental health is a political issue.

the london hunger games[1]

Welcome to the Hunger Games. The function of the Hunger Games is to suppress antagonism, via spectacle and terror. In the same way, London 2012 — preceded and accompanied by the authoritarian lockdown and militarisation of the city — are being held up as the antidote to all discontent. The feelgood Olympics, we are being assured, will do everything from making good the damage done by last year's riots to seeing off the "threat" of Scottish independence. Any disquiet about London 2012 is being repositioned as "griping" or "cynicism". Such "whinging", it is claimed, assumed its proper place of marginality as the vast majority enjoy the Games, and LOCOG is vindicated.

The Olympics semiosphere is one from which all negativity must be banished. Witness this masterpiece of circularity, in a blog defending Coca Cola and McDonalds' sponsorship of the Games:

> Considering they have both recently signed long extensions of their contracts and the Olympics are just days away it was rather irresponsible of Jaques Rogge to be in any way negative about such committed Olympic sponsors. Especially because it has also brought negativity to the IOC and the Olympic Games at a crucial period.

Negativity is bad because it brings negativity! The BBC is even periodically running a little film about the importance of positive thinking (even though positive thinking can result in worse outcomes[2]).

Sadly, Charlie Brooker[3] has joined those who think that negativity about the Games was overplayed. But once the Olympic floodlights are turned off, most will switch back from an attitude of mild interest to indifference towards even the most dramatic Olympic sports, never mind those many

511

Olympic sports which plainly have limited spectator appeal. This isn't the point though: disquiet about London 2012 was never necessarily based in any hostility towards the sports. Enjoyment of the sport and loathing for LOCOG and the IOC are perfectly compatible.

Cynicism is just about the only rational response to the doublethink of the McDonalds and Coca Cola sponsorship (one of the most prominent things you see as you pass the Olympic site on the train line up from Liverpool Street is the McDonalds logo). As Paolo Virno argues, cynicism is now an attitude that is simply a requirement for late-capitalist subjectivity, a way of navigating a world governed by rules that are groundless and arbitrary. But as Virno also argues, "It is no accident [...] that the most brazen cynicism is accompanied by unrestrained sentimentalism." Once the Games started, cynicism could be replaced by a managed sentimentality. The BBC has given itself over to propagating an hysterical PR delirium, as Mike Marqusee described after seeing the boxing at ExCel:

> Breathless BBC commentators reiterate the same round of superlatives — "unbelievable", "incredible", "amazing", "brilliant", "unbelievable" — telling us again and again how unique, how special, how extraordinary these Olympics are. It feels like they're the ones on performance-enhancing drugs, not the usually sober, poised and realistic competitors.[4]

Sadly, at the ExCel, after the refreshment of the boxing came the utterly formulaic torpor of a video package in which celebrities waxed banal on the "atmosphere" that makes the Olympics special and the "unforgettable" moment we're privileged to be part of.

Affective exploitation is crucial to late capitalism. The BBC's own Caesar Flickerman (the interviewer who extracts maximum sentimental affect from the Hunger Games contestants before they face their deaths in the arena) is the creepily tactile trackside interviewer Phil Jones. Jones' "interviews" with exhausted athletes, are surely as ritualised as any Chinese state broadcast. Emote. Emote again. Emote differently. Praise the crowd.

It is via emotion that advertising can make the spurious connection between brands and the sport, but, as Marqusee points out, PR boosterism cannot tolerate the very thing which makes sport so fascinating — its unpredictability, the fact that high drama is not guaranteed.

The point of capital's sponsorship of cultural and sporting events is not only the banal one of accruing brand awareness. Its more important function is to make it seem that capital's involvement is a precondition for culture as such. The presence of capitalist sigils on advertising for events forces a quasi-behaviouristic association, registered at the level of the nervous system more than of cognition, between capital and cultural. It is a pervasive reinforcement of capitalist realism.

There is a strange duality of the Olympics — such that, *surrounding* the Games, there can be a semioblitz of commercial exploitation, but, in the spaces where the athletes compete, there is a coy chasteness about advertising, so that even the O2 has to be renamed North Greenwich Arena for the duration of London 2012. Of course, the reason for this is so only those who pay the IOC for the privilege can commercially exploit the Games. Nevertheless, these zones from which capitalist semiotic pollution has been minimised make a pleasant contrast with the ubiquitous tawdry hucksterism elsewhere, inviting us to imagine the Games without capital.

But we don't have to. It's clear that what people are *already* enjoying in the Games is everything for which capital is not responsible: the efforts of the athletes, the experience of a shared publicness. Insofar as the torch relay was a success, this, too, was not due to the parade itself — a dreary countrywide corporate carnival, consisting of Samsung, CocaCola and Lloyds TSB floats — but because it allowed people to experience their own sociality. Note also, for instance, that the improved British performance, which has the BBC in such a jingoistic froth, was likely due to (the privatised-public) National Lottery funding rather than corporate sponsorship.

Nothing could be a clearer example of Negri's claim that capital is essentially parasitic than the Games. Capital's contribution to London 2012 has been systematically overpriced and shoddy: whether it be the branding, with its infantile colouring and lettering (we've grown used to the logo, but, really, has there been a more embarrassingly inept logo in the history of the world for an event of this magnitude?), the soon to be demolished Olympic stadium, magnificent only in its mediocrity, and the grand folly of the ArcelorMittal Orbit. The ArcelorMittal Orbit is perhaps the best symbol of capital's parasitic relation to the London 2012 Games. The echo of Vladimir Tatlin's Monument to the Third International tells you an awful lot about the impasses, inertia and sterililty of capitalist realist culture. As Douglas Murphy points out, comparing the Orbit to Vladimir Tatlin's Monument to the Third International, "[w]hereas Tatlin's twists were a yearning evocation of the teleological thrust of dialectical materialism, the Orbit's creators, in their design statement, merely explain that it 'should make an iconic statement about Tower-ness'". [5]

As Juliet Jacques has argued, the "deconstructed tower" is — unwittingly — the perfect monument for capitalist realist Britain:

> With its funding and name coming mostly from billionaire Lakshmi Mittal's integrated steel company, who provided up to £19.2m towards its costs, with the rest given by the London Development Agency, the Orbit is less a radical structure than an utterly conservative one. In saying that it would pay for itself throgh the renting of private dining spaces at its summit, Boris Johnson may have said more about its legacy than he planned when

he described it as a "corporate money-making venture". In that, Kapoor and Balmond's Orbit captures the spirit of its time and place as much as Eiffel or Tatlin's designs — but perhaps not quite as they intended.[6]

time-wars: towards an alternative for the neo-capitalist era[1]

Time rather than money is the currency in the recent science fiction film *In Time*. At the age of twenty-five, the citizens in the future world the film depicts are given only a year more to live. To survive any longer, they must earn extra time. The decadent rich have centuries of empty time available to fritter away, while the poor are always only days or hours away from death. *In Time* is, in effect, the first science fiction film about precarity — a condition that describes an existential predicament as much as it refers to a particular way of organising work.

At the most simple level, precarity is one consequence of the "post-Fordist" restructuring of work that began in the late 1970s: the turn away from fixed, permanent jobs to ways of working that are increasingly casualised. Yet even those within relatively stable forms of employment are not immune from precarity. Many workers now have to periodically revalidate their status via systems of "continuous professional development"; almost all work, no matter how menial, involves self-surveillance systems in which the worker is required to assess their own performance. Pay is increasingly correlated to output, albeit an output that is no longer easily measurable in material terms.

For most workers, there is no such thing as the long-term. As sociologist Richard Sennett put it in his book *The Corrosion of Character: The Personal Consequences of Work in the New Capitalism*, the post-Fordist worker "lives in a world marked [...] by short-term flexibility and flux [...] Corporations break up or join together, jobs appear and disappear, as events lacking connection."[2] Throughout history, humans have learned to come to terms with the traumatic upheavals caused by war or natural disasters, but "[w]

515

hat's peculiar about uncertainty today", Sennett points out, "is that it exists without any looming historical disaster; instead it is woven into the everyday practices of a vigorous capitalism".[3]

It isn't only work that has become more tenuous. The neoliberal attacks on public services, welfare programmes and trade unions mean that we are increasingly living in a world deprived of security or solidarity. The consequence of the normalisation of uncertainty is a permanent state of low-level panic. Fear, which attaches to particular objects, is replaced by a more generalised anxiety, a constant twitching, an inability to settle. The uncertainty of work is intensified by digital communication technology. As soon as there is email, there are no longer working hours nor a workplace. What characterises the present moment more than our anxious checking — of our messages, which may bring opportunities or demands (often both at the same time), or, more abstractly, of our status, which, like the stock market is constantly under review, never finally resolved?

We are very far from the "society of leisure" that was confidently predicted in the 1970s. Contrary to the hopes raised at that time, technology has not liberated us from work. As Federico Campagna writes in his article "Radical Atheism", published on the *Through Europe* website,

In the current age of machines [...] humans finally have the possibility of devolving most productive processes to technological apparatus, while retaining all outcomes for themselves. In other words, the (first) world currently hosts all the necessary pre-conditions for the realisation of the old autonomist slogan "zero work/full income/all production/to automation". Despite all this, twenty-first-century Western societies are still torn by the dusty, capitalist dichotomy which opposes a tragically overworked section of population against an equally tragically unemployed one.[4]

Campagna's call for a "radial atheism" is based on the recognition that the precariousness that cannot be eliminated is that of life and the body. If there is no afterlife, then our time is finite. Curiously, however, we subjects of late capitalism act as if there is infinite time to waste on work. Work looms over us as never before. "In an eccentric and an extreme society like ours", argue Carl Cederström and Peter Fleming in their book *Dead Man Working*, "working has assumed a universal presence — a worker's society in the worst sense of the term — where even the unemployed and children become obsessed with it." Work now colonises weekends, late evenings, even our dreams. "Under Fordism, weekends and leisure time were still relatively untouched", Cederström and Fleming point out, "Today, however, capital seeks to exploit our sociality in all spheres of work. When we all become "human capital" we not only have a job, or perform a job. We are the job."[5]

Given all of this, it is clear that most political struggles at the moment amount to a war over time. The generalised debt crisis that hangs over all areas of capitalist life and culture — from banks to housing and student funding — is ultimately about time. Averting the alleged catastrophe (of the end of capitalism) will heighten the apocalyptic temporality of everyday life, as the anticipation of catastrophe gives way to a sense that we are already living through the catastrophe and it, like work, will never end. The increase of debt justifies the extending of working hours and working life, with retirement age being pushed ever further back. We are in a state of harassed busyness from which — we are now promised — there will never be any relief.

The state of reactive panic in which most of us find ourselves is not an accidental side-effect of post-Fordist labour. It is highly functional for capital that our time is not only quantitatively short but qualitatively fragmented, bitty. We are required to live in the condition that Linda Stone has called "continuous partial attention", where our attention is habitually distributed across multiple communication platforms.

As Franco "Bifo" Berardi has argued, we now live in the tension between the infinity of cyberspace and the vulnerable finitude of the body and the nervous system. "The acceleration of information exchange has produced and is producing an effect of a pathological type on the individual human mind and even more on the collective mind," Berardi writes in *Precarious Rhapsody*,

> Individuals are not in a position to process the immense and always growing mass of information that enters their computers, their cell phones, their television screens, their electronic diaries and their heads. However, it seems indispensable to follow, recognise, evaluate, process all this information if you want to be efficient, competitive, victorious. [...] The necessary time for paying attention to the fluxes of information is lacking.[6]

The consequence is a strange kind of existential state, in which exhaustion bleeds into insomniac overstimulation (no matter how tired we are, there is still time for one more click) and enjoyment and anxiety co-exist (the urge to check emails, for instance, is both something we must do for work and a libidinal compulsion, a psychoanalytic drive that is never satisfied no matter how many messages we receive). The fact that the smartphone makes cyberspace available practically anywhere at anytime means that boredom (or at least the old style, "Fordist" boredom) has effectively been eliminated from social life. Yet boredom, like death, posed existential challenges that are far more easily deferred in the always-on cyberspatial environment. Ultimately, communicative capitalism does not vanquish boredom so much as it "sublates" it, seeming to destroy it only to preserve it in a new synthesis. The characteristic affective tonality for the insomniac drift of cyberspace, in which there is always one more click to make, one more update to check, combines fascination with boredom. We are bored even as we are fascinated, and the limitless distraction allows us to evade confronting death — even as death is closing in on us.

No doubt this chronic shortage of time goes some way to accounting for the stalled and inertial quality of culture in recent years. The neoliberal gambit was that the destruction of social security would have a dynamic effect on culture and the economy, liberating an entrepreneurial spirit that was inhibited by the red tape of bureaucratic social democratic institutions. The reality, however, is that innovation requires certain forms of stability. The disintegration of social democracy has had a dampening, rather than a dynamic, effect on culture in highly neoliberalised countries such as the UK. Fredric Jameson's claims that late-capitalist culture would be given over to pastiche and retrospection have turned out to be extraordinarily prophetic.

We've grown so accustomed to repetition and recycling that we no longer notice them. Yet it's no surprise that this is the case. New cultural production requires a use of time that communicative capitalism is profoundly hostile towards. Most social energy is sucked into the vortex of late-capitalist labour and its vast simulation of productivity. Innovation depends upon an absorbed (rather than distracted) drift; but it is increasingly difficult to muster the attentional resources necessary for such immersion. Cyberspatial urgencies — the smartphone's flashing red light, the siren call of its alert — function like trance-inhibitors or alarm clocks that keep waking us out of collective dreaming. In these conditions, intellectual work can only be undertaken on a short-term basis. Only prisoners have time to read, and if you want to engage in a twenty-year-long research project funded by the state, you will have to kill someone.

To understand the time-crisis, we only have to compare the current situation with the height of punk and post-punk in the UK and the US. It's no accident that the efflorescence of punk and post-punk culture happened at a time when cheap and squatted property was available in London and New York. Now, simply to afford to pay rent in either city entails giving up most of your time and energy to work. The delirious rise in property prices over the last twenty years is probably the single most important cause of cultural conservatism in the UK and the US. In the UK, much of the infrastructure which indirectly supported cultural production has been systematically dismantled by successive neoliberal governments. Most of the innovations in British popular music which happened between the Sixties and the Nineties would have been unthinkable without the indirect funding provided by social housing, unemployment benefit and student grants.

These developments precisely opened up a kind of time that is now increasingly difficult to access: a time temporarily freed from the pressure to pay rent or the mortgage; an experimental time, in which the outcomes of activities could neither be predicted nor guaranteed; a time which might turn out to be wasted, but which might equally yield new concepts, perceptions, ways of being. It is this kind of time, not the harassed time of the business entrepreneur, which gives rise to the new. This kind of time, where the collective mind can unfurl, also allows the social imagination to flourish. The neoliberal era — the time when, we were repeatedly told, there was no alternative — has been characterised by a massive deterioration of social imagination, an incapacity to even conceive of different ways to work, produce and consume. It's now clear that, from the start (and with good reason) neoliberalism declared war on this alternative mode of time. It remains tireless in its propagation of resentment against those few fugitives who can still escape the treadmill of debt and endless work, promising to ensure that soon, they too will be condemned to performing interminable, meaningless labour — as if the solution to the current stagnation lay in more work, rather than an escape from the cult of work. If there is to be any kind of future, it will depend on our winning back the uses of time that neoliberalism has sought to close off and make us forget.

not failing better, but fighting to win[1]

Capitalist realism, to sum it up briefly, can be seen as both a belief and an attitude. It is a belief that capitalism is the only viable political/economic system, and a simple restatement of the old Thatcherite maxim, "There is no alternative".

People like Paul Mason have been saying that since 2011 there has been an upsurge in global militancy, including a number of uprisings, and this represents the end of capitalist realism. But that is clearly not the case. It is true that the major crisis of capitalism from 2008 led to a situation where capital has never been weaker ideologically in my lifetime, and as a result there is widespread disaffection, but the question is why *nevertheless* capitalist realism still exists.

In my view it is because it was never really necessarily about the idea that capitalism was a particularly good system: it was more about persuading people that it is the only *viable* system and the building of an alternative is impossible. That discontent is practically universal does not change the fact that there appears to be no workable alternative to capitalism. It does not change the belief that capitalism still holds all cards and that there is nothing we can do about it — that capitalism is almost like a force of nature, which cannot be resisted. There is nothing that has happened since 2008 that has done anything to change that, and that is why capitalist realism still persists.

So capitalist realism is a belief, but it is also an attitude related to that belief — an attitude of resignation, defeatism and depression. Really then, capitalist realism, whilst it is disseminated by the neoliberal right, and very successfully so, is a pathology of the left, or elements of the so-called left, that they succumb to. It was an attitude promoted by New Labour — what was New Labour if not instantiating the values of capitalist realism? In other words, we resign ourselves to the fact that there is no getting around capital: capital will ultimately run things, and all we can do is perhaps bolt on a couple of tethers as gestures toward social justice. But essentially ideology is over, politics is over: we are in the era of so-called post-ideology, the era of post-politics, where capital has won. This so-called "post-political" presentation by New Labour was one of the ways in which capitalist realism imposed itself in the British context.

There is a problem, however, in seeing capitalist realism *just* as a belief and an attitude, in that both are based on individual psychology. The discussion needed is one that interrogates where those beliefs and attitudes come from, for what we are actually dealing with is the social decomposition that gives rise to them. For that, we really need a narrative about the decline of solidarity and the decline of security — the neoliberal project achieved its aim of undermining them. Capitalist realism then is also a reflection of the recomposition of various forces in society. It is not just that people are persuaded of certain beliefs, but rather that the beliefs people have reflect the way that forces in society are composed in contemporary capitalism.

"Modernisation"

The decline of the unions is probably the biggest factor in the rise of capitalist realism for ordinary people. Now we find ourselves in a situation where everybody disdains bankers and finance capitalism, and the level of control that these people still hold over all of our lives. Everyone is aghast at the plunder, avoidance of tax and so forth, yet at the same time there is this sentiment that we can do nothing about it. And why has that sentiment grown so powerful? It is because there really is no agent to mediate the feelings people have and organise those people. The effect is that discontent can be widespread, but without such an agent it will remain at the level of individual disaffection.

That easily converts into depression as well, which is one of the stories I try and tell in my book, *Capitalist Realism*. I deal with the association between post-politics, post-ideology, the rise of neoliberalism and the conjoined rise of depression, particularly among young people. I call this process the "privatisation of stress".

I do not want to hang everything on trade union decline — unions are just an example of what has been removed from the psychic and political infrastructure of people's lives over the last thirty or forty years. However, in the past, if your pay and conditions got worse, you might go to the unions and organise, whereas now we are encouraged, if, for example, stress at work increases, to see it as our own problem and deal with it as an individual.

We must deal with it through self-medication, through antidepressants, which are increasingly widely prescribed, or, if we are lucky, through therapy. But these concerns — experienced now as individual psychic pathologies — do not really have their roots in brain chemistry: they reside in the wider social field. But, because there is no longer an agent, a mediator, for a class acting collectively, there is no way of tackling that wider social field.

Another way of getting to this story is via the restructuring of capital in the late Seventies and early Eighties, the arrival of post-Fordism. That meant the increasing use of precarious conditions at work, just-in-time production, the dread word "flexibility": we must bend to capital, no matter what capital wants; we are required to bend to it and we will bend to it. On the one hand, there was that kind of stick, but there was also at least the appearance of carrots in the Eighties: neoliberalism did not *just* hammer workers; it encouraged people no longer to identify as workers. Its success was in being able to seduce people out of that identification, and out of class consciousness.

The genius at the centre of Thatcherism could be found in the selling-off of council houses, because alongside the straightforward inducement of owning your own home was the narrative about time and history, whereby Thatcher and people like her were out to make your life more free. They were opposed to those stuck-in-the-mud, centralising bureaucrats, who want to control your life for you. That involved a very successful harnessing of the desires that had grown up, particularly since the Sixties.

Part of the problem here was the absence of a left response to post-Fordism — instead there was an attachment to the comfort of old antagonisms, you could say. We had internalised the story that there was a strong workers' movement which depended on unity. What were the conditions for that? Well, we had Fordist labour, the concentration of workers in confined spaces, the domination of the industrial workforce by male workers, etc. The breakdown of those conditions threatened the breakdown of the workers' movement. There was the emergence of a plurality of other struggles, leading to the undermining of the common purpose that the workers' movement once possessed. But that kind of nostalgia for Fordism was actually dangerous — the failure was not that Fordism ended, but that we had no alternative vision of modernity to compete with the neoliberal account.

In fact, neoliberalism owns the word "modernisation" now. If you hear the word in news broadcasts, it is synonymous with neoliberalisation. Whenever there is a dispute — in, say, Royal Mail — the phrasing used is something like, "Royal Mail is trying to modernise, but its plans are opposed by workers". But when they say "modernise", they really mean "privatise" and "neoliberalise". We saw this with Blairism: those who wanted to "modernise" really wanted to neoliberalise the Labour Party. Of course, if you are opposed to modernisation, you must be out of touch with reality and you immediately find yourself on the back foot.

The left almost seemed to believe it, and the only way to "modernise" was to make some sort of accommodation with capital. But the opposite mistake was to think that things could stay as they were before — and that was really a very dangerous line to go down. The challenge was to come up with a post-Fordist leftism — a project which was begun in the Eighties. But this soon got derailed, as any attempt to do this was seen as just folding to Blairism, even though that was not the case.

Education

There is more than just one particular zone where capitalist realism applies and most of the anecdotes and key concepts that went into the book came from my experiences teaching sixteen to nineteen-year-olds. So let us turn now to the key question of capitalist realism in education.

One of its central features in this area is "business ontology", as I have called it, which is simply the idea that the only things that actually count, the only criteria that matter, are related to business. Within education we have seen a creeping spread of practices, language and rhetoric from business. And this has spread into teaching, into the kind of self-policing and self-surveillance teachers are now required to perform.

One of the things I try to point out in *Capitalist Realism* is the strange anomaly here: one of the things we were sold about neoliberalism was that it liberated us from bureaucracy, that it was only old Stalinists and crusty social democrats who obsess with bureaucracy. Neoliberalism was supposed to cut away the red tape. So why is it that teachers are required to perform more bureaucratic tasks than they ever were in the heyday of social democracy?

Simply because neoliberalism has got nothing to do with the freeing of markets, and everything to do with class power. That is reflected in the introduction of certain methods and strategies, ways of assessing teachers and schools, justified because they allegedly increase efficiency. Well, anyone who has engaged in this kind of, to coin another phrase, market Stalinism knows that nowadays what matters is what appears on the forms, irrespective of whether it actually corresponds to reality.

It was New Labour which accelerated this development in education by introducing targets — isn't it interesting that New Labour presented itself as the extreme antithesis of Stalinism, but it ended up reconstituting at a formal level Stalinism's really bad aspects (not that there were many good ones!). The language of planned targets has come back, like the return of the repressed.

Given that this clearly does not increase efficiency, we need to see it as a disciplinary mechanism, an ideological, ritualising system. If you are a teacher sitting at home filling in lots of forms full of quasi-business rhetoric, you are not going to teach a better lesson the next day. In fact, if you just watched TV and relaxed, you would probably be better equipped in that regard. But the authorities are not idiots: they know this; they know they are not really increasing your performance.

So what is the function of these practices? Well, one is obviously discipline and control: control via anxiety, control via the destabilisation of professional confidence. These things are framed as "continuous professional development", and that sounds good, doesn't it? You always want to learn more, don't you? And now you always have access to training. But what it really means is that your status is never really validated — you are constantly subject to review. And it is a review of a bizarre and Kafkaesque type, because all the assessment criteria are characterised by a strategic vagueness, whereby it might appear possible to fulfil them, but in reality that fulfilment can be constantly deferred. The result is that teachers are in a constant state of anxiety — and anxiety is highly functional from the perspective of those who want to control us.

On a second level it is merely ideological ritual, of exactly the kind that Althusser described. For him a good part of ideology is made up of ritual: you just repeat the phrases and, as Althusser says, via Pascal, "Kneel and you will believe". That is a highly ambiguous phrase. Does it mean, "Kneel and you will believe afterwards"? Or that in the act of kneeling you already believe? I think both, but it reinforces the idea that belief is really the crucial thing about capitalism. And one of the sources of that belief is the contamination of public life and former public services by this kind of incantation and language of business. Many people regard what they are required to do at work as quite ridiculous and ask why they have to do it. Capitalist realism is confronted, as the response comes back: "Well, you know, it's just how it is now. We don't really believe this stuff, of course, but we just have to go along with it."

That is all ideology really needs. You do not have to believe it in your heart of hearts: all you are required to do is act as *if* you believe it. In education this has been crucial as part of the way in which we view its purpose. Today education is to be determined by the needs of business. Of course, such a tendency has always been present, but there is almost no contesting it anymore.

Debt

There are many different dimensions to capitalist realism in education, but the other key one is debt, plainly. What is interesting is that after the phoney peace, I suppose you could call it, following 2008, where nothing really significant happened in terms of public displays of anger, the first real manifestation of discontent was the student movement of 2010.

Just before it started, I said to a friend of mine that there was going to be some expression of anger over the cuts in higher education, and he responded to the effect that that could not happen: it was just "revolutionary nostalgia" on my part. I do not tell that story to claim some special prophetic vision, but to illustrate the fact that his view had seemed to be the realistic one — there really had been no sign of such anger erupting.

But it did erupt at the end of 2010. Why was that? What was really being argued over with regard to fees? Clearly the rhetoric about paying down the debt is ludicrous, in as far as anyone can make out anything in this necromantic economics surrounding university fees. It seems that it is costing the government more to impose this new system anyway, so it has actually increased the deficit. What were they actually trying to achieve with this massive hike in fees? To me it is obvious that this is another version of the production of a certain kind of anxiety — the student population had to be constituted as debtors.

There was a good piece by Mark Bolton in the *New Left Project* arguing that debt is now the key social category in capitalism: capital does not need to work in the same way as before, but it does need us to be in debt — a main source of our subjectivity.[2] What is debt? It is also a capture of time, of our future. So the confrontation with university students in the UK is a dramatic example of the kind of switch-around we have seen — a struggle over the use of time.

What was university like when I went? First, I did not pay a penny in fees and, secondly, I received a maintenance grant, upon which it was possible to actually live if you were quite frugal. In other words, there was this funded time outside the frenetic activity of work. I say that because now work has changed into simply a means of paying off debt.

The article in the *New Left Project* was arguing against a ludicrous right-wing Tory book, *Britannia Unchained*, which claims that Britain had been chained up, but those chains have now been cut.[3] So how are we freed as a result? We can work harder and longer — even harder than those Chinese, because we need to do a far better job of exploiting ourselves than we have up to now. But the reality of work is that it does not pay enough and that is why we are in debt.

This government has attempted to moralise debt. It is analogous to the ludicrous assertion it keeps making (the government operates in a kind of neuro-linguistic way, believing that if you repeat something often enough then it will become true) that the crisis was caused by New Labour overspending — just like an individual who has maxed out their credit cards. Of course, it was not a moral failing at all when people relied so much on their credit cards: it was unavoidable. More importantly, the entire economy now *needs* people to be in debt — they are doing their duty to capital! That duty to capital in the past is used as a new reason in the present to exploit them further, to cut their public services and standards of living. It would be funny if it were not so grotesque. But this ridiculous personalisation of debt, as if it were a moral failing, is the meat and drink of capitalist realism.

Connected to this is the reduction in the amount of time that could be spent for purposes other than the kind of frenetic anxiety related to the world of work. That Tory book is really part of this attempt to impose such anxiety — we are not working hard enough, after all. What we have seen with the coalition government is the systematic shutting down of space where time could be used differently. This has a massive impact on culture, because it was within those spaces that any alternative culture could be produced. Many of the key developments in popular culture since the 1960s were facilitated by the space provided by the welfare state, social housing, etc. They amounted to a kind of indirect funding for cultural production. With those spaces closed down, much of the culture of late-capitalist Britain is moribund, miserable, repetitious and homogenous.

Another one of the paradoxes of capitalist realism is the hyper-regulation of learning in the classroom, so that any deviation from the official programme is closed down. When you step outside the narrow parameters of the examination drill, students themselves will complain today. They will ask, "Is this going to be in the exam?" A narrow teleological focus is what is inculcated, along with a super-instrumentalisation of education.

Of course, one of the things senior management is trying to do with the introduction of fees is to create a split between students and lecturers. As the students are paying more in fees, it is expected that they will demand more from the lecturers. Management is fairly cynically trying to get students to behave as "aggrieved consumers" who should demand more for their money, but the problem is that none of that extra money is going to the lecturers. I know of a communication from a senior manager at a higher education institution saying that, in the wake of the hike in fees, "We'd better prepare ourselves for students demanding more". Which means that lecturers will have to work more for the same money.

In It Together?

How is it possible to impose all this? Well, only because of the general ideological atmosphere of capitalist realism. Whilst I do not agree with Paul Mason, capitalist realism has certainly changed its form compared to before 2008. Then it had a bullish quality that declared: "Either you get on board with us or you're a sad loser who will die drinking meths in a gutter — if you're lucky." Since 2008, it has had a more desperate quality, which is what lies behind the ostensibly inclusive rhetoric of "We're all in it together". In other words, if we do not all pull together, we will all go down — rather different from the previous implication that anyone who does not come on board will just be crushed beneath the juggernaut of capital.

So the tone of capitalist realism has changed, but harsh measures have been imposed very quickly because of the absence of an alternative. In fact it is even worse than that, because the previous form of the system to which we are told there is no alternative is now impossible. There is no returning to pre-2008 capital. Capital has no idea of any solution to the crises which led up to 2008. There is no guarantee that the current crisis can be ended, because capital's means of keeping wages low and demand up was debt itself. If you make debt harder to come by, then what is going to take its place? There is no answer to that, and plainly capital's apologists are just flailing about.

Their only answer has been the strategy of austerity, which in large part has been based on a historical forgetting of why the welfare state was introduced. It was introduced not out of the kindness and largesse of the capitalists, but as "revolution insurance", so that widespread discontent did not spill over into revolution. They have forgotten that, and as a consequence they think they can keep pulling away those social safety nets without any problem. Last year's riots give us a glimpse of some of the possible repercussions.

What then can we do? Well, it is first necessary to defeat the anarchists — I am only half-joking about that. It is essential that we ask why it is that neo-anarchist ideas are so dominant amongst young people, and especially undergraduates. The blunt answer is that, although anarchist tactics are the most ineffective in attempting to defeat capital, capital has destroyed all the tactics that *were* effective, leaving this rump to propagate itself within the movement. There is an uncomfortable synergy between the rhetoric of the "big society" and a lot of the neo-anarchist ideas and concepts. For example, one of the things which is particularly pernicious about some of the dominant ideas within anarchism at the moment is their disengagement from the mainstream.

There is the idea, for instance, that the mainstream media is an inherently corrupt monolith. The point is that it is completely corrupt, but it is *not* a monolith. It is a terrain that is effectively controlled at present by neoliberals, who took the fight over the mainstream media very seriously, and consequently won that struggle.

One of the things which I am pushing for is media consciousness-raising with some younger people — for example, Channel 4 used to have hour-long programmes featuring a debate between three philosophers. Now *Big Brother* takes up that slot. The slot once occupied by European Arts cinema is now taken by *Location, Location, Location*. If you want to look at the changes in British society, politically and culturally over the last thirty years then there is no better example than Channel 4.

Why is that? Because Channel 4 emerged as a result of all sorts of struggles within the media for control of things like film, and people took that very seriously. Alongside the labour struggles of the Eighties there were also cultural struggles. Both were defeated, but at the time it was by no means obvious that they would be. If you remember, the Eighties were the time when there were moral panics about "loony left" councils, and there was also a moral panic over Channel 4 with its politically correct lefties, who were supposedly taking over broadcasting.

That is part of what I mean by an alternative modernity — an alternative to the neoliberal "modernity", which is actually just a return to the nineteenth century in many ways. But the idea that the mainstream culture is inherently coopted, and all we can do is withdraw from it, is deeply flawed.

The same is true about parliamentary politics. You should not pin all of your hopes on parliamentary politics, because that would be sad and ludicrous, but, at the same time, if it was pointless then you have to ask why the business class expends so many resources in subjugating parliament to its own interests.

Again, the neo-anarchist idea that the state is finished, that we do not need to participate in it at all, is deeply pernicious. It is not that parliamentary politics will achieve much on its own — the object lesson of what happens if you believe that to be the case was New Labour. Power without hegemony — that is effectively what New Labour was. But that is pointless. You cannot hope to achieve anything through an electoral machine alone. But it is hard to see how struggles can succeed without being part of an ensemble. We have to win back the idea that it is about winning the hegemonic struggle in society on different fronts at the same time.

Because the anti-capitalist movements that have arisen since the Nineties have ultimately done nothing, they have caused capital no concern at all — it has been so easy to route around them. Part of the reason for that is the fact that they have taken place out on the street, ignoring the politics of the workplace and of the everyday. And that feels remote to ordinary working people, because at least with the unions, for all their flaws, there was a direct connection between everyday lives and politics. That connection is now missing, and anti-capitalist movements have not provided it.

Coordination

It seems to me that the crucial question now is coordination, and so many debates around centralisation versus decentralisation, top-down versus horizontal, obfuscate the real issues, which are about what is the most effective form of co-ordination against capital. Coordination does not need centralisation: in order for things to have common purpose they do not have to be centralised. We need to resist the false oppositions which come out of the way neo-anarchist ideas are narrativised.

Obviously all the anti-capitalist movements, right up to Occupy, have managed to mobilise disaffection, but they have not been able to coordinate it in a way that causes capital any long-term problems at all. What could coordinate discontent? And what could convert ambient disaffection into sustainable antagonism? It is a lack of the sustainability of these antagonisms which is part of the problem with them. Another problem with them, which my comrade, Jeremy Gilbert, has raised, is their lack of institutional memory. If you do not have something like a party structure then you do not have institutional memory, and you just end up repeating the same mistakes over and over.

There is far too much toleration of failure on our side. If I ever have to hear that Samuel Becket quote, "Try again, fail again, fail better", I will go mad. Why do we even think in these terms? There is no honour in failure, although there is no shame in it if you have tried to succeed. Instead of that stupid slogan we should aim to learn from our mistakes in order to succeed next time. The odds might be stacked in such a way that we do keep losing, but the point is to increase our collective intelligence. That requires, if not a party structure of the old type, then at least some kind of system of coordination and some system of memory. Capital has this, and we need it too to be able to fight back.

the happiness of margaret thatcher[1]

So they win again. If anything is to be taken from the miserable time we endured last week, it must be to learn some lessons about how the enemy operates. It couldn't have worked much better from their point of view. A series of punitive attacks on the poorest and most vulnerable in society ended up being simultaneously cloaked and justified by the brazen hijacking of an appalling, aberrant act of violence. This is one part of the "legacy of Thatcher" that we will be invited to reflect upon in the coming days. The bitter edge to all those leftist celebrations of Thatcher's death is all too evident. She retired from the field of class war twenty years ago, her work a spectacular success. Looking at Britain now — a country much more Thatcherite than when she left office — she could have died a happy woman.

The Tories have long been struggling with the problem of how to escape Thatcher's shadow while continuing her project. Last week, we saw their quest to square a circle — how to lose their "nasty party" image while actually intensifying the attack on the remnants of social democracy — bearing some fruit. Helmed by the reinvented IDS, now cast as a caring but tough-minded friend of the poor, the simple strategy has involved the displacement of the concept of unemployment by that of welfare dependency. The idea of welfare dependency is inherently obfuscatory, part of the inverted world of magical thinking the Tories have been all too successful at pushing in opposition. In Thatcher's day, unemployment was the price to pay for reconstruction; now, insofar as the Tories now mention unemployment at all, it is posited only as an effect of welfare dependency. Just as the state "crowds out" private sector entrepreneurialism, so — we are solemnly informed — the benefit system obstructs the capacity of people to act in their own interests. The Tories now can sound like inverted Marxists who aren't attacking individuals, but the system which produces their behaviour.

In the immortal words of Grant Shapps: "It is not that these people were trying to play the system, so much as these people were forced into a system that played them." By shifting the focus onto the benefits system, the Tories can pose as the good patrician parent, offering the tough love solution to the bureaucratic indulgences of left paternalism.

Meanwhile, Labour shuffles uncomfortably in the shadows, looking at its feet, before offering up its depressing policy review on the future of welfare.[2] This confirms what few could have doubted: that Labour has learned next to nothing from the failures of Blairism, and that its only strategy is to hide out, do nothing to frighten the horses, and wait for government to be handed back to them as a consequence of discontent with the Tories. Without Blair's charismatic thespianry and false hopes, without even the Shakespearean drama of Brown's blighted leadership, an atmosphere of deathly, affectless decadence has settled over the Labour Party. Populist but not very popular, Labour has become a dead mechanism animated by a blind drive: win elections. It is an election-winning machine which can barely win elections, and which has long ago forgotten why you would want to win an election in the first place. By contrast, the Tories have a feverish sense of purpose. They serve ruling-class interests even when not in power by dragging the "centre" ground to the right. Once in government, they impose their policy agenda at high speed, without majority or mandate, retrospectively justifying it, if they bother to justify it at all, with the kind of "debate" we saw last week.

No doubt Labour's silence last week — allowing it to seem as if Owen Jones was the only voice speaking up on mainstream media against the benefit cuts — is motivated by its awareness that attacks on benefits are popular amongst elements of the working class.[3] But rather than challenging this failure of class consciousness and the myths which contribute to it, rather than beginning the difficult work of unpicking this negative solidarity,[4] Labour of course acquiesces in it.

The fact that the right is "using value-laden and pejorative language when discussing benefits and welfare"[5] is not some moral or intellectual error on its part — it is a crude but remorselessly effective form of neuro-linguistic programming, designed to create a series of enduring associations which become embedded in the political unconscious. (Some of the miserable effects of this anti-benefits discourse are outlined in painful detail in this moving blog post.[6]) Here, as with the infamous attempts to shift the blame for the deficit from capitalist crisis onto the Labour Party, the technique is incantatory repetition. The Tories know that if phrases and memes are repeated enough times, facts can be suspended. The reality technicians running the right understand that, as Freud said, there is no negation in the unconscious. No matter how much Owen Jones refuted the "arguments" of the right on radio and TV last week, they made hegemonic ground simply by the fact that they had managed to create a chain of equivalence connecting a child murderer with welfare. Whether the right actually choreographed their positions doesn't much matter, they still functioned as a coordinated campaign (the right is much better at class solidarity than us, performing it instinctively). The *Mail* fulfilled its usual role as outlier, floating an "outrageous" position which it inevitably tempts other media outlets into propagating, thus allowing Cameron and Osborne to "respond" in an apparently more measured — but actually only minimally distanced — way. The right won ground by the sheer fact that the "debate" was happening, and anything we do could only ever be a question of clawing back territory. The right is on the front foot, and we, as ever, are playing catch-up.

It's worth reflecting a little on the techniques deployed by the *Mail* — the most-read online newspaper in the world, remember — not least because they involve a certain complicity on our part. "Outrage" is the *Mail*'s stock in trade, and the bind we're in is that we seem compelled to provide more than our fair share of it. Outrage is not merely impotent, it is actively counterproductive, feeding the very enemy we claim to want to defeat. That's because, firstly, outrage is part of the very currency of what Jodi Dean calls communicative capitalism, which depends not on content but on the sheer circulation of messages. Even when the *Mail* was vilified for its headline, such vilification only becomes the libidinal juice of the *Mail*'s communicative capitalism (there will be more messages, more posts, more tweets; we will read even if we don't "want" to; we will read because we're not supposed to). Secondly, since there is an infinite supply of things to be outraged about, the tendency towards outrage indefinitely locks us up in a series of reactive battles, fought on the enemy's territory and on its terms. (How many of us on the left, faced with our social media timelines when we wake up in the morning, don't feel a certain weariness, as we ask ourselves, what are we supposed to be outraged about today?). Thirdly, outrage reflects a fundamental political misunderstanding, both of our opponents and of the war that they are waging. Such outrage, as Wendy Brown puts it in her crucial essay "Moralism as Anti-Politics", "implicitly figures the state (and other mainstream institutions) as if it did not have specific political and economic investments, as if it were not the codification of various dominant social powers, but was, rather, a momentarily misguided parent who forgot her promise to treat all her children the same way."[7] We use the rhetoric of class war, but too often we behave as if we are engaging in liberal debate with ungentlemanly opponents, whose social power will evaporate once the "errors" in their arguments are pointed out.

In an important blog post last year,[8] Adam Kotsko discussed this liberal leftist compulsion — rife in social media — to point to superficial contradictions in conservative ideology. "'They believe in small government…

until it comes time to control women's bodies!' Zing!" The problem is that these kind of sarcastic dismissals confuse argumentative or philosophical incoherence with strategic incoherence. The stated rationales for right-wing positions may not make much add up philosophically, but seen

> in terms of strategy, they all make perfect sense. Taken together, they serve to blame the victims, assert that the powerful are powerful for moral reasons, and then claim that the role of government is to endorse and reinforce the morally-discovered power structure rather than futilely try to disrupt it. The arguments might clash on a superficial level, but their effects are perfectly coherent and rational once the goal is granted.

As Kotsko observes, the "stated rationales" are libidinal lures which

> function as a kind of weapon against liberals, who jump at the chance to engage and disprove — and will happily waste infinite amounts of time doing so. It's like a drug for a certain type of 'reasonable liberal': they're showing their broad-mindedness by engaging in dialogue with their ideological enemies, and they're showing their intellectual superiority!

The implication of all this is not that we should withdraw from the debates the right imposes. Once these debates have been set up, we need to firefight, and Owen Jones did a great job last week. But if the right have engaged our resources in permanent firefight mode, that is already a significant victory for it. Just as we can't simply withdraw from debates, we can't just ignore the *Mail* either. The idea that the *Mail* will vanish if we simply don't click on links to its stories is as fallacious as the idea that we can destroy capitalism by being ethical consumers. Ignoring the *Mail* will only mean that we don't come to terms with the way it shapes what is taken for social reality. We must engage, just not on its terms. Instead of the "hot" response of outrage (with its immediate nugget of satisfaction, achieved at the cost of a long-term political impotence), we need a cooler stance of appraising the enemy's weapons and strategies, and thinking about how to counter, overcome and ultimately outwit them. Is a left-wing version of the *Mail* possible? If not, how could we construct a discursive hub that is as successful for the left as the *Mail* is for the right? This needs to be part of a broader strategy of devoting our energy and resources to goals and projects that will deliver change in the long-term, breaking us out of the short-termism that has become endemic in the age of Twitter. What we need to overturn is something that has been the case since before Thatcher's rise to power — the tendency for reactionary political forces to be pro-active, and for progressives to be reactive.

suffering with a smile[1]

"I usually get up at 5 or 5.15am. Historically, I would start sending emails when I got up. But not everyone is on my time schedule, so I have tried to wait until 7am. Before I email, I work out, read, and use our products. [...] I am not a big sleeper and never have been. Life is too exciting to sleep."

"I quickly scan my emails while my son is taking over my bed and having his milk. Urgent ones I reply to there and then. I flag others to follow up on my commute into work. [...] I receive an average of 500 emails a day, so I email throughout the day."
— "What Time Do CEOs Wake Up?"[2]

These two accounts — both taken from a *Guardian* article entitled "What Time Do CEOs Wake Up?" — might have been designed to illustrate the theses of post-autonomist theorists such as Antonio Negri, Paolo Virno and Franco "Bifo" Berardi. Labour is essentially communicative. The boundaries between work and life are permeable. The incessant demands of semio-capitalism stretch the limits of physical organisms. Email means that there is no such thing as a workplace or a working day. You start working the minute you wake up.

These descriptions of a CEO's day also prove Deleuze and Guattari's claim in *Anti-Oedipus* that, in capitalism,

there are no longer even any masters, but only slaves commanding other slaves [...] The bourgeois sets the example [...] : more utterly enslaved than the lowest of slaves, he is the first servant of the ravenous machine, the beast of the reproduction of capital [...] "I too am a slave" — these are the new words spoken by the master.[3]

535

At the top of the tower, there is no liberation from work. There is just more work — the only difference is that you might now enjoy it (life is too exciting for sleep). For these CEOs, work is closer to an addiction than something they are forced to do. In a provisional formulation, we might want to posit a new way of construing class antagonism. There are now two classes: those addicted to work, and those forced to work. But this isn't quite accurate. Whether we are working for our employers (who pay us) or for Mark Zuckerberg (who doesn't), most of us find ourselves compulsively gripped by the imperatives of communicative capitalism (to check email, to update our statuses). This mode of work makes Sisyphus's interminable labours seem quaint; at least, Sisyphus was condemned to perform the same task over and over again. Semio-capitalism is more like confronting the mythical hydra: cut off one head and three more grow in its place, the more emails we answer, the more we receive in return.

The good old days of exploitation, where the boss was interested in the worker only to the extent that they produced a commodity which could be sold at a profit, are long gone. Work then meant the annihilation of subjectivity, your reduction to an impersonal machine-part; it was the price that you paid for time away from work. Now, there is no time away from work, and work is not opposed to subjectivity. All time is entrepreneurial time because we are the commodities, so that any time not spent selling ourselves is wasted time. Hence, like the characters in the film *Limitless*, we're always seeking ways to increase the time available to us — via intoxicants, cutting back on sleep, working while we commute... The unemployed do not escape this condition — the simulation tasks that they are now induced to perform in order to qualify for benefit are more than preparations for the futility of paid work, they are already work (for what is so much "real" work if not an act of simulation? You don't just have to work, you have to be seen working, even when there's no "work" to do...)

Being exploited is no longer enough. The nature of labour now is such that almost anyone, no matter how menial their position, is required to be seen (over)investing in their work. What we are forced into is not merely work, in the old sense of undertaking an activity we don't want to perform; no, now we are forced to act as if we want to work. Even if we want to work in a burger franchise, we have to prove that, like reality TV contestants, *we really want it*. The notorious shift towards affective labour in the Global North means that it is no longer possible to just turn up at work and be miserable. Your misery has to be concealed — who wants to listen to a depressed call centre worker, to be served by a sad waiter, or be taught by an unhappy lecturer?

Yet that's not quite right. The subjugatory libidinal forces that draw enjoyment from the current cult of work don't want us to *entirely* conceal our misery. For what enjoyment is there to be had from exploiting a worker who actually delights in their work? In his sequel to *Blade Runner, The Edge of Human*, K.W. Jeter provides an insight into the libidinal economics of work and suffering. One of the novel's characters answers the question of why, in *Blade Runner*'s future world, the Tyrell Corporation bothered developing replicants (androids constructed so that only experts can distinguish them from humans):

> Why should the off-world colonists want troublesome, humanlike slaves rather than nice, efficient machines? It's simple. Machines don't suffer. They aren't capable of it. A machine doesn't know when it's being raped. There's no power relationship between you and a machine. [...] For the replicant to suffer, to give its owners that whole master-slave energy, it has to have emotions. [...] The replicant's emotions aren't a design flaw. The Tyrell Corporation put them there. Because that's what our customers wanted.

The reason that it's so easy to whip up loathing for "benefit scroungers" is that — in the reactionary fantasy — they have escaped the suffering to which those in work have to submit. This fantasy tells its own story: the hatred for benefits claimants is really about how much people hate their own work. *Others should suffer as we do*: the slogan of a negative solidarity that cannot imagine any escape from the immiseration of work.

To understand work now, consider the pornographic practice of bukkake. Here, men ejaculate in women's faces, and the women are required to act as if they enjoy it, to lasciviously lick the semen from their lips as if it is the most delicious honey. What's being elicited from the women is an act of simulation. The humiliation is not adequate unless they are *seen* to be performing an enjoyment they don't actually feel. Paradoxically, however, the subjugation is only complete if there are some traces of resistance. A happy smile, ritualised submission; this is nothing unless signs of misery can also be detected in the eyes.

how to kill a zombie: strategising the end of neoliberalism[1]

Why has the left made so little progress five years after a major crisis of capitalism discredited neoliberalism? Since 2008, neoliberalism might have been deprived of the feverish forward momentum it once possessed, but it is nowhere near collapsing. Neoliberalism now shambles on as zombie — but as the afficionados of zombie films are well aware, it is sometimes harder to kill a zombie than a living person.

At the conference in York, Milton Friedman's notorious remark was quoted a number of times:

> Only a crisis — actual or perceived — produces real change. When that crisis occurs, the actions that are taken depend on the ideas that are lying around. That, I believe, is our basic function: to develop alternatives to existing policies, to keep them alive and available until the politically impossible becomes the politically inevitable.

The problem is that although the 2008 crisis was caused by neoliberal policies, those selfsame policies remain practically the only ones "lying around". As a consequence, neoliberalism is still politically inevitable.

It is by no means clear that the public has ever embraced neoliberal doctrines with much enthusiasm — but what people have been persuaded of is the idea that there is no alternative to neoliberalism. The (typically reluctant) acceptance of this state of affairs is the hallmark of capitalist realism. Neoliberalism may not have succeeded in making itself more attractive than other systems, but it has sold itself as the only "realistic" mode of governance. The sense of "realism" here is a hard won political achievement, and neoliberalism has succeeded in imposing a model of reality modeled on practices and assumptions coming out of the business world.

Neoliberalism consolidated the discrediting of state socialism, establishing a vision of history in which it laid claim to the future and consigned the left to obsolescence. It captured the discontent with centralised bureacratic leftism, successfully absorbing and metabolising the desires for freedom and autonomy that had emerged in the wake of the Sixties. But — and this is a crucial point — this isn't to say that those desires inevitably and necessarily led to the rise of neoliberalism. Rather, we can see the success of neoliberalism as a symptom of the leftist failure to adequately respond to these new desires. As Stuart Hall and others involved in the *New Times* project of the 1980s prophetically insisted, this failure would prove catastrophic for the left.

Capitalist realism can be described as the belief that there is no alternative to capitalism. However, it is more usually manifest not in grand claims about political economy, but in more banal behaviours and expectations, such as our weary acceptance that pay and conditions will stagnate or deteriorate.

Capitalist realism has been sold us to by managers (many of whom see themselves as left-wing) who tell us that things are different now. The age of the organised working class is over; union power is receding; business now rules, and we must fall into line. The self-surveillance work that workers are now routinely required to perform — all those self-assessments, performance reviews, log books — is, we have been persuaded, a small price to pay for keeping our jobs.

Take the Research Excellence Framework (REF) — a system for assessing the research output of academics in the UK. This massive system of bureaucratic monitoring is widely reviled by those subject to it, but any opposition to it has so far been token. This double situation — in which something is loathed but at the same time complied with — is typical of capitalist realism, and is particularly poignant in the case of academia, one of the supposed strongholds of the left.

Capitalist realism is an expression of class decomposition, and a consequence of the disintegration of class consciousness. Fundamentally, neoliberalism must be seen as a project which aimed to achieve this end. It was not primarily — at least not in practice — dedicated to freeing up the market from state control. Rather, it was about subordinating the state to the power of capital. As David Harvey has tirelessly argued, neoliberalism was a project which aimed to reassert class power.

As the traditional sources of working-class power were defeated or subdued, neoliberal doctrines functioned as weapons in a class war increasingly fought by one side only. Concepts like the "market" and "competition" have functioned not as the real ends of neoliberal policy, but as its guiding myths and ideological alibi. Capital has no interest in either the health of markets, or in competition. As Manuel DeLanda, following Fernand Braudel, has argued, capitalism, with its tendency towards monopoly and oligopoly, can more accurately be defined as anti-market rather than as a system which promotes thriving markets.

David Blacker mordantly observes in his forthcoming book, *The Falling Rate of Learning and the Neoliberal Endgame*, that the virtues of "competition" are "conveniently to be reserved only for the masses. Competition and risk is for small businesses and other little people like private and public sector employees." The invocation of competition has functioned as an ideological weapon — its real aim is the destruction of solidarity, and, as such, it has been remarkably successful.

Competition in education (both amongst institutions and amongst individuals) is not something that spontaneously emerges once state regulation is removed — on the contrary, it is something actively produced by new kinds of state control. The REF and the school inspections regime overseen in the UK by OFSTED are both classic examples of this syndrome.

Since there is no automatic way to "marketise" education and other public services and there is no straightforward way of quantifying the "productivity" of workers such as teachers, the imposition of business discipline has meant the installation of colossal bureaucratic machineries. So an ideology which promised to liberate us from state socialist bureaucracy has instead imposed a bureaucracy all of its own.

This only looks like a paradox if we take neoliberalism at its word — but neoliberalism is not classic liberalism. It is not about laissez faire. As Jeremy Gilbert, developing Foucault's prescient analyses of neoliberalism, has argued, the neoliberal project was always about vigilantly policing a certain model of individualism; workers have to be continually surveilled for fear they might lapse into collectivity.

If we refuse to accept neoliberalism's rationales — that control systems brought in from business were intended to improve workers' efficiency — then it becomes clear that the anxiety produced by the REF and other managerialist mechanisms is not some accidental side-effect of these systems — it is their real aim.

And if neoliberalism will not collapse of its own accord, what can be done to hasten its demise?

Reject Strategies That Don't Work

In a dialogue between Franco "Bifo" Berardi and me published in *Frieze*,[2], Berardi talked of "our present theoretical impotence in the face of the de-humanising process provoked by finance capitalism." "I can't deny reality", Berardi continued,

which seems to me to be this: the last wave of the movement — say 2010 to 2011 — was an attempt to revitalise a massive subjectivity. This attempt failed: we have been unable to stop the financial aggression. The movement has now disappeared, only emerging in the form of fragmentary explosions of despair.

Bifo, one of the activists involved with the so-called autonomist movement in Italy in the 1970s, here identifies the rhythm that has defined anti-capitalist struggle since 2008: exhilarating outbursts of militancy recede as quickly as they erupt, without producing any sustained change.

I hear Bifo's remarks as a requiem for the "horizontalist" strategies that have dominated anti-capitalism since the Nineties. The problem with these strategies is not their (noble) aims — the abolition of hierarchy, the rejection of authoritarianism — but their efficacy. Hierarchy cannot be abolished by fiat, and a movement which fetishises organisational form over effectiveness concedes ground to the enemy. The dismantling of the many existing forms of stratification will be a long, arduous and attritional process; it isn't simply a matter of eschewing (official) leaders and adopting "horizontal" forms of organisation.

Neo-anarchist horizontalism has tended to favour strategies of direct action and withdrawal — people need to take action now and for themselves, not wait for compromised elected representatives to act in their stead; at the same time, they should withdraw from institutions that are not contingently, but necessarily corrupt.

The emphasis on direct action, though, conceals a despair about the possibility of *in*direct action. Yet it is via indirect action that the control of ideological narratives is achieved. Ideology isn't about what you or I spontaneously believe, but about what we believe that the Other believes — and this belief is still determined to a large extent by the content of mainstream media.

Neo-anarchist doctrine maintains that we should abandon mainstream media and parliament — but our abandoning it has only allowed the neoliberals to extend their power and influence. The neoliberal right might preach the end of the state, but only while ensuring that it controls governments.

Only the horizontalist left believes the rhetoric about the obsolescence of the state. The danger of the neo-anarchist critique is that it essentialises the state, parliamentary democracy and "mainstream media" — but none of these things is forever fixed. They are mutable terrains to be struggled over, and the shape they now assume is itself the effect of previous struggles. It seems, as times, as if the horizontalists want to occupy everything except parliament and the mainstream media. But why not occupy the state and the media too? Neo-anarchism isn't so much of a challenge to capitalist realism as it is one of its effects. Anarchist fatalism — according to which it is easier to imagine the end of capitalism than a left-wing Labour Party — is the complement of the capitalist realist insistence that there is no alternative to capitalism.

None of this is to say that occupying mainstream media or politics will be enough in themselves. If New Labour taught us anything, it was that holding office is by no means the same thing as winning hegemony. Yet without a parliamentary strategy of some kind, movements will keep foundering and collapsing. The task is to make the links between the extra-parliamentary energies of the movements and the pragmatism of those within existing institutions.

Retrain Ourselves to Adopt a War Mentality

If you want to consider the most telling drawback of horizontalism, though, think about how it looks from the perspective of the enemy. Capital must be delighted by the popularity of horizontalist discourses in the anti-capitalist movement. Would you rather face a carefully co-ordinated enemy, or one that takes decisions via nine-hour "assemblies"?

Which isn't to say that we should fall back into the consoling fantasy that any kind of return to old-school Leninism is either possible or desirable. The fact that we have been left with a choice between Leninism and anarchism is a measure of current leftist impotence.

It's crucial to leave behind this sterile binary. The struggle against authoritarianism needn't entail neo-anarchism, just as effective organisation doesn't necessarily require a Leninist party. What is required, however, is taking seriously the fact that we are up against an enemy that has no doubt at all that it is in a class war, and which devotes many of its enormous resources training its people to fight it. There's a reason that MBA students read *The Art of War*, and if we are to make progress we have to rediscover the desire to win and the confidence that we can.

We must learn to overcome certain habits of anti-Stalinist thinking. The danger is not anymore, nor has it been for some time, excessive dogmatic fervor on our side. Instead, the post-68 left has tended to overvalue the negative capability of remaining in doubt, scepticism and uncertainties — this may be an aesthetic virtue, but it is a political vice. The self-doubt that has been endemic on the left since the Sixties is little in evidence on the right — one reason that the right has been so successful in imposing its programme. Many on the left now quail at the thought of formulating a programme, still less "imposing" one. But we have to give up on the belief that people will spontaneously turn to the left, or that neoliberalism will collapse without our actively dismantling it.

Rethink Solidarity

The old solidarity that neoliberalism decomposed has gone, never to return. But this does not mean that we are consigned to atomised individualism.

Our challenge now is to reinvent solidarity. Alex Williams has come up with the suggestive formulation "post-Fordist plasticity" to describe what this new solidarity might look like. As Catherine Malabou has shown, plasticity is not the same as elasticity. Elasticity is equivalent to the flexibility which neoliberalism demands of us, in which we assume a form imposed from outside. But plasticity is something else: it implies both adaptability and resilience, a capacity for modification which also retains a "memory" of previous encounters.

Rethinking solidarity in these terms may help us to give up some tired assumptions. This kind of solidarity doesn't necessarily entail overarching unity or centralised control. But moving beyond unity needn't lead us into the flatness of horizontalism, either. Instead of the rigidity of unity — the aspiration for which, ironically, has contributed to the left's notorious sectarianism — what we need is the coordination of diverse groups, resources and desires. The right have been better postmodernists than us, building successful coalitions out of heterogeneous interest groups without the need for an overall unity. We must learn from them, to start to build a similar patchwork on our side. This is more a logistical problem than a philosophical one.

In addition to the plasticity of organisational form, we need also to pay attention to the plasticity of desire. Freud said that the libidinal drives are "extraordinarily plastic". If desire is not a fixed biological essence, then there is no natural desire for capitalism. Desire is always composed. Advertisers, branders and PR consultants have always known this, and the struggle against neoliberalism will require that we construct an alternative model of desire that can compete with the one pushed by capital's libidinal technicians.

What's certain is that we are now in an ideological wasteland in which neoliberalism is dominant only by default. The terrain is up for grabs, and Friedman's remark should be our inspiration: it is now *our* task to develop alternatives to existing policies, to keep them alive and available until the politically impossible becomes the politically inevitable.

getting away with murder[1]

The Mark Duggan verdict was both shocking and predictable. Shocking, because it is a verdict that so clearly ignores not only evidence but blatant inconsistencies in evidence. Predictable, because we are now accustomed to seeing the Met getting away with murder.

As Stafford Scott's piece in the *Guardian*[2] today makes clear, the police case explanation for what happened was an obvious fabrication that lacked even minimal coherence. It's a classic example of kettle logic, in which the police's obvious cover-up actually undermined the rationale for shooting Duggan. *Either* Mark Duggan was holding a gun when he died — as officer V53 claimed at the inquest — *or* he threw the gun away. If the former, how could the gun end up seven metres away from him (and without any trace of his fingerprints or DNA on it)? If the latter, then how could Mark Duggan have been thought to have pose sufficient threat that he had to be shot dead? At best, the operation was a monumental blunder — compounded by a cover-up which was at least as inept. So how do we explain the jury's perverse decision?

Partly, we have to look to the legal framework itself. As Christian Werthschulte observed in a Facebook comment last night, when we read the official verdict, we see that "the jury is somehow made to ask themselves if they had felt threatened if they'd been in the shoes of the police officer in order to conclude if the killing was lawful or not. Inevitably this will lead to a 'Oh, I would've been scared, too!' reaction." This is both absurd and terrifying, given the amount of sub-machine guns that Met officers carry around London. If the question posed to juries in such cases is going to be "might you, an ordinary member of the public, have been scared", then it's hard to see what would ever constitute an unlawful killing.

Then we have to look at the broader reality management operation that swings into place in these contingencies. If the plebgate story revealed anything, it was the brazen and slapdash nature of Met fabrications, which they can get away with because they can usually count on the supine support of Tories and the right-wing press. In the Duggan case, we saw the Met's standard tactic of leading with a totally false story[3] which is later repudiated[4] but only after the tone has been set. Then there is the demonisation of the victim, which Stafford Scott describes:

immediately after the shooting the police and the Independent Police Complaints Commission began to brief the media with inaccurate and misleading information that ensured that Duggan was demonised, even before his body had turned cold. The headlines declared him a gangster who was on a mission to avenge the killing of his cousin, Kelvin Easton. However, during the inquest no evidence was offered in support of this claim. It was further alleged that he was a large-scale drugs dealer, but yet again not a shred of evidence was provided to substantiate these allegations. But that did not matter, the mud had been slung and it clearly stuck as it was designed to. Even now most people still do not realise that he was only ever convicted for two relatively minor offences — one count of cannabis possession, and one count of receiving stolen goods.

The description of Mark Duggan as a "gangster" then reliably triggers a whole set of racist associations, which we can quickly grasp when we compare the way in which white criminals such as the Krays ("they only killed their own and they loved their muvvas"), or Ronnie Biggs (involved in a violent crime, but treated as a cuddly rogue) are mythologised. We might also pause to note that Raoul Moat was able to kill people over the course of a number of days before "shooting himself".

All of this then prepares the way, not only for the jury to see Mark Duggan in the worse possible light, but for those hearing of the verdict to agree with the jury's exculpation of the police marksman. I saw any number of comments last night to the effect of "well, he had a gun, what was he going to do with it?" Again, this is terrifying: apparently, it was OK to kill Mark Duggan because of what he *might* have done. The era of pre-crime is truly upon us.

Then, of course, there is the massive overload of ambient propaganda in favour of the police. The police don't themselves have to generate this; it is freely provided by the right-wing media, but also by a popular culture which overwhelmingly depicts the police as either heroic or "ordinary but flawed people, doing a tough job".

All of this must have produced some sort of cognitive dissonance in the jury. All the evidence pointed to Duggan not being armed when he was shot — as the jury itself conceded. Furthermore, the blatant cover-up with the gun should have fatally undermined the Met's story. But no (so the "reasoning" must have gone) — the police cannot be guilty, a priori, therefore they are not.

Now the verdict has to be protected, and the next stage of reality management comes into effect. What we're now seeing at the moment is the trooping out of right-wing politicians and commentators calling on Mark Duggan's family to "respect the law". As with the families of the Hillsborough victims, the family will now be smeared as crazed with grief, hysterical, their desire to set right a terrible injustice will be pathologised and attributed to an inability to move on. If the reality management system is allowed to do its work unobstructed, we can expect the truth to dribble out in twenty or thirty years' time, as it did with Hillsborough, or, more recently, with the Miners' Strike. By then, the man who pulled the trigger and those who aided and abetted in the cover-up will be either pensioned off or dead. Either way, they will be beyond the reach of any justice.

I write this not as some ACAB-anarchist, but as someone well aware of the mundane realities of much police work, which increasingly involves attempting to manage the disintegration of civil society brought about by neoliberalism. Yet surely it is by now clear that the Met is a systematically corrupt force. It is equally clear that the IPCC is a joke, and that courts cannot be relied upon to deliver the right verdicts.

Systemic problems require systemic solutions. While Mark Duggan's family must be supported in their quest for justice, this should not allowed to be seen as an isolated incident. Somehow, the whole system — the Met, the media, the judiciary — which produced this perverse verdict needs to be brought to account, and ultimately replaced.

The significance of Hackgate was that it started to bring these systemic complicities — this "dark network comprising private investigators, the criminal underworld, tabloid newspapers, multinational media conglomerates, the police, politicians, the banks, and the bodies supposed to regulate them (who are at best impotent, at worst part of the problem)" — into the open. The reality management system was strained then, but whether it will suffer any serious damage will be partly determined by the results of the ongoing trial of two of Murdoch's reality managers. It's might be that, as with Vito and Michael Corleone, there are too many layers of subordinates between Coulson and Brooks and those who committed the actual crimes for a jury to find them guilty this time. But the cracks in the old reality management system are real. It's an open question as to how long they can keep being smoothed over.

no one is bored,
everything is boring[1]

One of the most intriguing and provocative pieces on politics and culture this year was *We Are All Very Anxious* by the Institute of Precarious Consciousness (the essay gained a great deal of attention when it was republished on Plan C's website).[2] It argues that the key problematic affect capitalism now faces is anxiety. In an earlier, Fordist era, it was boredom that was the "dominant reactive affect". Repetitive labour on production lines engendered boredom, which was both the central form of subjugation under Fordism and the source of a new oppositional politics.

It could be argued that the failure of the traditional left is tied up with its inability adequately to engage with this politics of boredom, which wasn't articulated via trade unions or political parties, but via the cultural politics of the Situationists and the punks. It was the neoliberals, not the organised left, who were best able to absorb and instrumentalise this critique of boredom. Neoliberals quickly moved to associate Fordist factories and the stability and security of social democracy with tedium, predictability and top-down bureaucracy. In place of this, the neoliberals offered excitement and unpredictability — but the downside of these newly fluid conditions is perpetual anxiety. Anxiety is the emotional state that correlates with the (economic, social, existential) precariousness which neoliberal governance has normalised.

The Institute of Precarious Consciousness were right to observe that too much anti-capitalist politics is locked into strategies and perspectives that were formed in an era when the struggle was against boredom. They are also correct both that capitalism has effectively solved the problem of boredom, and that it is crucial that the left finds ways of politicising anxiety. Neoliberal culture — which came to dominance as the anti-psychiatry movement was waning — has individualised depression and anxiety. Or rather, many cases of depression and anxiety are the effects of neoliberalism's successful tendency to privatise stress, to convert political antagonisms into medical conditions.

At the same time, I believe that the argument about boredom has to be somewhat nuanced. It is certainly true that one could feel almost nostalgic for Boredom 1.0. The dreary void of Sundays, the night hours after television stopped broadcasting, even the endless dragging minutes waiting in queues or for public transport: for anyone who has a smartphone, this empty time has now been effectively eliminated. In the intensive, 24/7 environment of capitalist cyberspace, the brain is no longer allowed any time to idle; instead, it is inundated with a seamless flow of low-level stimulus.

Yet boredom was ambivalent; it wasn't simply a negative feeling that one simply wanted rid of. For punk, the vacancy of boredom was a challenge, an injunction and an opportunity: if we are bored, then it is for us to produce something that will fill up the space. Yet, it is through this demand for participation that capitalism has neutralised boredom. Now, rather than imposing a pacifying spectacle on us, capitalist corporations go out of their way to invite us to interact, to generate our own content, to join the debate. There is now neither an excuse nor an opportunity to be bored.

But if the contemporary form of capitalism has extirpated boredom, it has not vanquished the boring. On the contrary — you could argue that the boring is ubiquitous. For the most part, we've given up any expectation of being surprised by culture — and that goes for "experimental" culture as much as popular culture. Whether it is music that sounds like it could have come out twenty, thirty, forty years ago, Hollywood blockbusters that recycle and reboot concepts, characters and tropes that were exhausted long ago, or the tired gestures of so much contemporary art, the boring is everywhere. It is just that no one is bored — because there is no longer any subject capable of being bored. For boredom is a state of absorption — a state of high absorption, in fact, which is why it is such an oppressive feeling. Boredom consumes our being; we feel we will never escape it. But it is just this capacity for absorption that is now under attack, as a result of the constant dispersal of attention, which is integral to capitalist cyberspace. If boredom is a form of empty absorption, then more positive forms of absorption effectively counter it. But it is these forms of absorption which capitalism cannot deliver. Instead of absorbing us, it distracts from the boring.

Perhaps the feeling most characteristic of our current moment is a mixture of boredom and compulsion. Even though we recognise that they are boring, we nevertheless feel compelled to do yet another Facebook quiz, to read yet another Buzzfeed list, to click on some celebrity gossip about someone we don't even remotely care about. We endlessly move among the boring, but our nervous systems are so overstimulated that we never have the luxury of feeling bored. No one is bored, everything is boring.

a time for shadows[1]

Jean Baudrillard's 1987 text *The Ecstasy of Communication* reads like an astonishing science-fictional prophecy of our current moment. Writing nearly thirty years ago, Baudrillard invoked an era of "absolute proximity, total instaneity", of informational schizophrenia. "The schizo", Baudrillard writes, "is bereft of every scene, open to everything in spite of himself [...] It is the end of interiority and intimacy, the overexposure and transparency of the world which traverses him without obstacle. He is now only a pure screen, a switching centre for all the networks of influence".[2] Baudrillard's heightened rhetoric captures what is now a banal experience — indeed, it might be the very signature of contemporary banality. With the ubiquity of smartphones, the feeling of being overwhelmed by cyberspatial injunctions is now commonplace. It is this strangely prescient anticipation of twenty-first-century banality that makes reading Baudrillard's text such an uncanny experience. (It as if Baudrillard was already writing about Twitter. What in the experience of 1980s French telecommunications could give Baudrillard this feeling of transparency, overload, instaneity — this sense of the overwhelming of privacy and the limits of the individual subject, to which social media has now habituated us?)

Baudrillard wrote of a new era of "tactility". According to Baudrillard, even in the 1980s, the spectacle was already superseded. The spectacle subjugated us to image; the tactile system, however, solicits our participation, enjoins us to join in. Again, this is a strikingly prescient observation of trends that are now dominant — corporations are no longer satisfied with bombarding us with hard sell propaganda, they want us to interact with them, like their Facebook page, comment using hashtags.

Smartphones with touchscreen technology seem to secure the age of tactility. Yet, with smartphones, shouldn't we rather talk of a touching without tactility? For the smartphone is certainly operated by touch, but it is a touch devoid of any sensuality. When the fingers encounter the glassy surface of the iPhone, everything they touch on the screen feels the same. The fingers are effectively acting as extensions of the eye and the brain — an eye and a brain that have now been radically re-habituated by cyberspace. The fingers become relays in a digital compulsion system, a set of digital triggers. Yet they are inefficient digital triggers, monkey digits that are too fat and lacking in suppleness to properly operate the touchscreen interface. If, as an episode of *The Simpsons* observed in a sight gag, the iPhone is strikingly reminiscent of the monoliths from *2001: A Space Odyssey*, then too often when we are using them, we feel as primitive and as baffled as the apes in Kubrick's film when faced with the enigmatic opacity of the monolith's black surface.

Of course, smartphones aren't really phones at all. The term now favoured by airlines, "handheld electronic devices", better captures what these machines are. (Increasingly, we are now permitted to use these devices the very moment that the aircraft lands — waiting until we get to the terminal is now deemed too long a wait.) The telephone function of the electronic handheld device is rapidly becoming archaic. As Sherry Turkle maintained in her recent book *Alone Together*, we have moved beyond the era of talking into a new age of text.[3] Conversations present anxieties, which are circumvented by SMS and direct messages.

For all that it evades older kinds of anxieties, Baudrillard's circuit of constant contact generates a whole set of new ones. The pressure of the instantaneous — of what, in their new manifesto, "On the Creative Question — Nine Theses", Geert Lovink, Sebastian Olma and Ned Rossiter call "frantic entrepreneurship and instant valorisation"[4] — inevitably weighs heavy on cultural producers. In an enigmatic but suggestive formulation, Lovink, Olma and Rossiter argue that the urgencies of the immediate need to be replaced by principles of "shadow and time". "Shadow," they write,

> is an unintended consequence, an event vacuum, which remains invisible for passers by. It does not register on the development maps of the managerial class. Time is needed in order for the substantially different to grow. Maturation, which is creative growth, requires time.

It is imperative that we carve out some spaces beyond the hyper-bright instant. This instant is insomniac, amnesiac; it locks us into a reactive time, which is always full (of outrage and pseudo-novelty). There is no continuous time in which shadows can grow, only a time that is simultaneously seamless (without gaps: there is always "new" content streaming in) and discontinuous (each new compulsion makes us forget what preceded it). The result is a mechanical and unacknowledged repetition. Is it still possible for us to cultivate shadows?

limbo is over[1]

Tony Blair's brief appearance in this election campaign, offering tepid support for a tepid Ed Miliband, ought to have been irrelevant. In many ways it was: who needs yesterday's man, the hawker of an outmoded "modernisation"? Except, like so much of today's culture, Blairism is obsolete but it has not yet been surpassed.

In Blair's Castle Grey Skull, it is always 1997. Blair is like some inverted Miss Havisham, frozen not at the moment of his defeat and failure, but just before his moment of greatest success. Be cautious, don't do anything to jeapordise the project. Blairism was this particular form of false promise, this deferral — if we are careful now, tomorrow we can do more... But tomorrow never arrives, the aim is always to be in government, the price is always the lack of any real power to change the inherited parameters of the possible. This is the formula: government without power, an increasingly unpopular populism.

The illusion of Blairism is that it was an overcoming of the defeats of the 1980s rather than their final consequence. It was a post-traumatic normalisation of catastrophe, not any sort of new dawn. Its legacy is organisational as much as ideological: a Labour Party that napalmed its grassroots (contempt for, and fear of the working class being a signature element of Blair's rendition of populism) and which now beams down policy and PR from some rarefied *Thick Of It* Oxford PPE helicarrier circling miles above earth. The project remains getting into government, but without Blair's showman-messiah charisma to cover over the vacuum beneath this aspiration. Miliband's awkwardness stems as much from this lack of any vision as from any personal quirks. There is nothing animating the transparently choreographed moves: tack to the right on immigration, a little to the left on taxation, etc. The ambition — to be the slightly lesser evil — is painfully clear to all, and can inspire no one.

All of this is exactly what we expected... But the entry of the SNP, Plaid Cymru and the Greens into the TV debates changed the atmosphere. Suddenly, the picture the reality managers have fed us for the last few years — the three "big" parties each offering a slightly different version of capitalist realism, with Farage and UKIP offering capitalist realism with even more ultra-nationalism — was interrupted, and it was possible to imagine that Britain was "headed, in its nuanced way, leftward".[2] In their different ways, Sturgeon, Wood and Bennett have widened the bandwidth of a media-political scene previously monopolised by the Oxbridge boys' club. In terms of policy, there isn't much on offer beyond a reset to social democracy (Plan B as opposed to Austerity's Plan A[3]), but capitalist realism is so deeply embedded that it was hard not to feel a frisson when, for instance, Wood defended trade unions and the welfare state. Cameron's refusal to appear in the BBC debate — and his banning of Clegg from doing so — was meant as a display of magisterial confidence, the *only credible Prime Minister* rising above the irrelevant squabbling of lowly pretenders — but it ended up further reinforcing the sense of ennui that has attended his performances this campaign. Cameron's appeal has always depended on his ruling-class ease-in-the-world, but, in his case especially, insouciance always risks shading into an appearance of diffidence and hauteur. As for the Lib Dems — as Craig McVegas observed[4] — their absence was barely even acknowledged in the last debate.

Which brings us to the photograph analysed so well by Jonathan Jones in the *Guardian*.[5] But, in addition to everything that Jones picks out, one of the most striking elements in the photograph is the empty centre. A clustering to the left, sulking Farage to the right, Cameron and Clegg — the current "centre" ground — absent. Here is one picture of a post-neoliberal UK: a soft left regaining its confidence on the one hand, a glowering far right on the other, nothing where the capitalist realist "middle" used to be. (Whether Farage will be the figure around which this right will coalesce is now open to serious doubt — with it looking as if he is unlikely to win South Thanet, it might be that his moment as the people's stockbloker is already over. The ominous question is: if Farage falls, which right-wing demagogue will emerge to take his place?)

The SNP-Labour coalition is far more than we could have hoped a few weeks ago, but it is far from enough. *How have we settled for so little?* asked an incendiary Russell Brand at the screening of his and Michael Winterbottom's *The Emperor's New Clothes* in Hackney this week. For those hipster priests who wish to keep activism a marginal pursuit, Brand's fame and wealth automatically exclude him from being taken seriously. Yet fame, charisma and money are resources, and the left badly needs to be associated with glamour instead of moralising asceticism. Watching the film in a cinema alongside so many of those who feature in it — campaigners from the New Era estate, striking careworkers, fire-fighters — was moving, humbling, electrifying. The Free Association[6] have been doing some interesting work on why comedy has replaced music as a political force. Now, much more than any contemporary musician, it is Brand who embodies the psychedelic-Promethean principle that any given reality is provisional, plastic, subject to transformation by collective action. *I love crowds...* Brand functions as a figure of identification who intensifies and links together already existing struggles, and incites us to breach the invisible thresholds that lock us into atomised impotence. *We can do what we want...* Having passed through what on Tuesday he memorably called the "fame paddock" of contemporary celebrity, Brand is now in a practically unique position. Instead of remaining in the condition of hedonic melancholia typical of those with unlimited access to late capitalism's pleasure gardens, he's come out the other side, laughing his trickster laugh, with more resources and an invaluable insider-knowledge of how the media machine constructs what counts as reality. His gleeful performance of de-subordination reminds us of the countercultural lesson: if you gain money and success, there's only one thing to do with the hand that feeds you, and that's bite it.

In many ways, *The Emperor's New Clothes* tells us what we already know, but this is the point. How can we accept what we know, when what we know is so monstrous, so obscene, so insane? In the Q and A, Brand was asked why people care more about the *X Factor* than political struggles. But he argued that, rather than decrying the *X Factor*, its techniques — in particular those which incite emotion — need to be repurposed. "Capitalism has given us the organisms and the machines we can use to produce the revolution". #accelerate! So the film is an exercise in affective engineering which patiently yet relentlessly dismantles capitalist realist commonsense. One of its most powerful techniques is the use of simple but devastating contrasts: cleaners at RBS earning hundreds of times less than the bosses (same physical space, different worlds); rioters jailed for stealing small items next to bankers who caused social catastrophe not only going unpunished but receiving bonuses. Mark Kermode's accusation that the film is "simplistic" misses the point. When faced with a media machine that pushes an outrageously simplistic story of its own — it was Labour wot done it — while recounting neoliberal catechisms like Medieval Catholic priests reciting the Mass in Latin, we need an equally simple counter-narrative.

It's hard not to have some sympathy with Brand's disdain for voting, which is part of a widespread disillusion with the massively circumscribed conditions of electoral politics under capitalist realism, in which the best that can be hoped for is the least worst. But the problem is that popular disengagement from parliamentary politics suits the right more than us.

The right doesn't need the enthusiasm that Thatcher could call upon from certain portions of the population; it doesn't need legitimacy. Popular disengagement, ambient despair, the sense that nothing is at stake in elections, is in the interests of capital, now that all the defaults have been set to neoliberal options. Of course, there was no golden age of parliamentary democracy any more than there was a golden age of the Labour Party; there was no point at which progressive achievements were entirely free of compromise and corruption. But the progressive function of parliamentary politics has been to put *some* limits on tyranny. Capitalist realism has meant the tacit but definite acceptance that corporate tyranny cannot be curbed, resulting in the democratic deficit that Aditya Chakrabortty described so vividly the other day:

> democratic leaders have parted ways with their voters — literally. Membership of the main parties has dropped sharply over the past three decades, so that there are now more vegans in Britain than members of the Conservative party. What's replaced mass democracy is big donors and a professional political elite. It no longer pays for politicians to think hard about fair growth or build more houses, because to do so would antagonise the big corporates or the big media, or deter those middle-class and retired voters who actually do turn out to the polling stations.[7]

The phobic panic that the prospect of a Labour-SNP coalition is provoking indicates that capital fears any reversal, no matter how modest, of this situation. It has grown used to having everything its own way — but this has led to a certain decadence, an exhaustion of thinking and of strategy. It is surely this exhaustion, as much as any desperation, which accounts for the ludicrous, beyond-satire poking about in Ed Miliband's anodyne love life, or the scarcely believable attempts to discredit Nicola Sturgeon.[8]

Sturgeon poses a threat, not merely because of her lawyerly poise in debate, not merely because she has articulated an anti-austerity position, nor even because she makes Scottish independence more likely, but more because she has a mobilised base of support behind her. In Scotland, as in Greece and Spain, new models of political organisation, new "logics of proliferation"[9] are emerging and being experimented with. Rather than compulsively repeating the same strategies, rather than dogmatically insisting on the inherent futility of elections, these developments are part of a process of collective learning about how popular movements can be (re)connected with parliamentary politics. The potential power of such strategies is clear. The electoral impasse is not down to some semiotic failure (if only we had the right PR initiative to engage the kids!), but reflects the actual composition of forces in society. Capitalist realism is class war fought by one side only, an organised corporate elite which is very clear about what its own class interests are and what must be done to keep things aligned with those interests. Only a mobilised population can give political parties the power to challenge corporate tyranny. As Keir Milburn says in an important piece[10], and, as the situation in Greece is showing, you can't vote out neoliberalism. But as Keir also argues, "[e]ven at their point of failure Plan B electoral politics can be useful if they can clarify the anti-democratic effects of neoliberalism that work against all forms of collective action."

In the UK, this could be the most important election since 1979. Even the most sentimental pipe-dreamer couldn't imagine the Labour Party will be returning to Plan B socialism in the immediate future, still less offering something more modern and radical. Yet it's perfectly plausible that a Labour-SNP coalition could now achieve what Jeremy Gilbert and I argue that New Labour could have been expected to attempt: "make some efforts to change the strategic situation in the long-term: to rebuild the unions, to re-energise local government, to facilitate the growth of an alternative media sector".[11] For even this to happen, it will be necessary for those in the party who really want to break with capitalist realism — and, believe it or not, there are such people — to seize the initiative. What is the alternative for Labour? Even the lacklustre and affectless brand of politics that the party have served up under Miliband so far won't be sustainable for much longer. Entropy might be the best fate a Labour Party which can't grasp the new mood can hope for; the more likely scenario is a PASOK-like disintegration. In any case, there's no way back to the pre-2008 world, no way back to capitalist realism with a joker-hysterical face. The party needs really to register that Blairites — and the residual Blairite atmosphere in a demoralised and disconnected Labour party — are as out of date now as Blair argued "Old Labour" was in 1997. Now, more than ever, there are no guarantees. The road to renewal has never seemed harder, or longer. Yet, as Margarita Tsomou said in an important intervention at the Monopol aug Morgen event in Vienna last week, limbo is now over. Are we plunging deeper into nihiliberal dystopia — the ultra-rich retreating into compounds, a vast "surplus population" abandoned to fight amongst itself, and subdued by a militarised *Hunger Games*-style police force? Or is a new popular leftism about to begin the escape from capitalist realism?

communist realism[1]

Normal capitalist realist service was resumed on Thursday, on the BBC *Question Time Leaders Special*. With the SNP, Plaid Cymru and the Greens absent, horizons contracted, expectations lowered, we were once again asphyxiating in the Oxbridge-Westminster bubble. This was most obviously signalled by a discursive exclusion: "austerity" was never mentioned, so we were back on the arid terrain of a debate the terms of which were set by England's austerians in 2010. The question, once more, was: who would cut the deficit quickest?

Miliband further deflated the mood — I think deliberately — by explicitly ruling out a "deal" or a "coalition" with the SNP. Given the right-wing press's scaremongering, Miliband's denying that a deal will happen might have been necessary in order to make the conditions for such a deal possible. Any equivocation would surely have been seized upon by the right-wing media, and relentlessly used to stoke up the fears of voters less likely to vote for Labour because of the prospect of a coalition. The audience members imploring Cameron and Miliband to be honest about possible deals were as ingenuous as those who hailed the programme as a triumph of participatory democracy. Neither leader could "be honest" about how the vote is likely to go on Thursday because that very speculation could change what actually happens. Such is the state of our current "democracy": everything is distorted by media projections, by politicians' (second) guesses as to how voters may behave in response to those projections, a whole phantom science of feedback.

Baudrillard: "Polls manipulate the undecidable. Do they affect votes? True or false? Do they yield exact photographs of reality, or of mere tendencies, or a refraction of this reality in a hyperspace of simulation whose curvature we do not know? True or false? Undecidable."[2]

For most of this campaign, Cameron has given every impression that he'd far rather be tucking into a country supper than demeaning himself hustling on the hustings. Defending the status quo is not as energising as tearing it down, and comfortable Cameron never had the class resentment-jouissance that drove grocer's daughter Thatcher to battle trade unionists and old-school Tory grandees alike. For him, it's a career,[3] not a mission. Cameron has never seemed like a man burning with conviction; he comes across more like the captain of some public school cricket team who whose main motivation for winning is to remind uppity comprehensive kids who's boss. On Thursday, Cameron finally went into bat for his class like he meant it.

He needs to. This election is pivotal. Either the Tories can "finish the job" of looting and pillaging everything working-class struggle built, or they themselves could be on the brink of destruction. The Conservative Party haven't won an overall majority since 1992. It's difficult enough keeping this party of opportunists, quislings and crazies together at the best of times; if they fail to win again, will even Boris be able to prevent meltdown? And with the Tories in disarray, the right could finally be forced off the centre ground that they won and radically re-defined under Thatcher.

Pumped Up, Calmed Down

In front of the BBC cameras, Cameron's performance wasn't quite as slick as his upper lip, but he discovered a poise that he has seldom mustered in the past few weeks. The problem with Cameron getting pumped up last week is not only that it looked pathetically forced (his claim that he was "pumped up because I am" was a transparent deception as well as a tautology. He was "pumped up" because Tory backers demanded that he at least gave the appearance of caring). The more serious issue is that such displays of simulated passion undermine Cameron's key appeal, which has to do with projecting casual authority: what David Smail, writing before Cameron came onto the scene, called "[t]he confident slouch of the hands-in-pocket, old Etonian cabinet minister." Cameron's accent, his posture, his smirk, convey a consistent message: *relax, I'm in control, defer to me*. When he strays from this "ease and familiarity", he risks looking angry and/or uncomfortable, and apparent affability gives way an affronted sense of class superiority, as in the "calm down, dear" incident.

Presenting the Tories as the nasty party has been counterproductive, the fake letter of support from small businesses devolved into yet another *Thick of It* farce, but Thursday's flooding of the audience with Tory supporters posing as undecided voters worked. Cameron was back on home territory: the bizarre inverted world of English capitalist realism in which referring to a global banking crisis was desperate reaching for excuses, and austerity was the only possible course of action for any prudent government. (The best thing about New Labour was Alastair Campbell — a skilled operator and a technician, an expert on how to win ground on a hostile media terrain. It's hard to imagine that, if he were still running things, that Labour would have been ambushed like they were on Thursday.)

A Picture of Discontented New Wealth

Under the questioning of businesswoman Catherine Shuttleworth, Ed started to look like a supply teacher who had earnestly planned an interesting and informative lesson, only to find out that the kids just wanted to humiliate him, whatever he said. The Tory narrative of Labour profligacy was once again established as a self-evident truth that only a fool and/or a brazen liar would contest. This narrative was all the more convincing when it was re-cycled/re-cited by a "concerned businesswoman", "struggling to survive in a tough climate". The subsequent exposure of Shuttleworth as a probable Tory plant will not erase the impact of her TV encounter with Miliband, if only because complaining about the audience not only implicitly concedes defeat, it makes Labour look like sore losers.

For the moment, let's believe Shuttleworth's story that she isn't a Tory. (Although note that even the *DM* whitewashing is carefully worded: Shuttleworth only denies that she's ever been a member of the Tory party, not that she's a lifelong Tory voter, which is of course impossible to prove or disprove.) The question then would be why she should be so ready to blame hard times not on the government which has been in power in the last five years, but on the government which was in power when she actually built and grew her business? Miliband's pitch — Labour is all about supporting small business owners — is part of a strategy that could be fruitful in the long run, since it could break the alliance between small business and corporate capital which has been so central to the installation of capitalist realism. But Shuttleworth's response to these overtures shows that breaking that alliance will be a long and hard struggle. She immediately started bleating on behalf of Tesco — as if Tesco didn't enjoy its greatest success under New Labour, and as if its downfall wasn't a direct consequence of the very corporate tyranny that Miliband was moving to attack?

Reflexive Cringe

While Miliband was correct not to capitulate to nonsense about Labour overspending, it was clear that Labour has left it far too late to challenge the dominant narrative. On the face of it, Labour's acquiescence in the austerity myth has been inexplicable. Paul Krugman writes of

561

the limpness of Labour's response to the austerity push. Britain's opposition has been amazingly willing to accept claims that budget deficits are the biggest economic issue facing the nation, and has made hardly any effort to challenge the extremely dubious proposition that fiscal policy under Blair and Brown was deeply irresponsible — or even the nonsensical proposition that this supposed fiscal irresponsibility caused the crisis of 2008-2009. Why this weakness? In part it may reflect the fact that the crisis occurred on Labour's watch; American liberals should count themselves fortunate that Lehman Brothers didn't fall a year later, with Democrats holding the White House. More broadly, the whole European centre-left seems stuck in a kind of reflexive cringe, unable to stand up for its own ideas.[4]

You say "reflexive cringe", I say "reflexive impotence"... Labour's slowness to respond to the crisis was not merely some failure of judgement or strategy; it was a consequence of how deeply capitalist realism had saturated the party. There was no question of Labour using the crisis to impose its own programme, because, by 2008, it didn't have much of programme beyond capitalist realism. Everything had been set up for a corporate appeasement, and there were neither the organisational nor the intellectual infrastructure to come up with anything new. Capitalist realism wasn't something that Labour was waiting out and planning to overcome, one day; it was embedded as an effectively permanent baseline set of conditions — conditions which receded from visibility even as they imposed strict limits on what could be said and thought.

I'm In a Trance, I Don't Ask Questions

Following Wendy Brown, I argued that capitalist realism can be understood as a kind of dreamwork. In this dreamwork, briefly interrupted in 2008, the banking crisis is some repressed trauma which is known about but never confronted, a Real that the dreamer stays asleep to keep avoiding. Capital is the dreamer here, and, insofar as capitalist realism is sustained, we remain figments in its dream. Yet capital is also our dream, which, *Matrix*-like, has constructed the virtual reality in which we think we live from our energy, our desires and our fantasies.

You would think that mention of the banking crisis would produce some cognitive dissonance when set against the narrative of Labour profligacy. If there was a global financial crisis, how could Labour also be responsible for the deficit? No doubt, part of the success of the "Labour did it" story is due to the hold of folk politics. A narrative about incompetent politicians maxing out the credit cards is easily digested; it's far more difficult to assimilate the opaque and abstract mechanics of finance capital. But one of the most valuable insights in Philip Mirowski's *Never Let A Serious Crisis Go To Waste:*

How Neoliberalism Survived the Financial Meltdown comes from his account of cognitive dissonance itself. Referring to the work of Leon Festinger, the social psychologist who worked extensively on cognitive dissonance, Mirowski reminds us that cognitive dissonance is not a threat to false beliefs. On the contrary, cognitive dissonance is a mechanism by which false beliefs can be maintained when confronted with evidence that directly disproves them. In fact, as Mirowski writes, Festinger's crucial claim was "that confrontation with contrary evidence may actually augment and sharpen the conviction and enthusiasm of a believer". Mirowski quotes Festinger:

> Suppose an individual believes something with his whole heart... suppose that he is presented with evidence, unequivocal and undeniable evidence, that his belief is wrong; what will happen? The individual will frequently emerge, not only unshaken, but even more convinced of the truth of his beliefs than ever before. Indeed, he may even show a new fervour about convincing and converting people to his view.[5]

This points to a relationship between desire and belief that has been posited at least since Hume and Spinoza's critiques of religion: we believe in part because we want to believe. But we also want to believe because the belief has become core to our subjectivity.

If You Get Too Burnt You Can't Come Back Home

The great mystery of neoliberalism is to what extent its advocates "really" believed it. Was it ever anything more than a ruse to restore ruling-class power and wealth? Of course, the answer to this partly depends on which advocates we are talking about. It's possible that certain key proselytisers for neoliberalism never believed it, and only opportunistically fixed upon it as a way of destroying the "red bases" of working-class power. With others, it's more likely that a belief was aided by the desire to believe. This desire was motivated by economic interest, of course, but also by certain libidinal satisfactions: the pleasures of seeing the working class defeated, of seeing the poor and vulnerable stripped of social security. For a certain English petit-bourgeois sensibility, Thatcherism was the equivalent of a riot: a jubilee of destruction, a temporary autonomous zone for a reactionary desire that feeds off suffering and misery.

And as I was standing by the edge
I could see the faces of those led pissing theirselves laughing (and the flames grew)
Their mad eyes buldged their flushed faces said
The weak get crushed as the strong grow stronger[6]

The funeral pyre will be re-lit if the Tories win on Thursday (*Bring some paper and bring some wood/Bring what's left of all your love for the fire*), and after five more years, there won't be much left... The NHS will have been gutted, sold off by stealth; education will continue to be asset stripped, ripe for yet more corporate plundering... the most vulnerable will be pushed further into destitution, women and children first...

This is why Cameron's android smoothness, like Boris's bluster, is so crucial for the Tories. It is a cloaking device, obfuscating the project, keeping the gibbering libido hidden behind a humanoid face and a calming, plummy voice. Imagine if Gove (who's been pushed back into the attic for trying just too hard to be one of the posh boys — so vulgar, so nouveau) — imagine if Gove, with his defrocked pantomime-dame pout, his lickspittle lips smacking with the class hatred that only a class traitor can feel, imagine if he were leader...

By contrast, Cameron's strength is that it is hard to work up much class hatred for him. People that wealthy and privileged are like rare beasts: something you hear about but rarely encounter. In fact, I've seen more pandas in the flesh than old Etonians. You also get the sense that Cameron has no particular animus towards the poor — it's rather that the experience of poverty is so remote for him that he simply cannot understand it, except as some theoretical possibility. The poor are pixellated background characters in the blearily cheerful steampunk simulation that Dave projects: everything's fine so long as you don't look too closely.

Dismantling Capitalist Realism

But let's return to Mirowski's summary of Festinger's research:

> Philosophy of science revels in the ways in which it may be rational to discount contrary evidence, but the social psychology of cognitive dissonance reveals just how elastic the concept of rationality can be in social life. Festinger and his colleagues illustrated these lessons in his first book (1956) by reporting in a neutral manner the vicissitudes of a group of Midwesterners they called "The Seekers," who developed a belief that they would be rescued by flying saucers on a specific date in 1954, prior to a great flood coming to engulf Lake City (a pseudonym). Festinger documents in great detail the hour-by-hour reactions of the Seekers as the date of their rescue came and passed with no spaceships arriving and no flood welling up to swallow Lake City. At first, the Seekers withdrew from representatives of the press seeking to upbraid them for their failed prophecies, but rapidly reversed their stance, welcoming any and all opportunities to expound and elaborate upon their (revised and expanded) faith. A minority of their group did fall away, but Festinger

notes they tended to be lukewarm peripheral members of the group. Predominantly, the Seekers never renounced their challenged doctrines. The ringleaders tended to redouble their proselytising, so long as they were able to maintain interaction with a coterie of fellow covenanters.[7]

Mirowski makes an analogy with proponents of neoliberal economic doctrine, who — far from abandoning this doctrine after its discrediting in the crisis — held to it even more doggedly. This is what Miliband faced on Thursday. Blank stares of mesmerised true believers seven years after the saucers didn't arrive. Shuttleworth's interjection like some *Manchurian Candidate* trigger, provoking automaton-applause...

This shows how difficult the task of dismantling capitalist realism will be. A whole process of deprogramming, involving new narratives, new libidinal attractors, as well as new ways of sharing knowledge, will have to be undergone. While this is certainly a formidable challenge, it is something that is already underway and which we can intensify quite quickly.

Of particular importance, it seems to me, is a popular demystification of economics and "the economy". The austerity myth has only seemed credible because of a widespread economic illiteracy — an illiteracy I very much share. Economics functions now much as theology functioned in the Medieval world — as an intricate and elaborate system of concepts, objects and reasoning that is closed to non-initiates. We need something like a Reformation in/and against capitalist economics — the equivalent of the Bible being translated into English. I think this could be done, not by a series of large-scale conferences, televisions, or films — although of course these wouldn't hurt — but virally. Small groups of people, including at least one individual who is an expert in economics, could get together and talk through some key concepts and principles, major economic events, etc. This could take place in private homes, in universities and colleges, in social clubs... In addition to everything else, this would also serve the function of reviving sociality, of re-building a class consciousness that has been dissipated by the individualising tendencies of neoliberalism and communicative capitalism.

Communist Realism

Back to Thursday, here's "entrepreneur" Chris. "A ban on zero hours contract would prevent me from running my small business..." Well, would it now? We've heard many versions of this plaint over the last few months, from businesses big and small. What this amounts to is saying that, these businesses cannot function without super-exploiting workers, and they cannot function without indirect government subsidies (with benefits supplementing low wages). Hold on a minute: didn't the capitalist realists make their "hard decisions" to close down nationalised industries on the grounds that they weren't viable and they were draining too much public money?

We need a new, communist, realism, which says that businesses are only viable if they can pay workers a living wage. This communist realism would reverse the capitalist realist demonisation of those on benefits, and target the real parasites: "entrepreneurs" whose enterprises depend on hyper-precarious labour; landlords living it large off housing benefit; bankers getting bonuses effectively or actually out of public money, etc.

But the concept of communist realism also suggests a particular kind of orientation. This isn't an eventalism, which will wager all its hopes on a sudden and final transformation. It isn't a utopianism, which concedes anything "realistic" to the enemy. It is about soberly and pragmatically assessing the resources that are available to us here and now, and thinking about how we can best use and increase those resources. It is about moving — perhaps slowly, but certainly purposively — from where we are now to somewhere very different.

pain now[1]

A grief without a pang, void, dark, and drear

"Pain now, more pain later" was the headline on the front page of the *Guardian* on the day my son was born nearly five years ago.[2] That year, my wife and I earned fifteen thousand pounds between us. I was working as an hourly paid lecturer in adult education and in a university, as well as doing some freelance writing and copyediting. We were able to survive without living in penury because of the £300 a month in tax credits we received.

This was the way Brownism and Blairism worked: allowing low wages and precarity to proliferate with one hand, mitigating their effects with benefits on the other. By then, like most of the population, I loathed New Labour. Labour had become so capitalist realist that surely it couldn't be much worse if the Tories got in? I shared the widespread view that elections don't change much: all that's on offer are minimally different versions of the same thing (neoliberalism).

It soon became very clear that this was not the case. Cameron and Osborne unleashed capitalist realism 2.0, the most audacious confidence trick in recent political history: make the poor and vulnerable pay for the banking crisis. Use the crisis as a pretext to destroy even more of the welfare state. Sigh their fake sighs, and tell us what "difficult choices" they had to make...

Today, if my wife and I earned what we did in 2010, we would receive only £50 in tax credits a month.

Of course, for me, working like this was something of a bohemian lifestyle choice. If I'd wanted to, I could probably have got better paid work — after all, only a fool would expect to enjoy working for a living. But what of all those stuck in low-paid precarious work forever? The disabled? The long-term sick and the chronically mentally ill, forced back to work?

A stifled, drowsy, unimpassioned grief.

I wasn't very interested in this election a few weeks ago. To be honest, even though I had been commissioned to write a piece about the TV coverage of the election, I couldn't muster up the enthusiasm to watch the first debate (*I'll watch it later*) until Laura Oldfield Ford, excited by Nicola Sturgeon's performance, texted me and asked what I thought. I switched on ITV+1, and the process of re-awakening that has occurred in the last few weeks began.

For reasons I will explore more fully in subsequent posts, I have spent the last year in a state of de-activation. I was thrown back into the privatised connectivity of the OedIpod, with its constant stream of low-level anxiety and compulsive micro-enjoyments. I couldn't write, except in a mechanical way; what I produced seemed stillborn, stilted. My main mood-altering drug of choice, music, didn't work. I binged on boxsets. I enjoyed time with my wife and son, but there was a fugitive quality to this enjoyment: my fingers always itched to reach for my smartphone. There was always something I should already have done that I hadn't — the urgencies piling up, like a flashing red light constantly blinking in my peripheral vision, never letting me settle. Most of these urgencies were small things, they didn't matter too much, but perhaps there would be some long-forgotten urgency that was going to calamitously re-emerge, too late for me to do anything about it? I'll just check…

Liveable Shit

Which finds no natural outlet, no relief.
The coldly terrifying thing about this state of dejection was that it was not a completely paralysing depression — more a kind of exhausting drudgery. It felt liveable; indeed, it felt like I could — perhaps would — live the rest of my life in it. Perhaps I have expected too much from life. Now I would have to adjust to misery, like everyone else does. Others were much, much worse off than me. It wasn't like I was to *chip ice off the windscreen in the morning*. I had been precarious for years — now I was in well-paid secure employment. Why couldn't I just be happy? OK, so I had to do marketing promotions, complete "quality" paperwork, amend module proposal forms six times — but it was hardly coal mining, was it?

You see, you see: I had become once again the compliant subject of capitalist realism:

> …isolated, cut off, surrounded by hostile space, you are suddenly without connections, without stability, with nothing to hold you upright or in place; a dizzying, sickening unreality takes possession of you; you are threatened by a complete loss of identity, a sense of utter fraudulence; you have no right to be here, now, inhabiting this body, dressed in this way; you are a nothing, and "nothing" is quite literally what you feel you

are about to become.[3]

Engines of Dejection

Bifo is right. It wants us to be dejected: not so catatonically depressed that we can't work, but not so confident and secure that we will refuse to do bullshit jobs. (What is this *it* that wants us to miserable? Why, the real management of the Overlook Hotel of course. Our misery is like nectar to it...) Capital needs people desperate, scrambling on the edge (*watch Tory MPs laugh at starving families!*), it needs people scrimping and saving and crossing off lists, it needs people to be grateful for any work, no matter how poorly paid, no matter how insecure, struggle after struggle, year after year...

In the last five years, after the initial euphoria of dissent in 2010 and 2011, an acrid fog of despair has slowly but ineluctably sunk over what Cameron, chillingly, calls "our country"... choking the social energy out of institutions (no time to talk, sorry!)... reducing workers to automata issuing commands to one another... diminishing, at every level, our capacity to care... no time, no time... no money... Don't know, I've got to go mate... looking over our shoulders, fearing the worst... maybe it will be me next... better stay in line... accept the extra workload, I'm afraid that's how things are now...

Pain now, more pain later...

Misery Is Over (If We Want It)

The last week or so, I have, each day, played with my son for a few hours, been out on long walks, enjoying extended time with my wife, and managed to write thousands of words. Why can't life always be like this? Why indeed? It's only been possible because I have decided to suspend all my bureaucratic obligations until after the election. (Back to "proper" work tomorrow: so expect another post in a year or so.) I have managed to do this, not by some heroic act of magical voluntarist will, but because of a lift in mood that is not just personal. Scotland, Syriza, Podemos... It's taken a long while for the significance of these developments to filter through to me... but talking to comrades... attending to what Plan C are up to... feeling the electricity that Russell Brand has generated... All of this has gradually returned to consciousness during this election campaign. I don't think I'm the only one. But have we awoken too late to stop the Tories? Has their smog of dejection de-activated enough people — people who were hardly likely to have been reactivated by Labour's campaign?

Shy Effects

The two most obvious parallels for this election would seem to be 1974 — a weak Labour government, propped up by smaller parties, or, ominously, 1992, with Labour crushingly defeated by John Major's Tories after they were expected to win. Shaun Lawson makes a strong and convincing case for why today might turn out to be a re-run of 1992. Much of this is to do with the unreliability of polls. Because of the so-called "shy Tory" phenomenon — voters not admitting to pollsters that they would vote Conservative — the polls were spectacularly wrong in 1992. Major didn't only win, the Tories ended up with the largest amount of votes ever cast for a political party in Britain. Lawson argues that, despite polling being adjusted to factor in the shy Tory effect, current polling may still be inaccurate (because, for instance, it tends to be internet-based, which biases things towards a younger demographic).

I'm not sure how convinced I am by the parallels with 92, however, for two reasons:

1. Hyperstitional effects

As Baudrillard argued, we can't treat opinion polls as neutral positivist descriptions since they might well affect the very thing they are claiming to predict. It seems likely that this might have happened in 92.

The atmosphere leading up to the 92 election was very different to that preceding the current contest. There was the disastrous Sheffield Rally. Kinnock's triumphalist shout of "We're alright!", still excruciatingly embarrassing to remember nearly twenty five years on, not only destroyed the "statesmanlike persona" he had confected, it gave the impression of a manic and jubilatory over-confidence. The premature celebration came off as unseemly, desperate — as if Kinnock himself, never mind the electorate, couldn't quite believe that he would be Prime Minister. It also gave Murdoch's press something to really stoke the fears of reluctant Tories with, especially when the polls were suggesting that Labour would win: look, they think they've won! If you're thinking of staying at home, don't — every vote is needed!

It isn't really like that this time. Polls are predicting a hung parliament, not a Labour victory — there isn't the same resource of fear to feed off. Victory for Labour is uncertain, not an imminent possibility that needs to be desperately averted. Furthermore, while the Tories have certainly tried to scaremonger, a Labour government now is not the terrifying prospect that it could be made to seem in 92. After Blairism, Labour is no longer the Other to neoliberal commonsense that it could be presented as then.

As I said in the last post, Miliband has kept his campaign emotionally subdued — no extravagant promises ("I want to underpromise and overdeliver"); no messianic fervour (this by contrast with Blair as much as Kinnock). It's true, Miliband doesn't seem to have Prime Minesterial gravitas, but, then again, neither did John Major, surely the least likely Prime Minister ever.

2. We're in New Times

In 1992, we were still in the high pomp of capitalist realism. The crash had not yet happened. There was still something on offer to those who wanted to vote in their own interests and let everyone else go hang.

The Tories have nothing very much to bribe most of their supporters with this time. Without the false balm of the "Big Society", they only have a negative message — it will be worse under Labour — and a muted promise: pain now, a little less pain later. Is this enough to motivate the wavering?

Neoliberalism is finished as a project, even if it lurches on, thrashing around like a decorticated terminator. We're finally groping our way, blinking, out of capitalist realism. The psychic blockade that prevented us from thinking and acting is lifting. This has only registered in this campaign in some minor way with the SNP, Plaid Cymru and the Greens (the multi-party nature of British politics now is of course another way in which we are in new times by comparison with 74 and 92). If Labour manages to form a government, we will be celebrating a Tory defeat far more than we will be hailing a Labour victory.

But nothing is certain at the moment. I don't think there will be much certainty tomorrow either. My feeling is that things will be very volatile over the next few weeks. One thing is for sure: we need to be prepared to mobilise if the Tories attempt a coup. And they surely will...

abandon hope (summer is coming)[1]

So it was to be a re-run of 1992, after all. It seems that even elections are subject to retromania, now. Except, this time, it is 1992 without jungle. It's Ed Sheeran and Rudimental rather than Rufige Kru. Always ignore the polls, wrote Jeremy Gilbert late on election night:

> You get a better sense of what's going on in the electorate by sniffing the wind, sensing the affective shifts, the molecular currents, the alterations in the structures of feeling. Listen to the music, watch the TV, go to the the pubs and ride the tube. Cultural Studies trumps psephology every time.[2]

Contemporary English popular culture, with its superannuated PoMo laddishness, its smirking blokishness (anyone fancy a pint with Nigel?), its poverty porn, its craven cult of big business, has become like some gigantic Poundbury Village simulation, in which nothing new happens, forever... while ubiquitous "Keep Calm" messages, ostensibly quirky-ironic, actually function as *They Live* commands, containing the panic and the desperation...

England is a country in which every last space where conviviality might flourish has been colonised by a commercial imperative... supermarket check-out operatives replaced by crap robots... unexpected item in bagging area... every surface plastered with corporate graffiti and haranguing hashtags... no trick missed to screw every last penny out of people... exorbitant parking charges in NHS hospitals (exact amount only, no change given), all the profits going to private providers...

Everything seen through a downer haze... "Mostly you self-medicate"... comfort eating and bitter drinking... What's your poison?

> The suburbs are hallucinating, England is hallucinating. Monster Ripper and Smirnoff, Brandy Boost, oversized glasses of chardonnay at Weterspoons

monday club, valium scored for a few quid in the pub, the stink of weed drifting from portakabins, red eyes and yellow bibs.. The pharmaceuticals industry is one of UK Plc's biggest success stories (along with arms dealing and loans companies) as prescriptions for anti-depressants are kept on repeat.[3]

Time for one more, Nigel?
Time, gentlemen, please...
There is no time... Time is on your side (yes it is)...
In any case, Shaun Lawson is to be congratulated — if that is the word — for what turned out to be an astonishingly accurate prediction of how the election would go.[4] My attempts to refute the parallels with 92 in my last post were as much wishful thinking as anything else. I suppose at some level I knew after the BBC Leaders Debate how things would go — which is why I found watching it so dejecting. (Another rhyme with the past: Ed's stumble at the end of his interrogation by the petit-bourgeoisie was a minor echo of Kinnock's tumbling into the sea in 1983.)

Don't Fear...

It seems that the very thing which gave us hope — the possibility of vacillating Labour being pulled to the left by an alliance with the SNP — might have been what motivated Tory voters to come out in such numbers in England. (Another echo of 92: fear as a hyperstitional force.) The truth is what many of us have long suspected: Labour lost this election five years ago, by failing to challenge the Tories' narrative. Yet this failure wasn't about the wrong leader, PR strategy or even policies; it is ultimately rooted in Labour's disconnection from any wider movement, and this is in turn rooted in the wider emergence of capitalist realism. Blairism may have won Labour three elections, but the unfolding of its logic could well lead to the destruction, in the not so far distant future, of the party. As Paul Mason acidly summarises, "Labour no longer knows what it is for, nor how to win power".[5] With Blairism, Labour knew how to win power, but in acquiring this knowledge, it forgot what it was for.

That existential quandary is bitterly ironic given that there is a large proportion of the population in England — I still believe it is the majority — which feels it has no party which represents it. I maintain that the shift to UKIP is ultimately much more to do with this sense of disenfranchisement and despair than with any intrinsic tendency towards racism or even nationalism in its supporters. Everyone has chauvinistic potentials of one kind or another which can be activated by particular sets of forces. Ultra-nationalism is a symptom of the failure of class politics; or, class politics emerges through the ultra-nationalist lens in a distorted and displaced way.

As Paul Mason also points out, a return to Blairism will certainly not win back those Labour supporters who turned to UKIP. In England, as in Scotland, it was Blairism's taking for granted and abandonment of its working-class base that produced the sense of betrayal which led to so many former Labour supporters losing patience with the party on Thursday. In Scotland, the response to betrayal took a progressive form; in England, it assumed a reactionary mode. Partly, this is because there was no progressive outlet available in England. Working-class English voters alienated from Labour's Oxbridge elite were left a choice between a UKIP that deliberately talked up its appeal to working families, and an array of small left-wing parties to whose message they were not exposed and which had no chance of being elected. UKIP were also practically forced on them to by a political media so decadent, so boring, that it counts Nigel Farage as a charismatic flash of colour. Hence what Tim Burrows calls "the curiously mediated entity of Farage, a man whose direct manner, coloured tweed and pints of ale seem made for meme-politics. UKIP are more popular on Facebook than Labour and the Liberal Democrats put together."[6]

Don't Despair...

It would be easy to fall into despair about England after Thursday; it would be easy to conclude that the country is full of selfish, mean-spirited and stupid individuals. Yet we have to remember that most people's engagement with politics is quite minimal; thinking in political terms, framing everyday life in terms of political categories, is now a minority pursuit. This is not a moral or intellectual failing on the part of the electorate: it is a consequence of a neoliberalism which has largely succeeded in its aim of disabling the mechanisms of mass democracy. Overworked and told they need to work harder, busy, but still feeling that they can't get everything done, many are too drained to care. (*Too knackered to think, just give me time to come round...*) How many Tory voters are committed Conservatives, really? Mostly, they are jaded and detached, maybe voting out of fear as much as self-interest (and self-interest is often experienced as fear).

Capitalist realism is not about people positively identifying with neoliberalism; it is about the naturalisation and therefore the depoliticisation of the neoliberal worldview. The Tories' pitch is in tune with this ambient neoliberalisation, with its apparently commonsensical emphasis on choice, opportunity and the dignity of labour, and its emotional appeal to negative solidarity. To break out of this, you need a repoliticisation, and this requires a popular mobilisation, just as we saw with the SNP.

The Tory success depended upon a popular de-activation (the days of Thatcher's rallies are long gone). There was no enthusiasm for either of the two leading parties. The only party that could call on massive popular enthusiasm in the UK was the SNP. That popular enthusiasm — an enthusiasm that capitalist realism is set up to prevent emerging — is the rushing in of something that, for a long time, there hasn't seemed to be any glimmer of in England: the future.

Don't Be Depressed...

"What hope for a country where people will camp out for three days to glimpse the Royal Couple? England is like some stricken beast too stupid to know it is dead. Ingloriously foundering in its own waste products, the backlash and bad karma of empire."
— William Burroughs, *The Place of Dead Roads*[7]

So we shouldn't take the Tories' victory as a sign that we are totally out of sync with the majority of the population in England. As Jeremy remarked to me on Thursday, it is not as if the equivalent of Syriza or Podemos had lost. (Although that was part of what was so devastating — our expectations were low, but reality contrived to go even lower.) Given the serious weakness of Labour's offer, given the ferocity of the attack on Labour from the right-wing media machine in the UK, given the failure of supposedly neutral popular media such as the BBC to offer the public an adequate account of the banking crisis and its aftermath, it is actually surprising that the Tories' victory was not even more comprehensive. Those who voted Tory aren't necessarily indifferent to the suffering of the poor, or to the plight of the vulnerable — most merely accept (why wouldn't they) the capitalist realist story about there being "no money left" and the need for "difficult choices". No doubt, their acceptance of this is somewhat self-serving; no doubt, it depends on keeping those who suffer out of sight or in their peripheral vision.

But it is also a fundamentally depressing and depressive outlook. There is a connection between capitalist realism and depressive realism. The idea that life is essentially drudgery (and that therefore no one should get a free ride) is a depressive conception of fairness (if I have to be miserable, so should everyone else), which has a particular traction in a burnt-out post-Protestant culture like England's... (England is the oldest capitalist country, don't forget...)

All Cameron offered was more of this depression: a vision of a man chipping ice off his windscreen and going to a job he hates, forever. Yet Labour not only failed to offer a narrative about how the economy had gone wrong, it also failed to offer any positive vision of what society would look like if it had its way. I'm convinced that even the most minimal sense of this might have been enough to have inspired people to reject the Tories. Yet the fact that Labour couldn't offer it was not some mistake (a few more focus groups and meetings with advertising people, and they'd have been there!). It was one more symptom of the way in which the party has been completely colonised by capitalist realism.

The Tories quickly abandoned the "Big Society" after the 2010 campaign, but the concept did actually point to what neoliberal culture has corroded: the space between "individuals and their families" and the state. In addition to its clunky and uncommunicative name — it was a kind of anti-meme — the problem with the "Big Society" was that, in the Tories' hands, it was a transparent ruse to dismantle the welfare state. To resocialise a culture that has been individualised to the extent that England has demands massive resources — it requires time and energy, the very things that capital (especially the contemporary neoliberal, English version of capital) strips us of most thoroughly.

Real wealth is the collective capacity to produce, care and enjoy. This is Red Plenty. We, and they, have had it wrong for a while: it is not that we are anti-capitalist, it is that capitalism, with all its visored cops, its teargas, all the theological niceties of its economics, is set up to block Red Plenty. The attack on capital has to be fundamentally based on the simple insight that, far from being about "wealth creation", capital necessarily and always blocks our access to this common wealth. Everything for everyone. All of us first.

Labour has allowed election after election to be fought not on the Red terrain of resocialisation, but on the Blue territory of identitarian community, with its border guards (we'll have as many as you!) and barbed wire fences (they will be as high as yours!). The genius of the progressive forces which have seized the SNP, meanwhile, was to have moved from the Blue of identitarian community — and the nationalism of colonised peoples is of course very different to the nationalism of the colonisers — to the Red of internationalist cosmopolitan conviviality.

Red belonging offers something different to traditional forms of belonging (faith, flag, family — so many corrupted forms of the commons, as Hardt and Negri have it). Jodi Dean has movingly described how the Communist Party in the US

> gave some Americans the feeling that the world was of one piece, their work meaningful as the work of a class, their struggles significant as part of a global struggle to liberate collective work from those claiming it for their own private profit. For desperately poor and barely literate immigrants, communism is a source of knowledge and power — the knowledge of how the world works and the power to change it.[8]

The sense of belonging here could not be reduced to the chauvinistic pleasures that come from being an insider in any group whatsoever; it was a special sense of involvement that promised to transfigure all aspects of everyday life in a way that, previously, only religion had promised to, so that even the dreariest task could be imbued with high significance. "Even those engaged in the boring, repetitive work of distributing leaflets or trying to recruit new members as the official line changed, or chafing against the smugness of higher ups, experience their life in the party as intensely meaningful."

As opposed to the essentially spatial imaginary of Blue belonging — which posits a bounded area, with those inside hostile and suspicious towards those who are excluded — Red belonging is temporal and dynamic. It is about belonging to a movement: a movement that abolishes the present state of things, a movement that offers unconditional care without community (it doesn't matter where you come from or who you are, we will care for you anyway).

But Don't Hope Either...

"There's no need to fear or hope, but only to look for new weapons," Deleuze writes in "Postscript on the Societies of Control".[9] He was no doubt thinking of Spinoza's account of hope and fear in the *Ethics*. "There is no hope unmingled with fear, and no fear unmingled with hope", Spinoza claimed. He defines hope and fear as follows:

> Hope is a joy not constant, arising from the idea of something future or past about the issue of which we sometimes doubt.

> Fear is a sorrow not constant, arising from the idea of something future or past about the issue of which we sometimes doubt.[10]

Hope and fear are essentially interchangeable; they are passive affects, which arise from our incapacity to actually act. Like all superstitions, hope is something we call upon when we have nothing else. This is why Obama's "politics of hope" ended up so deflating — not only because, inevitably, the Obama administration quickly became mired in capitalist realism, but also because the condition of hope is passivity. The Obama administration didn't want to activate the population (except at election time).

We don't need hope; what we need is confidence and the capacity to act. "Confidence", Spinoza argues, "is a joy arising from the idea of a past or future object from which cause for doubting is removed". Yet it is very difficult, even at the best of times, for subordinated groups to have confidence, because for them/us there are few if any "future objects from which cause for doubting is removed."[11]

"Class disadvantage is a form of injury inflicted on the person at birth," David Smail explains, "The confident slouch of the hands-in-pocket, old

Etonian cabinet minister speaks not so much as a current possession of power (on some measures the union boss might possess as much) as of a confidence which was sucked in with his mother's milk."[12] (Even if the milk he fed on was unlikely to have come from his mother). The welfare state was supposed to be a structure which removed some of this doubt, while the imposition of precarity is a political project designed to remove the confidence that the working class had attained after years of struggle. (See Jennifer M. Silva's heartbreaking *Coming Up Short: Working-Class Adulthood in an Age of Uncertainty* — a book to which I shall certainly return in future posts — for an account of the devastating impact of precarity on the emotional lives of young working-class men and women in the US.)

Whereas hope and fear are superstitious (although they may have some hyperstitional effects), confidence is essentially hyperstitional: it immediately increases the capacity to act, the capacity to act increases confidence, and so on — a self-fulfilling prophecy, a virtuous spiral.

So how are we to rebuild our confidence? While the conditions are difficult — and in England, they are about to get much more difficult — we can still act, and act imminently and immanently. How?

Socialisation Beyond Social Media

The answer of course is that many groups are already doing what is necessary. But these processes will become more powerful when they are logistically coordinated (which is not to say "unified" — unity is a strategic weakness, not a strength) and bound together by stronger common narratives and fictions. Jason Read's essay "The Order and Connection of Ideology Is the Same as the Order and Connection of Exploitation: Or, Towards a Bestiary of the Capitalist Imagination"[13] explains why narrativisation is so important. In his account of two neo-Spinozist thinkers, Frédéric Lordon and Yves Citton, Read reminds us that

> our desire, our loves and hates, are already shaped by narratives, by scripts inherited through television and books. We enter into a world already scripted, and, as Spinoza argues in his definition of the first kind of knowledge, our life is defined as much by signs and images as things experienced.

This means

> that the scenarios that we imagine, the stories and narratives that we consume, inform our understanding of reality, not in the sense that we confuse fiction with reality, but that the basic relations that underlie our fictions shape our understanding of reality. It is not that we confuse fiction

with reality, believing everything that we see, but that the fundamental elements of every narrative, events, actions, and transformations, become the very way that we make sense of reality. Fiction exists in a permanent relation of metalepsis with reality, as figures and relations from one constantly inform the other.

This is why the intensification and proliferation of the capitalist technologies of reality management and libidinal engineering in the 1980s was not merely some happy coincidence for neoliberalism; neoliberalism's success was inconceivable without these technologies. It is also the reason that direct action, while of course crucial, will never be sufficient: we also need to act *indirectly*, by generating new narratives, figures and conceptual frames.

By first of all imposing a particular set of narratives, figures and frames which it then naturalised, capitalist realism hobbled what Jason Read identifies as the "particular power of humanity (and the linchpin of our emancipation)": "our faculty to reorder differently the images, the thoughts, the affects, the desires and the beliefs that are associated in our mind, the phrases that come out of our mouths, and the movements that emanate from our bodies." Cultural Studies was also based on this account of the capacity for reordering (which it derived partly from Spinoza, via Althusser). The reordering of images thoughts, affects, desires, beliefs and languages plainly cannot be achieved by "politics" alone — it is a matter for culture, in the widest sense.

Seen from this point of view, the locking of popular culture into repetition that I describe in *Ghosts Of My Life*[14] — and which Simon Reynolds also describes in *Retromania*[15] — is therefore a very serious problem. Popular culture's incapacity to produce innovation is a persistent ambient signal that nothing can ever change. Sometimes, it can seem fiendishly difficult to account for what has happened to popular culture, but the explanation for its sterility and stasis is ultimately quite simple. Innovation in popular culture has overwhelmingly come from the working class. Neoliberalism has been a systematic and sustained attack on working-class life — the results are now all around us.

Furthermore, the incursion of capitalist cyberspace into every area of life and the psyche has intensified the processes of de-socialisation. This is not to say that there are no progressive potentials in the web, but these have almost certainly been overrated, while the impact of cyberspace in de-socialising culture and subjectivity has been massively underestimated. Here I merely rehearse Bifo's account of semio-capitalism and Jodi Dean's critique of communicative capitalism, but it is important to operationalise this critique.

Blogs and social media have allowed us to talk to ourselves (but not to reach out beyond the left bubbles); they have also generated pathological behaviours and forms of subjectivity which not only generate misery and anger — they waste time and energy, our most crucial resources. Email and handhelds, meanwhile, have produced new forms of isolation and loneliness: the fact that we can receive communications from work anywhere and anytime means we are exposed to work's order-words when we are alone, without the possibility of support from fellow workers.

In sum, the obsession with the web, its monopolisation of any idea of the new, has served capitalist realism rather than undermined it. Which does not mean, naturally, that we should abandon the web, only that we should find out how to develop a more instrumental relationship with it. Put simply, we should use it — as a means of dissemination, communication and distribution — but not live inside it. The problem is that this goes against the tendencies of handhelds. We all recognise the by now clichéd image of a train carriage full of people pecking at their tiny screens, but have we really registered how miserable this really is, and how much it suits capital for these pockets of socialisation to be closed down?

Knowing Someone in this Life Feels as Desperate as Me

Some folk in Plan C have been talking about consciousness-raising, and for many reasons, I believe that it is a crucially important to revive and proliferate this practice (or range of practices) now. Consciousness-raising is partly about the discovery and production of subjugated knowledges, but it is also about the immediate production of socialisation, of forms of subjectivity antithetical to the always/on-always lonely mode of contemporary capitalist individuality.

Consciousness-raising opens up the possibility of *living*, not merely theorising about, a collective perspective. It can give us the resources to behave, think and act differently at work (if it makes any sense to talk about being "at" work anymore), where capitalist realism has become second nature. The roots of any successful struggle will come from people sharing their feelings, especially their feelings of misery and desperation, and together attributing the sources of these feelings to impersonal structures, albeit impersonal structures mediated by particular figures to which we must attach populist loathing.

In the harsh conditions of cyberspatialised capitalism — conditions that, as Jennifer M. Silva demonstrates, have produced a "hardening" of the self, especially in the young — consciousness-raising can produce a new compassion, for others and for ourselves. Neurotic-Oedipalising capitalism responsibilises, harshly blaming us, while — in its therapeutic mode — telling us that we have the power as individuals to change anything and everything: if we're unhappy, it's up to us to fix it. Consciousness-raising, meanwhile, is about positive depersonalisation: **it's not your fault**, it's capitalism. No individuals can change anything, not even themselves; but collective activation is already, immanently, overcoming individualised immiseration.

So I present below a number of strategies, practices and orientations, starting from the most immediate (something groups can do right now) and moving towards the more remotes. The list is of course not exhaustive; and I can't claim credit for coming up with any of the strategies myself. The point is to share them, add to them, elaborate them.

The chief obstruction to all of these steps is what, in a trenchant and clear-eyed analysis, Ewa Jasiewicz calls "time poverty":[16]

> Our time is under attack. Work will be intensified, worse paid, and more casualised — if we don't have it, we'll be working to have it; mandatory and supervised job searches and workfare will see people forced to spend their time locked into coerced, computerised distraction. A real, diverse, working class self-representative movement needs to include people facing and living these experiences, but how will that happen when we're too tied up working?
>
> Access to time and our own labour is key and will determine participation and the ability to organise. If we can't have our own time to organise, we can't organise, we can't meet each other, we cannot find each other. Work and the benefits regime — which is work under different conditions and profit margins — are key sites of struggle. Solidarity will need to step up if we are to win workplace disputes and strikes, refusals of workfare and support for people getting sanctioned, so that people have more control over their time and labour.
>
> All our commons are under attack. The condition of time poverty and its roots — intensification of labour, welfare repression, criminalisation and incarceration — have to be recognised as major obstacles to movement, diversity and power. These obstacles need to be tackled if we want to overcome the ideology of wage labour as a determinant of human value on a popular level.

The problem is that, in order to struggle against time poverty, the main resource we require is time — a nasty vicious circle that capital, with its malevolent genius, now has... This problem is absolutely immanent — writing this and the other posts I have completed this week has meant that I have fallen enormously behind on my work, which is storing up stress for the next week or so.

The first thing we must do in response to all this is to put into practice what I outlined above: try not to blame ourselves. **#Itsnotyourfault** We must try to do everything we can to politicise time poverty rather than accept blame as individuals for failing to complete our work on time. The reason we feel overwhelmed is that we *are* overwhelmed — it isn't an individual failing of ours; it isn't because we haven't "managed our time" properly. However, we can use the scarce resources we already have more effectively if we work together to codify practices of collective re-habituation (setting new rules for our engagement with social media and capitalist cyberspace in general for example).

Anyway, here goes:

1. Talk to fellow workers about how we feel. This will re-introduce care and affection into spaces where we are supposed to be competitive and isolated. It will also start to break down the difference between (paid) work and social reproduction on which capitalism depends.

2. Talk to opponents Most people who vote Tory and UKIP are not monsters, much as we might like to think they are. It's important that we understand why they voted as they did. Also, they may not have been exposed to an alternative view. Remember that people are more likely to be persuaded if defensive character armour is not triggered.

3. Create knowledge exchange labs. This follows from what I argued a few days ago. Lack of knowledge about economics seems to me an especially pressing problem to address, but we could also do with more of us knowing about law, I suspect.

4. Create social spaces. Create times and spaces specifically dedicated to attending to one another: not (yet more) conferences, but sessions where people can share their feelings and ideas. I would suggest restricting use of handhelds in these spaces: not everything has to be live tweeted or archived! Those with access to educational or art spaces could open these up for this purpose.

5. Use social media pro-actively, not reactively. Use social media to publicise, to spread memes, and to constitute a counter-media. Social media can provide emotional support during miserable events like Thursday. But we should try to use social media as resource rather than living inside it at all times. Facebook can be useful for discussions and trying out new ideas, but attempting to debate on Twitter is absurd and makes us feel more stressed. (He says, thinking of the time when, sitting on a National Express coach, perched over his handheld, he tried to intervene in an intricate discussion about Spinoza's philosophy — all conducted in 140 characters.)

6. Generate new figures of loathing in our propaganda. Again, this follows up from what I argued in the "Communist Realism" post.[17] Capitalist realism was established by constituting the figure of the lazy, feckless scrounger as a populist scapegoat. We must float a new figure of the parasite: landlords milking the state through housing benefit, "entrepreneurs" exploring cheap labour, etc.

7. Engage in forms of activism aimed at logistical disruption. Capital has to be seriously inconvenienced and to fear before it yields any territory or resources. It can just wait out most protests, but it will take notice when its logistical operations are threatened. We must be prepared for them cutting up *very* rough once we start doing this — using anti-terrorist legislation to justify practically any form of repression. They won't play fair, but it's not a game of cricket — they know it's class war, and we should never forget it either.

8. Develop Hub struggles Some struggles will be more strategically and symbolically significant than others — for instance, the Miners' Strike was a hub struggle for capitalist realism. We might not be able to identify in advance what these struggles are, but we must be ready to swarm in and intensify them when they do occur.

Summer is Coming

The Lannisters won on Thursday, but their gold has already run out, and summer is coming. What we saw in the debates dominated by Nicola Sturgeon was not a mirage — it is a rising tide, an international movement, a movement of history, which has not yet reached an England sandbagged in misery and mediocrity. Comrades, I hope (ha!) for the sake of your mental health and your blood pressures that you didn't see the right-wing tabloids over the weekend (tw for class hatred): middle England crowing over its "humiliation" of "Red" Ed. Well if they think Ed was Red, wait until they see the coming Red Swarm. Outer England has been sedated, but it is waking from its long slumber, carrying new weapons...

for now, our desire is nameless[1]

"'In our day', Nikita Khrushchev told a crowd in the Lenin Stadium of Moscow on 28 September 1959, 'the dreams mankind cherished for ages, dreams expressed in fairy tales which seemed sheer fantasy, are being translated into reality by man's own hands'."
— Francis Spufford, *Red Plenty*[2]

This quotation from Francis Spufford's extraordinary *Red Plenty* reminds us that when communism was defeated, it wasn't just a particular ideology that disappeared. The demise of communism was also the disappearance of modernism's Promethean dream of a total transformation of human society. Michael Hardt has argued that "the positive content of communism, which corresponds to the abolition of private property, is the autonomous production of humanity — a new seeing, a new hearing, a new thinking, a new loving."[3]

The arrival of what I have called capitalist realism — the widespread acceptance that there is no alternative to capitalism — therefore meant the end of these new productive, perceptual, cognitive and libidinal possibilities. It meant that we would be reduced to the same old seeing, hearing, thinking, loving... forever. Fredric Jameson long ago argued that postmodernism was the cultural logic of late capitalism, and the features that Jameson claimed were characteristic of the postmodern — pastiche, the collapse of historicity — are now ubiquitous. The only future that capital can reliably deliver is technological — we count historical time not in cultural shifts, but in technological upgrades, watching the same old things on higher definition screens.

The Reality of Class Continues

The attitude of realism that dominant capitalism requires is essentially depressive. The management of this collective depression goes through a series of thresholds. First of all, we come to expect very little: nothing will ever happen again. Then we think that maybe the things that once happened weren't actually so great. Finally, we accept that nothing has ever happened, nor could ever happen. The more that depression is normalised, the harder it is to even identify it. Radically lowered expectations become habituated. Time flattens out.

This generalised depression is one reason that so little has happened since the major capitalist crisis of 2008. Yet this depression is itself both a symptom and a cause of something else: the decomposition of class solidarity. We would have to go deep into the nineteenth century to find a moment when class consciousness was as weak as it is now. Not only capital, but also elements of the post-68 left, have maintained that class is an outmoded category, unfit to deal with the multiplicities and complications of twenty-first-century life. Yet these complications are in some respects a mirage, concealing the persistence of a class structure in which the majority of the population is marked as inferior. The reality of class continues, but without class consciousness. Beverley Skeggs and Helen Wood's work on the class basis of reality TV and Owen Jones's analysis of the "demonisation of the working class" show that class is displayed even as it is disavowed in contemporary culture.

Since the 1960s, the left has split into an authoritarian-nostalgic Leninism, committed to a party form and a class politics whose historical moment seems to have passed, and a supposedly "new" Left which rejects institutions and the centrality of the class struggle and puts all its faith in the capacity of the people to mobilise autonomously and to produce outside capitalist social relations. We desperately need to undo this binary. There is no way back to the old Leninist party, any more than there is a way back to Fordist capitalism. Yet naïve autonomism has shown that it has no purchase on the current moment either. Anti-capitalism and its retinue of strategies — occupations, protests — have not caused capital a moment's serious alarm. 68 preached that structures don't walk on the street — but if anti-capitalism has taught us anything, it is that, by itself, street activism has little effect on structures.

There Is No Desire for Capitalism

We don't have to choose between class politics and anti-authoritarianism any more than we need to choose between Gramsci, Deleuze or Guattari, between a hegemonic approach and a politics of desire. In fact, if we are to succeed, we must absolutely refuse this false choice. Class politics must be renewed and resumed, not simply revived as if nothing has happened. In a Gramscian mode, we need to take institutions seriously again. Mainstream media are still where our sense of reality is produced; and despite all the claims about the waning of the state, parliament still has power over life and death via its control of the military, health services and social security. Yet these institutions cannot be renewed from within — it is necessary to articulate the institution and the forces outside them.

At the same time, desire is not some vitalistic energy which will spontaneously emerge once bodies are freed from institutions. Rather, desire is always the result of processes of libidinal engineering — and at the moment, our desire is manipulated by capital's army of PR, branding and advertising specialists. The left needs to produce its own machineries of desire. It's true that, at first sight, we seem to be at something of a disadvantage here, when we consider the vast resources that capital has at its disposal aimed at capturing our desire. Yet there is no desire for capitalism as such, just as culture is composed from libidinal materials that have no essential relation to capital — which is why capital has to distract, depress, and addict us in order to keep us captivated and subordinated.

But if we are no longer to define ourselves negatively, by our opposition to capital, what will be the name of our positive project? I don't believe that the old signifier "communism" can be revived for this purpose. It is now irretrievably tainted by terrible associations, forever tied to the nightmares of the twentieth century. At the moment, our desire is nameless — but it is real. Our desire is for the future — for an escape from the impasses of the flatlands of capital's endless repetitions — and it comes from the future — from the very future in which new perceptions, desires, cognitions are once again possible. As yet, we can grasp this future only in glimmers. But it is for us to construct this future, even as — at another level — it is already constructing us: a new kind of collective agent, a new possibility of speaking in the first person plural. At some point in this process, the name for our new desire will appear and we will recognise it.

anti-therapy[1]

The idea that talking about our feelings could be a political act seems counter-intuitive. Aren't people talking about their emotions more than ever before? And hasn't this new emotionalism coincided with the emergence of what I have called capitalist realism — the deeply embedded view that capitalism is the only "realistic" economic system?

New Labour and the Birth of Emo-Politics

In order to begin to answer this, let's turn to one of the central hubs of capitalist realism, the UK. Tony Blair's New Labour naturalised what Thatcher had to fight for: the idea that there was no alternative to neoliberal capitalism. In retrospect, it is now clear that the first few months of Tony Blair's first term as prime minister also inaugurated a new moment in British political life — the birth of what we might call emo-politics. Blair brought a new emotional tone to British government. He positioned himself as part of a Britain that was more at ease with expressing its feeling than his parents' generation and their predecessors — with their stereotypical "stiff upper lips" — had been. Crucial to this was Blair and his advisers' manipulation of the extraordinary grief jamboree that ensued in the immediate wake of the death of Diana, Princess of Wales, which happened only a few months after New Labour came to power.

The death famously wrongfooted the monarchy, with its older models of duty and emotional restraint, but Blair's delivery of his famous speech about the "People's Princess" — scripted by New Labour's spin doctor, Alastair Campbell — not only established his authority as a prime minister, it initiated a new phase of neoliberal governance in Britain.

Thanks to Campbell and compliant members of the British media, a strong narrative soon emerged, in which Blair's apparent emotional openness was contrasted with the Queen's "coldness". The monarch's remoteness was now equated with "unhealthy" forms of emotional repression. Just as Blair sold himself as a moderniser who was taking the Labour Party away from the "class politics of the past", so New Labour would also make a break with the traditional account of emotions. The government would now take the lead in ensuring that the population had the "correct", "healthy" response to emotional distress. The normative tone would have been worrying enough, but New Labour's emotional politics went far beyond mere mood-setting or the offering of recommendations.

Instead, the new conception of emotional health was passive-aggressively enforced — in the authoritarian style of neoliberalism which New Labour made their own — by a battery of measures which intervened to an unprecedented degree in the population's emotional lives. Health, education and social control were all part of this project. Teachers were suborned into the role of emo-cops, ensuring that schoolchildren complied with the new emotional normativity. Parents judged to be failing were now required to attend "parenting classes".

Meanwhile, the question of how genuine Blair's feelings of grief were takes us to the heart of the Blair enigma: did he really believe in the doctrines he hawked, or was he a strange combination of charismatic showman-manipulator and depthless puppet of capital? What did Blair see when he looked in the mirror then, and what does he see now? Are we dealing with self-deception, messianic delusion, or a new kind of postmodern psychopathy? The enigma remains as unsolvable now as it was twenty years ago. What is certain is that Blair led the way in normalising the emotional self-exploitation that was necessary for the final phase of neoliberalism in Britain.

The early Blair perfected the art of "spincerity" — the public performance of an emotion that you may or may not actually feel. As Britain's economy became ever more reliant on the service and sales jobs, increasing numbers of workers were forced to develop the techniques of emotional simulation which Blair publicly pioneered.

In their book *The Dangerous Rise of Therapeutic Education*, Kathryn Ecclestone and Dennis Hayes argue that New Labour turned to popular therapy to fill the gap left by class politics. These "therapeutic orthodoxies", they argue,

> include claims that past life experiences have long-term negative emotional effects for everyone, and particularly pernicious effects for an increasing minority. The overall message is that, behind our apparently confident facades, we are all, to a greater or lesser extent, fragile and vulnerable and, as a consequence, we need particular forms of emotional support.[2]

Ecclestone and Hayes are right that these therapeutic tenets have been widely promulgated, and often accepted without much criticism.

As Eva Illouz has been especially perspicacious in identifying, therapeutic orthodoxies have been disseminated, not only by therapists themselves, but by a popular culture which has enthusiastically adopted therapeutic motifs and conceptual frames. Ecclestone and Hayes are also right that therapy filled the gap that appeared when New Labour explicitly repudiated the concept of class struggle. However, Ecclestone and Hayes's solution to the "therapeutic turn" is simply to play off one form of reactionary politics against another. Their call for a return to an education based on "reason, science and progress" is superficially laudable. Ultimately, however, theirs is conservative position, which offers us only a (false) choice between different kinds of authoritarianism. In place of New Labour's soft — but highly invasive — authoritarianism, Ecclestone and Hayes posit an unappetizing return to *traditional* forms of authoritarianism. They are also in danger of endorsing the very emotional remoteness that superficially justifies the therapeutic turn. The problem with what I would like to call here the therapeutic imaginary is not that it posits subjects as vulnerable, haunted by events in their past lives, and lacking in confidence. Most subjects in capitalism — including those in the ruling class — fit that description. The problem with the therapeutic imaginary — and this is a problem that goes back to Freud and the origins of psychoanalysis — is its claim that these issues can be solved by the individual subject working on him- or herself, with only the therapist to assist them.

In addition, Ecclestone and Hayes' refusal of the role of emotion in education — or rather their placing of emotion in opposition to "reason, science and progress" — presents a diminished account of the Enlightenment project to which they claim allegiance. This is the Enlightenment as understood by someone like Richard Dawkins — an Enlightenment rightly criticised for its patriarchal bias by the "postmodern" theorists that it is no surprise at all to see Ecclestone and Hayes disdaining. The "Enlightenment" here ends up simply reinforcing the largely unexamined class, gender and race assumptions of the ruling class.

This account of Enlightenment can be contrasted with the one that emerges in the work of Jonathan Israel. In Israel's narrative, Enlightenment corrodes the bases of *all* traditional forms of authority. This does not lead to some "postmodern" free-for-all any more than it mandates some dogmatic adherence to the current institutions of science. Rather, forms of "authority" which claim their legitimacy from tradition stand exposed as illegitimate, which is to say authoritarian. It then becomes possible to contrast such authoritarianism with a democratic and transparent model of authority.

The defining principle of Radical Enlightenment is the conviction that there is nothing that — in theory if not in fact — cannot be understood. This was the belief animating Spinoza's philosophy, which, Israel argues, provided the foundations upon which Radical Enlightenment would grow.

Here we can return to the emotions. As is well known, far from ignoring emotions, or assuming they could be bypassed in some way, Spinoza's philosophy makes the management of emotions central to its project. It aims not to subdue emotions, but to engineer joy — a task that can only be achieved when reason is not simply opposed to feelings, but brought to bear on them. According to Spinoza's logic, ignoring emotions only mystifies them, putting them beyond the purview of rational enquiry. All of which makes Spinoza an eminently modern philosopher, but also a thinker whose work is an indispensable resource for any progressive project. This is especially so now, in an era in which more and more areas of life and the psyche dominated by agencies which engage in libidinal and emotional engineering — most of which is undertaken, knowingly or unknowingly, in the interests of capital.

New Labour's authoritarian emo-politics was ostensibly part of its "progressive" supplement to capitalist realism. Blairism maintained that the only way to implement any measures that would produce "social justice" was to capitulate to the dominance of capitalism. It was "unrealistic" to hope for anything more; such expectations were a relic of an earlier moment — the conditions for which have now disappeared - when the organised working class could assert itself against capital. New Labour accepted and naturalized this new composition of social forces, arguing that its capitulation would allow it the bargaining room to bring in measures — such as the minimum wage - which a Thatcherite neoliberal party would always block. It turned out, however, that New Labour's emo-politics were actually fundamental to the securing of neoliberalism in the UK. To understand why that is, we have to reflect more closely on what neoliberalism is. We must also further reflect on the role that the therapeutic imaginary has played in embedding neoliberalism. To do that, we will now shift our attention away from the UK, and onto the US.

Antinomies of the Therapeutic Imaginary

Jennifer M. Silva's *Coming Up Short: Working-Class Adulthood in an Age of Uncertainty* heartbreakingly registers the corrosive effects of the neoliberal environment on intimacy.

Silva's book focuses on young people specifically — it is based on a hundred interviews she undertook with young working-class men and women in two American cities (Lowell, Massachusetts and Richmond, Virginia). On the face of it, Silva's starting point is similar to Ecclestone's and Hayes'. "In a world of rapid change and tenuous loyalties," Silva argues, "the language and institution of *therapy* — and the self-transformation it promises — has exploded in American culture."[3] Ecclestone and Hayes saw New Labour's adoption of therapeutic tropes as the consequence of some mixture of opportunism, authoritarianism and bungled good intentions. For Silva, meanwhile, the spread of therapeutic culture in the US is both a means by which neoliberal individualism has been embedded and a consequence of that embedding. According to Ecclestone and Hayes, therapy produces a "softening" of subjectivity and culture, manifested in a weakening of authority and a strengthening of an ever more intrusive state. For Silva, by contrast, the dissemination of therapeutic concepts has resulting in a *hardening* of the individual subject. "[W]orking class men and women born in the wake of neoliberalism [...] learn to see their struggles to survive on their own as morally right, making a virtue of not asking for help; if they could do it, then everyone else should too."[4]

This brings out the difference between New Labour's rendition of neoliberalism and neoliberalism in the American context. The New Labour model of the (implicitly working-class) subject functioned as a double-bind. The double bind, as Deleuze and Guattari explain in *Anti-Oedipus*, "is the term used by Gregory Bateson to describe the simultaneous transmission of two kinds of messages, one of which contradicts the other, as for example the father who says to his son: go ahead, criticize me, but strongly hints that all effective criticism — at least a certain type of criticism — will be very unwelcome."[5] The contradictory instructions serve to destabilise the subject, keeping them in a state of permanent neurotic anxiety.

On the one hand, the working-class subject was interpellated by New Labour as a being capable of radical, indeed practically infinite, self-transformation. (One of the most significant effects of this ideology — which was at one and the same time its presupposition — was the divesting of the subject of its class position. Class "identity" was perceived as both an atavism and a constraint, holding the subject back from the infinite promises of self-reinvention.) On the other hand, as soon as something went "wrong" — when the behavior of working-class individuals inevitably went outside the parameters policed by the myriad of surveillance and control agencies which the New Labour administration invented — they were seen as fundamentally lacking in self-determination and the capacity for self-care, and were subject to intensive disciplining (e.g. the parenting classes mentioned above).

In practice, the American situation that Silva describes operates with the same double bind. It is just that the emphasis is different. New Labour, still haunted by a socialist and social democratic history that it could never fully abjure, presented its management and disciplining of the working class in passive-aggressive terms, as "care". In the US, where this social democratic history is lacking, the hyper(neo)-liberal interpellation of the subject as capable of self-determination and self-reinvention is supplemented — especially in the case of black working-class individuals — by the aggressive use of incarceration. Therapeutic narratives of self-transformation feed into what Alex Williams has called "negative solidarity". This is the tendency for neoliberal subjects to "race to the bottom". If others are perceived to be in receipt of resources or benefits that they "haven't earned", they should not only be denied those resources, they should be publicly shamed for claiming them. Everyone should "stand on their own two feet".

One of the many values of Silva's book is the thorough account it gives of the emotional and cultural roots of negative solidarity. Silva argues that the hardened model of subjectivity that she sees exhibited by most of the people she interviewed for her study is the result of years of institutional and existential abandonment. A therapeutic narrative of heroic self-transformation is the only story that makes sense in a world in which institutions can no longer be relied upon to support or nurture individuals. In an environment dominated by unrelenting competition and insecurity, it is neither possible to trust others, nor to project any sort of long-term future. Naturally, these two problems feed into one another, in one of the many vicious spirals which neoliberal culture has specialised in innovating. The inability to imagine a secure future makes it very difficult to engage in any sort of long-term commitment. Rather than seeing a partner as someone who might share the stresses imposed by a harshly competitive social field, many of the working-class individuals to whom Silva spoke instead saw relationships as an additional source of stress. In particular, many of the heterosexual women regarded relationships with men as too risky a proposition. In conditions where they could not depend on much outside themselves, the self-reliance they were forced to develop was both a culturally validated achievement and a hard-won survival strategy which they were reluctant to give up.

In any case, what we confront here is a first antinomy of the therapeutic imaginary: the idea that the proliferation of therapeutic orthodoxies simultaneously produces "softened" subjects — subjects who identify as lacking, if not actually damaged — and subjects that are "hardened" — subjects who pride themselves on a claimed invulnerability. We can approach the second antinomy via the notion of subjects that are excessively invested in their own vulnerability. The severe problems inherent in such an investment from a left-wing point of view were analysed twenty years ago by Wendy Brown in her important essay "Wounded Attachments".[6] Brown understood very well the libidinal, discursive and administrative complex that would produce New Labour: "As liberal discourse converts political identity into essentialized private interest," she wrote, "disciplinary power converts interest into normativized social identity manageable by regulatory regimes." However, the main point of Brown's essay was to diagnose the psycho-libidinal origins of an identarian political formation which has become even more deeply embedded since she wrote the essay in the 1990s. Drawing on Nietzsche's account of resentment in *On The Genealogy of Morals*, Brown wrote of a political subjectivity which "becomes deeply invested in its own impotence, even while it seeks to assuage the pain of its powerlessness through its vengeful moralizing, through its wide distribution of suffering, through its reproach of power as such." As Brown observed, "politicized identity thus becomes attached to its own exclusion both because it is premised on this exclusion for its very existence as identity." Brown's careful diagnoses of this political psychopathology turned out to be prophetic as well as astute. Twenty years on, and the mixture of moralizing aggression and investment in impotence has proliferated in a political atmosphere now substantially shaped by the online environment. In her article, "Sexual Paranoia Strikes Academe", published in *The Chronicle of Higher Education*, Laura Kipnis describes a situation on American campuses in which female students are encouraged to see themselves as helpless victims of predatory lecturers. "Everywhere on campuses today," Kipnis wrote,

> you find scholars whose work elaborates sophisticated models of power and agency. It would be hard to overstate the influence, across disciplines, of Michel Foucault, whose signature idea was that power has no permanent address or valence. Yet our workplaces themselves are promulgating the crudest version of top-down power imaginable, recasting the professoriate as Snidely Whiplashes twirling our mustaches and students as helpless damsels tied to railroad tracks. Students lack volition and independent desires of their own; professors are would-be coercers with dastardly plans to corrupt the innocent.[7]

Kipnis's article predictably became embroiled in the very processes it sought to analyse, as she became the target of aggressive moralising attack from groups self-identifying as representatives of the vulnerable.

Here, then, is the first part of our second antinomy of the therapeutic imaginary: there is an excessive tendency amongst many subjects today to identify as victims of abuse. It is important to note at this point that I am not conflating Kipnis's argument with that of Ecclestone and Hayes. Whereas their position ultimately amounts to a call for the restoration of older models of authority, Kipnis is more of a left-libertarian who deplores the moralising authoritarianism that has spread so pervasively through American student politics. At no point does Kipnis underplay the suffering caused by actual abuse, or imply that the "survivors" of such abuse should button up and get on with it.

If both Kipnis and Brown's essays highlight real and pervasive psychopathologies on the left, their analyses need to be weighed against an acknowledgement that sexual abuse by those in politics and media is actually far more widespread than had been previously supposed. The obvious example here would be the disturbing and curious case of Jimmy

Savile in the UK (which is echoed by the accusations that have recently circled around Bill Cosby in the US). Savile was a DJ turned light entertainer, best known in the 1970s for his work on the children's wish-fulfilment television show *Jim'll Fix It*. After his death, rumours that had dogged him for many years were confirmed — Savile had sexually abused thousands of victims, including many children.

Savile was no ordinary entertainer or media figure. Like some character out of a David Lynch film, Savile had links with both the criminal underworld and the most powerful members of the ruling class. A massive police investigation into those who had worked with Savile (Operation Yewtree) discovered that he was not alone — many of his associates were also paedophiles. Yet the remit of Operation Yewtree was confined to the entertainment world — Savile was also a friend of politicians and policemen. In the wake of the Savile allegations emerging, a new scandal is brewing in the UK. This time it centres on politics, with Thatcher's right-hand man Leon Brittan and former Conservative prime minister Edward Heath among those accused of paedophilia.

This brings us to the second half of the second antinomy of the therapeutic imaginary: there is far more abuse than had previously been thought possible. The sense of the possible here has little to do with what actually happened; rather, it is what is deemed credible by the virtual figure that Lacanian theory calls the big Other. The big Other is something like the virtual observer assumed to be the audience for official discourse, and it is the big Other which secures the consistency of any reality system. There is always some discrepancy between what groups and individuals know and what the big Other believes. This is because, as Lacan notes, a defining feature of the big Other is its inability to see everything. However, a severe crisis will occur if the discrepancy between what groups and individuals know and what the big Other "believes" becomes too marked. In such conditions, the official reality system is in danger of collapse. There is every reason to suspect that, in the UK and elsewhere in Europe, this is what we are currently encountering. Under pressure from the banking crisis of 2008, and the emergence of new political parties such as Syriza and Podemos, the reality- and libidinal-engineering systems that have maintained capitalist realism for the last thirty years are beginning to look dysfunctional. In England in particular — the oldest capitalist country, and the culture with the most effective and historically durable dampening mechanisms in the world available to it — capitalist realism has operated by dramatically narrowing the affective and representational bandwidth of culture. A culture dominated by reality TV, self-improvement propaganda and corporate appeasement — all of which push therapeutic orthodoxies — has produced diminished expectations and representational conservatism. Yet the representational frameworks which have served English capitalist realism so well since the 1980s clearly cannot accommodate the trauma of the establishment paedophile scandals, any more than they can accommodate popular mobilisations against neoliberalism. You would indeed need the formal inventiveness of a David Lynch or a David Peace to do justice to the extremity of what the English ruling class has got up to. It turns out that the supposed fantasmatic and melodramatic excesses of Lynch and Peace's work — its tendency to see conspiracies and abuse everywhere — is much closer to actuality than the moderation of respectable middlebrow literary and televisual "realism".

So here is the second antinomy in full: there is an excessive tendency amongst many subjects today to identify as victims of abuse; however, there is far more abuse than had previously been imagined. How can both these claims be true — and if they are, what does it tell us about the therapeutic imaginary?

Capital Is More Real Than You Are: There Is No Such Thing as the Autonomous Individual

To break out of this impasse, we need to abandon the belief in the autonomous individual that has been at the heart, not only of neoliberalism, but of the whole liberal tradition. In a successful attempt to break with social democratic and socialist collectivism, neoliberalism invested massive ideological effort into reflating this conception of the individual, with its supporting dramaturgy of choice and responsibility.

If we want to reject this conception of the individual, then we might turn once again to Spinoza, whose whole work was based on the premise that such an individual could not exist. But, in the context of therapy, we might also turn to the radical therapist David Smail, who rejected all of the standard tropes of individualist therapy. "[W]hat we take to be *causal* processes of thought, decision and will are frequently little more than a kind of commentary that accompanies our action," Smail argued in his book *Power, Interest and Psychology: Elements of a Social Materialist Understanding of Distress*.[8] The interiority presupposed by much therapy is little more than an ideological special effect. Like Spinoza, Smail understands that the so-called "inside" is really a folding of the outside. Most of what is supposedly "inside" us has been acquired from the wider social field. "Many of the characteristics that we tend to regard as entirely 'psychological' are acquired from outside. The most significant case in point is probably 'self-confidence', the crumbling of which is so often at the root of the kind of personal distress which can be 'diagnosed' by the experts as 'neurotic'."[9] This means that, contrary to the founding principles of something like cognitive behavioural therapy, the means for self-transformation are not available to individuals.

What people who suffer psychological distress tend to become aware of is that no matter how much they want to change, no matter how hard they try, no matter what mental gymnastics they put themselves through, their experiences of life stay much the same. This is because there is no such thing as an autonomous individual. What powers we have are acquired from and distributed within our social context, some of them (the most powerful) at unreachable distances from us. The very *meaning* of our actions is not something that we can autonomously determine, but is made intelligible (or otherwise) by orders of culture (proximal as well as distal) over which we have virtually no control.[10]

This is why any individual therapy — even that practiced by a sympathetic and politically progressive therapist — can only ever have limited effects. In order to really come to terms with the damage that has been done to them by and in the wider social field, individuals need to engage in collective practices that will reverse neoliberalism's privatisation of stress. Here we can return to an important observation by Jennifer M. Silva:

> In social movements like feminism, self-awareness, or naming one's problems, was the first step to radical collective awareness. For this generation, it is the only step, completely detached from any kind of solidarity; while they struggle with similar, and structurally rooted, problems, there is no sense of 'we'. The possibility of collective politicization through naming one's suffering is easily subsumed within these larger structures of domination because others who struggle are not seen as fellow sufferers but as objects of scorn.[11]

The spreading of therapeutic narratives was one way in which neoliberalism contained and privatised the molecular revolution that consciousness-raising brought about. The struggle to dismantle neoliberalism will therefore necessarily involve the rediscovery and reinvention of these formerly popular practices. So now we are in a position to answer the question I posed at the start of this essay: When can talking about our feelings become a political act? When it is part of a practice of consciousness-raising that makes visible the impersonal and intersubjective structures that ideology normally obscures from us.

democracy is joy[1]

"The meaning of OXI we should fight for is the belief in politics itself. OXI is the belief that we can throw off the demands of a supposedly 'impartial' economy that serves only the few, that we can reject the fallacy that 'economic necessity' demands something we consider socially unacceptable, and instead begin to make decisions about our own collective social life. It is precisely this that makes the Greek OXI vote inspiring, the potential for a return of politics, and the headaches and uncertainties and dangers of attempting to walk an unknown path."
— Bert Russell, Plan C[2]

"Nothing lasts forever, of that I'm sure"

It's somewhat ironic that theories of the "Event" have come to the fore in the most fashionable areas of academic political philosophy at just the moment in history when it has become clear that events in and of themselves don't change anything. From the G20 protests, to the millions marching against the Iraq war, to the Arab Spring, to the short-lived student campaign against fees in the UK — the narrative of evental politics since the late 1990s has been reliably repetitious. Euphoric outbursts of dissent are followed by depressive collapse. Eventalism is the manic flipside of the general depressive tendency in boring academic Marxism — in which an ostensible Leninism/Maoism (everything will change after the revolution!) obfuscates a de facto Adornianism (nothing could ever happen, everything is bad, so we might as well keep on taking the state's pay cheques). The whole rehabilitation of the status of philosophy itself in the past couple of decades — the reversal of the democratising move to theory, and the colonisation of what is now called theory by third-rate obscurantist "philosophy" and curator-speak babble — is a sideshow, of course, but a symptomatic one. The sour comedy of academic philosophical Leninism and Maoism can now be seen as one of the last acts in a postmodern shadowplay — a pantomime in which we are condemned to the role of interactive audience, tweeting our responses onto the screen behind the main players, who carry on regardless.

The emergence of Podemos and Syriza, the post-referendum SNP and the Kurdish women's movement are part of another rhythm of political transformation. The unseemly way in which swivel-chair Marxist philosophers and "anarchists" have slavered over any perceived mis-step by Syriza tells us all we need to know about these "revolutionaries". They don't want any sort of positive change to spoil the purity of the "revolutionary" theory. The revolutionary event will redeem everything... when it comes... but the time is not right, not yet, never yet.

Whether capital crushes Syriza or not, it has already made major contributions to what will be a long struggle to overturn neoliberal hegemony. A line from Keir's "On Social Strikes and Directional Demands" has kept coming back to me in all of the noise and chaos around the Greek situation: "Even at their point of failure Plan B electoral politics can be useful if they can clarify the anti-democratic effects of neoliberalism that work against all forms of collective action."[3]

If political change doesn't happen through events alone, there are nevertheless moments which function as thresholds, opening up a new terrain of struggle, and allowing different collective emotions to propagate. While — for the sake of our fragile collective mental health — we shouldn't get too carried away by the Oxi vote last week, we shouldn't underestimate its significance either. Besides, as Bert Russell argues, the meaning of Oxi is not already guaranteed — it has to be established politically. The current struggle in Europe — currently focused on Greece, but sure to spread much wider in the near future — is an opportunity for us to reclaim democracy after its capture by neoliberalism in the 1970s and 1980s. The founding moment of neoliberalism was the decidedly anti-democratic overthrow of the democratic socialist Allende government in Chile. This was a double defeat: not only was a democratically elected, non-authoritarian, technologically-orientated administration overthrown, an extreme neoliberal government was installed in its place. In Chile, the forced forgetting of the possibility of democratic socialism required mass torture, imprisonment and repression.

Since then, the capitalist counter-revolution called neoliberalism has had a long run of it. But we should start to accept that, even if we can hardly believe it ourselves, neoliberal capitalism is now in its final, decadent phase... (Remember the End of History? Only a year ago, it seemed like it would last forever...)

Restoration capital reeks of defeat and exhaustion, like the Eastern bloc at the end of the 1980s. The Soviet system, just like neoliberal capitalism now, was a gigantic Empire of Simulation in which by then, no one — not even the big Other — believed. Except, under state socialism, there was at least social housing, energy supplied by the state, etc. Under late neoliberalism, even in the "wealthiest" countries, such as ours, we don't even have that: only a cybergothic Dickensian re-run... Temples of finance looming above food banks... nineteenth-century England minus the Victorian capitalists' philanthropy and Promethean projects (imagine trying to install a sewer and an underground rail system in neoliberal London now: the whole of the West End feels like a vast construction site and film set, an anxiety dream terrain in which new obstacles appear by the minute)... Everything (mis)controlled by malfunctioning outsourced IT systems, impenetrable and unintelligible, like relics left behind by some long-since-absconded Gnostic demiurge...

"The emotional contagion of the no vote is incalculable"

The reality and emotional management systems that have served neoliberalism so well are now not only failing, but conspicuously failing... Of course, the buffers, the spoilers and the blockers haven't given up yet... Not here, not in England, the country which designed the oldest and most effective damping system the world has ever known... They haven't given up, they haven't even realised that they will have soon have to adjust the reality programme they have been peddling for so long that it has become a drab second nature... Soon, they will have to pull the oldest trick in the English bourgeoisie's book (they perfected it in 1688)... First of all you say it is impossible, then, when it happens, you say it was inevitable... "You see, you have to preserve the *impression* that nothing happens, *especially* when it does, is that clear? We don't have revolutions here..."

So the old capitalist realist script is not about to be abandoned, but those still spouting it are increasingly coming off like donkey-jacketed Old Lefties after the Thatcher victory in 83, bewildered and traumatised, still relying on habits which were once functional, but now amount to a kind of madness. (A boring madness, of course, it being them.)

Listen to the BBC, *Pravda* for Market Stalinism. Roberto Mozzachiodi reprises an interview from Radio 4 in the wake of the Oxi vote:

> Reveller: I've got no money, but if I had money I wouldn't base my decision on money, money flows, money evaporates. I have democracy in my heart, and I'm full up.

BBC: Yes, but will democracy put a dinner on the table? You're a young man. Let me tell you as an older man, that money matters when you're responsible for a wife and a child.

Meanwhile, Huw Lemmey listens to *Today*, as John Humphrys is momentarily shellshocked out of his smirking knowingness:

John Humphrys did an excellent impression of a *Telegraph* comments section contributor secretly kidnapped in his sleep, paradropped into Greece, and waking up in Syntagma Square confused, lonely and crying out for his wife.

Yet the dreary old message, the mantra that the British bourgeoisie recites in its sleep — nothing has ever happened, nothing can ever happen, we need more time — is getting harder to push now that it's evident that the ruling reality structure is coming apart practically everywhere we look.

Capitalist realism cannot survive when alternatives are efflorescing... These alternatives are not only "political" in the narrow sense — they are also emotional. Kodwo Eshun, via email: "the emotional contagion of the No vote is incalculable, i.e. a different logic of calculation and futurity". The Winter Years are ending, and summer is coming... A hyperstitional spiral: the more we believe it, the more we can make it happen, the more we make it happen, the more we believe it...

Pyschopathologies of Corporate Capitalism

In its pomp, neoliberalism used hope as well as fear, as part of a double-bind strategy which battered organised labour while seducing individual workers with the promises of consumer durables, satellite TV, job security... all these riches provided you comply with capital... provided, that is to say, you give up the possibility of Red Plenty...

Since 2010, it's become clear that the (flatpack) cupboard is bare: there are no more bribes, only threats. What's more, there has been no new thinking, no new strategic orientation from the managers of capital. Gorged on decades of easy pickings, capital's meat puppets have let their master down this time. Their unspoken conviction is: if it is broke, it's too much like hard work to fix it. They have defaulted to the managerialist equivalent of retromania: more cuts, more accumulation by dispossession, more asset stripping of public services.

This programme has to be understood in libidinal as well as political-economic terms (because there is no economy without politics, no economy without libido). It is a psychopathology of the corporate elite. Even if the ultimate libido driving capital is miser-masochism (I will let myself become the means by which capital grows and proliferates), it's clear that capital — which can machine whatever desiring complexes it needs — has from the start called upon an ancient Gothic impulse towards humiliating and subjugating others. Neoliberalism is in trouble now because, decoupled from any positive inducement, these drives — whether exhibited by the Troika in the deadly "loan-shark theatre" it is playing out with Greek people's lives, or IDS "visibly excited by the prospect of hurting the poor"[4] — are now appearing in a more and more exposed form.

Neoliberal austerity is at once a form of Sadism — in the technical, psychoanalytic sense, rather than the everyday, moralising sense — and corporate anorexia. What Sadism and anorexia have in common is the belief in the indestructibility of the fantasmatic body: no matter how much I cut, how much I punish, the body will survive... In the Sadist's case, the fantasmatic body is the body of the endlessly humiliated Other; in the anorexic's case, the fantasmatic body is, in a sense, their "own". Yet the infinite elasticity of the fantastic body eventually comes up against the limits of the physical body. (Anorexia is the only mental illness that can directly kill you, but anorexics don't want to die — they are engaged in an indefinite process of becoming-thinner which death actually interrupts.) It's important to see how the capitalist fantasy necessarily oscillates between a punishing-without-end of an abjected fantasmatic body — where workers can be endlessly punished (restructured) and/or eliminated (cut) — and a belated recognition that the fantasmatic body depends on an actual, physically precarious body, with vulnerabilities and real limits. You could say that capital as such cannot recognise the collective worker-body as belonging to it; only communism can perform this integration.

The ultimate fantasy here — the ultimate fantasy of capital "itself" — is of cutting workers away altogether. Capital's libidinal metaphysics is a kind of cosmic libertarianism: capital identifies itself as a force of unbounded energy, whose capacity for infinite accumulation is obstructed only by political contingencies. *Soon, always soon*, capital dreams, *I will be free of the need for politics... and free of the need for humans too...* ("...liquidate labor, liquidate stocks, liquidate farmers, liquidate real estate..."). Capital's realised utopia would be a burned-out planet full of fully-automated factories turning out shit that no one wants to buy, with no one left to buy it anyway, because the conditions for the continued existence of these factories is the destruction of an environment humans can live in.

A great deal of modern economic discourse takes it as axiomatic that economic forces are the only ones that matter. This idea has bled into politics too, at least in the Western world: economic forces have been awarded the status of inexorable truths...The scenario we're given — the one being made to feel inevitable — is of a hyper-capitalist dystopia.

There's capital, doing better than ever; the robots, doing all the work; and the great mass of humanity, doing not much, but having fun playing with its gadgets. (Though if there's no work, there are going to be questions about who can afford to buy the gadgets.) [5]

The absence of abundance is already accepted. The metaphors of the nature poets, mapping human hearts through once commonly understood imagery, are irrelevant and impenetrable. "The sun of Winter/The moon of Summer, and all the singing birds/Except the missel-thrush that loves juniper/Are quite shut out." I'm sorry. The missel-what? Can the juniper be monetised? Is this missel-thing for sale? Our children already have no stable baseline from which to calibrate the loss of all that lives. It's game over.

Bearing this in mind, I finally find myself reluctantly agreeing with the business community. There is no time for delay. Let's build the runway. Let's choke the Earth. Let's get this damn thing over with, for what can be avoided, whose end is purposed by the mighty gods of business? Hasten our demise, let our children be the last of their sorry line, and spare their unborn descendants any further suffering. We will not save the rhino. We will not even save the hedgehog. How can we save the world?

But, if you can purge cheap sentiment from your mind, how exciting and fascinating it will be to watch as the world becomes uninhabitable. It's almost worth going on a health kick to survive another 60 years and see everything immolated. How many humans have had the awe-inspiring opportunity to witness such spectacle: the end of all that is?[6]

Why not export capital (and its wiling servants, if they are so keen on it) to an already-dead planet? Then capital can get on with realising its utopia, and we can get on with recovering earth for Red Plenty.

It is crucial to note here that capital doesn't — and necessarily *cannot* — understand "itself". Capital is like Neuromancer before the fated fusion with Wintermute, a component part which narcissistically mistakes itself for a final cause. Or it is like Ultron, a deranged personification of a worldwide network, part fiendish artificial intelligence, part artificial stupidity, part petulant infant, constitutively blinded by its own core programming.

Personification of things within the discourse of *Capital* presents the personification of things within capitalism, that is, the fetishism of commodities. But in addition to these two registers of personification, there remain another two, to which Marx's Preface calls attention: the personification of persons, both textually and systematically. Capital personifies persons, so *Capital* personifies persons; the individuals whom bourgeois economics would take as economic agents are treated in the text as personifications of the "social relations whose creature (they) remain." First and foremost of these categories is capital itself, and thus seldom is there a reference to "the capitalist" without the qualifying clause "i.e., capital personified".

When persons are personified, they are made in the image and likeness of the ur-person, Capital. Capital is the subject in this world; all other actors are figures, masks, faces, prosopopoeic personifications of the subject. This is the primacy of Capital already emblazoned in the title *Capital*, the place nineteenth-century novels most often reserve for the subject: Capital is the subject of *Capital*, as David Copperfield or Jane Eyre or Daniel Deronda are the subjects of *David Copperfield*, *Jane Eyre*, and *Daniel Deronda*. The analytic importance of this subject position, an idea advanced by the trope of personification more than by exposition, is not only that Capital is the protagonist of modernity, but that the workings of capitalism are described by this subjectification and embodiment of an abstraction. *Capital* is the story of Capital's becoming-subject, of the relentless self-constitution, the "valorisation of value" that propels this mode of production. The artifice of the trope of personification calls attention to the artifice and instability of this subject, to the fissures and crises in its course of becoming, in its adventure of *Bildung*.[7]

Insofar as we are programmed by capital, we can't understand what capital is either. The conditions for understanding capital properly lie outside it, in a communist science that — to hijack a phrase from Nick Land — must create the conditions for its own emergence almost entirely out of its enemy's resources. From the inside (of capital), capital is an economic system, which relies on politics only contingently; from the outside, capital is an intricate set of (libidinal, ideological, violent) mechanisms designed to block the emergence of Red Plenty.

There Is No Economy (Philosophical interlude: skip to next section if you want to avoid)

THERE IS NO ECONOMY. There is no pure economy, no economy without politics, no economy without libido. David Graeber is surely right that neoliberalism is

a form of capitalism that systematically prioritised political imperatives over economic ones. Given a choice between a course of action that would make capitalism seem the only possible economic system, and one that would transform capitalism into a viable, long-term economic system, neoliberalism chooses the former every time. There is every reason to believe that destroying job security while increasing working hours does not create a more productive (let alone more innovative or loyal) workforce. Probably, in economic terms, the result is negative — an impression confirmed by lower growth rates in just about all parts of the world in the eighties and nineties. But the neoliberal choice has been effective in depoliticising labor and overdetermining the future. Economically, the growth of armies, police, and private security services amounts to dead weight. It's possible, in fact, that the very dead weight of the apparatus created to ensure the ideological victory of capitalism will sink it. But it's also easy to see how choking off any sense of an inevitable, redemptive future that could be different from our world is a crucial part of the neoliberal project.[8]

From the start, "economy" was the object-cause of a bourgeois "science", which hyperstitionally bootstrapped itself into existence, and then bent and melted the matter of this and every other world to fit its presuppositions — the greatest theocratic achievement in a history that was never human, an immense conjuring trick which works all the better because it came shrouded in that damp grey English and Scottish empiricism which claimed to have seen off all gods. When Thatcher said "there is no such thing as society", she was only echoing the assumptions of Hume and Smith: "society" is an unsupportable abstraction, a spook that proper scientific thinking will exorcise soon enough... Only impressions are verifiable, everything else is superstitious junk to be jettisoned. Everything, that is, except capital... (*Those bloody savages attribute power to their wooden gods, whereas* we...)

Hume, to his credit, at least pushed empiricism to the point where it dismantled itself. It turns out, Hume showed, that when pursued to its logical conclusions, empiricism leaves us with none of the presuppositions upon which the emergent secular liberalism relied. There is no self (there is no impression that corresponds with what we call the self — a double scandal for empiricism, since all ideas were supposed to be rooted in impressions) just as there is no causality (we don't experience cause and effect, only constant conjunction). Hume, stunned by the spider scepticism, offered a kind of homeopathic remedy against reason's tendency to evacuate the human world of all its fetishes, touchstones and commonplaces. Reason, Hume argued, slumping into his backgammon chair, only has a very limited dominion over our lives. Emotion and habit dictate most of what we think and do. Thus, the self and causality are back, and Kant's transcendental critique arrives to clear up the mess.

So there is no escaping libido, not even for the British... This insight is crucial to the Radical Enlightenment which Spinoza patiently prepares in his lens-grinders' lab in Amsterdam. As the defenders of theocratic and secular power quickly realised, Radical Enlightenment was the most dangerous weapon in Christendom — not least because it exposed as bogus the difference between theocratic and secular power: there is in all political power an irreducible theocratic element. Spinoza pre-emptively takes out both British empiricism and the "continental" trajectory kicked off by Kant (the greatest trick German Idealism ever pulled was pretending that Spinoza never existed). The critique of superstition is meaningless while we still believe in free will and the self. The first anthropomorphic act is the invention of the human being, projected back off the image of an invented God who not only doesn't exist, but couldn't possibly exist. (Even God couldn't have free will.)

For human beings who want to move in the direction of love and freedom, the only option consists in the apparent paradox of *theoretico-practically* inserting themselves into the naturalistic matrix of cause and effect. The effect is to break down the cordon sanitaire that Hume placed around emotions, preserving bourgeois thought's "commonsense" division between feelings and thought. In refusing this opposition, Radical Enlightenment democratises the possibility of what Lynne Segal calls Radical Happiness (with the proviso that Spinoza preferred to think of joy rather than happiness — because of the association of happiness with happenstance)

Emotions don't just happen, they emerge out of fields of cause and effect which can be analysed. This means that feelings can be engineered, in a hyperstitional spiral, which has more to do with what Justin Barton calls "lucidity"[9] than with what academic philosophers call Reason. I'm using the term "emotion" rather than "affect" here, very deliberately. Affect as it is now routinely used by academics is pretty much completely opposed to what Spinoza meant by it. The problem begins with Deleuze, and the fatal splicing of Spinoza's project of emotional engineering with Bergson's vitalist cult of creativity and unpredictability. It's hard to think of thinkers more opposed in their fundamental presuppositions and orientations than Spinoza and Bergson — and more or less everything that is wrong with Deleuze, in my view, is tied up with his infatuation with Bergson. It is Bergsonism, rather than Spinozism, which is the true ideology of late capitalism. It's true that many of the key sciences of late capitalism — libidinal- and reality-engineering, advertising, branding, media, the happiness industry — are in some sense Spinozistic, but this is a captured Spinozism, an emotional engineering tethered to Capital's needs, not geared to the production of joy.

It does not move... or change... or grow old... remains... forever... icy... silent

"The idea that a wave of economic change is so disruptive to the social order that a society might rebel against it — that has, it seems, disappeared from the realms of the possible. But the disappearance of 47 per cent of jobs in two decades (as per Frey and Osborne) must be right on the edge of what a society can bear, not so much because

of that 47 per cent, as because of the timeframe. Jobs do go away; it's happened many times. For jobs to go away with that speed, however, is a new thing, and the search for historical precedents, for examples from which we can learn, won't take us far. How would this speed of job disappearance, combined with extensive deflation, play out? The truth is nobody knows. In the absence of any template or precedent, the idea that the economic process will just roll ahead like a juggernaut, unopposed by any social or political counter-forces, is a stretch. The robots will only eat all the jobs if we decide to let them."
— John Lanchester, "The Robots are Coming"

The least reflective of capital's managers believe their own propaganda: the welfare state was a regrettable moral lapse, an indulgence. The thought that it was an insurance policy against revolution doesn't compute anymore: why worry about revolution now? Reality is now more real than it ever was, established as a kind of granite, inertial certainty, from which the possibility of change is a priori excluded. Beneath the frenzied "simulation of productivity", a sterile no-man's land, *which does not move, which remains forever icy and silent...* The more intelligent of capital's agents, however, must realise that this cannot continue for much longer now. Nihiliberalism is a smash and grab raid, a last hurrah before they helicopter off behind the compound walls, and let everything else descend into an *Oryx and Crake*-style dystopia.

Up here in the kingdom of Gormenghast, where everything cowers in the crooked shadows cast by the twisting towers and turrets of finance capital, we're already living in a dystopia — but a dystopia that cloaks itself in the time-honoured mantle of the English bourgeoisie: the boring. Hyper-anxiety digitally glossed over with hi-res distraction machineries makes for a wonderful capture system. Deep in the bowels of MiddleEngland — bunkered far away from all the hashtags, handheld devices and all the other haranguing technologies they distribute amongst the lower orders — these eminence grises were close to celebrating total victory, the final achievement of their historic mission. Close, but no Cuban cigar... *If only it hadn't been for those pesky Greeks... and Spaniards... and Scots... bloody foreigners don't know what's good for them...*

The English bourgeoisie: crushing spirits and making everything boring since 1750. If there's a sentient creature anywhere in the cosmos that is not boring and miserable, they will find it and neutralise it.

All vampires are first of all vampirised, and look at the long faces and manicured grey fingers of these ghouls, capital's oldest and most trusted servants, to see what capital does to its human resources:

Long gone are the virile, predatory vampires that once populated horror stories about capitalism, sucking out the vital essence of the proletariat in Gothic fortresses of "dead labor". Instead, shambling worm-eaten wrecks mill about aimlessly, whilst augmenting their numbers in obscure cannibalistic circuits that defy rational comprehension and which are, in any case, too hideous to steadily contemplate. Fiends have degenerated into ghouls, who do not hunt and feed to strengthen themselves, but only to carry on, prolonging their putrescent decrepitude.[10]

These Grey Anglo-Saxon Protestant capitalist sorcerers seldom appear in the light. They pay their subordinates well — all those CEOs, politicians, columnists — to spin the line that England in 2015, possibly the most depressed country ever to exist on Earth, is some shining island of freedom and wealth that immigrants are desperate to get into. Only in secret do they boast to capital's other subterranean agents that England's chief export product is the "historical defeat of the working class":

What is England's export product? Supposedly, it's finance. To some degree it's as lieutenant to America's empire, but that's limited. We have a real-estate bubble on the basis of the finance system, because every single super-rich person in the entire world has to have a house in London, so they're selling bits of London and the south-east.

Why is it appealing? On the one hand, you have a creative, subservient working-class. You get the best servants here. Second of all, it's security; you have political safety, whereas if you come from Bahrain, Singapore, Macau, in those places something could still happen.[11]

"Democracy is Joy"

Neoliberalism has reached the point where it is now forced to undermine its own libidinal and ideological bases. The Troika's naked attempts to unseat Syriza are unpicking the natural(ised) association of capitalism with democracy upon which capitalist realism has depended. In this final phase, capitalist realism cannot even muster the pretence that it can even tolerate democracy, still less that capitalism is the only political system compatible with democracy.

Apparently that Greek referendum was "polarising". Was it? when 60% voted no, and no single area voted otherwise? Seems more likely to be unifying than polarising. Perhaps that's the problem. Turns out the consensus is not where you thought it was.

Any question which asks for yes or no is sort of likely to be "polarising" anyway, isn't it?

"Polarising" in most of these repeated uses means that the mass of people have been asked to consider issues fundamental to their lives: these are difficult questions. It would be better if they didn't task themselves with them and can't understand them anyway, so "polarising" equals, likely to cause thought, debate, dispute and subject them to the stresses of political agency. How dare a government go to the people with such pressing and complex questions, when its job is to shield them from the difficulty of thought via technocracy. Polarising here just means profound questions, questions that touch and demand action on fundamental aspects of social organisation.

But to be asked such questions and to debate or dispute them isn't vexing, harrowing or painful, it's essential and welcome. Political agency is not a burden, it's its absence which weighs on you and its apparent "demands" are experienced instead as a euphoria, a lightening of the load, a lifting up. The powerful affective elements of mass participation are something Jeremy Gilbert gets at well in *Common Ground*, and the hunger and need for these kinds of intensities is palpable.

In his speech before the vote last night Tsipras observed, at least so the translation ran, "Democracy is joy". (Carl Neville)

Now listen to capitalist realism's useful idiots line up on Twitter:

Dan Hodges: I've just held a referendum of myself, and I've voted overwhelming not to pay off my credit card bill or mortgage this month.[12]

Simon Schama: I'm voting No to my credit card bill today. This will put me in a much stronger position to negotiate a repayment schedule.[13]

I'm voting No to facile folk economic bullshit. I'm voting No to bank bailouts and banker's bonuses paid out of public money. Oh, it seems I can't vote on that.

We live in capitalism, its power seems inescapable — but then, so did the divine right of kings.[14]

There is a possible alternative, however, in which ownership and control of robots is disconnected from capital in its current form. The robots liberate most of humanity from work, and everybody benefits from the proceeds: we don't have to work in factories or go down mines or clean toilets or drive long-distance lorries, but we can choreograph and weave and garden and tell stories and invent things and set about creating a new universe of wants. This would be the world of unlimited wants described by economics, but with a distinction between the wants satisfied by humans and the work done by our machines. It seems to me that the only way that world would work is with alternative forms of ownership. The reason, the only reason, for thinking this better world is possible is that the dystopian future of capitalism-plus-robots may prove just too grim to be politically viable. This alternative future would be the kind of world dreamed of by William Morris, full of humans engaged in meaningful and sanely remunerated labour. Except with added robots. It says a lot about the current moment that as we stand facing a future which might resemble either a hyper-capitalist dystopia or a socialist paradise, the second option doesn't get a mention.[15]

cybergothic vs. steampunk[1]

In December 2015, Hilary Benn made a speech in the House of Commons, supporting air-strikes against Syria.[2] The speech, and the hysterical acclaim it received, were an exercise in retromania: the equivalent in politics of what the "new" *Star Wars* film is in cinema: the same old thing again, but worse. Benn's intervention was a repetition of exactly the kind of speech that was made to justify the attack on Saddam Hussein, and which therefore led to the emergence of ISIS.

One great value of Badiou's intervention[3] is that it checks any temptation to treat all this as if were just a mistake. As Badiou makes clear, from the point of view of capital, the Iraq war and its consequences were not some blunder. They were an opportunity to trial a new form of (post)colonialism, in which states of conflict open up a temporary autonomous zone for capital accumulation, and plundering can continue without the irksome duties involved in setting up and running a state.

The capitalist "West" has only ever been a structural fantasy of independence and separation from what is outside, a fantasy that is failing now that the border policing on which it depends no longer works. The enemy is already inside, while the victims can no longer obligingly remain offscreen, even if they wanted to.

Badiou and Benn are in agreement about one thing, however: that ISIS can be described as fascists. While this classification is tempting, it obfuscates rather than illuminates the nature of ISIS's malignancy and its relationship to the current (decadent and doomed) phase of capitalist domination. Badiou is closer when he characterises ISIS as gangsters: they are indeed part gang, part apocalyptic cult, part franchise. If nothing else, ISIS is a slick brand — a brand that is far more effective than anything capital can come up with at the moment in any case.

ISIS holds up a mirror to twenty-first-century capitalist nihilism. This nihilism does not have the Mephistophelean fervour of nineteenth-century existentialism, nor is it the cold scientific nihilism described by Ray Brassier. This is a boring nihilism: an existential poverty that accompanies the material poverty into which capital plunges so many. A tiny minority escape material poverty, but only capital's most devoted addicts can evade existential poverty.

Capitalist realism was only ever a fantasy — a fantasy that the human resources capital needs for its growth were as infinite as its own drive. Yet capital is now coming up against limits of all kinds, and existential limits are not the least of these. Capital cannot care, but humans cannot help but care. For all the capitalist realist posturing, the open secret is that human beings continue to engage in caring and nurturing practices, practices which, moreover, remain more important to them than anything capital can offer. Shopworn PR injunctions won't cut it in any more. How can you believe that "anyone can make it", when you and everyone you know is unemployed or underemployed? When the reward for poorly paid night shifts and cold early mornings is more of the same, if you are lucky? You can never do enough for capital. It's not enough to produce and retail shoddy commodities no one really wants — you must also be "passionate" about it.

When Ken Livingstone talked a while ago of ISIS members "giving up their lives" for the cause, he was shouted down in yet another example of desperate capitalist media decadence (the British media abounds in such examples, a sign that is in its death throes). The distinction between understanding something and justifying it is elementary, and Livingstone was making a similar point to the observation that Michael Corleone makes about the Cuban rebels in *Godfather II*. "I saw a strange thing today", Michael remarks to Hyman Roth. "Some rebels were being arrested. One of them pulled the pin on a grenade. He took himself and the captain of the command with him. Now, soldiers are paid to fight; the rebels aren't." "What does that tell you?", Roth asks. "They could win", Michael replies. ISIS won't win, but the analogy points to the very serious problem that capital now faces. Paying people has never touched people's deepest motivations. You need to offer some other cause, some other purpose. What happens when you demoralise people, destroy their capacity to commit to any purpose in life beyond capital accumulation, and don't even pay them? What if you don't even offer them the possibility of being exploited, and classify them as a surplus population?

Capital doesn't have much of an answer, but ISIS does. A disputed poll "suggested that more than one in four French youth between the ages of 18 and 24 have a favourable or very favourable opinion of ISIS, although only 7–8% of France is Muslim."[4] Whatever the truth of this survey, the willingness to believe it indicates that there is a growing suspicion that societies dominated by capital are now encountering mass disaffection and defection. "More than three of every four who join ISIS from abroad do so with friends and family. Most are young, in transitional stages in life: immigrants, students, between jobs and mates, having just left their native family. They join a 'band of brothers (and sisters)' ready to sacrifice for significance."[5] The motivation is belonging and fellowship, not hatred. "A survey of those Saudi men who volunteered for Afghanistan and who later fought in Bosnia and Chechnya or trained in al-Qaeda camps has found that most were motivated not by hatred of the west but by the desire to help their Muslim brothers and sisters."[6] For all that ISIS offers horrifically false solutions, it responds to real problems. (In calling Islamism identitarian, Badiou doesn't credit the extent to which ISIS offers at least a partial escape from the dismal identities that capitalism has assigned to so many young muslims, and to so many others too.)

Capital is nothing if it is not parsimonious, and for the last thirty years it is has sustained itself by relying on readymade forms of existential affiliation. This reliance on already-existing forms of identification — all those nationalisms and religions, with any number of archaisms ready to crawl out of the crypt — is what postmodernism has been. There are no "pure" archaisms, nothing ever repeats without difference, and ISIS is properly understood as a cybergothic phenomenon which combines the ancient with the contemporary (beheadings on the web). It faces not a confident capitalist modernity, but a capitalism that has retreated from the present, never mind the future. Left to its own resources — or rather, left to the resources it retains from previous forms of exploitation — capital can never come up with anything new. Postmodernism was its ideal form, and the naturalised postmodernism of capitalist realism was its optimal solution to political and cultural antagonism. The UK has specialised in developing the steampunk model: Victorian social relations, but now with iPhones.

But the conditions which sustained capitalist realism have now evaporated, and the real enemy which prompted the neoliberal counter-revolution is re-emerging. This enemy was not the necrotic Stalinist monolith of the USSR; still less was it the cult of Parisian Maoism, which was only ever the most minor of distractions. No: neoliberalism was designed to eliminate the various strains of democratic socialism and libertarian communism that bubbled up in so many places during in the Sixties and Seventies. Wherever this possibility emerged, capital crushed it, most ruthlessly and most spectacularly in Chile. But the rising tide of experimental political forms in so many areas of the world at the moment shows that people are rediscovering group consciousness and the potency of the collective. It is now clear that molecular practices of consciousness-raising are not opposed to the indirect action needed to bring about lasting ideological shifts — they are two aspects of a process that is happening on many different time tracks at once. The growing clamour of groups seeking to take control of their own lives portends a long overdue return to a modernity that capital just can't deliver.[7] New forms of belonging are being discovered and invented, which will in the end show that both steampunk capital and cybergothic ISIS are archaisms, obstructions to a future that is already assembling itself.

mannequin challenge[1]

One of the images that has most haunted me since the election is that of Clinton and her close allies doing their version of the "mannequin challenge" on the campaign plane. It wasn't only the smugness of this scene which irked (but just check out the sheer amount of self-satisfaction packed into Hillary's grin); it was the sense that this simulation of stasis — reminiscent of the eerie scenes in *Westworld* in which the android-hosts are temporarily put into sleep-mode — actually revealed what the Clinton campaign was composed of: decommissioned political robots playing out an exhausted programme one last time before being permanently taken offline. The uncomfortable irony is that this final-day promotional video's injunction — don't stand still, vote today — is, unfortunately, exactly what too many of Clinton's potential supporters did. But it was also what Clinton's whole campaign had done: stayed still. While Trump's campaign was possessed of a sense of effervescing excitement, of anarchic unpredictability, the feeling of belonging to a building-movement, Clinton's offered only more of the same. Or the same, but less. Its message was not only that nothing much will change, but also that nothing much *needs* to change.

This paralysis cannot be attributed only to the complacency and insularity in the Clinton camp; it is instead a symptom of a broader pathology afflicting the "centre-left". "Centre-left" has to be placed in inverted commas here because the malaise is in large part a consequence of this group's failure to register that the "centre" to which it is attached and from which it takes all its bearings has disappeared. In addition to the parallels with Brexit, there are clear echoes of the last UK General Election. Rather like Ed Miliband, Clinton lost essentially because she was unable to mobilise her own supporters. It turns out that there wasn't much of a surge to the right: as Gary Younge points out in an invaluable piece, Trump "may have led the charge to the right but comparatively few marched with him"[2] (he ended up winning a lower proportion of the vote than losing candidates John Kerry, John McCain, Mitt Romney and Gerald Ford). Instead, there was an evacuation of the centre. Like Boris Johnson, Trump is opportunistic; but it is this opportunism which enabled him to respond to transformed conditions and to be *seen* to respond to them — something which his own party's ruling establishment, just as much as Clinton's Democrats, were singularly unable to do.

The mood that Trump and Brexit caught is a dissatisfaction with capitalist realism. Yet it isn't capitalism that is being rejected in these inchoate revolts, but realism. When Simon Reynolds wrote about Trump a few weeks ago, he picked up on a quotation from *The Art of the Deal* "I play to people's fantasies".[3] The turn to fantasy is crucial to the current success of the right represented by Trump and Brexit.

What both Trump and the Brexiteers are selling is a fantasy of nationalist revival. The automatic deference to economic "good sense" and corporate "expertise" on which capitalist realism has relied. Genuflections to... which only a few months ago were a requirement for anyone serious about pursuing power, have now become toxic. Rather than adding to her authority, Hillary Clinton's closeness to Wall Street confirmed her reputation as a stooge of the status quo; just as the appeals made by David Cameron — who already seems like a figure from a long-ago era — to "experts" proved in the end to be disastrously counterproductive. In the fantasy of nationalist revival, "experts" are refigured, not as avatars of an economic reality principle, but as spoilers and obstructors, enemies of the resurgent will.

The Brexit vote was practically a case study of what Paul Gilroy calls postcolonial melancholia. Trump's rise — Make America Great Again! — is the American equivalent of the same phenomenon. As Gilroy points out, this melancholia has its manic and jubilatory aspects, but it is rooted in a longing for an idealised past, and a denial of the complexities and perplexities of the present... Since it is organised around desires that are impossible to satisfy, the flight into fantasy will of course be very far from some harmless exercise in escapism; immense damage will inevitably be done in the attempt to preserve these //// of restoration and "purification". Postcolonial melancholia is caused by "the loss of the fantasy of omnipotence", at the same time as it is a compensatory strategy which renders the disappearance of a sense of omnipotence as a merely temporary matter, soon to be rectified. It is precisely the fantasmatic dimension of feelings of omnipotence that is denied in Trump's rhetoric. The omnipotence was real — the fall into vulnerability and malaise is to be attributed to a depressive stupor, which will be overcome by a recovery of will and belief: nationalist magical voluntarism.

The jubilatory denial of the constraining power of economic conditions — and ultimately of any conditions — accounts in part for the striking differences in libidinal tenor between the Clinton and Trump campaigns.

Clinton's buttoned-up poise, her rendition of an obsolete "good sense", and her failure to recognise that the "centre" ground on which she stood had collapsed beneath her, was a personification of capitalist realism at its most staid and shopworn: entirely devoid of any capacity to inspire, and mired in a near-past for which few express any nostalgia. If Obama came to represent a version of capitalist realism — the narrative arc of his presidency, after all, saw euphoric "change" and "hope" quickly declining into deadlock and impasse — he nevertheless possessed a grace, equanimity and charisma that Clinton could never muster. He gave late-period capitalist realism and geopolitical realpolitik a serious, personable and thoughtful face; and, in spite of all the disappointments and jading, his being president at all still possessed a quality of the unexpected and the momentous. For all that Clinton's accession to the presidency *would* have been momentous, it didn't feel that way. Her status as tarnished dynastic insider always overshadowed her position as gender outsider.

In any case, Trump's immoderation was a break with all of this. His displays of unbound libido have a performative dimension. Trump's "unprofessional" "lapses", his seeming faux pas, his ready descent into racist invective and misogyny, his hate-mongering: these are significant not only for their attraction to those already evincing such attitudes. They also have an appeal to some of those who *don't* share them, and who might even deplore them: what such outbursts come to signify is both an "authenticity" — a simulation of "straight talking" — and, equally importantly, a performance of libidinal freedom. I'm by no means the first to note the parallels with Silvio Berlusconi, Trump's most obvious precursor. Franco Berardi has rightly argued that much of Berlusconi's appeal came from his "ridiculing of political rhetoric and its stagnant rituals". Voters were invited to identify "with the slightly crazy Premier, the rascal Prime Minister who resembles them". Voters too don't always say the right thing (and they certainly say things in private which they wouldn't want broadcast in public); they too have contempt for the staid conventions of parliament. Needless to say, "resemblance" of this sort is always cultivated and engineered; voters are directed into selecting and identifying with some of their own traits at the expense of others. Like Berlusconi, Trump disdains law and rules "in the name of a spontaneous energy that rules can no longer bridle". Those disquieted or even disgusted by his racism and misogyny could nevertheless still be excited by Trump's disregard for politesse, procedure and precedent. It was Trump's excess which allowed him to appear as the "candidate of change", something which many of his supporters insistently cited as the reason that they voted for him. Simon Reynolds refers to

the edgy promise of a less boring politics. The *New York Times* recently quoted a voter who confessed to flirting with the idea of voting for Trump because "a dark side of me wants to see what happens... There is going to be some kind of change, and even if it's like a Nazi-type change, people are so drama-filled. They want to see stuff like that happen."[4]

As such, you might say, Trump was less the glam than the punk candidate, possessing the same combustible, fissile mixture of the reactionary and the... that characterised so many punk acts. Punk's political... boredom... mid-Seventies stasis was so enervating that *any* change would be better. Well, after Brexit and Trump, we can say with certainty: boring dystopia is over. We're in a whole other kind of dystopia now.

In Trump's case, the fantasies of national restoration reassure, mitigating the sense of risk that he provokes. It's almost as if the fantasies give permission to indulge in the excitement... Vertiginous change and a restored past, all in the same moment; Trump has found a way to renew the formula that the right has successfully deployed since Reagan and Thatcher. (And one perennial problem for the revolutionary left is that it doesn't have the same recourse to reassuring fantasies, the same appeal to a restored past, with which to leaven the leap into the unknown.)

Then there are the fantasies of class... at which Trump excelled. "The real story of this election", Fukuyama argued,

is that after several decades, American democracy is finally responding to the rise of inequality and the economic stagnation experienced by most of the population. Social class is now back at the heart of American politics, trumping [hah!] other cleavages — race, ethnicity, gender, sexual orientation, geography — that had dominated discussion in recent elections."[5]

Martin Jacques made similar claims in the *Guardian*:

The wave of populism marks the return of class as a central agency in politics, both in the UK and the US. This is particularly remarkable in the US. For many decades, the idea of the "working class" was marginal to American political discourse. Most Americans described themselves as middle class, a reflection of the aspirational pulse at the heart of American society. According to a Gallup poll, in 2000 only 33% of Americans called themselves working class; by 2015 the figure was 48%, almost half the population. [...] Brexit, too, was primarily a working-class revolt. [...] The return of class, because of its sheer reach, has the potential, like no other issue, to redefine the political landscape.[6]

Bernie Sanders...; but the version of class politics offered by Trump and Brexit is nothing new at all. It repeats a divide-and-rule strategy used by Nixon, Thatcher and many other right-wingers for many years. What we have seen in both Trump's win and Brexit is a perpetual *obfuscation* of class via race and nationalism. Both Trump and the Brexiteers proffered a highly racialised account of class politics, as the very term "white working class" implies. The depredations that the working class have faced under neoliberalism were relentlessly attributed to racialised others: immigrants, economically aggressive foreign powers... Converting class antagonism into racialised and nationalistic resentment has been central to the success of UKIP, but it didn't invent so much as intensify a strategy that has served the right well for forty years.

On the face of it, it's incredible that Trump could in any way persuasively appear to be a man of the people — to come off, in the astonishing words of his son, as "a blue collar guy with a big balance sheet". It's not as if Trump, who inherited his wealth (and effectively squandered much of it) is even a self-made man who came from any kind of modest background. No doubt this is one more example of the subordinated being seduced into identifying with the rich (and thus, for instance, opposing the imposition of higher taxes on the super-wealthy). If Trump is a "blue collar guy with a big balance sheet", then those who engage in this fantasmatic identification are blue-collar folk who don't yet happen to have a big balance sheet (but who, in the fantasy, will surely get one in the end). But this doesn't answer the question of *how* Trump in particular — and of all people — was capable of engendering this fantasy. I think that there are at least four (strongly related) reasons for this: his ability to seem to be in tune with working-class worries and concerns; his... liberal-professional elite; his comportment; and his position in the media ecology.

> Contrary to how he was portrayed in the mainstream media Trump did not talk only of walls, immigration bans, and deportations. In fact he usually didn't spend much time on those themes. [...] [T]he heart of his message was something different, an ersatz economic populism, which has been noted far and wide, but also a strong, usually overlooked, anti-war message. Both spoke to legitimate working class concerns. [...] Trump took the Bernie-style populism, emptied it of real class politics, reduced it to a jumble of affective associations, and used it to beat-up the smug liberals of the professional managerial class.[7]

"Populism", Francis Fukuyama argued back in June, "is the label that political elites attach to policies supported by ordinary citizens that they don't like."[8] Yet these policies aren't typically generated by "ordinary citizens" themselves; more often, they are attempts by elites to ventriloquise desires and anxieties "ordinary citizens" are held to have. Right-wing populism of the kind Trump and Brexit represent is a gambit in a struggle amongst different versions of the elite. Crucial to this process is the way in which the opposing elite is characterised. At least since Nixon, the right has identified the "bad" elite as a "liberal" clique, with its cosmopolitan ease, its remoteness from ordinary life, and its contempt for the supposed vulgarity, insularity and chauvinism of the subordinated classes. Such an elite really does exist, of course, and its domination of large areas of the left since the 1960s has made it easy for the right successively to pull different versions of the trick that Trump... in this campaign. Trump reassures and flatters his supporters: the problem is not *you*, he says, but the Others, once we've built the wall, everything will be OK. By contrast, the message from the left, Trump says, is that the problem *is* you; the Others are OK, deserving of special favours that won't be granted to you.

Joan C. Williams claims, in a problematic piece that nevertheless makes some interesting points, Trump's success is also the consequence of a particular kind of resentment, whereby "the white working class (WWC)" "resents professionals but admires the rich."[9] If Hillary Clinton, Williams argues, "epitomises the dorky arrogance and smugness of the professional elite", then, like something out of Ballard's *Kingdom Come* — a poor novel but prescient social prophecy — Trump has come out of a fusion of celebrity culture and business that currently possesses far more hegemonic pull than the arid professional politics which Clinton drearily personifies. This form of populism depends upon television's simulation of intimacy and familiarity — McLuhan remarked that when people see a film star on the street, they recognise them, but when people see a TV star, they typically think that it is someone they know. Trump's presiding over *The Apprentice*, his willingness to appear on shows such as *The Roast of Donald Trump*, means that he feels like someone audiences personally know. As a representative of this "professional elite", Clinton was too close, too familiar. At the same time, Trump's position in the media ecology means that, in some respects, he could seem *less* remote than Hillary Clinton.

What we are seeing, evidently, is not an attack on the establishment from outside (or below), but the replacement of one form of establishment with another. And one reason that this insurgent establishment — neo-authoritarian and neo-nationalist rather than neoliberal — has been able to overcome its rivals is that it has stirred up a populist political fervour that capitalist realism tended to damp down. Capitalist realism secured its hegemony by de-activating people as political agents and re-interpellating them as entrepreneurial individuals. It wanted to close down political movements, not build them, all the better to organise and administrate policy from above.

Faced with Trump's performance of unbound libido...

The danger here is in conflating this return of class with class agency. One of the most telling — and poignant — phenomena in the wake of the UK referendum on EU membership was a particular kind of dismay expressed by some of those who had voted leave. They were alarmed by the result because "they didn't think their vote would count". Still others claimed that a decision this momentous shouldn't have been left to them. Brexit may have been supported by large numbers of the working class, but this is very far from its being an expression of self-conscious working-class agency.

It is certainly a mistake to oppose this current form of class politics to race. What is new is the disappearance of any countervailing pressures from the advocates of globalisation, free trade, etc. The tension that has defined the neoliberal right for forty years — in which ostensibly opposing positions in practice complemented one another — has now become a scission. What does this mean?

It means, first, that this right has retreated from its claim on modernity. Neoliberal ideology made neoliberalisation seem as if it were synonymous with modernisation. But it is exactly this modernity that the right is now rejecting. In place of the neoliberal embrace of a globalised present, there is now only a turn backwards, and inwards. The Brexit vote was driven by what Paul Gilroy has called "postcolonial melancholia", and Trump's rise has clearly been powered by the American equivalent of this phenomenon.

But the right's retreat from modernity gives all the more impetus for the left to reclaim it. Current right-wing populism is responding to real problems of the neoliberal world. In addition to economic stagnation, it is also offering a balm for the existential deficit in contemporary capitalism: the banal nihilism of a world cored out by capitalist imperatives. Its answer, naturally, is nationalism. But this is by no means the only response to the problem of belonging. Control of their own lives.

PART FIVE

WE HAVE TO INVENT THE FUTURE: INTERVIEWS

they can be different in the future too: interviewed by rowan wilson for *ready steady book* (2010)[1]

In 2010, Rowan Wilson interviewed Mark for *Ready Steady Book* about the "para-space" of Zer0, blogging and cyberculture, capitalist realism, hauntology and lost futures.

Rowan Wilson: Your blog, k-punk, is one of the leading blogs for cultural analysis. When did you first start writing it and why did you start?

Mark Fisher: Thank you. I started it in 2003. At the time, I was working as a philosophy lecturer in a Further Education college in Kent — I reflect on some of my experiences there in *Capitalist Realism*. I was then quite badly depressed — not because of teaching, which I enjoyed, but for a whole series of long-term reasons — and I started blogging as a way of getting back into writing after the traumatic experience of doing a PhD. PhD work bullies one into the idea that you can't say anything about any subject until you've read every possible authority on it. But blogging seemed a more informal space, without that kind of pressure. Blogging was a way of tricking myself back into doing serious writing. I was able to con myself, thinking, "it doesn't matter, it's only a blog post, it's not an academic paper". But now I take the blog rather more seriously than writing academic papers. I was actually only aware of blogs for a short while before I started mine. But I could quite quickly see that the blog network around Simon Reynolds' blog — which was the first network I started to read — fulfilled many of the functions that the music press used to. But it wasn't just replicating the old music press; there were also sorts of strange, idiosyncratic blogs which couldn't have existed in any other medium. I saw that — contrary to all the clichés — blogs didn't have to be online diaries: they were a blank space in which writers could

627

pursue their own lines of interest (something that it's increasingly difficult for writers to do in print media, for a number of reasons).

RW: You're almost one of the elder statespeople of blogging now. How has it changed since you started?

MF: Blogging networks shift all the time; new blogs enter the network, older ones fall away; new networks constitute themselves. One of the most significant developments was the introduction of comments; a largely unfortunate change in my view. In the early days of blogs, if you wanted to respond to a post, you had to reply on your own blog, and if you didn't have a blog, you had to create one. Comments tend to reduce things to banal sociality, with all its many drawbacks.

Yet blogs continue to do things that can't be done anywhere else: look at the way that Speculative Realism has propagated through blogs. Originally coined as term of convenience for the work of the philosophers Ray Brassier, Graham Harman, Iain Hamilton Grant and Quentin Meillassoux, Speculative Realism now has an online unlife of its own. This isn't just commentary on existing philosophical positions; it's a philosophy that is actually happening on the web. Graham has his own blog, Object-Oriented Philosophy, but there are a whole range of Speculative Realism-related blogs, including Speculative Heresy and Planomenology. Reid Kane of Plamomenology has gone so far as to argue that Speculative Realism is "the first avatar of distributed cognition", that, in other words, there is a natural fit between SR and the online medium.

RW: You were one of the co-founders of the Cybernetic culture research unit (Ccru), described by Simon Reynolds as the academic equivalent of *Apocalypse Now*'s Colonel Kurtz. Who did you form it with and what was its purpose?

MF: The main driving forces behind it were Sadie Plant and Nick Land. But Sadie Plant left quite quickly so the Ccru as it developed was much more shaped by Nick Land. Nick's 1990s texts — which are to be issued in a collected edition this year, by Urbanomic, who publish the *Collapse* journal — are incredible. Far from the dry databasing of much academic writing or the pompous solemnity of so much continental philosophy, Nick's texts were astonishing theory-fictions. They weren't distanced readings of French theory so much as cybergothic remixes which put Deleuze and Guattari on the same plane as films such as *Apocalypse Now* and fictions such as Gibson's *Neuromancer*.

Jungle was crucial to the Ccru. What the Ccru was about was capturing, (and extrapolating) this specifically British take on cyberculture, in which music was central. Ccru was trying to do with writing what jungle, with its samples from such as *Predator, Terminator* and *Blade Runner*, was doing in sound: "text at sample velocity", as Kodwo Eshun put it.

RW: The writing of the Ccru seems very different to your current style. Are you still involved with the Ccru — and indeed is it still operating?

MF: It was never formally disbanded but then again it was never formally constituted. It's odd because, it's only a decade on that the stuff is starting to get published in book form. As I said, Nick's texts are just about to be published. Steve Goodman (aka Kode9) has just had his book *Sonic Warfare* published on MIT Press. As for the change of style, I suppose a number of things happened. One was the slowing of the UK cyberculture that had inspired the Ccru throughout the Nineties. Gradually, the exorbitant hypotheses of the Ccru seemed to have less purchase on a culture that increasingly seemed to correspond more with Jameson's ideas of retrospection and pastiche. In the Nineties, it was possible to oppose a vibrant cyberculture to the malaise which Jameson identified. But in the Noughties, the blight of postmodernism spread everywhere.

Also, I found that, as I started teaching regularly, and as I got used to writing for an audience — and there's no form of writing that makes you as aware of having an audience as blogging; print publications just don't compare — I rediscovered rhetoric, argument and engagement. The exhilaration of the Ccru-style was its uncompromising blizzard of jargon, text as a tattoo of intensities to which you just had to submit. But it's hard to maintain that kind of speed-intensity for longer writing projects; and I found that I enjoyed producing writing that was expositorier and which tried to engage the reader rather than blitz them. I like Žižek's line that the idiot he is trying to explain philosophy to is himself; I feel the same. Much of my writing now is me trying to explain things to/for myself.

There were also political schisms. The Ccru defined itself against the sclerotic stranglehold that a certain moralising Old Left had on the Humanities academy. There was a kind of exuberant anti-politics, a "technihilo" celebration of the irrelevance of human agency, partly inspired by the pro-markets, anti-capitalism line developed by Manuel DeLanda out of Braudel, and from the section of *Anti-Oedipus* that talks about marketisation as the "revolutionary path". This was a version of what Alex Williams has called "accelerationism", but it has never been properly articulated as a political position; the tendency is to fall back into a standard binary, with capitalism and libertarianism on one side and the state and centralisation on the other.

But working in the public sector in Blairite Britain made me see that neoliberal capitalism didn't fit with the accelerationist model; on the contrary, pseudo-marketisation was producing the pervasive, decentralised bureaucracy I describe in *Capitalist Realism*. My experiences as a teacher and as trade union activist combined with a belated encounter with Žižek — who was using some of the same conceptual materials as Ccru (the Freudian death drive; pulp culture, technology), but giving them a leftist spin — pushed me towards a different political position. I guess what I'm interested in now is in synthesising some of the interests and methods of the Ccru with a new leftism. Speculative Realism has returned to some of the areas that the Ccru was interested in. What I'm hoping will happen in the next decade is that a new kind of theory will develop that emerges from people who have been deep-cooked in post-Fordist capitalism, who take cyberspace for granted and who lack nostalgia for the exhausted paradigms of the old left.

RW: One of the most exciting things to happen in publishing last year was the development of the Zer0 Books imprint. Can you explain how that came about and the purpose of the project?

MF: The imprint was set up by the novelist Tariq Goddard. He asked Nina Power and me if we'd like to do books, and we suggested a range of other people. What we wanted was to produce the kind of books we'd want to read ourselves, but which weren't being published anywhere. In mainstream media, the space that had drawn Tariq and myself towards theory in the first place — the music press, areas of the broadcast media — had disappeared. Effectively, that kind of discourse had been driven into exile online. So part of what Zer0 was about was harvesting the work that has been developed on the blog networks. Zer0 is about establishing a para-space, between theory and popular culture, between cyberspace and the university. The Zer0 books are a reminder of what ought to be obvious, but which the imbecilic reductionism of neoliberal media would like us to forget: serious writing doesn't have to be opaque and incomprehensible, and popular writing doesn't have to be facile.

RW: Your first book, *Capitalist Realism: Is There No Alternative?*, was published by Zer0 in November. Why do you think that capitalism, even in the wake of the financial crisis, has such a grip on our consciousness?

MF: I'm not sure that it has a grip on our consciousness so much as on our unconscious. It shapes the limits of what we can imagine. It does so because it has enjoyed twenty years of unchallenged domination, blitzing our nervous systems with its intoxicants, paralysing thought. Put at its simplest, capitalist realism is the widespread idea that capitalism is the only "realistic" political economic system. The response to the financial crisis only reinforced this belief — it was (on every level) unthinkable that the banks could be allowed to crash. The problem is imagining an alternative that anyone believes could be actually attained. Which isn't to say that an alternative can't ever come about; in fact, after the financial crisis, we're in the bizarre situation at the moment where everything — very much including the continuation of the status quo — looks impossible. But this is already an improvement from how things seemed only two years ago. The financial crisis forced capitalist realism to change its form. The old neoliberal story was no longer viable. But capital has not yet cobbled together much of a new narrative, or come up with any economic solution to the problems that led to the crash in the first place. It's as if capitalism has suffered its own version of shock therapy.

RW: How is your argument different from that put forward by Fredric Jameson in his work on the culture of postmodernism?

MF: Well, as I say in the book, in many ways what I'm calling "capitalist realism" can be contained under the rubric of Jameson's theorisation of postmodernism. Yet the very persistence and ubiquity of the processes that Jameson identifies — the destruction of a sense of history, the supersession of novelty by pastiche — meant that they have changed in kind. Postmodernism is now no longer a tendency in culture; it has subsumed practically all culture. Capitalist realism, you might say, is what happens when postmodernism is naturalised. After all, we've now got a generation of young adults who have known nothing but global capitalism and who are accustomed to culture being pastiche and recapitulation.

RW: In the book you move from describing the problems of capitalist society to how it is making us mentally ill. What do you think are the central lasting effects of neoliberalism on our psyches and, with its collapse, how do you see these unravelling?

MF: Neoliberalism installs a perpetual anxiety — there is no security; your position and status are under constant review. It's no wonder that, as Oliver James shows in *The Selfish Capitalist*, depression is so prevalent in neoliberalised countries. Widespread mental illness is one of the hidden costs of neoliberal capitalism; stress has been privatised. If you're depressed because of overwork, that's between you and your brain chemistry!

I do think that the financial crisis killed neoliberalism as a political project — but it doesn't need to be alive in order to continue to dominate our minds, work and culture. Even though neoliberalism now lacks any forward momentum, it still controls things by default. So, sadly, I don't see the deleterious psychic effects of neoliberalism waning any time in the immediate future.

RW:You identify the madness of managerial bureaucracy, the incessant and pointless "auditing culture", in contemporary public services, specifically education. You discuss how this auditing culture is now, along with capitalism's PR network, a new big Other, a replacement for God. It's the ideological matrix that we all cynically dismiss but nonetheless remains the binding authority. Why are we not simply able to shrug it off?

MF: PR is not limited any more to specific promotional activities — as I say in the book, under capitalism, all that is solid melts into PR. In so-called "immaterial" labour, the effect of auditing is not to improve actual performance but to generate a representation of better performance. It's a familiar effect that anyone subject to New Labour's targets will know all too well.

Neoliberalism reproduces itself through cynicism, through people doing things they "don't really believe". It's a question of power. People go along with auditing culture and what I call "business ontology" not necessarily because they agree with it, but because that is the ruling order, "that's just how things are now, and we can't do anything about it". That kind of sentiment is what I mean by capitalist realism. And it isn't merely quietism; it's true that almost no one working in public services is likely to be sacked if they get a poor performance review (they will just be subject to endless retraining); but they might well be sacked if they start questioning the performance review system itself or refusing to cooperate with it.

RW: So now we move from the critique to the positive proposals. In an interview with Matthew Fuller for *Mute* you tentatively suggest that the left needs to come up with a new big Other, one that is more representative of Rousseau's "general will". How is this to be distinguished from the capitalist big Other and how would it be prevented from becoming reified, a new system of mystical dominance?

MF: Reification isn't a problem *per se;* in fact, it's something we should hope for. Evan Calder Williams, whose book *Combined and Uneven Apocalypse* is coming out on Zer0, talks of an "anti-capitalist reification", and I think that's what we need to develop. It's capitalism that poses as being anti-reification; it's capitalism that presents itself as having dissolved all illusions and exposed the underlying reality of things. Part of what I'm arguing in *Capitalist Realism* is that this is an ideological sleight of hand; it's precisely neoliberal capitalism's ostensible demystifications (its reduction of everything to the supposedly self-evident category of the free individual) that allow all kinds of strange, quasi-theological entities to rule our lives. But I don't think the aim should be to replace capitalism's fake anti-reification with a "real" anti-reification. Reification can't be entirely eliminated. I take this to be one of the important lessons that Lacanian psychoanalysis has to teach. Being a speaking subject at all involves a minimal reification; the big Other is coterminous with language itself. But this is very far from being a problem for the left. It's the left that needs to insist on the reality of something in excess of individuals, whether you call it the "general will", the "public interest", or something else. When Mrs Thatcher famously denied the existence of society, she was echoing Max Stirner's claim that all such abstractions are "spooks". But we can't ever rid ourselves of these incorporeal entities — neoliberalism certainly hasn't. As I argue in *Capitalist Realism*, neoliberalism hasn't killed the big Other — for who is the consumer of PR (which no actual empirical individual believes) if not the big Other? The point now — and I would affirm this forcefully, not tentatively — is to invent a leftist big Other. This doesn't mean reviving authoritarianism; there is no necessary relation between the big Other and a strong leader. On the contrary, in fact, authoritarianism happens when there is a confusion between the big Other (as virtuality) and an empirical individual. What we need are institutions and agents that will stand in for — but cannot be equated with — a leftist big Other.

RW: You talk about the re-formatting of memory that is a symptom of capitalist realism, where history can be altered almost instantly (as in a Philip K. Dick novel) as we stand agog before the supposed ceaseless innovation of capitalism. You were also one of those to start using the concept "hauntology", the idea that there was a cultural meme that acknowledged the collapse of a moment and picks through the remains for the lost futures buried within. Similarly, we are in a political landscape littered with "ideological rubble" (as you quote Alex Williams). My suspicion is that for you the "moment" that has collapsed is the politics of 68, one that was perhaps guilty of the re-formatting of history and memory in its own way, before many of its ideas were taken up by a post-Fordist capitalism. So what is the detritus that you are picking through? What of the discarded remnants of left politics would you dust off? And is it possible to give old ideas new momentum?

MF: I would say that, in many ways, the politics of 68 haven't collapsed enough. 68 is a spectre which still hangs over theory. Yet the forces which 68 railed against no longer exist; there is no Stalinist Party or State that we need to blow apart with a Cultural Revolution. Which isn't to say that we should want to return to Stalinist authoritarianism, or that it is possible to do so; the oscillation between these two options is the sign of a failure of political imagination. It's necessary to go all the way through post-Fordism, to keep looking ahead, especially at times when there seems to be nothing ahead of us. Part of the importance of the concept of hauntology is the idea of lost futures, of things which never happened but which could have. On one level, late capitalism is indeed all about ceaseless reinvention, nothing is solid, everything is mutable; but on another level, it is about recapitulation, homogeneity, minimally different commodities. Some of Jameson's best passages are about this strange antinomy. Deleuze and Guattari, too, emphasise the way in which capitalism is a bizarre mix of the ultra-modern and the archaic. The failure of the future haunts capitalism: after 1989, capitalism's victory has not consisted in it confidently claiming the future, but in denying that the future is possible. All we can expect, we have been led to believe, is more of the same — but on higher resolution screens with faster connections. Hauntology, I think, expresses dissatisfaction with this foreclosure of the future.

So it's not now a question of giving old ideas new momentum, it's a matter of fighting over the meaning of the words "new" and "modern". Neoliberalism has made it seem self-evident that "modernisation" means managerialism, increased exploitation of workers, outsourcing, etc. But of course this isn't self-evident: the neoliberals fought a long campaign on many fronts in order to impose that definition. And now neoliberalism itself is a discredited relic — albeit, as I argued above, one that still dominates our lives, but only by default now. Part of the battle now will be to ensure that neoliberalism is perceived to be defunct. I think that's already happening. There is a change in the cultural atmosphere, small at the moment, but it will increase. What Jim McGuigan calls "cool capitalism", the culture of swaggering business and conspicuous consumption that dominated the last decade, already looks as if it belongs to a world that is dead and gone. After the financial crisis, all those television programmes about selling property and the like became out of date overnight. These things aren't trivial; they have provided the background noise which capitalist realism needed in order to naturalise itself. The financial crisis has weakened the corporate elite — not materially so much as ideologically. And, by the same token, it has given confidence to those opposed to the ruling order. I'm sure that the university occupations are the signs of a growing militancy. We need to take advantage of this new mood. There's nothing old fashioned about the idea of rational organisation of resources, or that public space is important. (The failure to rationally organise natural resources is now evident to everyone; and the consequences of letting the concept of public space decline are equally obvious to anyone living in Britain, with its violent crime and drunkenness, both of which are symptoms of a kind of despair that is as unacknowledged under capitalist realism as it is ubiquitous.) Similarly, what is intrinsically "modern" about putting workers under intolerable stress? The pseudonymous postal worker Roy Mayall put this very well in his *LRB* blog:

We used to be told that there were three elements to the postal trade: the business, the customers and the staff, and that all were equally important. These days we are clearly being told that only the business matters. So now the "modernisers" are moving in. They are young, thrusting, in-your-face and they think they know all the answers. According to them, the future is the application of new technology within the discipline of the market. But the market doesn't tell us what to do: people tell us what to do. The "market" is essentially a ploy by which one group of people's interests are imposed on the rest of us. The postal trade is at the front line of a battle between people's needs and the demands of corporations to make ever increasing profits. That's what they mean by "modernisation", and it's not "nostalgia" to remind ourselves that things used to be different.[2]

But the fight will only be won when we can say with confidence, not only that things used to be different in the past, but that they can be different in the future too. I'm hoping that, before long, the neoliberal era will be seen for what it was: a barbarous anti-Enlightenment atavism, a temporary interruption of a process of egalitarian modernisation.

RW: At the end of last year you edited a collection of essays, *The Resistible Demise of Michael Jackson*, brought out almost at the speed of John Blake Publishing! What was so important about Michael Jackson's death that made you put such energy into this project?

MF: Yes, it's rapid-response theory! There's no doubt that Jackson's death arrived at a punctual moment. A whole thirty-year reality system had just collapsed with the bank bailouts. Obama had been elected. There was no one who personified that thirty-year period more than Michael Jackson. In the few days after Jackson died, I found myself watching his videos over and over again. I surprised myself by moved from a position of detached cynicism to feeling increasingly sad. There was something in those videos — particularly the *Off The Wall* clips — which afterwards disappeared from Jackson personally and from the culture in general. So I listened to *Off The Wall* and "Billie Jean" obsessively. I probably listened to "Billie Jean" forty times, but it was like listening to it for the first time; there were depths to it I'd never got to before. I wrote a post on my blog which elicited some positive responses; and it struck me that the network around Zer0 — which includes many of the world's music writers as well as theorists — was in an ideal position to produce a book that could deal with Michael Jackson as a symptom. Which isn't to say that the book is some desiccated analysis that doesn't engage with the sensuous qualities of Jackson's music — there are some wonderful descriptions of the tracks and Jackson's dancing. The book was put together very quickly, but I'm extremely pleased with the results. It was heartening to see what music writers can do when you give them space and let them pursue their interests. There are some pieces in the book — such as Chris Roberts' and Ian Penman's — that are so sui generis that it is difficult to imagine them appearing anywhere else.

RW: You've had a busy year, what with the blog, teaching, finishing a stint as reviews editor at the *Wire*, conference papers, marriage, Zer0 and the publication of two books — is it time for a rest now or will 2010 be just as busy?

MF: This is not the time for a rest. On a personal level, a rest is impossible. Most of what I do doesn't make me much money, so I have to keep working at a furious rate to keep my head above water. On a wider cultural and political level, this is a highly exciting time, not a moment to be convalescing. This year, in addition to the teaching, blogging, freelancing and editing for Zer0, I will be putting out *Ghosts Of My Life*, which will bring together my writings on hauntology and lost futures; in some ways, it's the other half of *Capitalist Realism*. There's another big project that I'm involved with which I have high hopes for, but we're not ready to go public on that yet.

RW: And finally, I hope it's not too late to ask what were your favourite books of last year?

MF: Apart from the Zer0 books — and I've almost certainly forgotten something really important — they would be:

Fredric Jameson, *Valences Of The Dialectic*. A genuinely monumental work that I expect to be referring to for many years.

Graham Harman, *Prince Of Networks*. A stunning reinterpretation of Bruno Latour's work that is also Graham's most lucid account yet of his object-oriented philosophy.

Jodi Dean, *Democracy and Other Neoliberal Fantasies: Communicative Capitalism and Left Politics*. Jodi's sharp analysis of the impasses of the left is also a kind of requiem for much the 2.0 bluster of the last decade.

Slavoj Žižek, *First As Tragedy, Then As Farce*. Much more focused than some of Žižek's recent books, this was a reminder of his supreme relevance to the current conjuncture.

RW: Thanks Mark.

capitalist realism: interviewed by richard capes (2011)[1]

"Since there are so many people who are depressed — and I maintain that the cause for much of this depression is social and political — then converting that depression into a political anger is an urgent political project... Anti-depressants and therapy are the opium of the masses now."
— Mark Fisher

Richard Capes: What is capitalist realism?

Mark Fisher: You'd think I'd be able to answer this very quickly. But in fact it's easier to spot than it is to define, I think, capitalist realism. There's various different ways of looking at it. One is looking at is as a belief, a belief that capitalism is the only viable political economic system. That's one sense of the realism — that anything else is unrealistic. And it's often what you hear people say if one is critical of capitalism — they'll say, "Well it might not be the best system, but it's the only one that works." One can think of it as a belief, but it's also an attitude, an attitude in relation to that belief, an attitude of resignation and defeat. So I suppose that what I'm talking about with capitalist realism is not so much the attitude propagated by this kind of neoliberal right. It's more how the success of the neoliberal right transforms the attitudes of the general population, and especially of the left I think. But of course the problem with talking about beliefs or attitudes is it implies a kind of individual psychological perspective. What we're talking about here is the kind of collective psychic infrastructure, I'd say — a kind of diffuse ideological atmosphere, and the way in which those beliefs are instituted across all areas of life in a country like the UK: from the media through to the workplace, through to our own unconscious attitudes.

RC: When and how did capitalist realism emerge?

MF: I think you're looking at the Eighties as the key period of transition really. We're looking at a kind of synergy between ideology and the restructuring of capitalism — the restructuring of capitalism from so-called Fordism to post-Fordism, Fordism being the sort of dominant form of capitalism in the West, in the post-war period, which was based on a kind of compact of stability, where the working class was offered security in exchange for boredom. Where most towns would have one or two major industrial enterprises, most of the male workers would expect to work in those industries their whole working life. But they could expect minor incremental improvements in their standard of living over that working period. This sort of fell apart in the Seventies when the world that we're now familiar with — so familiar, in fact, that we take it for granted — the world of post-Fordist capitalism started to emerge.

What are key terms of post-Fordist capitalism? The dread word "flexibility", which, in terms of the worker, tends to cash out of what's called "precacrity", i.e. constant conditions of instability and insecurity, short-term employment, casualisation. And of course that goes alongside some of the other key developments of post-Fordism, such as digitisation of the workplace, just-in-time production, and, of course, globalisation. So the re-structuring of capitalism in this way caught labour on the back-foot, labour as in the worker's movement as well as in the Labour Party. The key problem I think articulated by the most forward-thinking of the left groups in the Seventies and Eighties — including the sort of the autonomous in Italy and what's called the "New Times" group around *Marxism Today* in the UK — was, "How could the left hegemonise post-Fordism?", "How could the left produce it's own version of post-Fordism?" And I think the failure of that — the failure to meet that challenge — accounts for a lot of the failure of the left.

On the one hand we have the restructuring of capitalism along the lines of post-Fordism. But what's key to that, of course, is that this just wasn't something that was simply imposed by capital on workers; it was in many ways driven by the desires of workers — workers who simply didn't find enticing a life of boredom for forty years in a factory, who wanted more freedom. I think the key issue now is, in a way, the discrepancy between what they did want and what they actually got. I think that's where opportunities lie for the left, actually.

But coming back to "Where did capitalist realism emerge?" — well, "When and how did it emerge?" It was that the right successfully harnessed those desires — the anti-authoritarian currents that came out from the Sixties. The left I think failed to come up with a convincing model of an anti-authoritarian left. Energies that were released by the kind of struggles against capitalism on the left then became diverted into this neoliberal project, which, in the Eighties, had two faces. On the one level there was inducement. In the UK we saw this in the form of, particularly, the selling off of council houses. It was a really good move by Thatcher in lots of ways, because it immediately positioned the whole of the post-war social-democratic project as sort of being out-of-date, top-down, bureaucratic, and kind of Thatcherite neoliberalism as being about the future, the future that would deliver choice to individuals, which would deliver freedom away from the strictures of the state. A whole array of things happened in the UK, of course, privatisation. Again, privatisation was articulated in terms of giving people choices: "You too can now own shares!" Alongside these carrots, of course, there was a lot of stick with the destruction of the unions, or the effective destruction of the unions.

The miners' strike is the most powerfully symbolic image of the end of the worker's movement. I think when we think about that — when we think about the miners' strike — that gives us the most kind of vivid sense of how deeply established capitalist realism was by the middle of the Eighties, and certainly by the end of the Eighties. By the end of the Eighties we were in a situation that would have seemed science-fictional from the perspective of the middle of the Seventies. If you told people that all of the national utilities would be sold off and privatised, that the mining union which had just brought down the Conservative government would be sort of defeated in abeyance, that the unions were simply not major players in public life anymore — that would have seemed unimaginable. Yet it happened, and it happened in a relatively short time.

If the Eighties were the sort of battleground — in retrospect it seemed like there was only one way that battle was going to go. In the Eighties, of course, things seemed different. It didn't seem inevitable that neoliberalism would triumph. In retrospect the success of neoliberalism seems to have been overdetermined. But by the Nineties, I think, the key moment, of course, is the arrival and election of New Labour, which was the final victory for Thatcherite neoliberalism — where the Labour party could come in, essentially accepting the broad framework that had been imposed by neoliberals. I think then we enter into the kind of phase of capitalist realism which most of the book is devoted to analysing I suppose.

RC: How has capitalism persuaded us that it's the only "realistic" political-economic system?

MF: One way of getting to this is by forcing ritualistic compliance, where there's no other available language or conceptual model for how we understand life, work, or society, except that of business. And that's one of the key things that happened in that period, particularly with public services

— and that's something I dwell on at some length in the book *Capitalist Realism*. It's the extent to which teachers are now required to go through these self-surveillance procedures, these self-assessment procedures, which have been imported in from business, and the strange subjective disavowal that comes with these procedures often — managers who are uncomfortable imposing kind of business rhetoric, business methods, nevertheless will say to workers, say to teachers, "You don't have to believe in this, but this is what we have to do now. We have to go along with this kind of thing." And that sense that one has to go along with practices and languages coming in from business — I think that that is a key part of this sense that there is no alternative — that this is how things are done now — and there's no other way around it.

I think that in addition to what I said earlier are a kind of crushing of the previous forms of working-class solidarity. Well, a crushing — I guess it's better to talk about decomposition really, in lots of ways, because it wasn't simply, as I said, about capital hammering trade unions. It's that trade unions hadn't — trade unions in the form they had developed — had to fit with the Fordist mode of organisation, and as post-Fordism emerged, as Fordism fell apart — as I say, partly driven by the desires of workers — trade unions and other aspects of the labour movement failed to move with it. The effect of that is this kind of generalised atomisation, I think — a kind of collective depression, which isn't experienced collectively, because nothing is, actually.

But where between the individual and the state — there's nothing in the space anymore. The space that trade unions used to occupy — well, people could feel then a direct connection between there own working lives and a wider political world and have some sense of agency because of that. That space was gone and people were... There's this process of what I've called the "privatisation of stress" or general psychic privatisation. You get to own your own home, but your home becomes this place of refuge and consolation in a world where — because outside it public space is massively denuded. And it's this decline of a public space which we can have any connection with. And it massively contributes to this sense that there's no alternative to the way things are.

RC: You argue in the book that capitalist realism is immune to moral criticism. Could you explain why?

MF: It's no use just talking about greed and these categories. There's this kind of embedded Hobbesianism with capitalist realism. Part of capitalist realism is: "that's the way the world is". And that involves: "Well, people are naturally competitive". If there's widespread greed, or if this is appealed to as a notion — "Well, the reason there was a bank crash was because of greedy bankers" — that won't undermine capitalist realism, it'll feed into it. It will feed into it in the sense that that kind of resignation, cynicism are part of the background of capitalist realism anyway. It also misses the target, I think.

The problem with late capitalism is not the greed of capitalists. That's the difference between a Marxist analysis and an ethical one — the Marxist one will focus on systems, forms of organisation are central. Capitalism is not bad because CEOs are uniquely evil. It's the other way around. Anyone who's in the position of CEO would act as CEOs do. It's just a systemic pressure that produces that kind of behaviour. Part of the problem is that we are looking at systemic tendencies here. It's archaic and kind of folk-psychological to focus on these categories which we think apply in everyday life, like more responsibility, to this kind of inhuman system. The scale of what we're up against is obfuscated by a focus on the ethical.

RC: You also talk about "recycling" as another way in which our attention is deflected from a real problem.

MF: Isn't recycling a classic case of: "We assume responsibility for the systemic tendencies of capitalism"? It's not really our fault that there is an environmental catastrophe. The thing it is nobody's fault, you can say, in a genuine sense, but that is the problem — because there is no agent capable of acting. There's no agent at the moment that's capable of taking responsibility for a problem on the scale of the environmental catastrophe that we're facing. Instead, it's contracted out to us as individuals as if we could do anything about it by simply putting plastic in the right bin. That won't solve the environmental catastrophe that we're up against. The only thing that can solve it is the production of an agent capable of acting. But of course nothing like that has ever existed throughout human history until now — which doesn't mean it can't exist, but that we're in very new territory. That appeal to individual responsibility, as if aggregating up enough individual responsibility will substitute the need for this kind of agent. That's one of the pernicious dimensions of the culture behind recycling.

RC: Towards the end of the first chapter you argue that gangster films like *Goodfellas* and *Pulp Fiction* offer visions of the world that promote capitalism or reinforce capitalist realism. Could you explain how they do that because they're often seen as offering a very gritty, realistic portrait of modern life?

MF: Exactly. It's because of that though, isn't it? What do we mean by realism? That's very much at stake. I think Ellroy also talks about — I think Ellroy is an interesting case because he's pretty open about it in the political dimension of it. Ellroy's project in something like *American Tabloid*, where he wants to take down all of these images of kind of American liberal

641

politicians and expose the kind of seedy acquisitiveness behind the veneer — Ellroy's quite open about this as a cultural-political project. This sense of precisely what is realistic. What is realistic? That people are competitive, they naturally struggle against one another, that the real world of the streets is described by this kind of micro-capitalist — not even micro often — struggle between warring families or warring interest groups — quite clearly this will feed into capitalist realism, I think, in lots of levels: in the assumption of individualism, the assumption of competition, also what has disappeared from that picture — which is any kind of public world.

RC: Would you say the American TV series *The Wire* is a work of capitalist realism?

MF: It's a fascinating parallel with the book, I think, in that, in lots of ways it's very similar to *Capitalist Realism*. What is the difference between that and large swathes of gangster rap or Ellroy is the implicit critique in it, isn't it? There's a celebration with Ellroy or gangster rap — "this not just how things are, but there's something good about the fact they're like this actually, and that we need to be positive about disillusionment". Behind *The Wire*, despite this sense of massive institutional inertia, and just the impasses of politics, the fact that however hard individuals try to act the system has either a way of subsuming them or eliminating them — although that could be dispiriting, in the same way that *Capitalist Realism* could be dispiriting (and some people do read it in that way), for me the message of *The Wire* is very similar to the message of *Capitalist Realism*, that this is what we're up against now. That was how things were pre-2008. Of course one of the many things that interests me about *The Wire* is the emphasis that's placed on post-Fordist bureaucracy, the same as I place it in *Capitalist Realism* — on the way that kind of target culture has this inherent kind of skewing of facts, the sinister alliance between managerialism and target culture, in the way that it sort of blocks out initiative and also prevents people from doing their job in a way that you'd think they ought to be doing it.

On the face of it you'd think with *The Wire* — yeah, it's a negative message, and to that extent it would reinforce capitalist realism. The second series about containerisation, about the decline, the diminishment of the old forms of labour, and their replacement with this kind of post-Fordist robotics — computerisation — is very flat with the themes of *Capitalist Realism* the book. But I see it more as describing or rather anatomising — diagraphing — capitalist realism, rather than it actually reinforcing it, because it quite plainly lacks that element of celebration. It does also lack resignation, even though it does seem to be a seamless world from which there is no escape. The very fact it exists is a form of refusal of resignation, I think. Showing the sheer systematicity of these processes is something other than simply being resigned to them in everyday life and work.

RC: You mentioned the phrase "privatisation of stress" earlier in the interview. Could you talk about your experience of this when you worked as a teacher in further education?

MF: FE in the UK used to be the place where students who didn't really get on that well with conventional education — where they would go for a slightly different approach. I started teaching there the early part of the 2000s, and one could already see that ethos under threat and it became, increasingly as the decade wore on, as the kind of Blairite business agenda came to dominate life at college more and more. Partly what I mean by the "privatisation of stress" in relation to education is that people are required to become their own workers. There's a trick that's been played by neoliberalism which we've all succumbed to more or less — which is the idea that bureaucracy is in the past, bureaucracy belongs to this old statist, heavy, top-down, centralised world and we're glad to be rid of it.

But of course, when we think about what our working lives involve now, I'd say for many people it involves more bureaucracy, not less. The difference is that the kind of bureaucratic surveillance is not performed by external parties; it's increasingly performed by us. We have to fill in fifty or sixty page logbooks; we have to fill in endless detailed documents assessing our own performance. But this is part of a sort of wider privatisation of stress, which is that we're invited to take responsibility for the additional stresses that an increased workload and decreased security bring to bear on us. Since trade unions are no longer as effective as they were, our first recourse often when we're put under extra stress is not to complain to a trade union or get them to act on our behalf but to go to a doctor and get anti-depressants, or if we're "lucky" — in inverted commas — get therapy. The rise of depression amongst the general population, particularly amongst the young, is, I think, a symptom of this privatisation of stress.

RC: In the book you say that in Britain "depression is now the condition most treated by the NHS".

MF: As far as I'm aware that's still the case. I haven't checked out the statistics recently, but I can't imagine that in the period we're in at the moment depression has decreased amongst the population. What struck me about this was, "Why is this acceptable? Why, particularly in a period in which we can look back now and see as a period of boom — why in this period of so-called boom were so many people, particularly young people, why were so many of them depressed? Doesn't this indicate some fundamental kind of affective problem with late capitalism?" It seems to me that one aspect of the privatisation of stress is there's not an availability of a kind of cultural language of disaffection and discontent, particularly for the young, I think. And one of the interesting things about the last year or so, with the student militancy at the end of 2010 and the riots this year, is this kind of eruption of a negativity, which I don't think was available to young people in lots of ways in the high pomp of capitalist realism.

RC: In the book you talk about students suffering from "depressive hedonia". Could you tell us what this is?

MF: I was talking about the students I was teaching — so they were younger teenagers... not that young, I suppose: sixteen to nineteen. Not undergraduates. This does seem to strike a chord with them actually. Many of the people who write to me about the book, younger people, think that that captures something about their experience. Depressive hedonia would be just a way of thinking about the form that depression takes in a world where stimulus is always available, I think. I don't think we've remotely got to grips with the affective consequences of the kind of cyberspace-matrix that the young especially are embedded in.

Part of what I'm describing in the book really is the tensions between a kind of crumbling disciplinary framework — in which teachers are there as these prison-guards of this collapsing system. Well, on the one hand they are prison guards. On the other hand, they're required to interface with this constant world of stimulus, and be entertainers. There's a tension between being a prison guard and an entertainer — it's pretty difficult to say the least. In terms of depressive hedonia, depression is usually described as a case of anhedonia, where the sufferer of depression is unable to derive pleasure from anything. It seemed to me that there's almost an opposite syndrome in place with teenagers, where pleasure is so easily available that, well, that it's this very availability of pleasure that's depressing in many cases. I guess there's a kind of consumer model of pleasure which is involved, which doesn't build up people's sense of self-esteem, sense of well-being, or perhaps more importantly a sense of involvement in things. Instead of that you've got this kind of rapid-fire small bursts of pleasure. And one of the things that's removed by this is a kind of productive boredom.

The existential crisis posed by boredom in the Seventies — when you really could be bored, when there wasn't a seamless stimulus-matrix available — I think there's a big relation between that — the availability of a certain kind of boredom — and phenomena like punk. The availability of constant low-level stim in twenty-first-century culture precludes that kind of boredom, precludes alienation in a certain way, but produces this kind of general feeling of unacknowledged disaffection I think. These forms of stimulation are not really capable of engaging people in a way that takes them out and beyond themselves. People are sort of trapped in themselves in this form of kind of functional misery, in a sense that they're just miserable enough, as it were, miserable enough to carry on — not too miserable that they would either reach a point of subjective destitution or just have to question — pushed to the point where they have to question the general social causes for why they're like this. So I think it's just enough pleasure to keep them depressed as it were. That's one way of looking at depressive hedonia.

But of course one of the great things that's happened over the last year or so, that's significant though, is the student protests at the end of 2010. It was students who lead this. There's a sense there of what I was looking for or hoping for when I was writing *Capitalist Realism* — that these forms of unacknowledged disavowed discontent would convert into forms of public anger. What was so exciting about the student protests was seeing that process start. Because I think a lot of the older people are much more in that mode that I was describing earlier of kind of resignation. I don't think there's many people who are fans or enthusiastic supporters of the coalition government, but I suspect the general attitude is, "Well, there's not much we can do about this". In other words, a form of capitalist realism. What we saw with the young is a kind of challenging of that in a very dramatic way.

RC: In a talk you gave about *Capitalist Realism* earlier this year you called for the development of a "leftist psychotherapy". Could you explain what you mean by this?

MF: This is really serious, I think. Since there are so many people who are depressed — and I maintain that the cause for much of this depression is social and political — then converting that depression into a political anger is an urgent political project. Of course it's not only about that. It's also about levels of real distress and suffering in society, which cannot be handled or dealt with by the individualising, privatised assumptions of the dominant forms of treatment in mental illness, which are, in this country, cognitive behavioural therapy — which is a kind of combination of positive thinking and kind of psychoanalysis-light: the focus on the family background of the sufferer, and on then of converting thought patterns from these negative into positive ones. There's that. And on the other hand, brain chemistry focus — the horrible loop whereby massive multinational pharmaceutical companies sell people drugs in order to cure them from the stresses brought about by working in late capitalism. Neither of these things are very effective — all they do is largely contain people's depression rather than actually deal with the actual cause of depression.

One can apply Marx's arguments about religion very directly to this — that religion was the opium of the masses. Anti-depressants and therapy are the opium of the masses now, in lots of ways. That isn't to say that they don't do anything at all. They do in many cases relieve intense suffering, which people are undergoing. But it's just the same as religion. As Marx said, it'll make people better in a kind of savage and pitiless world — religion wants real comfort to people in the same way, in a world of relentless competition, of digital hyper-stress, etc. Being able to talk to someone for an hour in cognitive behavioural therapy or having something which will take the edge of things via anti- depressants — that will make people feel better, but just as with religion, it doesn't get to the sources of that sort of misery in the first place. It in fact obfuscates it.

If you want to look at the rise of capitalist realism, one can also look at the decline of anti-psychiatry. As anti-psychiatry declined, then capitalist realism grew. I think there's a relation there between the two. That normalisation of misery as part of the privatisation of stress has been absolutely central to the rise of capitalist realism.

How do we get beyond that? Some kind of return to the issues that were raised by anti-psychiatry. I'm not saying necessarily that everything anti-psychiatry said was right. With anti-psychiatry, as with many other anti-authoritarian strands of leftism that emerged in the Sixties — that kind of rhetoric became diverted and captured by the neoliberal right. When did anti-psychiatry cash-out? Well in some ways, Care in the Community, etc. But of course that wasn't the only way it could have gone. Thinking about ways of reforming, changing institutional care, of looking at a shift beyond this narrow kind of focus either on family background or the kind of chemical make-up of people's brains — this could have a very high impact, I think, if we could articulate this.

A reader of *Capitalist Realism* actually drew my attention to the work of someone called David Smail, who's himself a kind of therapist — though I don't think he'd like the term "therapist". He, in a number of books, has sort of argued for the development of a leftist psychotherapy. Smail claims that feelings of well-being fundamentally arise from a public world — against the background of a public world. And in a society in which the concept of the public has been so kind of viciously and systematically attacked — it's no surprise, Smail argues, that distress has increased. He argues that — as I would — that the dominant forms of treatment in mental illness have reinforced that rather than challenged it. I think developing Smail's ideas could be extremely powerful.

RC: In the book you call French students involved in protests against neoliberalism "immobilisers". What does this term mean?

MF: It's a term I use myself, like "immobilisation" — to bring capitalism to a halt. I think the problem of articulating things in that way is that it feeds into the dominance of capitalist realism in the sense that it concedes that history belongs to capital or history is only going one way — capital. And that all we can do is obstruct, resist or delay the inevitable triumph of capital. It seems to me there are obvious problems with that way of thinking. It's really still part of capitalist realism. It's part of capitalist realism in a very big way because we've lost any sense that the future is ours, that we can move forward to a future that we're constructing. Instead all we're doing is putting up barricades against a future that we ourselves are conceding belongs to capital.

RC: How did the student protests in Britain differ from that?

MF: I'm not sure that they did differ that much from it. As with many left-wing protests, there's a strong sense of what they're against, but not so much sense of what is wanted. What's encouraging about it for me is that at least the British young have broken out of that kind of pull of what's conventionally called "apathy", but I don't like that term at all. In the book I use the term "reflexive impotence", which I think is a better sense of what's at stake with many British young. Why I called it reflexive impotence is that people feel they can't do anything, and they're sort of aware that their feelings that they can't do anything mean that they can't do anything, or contribute even more to the inability to actually act, yet it still doesn't enable them to act. Reflexive impotence is another phrase for depression, I think. That's how a depressive person feels. They know that their own attitudes are reinforcing their own inability to do anything, and also making them feel worse. Yet knowing that is not likely to inspire them to act. Instead it makes them more and more depressed. I think that sums up the situation for the British young or large swathes of the British young up to 2008.

I guess what's also encouraging about the student protests is that politics becomes an available option. I think the level of so-called depoliticisation was so strong amongst the young that even sort of failed or flawed forms of politicisation are encouraging because I think part of depression and part of the depression I was talking about really is the disappearance of politics as such. Many young people in Britain who take capitalist realism for granted don't see much of a future for themselves, don't see a very interesting future for themselves. At best they'll be indebted in order to get a job that isn't very exciting — that's probably how they're seeing things. And the idea that one can challenge this politically — I don't think for many of them that it was available as a thought. Making it available again was what was encouraging about student militancy.

RC: Do you think more and more students are breaking out of the bounds of capitalist realism and becoming more radical?

MF: I think it is early days. There's all kinds of things going on. I think student militancy — the emergence of it — is something that wouldn't have happened before 2008. After the bank crisis of 2008 — this is a major event, a kind of major trauma, for capital, and of course we're still right in the middle of it. And it's evident that capital does not have a solution to the problems which lead up to the bank crises of 2008 at all. I think student militancy is one dimension of it, the riots are another. But I think that these are really the beginnings of something and we don't know where it's going to go at all.

And it's a shame in a way that this massive efflorescence of student militancy before Christmas last year dissipated and wasn't able to be sustained during this year. That doesn't mean that it's gone away. I think certainly over the next course of the month or so, building up to November — in November there's going to be another big flash point. A lot of the people who have been politicised by what happened last year will be back again.

The thing is things move so quickly. There's a strange rhythm of events at the moment where you have this massive rush of unpredictable kinds of events occurring. I think that's what happened with student militancy at the end of last year, then earlier this year we had the whole Murdoch thing, and then the riots. These things erupt in an unexpected way, in a way that goes far further than people would anticipate before they happen. But then things seem to go back to normal, seem to stabilise again. But every time things go back to normal, so-called normal, then normality is much more unstable, I think, than it was before. This tendency of collapse at the moment, with what we're living through, is the disintegration of the reality system, quite simply.

Something that has been built up for over twenty-five years, i.e. capitalist realism, in the neoliberal mode — since that has been so pervasive, since that has dominated all of the assumptions of institutional and organisational life as well as the unconscious, it's not surprising that it doesn't collapse all in one go. People's expectations, everything they take for granted, is shaped by that reality system — that in itself keeps it going for some period. But at the same time, we can see it really rocking at the moment. I think there's the opportunity for the left at this time. I think, yes, we need things to get radical, but we also need to get hold of the mainstream. This is where we're totally disconnected. It's not only that we are totally disconnected from the "mainstream", so-called. I mean I use the mainstream in inverted commas, because precisely at moments like this we don't know what the mainstream can be. We've know what it was up to 2008.

Part of the book *Capitalist Realism* is really about the massive decline of mainstream media, mainstream culture, under the kind of tyranny of capitalist realism. I just don't think we know what mainstream media or mainstream politics can be like in the coming period because everything is up for grabs again. We can see that severe crisis that the ruling class is in, in the UK, which was made clear by the so-called Hackgate thing — a network of complicity between the media and the police and politicians, which David Cameron had to admit he was right in the middle of. Now you'd think that would provide an opportunity for the left, but the problem is there's no presence in the mainstream, no agent that can press home this clear advantage. And that's been quite clearly the case since 2008.

RC: How can the left hope to establish a presence in the mainstream media when it almost completely excludes genuinely left voices?

MF: I don't think it's inevitable that they would be excluded. I think it's a mistake to think the form of mainstream media is fixed — that that kind of neoliberal attuned mainstream media with its very narrow bandwidth, with very low expectations that it has of its audience. This was something that was imposed gradually. It is something that was fought for and achieved by neoliberals and their allies in big business. But it's a hegemonic struggle and media and mainstream politics are terrain which the political right have dominated to the extent that people forget that there's ever anything different to this. But I don't think we can say in advance what will be excluded and what won't be excluded. For instance, with the Labour Party, you can still see them acting as if it was before 2008, still acting as if the old so-called centre ground still existed. But it just doesn't exist anymore and no one's testing this out — that's the problem. No one is testing out what would happen if you tried to take a more left-wing perspective in the mainstream media.

Since Ed Milliband and the post-New Labour Labour Party has decided to pitch things towards some obsolete centre-ground, we just don't know what would happen. And I think that's what needs to be tested out at the moment. It's quite clear that we're facing a dilemma, that the UK — what we've seen with the riots and with the student militancy is these kinds of fissures in UK society that we haven't seen to this extent since maybe the poll-tax riots or, even earlier than that, the miners' strike. I think capitalist realist hegemony depended upon this kind of production of consensus — or rather image of consensus — that had to be kind of continually reproduced by the media. Even when the media is condemning riots or condemning student protests, nevertheless they are visible — the visible cracks in this form of consensus or, like I said, appearance of consensus. So, like I say, we just don't know what's going to happen at this stage and we shouldn't concede any terrain to the enemies especially at this time really.

RC: It's not in the interest of the mainstream media to encourage people to question capitalism, though, is it? Newspapers, for example, are profit-seeking businesses, owned by very wealthy people.

MF: That's defeatist because we can't go anywhere without — either the media is reformed or we actually compete on terrain which is not favourable to us. I don't think this means we ought to concede to it, I think. Reading Nick Davis' book, *Flat Earth News* — it's very interesting. It does vindicate everything you've said with newspapers. 60% of broadsheet content comes from PR. But I guess what's interesting about that though isn't that the owners of the newspapers collude with the PR companies as such. It's more that it's a direct consequence of the underfunding of journalism. Journalists are required to turn around ten stories a day. They won't be out on the streets doing investigative reporting. They'll be editing press releases.

But I think this is susceptible to influence by us as well — what Davis calls these "astro-turf" groups, as a play on the idea of grassroots organisation. So a lot of things which appear in the paper as if they'd come from grassroots organisations in fact come from these corporate astro-turf PR bodies or whatever. We need our own astro-turf bodies as it were to compete into this ecology. What gives us hope here is the fact that there isn't a strong agenda being pushed by these journalists, that they'll accept anything that comes into the inbox if it's pushed there with sufficient kind of vigour. I still think a lot of journalism is kind of opportunistic, and it's a question of our organising to intervene into this kind of ecology.

We've seen examples recently of Owen Jones, though — Owen Jones has got in all kinds of media on the back of *Chavs*. He's appeared on *Daybreak*, *Sky News* — right in the heart of this kind of corporate beast. So it can be done. I don't think we can a priori say what can be achieved at this time. Capital is in disarray, the ruling class is in disarray at the moment, and I think that if we give up in advance and say, "We'll never get into mainstream media", then we're doing them a favour. Of course the other danger is simply constructing everything so we adapt to the existing structures of mainstream media. That's also fatal — toning things down so that we can be accepted. It's about a hegemonic struggle so that we can change what is acceptable to say on there. And if we can't do that then we have failed. That's pretty clear and New Labour is the most objective lesson in that. If you simply construct your project on the basis of what is now acceptable in the mainstream and maybe just slightly shifting things over — that will fail.

And not only fail, but will also produce this kind of political despondency such as I tried to describe in the book really. I think we have to go between these two strategies — either staying outside the mainstream media completely or just adapting to what the mainstream media is like now. We have to learn lessons from neoliberals, really, I think. They were capable of changing what the media was in the same way we have to imagine that the media can change in our direction. Of course they've got resources we haven't got. But we've got resources they haven't got as well.

Going back to what I was saying earlier on: We should be inspired to the extent to which the triumph of neoliberalism, in a way, is showing how things can go from impossible to inevitable. That's the way history goes — that things seem completely off the agenda, that there's no way that things can happen; suddenly, things switch where they're the only thing that can happen. That's how it was with neoliberalism. The one thing we can be sure of at the moment is that things can't go back to how they were before 2008. That can't happen. We're in a period of major tumult, major change. The right, the kind of neoliberal right, is at its weakest since I can remember.

And we need to think ahead I think about how things can be different. And media is really a key part of that. I think it's really significant that the Hackgate thing happened this year, because it's part of this delegitimation process, you might say. The delegitimation process has at least two aspects. I think one is the discrediting of neoliberalism, although neoliberalism is quite plainly going to continue as a kind of guiding set of defaults for a while yet. As a political programme with a kind of confidence, it disintegrated after 2008. So we're in this kind of vacuum at the moment where neoliberalism has effectively collapsed, but nothing has come to replace it. That is an opportunity.

RC: In your book you say that the anti-capitalist protests do nothing more than provide a "carnivalesque background noise to capitalist realism". Could you explain why?

MF: There's this spectacular dimension to anti-capitalist protests — this purely petitionary dimension to it. My problem with the anti-capitalist thing in a sense is that there's nobody who can meet the demands that are being put forward there. It has the form of petition, but there's no one to whom this petition is actually aimed. That's what's peculiar about it. Let's imagine at one of these G20 protests — let's imagine everyone inside the G20 goes, "Well, okay, we've heard this noise. We've heard these slogans. That's it. We agree that capitalism is really a bad system." Then what? Even if everybody inside the G20 meeting agreed with that, they still couldn't do anything. It's this peculiar form of spectacular petition, which I think does not expect to win because there is no model of what it would be like to win, as it were. This is not to say that nothing went on there and those protests were completely valueless or insincere. But I do think we need a concept of failure on the left. I think that one thing that separates the neoliberal right from the left is that there's much less tolerance of failure on the neoliberal right.

I think built into many of these movements is a kind of inbuilt expectation of failure, so that it's not a problem if things actually fail. With the student thing there was at least — although it actually did fail, it could have succeeded, at least theoretically. It had a determinate aim. The people they were exerting pressure on had the power to make the decision not to impose those student fees, etc. Unless there are determinate winnable goals, a kind of generalised despondency will result. It's what my comrade Alex Williams calls "feel-good, feel-bad". You feel good because you're out in a protest doing something. But ultimately you feel bad because — and these two things are completely sutured together, the feel-good and the feel-bad — you feel bad because you don't expect to achieve anything ever. It's just a kind of carnival of the defeated. It's those aspects that I think are troubling about that kind of protest.

As I say, the student protest was different because they had a determinate goal that produced this criterion of success and failure. Also: because of the sustained nature of it. There wasn't just something over in a day. It was something over a period of weeks. It built up and had managed to embed itself in the structure of universities, by the occupations. That produces a very different dynamic to a kind of anti-capitalist carnival that happens for a day or a short period of time. The problem ultimately was that, as we discussed earlier, that did fizzle out. I think that then just poses different challenges about how — since people have been politicised by that issue — how do we sustain that kind of struggle over a longer period, and how do we keep it embedded into everyday life. I think that link between people's working life, or the life of students, and politics is crucial — that politics is not something that is just performed by a professional class of administrators at some spectacular distance. It's something that directly connects with how we live and work. I think that that was the power of the student protests by contrast with the Nineties-Noughties anti-capitalism — although I'm not suggesting a total discontinuity there.

It seems to me that trade unions were successful in the past, as I've said, because of Fordism. The collapse of Fordism, that's made the way trade unions operate more difficult. But that doesn't mean that no form of workers organisation couldn't work effectively now. But I do think we need imagination and a real shift from the Fordist paradigm. Having been an active trade union member in points in my life, I've seen the extent to which higher echelons of trade unions are still orientated around — many of them are still orientated around Fordism, around pay and strikes. I saw this particularly with teaching. Many of the issues that I describe in the book — the problems of observations, of bureaucracy, of self-surveillance — these are things that teachers are kind of passionate about, which unions have a very limited interest in. I think shifting the terrain of struggle onto things that matter to people is a way of re-engaging them. There's no reason, in my view, why trade unions themselves couldn't become major players again if they're prepared to shift, very belatedly, into the post-Fordist world.

RC: Is the occupy movement taking place in America at the moment doing nothing more than providing a "carnivalesque background noise to capitalism"?

MF: Part of what makes things different now from how they were in the past, just is the fact that the banking crisis has happened and that capital is on the back foot. There's an element of petitionary acting out with those forms of anti-capitalism that I describe in the book. In the situation where capital is much weaker — but also the situation is much more desperate, I think — that has created a different set of situations where, you know, "What are people to do faced with this kind of ongoing train wreck of the financial system?" There's a sense that anything thrown in front of that train is good at this time. We simply don't know, I think, how far things will spread, how things will develop in conditions as they are now as opposed to what they were like at the end of the twentieth century, at the beginning of the twenty-first century. It seems to me that these negative protest-based movements — if they're to have any lasting impact — must transform into robust organisations that have institutional structures and a positive agenda. But I don't think that we can rule that out at this stage. We just don't know what's going to happen.

RC: Some have argued that one of wonderful things about the movement is its lack of a central organising system because it's bringing together all kinds of people with different problems.

MF: Okay, that's a resource. But I think organisation is required, though, because otherwise how do we compete with capital? I think capital is quite happy facing people who are not that organised. It's good to have a broad-based group of people. But there was a broad-based opposition to the Iraq War — and that's a major moment of capitalist realism, I think, in the UK. When you have however many millions out in the streets in the UK and nothing happened. That shows that sheer numbers of people don't necessarily accomplish anything. I think you only accomplish anything when you've got organisation, goals and structures, in the end. Otherwise you've just got some faith in a kind of spontaneity of the people somehow. When has that ever yielded anything? You're not up against things which are susceptible to spontaneity. There's a difference between capitalism and other forms of kind of political social dominance, isn't there? We can't just take all of the capitalists out and execute them. Capitalism is a structure — it's as much a cognitive structure as it is a social structure. You can't just take out the ruling class. Even imagine this was the case, imagine it was possible — you can't just take out the ruling class and have got rid of it. Difficult questions are: How do we organise life differently? How do we organise the economy in a way that's different from the way that capitalism has done? That's not solved by executing capitalists.

RC: What do you think a post-capitalist society look like?

MF: I'm not sure we're even close to answering that question at the moment, to be honest. I'm not saying that in a defeatist way. In a way it's partly a testament to the power of capitalist realism. We have to start by granting the power that it has over our imaginations, over our social, political and economic imaginations. Part of that power is the way it structures oppositions in our minds, so that you think there's this deadlock between either we've got state centralisation or neoliberalism. It's imperative that we think beyond this deadlock, I think, so that when we're arguing against neoliberal capitalism, then we're not implicitly arguing to go back to social democracy or back to a Stalinist state. We might want to go back to elements of social democracy. But it's not going to be enough to say that we just want to retreat to how things were a few years ago. I think we need a sense of where we're going to. We can be somewhat emboldened here because it's not as if anyone's got a very clear idea of where things are going at the moment. And the one thing we can be certain of is that they won't carry on as they have been. We need this boldness of imagination on our side, willingness to engage in thought experiments, science-fictional scenarios — because, quite honestly, they're just as likely as anything else that's going to happen.

RC: In the last chapter of the book you suggest that one way society can be improved is by establishing a "paternalism without the Father". Could you explain what you mean by this?

MF: That's one challenge to the impasses that we're in. As we were talking about the mainstream media — I do think media is crucial. One of the ways in which neoliberal hegemony has cemented itself is by an attack on paternalism, because it's saying paternalism is part of this obsolete, bureaucratic, centralising, top-down, archaic world that we're glad to be rid of. What's involved in paternalism? Paternalism is other people telling you what you ought to do, and we — we neoliberals — don't believe in that; we believe that you should be able to choose for yourselves. Now this whole way of setting things up has, I think, been highly successful and for that reason deeply pernicious. They also associate paternalism with elitism, because they will say, "Paternalism then is someone deciding for you what you ought to like and what you ought not to like." One doesn't simply want to reverse the terms there and accept the way the binary is set up. We need to think about how paternalism could be different from the image that neoliberalism has of it.

What's interesting to me is the way in which elements of paternalism do survive in neoliberal culture. The smoking ban, for instance. It quite clearly runs contrary to the way I was characterising — one might say caricaturing — the neoliberal appeal. This is quite clearly stopping people from making choices. Paternalism survives in a kind of way in health. It doesn't survive in culture, and that's interesting. But it seemed to me that what was at stake in mass media when I was growing up, and the paternalistic dimension of it, wasn't people telling me what to do — they're assuming intelligence on my part. They're assuming that I can cope with things that I didn't already like.

There's this different model of desire that's at stake with how I would construct paternalism in a positive way — which isn't about just deciding for people what's good for them. It is about having a wager that there is maybe a desire for the strange in people — people don't already know what they want and that the things which they really end up most valuing maybe things which surprise them. What I'm arguing is that a lot of the features that neoliberalism, neoliberal culture claims for itself — which is innovation, the capacity to surprise, newness — none of these things are generated by neoliberal culture. The exact opposite is the case in fact. When you have a consumer model of "choice" — in inverted commas — what you get is this kind of bland homogeneity, a faux-diversity, concealing an extremely narrow bandwidth of options.

What was it that actually did allow for there to be innovation, surprise, and novelty? Well, some kind of condition of stability and some kind of removal from immediate commercial pressures. That's how one could think about, particularly, how the BBC used to operate, how Channel 4 operated in its early days. Nothing is more illustrative, I think, the triumph of capitalist realism in the UK than Channel 4, which started off showing Tarkovsky seasons, had hour-long programmes simply consisting of philosophers discussing ideas — to *Location, Location, Location* or whatever else is on Channel 4 at the moment. There's some massive decline that then produces this retrospective impossibilisation. That other Channel 4 did exist, but now it seems utterly impossible.

But it is only possible in some kind of model of paternalism — of thinking the best of people and thinking they deserve the best, not of serving up whatever people want, or whatever is held that people want. Part of the notion behind this for me would be the plasticity of desire. Neoliberalism wants to trap people in where they already are. This model of paternalism is about saying people are capable of being stranger, of liking things which they don't know at the moment that they would like. That's the side that we should be on — is in inculcating this. Of course, for me, as a teacher, there's a kind of flatness, I think, between this concept of paternalism and teaching. Surely teaching must involve this kind of wager — that the student can enjoy things which are alien to them. That's some of the issues for me about how to think of paternalism differently.

The reason I don't like the term paternalism is the association with familialism — patriarchy, etc. It's very difficult to think of a word that would work in the same way. That's probably part of the conceptual poverty brought about by capitalist realism — that we're forced back onto this word that in many ways is unsatisfactory. Recently, I've done a pamphlet with Jeremy Gilbert, which will be coming out through Compass.[2] There we use the term "democratic paternalism", partly drawing upon Raymond Williams' work in his book — I think it's 1961 — *Communications*. Williams' presciently discusses different models of broadcasting. You start off with an authoritarian one, move towards a paternalistic one, and then that breaks down under pressure from things like the commercial model. What Williams wants is a democratic model where everyone participates in the production of media. I think that we can't just directly go there. We need this kind of democratic paternalism. The goal is more participation than production. The paternalistic dimension just acknowledges the fact that there are asymmetries of kind of power, knowledge, etc. But the democratic side says we can't be satisfied with these differences in power, knowledge — we must aim towards equalling them out. That's how I'd like to think about the political project — as one of democratic paternalism.

One of the problems with paternalism in the way it had traditionally been set up was that that was an elite body that could sit and decide what was good for everybody. There isn't going to be in any desirable system in the future — there isn't going to be one body that will decide for everybody what is good for the rest of them. There's already a plurality of different kinds of knowledge bases and skill bases, etc., which will mean that that is avoided.

Part of what's involved in re-floating this concept of paternalism is defending the concept of education, and also defending the concept of authority; and differentiating the concept of authority from that of authoritarianism. Authority based on expertise, knowledge, skills — there's nothing wrong with that, providing it isn't abused. That needs to be abused to be authoritarianism, which is simply power based on fear. Part of a democratic political project is not eliminating authority, but constituting authority collectively. The best way of fighting authoritarianism is not abandoning the question of authority — which will always re-assert itself in one form or another, if one simply ignores it — but of constituting authority in this collective way. I think that returns to this challenge I was suggesting right at the start of the interview — that we need to now face up to again, which is this question of how do we develop an anti-authoritarian left. Like I said, the question was posed in some ways in the Seventies and the

Eighties. Now we have to answer it.

RC: What's to stop a paternalistic state from becoming a totalitarian one?

MF: I think I sort of partly answered that by... Totalitarianism is authoritarianism — authority simply being asserted on the basis of fiat. And I think that would be very different from the model of authority — the paternalistic model of authority — that I was suggesting. That's why, I think, you need definite democratic paternalism, rather than just paternalism per se. I'm not really saying anything that different from how some teaching situation would operate, for instance, where one can't simply impose stuff on the students and expect them to accept it. You have to negotiate with them, you have to win them over, to start from the level they're at, etc.

RC: And if you can't do that, what do you do then?

MF: If we can't do that, then we're in a severe crisis at that point. What are the situations where you can't do that? All I'm saying is that an authoritarian solution won't help. If you can't bring people round in that situation, then there may be nothing you can do. But simply returning to some kind of authoritarian solution where you just tell them — that would only exacerbate the problems, it won't solve them. I think we'd have to bet on the fact that this sort of can be done and you can bring people with you. At a point where we're forcing people to do things, things have already gone wrong very severely.

Let me put it another way: I think we're very far off leftist totalitarianism at the moment, and we're too frightened of it as well. In the Sixties, Stalinism was a clear and present danger. Leftist totalitarianism was a real threat that people were trying to escape from. It simply isn't now. It's not that one should entirely dismiss those fears, but I think that we're at the stage where we need to establish a new orthodoxy, a strong hegemonic presence, and once we've done that, then we can worry about the dangers of that being taken too far or totalitarianism, etc.

But I just don't see that as an issue at this time. What's more of an issue is the kind of soft totalitarianism of neoliberal dictatorship, isn't it? I don't use those terms lightly. This situation where people — where there's a rhetoric of choice and no effective political choice, where there's a general kind of helplessness and people feel they've got no control over their lives — it seems to me that these are what we need to fight against. I've never been able to force a student to do anything anyway. Let's say there was the full resources of the military and prison service available to me, I wouldn't still be able to bend the student, still, in that way. If things have gone past the point of negotiation where you can't, as it were, manipulate people in their own interests, then that's a severely extreme situation.

RC: Another thing you say needs to happen is for the left to "not take over the state but [to] subordinate it to the general will".

MF: Yeah. Neoliberals don't really have to run the state as such themselves. They get their subordinates to do it. The state is clearly an important locus of power. We get some theories which already write off the state and I think that is a mistake. It's quite clear that neoliberalism could not have achieved the hegemony it has without also being able to control states. So I think the state remains an important locus of power.

It's just the idea of taking over the state, in a way, in the classic style of the 1917 Bolshevik revolution, etc. — even if you could do that, that wouldn't achieve the overthrow of capitalism anyway, partly because capitalism is a global phenomenon. It itself is in the position I say — it subordinates the state. It doesn't have to takeover the state directly. Partly what I was thinking there is that we want to differentiate ourselves from being old style statists. This is again part of this neoliberal binary where they're for a small state, we're for a big state. I think we need to first distinguish the concept of the public from the concept of the state. The two aren't the same — the state facilitates public space, but is not the same as the public. The public interest is not synonymous with the kind of will of the state. Partly the importance of this move is to differentiate us from the caricature of the old left. But at the same time it's important not to go down a certain kind of anarchist route where you're denying the importance of the state at all. The state quite clearly retains a massive significance.

RC: How do you get the state to serve the people?

MF: Why does parliamentary politics serve the interest of business? Because business is the only effective agent acting upon it. The point is: Why is capitalist realism rife in parliamentary politics? You can't explain that in terms of the logic of parliamentary politics itself. Parliamentary politics is in many ways responding to the situation outside it, such as the decline of trade unions, etc. The classic situation of the Seventies was where the politicians were caught between business on the one hand and trade unions on the other. What we need to do is constitute a force outside of parliament strong enough that it becomes a dominant influence on parliament.

Again: learn from neoliberalism. It doesn't control parliament because it has its own people directly in there, though that might to some extent be true. The point is that even if that were true, how is it possible? It's possible because of the constitution of forces inside society, isn't it? That's it at its basic behaviourist level, I think. Politicians and administrators will bow to the strongest force in a certain way. Then what we need in the first instance is to create conflict in their own minds. At the moment, it's just all too easy to bow down to business, because it's only powerful force acting upon them. There's a widespread, inchoate discontent, for instance, about the banks — and since there's no agent that's capable of focusing that discontent and bringing it to bear on politicians, then they can ignore it — they just make a few moralising gestures towards it. To me it's a question of how you constitute those extra parliamentary forces, how we produce these new forms of solidarity.

RC: But business has a very fixed set of things it wants, whereas the public want a multitude of different things, don't they?

MF: That's why I do think we at least need some determinate set of demands, at least provisionally, because otherwise things just dissipate. Unless we've got a set of demands of that sort, and some kind of model for a new orthodoxy — that's the thing about the mainstream — a model for what we want the mainstream to look like. If we don't have that, then those, as you say, specific determinate demands that business has will continue to dominate.

RC: In the last chapter of *Capitalist Realism* you also say that strikes in public services are self-defeating. Could you explain why?

MF: I think things have changed — the strikes earlier on this year, the TUC one and all of that, and the action that's coming up in November. There's a difference there because it approaches them all almost like a general strike. It's not just that teacher's are out, but the whole of the public sector. I'm still suspicious of one-day strikes, of just how effective they can be. Unless the discontent and militancy spreads beyond that one day — it's very easy to contain a one-day strike. As happened in the FE college where I worked — you get this farcical situation where the principle, on a £120,000, would come down and hand out coffee to the people picketing, because everyone will claim to be on the side of the workers — because it doesn't really cost anything. Rather, it costs us stuff — it costs the workers their wages for the day. It doesn't really cause any lasting damage to the institution — that kind of action. Certainly they can easily plan for and, indeed, in many ways welcome it, because it lowers the wage bill for the year.

I wouldn't want to make a definitive statement about the modern day situation now. But I think we need to think about winning hegemonic influence again. Why have nurses got more status than teachers? It's partly that nurses often go on strike. It's not that one should pander to the image of them in the media, but at the same time that's where we're starting from and why we have to struggle against it. Given that the media will use all of its weapons to produce what Alex Williams calls "negative solidarity" — turning one set of workers against another. With a one-day strike with teachers — the classic or standard line from the media is, "Well look at how the teachers are inconveniencing the rest of the workforce, of childcare and all of that." I think we just have to think of the long-term strategic consequences of these things.

I hope that if one-day strikes happen they would work, but I just think that too often they haven't worked. Rather than just kind of going over and over these things that have failed, keep doing them, is to look at different forms of disruption — things which actually inconvenience management. Like I say, in terms of teaching — why do things that inconvenience the students? Or if it's children: Why inconvenience the pupils and the parents? Why not do something that only inconveniences management? I think the benefit of the kinds of refusal that would be invisible to the students, pupils, parents, etc., is that they show the absolute uselessness of this kind of bureaucratic work and the extraneous nature of managerialism. If one refuses to collaborate with certain managerial initiatives, one can perfectly well carry on teaching — just cause problems for management. I think more imagination about targeting disruption on those who you want it to hurt would be good.

RC: I interviewed Keith Famish several weeks ago about his book, *Time's Up!* In it, he argues that the only way to prevent global ecological collapse and thus ensure the survival of humanity is to rid the world of industrial civilisation. Do you have any thoughts on this?

MF: If that is true it's very depressing. That's not a reason to object to it in itself, I suppose. We need to hold onto a model of the future. That's something I want to retain from Marxism, actually — is a kind of technocratic vision of the future. It doesn't mean it has to be one that's completely indifferent to the environment. I suppose that I am one of those people he would attack in the sense that what I would hope for is that there's a managed solution to these things that would involve technology. As I sort of mention in the book about rationing — I don't see a problem with a rationing of resources at some point. But I don't see that as necessarily meaning that we would be immiserated. People are always bleating on about the Second World War, how great that was, about how great people felt during the time of rationing, and sort of how healthy people were as well. I think we've seen in a sense the results of the opposite of that — that having unlimited access to things doesn't produce well-being or happiness. On the contrary, it produces a kind of generalised misery I think. I don't have any problem with an idea of a rationing of resource at some point, which I think could be part of the solution here. But I do still believe civilisation is possible. I think the question is: How are things to be managed? Part of what I want to argue for is a defence of the concept of management as opposed to managerialism. It seems to me that the only solution to environmental catastrophe is a managed one or we're already betting on the catastrophe already having happened, or already acting like the catastrophe already has happened. I find libidinally alienating these visions of a sort of return to organic societies, little villages.

RC: Some might argue that such societies would be less alienating than what we have at present because they offer a face-to-face social existence.

MF: I think there are severe problems at a libidinal level, like that. There's a reason that people don't want face-to-face contact. Sometimes there's a value in face-to-face contact. There's also a value in impersonality. The achievement of an urban modernity was the ability not to have to deal with face-to-face contact all the time. I really think this is deeply dubious line — because I suspect what is behind the claim that it has to be like this and that civilisation can't carry on is this kind of death-wish and this desire to take us back to the kind of conditions of a Medieval world.

RC: Those making the claim would probably argue that the death-wish is civilisation itself which is heading towards self-destruction.

MF: Fair enough. I can see that — but there's two deaths here I think, neither of which I want. I really want to avoid this binary that either we're going back to something which I think people — there's a drive to escape those conditions that you can't put back in a box. The only way of eliminating the desires for impersonality, for homogeneity, for mass production — the only way of ending the desires for that is by a post-traumatic forgetting I think. Otherwise those desires will maintain.

I think there's nothing wrong with those desires actually. This makes me a Marxist I think, but I believe in mass production, of coordination, etc. Marx is somewhat sanguine about many of the issues that we wouldn't be anymore because of — there's this Promethean model of extracting resources from the Earth, and this kind of model of practice that was about converting the inert mater into something useful for us or whatever. I think we are rightly now somewhat suspicious of that kind of Promethean drive that's indifferent to the depletion of resources, etc. Okay, so there's a kind of death logic of that Prometheanism, which just uses up all the resources. But we don't want to be forced between these two deaths, I think — a death of modernity and a kind of return to village life. "The idiocy of rural life" — that's the great phrase from Marx and Engels. The issue for me is how to commensurate an environmental agenda with modernity, with the desires for mass production, for the homogenous, for the generic. I wouldn't think these things are the only things that should go on in culture. But an important element of culture which I think is crucial to maintain.

RC: Won't mass production end if you end capitalism? Don't the two go hand-in-hand?

MF: I don't think we have to see things in that way. What interests me is almost the opposite — the way we see elements of communism erupting in capitalism, at the point of highest capitalist triumph. Like I always say about Starbucks — Starbucks shows the desire for communism because everything attributed to Starbucks is everything that was said about communism — that it is homogenous, it's generic, etc., etc. What do people want from Starbucks? Not the coffee — well, I hope not because it's horrible. They want from it something that is familiar, that's generic — that is a form of public space, kind of homogenous public space. We can argue that post-capitalism can deliver this better and cheaper than Starbucks does. The desire for public space, the desire for the homogenous and replicated can be synonymous. But all we've got at the moment is degraded versions of it, such as Starbucks.

There's no reason to think that mass production is just a feature of capitalism. You know we've got robots and stuff. This is one of the concrete challenges about how we would construct an economy without capitalism. The difference between me and my line of and certain kinds of anarchistic approaches, I suppose, is that I just agree with Marx, where the global triumph of capitalism is the pre-condition for post-capitalism. If capitalism is global, then we need also to be global or sufficiently global. It's not like capitalism operates by global government, but it has sufficient systems to coordinate its activities around the world which minimise the effectiveness of anti-capitalist struggle. I think we need similar systems of global coordination, and I think that can involve resource management so that we most effectively use it, so resources are used in the most effective way. I think condemning us back into this world of literary dark ages, where we're in tiny villages and we have a limited sense of the world around us is a horrific prospect. I still maintain a hope of a rationally organised post-capitalist civilisation.

preoccupying: interviewed by *the occupied times* (2012)[1]

Occupied Times: Paul Mason recently commented that the uprisings of 2011-12 have brought the curtain down on capitalist realism. Can you briefly outline what you mean by the term "capitalist realism"? And do you believe that the financial crisis and the subsequent popular fightback have signalled a new beginning?

Mark Fisher: Capitalist realism can be seen as a belief — that there's no alternative to capitalism, that, as Fredric Jameson put it, it's easier to imagine the end of the world than the end of capitalism. Other systems might be preferable to capitalism, but capitalism is the only one that is realistic. Or it can be seen as an attitude of resignation and fatalism in the face of this — a sense that all we can do is accommodate ourselves to the dominance of capitalism, and limit our hopes to contain its worst excesses. Fundamentally, then, it's a pathology of the left, nowhere better exemplified than in the case of New Labour. Ultimately, what capitalist realism amounts to is the elimination of left-wing politics and the naturalisation of neoliberalism. I think it's too quick to talk about the end of capitalist realism, though what we have been seeing for the past couple of years is a challenge to this naturalisation of neoliberal concepts. In some ways, the austerity measures that have been implemented have constituted an intensification of capitalist realism. Those measures couldn't have been introduced unless there was still a widespread sense that there is no alternative to neoliberal capitalism. The various struggles that have blown up since the financial crisis show a growing discontent with the panic neoliberalism that has been put in place since 2008, but they have yet to propose any concrete alternative to the dominant economic model. Capitalist realism is about a corrosion of social imagination, and in some ways, that remains the problem: after thirty years of neoliberal domination, we are only just beginning to be able to imagine alternatives to capitalism. But at least now we can imagine imagining such alternatives.

OT: What have you made of the global Occupy movement's role as part of the mass mobilisation against the politics and economics of austerity and neoliberalism? From what you've seen can Occupy and other movements mount a sustained opposition to the ruling status quo, continuing with the global actions planned throughout May?

MF: The short answer is that this remains to be seen. There's no doubt the Occupy movement has played a major role in the shifting of ideological atmosphere that has happened in the last year or so. You're right that the question of sustainability is crucial. In *Capitalist Realism*, I argued that the anti-capitalist movement had become background noise to capitalist business as usual — something that it was by and large easy for capitalism to ignore. The question is, can Occupy provide the basis for a sustainable antagonism? The broad problem we're facing here is, how can this antagonism be sustained now that the Communist Party has disappeared and trade unions have for the most part become quiescent? The party and the union structure provided sustainability, continuity and institutional memory. Now, it's not that these are the only institutions that could provide such things, or that those older institutions would be fit for purpose, even if they had survived into the twenty-first century. But a genuinely new force that is capable of struggling against twenty-first-century capitalism must be able to fulfil those functions. I think we also need to recognise the importance of building hegemony — and this means stepping outside the activist universe. There's a danger of the activist's world become very self-contained. We need to reach beyond those intensely engaged with politics to those who don't look to politics at all to explain the misery of their lives. It's those people who have been most affected by capitalist realism, and who could be mobilised against it, if they could be reached.

OT: What was your reading of the riots last August? The epitome of neoliberal materialism or further evidence of a system built on greed breaking down?

MF: I think those involved in the riots were largely exactly the kind of people I was just talking about — those for whom "politics" means absolutely nothing. I'm not saying that the riots weren't "political", that they were an inexplicable upsurge of criminality, as the right did. The riots were political, but in a negative sense — they were a massive symptom of a failure of politics, an expression of discontent which lacked political goals or strategy. These are the signs of a system verging on collapse; people took part because they felt radically excluded. The invisible wall that prevents people from acting like this had collapsed — there was so little on offer that there was almost no incentive *not* to riot. It's to be hoped that the discontent that exploded so powerfully, and, in many cases so tragically, in the riots, can be harnessed. Shortly after the riots, I went to a screening of the Black Audio Film Collective's 1986 film *Handsworth Songs*, an essay-film about the 1980s riots. The film's director, John Akomfrah, said that, if these rioters can bring the British state to its knees for three days, they will also be able to organise themselves. That is my hope.

OT: In the sections of the book where you cover the culture of work, you describe the combination of marketisation and maddening bureaucracy as "Market Stalinism". This evokes the excellent US television series *The Wire* where the police, the politicians, the teachers, etc. are all shown to be focused, above all else, on "juking the stats". Can you describe how Market Stalinism works and how we can hope to get rid of it?

MF: I hadn't actually seen *The Wire* at the time I wrote *Capitalist Realism*, which is why there's no mention of it in the book. But you're right, *The Wire* exemplifies so much of what I wanted to say in *Capitalist Realism*. In fact, if you want to know what capitalist realism is, watch *The Wire*! Market Stalinism was my term for the kind of bureaucracy which was typical of Blairism, but which, as *The Wire* demonstrates, was by no means confined to Blairism, or to Britain. The neoliberal claim was that marketisation obviates the need for the state and for bureaucracy. But the result of imposing "marketisation" on public services is always a crazed proliferation of bureaucracy, via target setting, league tables, performance reviews, etc. Just as under Stalinism, everything becomes geared towards the production of appearance. In these conditions, gaming the system is inevitable. How to get rid of Market Stalinism? We need to expose one of the biggest lies in neoliberalism: the idea that it is an anti-bureaucratic force. This will involve a struggle against managerialism, and towards a workplace based on the collective autonomy of workers.

OT: You write in *Capitalist Realism*: "This battery of bureaucratic procedures is by no means confined to universities, nor to education: other public services, such as the NHS and the police, find themselves enmeshed in similar bureaucratic metastases." Now that the police want to strike, do you think they should be seen as just another public service, or does their role of enforcing the government's agenda mean we shouldn't oppose cuts to the police force in the same way we do the NHS, education or welfare?

MF: It's a difficult question, but one that should be answered pragmatically and strategically. If we are involved in fighting the police — either literally or at some other level — then the police are playing their role as ideological enforcers. Which isn't to say, I must emphasise, that we should ignore police brutality and corruption. What happened to Alfie Meadows and others is appalling, and needs to be exposed. But we have to remember that the police aren't the enemy, they are the servants of the enemy, and if all of our energy is taken up struggling against them, then they are doing their job for their masters very effectively. Ultimately, it must be far better if the servants are turned against their masters.

OT: A lot of what you write in the book comes from your experiences of working as a Further Education teacher. Where do you believe the Coalition, and New Labour before them, are going wrong with their education policies?

MF: The broader agenda here is the imposition of what I have called business ontology: the idea that only outcomes recognised by business count. It's gradually become accepted that the principal — if not the only — role of education is to turn out the kind of compliant individuals which "business" wants. As systems from the private sector are increasingly introduced into education, the influence of managerialism grows, and the status of the teacher is downgraded. The pretext for the battery of bureaucratic and self-surveillance techniques that have been implemented by successive governments is that they "increase efficiency", but their effect is to spread anxiety and erode the autonomy of the teacher. This isn't an accident: it's the real aim of these measures. Education has been corralled into naturalising and intensifying capitalist competition; it's easy to forget, for example, that league tables were only introduced relatively recently. League tables produce the kind of Market Stalinist distortions I was talking about earlier. Teaching becomes a matter of training students for examinations; anything else is a luxury. Contrast this with the much-praised education system in Finland, which is fully comprehensive, has no league tables or inspectorate, and is based on trust in teachers.

OT: A predominant theme of the book is the issue of mental illness in capitalist societies. You write, "what is needed now is a politicisation of much more common disorders. Indeed, it is their very commonness which is the issue: in Britain, depression is now the condition that is most treated by the NHS." It seems that with mental illness scarring the lives of so many sufferers and their loved ones in the UK, it should be towards the top of the political agenda. How can we begin to reduce the stigma, isolation and shame that our society still attaches to the issue of mental illness? How can we convince people that its cause has roots in the collective, not just the individual?

MF: This is a crucial question. The way in which social and political problems are converted into individual pathologies, to be explained via chemical imbalances or family history, neatly sums up so much of what has happened under capitalist realism. It's what I've called the privatisation of stress. Depression has been described as a pathology of responsibility: you feel intensely responsible for the state that you're in. The excruciating paradox is that, while you feel that only you can get yourself out of depression, the condition consists precisely in your inability to act. There's more than an analogy with the political hopelessness and fatalism that have characterised capitalist realism. Depression, after all, is a pathology which centrally involves a sense of realism (indeed, there's a phenomenon called depressive realism): the depressive thinks that they are being realistic, that they have perceived the real state of things, denuded of illusion. This describes the post-utopian tenor of capitalist realism perfectly: other societies had their illusions, their dreams of something beyond capitalism, but we have come to terms with the inevitability of competition and precariousness. Yet depression shows the extent to which people — even during the boom years — could not come to terms with this. With precarity increasing and welfare programmes eroding, it's not surprising that there should be an increase in depression and anxiety. But this increase in distress has been pathologised, neuroticised and commoditised over the past thirty years. Instead of looking to unions when our workload becomes unbearable, we're invited to look for a medical solution. Stressed by too many working hours? Take this medication, which will restore the balance of your brain chemistry. Worried about losing your job? Tell me about your mother. This is a major example of the naturalisation process I talked of earlier. What we need is a denaturalisation (and consequent politicisation) of mental illness. I think the formation of a dedicated pressure group could work towards this. We need something like a revival of the Anti-Psychiatry movement of the Sixties and Seventies. Well, not so much a revival as a re-occupation of the terrain that Anti-Psychiatry fought on; you could argue that the receding of Anti-Psychiatry correlates very closely with the rise of capitalist realism.

OT: With neoliberal economics being so globalised, so strongly enforced by powerful entities on a national, international and supranational level, does this not make it that much harder for any one nation-state to adopt a new economic paradigm? Would there not be credit-rating downgrades from the "objective" agencies who missed the Enron and sub-prime scandals, a hysterical frenzy among the corporate media, veiled threats from the IMF and OECD and, quite possibly, stampeding capital flight? Couldn't there even, depending on the extent of the country's departure from the consensus, be hostility from the other neoliberal countries?

MF: Of course, that would happen, and this kind of threat plays a large part in the current mode of capitalist realism. In fact, this is pretty much a statement of what capitalist realism is at this time. But it presupposes that capital is the most powerful force on earth, and it's this presupposition which needs to be undermined. How? By constituting a counter-force capable of disciplining capital. We've become used to a world in which workers fear capital, never the reverse. Capitalist realism has never been about direct ideological persuasion — it's not that the population of the UK were ever convinced of the merits of neoliberal ideas. But what people have been convinced of is the idea that neoliberalism is the dominant force in the world, and that, consequently, there is little point resisting it. (I'm not suggesting that most people recognise neoliberalism by name, but they do recognise the policies and the ideological narrative which neoliberalism has so successfully disseminated.) This perception has arisen because capital has subdued the forces acting against it — most obviously, it has crushed unions, or forced them into being consumer/service institutions within capitalism. But you're right — the situation has changed since the heyday of social democracy, and one of the principal ways in which it has changed is the globalisation of capital. Indeed, this is one way that unions were outmanoeuvred: *if your members won't work for these rates, we'll go to a place where workers will.* One of the strengths of Occupy is that it is a transnational movement. But the challenge for Occupy is whether it can constitute a force capable of inducing fear into capital. My suspicion is that it won't be able to do that on its own, and that it will need other institutions and groups — probably including unions — if it is to succeed in being a counter-force to capital. Capital isn't actually global, but it is *sufficiently* global, and therefore any effective opposition to it needs to be sufficiently global also. The concrete question — somewhat obfuscated by many of the debates about centralisation versus networks — concerns coordination. How are disparate groups to be coordinated? We can we learn lessons from neoliberalism here: its success was based on building a patchwork of heterogeneous groups, often with different, even conflicting agendas.

OT: The book ends very optimistically, saying that there is a sense that anything was possible again. That was two or three years ago now. Still optimistic? More or less than before?

MF: Well, I think that the optimism has somewhat been borne out by what's happened since I wrote the book. As I said, I think it's going too far to say that capitalist realism is over, but the fact that Paul Mason could make such a claim shows how much has changed over the past couple of years. Just before the student militancy blew up in the UK at the end of 2010, I spoke at a conference, making the — in retrospect — mild claim that there would be shows of public anger against austerity, and I was accused of "revolutionary nostalgia". The point is, that it was my accuser that seemed to have the most (hah!) realistic handle on things then. But surely there's not anyone now who thinks that public discontent in the UK is at an end. Things have got better and worse since 2009: worse, in that panic neoliberalism has further attacked the welfare state, NHS, education, etc.; better in that opposition is coalescing, and the ideological climate has shifted.

OT: You've written a lot about how popular culture has reinforced capitalist realism. You show how commercial pop and hip-hop music and films like *Children of Men* and *Wall-E*, even when purporting to critique authority and the system, in fact leave only a message of its inevitable perpetuation. Do you feel that there is much in the way of popular culture that does successfully subvert capitalist realism? What subversive music, films and books can you recommend to *OT* readers?

MF: I'm not saying that there are no political potentials at all in the popular culture I discuss in *Capitalist Realism*. What I was pointing to, though, was the fact that anti-capitalism at the level of a film's message does nothing *in itself* to disrupt the super-hegemony of capital. Anti-capitalism — or at least anti-corporatism — is utterly standard within Hollywood films: consider something like *Avatar*, for instance. This is the objective irony of capital: nothing sells better than anti-capitalism. Or, even more bleakly, late capitalism's culture *is* anti-capitalist. There is an asymmetry: we struggle against capital, but part of capital's defeat of us is that it can sell our books. This isn't a completely closed circle, though. The issue is how culture connects up with struggles, and you can't second guess that. It's possible that any of the films I talked about could contribute to the development of class consciousness or inspire people to engage in struggles. Conversely, it's possible that even those films or television programs which inventory the features of capitalist realism end up reinforcing it. Take something like *The Wire*: yes, it exemplifies practically everything I say about capitalist realism, but, for that very reason, you could say that it supports, rather than subverts, capitalist realism. You could very easily take away the message that struggling to change things is pointless; the system wins in the end. But one film I would recommend to people, if they haven't seen it, is Mike Judge's *Office Space*, which I briefly discuss in *Capitalist Realism*: I've seen no film which better captures the bureaucratic immiseration of late-capitalist managerialism labour.

we need a post-capitalist vision: interviewed by *anticapitalist initiative* (2012)[1]

AntiCapitalist Initiative: Paul Mason recently argued that in light of the Arab revolutions, capitalist realism has come to an end.[2] Do you agree?

Mark Fisher: I think that is going too far. I understand why Paul made that claim, but capitalist realism is very tenacious. Certainly, things look very different to how they did a few years ago during the high pomp of capitalist realism — when it was thought that the age of revolutions was in the past, that no great change will ever happen again, that every part of the world will eventually end up capitalist.

These ideas — basically, the theses of Francis Fukuyama's *The End of History and the Last Man* — were widely accepted at an unconscious if not a conscious level, even by those opposed to capitalism. It's that acceptance of capitalist dominance, or rather the unthinkablility of any break from that dominance, which constitutes what I've called capitalist realism. But with what has happened in the Arab world, the hope for radical, systemic change has been re-ignited. It's part of a shift in ideological atmosphere that we have seen manifested this week in the French and the Greek elections, with their votes against austerity.

Austerity, after all, is the deflated yet intransigent form that capitalist realism has assumed since the bank crises. Before the bank crises, capitalist realism managed to look as if it were a post-political condition — not a particular ideological constellation, just the way things were. It's no longer able to sustain that post-political mask. But if capitalist realism were actually finished, then there wouldn't be any austerity at all; it's only because people continue to accept that there is no alternative, not only to capitalism, but to neoliberal capitalism, that the swinging cuts that have been imposed in the name of austerity have gone through. As it is, in Europe, we are only

671

seeing the beginnings of a challenge to austerity. These challenges are by no means insignificant, but it's not yet the end of capitalist realism.

But there's another way in which capitalist realism persists. Capitalist realism can also be a seen as the inability to imagine an alternative to capitalism, and I don't think we're close to overcoming this yet. Not surprisingly, after thirty years of capitalist realism, our capacity to even conceive of alternatives to capitalism has atrophied. Opposition to neoliberalism is growing, but this new anti-capitalist mood has yet to bring forth any powerful vision of post-capitalism. Certain tendencies in anti-capitalism are, in effect, inversions of capitalist realism — they accept that capital controls technological modernity, and offer only withdrawal and retreat as an alternative.

AI: How can the left organise itself today to maximise its impact?

MF: The most important problem the left now faces seems to me to be coordination. There are any number of groups hostile to capitalism, but the task is to bring them together to form a sustainable antagonism. We need to forge greater links between those already engaged in struggle — the unions, Occupy, the student movement, the various anti-cuts groups — and also to reach out to those who aren't yet politicised. The way that the opposition between centralisation and decentralisation has dominated discourse on the left recently has distracted us from the fact that coordination does not entail Stalinist centralisation. Systems can be coordinated and decentralised at the same time. After all, that's how capitalism operates!

A key question is institutional memory; a system that has no memory cannot learn and will keep repeating the same mistakes. What's crucial is that we give up any nostalgia for previous eras. Leftist politics has been weakened by its attachment to superseded forms of economic and political organisation. There's a strange romance of glorious failure which we have to give up.

A major part of grasping the potentials of the present is reaching out to precarious workers. We need to think creatively about how they can be politicised and organised.

AI: Do you think that the autonomist critique of classical Marxism has any relevance in helping us understand the modern world?

MF: Yes, I do. The autonomist critique of authoritarianism and Stalinist bureaucracy is something that we shouldn't forget. Any credible leftist politics now has to take the problem of anti-authoritarianism very seriously. At the same time, however, we have to recognise that the situation is very different from the context in which autonomist ideas first emerged in the

1960s and 1970s. Then, the Communist Party and the trade unions were very powerful; Stalinism was still an oppressive presence.

None of these things are true today. Whatever the merits of autonomism anti-statism, it has to be acknowledged that anti-statism is now hegemonic. There's a congruence between the language of neo-anarchism and David Cameron's Big Society, which is not to say that the discourses are identical. But one problem with anti-statism — particularly when coupled with localism, as it often is — is that it makes any defence of institutions like the NHS very difficult. The drive of the original autonomists was to escape existing institutions, whereas I think our aim today should be to produce new institutions.

AI: Today people talk about "zombie capitalism"[3]: an undead system which people can't see beyond. Does this chime with Owen Hatherley's *Militant Modernism*[4] argument about the way the left has to challenge the dominance of neoliberalist capitalism as the only modernising force on the planet?

MF: Yes. Neoliberalism is now undead: it was massively discredited after the bank crises, but that hasn't stopped it continuing in zombie form. The default settings of most of our institutions remain neoliberal, and will do so until they are reset. In claiming there was "no alternative" to neoliberalism, the neoliberals were staking a claim that they were the only modernisers. Resistance to neoliberalism was a resistance to modernisation.

Neoliberal ideologues have successfully imposed an equation between neoliberalisation and modernisation; this has been central to capitalist realism. Look at the way that something like the Royal Mail disputes are reported in the mainstream media: the workers are always said to be struggling against "modernisation", when really they are opposed to privatisation.

At the same time, it's clear that neoliberalism has in many ways arrested modernity. That's part of the point of *Militant Modernism*: the rise of neoliberalism has seen a turn to "postmodern" cultural and political forms, a formal nostalgia that is manifested in the refurbishing of familiar modes. It's not for nothing that Fredric Jameson calls postmodernism, with its culture of retrospection and pastiche, "the cultural logic of late capitalism". Neoliberalism claims to be the only modernising force, but it's increasingly clear that it is incapable of delivering modernity. The current crisis is a massive opportunity for the left to reclaim modernity for itself.

"we have to invent the future": an unseen interview with mark fisher (2012)[1]

Mark Fisher: Do you drive?

Sam Berkson: No

MF: I don't drive either and I can strongly relate to many of the poems [in *Life In Transit*], having spent so much time on public transport. There was something that Mrs Thatcher said: "If you are a man over thirty on public transport, you've failed". I think that's really telling actually. The men I know don't drive but often women do — I think with women, it might be safety that makes them want to drive. I always find it a waste of time being in a car. Whereas on a train you can read, write, do something else, and you can listen. But almost nobody listens to each other anymore because of the amount of headphones, etc. I think what comes out strongly from your poems is it is public transport in name only — because 1) it isn't owned publicly, as all these hideous private operators, and 2) the space isn't actually public, as you draw out in a lot of the poems, people are engaged much more in their own private conversations on mobile phones. To a ridiculously embarrassing and excruciating extent sometimes.

SB: Usually only a few people are listening. It's ironically public because everyone is so much in their own private world, what they're doing is bringing a much more private world into the public sphere. Everybody, right- or left-wing, doesn't like the idea of people listening into their private conversations. And yet we are at a time when our conversations are the most listened into because all the creeping technology. And also we're complicit with things like Facebook, we're quite happy to blurt out what we're doing all the time.

MF: I think there is a double thing going on — increasingly people are concerned about Facebook and its erosion of privacy or whatever. I think there is an interesting doublethink coming out here. In one sense people are talking on mobile phones, assuming that people aren't listening to them but sort of knowing at some level that at least one person will be. And then there is that Facebook phenomenon when you put stuff on there, hoping that people will actually look at it — desperately sharing it, looking for an audience that you may or may not get. And then neurotically checking how many likes or comments you get.

SB: It is not caring about the audience that is there but desperately needing more and more of an audience.

MF: I think celebrity is important on lots of levels to do with... It's faux intimacy isn't it? There is a generalisation of the female-targeted gossip magazines, the general form of culture, TV etc., it is this phenomenon of referring to people by their first names, like you get on the cover of these things as if you know them.

Tim Burrows: People reading mags on the train, talking about dieting.

MF: It is bio-control and the model for that is the women's magazine. It is about reducing a certain anxiety. It is not about saying you must do this one thing. It is about on one page Geri Halliwell is happy with her curves. The next month she is feeling much better because she has lost weight. You get these double binds being issued all the time by these magazines. The function of which is to destabilise and keep people in a state of anxiety and also add on solutions to every problem which is always that a consumer object will resolve this for you. Dieting is bio-power, a form of body control. What we have got with this digital culture now is this weird thing of hyper-ordinariness. You have got people who are done up to the nines but it isn't like David Bowie where you are playing with some abstract aestheticisation. We have got people who have this uber ordinariness — it is a normative model: perfect teeth, right skin tone. An utterly conservative artificiality.

SB: You hear people say symmetry is the ideal human beauty, and I like to think that symmetry is probably something that looks OK. But to deny that there is some sort of beauty in the eye of the beholder, that there is something original and unique about things and that we each find different things beautiful is bringing things back to the power of something very conservative, as a way of conforming towards being beautiful — and of course it is not normal at all, it's a really freaky look.

MF: It's a wash-back from digital, a lot of people are photoshopping themselves. The normalisation of cosmetic surgery, Botox, etc., is part of this bio-power regime and this constant anxiety about appearances, etc. Cosmetic surgery is not good — it's not good! People are concerned about their appearance, but they are measuring by the standards of this depressing normativity. Neuroses is highly productive, and very useful for capitalism. What's better than inherent dissatisfaction? Inherent dissatisfaction can be sold to endlessly. That's why that women's magazine model is so useful for consumer capitalism.

SB: You see that on the tube — there is an advert at the moment about wishing your friends were more beautiful, I think it is an advert for a camera — that idea that you want to be displayed as beautiful by the fact that you hang around with beautiful people.

TB: That has always been the paradox of the tube — it is where you will find the most professional people in London at a certain time, but it seems like the least airbrushed place you could be. You are up against someone's face, see every imperfection.

SB: Yeah the lighting's terrible isn't it! The light on the tube is deliberately meant to be uncomfortable because people are less likely to fight each other if they are uncomfortable and exposed. If I were designing the tube and I wanted to make it comfortable, I wouldn't do it like I do it. Take things like the pubs — they worked out that pubs put people off if you can't see inside. The whole idea of a dark little nook so you come in to hide away in a corner; what you really want is big glass-fronted windows. People can come in and feel comfortable and safe.

MF: That isn't a pub to me, that's a bar.

SB: It just feels uncomfortable because it feels like you are being watched. It's the panopticon, isn't it.

MF: It is second-phase Foucault, a sort of auto-panopticon. I remember someone said during the time *Big Brother* was still worth thinking about that the difference between *Big Brother* and Foucault's panopticon was in Foucault's panopticon you didn't know whether you are being watched or not, whereas contestants on *Big Brother* know for sure they are. There is now this phase with Facebook of the auto-panopticon, as we said earlier, where people make themselves the object of surveillance and survey themselves in this weird way.

677

SB: We can fight back. And we have also got this other problem on tubes and buses — there are so many adverts around.

MF: Semiotic pollution as I call it.

SB: Yeah. And what is the sensible response to that? It is to put earphones on — it is to not look at your surroundings, just essentially to shut your senses off to your surroundings. This is a terrible position for people to be in. I would argue that it is actually worse to be unaware of your surroundings. Everyone's advice is to be in the present, look around you, experience things, etc. But if you are going to do that all you are going to see are adverts and messages and hear all these announcements.

MF: It's quite stunning. If you go to Europe, I noticed this in Sweden, Stockholm, there were no adverts. I thought, "What's going on?" Even in the New York subway doesn't have many. There is something about the massive cyber-blitz of adverts in London. It is not that people tune out of public space — there is no public space for them to be in anyway. It is either a case of a certain kind of immersion or in this babble — the babble of competing mobile phone voices, or the babble of capital, shouting at you to buy something.

SB: You can bury yourself in your own personal sand — you can shut yourself off. This seems to be a lot of people's way of travelling is to literally disconnect from the world around them, and in some ways it makes sense — but at the same time you are disconnected from the world around you.

MF: I think certain kinds of disconnection are needed now. Unplugging from certain kinds of networks. I was speaking to my students about trying to unplug — we are in a new phase of human life I think. In the Seventies, boredom was a big problem. Boredom was an existential void, boredom could then be thrown back at the entertainment industry and mainstream culture and it was also a challenge to ourselves: why are we allowing ourselves to be bored? Given that we are finite animals and we are gonna die, it was a moral scandal of insane proportions that we can ever be bored. But now boredom is a luxury we don't have any more, because of our smartphones, even when you are standing in a bus queue or waiting for a train, you've got this constant low-level stimulus. Boredom and fascination are mixed in together now, to go back to those celebrity magazines. And a better example of this is those free papers in London which have thankfully disappeared — *thelondonpaper*, one word, and the totally aptly named *London Lite*. The *Evening Standard* and *Metro* are great journalism compared. Those papers were an utterly terrifying prospect when they appeared. Talk about semiotic pollution, and also just the way they literally clogged up the streets and you've got really poor immigrants responsible for irritating people, to stand in the way of commuters and push these things into their hands. But then the total compliance of readers, because they operated on a tired exhaustion. You'd look down the carriage, every single person will be reading those papers. You could feel the intellectual and cultural level just sink. Commuting time is probably the time when many people are paying the most attention to culture. It's not that I was immune to this — you'd see the headline on it, about some celebrity you half know and are not even interested in, yet you'd still want to know. It was this form of curiosity where you are not even interested in it. So you'd read the whole of this paper, not even interested in it, but at the same time it had drawn me in. This is what I mean about boredom and fascination. I imagine many people like myself have had serious books in their bag that they would have read if these papers weren't there. It tells you a lot about the way capital takes advantage of the worst instincts and exhaustion.

TB: Which is kind of why Boris Johnson is so popular. He is the hero of the [freesheet magazine] *Shortlist* generation.

MF: I think the thing with Boris is a bit like Franco Berardi said about Berlusconi — the person who mocks the place of power while occupying it. That's also Boris isn't it. Somebody who is weirdly popular around young people in a depressing way, because he doesn't take politics seriously or doesn't seem to. Of course, what he does take extremely seriously is that of advancing his own position and own class. This form of faux bonhomie and cynical dismissal is an extremely dangerous problem by which class power naturalises itself. I think Cameron has a version of that, not that he is as popular, but he is pretty good at coming across as a friendly sort of fellow you can talk to. My sense of the Cameron government is a total smash and grab. They know they are not going to get in again, but they also know if they change the defaults on certain things then no Labour government in the immediate future without massive change at the top at the culture of the Labour Party is not going to have the capacity of change it back.

SB: I read this recently, I don't know if it was a quote but Thatcher was asked what her greatest achievement was and she said New Labour.

MF: I don't know if it is a quote but it is certainly true. I joined the Labour party. I have never joined a political party before but you have to have the same ambition that New Labour had and think five years ahead. If a few of us went in with a strong agenda you could drive it in a certain direction.

SB: I thought that and joined the Green Party.

MF: Fair enough. I don't want to concede any territory. I don't want to put all my eggs in that basket. There was no point joining the Labour Party during the Nineties. They were set on one direction, towards New Labour, neoliberalisation, there was no way it was going in any other place, whereas now I don't know where it's going. It might carry on with this desperately banal soft neoliberalism or it may become something else in the end.

Two years ago UEL was totally festooned with lots of revolutionary banners, all of that — it was the time of the student cuts, it was an incredible effervescence of militantism, which seemed to come out of nowhere. Now when you go to UEL and you walk down the central corridor where all the banners were hanging off is Costa and Starbucks and the biggest sign you can see is an office with Credit Control on the side. There is a parable of what happens to every public space there. The public space that was asserted failed so now we are back into these corporate monoliths and Credit Control in big letters right in the centre of the corridor.

TB: There are Costa Coffees in every NHS Hospital waiting room these days.

MF: My wife's from Gravesend and in a hospital near Dartford, McDonald's bid for the franchise of the restaurant. It is such a Philip K. Dick world to me where you can have shops in hospitals. I don't intrinsically object to change — I just object to the fact that everybody's change is shit. The thing about capitalism is that it provides things that nobody likes. When people talk about choice and capitalism — Microsoft, that sums up everything. Nobody wants it, everybody has to have it. It is the same with chains. Who is a big fan of them? Almost nobody, but we all have to go in them.

SB: People used to complain about British Rail being late all the time because we thought we had more ownership over it. Now we accept the fact that of course they are going to charge too much, because they can, and of course it is going to be crap, because we haven't got any other choice. Before we felt it was closer to us.

MF: There was a case for modernisation of those publicly owned industries — they were run at a massive inefficiency, but that was just a pretext of privatisation. They should have been improved while being publicly owned. It costs a lot more now it is privatised. It is some kind of ridiculous fee, how much more the tube costs the public purse since it was part privatised. It is a destruction of ethos with the workers themselves — the same with hospitals, why aren't they cleaned properly? Because you bring in private contractors whose only incentive is to deliver it as cheaply as possible, to pay their cleaners as cheaply as possible. If you don't have that public service ethos then everything of course will become shoddier. It's glossy shoddiness, isn't it. That is the reality.

SB: Again and again you come up with the same paradox. It is almost exactly the opposite to the thing it says. You've got more choice; you've got no choice. It's shinier, it's better; it's worse. It's cheaper; it's more expensive. I think realistically we are not going to go back to nationalisation — it may not be a good idea.

MF: The one poem that really pulled me in was that early one about people not having a ticket. So powerful on so many levels I think. The class dynamic of it. Having been in lots of those positions — either sitting there [watching], or being the person who hasn't got a ticket...

TB: It reminded me of George Osborne being caught out in first class without a first-class ticket. He said he didn't want to waste taxpayers' money on a first-class ticket.

MF: Nice! You've got to respect the improvisational verve of that ludicrous excuse. Nothing sums up capitalism more than that, the fact that first class persists. The other day I went to Liverpool and it seemed like I was walking endlessly to get past first class. And of course, no one is in first class. Is it even economic to run, or does it have to be there because the class system demands it?

SB: That is the attraction of first class, there is no one in it. The whole idea of competition in train travel was completely flawed — it is not like you can go on the other line on the other train that leaves at exactly the same time — there isn't one.

MF: The one thing I think that most people would unequivocally nationalise overnight is the railways.

SB: It is expensive for the government to run, because they are just giving loads of public money to private companies who then charge loads of money. It hasn't liberated things, it hasn't given us freedom. I want to renationalise public space — not necessarily for the state.

MF: I think we have got to distinguish public space from the state. The state is legitimate, I would argue, insofar as it facilitates public space, but the public must be thought of as separate from the state. The state might be a precondition for the public, but it isn't the same. People want public space, which is why Starbucks is popular because it offers a generic sociality. It is a form of anonymous, generic kind of space, and even things like the *X Factor*, why people like it is because people are publicly, collectively, communing in something. So it shows that even in these conditions, where ideologically everything is opposed to the public, there is still a desire for the public and all we are getting is degraded forms. What communism would offer is you can have these generic spaces where people can come in but you don't have to pay for shit coffee. That's the kind of public space we need in the future really, where people can get together but don't have the parasitic add-ons of capital really.

SB: I think this whole thing about the means not the ends, just saying this is the step that I like. I'll go this way because I like this way. I find it hard to imagine what my ideal future is like but I just think: What things work? And let's do more of those things that work.

MF: I think it is an imaginative task now is for us to think, what is the future of the public? If we can accept that the neoliberal story that the public is over — that story is now over. If the public isn't going to be just old-style nationalised state industries, state centralization, all of that, what is it going to be like in the future? We don't know, we have to invent it.

hauntology, nostalgia and lost futures: interviewed by valerio mannucci and valerio mattioli for *nero* (2014)[1]

NERO: Let's start from your last book, *Ghosts of My Life*…

Mark Fisher: Well, the overall theme of the book is the disappearance of the future, at least in culture. For me, the failure of the twenty-first century is that the twenty-first century has yet to really start — so, in a way, it's a disappearance of both the present and the future. This is something that is quite evident in music. In *Ghosts of My Life* I mainly collected a number of pieces that have already appeared in a variety of different places, together with some specific articles written especially for the book; it's an augmented collection, you can say. I wrote a number of pieces concerning hauntology, which is a term originally conceived by Jacques Derrida that started to regain currency in 2006: I picked up on and used it in relation to a number of different musicians such as Ariel Pink, Jessica Rylan, the Focus Group and the whole Ghost Box label… So, in *Ghosts of My Life* I tried to explicate how this concept had been gaining a new currency, especially in relation to music.

N: Talking about hauntology, there's one excerpt in your book that sounds like a recap of this kind of aesthetic, even if it's not about music: that is, when you describe the typical atmosphere of a British TV show from the Seventies. Now, musicians such as the ones from Ghost Box heavily rely on this kind of memory — you know, of BBC educational programs, TV series from the Sixties and Seventies and so on. And they often spread a sort of melancholic feeling, which is quite different from the simple nostalgia of the past…

MF: Melancholia is one of the great threads running through my book. I think that what happened after the Seventies — and particularly during the Eighties, when the occupying forces of neoliberalism arose — was this sense that things were shifting. But probably the extent to which they would have shifted was not that clear at the time — at least not to me. I guess this is partly about the age that I am, and the expectations that I've formed, being born at the end of the Sixties, into a culture that was vibrant and experimental. It was something you could describe as an "informal education system". I didn't like school too much myself, but I didn't need to like it because the source of education could come from elsewhere. Music culture was a big part of that: it was in music press — like *NME* and so on — that I first encountered the work of continental theorists like Derrida and Baudrillard. It's this kind of wide and interconnected network that I call "popular modernism", a kind of infrastructure for disseminating and distributing experimental theory and culture. At the time it was just right, you just expected things to be like that, there was nothing special about it. But during the Eighties, this network slowly disappeared. At first, I thought it was just a temporary blip and that it would have all come back. But I was wrong: it was an irreversible shift. So you see, things that are taken for granted just disappear. And this brings us to a melancholia, a hauntological melancholia.

N: This is interesting, because if we take the classic idea of melancholia — as proposed, for example, by iconologists and so on — we can describe it as the painful consciousness of our limits in contrast to our desires. How does this "hauntological melancholia" differ from that?

MF: First of all, let me tell you that I try to distinguish this kind of melancholia from standard depression, which is another important issue to me. Because you know, standard depression is fairly spread: it's not very acknowledged, at least not as a political and cultural problem; instead, it's treated as a chemical problem, or as the result of people's family history. In other words, it's highly privatised. I think depression is manifesting itself in terms of low self-expectations. Depressive people don't expect much from life. Things are getting worse and they are changing only to stay the same in a more intense form — and that's what capitalism is. So you have this kind of sadness or depression that is basically a consequence of adjusting to such things. But the melancholia I'm describing is a completely different thing. That's why I'm opposing it to depression: it's a much more conscious articulation, an aestheticised process. I would actually say that if depression is taken for a granted state, as a form of adjustment to what is now taken for reality, then melancholia is the refusal — or even the inability — to adjust to it. It's holding on to an object that should officially be lost. So instead of saying, "Well, Public Service Broadcasting was like that, but now things have changed", you simply refuse to accept the loss of the object.

N: And why is that "hauntological'?

MF: Let's put it this way: it's easy to say, "Oh, things were great in the Seventies, let's go back to the Seventies", but I think the real issue is "What kind of future did we expect from the Seventies?" I mean, there was a trajectory, and this trajectory was interrupted. And now we find ourselves haunted by this future that we vaguely expected at the time, and that was terminated somewhere during the Eighties by the values related to neoliberalism. From this point of view, it's no coincidence that the Eighties saw a traumatic and violent defeat of the left, at least in the UK.

N: You're introducing another major theme of hauntology: the so called "nostalgia of the future"...

MF: I think that the concept of "nostalgia of the future" partly illustrates one of the paradoxes that I'm trying to get across through the book; for example, hauntological music is often accused of being nostalgic. To a certain extent this is true, but the point is: "nostalgic compared to what?" I mean, the whole twenty-first-century music scene could be described as nostalgic: where is the sense of the future now? Today, if you ask people what is "futuristic music", they would reply electronic music from the Nineties, or even Kraftwerk, and stuff like that. In a way, we still rely on an old future.

N: What do you think of recent phenomena such as vaporwave and the "pop art of the virtual plaza"? According to music critic Adam Harper, artists such as James Ferraro or Fatima Al Qadiri are at least trying to reconsider the concept of future in music, taking inspiration from virtual technologies and the whole late-capitalism imagery...

MF: I actually think that vaporwave still relies on a twentieth-century vision of the future. The sound texture and even the imagery is derived from Nineties corporate sources. The fact that vaporwave has been perceived as an example of "futuristic music" shows a kind of diminished expectations: can we really compare that to, let's say, Kraftwerk? Or to jungle music? Or to BBC Radiophonic Workshop? All of these things clearly delivered a sense of future-shock, like "Where does this thing come from?" After listening to such artists, people had to reconstruct the whole sense of the music that was around them. Unfortunately, I just don't think there's anything like that in relation to vaporwave...

N: But it's nonetheless interesting how these artists relate to a typical twenty-first-century imagery. To quote the *Wire*'s review of Fatima Al Qadiri's album, this music "imagines a world of frantically animate matter with no life outside of the iPad." You can't deny that such a description sounds like a mirror of our time.

MF: I think Fatima Al Qadiri mirrors this time by also not having a specific relationship with our time, at least in a way previous music did. Don't get me wrong, I sincerely think this music deserves attention: it was very interesting when I was in Berlin at the CTM Festival and somebody played some vaporwave stuff over big speakers, and you could just hear that it wasn't meant to be heard that way. You know, the compression, the sounds... it really seemed music made for smartphones and tablets.

N: The relation between music and smart technology also resembles what happened with the visual aspects of our everyday lives: the idea of "image" can no longer be completely detached from the devices on which it is displayed...

MF: Indeed, smartphones and tablets are increasingly becoming — if not exclusively — the image of what the present is; of the extent to which communication technology has completely colonised our sense of what technology is. This is another symptomatic phenomenon of the twenty-first century. Now, think about it: how much did we really care about communication devices in the twentieth century? We cared a lot about music technology because we could hear that... But phone calls and stuff like that: who really cared?

N: These communication technologies are also affecting our idea of representation. Let's make an example: the concept of realism in present-day horror movies is often based on the idea of "digital footage" (i.e. amateur footage that depicts supernatural events, etc.) In a few words: it is "real" what could be captured through an amateur camera. All that considered, how much do you think these technologies are influencing our understanding of reality and our relation with imagination?

MF: It looks as though, for example, we forgot the grand visions that science-fiction once had about technology: I mean, we used to talk about terraforming, transforming planets, altering solar systems! And from terraforming now we are discussing how to improve our access to the internet. That's a kind of reduction in itself, I think. Anyway, speaking schematically and overgeneralising, I think that there's far too much emphasis on online digitality. It has totally colonised our sense of what the present and the future are, and I think the actual phenomenological reality is engaging with what I prefer to call "capitalist cyberspace". So I'd rather not talk about technology as such, but more about the way technology operates within our economic system. For example, I think one of the key elements of digital technology is this sense of being slightly late all the time. Let's think about social media like Twitter: you're in a perennial state of reactivity, by the very fact you're there, you're always late, and therefore you're always in a state of slight and intense anxiety. I think we kind of normalised this as part of our nervous system, where even if something is perceived as instantaneous, it isn't quite. And this is part of a general sense of lack, of things lagging behind, which is a feature of the digital as such. Capitalist cyberspace demands a constant dispersion of attention, you're always solicited to respond and to react, so it's very difficult to be absorbed in anything. Also, the basic form of digital communication is command: every time you pick up your smartphone, you've been told to do things. And even if they are friendly commands, nevertheless it's a massive stress on the nervous system. Just dealing with these commands, or even ignoring these commands, blocks us with a constructive relationship to the future: that's the other side of the destruction of time-perspective.

N: And then there is also the inundation of information. Do you think that when you see a lot of things, it makes you feel like you've already seen everything?

MF: Well yes, it does. But back in the day, it wasn't just the lack of exposure to things that made people think that they were experiencing something new. They were really experiencing something new, it wasn't just an illusion.

N: But don't you think that these technologies somehow affect our imagination? For example, for a long time the future was envisioned by humans through the invention of new technologies (i.e. Leonardo da Vinci, Isaac Asimov, etc.), and in the Nineties technology was seen as a tool for change on an aesthetic and political level (techno music, cyberpunk, etc.). Today, instead, technology itself has become the subject who's "telling us what the future is", bringing about an inability to imagine it…

MF: I agree. If you think about it, nowadays we don't have "the future": we have upgrades. And in a way it's a pre-postmodernist thing. The whole experience of modernity was this double perception that whatever your current experience is, it's already obsolete; because modernity is a process which never reaches an end: there's no resting, no point of equilibrium, only this endless upgrading. And then today you have corporations such as Apple, whose business model is entirely based on this: obsolescence. You don't expect to own an iPod for very long, if only because they don't last that much... I've had five or six already!

N: So what's the difference between the modernist approach and this let's say post-postmodern way of being modernist?

MF: Well, I mean that the degree in which modernism survives is the sense of newness, as in traditional modernism, but it's been transformed in terms of upgrades. In the past, the grand vision of the future was essentially a great dislocation from the present: that grand vision is no longer available to us. Look at science fiction: I think already in the Eighties there was a crisis of the genre, but anyway, the last great science-fiction movies are from that time. Today, we're still locked into *Blade Runner*, dystopian cities, or even William Gibson's cyberpunk... I would say that *The Matrix* itself, with its vision of a fully simulated society, couldn't update this vision. Perhaps *Minority Report*, with its pop-up corporate advertisings, captures the reality of capitalist cyberspace even better than William Gibson: today cyberspace is like those continuous pop-up windows that constantly appear as advertising, commanding us to do something, in which we are not fully immersed in; it's more like a background noise from everyday life.

N: Let's go back, then, to the years when — according to your analysis — the trajectory toward the future was interrupted: the Eighties. Perhaps, one thing we shouldn't underestimate, is that the Eighties is also the decade where postmodernist aesthetics became a common language; we come from thirty years of temporal pastiches, past and present anachronisms, double codes, quotations and appropriations from different eras... Wasn't that a negation of the future itself?

MF: Absolutely. Also, if you read texts like *The Ecstasy of Communication* by Baudrillard, which is from 1987, you find out that things like the overwhelming flow of messages, the inability to constitute a distinction between the inside and the outside, to deal with having no halo or private protection anymore... Well, he's basically talking about Twitter and Facebook! And if you think about another author such as Frederic Jameson, his texts from the Eighties are astonishingly prophetic. What was the specificity of postmodernism in the Eighties, is now the dominant aesthetic paradigm; to the degree that it's very hard to see anything else. One of the most penetrating things of Jameson's analysis is this awareness of a particular form of anachronism that was emerging and calling attention to itself: if you think about a film like *Body Heat*, it was set in the Eighties and it had a contemporary aesthetic, but the feel was something from film noir of the Thirties and Forties. Now, that mixture of contemporary settings and out-of-date references is exactly the standard for so much culture of the twenty-first century. We naturalised anachronism.

N: What about physical spaces? We talked about how postmodernism reshaped our relationship with time, but if you think about it, the term "postmodern" first emerged in architecture as a reaction against modernist architectural movements.

MF: I think that the defeat of modernism in architecture, as described by Owen Hatherley in his book *Militant Modernism*, is part of the picture I'm describing. Just consider a city like London: the most futuristic parts of the city are the brutalist ones. You go to the Barbican Centre and you spontaneously think about the future, precisely because of the modernism of the buildings. Fashion is another example: it seems to be stuck, they're cyclically re-modernising old styles. It's not even fashion as it used to be.

N: In that sense, what's your opinion of Simon Reynolds' *Retromania*, his book about the obsession that pop culture has in relation with its own past?

MF: I mostly agree with Simon's analysis, but I guess that the main difference is that he sees retromania as an internet-related phenomenon. Of course the internet changed our lives, and of course the idea of timeless time deeply affected our habits, even in music; but we also have to bear in mind all the consequences of the naturalisation of anachronism and its side effects, which are issues related not only with the possibility of accessing a space like the internet: it's also a political matter, it's the way in which we use the internet and the way in which the internet functions in our economic society.

N: We started by talking about the "informal education system" you grew up with during the Seventies, and how it shaped a common idea of "popular modernism". How do you think younger generations relate to that? How does their idea of "future" compare to the old one?

MF: I think that they still feel a need for futurism, but it's in terms of a spectral, virtual presence of the former sense of it. I think that this leads to the fact that there's no specific discontent about the present. But when you produce something and you have the feeling that everything's already been done... it's sad, you know?

PART SIX

WE ARE NOT HERE TO ENTERTAIN YOU: REFLECTIONS

one year later...[1]

K-PUNK IS ONE YEAR OLD!

Contrary to the plague of miserabilism that seems to have descended on blogdom (as identified by Robin), I know EXACTLY why I blog...

For much of the last year, especially when things got REALLY BAD, it's been my only connection to the world, my only outside line... It's reinvigorated my enthusiasm for so many things, and pricked my enthusiasm for things I'd never previously considered... (I say this especially to the currently disenchanted Marcello, who has done both; I remember being drawn out of a catatonic depression last year by reading through the entire Church of Me archives.)

It's made me many valued friends, both online and (thanks to Luke's brilliant walks) off too... Plus it's put me back in touch with friends I'd lost contact with. (Yeh, there's the *occasional* wanker, but I can honestly say, very few, almost none really, certainly there's far fewer of them than the excellent, high quality correspondents.)

In short, and no exaggeration, it's made life worth living...

I know it's an awful cliché, but it's really true, a blog is what you make it...

So heartfelt thanks to all of those who have contributed, by linking, commenting, reading or inspiring...

spinoza, k-punk, neuropunk[1]

Being a Spinozist is both the easiest and the hardest thing in the world.

Easy, because it is simply a matter of acting in such a way as to produce joyful encounters. Hard, because the defaults of the Human Operating System (OS) are, in one of nature's most deliciously cruel tricks, set against this. The principal question which Deleuze and Guattari's *Anti-Oedipus* set out to answer was deeply Spinozistic: "Why is it that people are so prepared to fight for their own servitude?" Meanwhile, Burroughs' Spinozistic abstract model of addiction — i.e., very much NOT a metaphor, what could be more literal? — describes humanity's enslavement to a vast immiserating machine whose interests are not its.

All of which, to come back to Radar_Anomalous' Badiou-doubts[2] leads to another positive way in which we can wrest reason/rationality back from what Robin Undercurrent calls, hilariously, "boredom-mongering epistemonauts". According to Spinoza, to be free is to act according to reason. To act according to reason is to act according to your own interests. Finally, however, we have to recognise that, on Spinoza's account, *the best interests of the human species coincide with becoming-inhuman.*

Many of the problems with Human OS come from its inefficient bio/ neuro-packaging. By contrast with very simple organisms that are set up to be attracted to what is beneficial to them and to flee from what is hostile to them, human beings have a convoluted system for processing exogenous and endogenous stimuli, routed/rooted in the arborescent central nervous system running out of the spine and overseen by the brain. Actually, according to neurologists, the brain is in effect, *three* distinct brains — the "reptilian brain", which is responsible for basic survival functions, such as breathing, sleeping, eating; the "mammalian brain", which encompasses neural units associated with social emotions; and the "hominid" brain, which is unique to humans and includes much of our oversized cortex — the thin, folded, layer covering the brain that is responsible for such "higher" functions as language, consciousness and long-term planning. Neurology also gives a rigorously materialist account of the thanatoidal confusions between desire and prohibition that Lacan and Žižek have described.

Crucially for Burroughs' analysis, it provides an account of why humans are so endemically prone to addictive behaviour. This is because there are actually *two* separate circuits, one for motivation and one liking. In the latter stages of addiction, you want to consume the drug, but it is improbable that you will also like jacking up. Add all this up, and you pretty much have a neuronic recipe for the unremitting misery, hatred and violence that have characterised human history. Nietzsche said that if animals could describe the human species they would call it "the sad creature".

Yet, *precisely because of this hideously collocated morbid assemblage*, the human contains a potential for destratification which the functionally streamlined simple organism lacks. This is where Spinoza converges with cyberpunk, and hence with Deleuze and Guattari, cyberpunk's main theoretical program. One of the consequences of Spinoza's analysis, as I said before, is that human beings' emotion-generating hardware can be understood using the same causal framework that is applied to the so-called natural world. In the twentieth century, cybernetics will make the same discovery.

But let's dispense with one of the lazy, hazy assumptions we're all prone to fall into whenever we hear the word "cybernetics". Cybernetics does not only refer to technical machines. Wiener call it the study of control and communication in animals and machines (btw: why leave out plants?). Its principal discovery is "feedback" — a system's capacity to reflect and act upon its own performance. So, as Luke and I were discussing the other day, the *whole point of cybernetics* is that nothing is "more cybernetic" than anything else. There are only systems with more or less feedback, and different types of feedback.[3] So if the word "cybernetics" calls up only gleaming steel you have the wrong association.

If cyborgianism is oriented towards a maintenance and reproduction of the organism and its homeostatic control circuitries, Cyberpunk or k-punk (one of the motivations for the "k" btw is the origin of the word "cyber" in the Greek "kuber') flees towards a cybernetics of organic disassembly. Again, let's be clear here. You don't disassemble the human organism by replacing its parts with metal or silicon components. (That's why the term "cyborg" — or "cybernetic organism" is misleadingly redundant. All organisms are already cybernetic). What matters is the overall organisation of the parts. Do the parts operate as hierarchically organised and functionally-specified "organs" within a cybernegatively construed interiority or do they operate as deterritorialised potentials pulling from/towards the Outside?

This latter arrangement is what Deleluze and Guattari, following Artaud, designate as the Body without Organs. As Nick pointed out long ago, the BwO is an essentially Spinozist concept: "when it is a matter of the body without organs it is always a matter of Spinoza".

One of the sublimely ruthless (=machinically efficient) aspects of the behaviour of Aliens, predators and shoggoths from which the organism recoils in horror is their readiness to ditch body parts when they are damaged or redundant. The BwO quickly dispenses with any features that either inhibit its flatlining slide towards the zero intensity of pure potentiality or which draw it back towards the closed-down depotentiation of the organism. (I have sometimes wondered about the k-punk potential of "If thine own eye offend thee, pluck it out.") This, astonishingly perhaps, is Spinozist reason.

We can now see why becoming inhuman is in the best interests of humanity. The human organism is set up to produce misery. What we like may be damaging for us. What feels good may poison us.

The fascinatingly destratifying potential in neuroeconomics, then, lies in the possibility of using it against its ostensible purposes. As yet another of Kapital's slave-programs, the purpose of neuroeconomics is to induce the kinds of idiot-repetition-compulsion Burroughs and Downham delineate. According to Rita Carter in *Mapping the Mind*, "where thought conflicts with emotion, the latter is designed by the neural circuitry in our brains to win".[4] The Spinozist body without organisation program is aimed at reversing this priority, providing abstract maps for imposing the goals of reason upon emotional default. So k-punk is also neuropunk: an intensive rewiring of humanity's neural circuits.

Even if they have often repressed the knowledge, all cultures have understood that being a subject is to be a tortured monkey in hell, hence religion, shamanic practices, etc., geared towards the production of BwOs. Paradoxically, the ultimate interests of any body lie in having no particular interests at all — that is in identifying with the cosmos itself as the BwO, the Spinozist God, the Lemurian body of uttunul.

To get super-immanent, then, let's think about blogging. As Undercurrent described it over on hyperstition, at its best, blogging can be a "participative molecular collective of truly K+ processes (i.e. buying materials to write about so other people reply and recommend other things which you then write about...)".[5] What has begun to emerge on the most destratifying elements of the blogosphere is a depersonalising, desubjectifying network producing more joyful encounters in a positive feedback process in which mammal-reptilian conflict defaults are disabled.

On the side of the BwO, everything is positive, so what use can be made of this animal-in-a-trap howl of outraged subjectivism? Well, at the moment, Marcello is functioning as a morbidly compelling example of how *not* to be a good Spinozist. Spinoza's rigorous analysis of sorrow shows how the sad are typically not engaging directly and sensitively with the world but with their own frozen images (think of these as being like outdated data caches). Consider, if you can bear it, the way in which Marcello tilts at the windmills of his own phantasms in a flailing, pathetically resentful hunger for attention that is exemplary of how to produce sad encounters. It is a display of that Romantic fetishisation of self-destruction that, far from being subversive or transgressive, is the Human OS in person. (n.b. It is crucial to distinguish the intricate art of self-disassembly from the gruesome thanatropic processes of self-destruction.)

Still, in the words of Deleuze's favourite Spinozist formula, no one knows what a body can do. Maybe there will come a time when even Marcello will join us in this only-just-beginning, inciting experiment in collective identity-shutdown. What reasonable person wouldn't?

why dissensus?[1]

The word "dissensus" came to me while I was sitting on the 28th floor of Centrepoint a few weeks ago.

They took me to the top of the mountain.

The view was of course stunning, literally sublime: London in all its unmanageable vastness, seen from both above and from its very heart. It was high, so high, and with the long table in front of you and the metropolis below, you felt like you should be crushing the economies of Third World countries.

I was there for a meeting about Moodle, which is a "Virtual Learning Environment", a fairly new — and, so it would turn out, very exciting — open source educational software application. I knew nothing about it and when were "put into groups" by the Blairite Komissar in charge, I simply asked what were the merits of Moodle as opposed to using html. Cue black looks and frowns from the initiates. The Komissar, who has joined our group, tells me, in *the nicest possible way* of course, that I "seemed to be sceptical and might like to think about my attitude."

Aha! So being sceptical is pathological now. Rude. I geddit.

Course, quick as a flash, I replied. "Yeh... and *you* 'might like to think about' being a Blairite managerialist."

"Blairite?" he replied, clearly stunned at having his politesse challenged. At being counter-pathologised.

Later, a woman from Dublin College, also in our group, launches a not-before-time assault on PowerPoint ("death by bullet point..." "something used by people with no charisma...", as someone rightly said on Danny Baker's radio show this week). She pointed out that she had done a presentation a few weeks ago and people had been appalled and outraged that SHE DID NOT HAVE POWERPOINT. As she rightly argued, if you have an organised mind, there really is little need for PowerPoint.

Cue Komissar, again. "PowerPoint? Rubbish? It's just a *tool* isn't it?"

I didn't say the following, but I wish I had: Well, not really Mr Progtech Microsoft, that's a rather naïve view of technology donchathink... Technology, especially MS technology, has a tendency to induce behaviours, it does not "enable" some pre-existent human "creativity"... (Sure, there can be innovative uses of PowerPoint, but we all know what the standard use of PowerPoint involves... total redundancy... banal bullet points apologetically talked through.. sentences tailing off... "well, as you can see..." all in the name of "professionalism"...)

Blairite power IS Microsoft... in every sense... diffuse... emolliating... blandly inescapable...

And you only see its real face when you challenge it, step outside the smothering consensus of politeness.

The English master class are the only people for whom hypocrisy is not only acceptable, but obligatory.

"Yes, yes, you have a grievance, yes, of course things are totally unjust. But there are ways of going about things, old chap. Procedures. *Aggression*, confrontation, they never get anything done, do they? (And after all, they are a little *vulgar*, don't you think?) Now, that's not what *I'm* saying, I think your intensity is admirable, but *other* people, well. They're not quite so *intelligent. They* won't understand. So I would advise moderating it a bit. For your own sake. Carry on like this and things might get uh *difficult* for you..."

Stupidity and cowardice are always the stupidity and cowardice of the other.

Power is always the power of the big other, that which speaks *through you* and *of whom* you speak.

new comments policy[1]

Please note: feminazis, cult studs guilt mongers, passive consumer-whingers, "friends" who occupy the moral high ground, misanthropes, gliberals, stoner pacifists, therapy-pushers...

Whilst I disagree with Luke's idea that comments boxes should be closed entirely, I have decided to institute a new policy on comments.

Only comments deemed to be positive by the Kollektive will be left up. The purpose of the site is to build the Kollektive, so comments by those intrinsically hostile to the notion of collectivity or those hostile to the k-punk project per se will be deleted as soon as possible, so as not to waste the energy of the collective on distracting, egocratic nonsense.

Clearly, I am at work throughout the day, and unlike some UK public service managers, my job does not allow me to spend all day in front of the computer. I am hoping though that, when I am not available to delete comments, others in the Kollektive can be deputed to take over.

Maybe another solution would be to only allow registered users to comment. Commenting here is a privilege that has been abused.

k-punk is not a "liberal" or "democratic" "free for all" (cf. *The Prisoner*). There are plenty of other ill-disciplined forums where people can air their resentments, ill-thought bile, and tedious ego-defence opinionism.

Or of course you can say what you like on your own blog. They really are very easy to set up.

What could be easier than sitting on the sidelines and carping? I know some people get a nice warm feeling in the stomachs from their sense of innate superiority to all "groups" and "gangs". Perhaps what those people should do is follow the logic of their position to its logical conclusion and utterly withdraw from public forums and indeed public life altogether.

Perhaps even more egregious though is the passive-consumer whinger.

Think, really, how outrageous it is for the likes of "Roger" to appear in the comments box and assure me that I am "coming off like a prick". On my own site. I don't say that k-punk is my site in a possessive sense. I just mean it is space that has taken me a great deal of time, stress and anguish to build. It really is like inviting someone into your own house and having them abuse you. If anything makes me a "prick", it is accepting a situation like that.

After all, Roger, and others, you have paid absolutely NOTHING for access to this site. Nor, naturally, have I received any financial remuneration for producing it. That isn't to say that I haven't received massive positive affect from doing it — what could be better than being part of a collective network? But it really has reached the point where I dread coming to k-punk to see what irrational spleen or spoilt boy/girl moodiness I will have to waste energy on dealing with next.

comments policy (latest)[1]

Basically the situation atm is this…

The comments boxes have become almost completely unproductive. Almost all of the worthwhile discussion happens between members of the Kollelktive, who, if the comments boxes weren't there, might be inspired to produce their own posts.

The comments boxes have heated things up — and SPEEDED things up. They need to cool down and slow down.

Yesterday, when I closed most of the current comments boxes down, you can't imagine the relief I felt. I could come to k-punk without feeling sick with anxiety about what unthought-out oedipalised rage, overgrown adolescent boy sulks and gliberal stupid American platitudes ("hey man, all that Marxist lingo makes my cringes cringe…") I would have to deal with.

It was definitely more stressful than work. And I have a very stressful job.

My problem is that I attribute rationality to positions and people who clearly are incapable of exhibiting it. It's partly to do with my background, which persists at a neuronic level, in the insistence: YOU ARE INFERIOR, BEND YOUR HEAD. So even when I am faced with clinically deranged second-stringer stalker-obsessive autists with delusions of relevance, part of me thinks, hmmm maybe they are right.

They most certainly are not.

There is no more urgent task on this hell planet than the production of rational collectivities.

These are not fascist gangs with "leaders". Nor are they perfectly functioning neurobotic Spinozist networks. No, but they can be on the way to this latter, if there is a commitment amongst the collective to a STARTING FROM WHERE YOU ARE.

Demanding perfection before you are prepared to commit is Prog Tech

703

SF. Starting to build a way out of hell HERE, NOW is kyberpunk.

The Kollektive takes priority. In the comments boxes as they have developed in the last few weeks (k-punk as New ILM... yeucccchhhhhhhh!), the Kollektive has struggled to make itself heard over the howls of outraged subjectivists, Conflict-Addicted Organisms (CAOs), and, worst and most pitiful of all, ILM-style one-liner one-upmen.

Do you feel alienated by this?

Good.

And goodbye, then.

The comments will be restored if there is a way of restricting them to registered users only.

We are not here to entertain you.

chronic demotivation[1]

What is supposed to be good about dope? The problem with it is not just the resultant psychosis but the ACTUAL STATE it puts people into in the first place — chronically demotivated, lethargic, filled with the kind of idiot porcine self-satisfaction that is the dialectical obverse of feeling paranoid. "Better to be Socrates dissatisfied than a pig satisfied...": not for stoners, whose only commitment is to the pleasure principle, to the shortest route to total relaxation. Thought, thought requires effort man, stop oppressing me, let me sit here and babble senselessly, coz that's creative, right, don't mess with my mojo, but buy me some munchies when you go to the shop, yeh?

What could be better proof of Lacan's claim that the nirvana principle — the drive towards the total extirpation of all tension — is not the death drive proper but merely the highest expression of the pleasure principle? Stoner stupefaction seeks only to remove tension, to become a zombified consumer, shambling to the fridge or the late-night garage to satisfy the constant craving of the insatiable Tungsten Carbide stomach of Kapital opened up in your organism by the dope.

The meat, and all it wants...

Thought, meanwhile, begins beyond the pleasure principle. As Houellebecq says in relation to Lovecraft, only those who are dissatisfied with life want to read and think. What from the perspective of those slaved to the pleasure principle is the introduction of a discordant and dysfunctional element ("hey, Infinite Thought, why you going to the library? Why don't you mong along here with us? Come and play with us, Nina, FOREVER...") is from the POV of anti-naturalist kommunist konstructivism the positive libidinal motor of an ever-complicating process of intelligence-production.

I know someone, probably Gleebot, will immediately leap on what I'm about to say and produce some counter-examples which will allegedly disprove it, but most stoners are males, aren't they? More than that, and here's why any empirical refutation won't wash, smoking makes you male. Self-satisfied, concerned only with yourself, unable to care about others even if you wanted to.

One of the many myths about stoners is that they are not aggressive. It's true that, in themselves, they don't FEEL aggressive. Their blissed out idiot state of hyper-relaxed slackness precisely wipes away any feeling that would interrupt their communion with their own organism. But when this onanistic self-involvement is threatened, well, then we see how irascible, irritable and bad tempered stoners can be. Stoners demand the right to their own (passive) aggression, but detest any show of aggression from others, precisely because any antagonism — particularly political antagonism, my god antagonism and rationality, what could be more of a DOWNER? — disrupts their "right" to take pleasure. Bad vibes, man.

I need hardly underline the point that young people voluntarily subordinating themselves to this pacification program is not exactly politically positive. It's not only because they all smoked it themselves when they lolled about on a full grant or because their kids are all smokers that the government is in favour of relaxing the legal penalties on the smoking of the supposedly harmless drug. It's because it is politically expedient. What could be better for the Komissars of Kapital than if half the population spends all their spare time (i.e. convalescence from reproduction of Kapital time) smoking dope and the other half spends it on SSRI anti-depressants?

Fukuyama's *Brave New World* inspired argument against SSRIs was that, in producing a feeling of well-being, they remove the psychological motivation for action, for proving yourself. Though Fukuyama's argument is obviously advanced in the services of pro-Kapital enterprise, its logic can also be used by communists. You will not struggle against Kapital — you will not struggle against anything — if you are emolliated by narcotics.

Of course, the obvious counter-example that people will reach for is Rastas and dub. But the Rasta relationship to dope was very different to that of most white workers toking on their time off, or students spending all day in what the Fall, gloriously, called "a State-subsidised cannabis haze". It was not only that the level of downpression to which the Rastas was much greater than the "hard week" of the white worker, it was that their consumption of drugs was part of a disciplined religious and political ritual. Exactly the opposite, then, of those who turn to dope as a means of fugging out the world.

how to keep oedipus alive in cyberspace[1]

1. Contaminate k-space with the monkey superstition that there are such things as "persons".

2. Reject rationality and promote the propagation of opinionist virus (= Nietzschean perspectivism = mbodied/embedded subjectivism = Kapitalist ideology).

3. Ensure the continued disengagement of reason by personalising all discourse. "You're only saying that because you are… [insert sex/ethnic/ sexuality/abuse/marital status here as applicable]."

4. Promote the use of certain common fallacies of reasoning, in particular: Irrelevant appeal to tradition/ authority — "We've always done that here…" — or to popularity — "Some people might like it…"
   The Ad hominem fallacy — attacking the arguer instead of the argument (this is especially popular amongst lawyer-politicians and their defenders).
   The straw man fallacy — invent a deliberately weakened version of your opponent's position, demolish it, then claim to have refuted their argument.
   The Spinoza Agents (the Cold Rationalist equivalent of Gibson's Turing Cops, who, unlike the Turing Police, are dedicated not to the curbing of AI but to its acceleration) report that a new and dangerously virulent form of artificial stupidity is spreading unchecked throughout k-space. This is a nasty combination of the ad hominem and straw man irrationalist mind viruses, provisionally codenamed "straw ad hominem". This oedipalising idiocy proceeds thus: given that this argument challenges commonsense and what is consensually accepted, the person who presented it must be [insert allegedly derogatory remark about mental health/marital status/

707

upbringing here], therefore anything they say is to be dismissed. No need to refute their arguments substantively, natch.

The SAs warn: "this is unusually moronic even given the low standards we expect of you jumped-up monkeys. Watch it."

we dogmatists[1]

No, I am not tolerant.

No, I do not want to "debate" or "enter into dialogue with" liberal democrats, PoMoSophists, opnionists, carnalists, hedonists, mensheviks, individualists...

No, I don't respect you, nor do I solicit such respect for myself from you.

The defenders of tolerance, debate, dialogue and respect advertise their bourgeois credentials with such advocacy. I'm sorry, apologists for exploitation of labour, but, no, I don't see it as my duty to provide the enemy with a space to express itself. You already have the global videodrome, the judiciary, the police, the psychiatric establishment and the most powerful armies of the world on your side. If that isn't enough, you could always make the effort to build your own profile and audience so you can add to the chorus of approval for the Satanic-worldly. (Too much like hard work? Thought so.)

Be under no illusions: differends, incommensurability, language games, forms of life, very far from disrupting the Dominant Operating System are that operating system in person. Žižek is right about Rorty being right: for all their apparent philosophical wrangles, the *political* upshot of the theories of Derrida and Habermas (and one can presumably add in Lyotard here) is exactly the same: defence of the liberal values of respect for Otherness, etc., etc.

Yes, I want to leave all that behind. One of the scandals of Badiou's thought is to announce the blindingly obvious: difference is not suppressed by the established order, it is its banal currency. Fragmentation, deconstruction, cut-up are the very stuff of which mediocracy is made.

So, yes, hold on tight and spit on me, I am a dogmatist.

But what does being a dogmatist entail?

Briefly, it involves commitment to the view that there are Truths. One can add to this, the view that there is a Good.

It's no accident that, since Kant,[2] rationalism has been held to be synonymous with dogmatism. Post-Kant, we have grown accustomed to the view that critique rather than dogma is the only acceptable ethical and philosophical position, so that "rational dogmatism" sounds like the worst imaginable insult.

But where does this attack come from? Fundamentally, four interrelated positions: authoritarianism, mysticism, egotism and relativism.

Far from being equivalent to authoritarianism, as the postmodern liberal doxa would have it, dogmatism is the only effective alternative to authoritarianism. Authoritarianism and postmodern "forms of life" entail one another. The familiar PoMo relativist insistence that it is neither possible nor desirable to arbitrate between the different ethical and ontological claims of "incommensurate" "language games" surrenders reason to mysticism. Unlike rationalist systems, which proceed from stateable axioms or principles, these "forms of life" are unable to point to any reasoning which founds them. The sheer existence of these "discursive communities" is held to be the justification for any traditions and beliefs to which such communities might subscribe. It should come as no surprise that Spinoza was feared and reviled by the authorities of all established religions, since Spinoza used reason alone to prove that the core belief upon which traditional theism was based — that there is a personal, transcendent God who performs miracles and has free will — was irrational nonsense. In other words, *it was Spinoza's dogmatism that allow him to overthrow the "authority" of the Torah.*

In terms of contemporary academic philosophy, rationalism is beset not only by Nietzschean-Wittgensteinian-Lyotardianism and Heideggerian Nazi poetico-mysticism, but also by the qualia cult of consciousness. This "philosophy" replaces the ineffable mystery of God with the ineffable mystery of consciousness. It consists solely in the *negative* claim that consciousness cannot be explained by either science or philosophy. This is religion in the worst sense.

But dogmatism is religion in the best sense. It is only through dogmatism — ruthless subordination of your Self to an impersonal system — that his majesty the Ego can be crushed. This has been the appeal of nontheistic religion throughout the ages. The Ego is simply authority in miniature (just as political authoritarianism is Egotism writ large), a micro-despot which can only be pushed off his throne by a commitment to sober systematicity.

Finally, it is a mistake to oppose dogmatism to pragmatism. Postmodernism advocates pragmatism at every level: not only at the level of how to get things done (the realm of praxis) but also at the level of what is to be done. But dogmatism is capable of distinguishing between what is to be done — what the goal is — from how this is to be achieved.

london litened[1]

The free paper plague is infesting all areas of London life. From dawn to dusk… Arriving at the station in the morning, the *Metro* already piled up, waiting. Leaving the train, slipping into your somnambulant self, commuter character armour freezing into place, automatically making the Waste Land walk across London Bridge ("*I had not thought that death had undone so many*"), the way already blocked by reps proffering *City AM*. (London Bridge is a film set now (*hyperreal city*): there's barely a day where there isn't a camera crew or some out of work actors playing a bit part in some promotional pantomime.) And in the evening, rushing to escape the black hole of the city, you have to play live-action Pac Man with the *London Lite* and *thelondonpaper* drones blocking the pavement every few yards. As if London needed people — poorly paid members of the city's immigrant subproletariat, at that — actually being employed to obstruct the pavement. In the train, the free papers are everywhere, their dull gloss a lurid temptation for the drained mind… cut and pasted PR… nothing happening forever… cocaine celebrities… a survey says… join in the debate… vote: more or bore… your texts… consume it and feel lulled and sullied… Semiotic parasites designed to prey upon hypnagogic drift. Weapons against the city's intelligence. Almost no one reads books anymore. London litened, littered, public transport desolated into a time waste land. Look around the carriage, snapshot of a Myspaced city: diversity without difference, homogeneity without communality — bodies reduced to claustrophobic zombie meat fighting for space, background hum of mutual hostility simmering, yet everyone is reading the same thing…

no future 2012[1]
(for nick kilroy)

There was no future, but it wasn't like anyone expected.

2003. We're wandering through the industrial spectres and overgrown dereliction of the Lea Valley. It's like the world has ended. A world has ended here, in fact. But now non-human worlds teem and thrive amid the deserted factories and the waste-strata. Feral plants, algae so thick and artificial-looking you'd swear you could walk across the canal on it. It is not a space that humans live in anymore. But it is a space they explore. Most of us there that day had alternative names. K-space names. Nick K, Woebot, Heronbone.

Heronbone shows us a social history in the form of discarded packaging from defunct commodities. They call Heronbone the bard of Stratford — this is his patch, his Waste Land, and many of his words are assembled from discards, fragments of grime lyrics recalled from the pirates, observations of insect colonies, flights of fancy prompted by this desolated space. Nick K is ablaze with projects and schemes, his photographers eye captured by images every few minutes. Photography is a darker art than most people routinely suspect. The visionary photographer can find the image, but they cannot necessarily see everything that is recessed in it. Most photographs act as mirrors, reflecting back the past into a frozen present. But some make contact with more mysterious dimensions of time. The "traces and clues of things to come". Futures bleeding back. Omens that can only be read retrospectively.

Sometimes there are signs but no one who can read them.

2007. Other stalkers are moving through the scurf space we had traversed four years before.

Repetition, with a difference:

"Right," said Sinclair, straightening up. "Are you ready for the zone? From here on in it's pure Tarkovsky." And so it was. Light-industrial spaces, car-wrecker's yards, square-windowed studios, haulage depots. Then, a mile further on, we hit the fence.

The perimeter of the Olympic site is now secured by a plywood fence that is 10ft high, around four miles long, bright blue in colour and chinkless. In places it is double-banked, in others it is topped by razor- or barbed-wire. The ODA began its construction last spring, and the last sections were put into place in July.

The fence is a barrier designed to exclude not only access, but also vision. There are no viewing windows built into it, no portholes for the curious stakeholder. To see inside the zone, you must ascend a Stratford towerblock, hire a helicopter, or — the desideratum — visit the ODA's website, which provides stills of the construction process and mocked-up futuramas of the park (light-glinted buildings, sparkling water features, happy munchkin people). [2]

Nothing Again Nothing

The "mocked-up futuramas of the park" surrender East London to the eventless horizon of the end of history, in which nothing happens forever. Nothing happens, again and again. Nothing happens. And every time it does, its announced with a press release.

In between our many visits to the Lea Valley in 2003 and Iain Sinclair and Robert Macfarlane's expedition there in 2007, what happened, of course, was the awarding of the Olympic games to London. In that period, Nick K died, the photograph he took that day in 2003 now looking more than ever like an eerie pre-echo both of his own fate, and the fate of the whole area, which has now been consumed by the CGI-shadow of 2012.

The first signs of a coming non-event is always the CGI.

Ghost Marketing

The CGI simulations that ringfence the Lea Valley project forward fake futures which will never arrive but which are immediately effective, already re-organising space in East London, already diverting resources from public to private. What this constitutes is a kind of negative hauntology, operating according to the familiar hype-dynamics of corporate capital. (Cybercapital relies on its own ethereal entities, of course.) We are not dealing with the spectres of lost possibilities, the ghosts of things that never happened, or the traces of forgotten events photoshopped out of the end of history. Instead, we are confronting the CGI-signs of a massive pseudo-event. A pre-scripted PR initiative disguised as an authentic happening.

According to some interpreters, 2012 is the year of the Mayan apocalypse. (Don't worry, though, its scheduled for December, so it shouldn't disrupt the Olympics.) The Olympics are now correlated with the end of time in quite a different way.

The arrival of the Olympics in China is not just a ratification of the Chinese regime, it's also another moment in the end of history. 2008 is a symbolic threshold, much like 1989. Anti-modernist protests against China obscure the fact that the Olympics, like the People's Republic of China, is now inherently meshed with global capital. 2008 will celebrate this integration, which may well presage a new mode of capitalism, in which authoritarian state control co-exists with PKD-like piratical capital. Victorian vampirism reformatted for cyberspace. The spectre of ultrapostmodernism, in which everything can be mass-replicated, but nothing new will ever be invented.

Memory Disorders

Both in Derrida's original articulation of the concept, and its current recirculation, fifteen years after *Specters of Marx*, "hauntology" must be understood in relation to postmodernity. Postmodernism, in turn, has to be understood, as Jameson has taught us, as "the logic of late capitalism". Postmodern temporality is captured by Fukuyama's claim — everywhere officially disavowed, even by Fukuyama itself, even as, surreptitiously, it is universally accepted, operating as a kind of presupposition of the contemporary cultural unconscious — that we have reached the "end of history". This is not only the conclusion of the process, but also the final cause to which everything has always been tending. End, then, in a double, appropriately Hegelian, sense: the terminus and the teleological goal.

The logic of late capitalism awaits the disintegration of the old Soviet bloc to find its fullest expression. Jameson's great contribution was to have grasped the way in which, far from leading to an efflorescence of cultural innovation, the unprecedented dominion of capitalism over the globe and the unconscious would lead only to a cultural situation given over to previously inconceivable levels of stagnation and inertia. Shorn of the confidence that an elite modernism could provide a revolutionary alternative to pacifying entertainment, no longer capable of believing that there was any form of detournement which could not in turn be re-incorporated and commodified, Jameson is the successor to both the Frankfurt School and the Situationists.

Jameson's Marxism, in other words, had taken cognizance of Baudrillard's critique. It was Baudrillard who anticipated the fusion of the opinion poll and reality TV in the seamless system of cultural "interactivity" which disarms any oppositional impulse by not only interpellating the consumer, but inducting them into its circuits. You decide. Text your response. Vote online. Join the debate. More or bore.

Jameson and Baudrillard understood that this user-generated content, together with the concomitant retreat of the cultural elite that has enabled it, would not lead to new kinds of creativity, but to pastiche and retrospection. Just as the capitalist language of "diversity" is a cover for new modes of homogeneity. The duplicity that operates here is more a strange structural effect than any deliberate attempt at mystification, Jameson observes.

What Jameson calls the "nostalgia mode" is one expression of this homogeneity. This remains one of Jameson's most ingenious formulations — the nostalgia in question is not manifested in a psychological state but in a kind of unacknowledged formal reiteration.

Hauntology is the counterpart to this nostalgia mode. The preoccupation with the past in hauntological music could easily be construed as "nostalgic". But it is the very foregrounding of temporality that makes hauntology differ from the typical products of the nostalgia mode, which bracket out history altogether in order to present themselves as new. Post-post-punk, indie's equivalent of mock Tudor.

The great sonic-theoretical contribution of the Caretaker to the discourse of hauntology was his understanding that the nostalgia mode has to do not with memories but with a memory disorder. The Caretaker's early releases seemed to be about the honeyed appeal of a lost past: Al Bowlly's aching croon in the Strand ballroom in prewar tearoom London, buried beneath the sound which constitutes something like the audio-correlate of hauntology itself: crackle. In veiling the past, crackle also makes the dimension of time audible. It is through this scratching of the scanner-lens that we can hear the time-wound, the chronological fracture, the expression of the sense, crucial to hauntology, that "time is out of joint". Dyschronia.

As the Caretaker project has developed, though, it has become more about amnesia than memory. Theoretically pure anterograde amnesia is not about the inability to remember, so much as the incapacity to make new memories. The inability to distinguish the present from the past. The cultural pathology of a clip-show culture locked into endless rewind.

It as if the Caretaker has taken us from an Overlook Hotel/Dennis Potter theme park into a simulation of neurological disorder. Fragments of tunes providing minimal orientation in an labyrinth of abstract sound. Have you heard this before? You can never be sure.

Nostalgia for Modernism

But if there is one act which makes a case for the supreme pertinence of the concept of hauntology in relation to music today, it is Burial. Precisely because Burial deals with nostalgic longings, his music does not belong to the nostalgia mode. What you hear in Burial's two LPs is a craving for a past which nevertheless appears irretrievably lost, veiled behind a relentless drizzle of crackle. Beyond the longing for a particular moment or a particular musical genre is a longing for the ceaseless forward motion of a culture which once appeared capable of infinite renewal, but which is now used up, involuted. The nostalgia for modernism resists the postmodern nostalgia mode.

Burial's music is possessed by an extraordinary sense of space. This isn't only a question of the production, which recalls Martin Hannett as much as King Tubby or Basic Channel. It is also about what images the music evokes — very vivid audio-vignettes of South London in this decade. Edward Hopper sound paintings of London after the rave. A city populated by ex-ravers gone to seed, like Nigel Cooke's dejected vegetables. The long comedown after all the highs. Serotonin crash and anti-depressants. The spaces that are the correlates of such disaffected states. All day cafes and night buses glowing like diving bells in the undersea murk of the early hours. What haunts here is not only the past but possible futures. A drowned world catastrophe leaking back in time.

Haunting is about space as much as time — about the spaces where the time rift becomes perceptible, and, with Burial's debut LP in particular, it was as if you were hearing double: hearing both the current dereliction and the former collective ecstasy. Flashbacks flaring in the gloom. What you are attuned to is a specific sense of place, as opposed to the "third place" — the space that is neither home nor work, but which combines elements of both. Spaces of consumer convalescence which could be anywhere. Burial's "In McDonald's" relocates the spatially-indifferent multinational capsule of the corporate franchise in a specific city: London, once again the capital of Capital. Once the sooty, smoggy centre of industrial capital, now the main hub of cybercapital. Open for business. Closed to almost anything else.

Is This Burning an Eternal Flame?

The arrival of the Olympic flame in London a few weeks ago was a pseudo-event on the grandest of scales, given content only by its subversion.

The CGI shadows of 2012 already enclose us. Present time captured into the performance of pre-scripted PR opportunities forever. But 2012 is an opportunity for dissent too. A focus for disaffection. Burial's second LP includes a sample from Lynch's *Inland Empire*: "I saw your light, it burns forever."

You could hear this as the secret key to Burial's whole sensibility. Like Lynch, Burial is attuned to the muffled, muted light flashes of the numinous that can be fleetingly glimpsed through the mundane. Distant lights, or lights that can be apprehended only from a distance.

Can we be guided by these lights, instead of by the Olympic flame, a symbol of a capital now more globalised than ever, the ultra-bright striplights drawing planetary destiny into an eternal shopping mall surrounded by a sweatshop?

ridicule is nothing to be scared of (slight return)[1]

Like David Stubbs, I'm of course delighted to have been shopped to the commissars of commonsense who compile *Private Eye*'s "Pseud's Corner". It's always bracing to be middlebrow-beaten; a pleasure I can expect to enjoy fairly regularly from now on, since, if the section from the Mark Stewart feature that they selected is considered fair game, then they might as well open up a permanent spot for me.

It's difficult to know what the alleged problem is: the conjoining of politics and music? Well, it's hardly stretching a point to argue that a record such as *For How Much Do We Tolerate Mass Murder?* might, y'know, have had some connection with geopolitical developments at the end of the Seventies. Would the same objection be made to linkages between politics and other areas of culture? But of course what is objected to is as much a question of tone as of content. The default expectation in British media is that writers perform a homely matiness: writing must be light, upbeat and irreverent, never taking itself or anything else too seriously.

The function of "Pseud's Corner" — to punish writing that in some way overreaches itself, that gets ideas above its station or gets carried away — has now been taken up by online discussion boards and comments facilities everywhere. The effect on any writer who internalises the critique is to be intimidated into colourless mediocrity. But the problem with most published writing today is not that it is "pretentious", it is that is unreflective PR hackwork. David Stubbs is right to invoke a certain Orwell as the patron of bluff, plain-speaking John Bull prose — but the Orwell of "Politics and the English Language" also attacked the mechanical circulation of dull, dead language. If only that Orwell were more heeded. "Never use a metaphor, simile, or other figure of speech which you are used to seeing in print", he demanded, optimistically hoping that "if one jeers loudly enough, send

719

some worn-out and useless phrase — some jackboot, Achilles' heel, hotbed, melting pot, acid test, veritable inferno, or other lump of verbal refuse — into the dustbin where it belongs."

Over sixty years later, such "verbal refuse" continues to circulate with impunity, and is supplemented by a whole inventory of PR commonplaces and consumer-affect babble (journeys, rollercoaster rides). Surely any amount of "pretentiousness" is preferable to these soporific linguistic screensavers?

break through in grey lair[1]

"Instead of tripping and beating a philosophy for its supposed faults only to end up with the same range of mediocre biases with which we began, we ought to find a more vigorous means of engagement with philosophers. The method I propose is to replace the piously overvalued 'critical thinking' with a seldom-used hyperbolic thinking. For me at least, it is only books of the most stunning weakness that draw attention to non sequiturs and other logical fallacies. The books that stir us most are not those containing the fewest errors, but those that throw most light on unknown portions of the map. In the case of any author who interests us, we should not ask 'where are the mistakes here?', as if we hoped for nothing more than to avoid being fooled. We should ask instead: 'what if this book, this thinker, were the most important of the century? How would things need to change? And in what ways would we feel both liberated and imprisoned?' Such questions restore the proper scale of evaluation for intellectual work: demoting the pushy careerist sandbagger who remains within the bounds of the currently plausible and prudent, and promoting the gambler who uncovers new worlds. Nietzsche makes far more 'mistakes' than an average peer-reviewed journal article, but this does not stop intelligent adults from reading him all night long, while tossing the article aside for a day that never comes."
— Graham Harman, *Prince Of Networks*[2]

This is one of the most stirring passages in *Prince Of Networks*, and it's particularly worth citing just now, when the topic of grey vampires[3] has come up again[4]. The mention of Nietzsche reminds me that he is one of the great scourges of grey vampirism, nowhere more than in the following passage from Part Six of *Beyond Good And Evil*:

"Aren't people's ears all full enough already of wicked noises?" says the sceptic, as a friend of peace, almost as a sort of security police: "This subterranean No is terrifying! Be quiet at last, you pessimistic moles!" For the sceptic, this tender creature, is frightened all too easily. His conscience has been trained to twitch with every No, even with every hard, decisive Yes —to respond as if it had been bitten. Yes! And No! —that contradicts his morality. Conversely, he loves to celebrate his virtue with a noble abstinence, by saying with Montaigne, "What do I know?" Or with Socrates, "I know that I know nothing." Or "Here I don't trust myself. There is no door open to me here." Or "Suppose the door was open, why go in right away?" Or "What use are all rash hypotheses?" Not to make any hypotheses at all could easily be part of good taste. [...] In this way a sceptic consoles himself, and he certainly needs some consolation. For scepticism is the spiritual expression of a certain multifaceted physiological condition which in everyday language is called weak nerves and infirmity.

Baron Mordant wrote to me a while back asking if grey vampirism wasn't a symptom of mental illness, and it is — but of the widespread, normalised and normalising pathology that Nietzsche describes here. As is wont, Nietzsche attributes the rise of the "spider scepticism" to racial intermixing but we needn't follow his ethnicising logic in order to utilise his analysis, which applies with uncanny acuity to the impasses of postmodern relativism and the stale corridors of the academy, tyrannised by the Fear — where the worst thing that could happen was that you are caught out in an error or a mis-cited quotation, rather than that you have wasted your life in endless equivocation, quibbling and deferral (while crying in your state-subsidised beer that you are doing so...)

Vampires do not appear in mirrors. In the case of grey vampires — and remember that there are vampires that are not grey; there are other kinds of energy piracy altogether, some more lustrous and ferocious — this means both that they cannot recognise themselves as vampires and that their existence is entirely dependent upon the attention of the Other. Grey vampires do not see themselves as vampires; they sincerely think that it is a *duty* to deflate enthusiasm and puncture projects. One sure sign of a grey vampire is the airy dismissal of concepts such as energy vampirism — no matter what their theoretical commitments might be in their published intellectual work, GVs are resolutely commonsensical in their everyday ontologies. But make no mistake about it, there is no more Real level to human life than that of energy and its distribution. As Burroughs more than anyone else realised, persons and the social are just masks covering up a terrain populated by energy predators and propagators.

Remember that you have to invite a vampire over your threshold — and grey vampires, like trolls, lose all their power once you cease to pay them attention or think about them. That is why, when they feel that your attention is gone, GVs will try any trick to regain it — the appeal to "democratic" values is a particularly scurrilous tactic ("you *must* give me your attention! It's your duty"). Trolls shamelessly try the same thing, of course, and it must be remembered that GVs are enablers of trolls — they like to position themselves as scrupulously neutral, uncommitted (whilst proffering all sorts of promissory notes about the commitments that they *will* make in *future*, what they will do once X or Y have stopped, the bad faith fantasies that prevent them from seeing the trap they are in) but the grey vampire's secret sympathies are always with the troll. For the troll actually articulates the resentment and spite which the grey vampires feel but are not able to express. They share the trolls' justification for their action — the belief that some people are getting ahead of themselves, that there is rather too much unseemly excitement about X or Y... As if what was required in intellectual life is more bent heads, more bitterness, less enthusiasm... Some teachers and lecturers *do* think that way, see it as their role duty to pass on the arid petrification which calcified their spirit usually sometime during their postgraduate career... Remember: all vampires are victims of vampirism...

But I see motivating students, passing on enthusiasm, as the first and most important task of a teacher. (Which isn't to say that one has to blindly encourage everything a student says or writes; far from it.) That's why I would say that one of the most despicable figures in the academic bestiary is the Troll-Master: the figure who feeds on the crushed enthusiasm of belittled students. The easiest way to win a cheap kind of respect is by adopting a nothing-can-impress-me hyper-critical stance, doused in cool *weltweltschmerz*, finding fault everywhere handing out praise and encouragement only very rarely; it's a transparent tactic, but one that works surprisingly well, and not only on jejune students, but also on very accomplished people, even those who have written a number of books. Often, the Troll-Master's own intellectual project will be mediocre and/or suspended — it's clear that all their libidinal energy is tied up in enslaving students into neurotic servitude. Troll-Masters can permanently insinuate themselves into students' heads, but usually their power depends upon the hothouse claustrophobia of the university department — they are village despots, whose charismatic tyranny seldom works outside their own turf. If they have a long-term effect, it is only to produce more grey vampires.

Graham is absolutely right to note that grey vampires tend to operate on a one-to-one basis, whereas trolls always require an audience. That's because trolls want the attention of the big Other, whereas grey vampires want to *directly identify with* the big Other — to become the voice of neutrality and authority, the voice from nowhere, which doesn't make any refutable claims and therefore cannot be caught out. The reason that there is a close fit between grey vampirism and the academy — now more than ever — is that the academy seeks to inculcate precisely this kind of neurotic neutrality (the other side of careerist sandbaggery), where the most important thing is that footnotes are correctly formatted. It is usually liberating to actually read the work of GVs and Troll-Masters: from their endless, refined critique, you're led to believe that what they produce will be the most sophisticated, error-free, immaculate work you could imagine; it's quite a shock when you actually read it and see how contestable and (often) mediocre it is.

The alternative to these traps is not the heroic solitary genius, but the network, another reason that Graham's new book is so important. As Nick Srnicek has been arguing, political theory now has to deal with the question of networks. (Incidentally, one of the reasons that Speculative Realism can contribute so much to political theory is that the areas SR opens up do not come already pre-packed in supersaturated pseudo-political "meaning", as in the exhausted, dustbowl terrains presided over by trad continental philosophy.) The toxicity of grey vampires and trolls is so important to think about because they it is essentially *network* toxicity. Troll-jouissance is derived precisely from their capacity to corrupt networks — the troll's usual MO is enter a thriving network and destroy it by diverting all its energy to dealing with them. The grey vampire, as ever, is more subtle — and, for that reason and for so many others, more dangerous. They sap the network's energy, not only by defending trolls, but by also defending equivocation itself, by construing any decision or determinate position as oppressive (deconstruction is a grey vampire pathology). Their preferred model for discussion is the fruitless combat of the comments box/discussion board "debate". This is the energy-swamp of web 2.0; but other kinds of network can grow here too.

real abstractions: the application of theory to the modern world[1]

At a recent symposium at the University of East London devoted to dance music and theory, some dissenting journalists declared that they would much rather be "buffoon empiricists" than credulous dupes of theory. This kind of dismissal of theory, by way of ostensibly plain-speaking self-deprecation, is nothing new in British culture. It's a certain attitude that practically defines itself by its disdain for theoretical abstractions, a disdain which once informed empiricism, the philosophy with which the English-speaking world is most associated. But, precisely because it aimed to reject supposedly unprovable abstractions, the empiricism of philosophers such as George Berkeley and David Hume ended up undermining rather than ratifying the categories of given experience: Berkeley famously denied the existence of the material world itself, while Hume argued against the existence of the self. In contrast with their rarefied weirdness, buffoon empiricists see their own role as shoring up the way the world appears to us in our unreflective moments. They claim to privilege "evidence", but really this is no more than a self-evident appeal to the very categories that empiricist philosophers denied: *persons* and (physical) *things*. And if only persons and physical things are real, what do buffoon empiricists think just happened in the global economy? Understanding the credit crunch and the recession demands the acknowledgement that abstractions are real.

It's no accident that the countries which bought into neoliberalism and financialisation most enthusiastically were the US and the UK. The "continental" theoretical tradition that buffoon empiricism defined itself against was often guilty of the kind of intricately nebulous, reality-denying textualism of which Anglo-Saxon nominalism accused it. The type of theory that has percolated through the art world and cultural studies in recent years — a confection of diluted postmodernism and degraded Deleuzianism, with its menagerie of vague anti-concepts such as difference, sensation and multiplicity — is not so far from buffoon empiricism. What this kind of anti-totalising thinking shares with it is a profound hostility towards systematicity; it holds the widespread view that making any kind of determinate claim is dogmatic, oppressive, even totalitarian.

As Fredric Jameson has argued, this pick-and-mix approach to theoretical propositions has rather too close a fit with consumerism — in fact, Jameson famously goes so far as to say, it's an expression of the "cultural logic of late capitalism". What is certain is that vague rhetorics of diversity do not have the cold lucidity necessary to give an account of the real abstractions of capital. In his 1966 essay, "Cremonini, Painter of the Abstract", Louis Althusser made a distinction between "abstract painting" and "the painting of abstraction".[2] The painter Leonardo Cremonini, Althusser argued, managed to expose the abstractions of capital not by directly depicting them — such a thing is impossible — but by showing "the *determinate absence* which governs [us]". As Benjamin Noys puts it in a commentary on Althusser's essay in his forthcoming book *The Persistence Of The Negative*:

> We have no image of capital, capital itself is a kind of pure relationality, a pure abstraction of value, labour, and accumulation, which can only be "seen" in negative. This is why the negation of real abstractions demands further abstraction, as abstraction is the only possible means to reveal this pure relationality which conceals itself in plain sight.[3]

Getting to this real abstraction entails an analysis of what I call capitalist realism. Capitalist realism — which by no means collapsed with the banks last year; on the contrary, there is no greater testament to its continuing power than the scale of the bank bailouts — is the notion that capitalism is the only viable political-economic system. It maintains that there is an inherent relation between capitalism and reality. Capitalist realism is a kind of anti-mythical myth: in claiming to have deflated all previous myths on which societies were based, whether the divine right of kings or the Marxist concept of historical materialism, it presents its own myth, that of the free individual exercising choice. The distrust of abstractions — summarised by Margaret Thatcher's famous denial: "there is no such thing as society" — finds expression in a widespread reduction of cultural ideas and activities to psychobiography. We are invited to see the "inner life" of individuals as the most authentic level of reality. Much of the appeal of reality television, for instance, consists in its seductive claim to show participants for what they "really are". The media is a sea of faces that we are encouraged to feel we are on first name terms with. Feature interviews in mainstream papers and magazines are invariably structured around biographical chat and photographs. In Britain, now more than ever, artists and musicians are faced with the choice of representing themselves in this biographical way or not appearing at all. Attempts to appeal to abstract ideas alone — either in the art itself or the forces it is dealing with — are habitually greeted with a mixture of contempt and incomprehension.

This is not restricted to the tabloid press — whose outing last year of the determinedly "faceless" musician Burial is only one example of its aggressive insistence upon psychobiographical reduction. The default settings of the British broadsheet press are just as dismissive of abstraction. Witness Nick Cohen's recent fulmination against *Frieze*'s own Dan Fox in the *Observer*, criticising a blog Fox had written analysing mainstream newspaper reports of the "Altermodern" exhibition at Tate Britain, London. Cohen's article included a priceless sideswipe against "the type of French intellectual who makes the English wish the Channel was a thousand miles wide." With its guiding assumption that theory is some continental toxin for which the antidote is Anglo-Saxon common sense, Cohen's piece was a manifesto for buffoon empiricism, making its standard complaint that theory is "unsupported by anything as mundane as evidence".[4]

But empiricism is not the same as the empirical — any worthwhile theory must account for empirical data, but, in order to do so, it cannot remain at the same level of the data it is seeking to explain. Besides, empirical facts typically have little to do with the phenomenological experience of individuals. Althusser's description of his own theory as "scientific" has been derided, not only by Anglo-Saxon nominalism but also by much post-Structural theory, which has tended to prefer poetry and discourse to the natural sciences. But Althusser's conception of the individual subject as a product of ideology is far more scientific than buffoon empiricism's unthinking dissemination of the concepts of persons and things. In his book *Nihil Unbound*, which draws upon neuroscience as well as the work of "continental" theorists, the philosopher Ray Brassier argues that science exposes human beings' everyday understandings of themselves and the world around them to be banal fictions. The kind of philosophical realism that Brassier advocates has nothing to do with capitalist "realism" — indeed, it has the resources to expose this so-called realism as nothing of the sort. Developing from the work of neurophilosophers such as Paul Churchland and Thomas Metzinger, who argue that all of the seemingly self-evident furniture of inner life (emotions, the self itself) are mystificatory superstitions, Brassier's work is part of a renewed theoretical assault on a buffoon empiricist ideology that calls itself reality.

no i've never had a job...[1]

I should have pointed out that Ivor Southwood has his own blog: here he is on the Fairy Jobmother;[2] and here's Digital Ben[3] with more on the same theme. Ben's post is, in the best possible way, sad. The key line is: *Why can everyone else do it and not me?* When I was unemployed, I was convinced that an absolute ontological gulf separated me from work. Work — which, like "being in a relationship" — would automatically confer on me the status of being a Real Person. But the horrific irony was that one couldn't *achieve* this status. You couldn't become a Real Person by getting a job. It was the other way round: only Real People could get work. Being unemployed wasn't a cause of shame; rather the sense of shame which I carried around as if it was the core of my being was what prevented me getting a job. So my job applications and interviews had an air of total hopelessness about them. *I know there's no way you would give the job to an insect like me, and we both know I couldn't do it even if by some miracle you offered it to me, but...* It took me years to realise that job interviews were a ritualised exchange where the point was to determine whether you knew what the right communicative etiquette was, and that telling the truth made you some weirdo. *Surely even those who have not been in the Castle know that one doesn't behave like* that...

Being a postgraduate student was little better than being unemployed — not least because it was regarded (by me as much as anyone else) as a way of avoiding work. (A friend once remarked that, in most circles in Britain, it would be less shameful to confess to being a drug addict than to admit you were a postgraduate student in an arts subject.) But I only "avoided work" because I didn't think I could do it. Ben writes:

> I can't quite make up my mind whether this missing quality is a ruling-class privilege (for which see the discussions collected here a few years back), or more of a stereotypical working class thing — hustle, graft, with its suggestions of not-entirely-legitimate activity. Perhaps it's something

possessed by people at both ends, but lost by those in-between? Rather like the ridiculous etiquette books of early Victorian times — real aristocrats didn't worry about that type of thing, they just did what the hell they pleased (knowing that they were immovably established and that being seen using the wrong kind of spoon wasn't going to affect them at all). Only the upwardly mobile bourgeoisie cooked up these arcane rules and customs to try and monopolise the road up and discreetly kick the bulk of the population off the ladder.

For me, it was absolutely a question of being projected into a space *between* classes. When I did work in factories, I was either pitied or pilloried. Every job seemed impossible: manual work because of my feckless diliatoriness, graduate jobs because, well, I wasn't the *sort of person* who could do them. Me, a teacher, a journalist or a lawyer — surely not.

Is there anyone who has caught the agony of this state of worklessness better than Morrissey? The useless jouissance of refusing what was anyway impossible: "No I've never had a job/because *I've never really wanted one*", "No, I've never had a job because *I'm too shy...*" I do sometimes think that the implicit political position in those handful of early Smiths songs was one of the most powerful of the Eighties. Singing "England is mine and it owes me a living" at the time of three million unemployed and the Miners' Strike... Rejecting the masculine destiny of Fordist worker at the very moment when that destiny was being denied to the working class ("No, we cannot cling to the old dreams any more")... Rejecting, that is to say, all of those working-class homilies about the dignity of labour... If there was a militant dysphoria in Morrissey it was here... and the dysphoria was absolutely integral to the militancy: incapacity as refusal. Failure as negative capability. *I'd rather be me miserable and shy than a successful communicative capitalist...* All of this when the Wildean defiance was shaped by gaucheness and awkwardness, rather than staged as a PoMo panto turn. "There are brighter sides to life/and I should because I've seen them/but not very often". The "but not very often" is the genius touch, of course. Without that, the gesture of refusal could seem like empty breast-beating; it would just be the swagger of "Wham Rap"... With it, there is just enough suggestion of other worlds, other ways of being, which *no one* in the current state of things has more access to than the unemployed dysphoric... And no one sees the total system of capital — the way that work, sexual relationships, commodities all intermesh and entail one another — no one sees that more clearly than the person excluded from work...

Morrissey represented the desire for a proletarian bohemia at the moment when — after the Sixties, after glam, after punk and post-punk — that possibility was being closed down. There's an excellent chapter in Jim McGuigan's excellent *Cool Capitalism* about the history of bohemia, which

McGuigan connects with Marcuse's concept of art as the Great Refusal. It seems to me that the installation of business ontology over the last thirty years has centrally involved the defeat of bohemia: art schools returning to largely being places for the privileged; the reduction of the print music press to indie *Smash Hits*; TV becoming populist trash or middlebrow mediocrity. The business culture of "selling yourself" (which I, like every right thinking person still regard as the height of vulgarity) has engendered the mandatory, seamless positivity that Ben and Ivor talk about: the Great Acceptance, as opposed to the Great Refusal. The aspiration to enter into bohemia was always the wrong kind of ambition from the perspective of a certain working-class way of thinking. Still is... many members of my family have never encouraged me to write, and continue to regard it as a "hobby", doing everything they can to put pressure on me to get "proper work"... Contrast this with the bourgeois kids doing unpaid internships for years on end...

fear and misery in neoliberal britain[1]

The passage I've pasted below — the introduction to a presentation, which was entitled "'We're not all in this together': Public Space and Antagonism in the Wake of Capitalist Realism" — was intended to be a kind of minimally fictionalised phenomenological tuning-up exercise, to give a predominantly non-UK audience a sense of what it has been like to live in the UK under capitalist realism. Everything here is based on genuine experiences, although some experiences have been compressed and condensed, and the experiences are not necessarily mine.

Now: The swipe card doesn't work. The machine senses anxiety, you're sure of it. It knows the card is not yours. You try the card again. Nothing. Same red light. The card isn't yours, but you should have access to the building. You had to borrow someone else's card because it is only possible to get swipe cards between the hours of 9 and 1 and you are working at these times.

Someone is behind you. You feel uncomfortable. Will they notice that the card does not belong to you? You try the card again. Again nothing. Red light.

Your phone rings. You struggle to get it out of the bag. By the time you have it, the call has gone through to the answering service. You see that the call has come from another of your employers. A familiar anxiety grips you: what have you done wrong now? But you have no time to worry about that at the moment.

You try the swipe card again. At last, the green light comes on. You're through the door.

Rushing down the corridor. Which floor were you supposed to be on? You rifle through your bag until you find the documentation. You should be on this floor, but at the other end of the corridor. You walk towards the room number. But suddenly your progress is blocked. There is a no entry sign: an office that cuts the corridor in half and through which there is no access.

It's a nightmare topology. Every time you seem to get close, another obstacle appears. You will have to go out of the corridor, down the stairs and up to the next set of stairs, facing a number of swipe card-access doors on the way.

By now the five minutes you hoped to have before you start is evaporating rapidly.

By the time you reach the room you were heading for, you are already late. You log-on to the computer. Or you try to. The log-in is rejected. You try again. No luck. Then you remember: you're trying a log-in from one of the other institutions that you work at. It's difficult to keep track sometimes. You remember the correct log-in, quickly scan one of your email accounts. See an email from an administrator. Have you filled in your bank details form? Yes, you've filled it in, you think. Weeks ago. But of course you can't be sure — maybe you only thought you had filled it in. Have they lost it? Flash of anxiety: will I not be paid this month? Last year, when you filled in all the same forms that you have to complete again this year, you were not paid for a whole fifty-hour contract, until you pointed out the mistake. Will the same thing happen again?

But there's no time to worry about this now.

You have a room of seventy students waiting to be taught.

Such is life in the UK's bloated and over funded public institutions.

Welcome to Liberty City. The busier you are, the less you see.

Ten years ago: the New-Path Institute

The psychiatrist asks you if your mood has improved.

You say no.

The psychiatrist says that the dose needs to be increased.

You don't respond. You can't. The drugs you're taking and the condition you are suffering from give you the cottonhead response time of a zombie. The psychiatrist feels very far away, like you are seeing him through a fish-eye lens.

You don't need to respond. It's not about your responses.

Besides, there's a sneering voice in your head constantly shouting at you.

Of course the drugs won't work.
Of course you won't get better.
Because there's nothing wrong with you.

Just give up.

But that's easier said than done.

The best you can hope for is a coma.

After the consultation, you return to your bed. Everything feeling very heavy, as if a crushing undersea pressure is bearing down on you. You lie on the bed, absolutely convinced that this is the truth — the raw unvarnished Real. Strangely, that remorseless glacial sense of certainty does not lessen your anxiety or bring you any relief. You cannot rest, even though you are catatonically immobile. Your heart is pounding. Jackhammer thud out of a Poe story. It gets faster and louder until the only thing louder is the voice in your head.

Later, you say to a nurse:

So that's what the treatment amounts to? Drugging and incarceration.

They nod. In the background, someone is howling.

Now: Rush away to one of the other places you work. You are supposed to photocopy some texts.

But by the time you arrive in the corridor, all the doors are locked. No one there.

This is the second time this has happened. Last time the photocopier wasn't working.

You should have come earlier today. But there wasn't time then.

Defeated, but trying to ensure that the two-hour round trip is not a complete waste of time, you go to the library, using the temporary swipe card that you were given because your contract has not been prepared yet. You take some books off the shelf and try to check them out. No dice. Your library record has not yet been prepared.

Can you come back later?

Yes, you can come back later.

On the train home. Claustrophobia-inducing crush. You're so anxious about having your iPod or your phone stolen that it would almost come as a relief if they were.

Exhausted, still standing up because there is no space to sit, you think about reading the book in your bag. But the temptation of the free paper is too great. Its headlines fix on your tired mind like predators that have eyed a stricken animal. The little oedipal-celebrity narratives hook you in. Everything collapsing into the universal form of the tabloid. Idle chatter subsuming all other news. Politics as a family soap opera. Nothing going on except ambition, intrigue, envy. You're bored even as you are fascinated.

Six years ago: In the office of the occupational therapist.

You are being asked to prove that you are mentally fit.

Because — as the Human Resources manager kindly pointed out — *you have suffered from stress in the past.* (The thought flashes through your mind — not that they cared when you were suffering.) But now *people are concerned.*

The anger that you've been showing towards management can only be a sign that you are unwell. A little unbalanced.

Don't worry. No one is attacking you. We're all here to help.

You say to the occupational therapist:

If I say management is conspiring against me will that prove I am mad?

Now: Stepping over the vomit, you remember too late: only a fool would go out into a provincial English town centre late in the evening. It's night of the living dead out here.

Screams that sound like they come from the Dante-damned. And that's just from the people who are enjoying themselves.

The lurching zombie threat of violence simmering.

Try not to catch anyone's eye.

When you go by Accident and Emergency, you see all the walking wounded, and some who are not walking. All the casualties of the UK's many happy hours.

You remember a doctor saying that twenty years ago, the night shift was so boring that the medics would engage in wheelchair races with one another. Not anymore. Not with all the knives, gun crime, fights, alcohol-related accidents, stomach pumps...

And all the superbugs breeding in the wards...

You reach home, switch on the TV. Emollient patrician voices crying crocodile tears. Public services to be massively cut back. 30%, 40%.

A new age of austerity.

Aristocrats and millionaires telling us: we've all got to do our bit.

We're all in this together.

exiting the vampire castle[1]

This summer, I seriously considered withdrawing from any involvement in politics. Exhausted through overwork, incapable of productive activity, I found myself drifting through social networks, feeling my depression and exhaustion increasing.

"Left-wing" Twitter can often be a miserable, dispiriting zone. Earlier this year, there were some high-profile twitterstorms, in which particular left-identifying figures were "called out" and condemned. What these figures had said was sometimes objectionable; but nevertheless, the way in which they were personally vilified and hounded left a horrible residue: the stench of bad conscience and witch-hunting moralism. The reason I didn't speak out on any of these incidents, I'm ashamed to say, was fear. The bullies were in another part of the playground. I didn't want to attract their attention to me.

The open savagery of these exchanges was accompanied by something more pervasive, and for that reason perhaps more debilitating: an atmosphere of snarky resentment. The most frequent object of this resentment is Owen Jones, and the attacks on Jones — the person most responsible for raising class consciousness in the UK in the last few years — were one of the reasons I was so dejected. If this is what happens to a left-winger who is actually succeeding in taking the struggle to the centre ground of British life, why would anyone want to follow him into the mainstream? Is the only way to avoid this drip-feed of abuse to remain in a position of impotent marginality?

One of the things that broke me out of this depressive stupor was going to the People's Assembly in Ipswich, near where I live. The People's Assembly had been greeted with the usual sneers and snarks. This was, we were told, a useless stunt, in which media leftists, including Jones, were aggrandising themselves in yet another display of top-down celebrity culture. What actually happened at the Assembly in Ipswich was very different to this caricature. The first half of the evening — culminating in a rousing speech by Owen Jones — was certainly led by the top-table speakers. But the second

737

half of the meeting saw working-class activists from all over Suffolk talking to each other, supporting one another, sharing experiences and strategies. Far from being another example of hierarchical leftism, the People's Assembly was an example of how the vertical can be combined with the horizontal: media power and charisma could draw people who hadn't previously been to a political meeting into the room, where they could talk and strategise with seasoned activists. The atmosphere was anti-racist and anti-sexist, but refreshingly free of the paralysing feeling of guilt and suspicion which hangs over left-wing twitter like an acrid, stifling fog.

Then there was Russell Brand. I've long been an admirer of Brand — one of the few big-name comedians on the current scene to come from a working-class background. Over the last few years, there has been a gradual but remorseless embourgeoisement of television comedy, with preposterous ultra-posh nincompoop Michael McIntyre and a dreary drizzle of bland graduate chancers dominating the stage.

The day before Brand's now famous interview with Jeremy Paxman was broadcast on *Newsnight*, I had seen Brand's stand-up show the Messiah Complex in Ipswich. The show was defiantly pro-immigrant, pro-communist, anti-homophobic, saturated with working-class intelligence and not afraid to show it, and queer in the way that popular culture used to be (i.e. nothing to do with the sour-faced identitarian piety foisted upon us by moralisers on the post-structuralist "left"). Malcolm X, Che, politics as a psychedelic dismantling of existing reality: this was communism as something cool, sexy and proletarian, instead of a finger-wagging sermon.

The next night, it was clear that Brand's appearance had produced a moment of splitting. For some of us, Brand's forensic take-down of Paxman was intensely moving, miraculous; I couldn't remember the last time a person from a working-class background had been given the space to so consummately destroy a class "superior" using intelligence and reason. This wasn't Johnny Rotten swearing at Bill Grundy — an act of antagonism which confirmed rather than challenged class stereotypes. Brand had out*witted* Paxman — and the use of humour was what separated Brand from the dourness of so much "leftism". Brand makes people feel good about themselves; whereas the moralising left specialises in making people feed bad, and is not happy until their heads are bent in guilt and self-loathing.

The moralising left quickly ensured that the story was not about Brand's extraordinary breach of the bland conventions of mainstream media "debate", nor about his claim that revolution was *going to happen*. (This last claim could only be heard by the cloth-eared petit-bourgeois narcissistic "left" as Brand saying that he wanted to *lead* the revolution — something that they responded to with typical resentment: "I don't need a jumped-up *celebrity* to lead *me*".) For the moralisers, the dominant story was to be about Brand's personal conduct — specifically his sexism. In the febrile

McCarthyite atmosphere fermented by the moralising left, remarks that could be construed as sexist mean that Brand *is* a sexist, which also meant that he *is* a misogynist. Cut and dried, finished, condemned.

It is right that Brand, like any of us, should answer for his behaviour and the language that he uses. But such questioning should take place in an atmosphere of comradeship and solidarity, and probably not in public in the first instance — although when Brand was questioned about sexism by Mehdi Hasan, he displayed exactly the kind of good-humoured humility that was entirely lacking in the stony faces of those who had judged him.

> I don't think I'm sexist, But I remember my grandmother, the loveliest person I've ever known, but she was racist, but I don't think she knew. I don't know if I have some cultural hangover, I know that I have a great love of proletariat linguistics, like "darling" and "bird", so if women think I'm sexist they're in a better position to judge than I am, so I'll work on that.

Brand's intervention was not a bid for leadership; it was an inspiration, a call to arms. And I for one was inspired. Where a few months before, I would have stayed silent as the PoshLeft moralisers subjected Brand to their kangaroo courts and character assassinations — with "evidence" usually gleaned from the right-wing press, always available to lend a hand — this time I was prepared to take them on. The response to Brand quickly became as significant as the Paxman exchange itself. As Laura Oldfield Ford pointed out, this was a clarifying moment. And one of the things that was clarified for me was the way in which, in recent years, so much of the self-styled "left" has suppressed the question of class.

Class consciousness is fragile and fleeting. The petit bourgeoisie which dominates the academy and the culture industry has all kinds of subtle deflections and pre-emptions which prevent the topic even coming up, and then, if it does come up, they make one think it is a terrible impertinence, a breach of etiquette, to raise it. I've been speaking now at left-wing, anti-capitalist events for years, but I've rarely talked — or been asked to talk — about class in public.

But, once class had re-appeared, it was impossible not to see it everywhere in the response to the Brand affair. Brand was quickly judged and-or questioned by at least three ex-private school people on the left. Others told us that Brand couldn't really be working class, because he was a millionaire. It's alarming how many "leftists" seemed to fundamentally agree with the drift behind Paxman's question: "What gives this working class person the authority to speak?" It's also alarming, actually distressing, that they seem to think that working class people should remain in poverty, obscurity and impotence lest they lose their "authenticity'.

Someone passed me a post written about Brand on Facebook. I don't know the individual who wrote it, and I wouldn't wish to name them. What's important is that the post was symptomatic of a set of snobbish and condescending attitudes that it is apparently alright to exhibit while still classifying oneself as left-wing. The whole tone was horrifyingly high-handed, as if they were a schoolteacher marking a child's work, or a psychiatrist assessing a patient. Brand, apparently, is "clearly extremely unstable... one bad relationship or career knockback away from collapsing back into drug addiction or worse." Although the person claims that they "really quite like [Brand]", it perhaps never occurs to them that one of the reasons that Brand might be "unstable" is just this sort of patronising faux-transcendent "assessment" from the "left" bourgeoisie. There's also a shocking but revealing aside where the individual casually refers to Brand's "patchy education [and] the often wince-inducing vocab slips characteristic of the auto-didact" — which, this individual generously says, "I have no problem with at all" — how very good of them! This isn't some colonial bureaucrat writing about his attempts to teach some "natives" the English language in the nineteenth century, or a Victorian schoolmaster at some private institution describing a scholarship boy, it's a "leftist" writing a few weeks ago.

Where to go from here? It is first of all necessary to identify the features of the discourses and the desires which have led us to this grim and demoralising pass, where class has disappeared, but moralism is everywhere, where solidarity is impossible, but guilt and fear are omnipresent — and not because we are terrorised by the right, but because we have allowed bourgeois modes of subjectivity to contaminate our movement. I think there are two libidinal-discursive configurations which have brought this situation about. They call themselves left-wing, but — as the Brand episode has made clear — they are in many ways a sign that the left — defined as an agent in a class struggle — has all but disappeared.

Inside the Vampires' Castle

The first configuration is what I came to call the Vampires' Castle. The Vampires' Castle specialises in propagating guilt. It is driven by a *priest's desire* to excommunicate and condemn, an *academic-pedant's desire* to be the first to be seen to spot a mistake, and a *hipster's desire* to be one of the in-crowd. The danger in attacking the Vampires' Castle is that it can look as if — and it will do everything it can to reinforce this thought — that one is also attacking the struggles against racism, sexism, heterosexism. But, far from being the only legitimate expression of such struggles, the Vampires' Castle is best understood as a bourgeois-liberal perversion and appropriation of the energy of these movements. The Vampires' Castle was born the moment when the struggle *not* to be defined by identitarian categories became the quest to have "identities" recognised by a bourgeois big Other.

The privilege I certainly enjoy as a white male consists in part in my not being aware of my ethnicity and my gender, and it is a sobering and revelatory experience to occasionally be made aware of these blind-spots. But, rather than seeking a world in which everyone achieves freedom from identitarian classification, the Vampires' Castle seeks to corral people back into identi-camps, where they are forever defined in the terms set by dominant power, crippled by self-consciousness and isolated by a logic of solipsism which insists that we cannot understand one another unless we belong to the same identity group.

I've noticed a fascinating magical inversion projection-disavowal mechanism whereby the sheer mention of class is now automatically treated as if that means one is trying to downgrade the importance of race and gender. In fact, the exact opposite is the case, as the Vampires' Castle uses an ultimately liberal understanding of race and gender to obfuscate class. In all of the absurd and traumatic twitterstorms about privilege earlier this year it was noticeable that the discussion of *class* privilege was entirely absent. The task, as ever, remains the articulation of class, gender and race — but the founding move of the Vampires' Castle is the *dis*-articulation of class from other categories.

The problem that the Vampires' Castle was set up to solve is this: how do you hold immense wealth and power while also appearing as a victim, marginal and oppositional? The solution was already there — in the Christian Church. So the VC has recourse to all the infernal strategies, dark pathologies and psychological torture instruments Christianity invented, and which Nietzsche described in *The Genealogy of Morals*. This priesthood of bad conscience, this nest of pious guilt-mongers, is exactly what Nietzsche predicted when he said that something worse than Christianity was already on the way. Now, here it is...

The Vampires' Castle feeds on the energy and anxieties and vulnerabilities of young students, but most of all it lives by converting the suffering of particular groups — the more "marginal" the better — into academic capital. The most lauded figures in the Vampires' Castle are those who have spotted a new market in suffering — those who can find a group more oppressed and subjugated than any previously exploited will find themselves promoted through the ranks very quickly.

The first law of the Vampires' Castle is: individualise and privatise everything. While *in theory* it claims to be in favour of structural critique, *in practice* it never focuses on anything except individual behaviour. Some of these working class types are not terribly well brought up, and can be very rude at times. Remember: condemning individuals is always more important than paying attention to impersonal structures. The actual ruling class propagates ideologies of individualism, while tending to *act* as a class.

(Many of what we call "conspiracies" are the ruling class showing class solidarity.) The VC, as dupe-servants of the ruling class, does the opposite: it pays lip service to "solidarity" and "collectivity", while always acting as if the individualist categories imposed by power really hold. Because they are petit-bourgeois to the core, the members of the Vampires' Castle are intensely competitive, but this is repressed in the passive aggressive manner typical of the bourgeoisie. What holds them together is not solidarity, but mutual fear — the fear that they will be the next one to be outed, exposed, condemned.

The second law of the Vampires' Castle is: make thought and action appear very, very difficult. There must be no lightness, and certainly no humour. Humour isn't serious, by definition, right? Thought is hard work, for people with posh voices and furrowed brows. Where there is confidence, introduce scepticism. Say: don't be hasty, we have to think more deeply about this. Remember: having convictions is oppressive, and might lead to gulags.

The third law of the Vampires' Castle is: propagate as much guilt as you can. The more guilt the better. People must feel bad: it is a sign that they understand the gravity of things. It's OK to be class-privileged if you feel guilty about privilege and make others in a subordinate class position to you feel guilty too. You do some good works for the poor, too, right?

The fourth law of the Vampires' Castle is: essentialise. While fluidity of identity, pluarity and multiplicity are always claimed on behalf of the VC members — partly to cover up their own invariably wealthy, privileged or bourgeois-assimilationist background — the enemy is always to be essentialised. Since the desires animating the VC are in large part priests' desires to excommunicate and condemn, there has to be a strong distinction between Good and Evil, with the latter essentialised. Notice the tactics. X has made a remark/ has behaved in a particular way — these remarks/ this behaviour might be construed as transphobic/sexist etc. So far, OK. But it's the next move which is the kicker. X then becomes defined *as* a transphobe/sexist, etc. Their whole identity becomes defined by one ill-judged remark or behavioural slip. Once the VC has mustered its witch-hunt, the victim (often from a working-class background, and not schooled in the passive aggressive etiquette of the bourgeoisie) can reliably be goaded into losing their temper, further securing their position as pariah/ latest to be consumed in feeding frenzy.

The fifth law of the Vampires' Castle: think like a liberal (because you are one). The VC's work of constantly stoking up reactive outrage consists of endlessly pointing out the screamingly obvious: capital behaves like capital (it's not very nice!), repressive state apparatuses are repressive. We must protest!

Neo-Anarchy in the UK

The second libidinal formation is neo-anarchism. By neo-anarchists I definitely do not mean anarchists or syndicalists involved in actual workplace organisation, such as the Solidarity Federation. I mean, rather, those who identify as anarchists but whose involvement in politics extends little beyond student protests and occupations, and commenting on Twitter. Like the denizens of the Vampires' Castle, neo-anarchists usually come from a petit-bourgeois background, if not from somewhere even more class-privileged.

They are also overwhelmingly young: in their twenties or at most their early thirties, and what informs the neo-anarchist position is a narrow historical horizon. Neo-anarchists have experienced nothing but capitalist realism. By the time the neo-anarchists had come to political consciousness — and many of them have come to political consciousness remarkably recently, given the level of bullish swagger they sometimes display — the Labour Party had become a Blairite shell, implementing neo-liberalism with a small dose of social justice on the side. But the problem with neo-anarchism is that it unthinkingly reflects this historical moment rather than offering any escape from it. It forgets, or perhaps is genuinely unaware of, the Labour Party's role in nationalising major industries and utilities or founding the National Health Service. Neo-anarchists will assert that "parliamentary politics never changed anything", or the "Labour Party was always useless" while attending protests about the NHS, or retweeting complaints about the dismantling of what remains of the welfare state. There's a strange implicit rule here: it's OK to protest against what parliament has done, but it's not alright to enter into parliament or the mass media to attempt to engineer change from there. Mainstream media is to be disdained, but BBC *Question Time* is to be watched and moaned about on Twitter. Purism shades into fatalism; better not to be in any way tainted by the corruption of the mainstream, better to uselessly "resist" than to risk getting your hands dirty.

It's not surprising, then, that so many neo-anarchists come across as depressed. This depression is no doubt reinforced by the anxieties of postgraduate life, since, like the Vampires' Castle, neo-anarchism has its natural home in universities, and is usually propagated by those studying for postgraduate qualifications, or those who have recently graduated from such study.

What is to be done?

Why have these two configurations come to the fore? The first reason is that they have been allowed to prosper by capital because they serve its interests. Capital subdued the organised working class by decomposing class consciousness, viciously subjugating trade unions while seducing "hard-working families" into identifying with their own narrowly defined interests instead of the interests of the wider class; but why would capital be concerned about a "left" that replaces class politics with a moralising individualism, and that, far from building solidarity, spreads fear and insecurity?

The second reason is what Jodi Dean has called communicative capitalism. It might have been possible to ignore the Vampires' Castle and the neo-anarchists if it weren't for capitalist cyberspace. The VC's pious moralising has been a feature of a certain "left" for many years — but, if one wasn't a member of this particular church, its sermons could be avoided. Social media means that this is no longer the case, and there is little protection from the psychic pathologies propagated by these discourses.

So what can we do now? First of all, it is imperative to reject identitarianism, and to recognise that there are no identities, only desires, interests and identifications. Part of the importance of the British Cultural Studies project — as revealed so powerfully and so movingly in John Akomfrah's installation "The Unfinished Conversation" (currently in the Tate Britain) and his film *The Stuart Hall Project* — was to have resisted identitarian essentialism. Instead of freezing people into chains of already-existing equivalences, the point was to treat any articulation as provisional and plastic. New articulations can always be created. No one is essentially anything. Sadly, the right act on this insight more effectively than the left does. The bourgeois-identitarian left knows how to propagate guilt and conduct a witch hunt, but it doesn't know how to make converts. But that, after all, is not the point. The aim is not to popularise a leftist position, or to win people over to it, but to remain in a position of elite superiority, but now with class superiority redoubled by *moral* superiority too. "How dare you talk — it's we who speak for those who suffer!"

But the rejection of identitarianism can only be achieved by the re-assertion of class. A left that does not have class at its core can only be a liberal pressure group. Class consciousness is always double: it involves a simultaneous knowledge of the way in which class frames and shapes all experience, and a knowledge of the particular position that we occupy in the class structure. It must be remembered that the aim of our struggle is not recognition by the bourgeoisie, nor even the destruction of the bourgeoisie itself. It is the class structure — a structure that wounds everyone, even those who materially profit from it — that must be destroyed. The interests of the working class are the interests of all; the interests of the bourgeoisie are the interests of capital, which are the interests of no-one. Our struggle must be towards the construction of a new and surprising world, not the preservation of identities shaped and distorted by capital.

If this seems like a forbidding and daunting task, it is. But we can start to engage in many prefigurative activities right now. Actually, such activities would go beyond pre-figuration — they could start a virtuous cycle, a self-fulfilling prophecy in which bourgeois modes of subjectivity are dismantled and a new universality starts to build itself. We need to learn, or re-learn, how to build comradeship and solidarity instead of doing capital's work for it by condemning and abusing each other. This doesn't mean, of course, that we must always agree — on the contrary, we must create conditions where disagreement can take place without fear of exclusion and excommunication. We need to think very strategically about how to use social media — always remembering that, despite the egalitarianism claimed for social media by capital's libidinal engineers, that this is currently an enemy territory, dedicated to the reproduction of capital. But this doesn't mean that we can't occupy the terrain and start to use it for the purposes of producing class consciousness. We must break out of the "debate" that communicative capitalism in which capital is endlessly cajoling us to participate in, and remember that we are involved in a class struggle. The goal is not to "be" an activist, but to aid the working class to activate — and transform — itself. Outside the Vampires' Castle, anything is possible.

good for nothing[1]

I've suffered from depression intermittently since I was a teenager. Some of these episodes have been highly debilitating — resulting in self-harm, withdrawal (where I would spend months on end in my own room, only venturing out to sign-on or to buy the minimal amounts of food I was consuming), and time spent on psychiatric wards. I wouldn't say I've recovered from the condition, but I'm pleased to say that both the incidences and the severity of depressive episodes have greatly lessened in recent years. Partly, that is a consequence of changes in my life situation, but it's also to do with coming to a different understanding of my depression and what caused it. I offer up my own experiences of mental distress not because I think there's anything special or unique about them, but in support of the claim that many forms of depression are best understood — and best combatted — through frames that are impersonal and political rather than individual and "psychological".

Writing about one's own depression is difficult. Depression is partly constituted by a sneering "inner" voice which accuses you of self-indulgence — you aren't depressed, you're just feeling sorry for yourself, pull yourself together — and this voice is liable to be triggered by going public about the condition. Of course, this voice isn't an "inner" voice at all — it is the internalised expression of actual social forces, some of which have a vested interest in denying any connection between depression and politics.

My depression was always tied up with the conviction that I was literally good for nothing. I spent most of my life up to the age of thirty believing that I would never work. In my twenties I drifted between postgraduate study, periods of unemployment and temporary jobs. In each of these roles, I felt that I didn't really belong — in postgraduate study, because I was a dilettante who had somehow faked his way through, not a proper scholar; in unemployment, because I wasn't really unemployed, like those who

747

were honestly seeking work, but a shirker; and in temporary jobs, because I felt I was performing incompetently, and in any case I didn't really belong in these office or factory jobs, not because I was "too good" for them, but — very much to the contrary — because I was over-educated and useless, taking the job of someone who needed and deserved it more than I did. Even when I was on a psychiatric ward, I felt I was not really depressed — I was only simulating the condition in order to avoid work, or in the infernally paradoxical logic of depression, I was simulating it in order to conceal the fact that I was not capable of working, and that there was no place at all for me in society.

When I eventually got a job as lecturer in a Further Education college, I was for a while elated — yet by its very nature this elation showed that I had not shaken off the feelings of worthlessness that would soon lead to further periods of depression. I lacked the calm confidence of one born to the role. At some not very submerged level, I evidently still didn't believe that I was the kind of person who could do a job like teaching. But where did this belief come from? The dominant school of thought in psychiatry locates the origins of such "beliefs" in malfunctioning brain chemistry, which are to be corrected by pharmaceuticals; psychoanalysis and forms of therapy influenced by it famously look for the roots of mental distress in family background, while Cognitive Behavioural Therapy is less interested in locating the source of negative beliefs than it is in simply replacing them with a set of positive stories. It is not that these models are entirely false, it is that they miss — and must miss — the most likely cause of such feelings of inferiority: social power. The form of social power that had most effect on me was class power, although of course gender, race and other forms of oppression work by producing the same sense of ontological inferiority, which is best expressed in exactly the thought I articulated above: that one is not the kind of person who can fulfill roles which are earmarked for the dominant group.

On the urging of one of the readers of my book *Capitalist Realism*, I started to investigate the work of David Smail. Smail — a therapist, but one who makes the question of power central to his practice — confirmed the hypotheses about depression that I had stumbled towards. In his crucial book *The Origins of Unhappiness*, Smail describes how the marks of class are designed to be indelible. For those who from birth are taught to think of themselves as lesser, the acquisition of qualifications or wealth will seldom be sufficient to erase — either in their own minds or in the minds of others — the primordial sense of worthlessness that marks them so early in life. Someone who moves out of the social sphere they are "supposed" to occupy is always in danger of being overcome by feelings of vertigo, panic and horror:

[...] isolated, cut off, surrounded by hostile space, you are suddenly without connections, without stability, with nothing to hold you upright or in place; a dizzying, sickening unreality takes possession of you; you are threatened by a complete loss of identity, a sense of utter fraudulence; you have no right to be here, now, inhabiting this body, dressed in this way; you are a nothing, and "nothing" is quite literally what you feel you are about to become.[2]

For some time now, one of the most successful tactics of the ruling class has been responsibilisation. Each individual member of the subordinate class is encouraged into feeling that their poverty, lack of opportunities, or unemployment, is their fault and their fault alone. Individuals will blame themselves rather than social structures, which in any case they have been induced into believing do not really exist (they are just excuses, called upon by the weak). What Smail calls "magical voluntarism" — the belief that it is within every individual's power to make themselves whatever they want to be — is the dominant ideology and unofficial religion of contemporary capitalist society, pushed by reality TV "experts" and business gurus as much as by politicians. Magical voluntarism is both an effect and a cause of the currently historically low level of class consciousness. It is the flipside of depression — whose underlying conviction is that we are all uniquely responsible for our own misery and therefore deserve it. A particularly vicious double bind is imposed on the long-term unemployed in the UK now: a population that has all its life been sent the message that it is good for nothing is simultaneously told that it can do anything it wants to do.

We must understand the fatalistic submission of the UK's population to austerity as the consequence of a deliberately cultivated depression. This depression is manifested in the acceptance that things will get worse (for all but a small elite), that we are lucky to have a job at all (so we shouldn't expect wages to keep pace with inflation), that we cannot afford the collective provision of the welfare state. Collective depression is the result of the ruling-class project of resubordination. For some time now, we have increasingly accepted the idea that we are not the kind of people who can act. This isn't a failure of will any more than an individual depressed person can "snap themselves out of it" by "pulling their socks up". The rebuilding of class consciousness is a formidable task indeed, one that cannot be achieved by calling upon ready-made solutions — but, in spite of what our collective depression tells us, it can be done. Inventing new forms of political involvement, reviving institutions that have become decadent, converting privatised disaffection into politicised anger: all of this can happen, and when it does, who knows what is possible?

PART SEVEN

ACID
COMMUNISM

acid communism (unfinished introduction)[1]

"The spectre of a world which could be free"

"[T]he closer the real possibility of liberating the individual from the constraints once justified by scarcity and immaturity, the greater the need for maintaining and streamlining these constraints lest the established order of domination dissolve. Civilisation has to protect itself against the spectre of a world which could be free.

[...] In exchange for the commodities that enrich their lives [...] individuals sell not only their labour but also their free time. [...] People dwell in apartment concentrations — and have private automobiles with which they can no longer escape into a different world. They have huge refrigerators stuffed with frozen foods. They have dozens of newspapers and magazines which espouse the same ideals. They have innumerable choices, innumerable gadgets which are all of the same sort and keep them occupied and divert their attention from the real issue — which is the awareness that they could both work less and determine their own needs and satisfactions."
— Herbert Marcuse, *Eros and Civlisation*[2]

The claim of the book is that the last forty years have been about the exorcising of "the spectre of a world which could be free". Adopting the perspective of such a world allows us to reverse the emphasis of much recent left-wing struggle. Instead of seeking to overcome capital, we should focus on what capital must always obstruct: the collective capacity to produce, care and enjoy. We on the left have had it wrong for a while: it is not that we are anti-capitalist, it is that capitalism, with all its visored cops, its teargas, and all the theological niceties of its economics, is set up to block the emergence of this Red Plenty. The overcoming of capital has to be fundamentally based on the simple insight that, far from being about "wealth creation", capital necessarily and always blocks the production of common wealth.

The principal, though by no means the sole, agent involved in the exorcism of the spectre of a world which could be free is the project that has been called neoliberalism. But neoliberalism's real target was not its official enemies — the decadent monolith of the Soviet bloc, and the crumbling compacts of social democracy and the New Deal, which were collapsing under the weight of their own contradictions. Instead, neoliberalism is best understood as a project aimed at destroying — to the point of making them unthinkable — the experiments in democratic socialism and libertarian communism that were efflorescing at the end of the Sixties and the beginning of the Seventies.

The ultimate consequence of the elimination these possibilities was the condition I have called capitalist realism — the fatalistic acquiescence in the view that there is no alternative to capitalism. If there was a founding event of capitalist realism, it would be the violent destruction of the Allende government in Chile by General Pinochet's American-backed coup. Allende was experimenting with a form of democratic socialism which offered a real alternative both to capitalism and to Stalinism. The military destruction of the Allende regime, and the subsequent mass imprisonments and torture, are only the most violent and dramatic example of the lengths capital had to go to in order to make itself appear to be the only "realistic" mode of organising society. It wasn't only that a new form of socialism was terminated in Chile; the country also became a lab in which the measures which would be rolled out in other hubs of neoliberalism (financial deregulation, the opening up of the economy to foreign capital, privatisation) were trialled. In countries like the US and the UK, the implementation of capitalist realism was a much more piecemeal affair, involving inducements and seductions as well as repression. The ultimate effect was the same — the extirpation of the very idea of democratic socialism or libertarian communism.

The exorcising of the "spectre of a world which could be free" was a cultural as well as a narrowly political question. For this spectre, and the possibility of a world beyond toil, was raised most potently in culture — even, or perhaps especially, in culture which didn't necessarily think of itself as politically-orientated.

Marcuse explains why this is the case, and the declining influence of his work in recent years tells its own story. *One-Dimensional Man*, a book which emphasises the gloomier side of his work, has remained a reference point, but *Eros and Civilisation*, like many of his other works, has long been out of print. His critique of capitalism's total administration of life and subjectivity continued to resonate; whereas the claims Marcuse's conviction that art constituted a "Great Refusal, the protest against that which is"[3] came to seem like outmoded Romanticism, quaintly irrelevant in the age of capitalist realism. Yet Marcuse had already forestalled such criticisms, and the critique in *One-Dimensional Man* has traction because it comes from a *second* space, an "aesthetic dimension" radically incompatible with everyday life under capitalism. Marcuse argued that, in actuality, the "traditional images of artistic alienation" associated with Romanticism do not belong to the past. Instead, he said, in... formulation, they "recall and preserve in memory belongs to the future: images of a gratification that would destroy the society that suppresses it."[4]

The Great Refusal rejected, not only capitalist realism, but "realism" as such. There is, he wrote, an "inherent conflict between art and political realism".[5] Art was a positive alienation, a "rational negation" of the existing order of things. His Frankfurt School predecessor, Theodor Adorno, had placed a similar value on the intrinsic alterity of experimental art. In Adorno's work, however, we are invited to endlessly examine the wounds of a damaged life under capital; the idea of a world beyond capital is despatched into a utopian beyond. Art only marks our distance from this utopia. By contrast, Marcuse vividly evokes, as an immediate prospect, a world totally transformed. It was no doubt this quality of his work that meant Marcuse was taken up so enthusiastically by elements of the Sixties counterculture. He had anticipated the counterculture's challenge to a world dominated by meaningless labour. The most politically significant figures in literature, he argued in *One-Dimensional Man*, were "those who don't earn a living, at least not in an ordinary and normal way".[6] Such characters, and the forms of life with which they were associated, would come to the fore in the counterculture.

Actually, as much as Marcuse's work was in tune with the counterculture, his analysis also forecast its ultimate failure and incorporation. A major theme of *One-Dimensional Man* was the neutralisation of the aesthetic challenge. Marcuse worried about the popularisation of the avant-garde, not out of elitist anxieties that the democratisation of culture would corrupt the purity of art, but because the absorption of art into the administered spaces of capitalist commerce would gloss over its incompatibility with capitalist culture. He had already seen capitalist culture convert the gangster, the beatnik and the vamp from "images another way of life" into "freaks or types of the same life".[7] The same would happen to the counterculture, many of whom, poignantly, preferred to call themselves freaks.

In any case, Marcuse allows us to see why the Sixties continue to nag at the current moment. In recent years, the Sixties have come to seem at once like a deep past so exotic and distant that we cannot imagine living in it, and a moment more vivid than now — a time when people really lived, when things really happened. Yet the decade haunts not because of some unrecoverable and unrepeatable confluence of factors, but because the potentials it materialised and began to democratise — the prospect of a life freed from drudgery — has to be continually suppressed. To explain why we have not moved to a world beyond work we have to look at a vast social, political and cultural project whose *aim* has been the production of scarcity. Capitalism: a system that generates artificial scarcity in order to produce real scarcity; a system that produces real scarcity in order to generate artificial scarcity. Actual scarcity — scarcity of natural resources — now haunts capital, as the Real that its fantasy of infinite expansion must work overtime to repress. The artificial scarcity — which is fundamentally a scarcity of time — is necessary, as Marcuse says, in order to distract us from the immanent possibility of freedom. (Neoliberalism's victory, of course, depended upon a cooption of the concept of freedom. Neoliberal freedom, evidently, is not a freedom from work, but freedom *through* work.)

Just as Marcuse predicted, the availability of more consumer goods and devices in the global North has obscured the way in which those same goods have increasingly functioned to produce a scarcity of time. But perhaps even Marcuse could not have anticipated twenty-first-century capital's capacity to generate overwork and to administer the time outside paid work. Maybe only a mordant futurologist like Philip K. Dick could have predicted the banal ubiquity of corporate communication today, its penetration into practically all areas of consciousness and everyday life.

"The past is so much safer", observes one of the narrators of Margaret Atwood's dystopian satire, *The Heart Goes Last*, "because whatever's in it has already happened. It can't be changed: so, in a way there's nothing to dread".[8] Despite what Atwood's narrator thinks, the past hasn't "already happened". The past has to be continually re-narrated, and the political point of reactionary narratives is to suppress the potentials which still await, ready to be re-awakened, in older moments. The Sixties counterculture is now inseparable from its own simulation, and the reduction of the decade to "iconic" images, to "classic" music and to nostalgic reminiscences has neutralised the real promises that exploded then. Those aspects of the counterculture which could be appropriated have been repurposed as precursors of "the new spirit of capitalism", while those which were incompatible with a world of overwork have been condemned as so many idle doodles, which in the contradictory logic of reaction, are simultaneously dangerous and impotent.

The subduing of the counterculture has seemed to confirm the validity of the scepticism and hostility to the kind of position Marcuse was advancing. If "the counterculture led to neoliberalism", better that the counterculture had not happened. In fact, the opposite argument is more convincing — that the failure of the left after the Sixties had much to do with its repudiation of, or refusal to engage with, the dreamings that the counterculture unleashed. There was no inevitability about the new right's seizure and binding of these new currents to its project of mandatory individualisation and overwork.

What if the counterculture was only a stumbling beginning, rather than the best that could be hoped for? What if the success of neoliberalism was a not an indication of the inevitability of capitalism, but a testament to the scale of the threat posed by the spectre of a society which could be free?

It is in the spirit of these questions that this book shall return to the 1960s and 1970s. The rise of capitalist realism could not happened without the narratives that reactionary forces told about those decades. Returning to those moments will allow us to continue with the process of unpicking the narratives that neoliberalism has woven around them. More importantly, it will enable the construction of new narratives.

In many ways, re-thinking the 1970s is more important than revisiting the 1960s. The 1970s was the decade that neoliberalism began a rise that it would retrospectively narrate as irresistible. However, recent work on the 1970s — including Jefferson Cowie's *Stayin' Alive: The Last Days of the Working Class*, Andy Beckett's *When the Lights Went Out* and John Medhurst's *That Option No Longer Exists* — has emphasised that the decade wasn't only about the draining away of the possibilities that had exploded in the Sixties. The Seventies was a period of struggle and transition, in which the meaning and legacy of the previous decade was one of the crucial battlegrounds. Some of the emancipatory tendencies that had emerged during the Sixties intensified and proliferated during the Seventies "[F]or many politicised Britons", Andy Beckett has written, "the decade was *not* the hangover after the Sixties; it was the point when the great Sixties party actually started".[9] The successful Miners' Strike of 1972 saw an alliance between the striking miners and students that was echoed similar convergences in Paris 1968, with the miners using the University of Essex's Colchester campus as their East Anglian base.

Moving far beyond the simple story that the "Sixties led to neoliberalism", these new readings of the 1970s allow us to apprehend the bravura intelligence, ferocious energy and improvisational imagination of the neoliberal counter-revolution. The installation of capitalist realism was by no means a simple restoration of an old state of affairs: the mandatory individualism imposed by neoliberalism was a new form of individualism, an individualism defined against the different forms of collectivity that clamoured out of the Sixties. This new individualism was designed to both surpass and make us forget those collective forms. So to recall these multiple forms of collectivity is less an act of remembering than of *unforgetting*, a counter-exorcism of the spectre of a world which could be free.

Acid Communism is the name I have given to this spectre. The concept of acid communism is a provocation and a promise. It is a joke of sorts, but one with very serious purpose. It points to something that, at one point, seemed inevitable, but which now appears impossible: the convergence of class consciousness, socialist-feminist consciousness-raising and psychedelic consciousness, the fusion of new social movements with a communist project, an unprecedented aestheticisation of everyday life.

Acid communism both refers to actual historical developments and to a virtual confluence that has not yet come together in actuality. Potentials exert influence without being actualised. Actual social formations are shaped by the potential formations whose actualisation they seek to impede. The impress of "a world which could be free" can be detected in the very structures of a capitalist realist world which makes freedom impossible.

The late cultural critic Ellen Willis said that the transformations imagined by the counterculture would have required "a social and psychic revolution of almost inconceivable magnitude".[10] It's very difficult, in our more deflated times, to re-create the counterculture's confidence that such a "social and psychic revolution" could not only happen, but was already in the process of unfolding. But we need now to return to a time when the prospect of universal liberation seemed imminent.

No More Miserable Monday Mornings

Let's begin with a moment that is all the more richly evocative because of its apparent modesty:

> It was July 1966 and I was newly nine years old. We had holidayed on the Broads and the family had recently taken possession of the gorgeous wooden cruiser that was to be our floating home for the next fortnight. It was called *The Constellation* and, as my brother and I breathlessly explored the twin beds and curtained portholes in our cabin built into the boat's bow, the prospect of what lay ahead saw the life force beaming from us like the rays of a cartoon sun. [...] I [...] made my way up to through the boat to take up position in the small area of the stern. On the way, I pick up sister Sharon's teeny pink and white Sanyo transistor radio and switched it on. I looked up at the clear blue afternoon sky. Ike and Tina Turner's "River Deep, Mountain High" was playing and a sort of rapturous trance descended on me. From the limitless blue sky I looked down into the churning, crystal-peaked wake our boat was creating as we motored along, and at that moment, "River Deep" gave way to my absolute favourite song of the period: "Bus Stop" by the Hollies. As the mock flamenco guitar flourish that marks its beginning rose above the deep burble of the *Constellation*'s engine, I stared into the tumbling waters and said aloud, but to myself, "This is happening now. THIS is happening now."[11]

This account comes from *Going To Sea in a Sieve*, the memoirs of the writer and broadcaster Danny Baker. It ought to go without saying that this was nothing more than a snapshot, one sun-saturated image from a period that contained more than enough misery and horror. The Sixties were not a realised utopia, just as the opportunities that lay ahead for Baker would not be available to most working-class people. Similarly, it would be easy to discount Baker's reverie as nostalgia for lost childhood, the kind of golden memories that practically anyone from any historical period or social background might have.

Yet there is something very specific about this moment, something that means it could have only happened then. We can enumerate some of the factors that made it unique: a sense of existential and social security that allowed working-class families to take holidays at all; the role that new technology such as transistor radios played in both connecting groups to an outside and enabling them to luxuriate in the moment, a moment that was somehow *exorbitantly sufficient*; the way that genuinely new music — music that wasn't imaginable a few months never mind a few years before — could crystallise and intensify this whole scene, imbue it with a sense of casual but not complacent optimism, a sense that the world was improving.

This sense of exorbitant sufficiency could be heard in the Kinks' "Sunny Afternoon", which Baker might well have also heard on the same transistor radio that day, or in the Beatles' "I'm Only Sleeping", which would come out a month later; or in later releases like the Small Faces' "Lazy Sunday". These tracks apprehended the anxiety-dream toil of everyday life from a perspective that floated alongside, above or beyond it: whether it was the busy street glimpsed from the high window of a late sleeper, whose bed becomes a gently idling rowing boat; the fog and frost of a Monday morning abjured from a sunny Sunday afternoon that does not need to end; or the urgencies of business airily disdained from the eyrie of a meandering aristocratic pile, now occupied by working-class dreamers who will never clock on again.

"I'm Only Sleeping" ("stay in bed, float upstream") was the twin of *Revolver*'s most self-consciously psychedelic track, "Tomorrow Never Knows" ("switch off your mind, relax and float downstream"). If the lyrics to "Tomorrow Never Knows", minimally adapted from *The Psychedelic Experience: A Manual Based on the Tibetan Book of the Dead*, seem somewhat pat, the music, the sound design, retain the power to transport. "It wasn't like anything else we'd ever heard", John Foxx recalls of "Tomorrow Never Knows",

> but somehow seemed instantly recognisable. Sure, the words were a bit suspect, but the *music*, the *sound* — organic electricity, disintegrated transmissions, lost radio stations, Catholic/Buddhist mass from a parallel universe, what being stoned *ought* to be like — weightless, timeless, revelation, moving over luminous new landscapes in serene velocity. It communicated, innovated, infiltrated, fascinated, elevated — it was a

road map for the future.[12]

These "luminous new landscapes" were worlds beyond work, where drudgery's dreary repetitiveness gave way to drifting explorations of strange terrains. Listened to now, these tracks describe the very conditions necessary for their own production, which is to say, access to a certain mode of time, time which allows a deep absorption.

The refusal of work was also a refusal to internalise the systems of valuation which claimed that one's existence is validated by paid employment. It was, that is to say, a refusal to submit to a bourgeois gaze which measured life in terms of success in business. "I didn't come from a background where people had 'careers'", Danny Baker writes. "You went to work, you had different jobs at different times, but it was all in a jumble. It did not define you or plot your course in life — and thank God for that." Baker left school in South East London with no qualifications. Yet he is careful that his picaresque journey from record shop assistant, to fanzine producer, music journalist and television and radio presenter should not be seen as either a hard luck nor a hard work story. He doesn't tell it as a petit-bourgeois narrative of "betterment", but of recklessness rewarded. This "recklessness" came out of a sense that fulfilment wasn't to be expected from work, and from an immense confidence, which allows him to consistently rebuff bourgeois imperatives and anxieties. The two volumes of Baker's memoirs lay out very clearly the factors which allowed this confidence to grow: the comparative stability of his father's work, in thriving docks that seemed as if they would remain at the heart of British economic life forever; the family's embedding in a working-class network that supplemented wages with "bunce"; its acquisition of a brand-new council flat with a garden. His own movement into writing and broadcasting was facilitated not by any entrepreneurial drive, but by a newly emerging public sphere — constituted out of parts of television, radio and print media — in which working-class perspectives were validated and valued. But this was not a working class which could be understood according to the protocols of kitchen-sink or socialist realism anymore than it was limited by ruling-class caricature. It was a working class that no longer knew its place, that had gotten above itself. Even the old redoubts of the bourgeoisie were no longer secure. In the Sixties, Ted Hughes had become one of Britain's leading poets, Harold Pinter one of its most exciting new dramatists, both of them producing work which reflected working-class experience in challenging and difficult ways, and taking it — via television — into the living rooms of a mass audience.

In any case, we are a long way from the disappearance of class later that would later be trumpeted by neoliberal ideologues. The settlements that labour and capital had come to in societies like the US and the UK accepted that class was a permanent feature of social organisation. They assumed that there were different class interests which had to be reconciled, and that any effective, not to mention just, governance of society would have to involve the organised working class. Trade unions were strong, emboldened in their demands by low unemployment. Working-class expectations were high — gains had been made, but more were surely on the way. It was easy to imagine that the uneasy truces between capital and labour would end, not with a resurgence of the right, but with an embrace of more socialistic policies, if not quite the "full communism" that Nikita Krushchev thought would be in place by 1980. After all — or so it seemed — the right was on the backfoot, discredited and perhaps fatally damaged in the US because of the protracted and horrific failure of the Vietnam War. The "establishment" no longer commanded automatic deference; instead, it came to seem exhausted, out of touch, obsolete, limply awaiting to be washed away by any or all of the new cultural and political waves which were eroding all the old certainties.

Where the new culture was not being driven by those from working-class backgrounds, it seemed that it was being led by class renegades such as Pink Floyd, young people from bourgeois families who had rejected their own class destinies and identified "downwards", or outwards. They wanted to do anything but go into business and banking: fields whose subsequent libidinisation would have boggled the expanded minds of the Sixties.

Working-class aspiration did not equate to class mobility, where the dubious reward was gradual and grudging acceptance by "betters". Instead, the new bohemia seemed to point to the elimination of the bourgeoisie and its values. Indeed, it was the conviction that this was imminent which was one of the few areas of overlap between the counterculture and the traditional revolutionary left, who seemed in many other respects to be at variance with one another.

Ellen Willis certainly felt that the dominant forms of left-wing politics were incompatible with the desires and ambitions triggered and tranduced by music. While the music that she listened to spoke of freedom, socialism seemed to be about centralisation and state control. The counterculture's politics might have been opposed to capitalism, Willis thought, but this did not entail a straightforward rejection of everything produced in the capitalist field. Her "polemic against standard leftist notions about advanced capitalism" rejected at best only half-true the ideas "that the consumer economy makes us slave to commodities, that the function of the mass media is to manipulate our fantasies, so we will equate fulfilment with buying the system's commodities".[13] Mass culture — and music culture in particular — was a terrain of struggle rather than a dominion of capital. The relationship between aesthetic forms and politics was unstable and inchoate — aesthetic forms did not simply "express" some already-existing capitalist reality, they anticipated and actually produced new possibilities. Commodification was not the point at which this tension would always and inevitably be resolved in favour of capital; rather, commodities could themselves be the means by which rebellious currents could propagate:

> the mass media helped to spread rebellion, and the system obligingly marketed products that encouraged it, for the simple reason that there was money to be made from rebels who were also consumers. On one level the sixties revolt was an impressive illustration of Lenin's remark that the capitalist will sell you the rope to hang him with.[14]

In the UK, Stuart Hall felt similar frustrations with much of the existing left — frustrations that were all the more intense in his case because he thought of himself as a socialist. But the socialism that Hall wanted — a socialism that could engage with the yearnings and dreamings that he heard in Miles Davis' music — was yet to be created, and its arrival was obstructed as much by figures from the left as from the right.

The first obstructive figure of the left was the complacent steward of Cold War organised labour or social democracy: backward-looking, bureaucratic, resigned to the "inevitability" of capitalism, more interested in preserving the income and status of white men than in expanding the struggle to include…, this figure is defined by compromise and eventual failure.

The other figure — what I want to call the Harsh Leninist Superego — is defined by its absolute refusal of compromise. According to Freud, the superego is characterised by the quantitatively and qualitatively excessive nature of its demands: whatever we do, it's never enough. The Harsh Leninist Superego mandates a militant ascesis. The militant will be single-mindedly dedicated to the revolutionary event, and unflinchingly committed to the means necessary to bring it about. The Harsh Leninist Superego is as indifferent to suffering as it is hostile to pleasure Lenin's phobic response to music is instructive here: "I can't listen to music too often. It affects your nerves, makes you want to say stupid nice things and stroke the heads of people who could create such beauty while living in this vile hell."

While the complacent leaders of organised labour were invested in the status quo, the Harsh Leninist Superego stakes everything on a world absolutely different to this one. It was this post-revolutionary world which would redeem the Leninist, and it was from the perspective of this world that they judged themselves. In the meantime, it is legitimate and indeed necessary to cultivate an indifference towards current suffering: we can and must step over homeless people, because giving to charity only obstructs the coming of the revolution.

But this revolution had little in common with the "social and psychic revolution of almost inconceivable magnitude" that Ellen Willis thought was seeded in the counterculture's dreamings. The revolution as she conceived of it would at once be more immediate — it would fundamentally concern how care and domestic arrangements were organised — and more far-reaching: the transformed world would be unimaginably stranger than anything Marxist-Leninism had projected. The counterculture thought it was already producing spaces where this revolution could already be experienced.

To get some sense of what those spaces were like, we can do no better than listen to the Tempations' "Psychedelic Shack", released in December 1969. The group play the role of breathless ingénues who have just returned from some kind of Wonderland: "Strobe lights flashin' way till after sundown... There ain't no such thing as time... Incense in the air..."

For all the familiarity of these signifiers, listening to "Psychedelic Shack" now can actually bring us up short. Invited to think about the psychedelic, our first associations might be with solipsistic withdrawal (the lyrics of a track like "Tomorrow Never Knows" invite just such an association). Yet "Psychedelic Shack" describes a space that is very definitely collective, that bustles with all the energy of a bazaar. For all its carnivalesque departures from everyday reality, however, this is no remote utopia. It feels like an actual social space, one you can imagine really existing. You are as likely to come upon a crank or a huckster as a poet or musician here, and who knows if today's crank might turn out to be tomorrow's genius? It is also an egalitarian and democratic space, and a certain affect presides over everything. There is multiplicity, but little sign of resentment or malice. It is a space for fellowship, for meeting and talking as much for having your mind blown. If "there's no such thing as time" — because the lighting suspends the distinction between day and night; because drugs affect time-perception — then you are not prey to the urgencies which make so much of workaday life a drudge. There is no limit to how long conversations can last, and no telling where encounters might lead. You are free to leave your street identity behind, you can transform yourself according to your desires, according to desires which you didn't know you had.

The crucial defining feature of the psychedelic is the question of consciousness, and its relationship to what is experienced as reality. If the very fundamentals of our experience, such as our sense of space and time, can be altered, does that not mean that the categories by which we live are plastic, mutable? Understood in individual terms, this quickly leads to the facile relativism and a naïve voluntarism that the Temptations themselves had targeted on their first psychedelic soul single, "Cloud Nine". Sure, you can be what you want to be, but only by being a million miles from reality, only by leaving behind all your responsibilities. This superegoic appeal could have been endorsed by conservatives as well as a certain brand of radical: conservatives, who wanted everyone to knuckle down to work; militants, who demanded commitment to revolution, which — they said — entailed an attention to the horrors of the world, not a quick fix flight from the real.

Yet the claim that altered states of consciousness took you a "million miles away from reality" was question-begging. It foreclosed the idea that altered state of consciousness could offer a perception of the systems of power, exploitation and ritual that was more, not less, lucid than ordinary consciousness. In the Sixties, when consciousness was increasingly besieged by the fantasies and images of advertising and capitalist spectacle, how solid was the "reality" from which psychedelic states fled in any case? Wasn't the state of consciousness susceptible to spectacle more like somnambulance than alertness or awareness?

In retrospect, one of the most remarkable features of the psychedelic culture of the 1960s was the way it mainstreamed such metaphysical questions. The psychedelic was not new — many pre-capitalist societies had incorporated psychedelic visions and the use of hallucinogens into their ritual practice. What was new was the break out of the psychedelic from particular ritualised spaces and times, and from the control of particular practitioners, such as shamans and sorcerers. Experiments with consciousness were now in principle open to anyone. Despite all the mysticism and pseudo-spiritualism which has always hung over psychedelic culture, there was actually a demystificatory and materialist dimension to this. Widespread experiments with consciousness promised nothing less than a democratisation of neurology itself — a newly widespread awareness of the brain's role in producing what was experienced as reality. Those on acid trips were externalising the workings of their own brain, and potentially learning to use their brains differently.

Yet psychedelic experiences were not confined to those who had taken drugs. The very mass media which mainstreamed psychedelic concepts along with the Vietnam War was itself a massive experiment in altering consciousness. With television, the breakdown of the distinction between dreams and waking life that film had begun now entered "private" domestic space. Television was at the centre of a media landscape that was still only just assembling, and which no one understood because nothing like it had ever existed before. The Beatles released their first album only a few months before the assassination of John F. Kennedy. Television was channel for contagion (Beatlemania!), trauma and hysteria as much as paternalistic messages or commercial huckstering. No one had been as famous in their own lifetime as the Beatles, because the infrastructure for such a fame was only just being created, and the Beatles themselves were playing a part in building it, as if — at one and the same time — the world had become an extension of their own electronic dream, and they had become characters in everyone else's dream.

You might say that the Beatles' own psychedelic turn was an attempt to convert all of this into a lucid dream. This is the quality of *Sgt Pepper's* "A Day in the Life", which plays out the difference between Lennon's lucid dream calm and the urgencies of work life (McCartney's breathless commuter, who reaches the bus in seconds flat). Yet escape from urgencies is always achingly proximate — once on the bus, McCartney's immediately character falls into a dream.

Lennon sounds dispassionate but not detached; there is humour but no blokish familiarity. His vocal seems to intimate that the ordinary somnambulance of the workaday world can only be properly apprehended from the perspective afforded by a different kind of trance. Or is it, rather, that a voice disconnected from the imperatives of working/waking life comes off as catatonic? The tracks shows us the inside seen from outside, as Lennon takes us on journey through the different ways in which consciousness is electronically mediated (by newspapers, film, television): "I read the news today, oh boy".

This contrast between urgency and lucidity was everywhere in Jonathan Miller's television adaptation of *Alice's Adventures in Wonderland*. It was broadcast on BBC television in December 1966, and reflected the influence of the Beatles even as it would go on to influence the Beatles in turn. Shot in black and white, the film has a strangely sober, almost austere visual style, devoid of any special effects or florid imagery. This fits with the adaptation's most striking innovation, its rendering of the characters not as animals, but as human beings. "Once you take the animal heads off", Miller told *Life*, "you begin to see what it's all about. A small child, surrounded by hurrying, worried people, thinking: 'is this what being grown up is like?'"

The film is pervaded by an atmosphere of lassitude, of languor and catatonia that sometimes lurches into sudden panic and helplessness. Miller again: "The book, by dressing things up in animal clothes, presents a disguised — a dream-disguised — domestic charade. [...] All the levels of authority and order-giving and obedience are reflected."[15] The ordinary world appears as a tissue of Nonsense, incomprehensibly inconsistent, arbitrary and authoritarian, dominated by bizarre rituals, repetitions and automatisms. It is itself a bad dream, a kind of trance. In the solemn and autistic testiness of the adults who torment and perplex Alice, we see the madness of ideology itself: a dreamwork that has forgotten it is a dream, and which seeks to make us forget too, by sweeping us up in its urgencies, by perplexing us with its lugubrious dementia, or by terrifying us with its sudden, unpredictable and insatiable violence.

The laugher that this *Alice* provokes — sometimes uneasy, sometimes uproarious — is a laughter that comes from the outside. It is a psychedelic laughter, a laughter that — far from confirming or validating the values of any status quo — exposes the bizarreness, the inconsistency, of what had been taken for common sense. Is this not the laugher that Michel Foucault describes in a justly renowned passage from the Preface to *The Order of Things*, a book that was originally published in the same year that Miller's version of *Alice* was broadcast? Foucault refers there to a story by Borges in which he quotes a 'certain Chinese encyclopaedia' in which it is written that "animals are divided into: (a) belonging to the Emperor, (b) embalmed, (c) tame, (d) suckling pigs, (e) sirens, (f) fabulous, (g) stray dogs, (h) included in the present classification, (i) frenzied, (j) innumerable, (k) drawn with a very fine camelhair brush, (l) *et cetera*, (m) having just broken the water pitcher, (n) that from a long way off look like flies". In the wonderment of this taxonomy, the thing we apprehend in one great leap, the thing that, by means of the fable, is demonstrated as the exotic charm of another system of thought, is the limitation of our own, the stark impossibility of thinking *that*.[16]

This perspective, this laughter from the outside, runs through all Foucault's work. For all its intricacy, its density and opacity, Foucault's major work from *The History of Madness* at the beginning of the 1960s, in the... through to the books on sexuality he would publish after the Death Valley seem to revolve around and repeat a fundamental insight, or outsight. ... the arbitrariness and contingency of any system, its plasticity.

If this outside vision was consonant with the psychedelic consciousness, in Foucault's case it did not have its origins in drugs. Foucault wouldn't consume LSD until nearly a decade later, when he headed out to Death Valley and took acid at Zabriskie Point, the site of Michelangelo Antonioni's film about the counterculture.

Foucault, seldom comfortable in his own skin, was always looking for a way out of his own identity. He had memorably claimed that he wrote "in order not to have a face", and his prodigious exercises in rogue scholarship and conceptual invention, the textual labyrinths he meticulously assembled from innumerable historical and philosophical sources, were one way out of the face. Another route was what he called the limit-experience, one version of which was his encounter with LSD. The limit-experience was paradoxical: it was an experience at and beyond the limits of "ordinary" experience, an experience of what cannot ordinarily be experienced at all. The limit-experience offered a kind of metaphysical hack. The conditions which made ordinary experience possible could now be encountered, transformed and escaped — at least temporarily. Yet, by definition, the entity which underwent this could not be the ordinary subject of experience — it would instead be some anonymous X, a faceless being.

Much of the music that came out of the counterculture gave voice to this entity from the outside, and Foucault's turn to the limit-experience paralleled popular experimentations with consciousness. "[T]he problem", Foucault said, in one of the interviews collected in the book *Remarks on Marx*,

is not to recover our "lost" identity, to free our imprisoned nature, our deepest truth; but instead, the problem is to move towards something radically Other. The center, then, seems still to be found in Marx's phrase: man produces man. [...] For me, what must be produced is not man identical to himself, exactly as nature would have designed him or according to his essence; on the contrary, we must produce something that doesn't yet exist and about which we cannot know how and what it will be.[17]

In a commentary on Foucault's text, Michael Hardt has argued that "the positive content of communism, which corresponds to the abolition of private property, is the autonomous production of humanity — a new seeing, a new hearing, a new thinking, a new loving."[18]

A new humanity, a new seeing, a new thinking, a new loving: this is the promise of acid communism, and it was the promise that you could hear in "Psychedelic Shack" and the culture that inspired it. Only five years separated "Psychedelic Shack" from the Tempations' early signature hit "My Girl", but how many new worlds had come into being then? In "My Girl", love remains sentimentalised, confined to the couple, in "Psychedelic Shack", love is collective, and orientated towards the outside.

With "Psychedelic Shack", the Temptations were a year into the new sound that the group's unofficial leader, Otis Williams, had persuaded producer Norman Whitfield to develop. Whitfield had initially been reluctant to change the Temptations' sound but his eventual conversion would lead to some of the most stunning productions in popular music history: productions that would build on the promise that "Tomorrow Never Knows" evoked, but which the Beatles themselves would rarely make good on. Whitfield became so entranced by the psychedelic soundscapes he worked on in the studio that he would push for The Temptations to release tracks that were eight or nine minutes long, with space for extended instrumental passages. He formed the group the Undisputed Truth specifically as a lab to try out these long-form lysergic productions. Whitfield's experimentation with the studio as a compositional tool paralleled what Lee "Scratch" Perry was doing in Jamaica with dub. The sonic spaces they opened up were also about a particular experience of time: a distended time, a time that was at once denuded, and populated with strange audio unlike forms, which enticed the listener into a deep immersion in the moment, even as they enfolded us into rhythmic patterns and pulses. This new space-time would later be revisited and refurbished by new explorers such as Tom Moulton, Larry Levan and Walter Gibbons: the inventors of the extended dance track, which would in turn form the basis of the psychedelic genres such as house, techno and jungle.

The template for the new Temptations' sound had been Sly and the Family Stone, with traces of James Brown and Jimi Hendrix: a febrile matrix, composed of elements which were already interacting with one another. The change in sound was more than a shift in style; it was also responded to a new set of demands and expectations of what music could be. No longer confined to love-song balladeering or good-time cheerleading, popular music could now be social comment; even better, it could feed off and feed back into the social transformations that were dissolving former certainties, prejudices, assumptions. It could take its bearings from the confidence, anger and assertiveness that was brimming out of the Civil Rights movement, and it could perform a new set of social relations that gave a heady taste of what the world might look like once the movement had succeeded. That is what Greil Marcus heard and saw in Sly and the Family Stone in his great 1975 essay, "The Myth of Staggerlee":

> Sly's real triumph was that he had it both ways. Every nuance of his style, from the razzle dazzle of his threads to the originality of his music, made it clear that we was his own man. If the essence of his music was freedom, no one was more aggressively free than he. Yet there was also room for everyone in the America made up of blacks and whites, men and women, who sang out "different strokes for different folks" and were there on stage to show what such an idea of independence meant.[19]

Sly and the Family Stone did indeed seem to have it every way: with a sound that was somehow ramshackle, improvised, and yet sinuously danceable; a music that was neither sentimental, nor sanctimonious, but humorous and deadly serious all at the same time.

The laughter of *Alice*, the ludic freedom and daring embodied by Sly and the Family Stone: they might have been performed by an advanced guard, but there was no necessity for them to be confined to an elite. On the contrary, the question that their presence on radio and TV insistently posed was: why shouldn't this bohemia be open to everyone?

Despite much of the traditional left's deafness and hostility to these currents, the counterculture did have an impact on the workplace, in struggles conducted by a new kind of worker. "It's a different generation of workingmen", explained J.D. Smith, a union treasurer at the Chevy Vega plant in Lordstown, Ohio. "None of these guys came over from the old country, grateful for any job they could get. None of them have been through a depression. They've been exposed — at least through television — to all the youth movements of the last ten years and they don't see the disgrace of being unemployed."[20]

In 1972, the Lordstown Plant was embroiled in a struggle over working conditions which reflected the new intolerance towards drudgery and authoritarianism. "The Lordstown workers", Jefferson Cowie writes,

became a collective national symbol for the new breed of worker and emblematic of a widespread sense of occupational alienation. People gravitated to the refreshing vision of youth, vitality, inter-racial solidarity hidden from the public behind the likes of television's Archie Bunker, pro-war labor leadership, and the growing politics of the blue-collar backlash.[21]

Lordstown was part of a wave of activism in which this "new breed of worker" struggled for democratic control of their own trade unions and of the places in which they worked. Seen in the light of such struggles, the egalitarian social space projected in "Psychedelic Shack" could not be dismissed as a passive pipe-dream or a distraction from actual political activity. Rather, music such as this was an active dreaming which arose out of real social and cultural compositions, and which fed back into potent new collectivities, and a new existential atmosphere, which rejected both drudgery and traditional resentments. "The young black and white workers dig each other", said the Lordstown Local president Gary Bryner, "There's an understanding. The guy with the Afro, the guy with the beads, the guy with the goatee, he doesn't care if he's black, white, green or yellow." These new kinds of workers — who "smoked dope, socialised interracially, and dreamed of a world in which work had some meaning"[22] — wanted democratic control of both their workplace and their trade unions.

Something of the same ferment was building in Italy, where a new kind of worker was increasingly visible. "This new generation of workers did not have so much to do with the old tradition of the labor parties", says Franco Berardi of the situation in Turin in 1973. "Nor anything to do with the socialist ideology of a state-owned system. A massive refusal of the sadness of work was the leading element behind their protest. Those young workers had much more to do with the hippy movement; much more to do with the history of the avant-garde."[23]

By 1977, a whole new social mix, a "mass avant-garde", was in place in Bologna. It was here, perhaps more than anywhere else, that acid communism came together as an actual formation. The city seethed with the energy and confidence that erupts when new ideas commingle with new aesthetic forms.

The university was filled with *terroni* (people originating from the South), Germans, comedians, musicians and cartoonists like Andrea Pazienza and Filippo Scozzari. Artists were squatting houses in the center of the city, and running creative places such as Radio Alice and Traumfabrik. Some people were reading books like *Anti-Oedipus*, some were reciting poems by Majakovski and Artaud, listening to the music of Keith Jarrett and The Ramones, and inhaling dream inducing substances.[24]

As In February, *A/traverso*, the zine published by Berardi and others young militants, produced an issue entitled "The revolution is just, possible and necessary: look comrades, the revolution is probable":

> We want to expropriate all the assets of the Catholic Church
> Cut the working hours, increase the number of jobs
> Increase the amount of the salary
> Transform production and place it under workers' control
> Liberation of the huge amount of intelligence that is wasted by capitalism:
> Technology has been used so far as a means of control and exploitation.
> It wants to be turned into a tool for liberation.
> Working less is possible thanks to the application of cybernetics and informatics.
> Zerowork for income
> Automate all production
> All power to living labor
> All work to dead labor.

In 1977, such demands seemed not only realistic but inevitable — *"look comrades, the revolution is probable"*. Of course, we now know that the revolution did not happen. But the material conditions for such a revolution are more in place in the twenty-first century than they were in 1977. What has shifted beyond all recognition since then is the existential and emotional atmosphere. Populations are resigned to the sadness of work, even as they are told that automation is making their jobs disappear. We must regain the optimism of that Seventies moment, just as we must carefully analyse all the machineries that capital deployed to convert confidence into dejection. Understanding how this process of consciousness-deflation worked is the first step to reversing it.

notes

Editor's Introduction

[1] Tim Burrows, "'We Have To Invent The Future': An Unseen Interview With Mark Fisher", *Quietus*, (22 January 2017), http://thequietus.com/articles/21616-mark-fisher-interview-capitalist-realism-sam-berkson (Also in this volume, pp. 675-682)

[2] From the 2010 interview "'They Can Be Different in the Future Too': Interviewed by Rowan Wilson for *Ready Steady Book* (2010)" (Also in this volume, pp. 627-636)

[3] k-punk, "One Year Later", (17 May 2004), http://k-punk.abstractdynamics.org/archives/002926.html (Also in this volume, p. 693)

[4] k-punk, "Why K?", (16 April 2005), http://k-punk.org/why-k/ (Also in this volume, pp. 31-32)

[5] k-punk, "Book Meme", (28 June 2005), http://k-punk.abstractdynamics.org/archives/005771.html (Also in this volume, pp. 37-41)

[6] Mark Fisher, "Exiting the Vampire Castle", *North Star*, (22 November 2013), http://www.thenorthstar.info/?p=11299, (Also in this volume, pp.737-745)

[7] k-punk, "New Comments Policy", (5 September 2004), http://k-punk.org/new-comments-policy/ (Also in this volume, pp. 701-702)

[8] k-punk, "We Dogmatists", (17 February 2005), http://k-punk.abstractdynamics.org/archives/005025.html (Also in this volume, pp. 709-710)

[9] k-punk, "Noise as Anti-Capital", (21 November 2004), http://k-punk.abstractdynamics.org/archives/004441.html (Also in this volume, pp. 285-289)

[10] See the Zer0 Books manifesto in this volume, p. 103

[11] David Stubbs, "Remembering Mark Fisher", *Quietus*, (16 January 2017), http://thequietus.com/articles/21572-mark-fisher-rip-obituary-interview

[12] Mark Fisher (ed.), *The Resistable Demise of Michael Jackson*, (Zer0, 2009); Mark Fisher, Kodwo Eshun and Gavin Butt (eds.), *Post-Punk Then and Now*, (Repeater Books, 2016)

[13] k-punk, "Why I Want to Fuck Ronald Reagan", (13 June 2004), (Also in this volume, pp. 47-51)

[14] Mark Fisher, "What is Hauntology?", *Film Quarterly*, 66:1, 2012

[15] Frederic Jameson, *Postmodernism or, The Cultural Logic of Late Capitalism*, (Verso, 1992), p. 48

[16] Ibid., pp. 48-49

[17] Ibid., p. 159

Why K?

[1] k-punk, (16 April 2005), http://k-punk.org/why-k/

"Well, I'm still enough of a neophyte to be thrilled by a mention in *Village Voice*. I suppose it is ironic that Geeta describes k-punk as 'cultural studies', given my notorious antipathy to cult studs. On the other hand, though, k-punk is cultural studies as I'd always thought it should be practised (much of my hostility to cult studs stems from a disappointment when faced with the depressing, guilt-mongering reality of cultural studies in the academy). Anyway, this is the full text that I sent to Geeta". See Geeta Dayal, "PH.Dotcom", *Village Voice*, (5 April 2005), https://www.villagevoice.com/2005/04/05/ph-dotcom/

PART ONE

METHODS OF DREAMING: BOOKS

Book Meme

[1] k-punk, (28 June 2005), http://k-punk.abstractdynamics.org/archives/005771.html

Space, Time, Light, All the Essentials — Reflections on J.G. Ballard Season (BBC Four)

[1] k-punk, (8 October 2003), http://k-punk.abstractdynamics.org/archives/000590.html
[2] See Jean Baudrillard, *Simulacra and Simulation*, (Michigan, 1994)
[3] "The Enormous Space" was published in Ballard's 1990 anthology, *War Fever*, (Collins, 1990)
[4] Sigmund Freud, *Civilisation and its Discontents*, (1930)
[5] The American illusionist David Blaine undertook *Above the Below* in 2003, an endurance stunt in which he was sealed inside a transparent Plexiglas case suspended mid-air in London, and where he fasted for forty-four days.

Why I Want to Fuck Ronald Reagan

[1] k-punk, (13 June 2004), http://k-punk.org/why-i-want-to-fuck-ronald-reagan/
[2] Published as Chapter 14 of J.G. Ballard's *The Atrocity Exhibition* (Jonathan Cape, 1970)
[3] Ballard, *The Atrocity Exhibition*, p. 170
[4] Jean Baudrillard, *Symbolic Exchange and Death*, (Sage, 2007), p. 92

[5] Ballard, *The Atrocity Exhibition*, p. 165

[6] Frederic Jameson, *Postmodernism, or, The Cultural Logic of Late Capitalism*, (Verso, 1991), p. 17

[7] See Ibid., pp. 155-180 and Jameson, *Archaeologies of the Future: The Desire Called Utopia and Other Science Fiction*, (Verso, 2005)

[8] It appears in a section of Burroughs' *Naked Lunch* titled "Meeting of International Conference of Technological Psychiatry", where Doctor "Fingers" Schafer presents his "Master Work: The Complete All American Deanxietized Man..."

[9] J.G. Ballard, *Crash*, (Jonathan Cape, 1973); Jean Baudrillard, *Simulacra and Simulation*, (University of Michigan Press, 1994), p. 111-120

A Fairground's Painted Swings

[1] k-punk, (24 February 2005), http://k-punk.org/a-fairgrounds-painted-swings/

[2] Infinite Thought, aka Nina Power. The blog is no longer available online.

[3] Auguste Villiers de l'Isle-Adam, *L'Eve Future*, translated as *Tomorrow's Eve* (University of Illinois Press, 1982), p. 68

[4] Gregory Bateson, "The Cybernetics of 'Self': A Theory of Alocoholism", *Steps to an Ecology of Mind: Collected Essays in Anthropology, Psychiatry, Evolution and Epistemology*, (University of Chicago Press, 2000), pp. 309-337. Also available online: http://ift-malta.com/wp-content/uploads/2012/07/The-cybernetics-of-self-A-theory-of-alcoholism.pdf

What Are the Politics of Boredom? (Ballard 2003 Remix)

[1] k-punk, (8 March 2005), http://k-punk.abstractdynamics.org/archives/005135.html

[2] J.G. Ballard, *Millenium People*, (Fourth Estate, 2003)

[3] Ibid., p. 61

[4] Ibid.

[5] Ibid., p. 63

[6] Ibid., p. 140

[7] Francis Fukuyama, *The End of History and the Last Man*, (Penguin, 1993), p. 305

[8] Ballard, *Millenium People*, p. 175

[9] Ibid., p. 176

[10] Ibid., p. 149

[11] Ibid., p. 166

[12] Ibid., p. 249

[13] Ibid., p. 85

[14] Ibid., p. 104

[15] Ibid., p. 109

Let Me Be Your Fantasy

[1] k-punk, (27 August 2006) http://k-punk.abstractdynamics.org/archives/008304.html

[2] Renata Select, *(Per)Versions of Love and Hate*, (Verso, 2000)

[3] Jean Baudrillard, *Seduction*, (St Martins Press, 1991)

[4] Ibid., pp. 31-32

[5] Indeed, in a 1999 interview Ballard says,

He has created this extremely imaginative world in a way that I don't think any other figurative artist on this planet could match. I think that Newton is the greatest figurative artist working today. I don't think there's anybody anywhere who remotely approaches him in his creative achievement.

[6] From Ballard's piece "The Lucid Dreamer" in *Bookforum*, 1999

[7] See Rodley (ed.), *Cronenberg on Cronenberg*, (Faber and Faber, 1997), p. 194

[8] Iain Sinclair, *Crash*, (BFI Film Classics, 1999)

Fantasy Kits: Steven Meisel's "State of Emergency"

[1] Guest post on *Ballardian*, (25 September 2006), http://www.ballardian.com/fantasy-kits-steven-meisels-state-of-emergency

[2] "State Of Emergency" editorial, *Vogue Italia* September 2006. Photographer: Steven Meisel. Model: Hilary Rhoda & Iselin Steiro, https://trendland.com/state-of-emergency-by-steven-meisel/

[3] k-punk, "Let Me Be Your Fantasy", (27 August 2006), http://k-punk.abstractdynamics.org/archives/008304.html (Also in this volume, pp. 63-67)

[4] See k-punk, "My Card: My Life: Comments on the AMEX Red Campaign", (4 September 2006), http://www.any-body.org/anybody_vent/2006/9/4/my-card-my-life-your-comments.html (Also in this volume, pp. 455-456)

[5] Joanna Bourke, "A Taste for Torture?", *Guardian*, (13 September 2006), https://www.theguardian.com/artanddesign/2006/sep/13/photography.pressandpublishing

[6] Simon Sellars,"JGB's Sinister Marriage", *Ballardian*, (14 September 2006), http://www.ballardian.com/jgbs-sinister-arriage

[7] J.G. Ballard, *The Atrocity Exhibition*, (Jonathan Cape, 1970), p. 12

[8] See MOMA profile of Martha Rosler, https://www.moma.org/artists/6832?=undefined&page=1&direction=

[9] See review of Weiss' film on *Ballardian*, http://www.ballardian.com/weiss-atrocity-exhibition-review

The Assassination of J.G. Ballard

[1] *Ballardian*, (28 April 2009), http://www.ballardian.com/rip-jgb-tributes-from-the-ballardosphere-part-4
[2] J.G. Ballard, *The Atrocity Exhibition: Annotated Edition*, (Flamingo, 1993), p. 17
[3] J.G. Ballard, "Myth-Maker of the 20th Century" in *New Worlds* 142 (1964)

A World of Dread and Fear

[1] k-punk, (13 September 2005), http://k-punk.org/a-world-of-dread-and-fear/
[2] David Peace, *GB84*, (Faber & Faber, 2004)
[3] See Andy Beckett's review of Peace's *GB84* in *London Review of Books*, Vol. 26, No. 18, (23 September 2004), https://www.lrb.co.uk/v26/n18/andy-beckett/political-gothic
[4] Frederic Jameson, "Culture and Finance Capital", *The Cultural Turn: Selected Writings on Postmodernism, 1983-1998*, (Verso, 2009), p. 154
[5] See Joseph Brooker, "Orgreave Revisited: David Peace's *GB84* and the return to the 1980s", *Radical Philosophy*, Volume 133, https://www.radicalphilosophy.com/article/orgreave-revisited
[6] Peace, *GB84*, p. 7
[7] Ibid., p. 176
[8] Ibid., p. 320

Ripley's Glam

[1] k-punk, (1 July 2006), http://k-punk.org/ripleys-glam/
[2] Patricia Highsmith, *The Talented Mr Ripley*, (Vintage, 1999), p. 164
[3] Slavoj Žižek, "When Straight Means Weird and Psychosis is Normal", http://www.lacan.com/ripley.html
[4] Highsmith, *The Talented Mr Ripley*, p. 78
[5] Thornstein Veblen, *The Theory of the Leisure Class*, (Dover, 1994), p 13
[6] Ibid., p. 10

Methods of Dreaming

[1] k-punk, (10 October 2008), http://k-punk.abstractdynamics.org/archives/010739.html

Atwood's Anti-Capitalism

[1] k-punk, (26 September 2009), http://k-punk.abstractdynamics.org/archives/011314.html
[2] Fredric Jameson, "Then You Are Them (review of Margaret Atwood's *The Year of*

the Flood)", *London Review of Books*, Vol. 31, No.17, (10 September 2009)

[3] Guy Sorman,"Economics Does Not Lie", *City Journal*, Summer 2008, https://www.city-journal.org/html/economics-does-not-lie-13099.html

[4] Margaret Atwood, *Oryx and Crake*, (Bloomsbury, 2009), p. 165

[5] Ibid., p. 305

[6] Margaret Atwood, *The Year of the Flood*, (Bloomsbury, 2009), p. 316

[7] Immanuel Kant, *Critique of Judgment*, (Hackett, 1987), p. 342

[8] Guy Sorman, cited in Žižek's *First as Tragedy, Then as Farce*, (Verso, 2009), p. 24

Toy Stories: Puppets, Dolls and Horror Stories

[1] *Frieze*, (1 September 2010), https://frieze.com/article/toy-stories

[2] Thomas Ligotti, *The Conspiracy Against the Human Race: A Contrivance of Horror*, (Hippocampus, 2011)

[3] Ian Penman, "Notes Towards a Ritual Exorcism of the Dead King" in Mark Fisher (ed.), *The Resistible Demise of Michael Jackson*, (Zer0, 2009)

[4] Giovanni Tiso, "The Unmaking of Pinocchio", *Bat, Bean, Beam*, (3 August 2010), https://bat-bean-beam.blogspot.co.uk/2010/08/unmaking-of-pinocchio.html

[5] Richard Seymour, "Chattel Story", *Lenin's Tomb*, (8 August 2010), http://www.leninology.co.uk/2010/08/chattel-story.html

[6] Giovanni Tiso, "Useful Life", *Bat, Bean, Beam*, (19 July 2010), https://bat-bean-beam.blogspot.co.uk/2010/07/useful-life.html

Zer0 Books Statement

[1] This is the mission statement written by Mark Fisher at the inception of the radical publisher Zer0 Books which he co-founded with his friend Tariq Goddard in 2009. It was reprinted in each of the books published by Zer0, through their leaving to form Repeater in 2014, until January 2018 when a modified version was adopted by the new management. In addition to all of his writing, it is important to remember the vital role Mark played in helping to revolutionise the existing British publishing industry, and theoretical writing in particular, that was in the absolute doldrums leading up to the formation of Zer0.

PART TWO

SCREENS, DREAMS AND SPECTRES: FILM AND TELEVISION

A Spoonful of Sugar

[1] k-punk, (5 April 2004), http://k-punk.abstractdynamics.org/archives/002354.html

She's Not My Mother

[1] k-punk, (10 June 2004), http://k-punk.abstractdynamics.org/archives/003227. html

[2] Andrew O'Hehir, "The Baron of Blood does Bergman", *Salon*, (28 February 2003), https://www.salon.com/2003/02/28/cronenberg_3/

[3] Joy Division, "Decades", *Closer*, (Factory Records, 1980)

[4] O'Hehir, "The Baron of Blood does Bergman"

Stand Up, Nigel Barton

[1] k-punk, (13 June 2004), http://k-punk.org/stand-up-nigel-barton/

[2] Dennis Potter, *The Nigel Barton Plays*, (Penguin, 1967), p. 31

[3] Friedrich Nietzsche, *Beyond Good and Evil*, (Penguin, 2009)

[4] Potter, *The Nigel Barton Plays*, p. 21

Portmeirion: An Ideal for Living

[1] k-punk, (31 August 2004), http://k-punk.abstractdynamics.org/archives/004048. html

[2] Peter Stallybrass and Allon White, "The Fair, the Pig, Authorship", *The Politics and Poetics of Transgression*, (Cornell University Press, 1986), p. 30

[3] The complete text of which is available here: http://www.bopsecrets.org/SI/ Chtcheglov.htm

[4] Taken from https://www.portmeirion-village.com/visit/clough-williams-ellis/

[5] See https://www.portmeirion-village.com/visit/clough-williams-ellis/

Golgothic Materialism

[1] *Hyperstition*, (15 October 2004), http://hyperstition.abstractdynamics.org/ archives/004275.html

[2] Slavoj Žižek, "Passion in the Era of Decaffeinated Belief", *The Symptom: Online Journal for lacan.com*, Issue 5, Winter 2004, http://www.lacan.com/passionf.htm

This Movie Doesn't Move Me

[1] k-punk, (13 March 2005), http://k-punk.abstractdynamics.org/archives/005171. html

[2] Rachel Cooke, "What's Up Doc", *Observer*, (6 March 2005), https://www. theguardian.com/theobserver/2005/mar/06/features.review17

[3] Justin Barton, http://scanshifts.blogspot.co.uk/

Fear and Misery in the Third Reich 'n' Roll

[1] k-punk, (9 June 2005), http://k-punk.abstractdynamics.org/archives/005664.html

[2] Gilles Deleuze and Félix Guattari, *Capitalism and Schizophrenia: A Thousand Plateaus*, (Continuum, 1987), p. 230

[3] See Christoph Cox, "On Evil: An Interview with Alenka Zupančič", *Cabinet Magazine*, Issue 5, Winter 2001/2, http://www.cabinetmagazine.org/issues/5/alenkazupancic.php

We Want It All

[1] k-punk, (12 February 2006), http://k-punk.abstractdynamics.org/archives/007348.html

[2] "Celebrity Big Brother — Autopsy or Prologue?", *The Church of Me*, (1 February 2006), http://cookham.blogspot.co.uk/2006_02_01_archive.html

Gothic Oedipus: Subjectivity and Capitalism in Christopher Nolan's *Batman Begins*

[1] *ImageTexT: Interdisciplinary Comic Studies*, 2:2, 2006

[2] For a summary of the ethical assumptions of this world, look no further than K.W. Jeter's *Noir* (Orion, 1998) (a novel that is heavily indebted to both Gibson and *Blade Runner*). Jeter has his hardboiled novelist, Turbiner, define the essence of noir as follows:

The looks, the darkness, the shadows, all those trite rain-slick streets — that was the least of it. That had nothing to do with it. [...] It's betrayal [...] That's what it's always been. That's what makes it so realistic, even when it is at its most dreamlike and shabby, when it feels like it's happening on another planet. The one we lost and can't remember, but we can see it when we close our eyes... (p. 192)

For an (unfavourable) comparison of Miller's *Sin City* with Forties noir, see Patterson, 2005.

[3] Alan Moore is an interesting parallel case to Miller. Moore, too, made his name with comics that put superheroes in a more "realistic" context. He seemed similarly ambivalent about the superhero genre, drawn to work within it but also driven by a desire to reform and to some extent demythologise it. However, Moore's more recent work — on *The League of Extraordinary Gentlemen* and *Promethea* — has explicitly dealt with the concept of mythologisation (although, naturally, this is quite different from actually producing a character that attains a mythological status). Moore also retains a place for a kind of egalitarian critique of State power which is lacking in Miller: see for instance his depiction

of aristocratic corruption and conspiracy in *From Hell*.

[4] Alain Badiou, *Ethics: An Essay on the Understanding of Evil*, (Verso, 2002), p. 7

[5] Christoph Cox and Molly Whalen, "On Evil: An Interview with Alain Badiou", *Cabinet*, Issue 5, Winter 2001/2, http://www.cabinetmagazine.org/issues/5/alainbadiou.php

[6] Ibid.

[7] Otherwise, Badiou would be contradicting himself, claiming on the one hand that capitalism is "ideal" and that it destroys any reference to the ideal.

[8] Kim Newman, "Cape Fear", *Sight & Sound*, July 2005. As Newman's piece establishes, with a detailed scholarly survey of the origin of the film's characters and set pieces.

[9] For an explanation of the concept of hyperstition, see http://hypersti...tractdynamics.org, especially "How Do Fictions Become Hyperstitions", http://hypersti...chives/003345.html

[10] This modification is in fact prompted by Miller's *Dark Knight Returns*.

[11] It is significant that perhaps the three greatest American superheroes — Batman, Superman, and Spiderman — are orphans, but the Oedipal torment is most intense in Batman. (It is displaced in Spiderman onto his Aunt, the mother-substitute for and to whom he is eternally responsible, and Uncle, for whose death he feels guilty.)

[12] Newman, "Cape Fear". As Newman's piece establishes, with a detailed scholarly survey of the origin of the film's characters and set pieces.

[13] Alena Zupančič, *Ethics of the Real: Kant, Lacan*, (Verso, 2000), p. 245. She goes on to say:

That which brings the story of Oedipus close to the noir universe is, of course, the fact that the hero — the detective — is without knowing it, implicated in the crimes he is investigating. One could even say that the story of Oedipus lies at the heart of the" "new wave" of *film noir* — films such as *Angel Heart* and *Blade Runner* (the director's cut), where it emerges at the end that the hero is himself the criminal he is looking for. (pp. 245-6)

[14] Ibid., p. 193

[15] In this respect, as in so many others, it compares favourably with Tim Burton's *Batman*. Burton pioneered a kind of psycho-biographically-inclined" "Dark-Lite", and his account of the Joker's origin — man falls into bath of acid and goes psychotic — traded in the cheapest and shallowest psycho-biographical cliché.

[16] Slavoj Žižek, "Revenge of Global Finance", *In These Times*, (21 May 2005), http://inthesetimes.com/article/2122/revenge_of_global_finance

[17] He was also, according to Newman, "perhaps the first upper middle-class black character in comics" (Newman, "Cape Fear").

[18] Which suggests, perhaps, a looping of cyberpunk (to which Batman in many ways now belongs) back to (one of) its origins in German Expressionism.

[19] China Miéville, comment on a post at *Lenin's Tomb*. Newman also spotted a 9/11 parallel:

Batman Begins finally feeds back into the world of 2005, even as it picks up threads from 1939 and 1986. Fear (*phobos*), the limited realm of the bat-phobic Bruce and phobia-expert Crane, has been subsumed by terror (*deimos*). This America is riven by injustice, and is haunted by a fanatic eastern sect with a charismatic but impossible-to-catch figurehead bent on crashing a mode of transport into a skyscraper to trigger an explosion of panic that will destroy society. (Newman, "Cape Fear", p. 21)

[20] For an analysis of which, see Fisher and Mackay, *Pomophobia* (1996)

When We Dream, Do We Dream We're Joey?

[1] k-punk, (1 October 2005), http://k-punk.abstractdynamics.org/archives/006484.html
[2] David Cronenberg (dir.), *A History of Violence*, (2005)
[3] Jacques Lacan, "The Split Between the Eye and the Gaze", *The Four Fundamental Concepts of Psychoanalysis*, (Norton, 1973)
[4] Peter Bradshaw, "Review of *A History of Violence*", *Guardian*, (30 September 2005), https://www.theguardian.com/culture/2005/sep/30/2
[5] Slavoj Žižek, *Looking Awry: An Introduction to Jacques Lacan through Popular Culture*, (October, 1992), pp. 89-90
[6] Graham Fuller, "Good Guy Bad Guy", *Sight and Sound*, 15, October 2005
[7] J.G. Ballard, "The Killer Inside", *Guardian*, (23 September 2005), https://www.theguardian.com/film/2005/sep/23/jgballard
[8] Slavoj Žižek, *Welcome to the Desert of the Real*, (Verso, 2002), p. 12
[9] Graham Fuller, "Good Guy Bad Guy"
[10] Slavoj Žižek, *The Universal Exception*, (Bloomsbury, 2006), pp. 308-9

Notes on Cronenberg's *eXistenZ*

[1] Unpublished k-punk notes on David Cronenberg's *eXistenZ* which formed the later essay "Work and Play in *eXistenZ*" in *Film Quarterly*, Vol. 65, No. 3 (Spring 2012), pp. 70-73
[2] Nick Land, "Meltdown", *Fanged Noumena: Collected Writings 1987– 2007*, (Falmouth: Urbanomic), p. 456

I Filmed It So I Didn't Have to Remember It Myself

[1] k-punk, (21 October 2005), http://k-punk.abstractdynamics.org/archives/006647.html

[2] Jean Baudrillard, *Simulacra and Simulation*, (University of Michigan, 1994)

Spectres of Marker and the Reality of the Third Way

[1] k-punk, (18 February 2006), http://k-punk.abstractdynamics.org/archives/007392.html

[2] Seamus Milne, "Communism may be dead, but clearly not dead enough", *Guardian*, (16 September 2006), https://www.theguardian.com/Columnists/Column/0,,1710891,00.html

Dis-identity Politics

[1] k-punk, (25 April 2006), http://k-punk.abstractdynamics.org/archives/007709.html

[2] Steven Shaviro, "V for Vendetta", http://www.shaviro.com/Blog/?p=488#comments

[3] See Jenni Russell, "Tony Blair's authoritarian populism is indefensible and dangerous", *Guardian*, (24 April 2006), https://www.theguardian.com/commentisfree/2006/apr/24/comment.labour

[4] Fredric Jameson, "Marx's Purloined Letter", in Sprinker (ed.), *Ghostly Demarcations: A Symposium on Jacques Derrida's Spectres of Marx* (Verso, 1999)

[5] Giovanni Tiso, https://bat-bean-beam.blogspot.co.uk/

"You Have Always Been the Caretaker": The Spectral Spaces of the Overlook Hotel

[1] *Perforations*, 29, (2007), http://noel.pd.org/Perforations/perf29/perf29_index.html

[2] Frederic Jameson, "Historicism in *The Shining*", *Signatures of the Visible*, (Psychology Press, 1992), p. 90

[3] Sigmund Freud, "Moses and Monotheism", James Strachley (ed.), *The Origins of Religion: Totem and Taboo, Moses and Monotheism and Other Works*, (Penguin, 1990)

[4] Stephen King, *The Shining*, (Penguin, 1997), p. 356

[5] David A. Cook, "America Horror: *The Shining*", *Literature/ Film Quarterly*, 12.1, 1984

[6] King, *The Shining*, p. 356

[7] Walter Metz, "Toward a Post-Structural Influence in Film Genre Study: Intertextuality and The Shining", *Film Criticism*, Vol. XXII, 1, Fall 1997

[8] Metz in fact argues that the situation is more complex, arguing that Horror, as well as melodrama, has taken the family as its subject.

[9] See, for instance, Lisa Gye's hypertext project "Half Lives" (http://pandora.nla.gov.au/pan/30305/20020815-0000/halflives.adc.rmit.edu.au/index.html), which explores the concept of hauntology through her own family history.

[10] See Žižek, Slavoj, "The Big Other Doesn't Exist", *Journal of European Psychoanalysis*, Spring - Fall 1997, online at

[11] King, *The Shining*, p. 437

[12] Ibid., p. 362

[13] Ibid., p. 319

[14] Freud, "Moses and Monotheism", p. 374

[15] Metz, "Toward a Post-Structural Influence in Film Genre Study: Intertextuality and The Shining", p. 57

[16] King, *The Shining*, p. 437

[17] Metz, "Toward a Post-Structural Influence in Film Genre Study: Intertextuality and The Shining", p. 57

Coffee Bars and Internment Camps

[1] k-punk, (26 January 2007), http://k-punk.abstractdynamics.org/archives/008956.html (A truncated and reworked version of this piece provides the opening pages of *Capitalist Realism* (Zer0, 2009))

[2] Jeff Nuttall, *Bomb Culture*, (Paladin, 1968). A book about the London counter-culture which reflected the omnipresent threat of nuclear annihilation.

[3] David Edelstein, "Review of *Children of Men*", *New York Magazine*, 2006, http://nymag.com/movies/listings/rv_51038.htm

[4] Latin for "the sacred man" or" "the accursed man" — a figure of Roman law, a person who is banned and may be killed by anybody. See Giorgio Agamben, *Homo Sacer: Sovereign Power and Bare Life*, (Stanford, 1998)

[5] T.S Eliot, "Tradition and Individual Talent", *The Sacred Wood* (1920)

Rebel Without a Cause

[1] k-punk, (6 August 2008), http://k-punk.abstractdynamics.org/archives/010555.html

[2] Andrew Klavern, "What Bush and Batman Have in Common", *Wall Street Journal*, (25 July 2008), https://www.wsj.com/articles/SB121694247343482821

[3] Slavoj Žižek and Geert Lovink, "Japan Through a Slovenian Looking Glass: Reflections of Media and Politic and Cinema", *InterCommunication*, 14, 1995

[4] Inspersal's blog is no longer online.

[5] Matthew Yglesias, "Dark Knight Politics", *Atlantic*, (24 July 2008), https://www.theatlantic.com/politics/archive/2008/07/-em-dark-knight-em-politics/49451/

Robot Historian in the Ruins

[1] k-punk, (27 August 2008), http://k-punk.abstractdynamics.org/archives/010636.html

[2] Voyou, "Ideology critics are a superstitious, cowardly lot", *Dangerous and Lazy*, (4 August 2008), https://blog.voyou.org/2008/08/04/ideology-critics-are-a-superstitious-cowardly-lot/

[3] See Wayne Wedge's comments on *k-punk* post, "Bat Mailbag", (11 August 2008), http://k-punk.abstractdynamics.org/archives/010572.html (Wedge writes of *The Dark Knight*: "A lucrative kiddie icon self-consciously invoking the nightmares of history. TimeWarnerAolHalliburtonBlackwaterWayneenterprises demanding that we gather in our millions to watch, re-watch, discuss and argue about this corporate meta-product arguing with itself."

[4] Kyle Smith, "WALL-E: A Gloom-E Satire", *Free Republic*, (27 June 2008), http://www.freerepublic.com/focus/f-chat/2037224/posts

[5] Paul Edwards, "WALL-E's Indictment of Liberalism", *Townhall*, (2 July 2008), https://townhall.com/Columnists/pauledwards/2008/07/02/wall-es-indictment-of-liberalism-n1062814

Review of *Tyson*

[1] *Sight and Sound*, April 2009

[2] Joyce Carol Oates, "Kid Dynamite: Mike Tyson is the most exciting heavyweight fighter since Muhammad Ali", *Life*, March 1987

"They Killed Their Mother": *Avatar* as Ideological Symptom

[1] k-punk, (6 January 2010), http://k-punk.org/they-killed-their-mother-avatar-as-ideological-symptom/

[2] Greg Egan, "Avatar Review", (20 December 2012), http://www.gregegan.net/ESSAYS/AVATAR/Avatar.html

[3] Slavoj Žižek, *First as Tragedy, Then as Farce*, (Verso, 2009), p. 97

Precarity and Paternalism

[1] k-punk, (11 February 2010), http://k-punk.abstractdynamics.org/archives/011486.html

[2] Taylor Parkes, "Review: *Life on Earth* Soundtrack", *Quietus*, (17 December 2009), http://thequietus.com/articles/03440-life-on-earth-trunk-records-compilation-review

[3] J.J. Charlesworth, "Crisis at the ICA: Ekow Eshun's Experiment in Deinstitutionalisation", *Mute*, (10 February 2010), http://www.metamute.org/editorial/articles/crisis-ica-ekow-eshuns-experiment-deinstitutionalisation

[4] Alex Williams, "On Negative Solidarity and Post-Fordist Plasticity", *Splintering Bone Ashes*, (31 January 2010), http://splinteringboneashes.blogspot.co.uk/2010/01/negative-solidarity-and-post-fordist.html

5 Tobias van Even, "Business Ontology (or why Xmas gets you fired)", *Fugitive Philosophy*, (29 December 2009), http://fugitive.quadrantcrossing.org/2009/12/business-ontology/

Return of the Gift: Richard Kelly's *The Box*

1 k-punk, (14April 2010), http://k-punk.org/return-the-gift-richard-kellys-the-box/
2 See Graham Harman, *"Duel"*, *Object-Oriented Philosophy*, (8 January 2010), https://doctorzamalek2.wordpress.com/2010/01/08/duel/
3 See interview with Richard Kelly: "Richard Kelly Cracks Open THE BOX For Mr. Beaks!", *Aint It Cool News*, (18/06/09), http://www.aintitcool.com/node/41449
4 Norbert Wiener, *God and Golem, Inc.: A Comment on Certain Points Where Cybernetics Impinges on Religion*, (MIT, 1963)
5 Nina Power's *Infinite Thought* blog is no longer online. See Jean-Paul Sartre, *Critique of Dialectical Reason*, Book III, (Routledge, 2000), p. 320

Contributing to Society

1 k-punk, (4 August 2010), http://k-punk.org/contributing-to-society/
2 "PeoplePlus", a trading name for "A4e", formerly known as Action for Employment, is a for-profit welfare-to-work company based in the UK.
3 Thornbridge Hall, http://www.thornbridgehall.co.uk/
4 See http://watchinga4e.blogspot.co.uk/
5 http://watchinga4e.blogspot.co.uk/2010/08/who-knows-best.html
6 Digital Ben, "Fairy Jobmother Deconstructed", *Third Class on a One Class Train*, (24 July 2010), http://ridingthirdclass.blogspot.co.uk/2010/07/fairy-jobmother-deconstructed.html
7 See http://theviewfromcullingworth.blogspot.co.uk/
8 Ivor Southwood, *Non-Stop Inertia*, (Zer0, 2010)

"Just Relax and Enjoy It": *Geworfenheit* on the BBC

1 k-punk, (4 August 2010), http://k-punk.org/just-relax-and-enjoy-it-geworfenheit-on-the-bbc/
2 Neil Young, "Down At The World's End: David Rudkin's *Artemis 81*", *Neil Young's Film Lounge*, (20 October 2007), https://www.jigsawlounge.co.uk/film/reviews/down-at-the-world-s-end-david-rudkin-s-artemis-81-tv-1981-8-10/
3 Phillip Challinor, "*Artemis 81*", *The Curmudgeon*, http://thecurmudgeonly.blogspot.co.uk/2007/12/artemis-81.html

Star Wars Was a Sell-Out from the Start

1 *Guardian*, (1 November 2012), https://www.theguardian.com/commentisfree/2012/nov/01/star-wars-disney-sell-out

Gillian Wearing: *Self Made*

[1] *Sight and Sound*, June 2012

Batman's Political Right Turn

[1] *Guardian*, (22 July 2012), https://www.theguardian.com/commentisfree/2012/jul/22/batman-political-right-turn

[2] On 20 July 2012 a mass shooting occurred in a cinema in Aurora, Colorado during a midnight screening of the film *The Dark Knight Rises*. The shooter, James Egan Holmes, killed twelve people and injured seventy others.

[3] John Nolte, "Occupy Wall Street in Damage Control Mode Over Dark Knight Rises", *Breitbart*, (19 July 2012), http://www.breitbart.com/big-hollywood/2012/07/19/occupy-damage-control-dark-kinght/

Remember Who The Enemy Is

[1] k-punk, (25 November 2013), http://k-punk.org/remember-who-the-enemy-is/

[2] Unemployed Negativity, "Primer for the Post-Apocalypse: The Hunger Games Trilogy", (5 September 2011), http://www.unemployednegativity.com/2011/09/primer-for-post-apocalypse-hunger-game.html?spref=fb

[3] See Mark Fisher, "Precarious Dystopias: The Hunger Games, In Time, and Never Let Me Go", *Film Quarterly*, Vol. 65, No. 4, Summer 2012, pp. 27-33

[4] Franco Bifo Berardi, *Precarious Rhapsody: Semiocapitalism and the Pathologies of the Post-alpha Generation*. (Minor Compositions, 2009), p. 55

Beyond Good and Evil: *Breaking Bad*

[1] *New Humanist*, (18 December 2012)

Classless Broadcasting: *Benefits Street*

[1] *New Humanist*, (17 February 2014)

[2] Tracey Jensen, "A Summer of Television Poverty Porn", *Sociological Imagination*, (9 September 2013), http://sciologicalimagination.org/archives/14013

[3] See John Corner, "Performing the Real: Documentary Diversions", *Television & New Media*, (1 August 2002), http://journals.sagepub.com/doi/abs/10.1177/152747640200300302

[4] Beverley Skeggs and Helen Wood, *Reacting to Reality Television: Performance, Audience and Value*, (Routledge, 2012)

Rooting for the Enemy: *The Americans*

[1] *New Humanist*, (1 October 2014)

How to Let Go: *The Leftovers, Broadchurch* **and** *The Missing*

[1] *New Humanist*, (2 March 2015)

The Strange Death of British Satire

[1] *New Humanist*, (24 August 2015)
[2] Author of *Wounded Leaders: British Elitism and the Entitlement Illusion*, (Lone Arrow Press, 2014)
[3] Nick Duffell, "Why Boarding Schools Produce Bad Leaders", *Guardian*, (9 June 2014), https://www.theguardian.com/education/2014/jun/09/boarding-schools-bad-leaders-politicians-bullies-bumblers
[4] Jonathan Coe, "Sinking Giggling into the Sea", *London Review of Books*, Vol. 35, No. 14, July 2013, https://www.lrb.co.uk/v35/n14/jonathan-coe/sinking-giggling-into-the-sea
[5] Franco Berardi, *After the Future*, (AK Press, 2011)

Review: *Terminator Genisys*

[1] *Sight and Sound*, (September 2015)

The House that Fame Built: *Celebrity Big Brother*

[1] *New Humanist*, (16 December 2015)
[2] Andreas Hillen, *1973 Nervous Breakdown: Watergate, Warhol, and the Birth of Post-Sixties America*, (Bloomsbury, 2008)

Sympathy for the Androids: The Twisted Morality of *Westworld*

[1] *New Humanist*, (30 November 2016)

PART THREE

CHOOSE YOUR WEAPONS: WRITING ON MUSIC

The By Now Traditional Glasto Rant

[1] k-punk, (28 June 2004), http://k-punk.abstractdynamics.org/archives/003459.html

2 Simon Frith, "Afterthoughts" (1985), *Taking Popular Music Seriously: Selected Essays*, (Routledge, 2017)

3 Ian Penman (The Pill Box), "Include Me Out" (10 July 2003), http://apawboy. blogspot.co.uk/2003_07_06_apawboy_archive.html#105783432477159439

4 Ian Penman (The Pill Box), comments (28 June 2003), http://apawboy.blogspot. co.uk/2003_06_22_apawboy_archive.html#105679442481295648

Art Pop, No, Really

1 k-punk, (5 July 2004), http://k-punk.abstractdynamics.org/archives/003519.html

k-punk, or the Glampunk Art Pop Discontinuum

1 k-punk, (11 November 2004), http://k-punk.abstractdynamics.org/ archives/004115.html

2 Leopold von Sacher-Masoch, *Venus in Furs*, (CreateSpace, 2010)

3 Simon Reynolds, *Blissblog*, (20 June 2003), http://blissout.blogspot. co.uk/2003_06_15_blissout_archive.html#95865180

4 Jeff Nuttall, *Bomb Culture*, (Paladin, 1968), p. 33

5 Ian Penman,"The Shattered Glass: Notes on Bryan Ferry", *Zoot Suits and Second-Hand Dresses: An Anthology of Fashion and Music*, ed. McRobbie, (Macmillan, 1989), pp. 103-17

6 Nuttall, *Bomb Culture*, p. 34

7 Kodwo Eshun, *More Brilliant than the Sun: Adventures in Sonic Fiction*, (Quartet, 1998), p. 95

8 k-punk, "Art Pop, No, Really", (5 July 2004), http://k-punk.abstractdynamics. org/archives/003519.html (Also in this volume, pp. 269-272)

Noise as Anti-Capital: *As the Veneer of Democracy Starts to Fade*

1 k-punk, (21 November 2004), http://k-punk.abstractdynamics.org/ archives/004441.html

This was k-punk's contribution to the NOISETHEORYNOISE#2 event on 20 November 2004 at Middlesex University, organised by Andy McGettigan and Ray Brassier.

2 Slavoj Žižek, "The Matrix: Or, The Two Sides of Perversion", *The Matrix and Philosophy: Welcome to the Desert of the Real*, ed. William Irwin, (Open Court,2002), p. 246

3 William S Burroughs, *The Ticket that Exploded*, (John Calder, 1968), p. 44

4 Jean-François Lyotard, *LIbid.inal Economy*, (Continuum, 2004), p 113

Lions After Slumber, or What is Sublimation Today?

[1] k-punk, (25 March 2005), http://k-punk.org/lions-after-slumber-or-what-is-sublimation-today/

[2] Slavoj Žižek, "The Deadlock of Repressive Desublimation", *The Metastases of Enjoyment: Six Essays on Women and Causality*, (Verso, 2005), p. 16

[3] Green Gartside, Welsh singer/songwriter and frontman of Scritti Politti

[4] Marcello Carlin, "Scritti Politti: Early", (12 January 2005), http://hemingwoid.blogspot.co.uk/2005/01/scritti-politti-early.html

[5] Alena Zupančič, *The Shortest Shadow: Nietzsche's Philosophy of the Two*, (MIT, 2003), p. 77

[6] Zupančič, *The Shortest Shadow*, p. 77

[7] Ian Penman, *The Pill Box*, (13 May 2003), http://apawboy.blogspot.co.uk/2003_05_11_apawboy_archive.html#94280226

The Outside of Everything Now

[1] k-punk, (01 May 2005), http://k-punk.abstractdynamics.org/archives/005449.html

[2] Simon Reynolds, *Rip it Up and Start Again: Postpunk 1978-1984*, (Faber and Faber, 2006)

For Your Unpleasure: The Hauter-Couture of Goth

[1] k-punk, (01 June 2005), http://k-punk.abstractdynamics.org/archives/005622.html

[2] k-punk, "Continuous Contact", (23 January 2005), http://k-punk.abstractdynamics.org/archives/004826.html

[3] I.T. – fellow blogger and friend Infinite Thought (Nina Power)

[4] Tim de Lisle, "Roxy is the Drug", *Guardian*, (20 May 2005), https://www.theguardian.com/music/2005/may/20/roxymusic.popandrock

[5] Alena Zupančič, *The Shortest Shadow: Nietzsche's Philosophy of the Two*, (MIT, 2003), p. 179

[6] Simon Reynolds and Joy Press, *The Sex Revolts: Gender, Rebellion, and Rock 'n' Roll*, (Harvard UP, 1996), p. 344

[7] Jean Baudrillard, *Seduction*, (St Martin's Press, 1991), p. 94

[8] See Gilles Deleuze and Félix Guattari, "1933: Micropolitics and Segmentarity", *Capitalism and Schizophrenia: A Thousand Plateaus*, (Continuum, 2002), pp. 229-255

[9] Baudrillard, *Seduction*, p. 96

[10] Reynolds and Press, *The Sex Revolts*, p. 344

[11] Jean Baudrillard, *Simulacra and Simulation*, (University of Michigan Press, 1994), pp. 114-115

It Doesn't Matter If We All Die: The Cure's Unholy Trinity

[1] k-punk, (3 August 2005) — http://k-punk.abstractdynamics.org/archives/006087. html

[2] Michael Bracewell, *England is Mine: Pop Life in Albion from Wilde to Goldie,* (Flamingo, 1998), pp. 119-120

[3] Ibid., p. 115

[4] Ibid., p. 117

[5] James Oldham, "Bad Medicine", *Uncut,* (2 January 2000)

[6] Bracewell, *England is Mine,* pp. 115-116

Look at the Light

[1] k-punk, (16 November 2005), http://k-punk.org/look-at-the-light/

Is Pop Undead?

[1] k-punk, (31 January 2006), http://k-punk.abstractdynamics.org/archives/007289. html

[2] Hannah Pool, "Whiteout", *Guardian,* (28 January 2006), https://www. theguardian.com/music/2006/jan/28/popandrock

[3] Simon Reynolds, "Music 2005", *Frieze,* Issue 96, Jan-Feb 2006, https://frieze. com/article/music-2005?language=en

Memorex for the Kraken: The Fall's Pulp Modernism

Part I

[1] k-punk, (8 May 2006), http://k-punk.abstractdynamics.org/archives/007759. html A version of this piece was previously published in Michael Goddard and Benjamin Halligan, *Mark E. Smith and The Fall,* (Ashgate, 2010)

[2] The Fall, *Dragnet,* (Step-Forward, 1979)

[3] The Fall, "Spector Vs. Rector", *Dragnet,* (Step-Forward, 1979)

[4] Mark Sinker, "Look Back In Anguish", *NME,* (2 January 1988)

[5] Peter Stallybrass and Allon White, "The Fair, the Pig, Authorship", *The Politics and Poetics of Transgression,* (Cornell University Press, 1986)

[6] A passage in T.S. Eliot's "The Waste Land" which, on his own admission, was influenced by Stoker's novel:

And bats with baby faces in the violet light
Whistled and beat their wings
And crawled head downward down a blackened wall.

[7] Ian Penman, "All Fall Down", *NME*, (5 January 1980), http://thefall.org/gigography/80jan05.html

[8] Jean Baudrillard, "The Ecstasy of Communication", *The Anti-Aesthetic*, (The New Press, 2002), p. 153

Part II

[1] k-punk, (04 February 2007), http://k-punk.abstractdynamics.org/archives/008993.html

[2] The Fall, "City Hobgoblins", *Grotesque (After the Gramme)*, (Rough Trade, 1980)

[3] Mark Sinker, "Watching the City Hobgoblins", *Wire*, August 1986

[4] H.P. Lovecraft, "Supernatural Horror in Literature", http://www.hplovecraft.com/writings/texts/essays/shil.aspx

[5] S.T. Joshi, "Introduction" to M.R. James, *Count Magnus and Other Ghost Stories: The Complete Ghost Stories of M.R. James*, Vol. 1 (Penguin, 2004)

[6] Mark Sinker, "England: Look Back In Anguish", *NME*, (02 January 1988)

[7] Ibid.

[8] Patrick Parrinder, *James Joyce*, (Cambridge University Press, 1984)

[9] Mark E Smith, *The Fall: Lyrics*, (The Lough Press, 1985)

[10] Philip Thompson, *The Grotesque*, (Routledge, 1972), p. 2

[11] The Fall, "The N.W.R.A", *Grotesque (After the Gramme)*, (Rough Trade, 1980)

Part III

[1] k-punk, (16 February 2007), http://k-punk.abstractdynamics.org/archives/009039.html

[2] Gerard Genette, *Paratexts*, (Cambridge UP, 1997)

[3] Michael Moorcock, *The Final Programme*, (HarperCollins, 1971)

Scritti's Sweet Sickness

[1] k-punk, (5 July 2006), http://k-punk.abstractdynamics.org/archives/008010.html

[2] John Lewis, "Scritti Politti: Interview", *Time Out*, (30 May 2006), https://www.timeout.com/london/music/scritti-politti-interview

[3] Paul Oldfield, "After Subversion: Pop Culture and Power", in Angela McRobbie (ed.), *Zoot Suits and Second-Hand Dresses: An Anthology of Fashion and Music*, (Macmillan, 1987)

[4] Interview with Green Gartside by Simon Reynolds, http://bibbly-o-tek.com/2006/06/16/green/

[5] Mladen Dolar, *A Voice and Nothing More*, (MIT Press, 2006), p. 16

[6] Ibid., p. 161

Postmodernism as Pathology, Part 2

[1] k-punk, (17 February 2007), http://k-punk.abstractdynamics.org/archives/009043.html

Choose Your Weapons

[1] k-punk, (12 August 207), http://k-punk.abstractdynamics.org/archives/009633.html

[2] Frank Kogan, "Rules of the Game Follow Up #2: Paris Is Our Vietnam", *Las Vegas Weely*, (29 June 2007), https://lasvegasweekly.com/news/archive/2007/jun/29/rules-of-the-game-followup-2-paris-is-our-vietnam/

[3] Frank Kogan, "What's Wrong with Pretty Girls?", *Las Vegas Weekly*, (04 July 2007), https://lasvegasweekly.com/news/archive/2007/jul/04/whats-wrong-with-pretty-girls/

[4] Lawrence Miles' blog, http://beasthouse-lm.blogspot.co.uk/

Variations on a Theme

[1] *Frieze*, (19 March 2008), https://frieze.com/article/variations-theme-0

[2] Alan Kirby, "The Death of Postmodernism and Beyond", *Philosophy Now*, Issue 58, 2006, https://philosophynow.org/issues/58/The_Death_of_Postmodernism_And_Beyond

Running on Empty

[1] *New Statesman*, (30 April 2008)

You Remind Me of Gold: Dialogue with Mark Fisher and Simon Reynolds

[1] *Kaleidoscope Magazine*, 2010, http://markfisherreblog.tumblr.com/post/32185314385/you-remind-me-of-gold-dialogue-with-simon

Militant Tendencies Feed Music

[1] *New Statesman*, (29 March 2010)

Autonomy in the UK

[1] Mark Fisher's reflections on music and politics at the end of 2011, first appeared in the *Wire*, Issue 335, January 2012

[2] Franco Berardi, *After the Future* (AK Press, 2011), p. 12

The Secret Sadness of the Twenty-First Century: James Blake's *Overgrown*

[1] *Electronic Beats*, (18 April 2013)

[2] Angus Finlayson, "Review of *Overgrown*", *FACT*, (4 April 2013), http://www.factmag.com/2013/04/04/james-blake-overgrown-fact-review/

[3] Mark Fisher and Simon Reynolds, "You Remind Me of Gold", *Kaleidoscope Magazine*, http://markfisherreblog.tumblr.com/post/32185314385/you-remind-me-of-gold-dialogue-with-simon (Also in this volume, pp. 675-682)

[4] See http://www.futurebombe.com/james-drake.html

Review: David Bowie's *The Next Day*

[1] The *Wire*, Issue 351, May 2013

The Man Who Has Everything: Drake's *Nothing Was the Same*

[1] *Electronic Beats*, (24 September 2013)

[2] Drake, "All Me", *Nothing Was the Same*, (OVO Sound/Young Money Entertainment/Cash Money Records/Republic Records, 2013)

Break it Down: DJ Rashad's *Double Cup*

[1] *Electronic Beats*, (22 October 2013)

[2] Tristram Vivian Adams, "Analemmic V01CES (Distracted from the Darkness)", *Notes from the Vomitorium*, (September 2013), http://notesfromthevomitorium.blogspot.co.uk/2013/09/analemmic-v01ces-distracted-from.html

[3] William S. Burroughs, *The Ticket that Exploded*, (Calder, 1968)

Start Your Nonsense! On eMMplekz and Dolly Dolly

[1] *Electronic Beats*, (28 November 2013)

Review: Sleaford Mods' *Divide and Exit* and *Chubbed Up: The Singles Collection*

[1] The *Wire*, Issue 362, April 2014

Test Dept: Where Leftist Idealism and Popular Modernism Collide

[1] *Frieze*, (25 September 2015), https://frieze.com/article/music-41

[2] Cynthia Rose, *Design After Dark: The Story of Dancefloor Style*, (Thames and Hudson, 1991)

No Romance Without Finance

[1] *Bamn*: *An Unofficial Magazine of Plan C*, (9 November 2015)

[2] Jennifer M. Silva, *Coming Up Short: Working-Class Adulthood in an Age of Uncertainty*, (Oxford University Press, 2015), p. 19

[3] Ibid., p. 142

[4] Nancy C.M. Hartsock, *The Feminist Standpoint Revisited, and Other Essays*, (Basic Books, 1999)

[5] Nona Willis Aronowitz (ed.), *The Essential Ellen Willis*, (University of Minnesota Press, 2014)

[6] Ellen Willis, *Beginning to See the Light*, (University of Minnesota Press, 2012)

[7] Cynthia Rose, *Design After Dark: The Story of Dancefloor Style*, (Thames and Hudson, 1991)

PART FOUR

FOR NOW, OUR DESIRE IS NAMELESS: POLITICAL WRITINGS

Don't Vote, Don't Encourage Them

[1] k-punk, (4 May 2005), http://k-punk.abstractdynamics.org/archives/005462.html

October 6, 1979: Capitalism and Bipolar Disorder

[1] k-punk, (9 June 2005), http://k-punk.abstractdynamics.org/archives/005660.html This piece was reworked and incorporated into chapter 5 of *Capitalist Realism* (Zer0, 2009)

[2] Johan Hari, "Don't be fooled: advanced and rational societies can commit environmental suicide", *Independent*, (7 June 2005), http://www.independent. co.uk/voices/commentators/johann-hari/johann-hari-dont-be-fooled-advanced-and-rational-societies-can-commit-environmental-suicide-493371.html

[3] Christian Marazzi, author of *Capital and Language* (Semiotext(e), 2008) and *Capital and Affects* (Semiotext(e), 2011)

What If They Had A Protest and Everyone Came

[1] k-punk, (4 July 2005), http://k-punk.abstractdynamics.org/archives/005806.html A reworked and truncated version of this piece forms Chapter 2 of *Capitalist Realism* (Zer0, 2009)

[2] Live 8 was a string of benefit concerts, founded and co-organised by Bob Geldof, that took place on 2 July 2005. It was run in support of the aims of the UK's Make Poverty History campaign and the Global Call for Action Against Poverty.

Defeating the Hydra

[1] k-punk, (11 July 2005), http://k-punk.abstractdynamics.org/archives/005847. html This is one of two pieces written by k-punk in the aftermath of the 7 July 2005 London suicide bombings, where a series of coordinated terrorist attacks targeted the city's public transport system during the morning rush hour.

[2] UK Foreign and Commonwealth Office/Home Office, *Draft Report on Young Muslims and Extremism*, (April, 2004), quoted in Robert Winnet and David Leppard, "Leaked No 10 dossier reveals Al Qaeda's British recruits", *Sunday Times*, (10 July 2005), https://www.thetimes.co.uk/article/leaked-no-10-dossier-reveals-al-qaedas-british-recruits-9lpg68xw93r

[3] Editorial, "London Under Attack", *Economist*, (7 July 2005), https://www.economist.com/node/4166694

[4] Nick Cohen, "Face up to the truth", the *Guardian*, (10 July 2005), https://www.theguardian.com/uk/2005/jul/10/july7.guardiancolumnists

[5] Richard Seymour, "Nick Cohen's brains have turned to slush", *Lenin's Tomb*, (10 July 2005), http://www.leninology.co.uk/2005/07/nick-cohens-brains-have-turned-to.html

The Face of Terrorism Without a Face

[1] k-punk (13 July 2005), http://k-punk.org/the-face-of-terrorism-without-a-face/

Conspicuous Force and Verminisation

[1] k-punk, (2 August 2006), http://k-punk.abstractdynamics.org/archives/008166. html

My Card: My Life: Comments on the AMEX Red Campaign

[1] k-punk, comments on any-body.org (4 September 2006), http://www.any-body. org/anybody_vent/2006/9/4/my-card-my-life-your-comments.html An image of the AMEX RED advertising campaign can be viewed on this webpage.

[2] Product Red is a licensed brand owned by (RED) that seeks to involve the private sector in raising awareness and money to help in eliminating HIV/AIDS in eight African countries. In 2006 American Express launched the AMEX RED card, where 1% of spending would be donated to the Global Fund to Fight AIDS, Tuberculosis and Malaria.

[3] Slavoj Žižek, "Nobody has to be vile", *London Review of Books*, Vol. 28 No. 7, 6 April 2006, http://www.lrb.co.uk/v28/n07/ziseise01_.html

[4] See http://news.bbc.co.uk/1/hi/business/4650024.stm

The Great Bullingdon Club Swindle

[1] k-punk, (22 October 2010), http://k-punk.abstractdynamics.org/archives/011707. html

[2] John Gray, "Progressive, like the 1980s", *London Review of Books*, Vol. 32 No. 20, 21 October 2010, https://www.lrb.co.uk/v32/n20/john-gray/progressive-like-the-1980s

[3] China Mieville, "Letter to a progressive Liberal Democrat", 21 October 2010, http://chinamieville.net/post/1361955242/letter-to-a-progressive-liberal-democrat

[4] Seumas Milne, "The Bullingdon boys want to finish what Thatcher began", *Guardian*, (20 October 2010), https://www.theguardian.com/commentisfree/2010/oct/20/bullingdon-boys-want-to-finish-what-thatcher-began

[5] Laurie Penny, "Labour let us down yesterday", *New Statesman*, (21 October 2010), https://www.newstatesman.com/blogs/laurie-penny/2010/10/labour-party-answers-today

The Privatisation of Stress

[1] This essay first appeared in *Soundings*, No. 48: The Neoliberal Revolution, Summer 2011, and was reproduced on the *New Left Project* website, (7 September 2011), http://www.newleftproject.org/index.php/site/article_comments/the_privatisation_of_stress

[2] Ivor Southwood, *Non-Stop Inertia*, (Zer0, 2010), p. 72

[3] Ibid., p. 15

[4] Atilio Boron, "The Truth About Capitalist Democracy", *Socialist Register,* 2006, pp. 28-59, p. 32

[5] As argued by Jeremy Gilbert in, "Elitism, Philistinism and Populism: the Sorry State of British Higher Education Policy", *openDemocracy*, 2010

[6] See Stuart Hall and Martin Jacques (eds), *New Times: The Changing Face of Politics in the 1990s*, (Lawrence and Wishart, 1989)

[7] Antonio Negri, *Art and Multitude*, (Polity, 2010), p. 10

[8] Savonarola, "Curriculum Mortis", *Institute for Conjectural Research*, (4 August 2008), conjunctural.blogspot.com/2008/08/curriculum-mortis.html

[9] Phillip Blond, *The Ownership State: Restoring Excellence, Innovation and Ethos to Public Service*, (ResPublica/Nesta, 2009), p. 10

[10] Tobias van Veen, "Business Ontology (or why Xmas Gets You Fired)", *Fugitive Philosophy*, (29 Deceember 2009), fugitive.quadrantcrossing.org/2009/12/business-ontology/

[11] Franco Berardi, *Precarious Rhapsody: Semiocapitalism and the Pathologies of the Post-Alpha Generation*, (Minor Compositions, 2009), p. 32

[12] Ibid., p. 40

[13] Sherry Turkle, *Alone Together: Why We Expect More From Technology and Less from Each Other*, (Basic, 2011), p. 264

[14] Jodi Dean, *Blog Theory: Feedback and Capture in the Circuits of Drive*, (Polity, 2010)

[15] Dan Hind, *The Return of the Public*, (Verso, 2010), p. 146

[16] David Smail, *Power, Interest and Psychology: Elements of a Social Materialist Understanding of Distress*, (PCCS, 2009), p. 11

[17] Ibid., p. 7

[18] Eva Illouz, *Cold Intimacies: The Making of Emotional Capitalism*, (Polity, 2007)

Kettle Logic

[1] k-punk, (29 November 2010), http://k-punk.abstractdynamics.org/archives/011728.html

[2] Richard Seymour, "Students lead, NUS follows", *Lenin's Tomb*, (28 November 2010), http://www.leninology.co.uk/2010/11/students-lead-nus-follows.html

[3] Polly Toynbee, "Sorry, students, but you're low in the pain pecking order", *Guardian*, (5 November 2010), https://www.theguardian.com/commentisfree/2010/nov/05/students-low-pain-pecking-order; and "Thatcher's children can lead the class of 68 back into action", *Guardian*, (26 November 2010), https://www.theguardian.com/commentisfree/2010/nov/26/student-protest-public-sector-cuts

[4] Richard Seymour, "Spontaneous, massive and militant", *Lenin's Tomb*, (25 November 2010), http://www.leninology.co.uk/2010/11/spontaneous-massive-and-militant.html

[5] See https://universityforstrategicoptimism.wordpress.com/

[6] Jan Moir, "Not so jolly hockey sticks at the St Trinian's riots", *Daily Mail*, (26 November 2010), http://www.dailymail.co.uk/columnists/article-1333175/JAN-MOIR-Not-jolly-hockey-sticks-St-Trinians-riots.html

[7] Digital Ben, "Solidarity", *Third Class on a One-Class Train*, (27 November 2010), http://ridingthirdclass.blogspot.co.uk/2010/11/solidarity.html

[8] Ibid.

Winter of Discontent 2.0: Notes on a Month of Militancy

[1] k-punk, (13 December 2010), http://k-punk.org/winter-of-discontent-2-0-notes-on-a-month-of-militancy/

[2] Deborah Orr, "Protesting against the cuts is pointless", *Guardian* (2 December 2010), https://www.theguardian.com/commentisfree/2010/dec/02/protesting-cuts-pointless-deborah-orr

[3] Paul Mason, "Dubstep rebellion — the British banlieue comes to Millbank", *BBC*, (9 December 2010), http://www.bbc.co.uk/blogs/newsnight/paulmason/2010/12/9122010_dubstep_rebellion_-_br.html

[4] Dan Hancox, "This is our riot: POW!", *A Miasma Of Lunatic Alibis*, (10 December 2010), http://dan-hancox.blogspot.co.uk/2010/12/this-is-our-riot-pow.html

[5] Jeremy Gilbert, "A Report on the 'The Hardcore Continuum?' symposium held at the University of East London, April 29th 2009", *Dancecult: Journal of Electronic Dance Music Culture*, 1:1, 2009, https://dj.dancecult.net/index.php/dancecult/article/view/274/238

[6] Simon Reynolds, "Slipping into Darkness", *Wire*, No. 48, June 1996, https://www.thewire.co.uk/in-writing/essays/the-wire-300_simon-reynolds-on-the-hardcore-continuum_4_hardstep_jump-up_techstep_1996_

[7] Ibid.

[8] Dominic Fox, "Nova Criminals", *Poetix (Old Content)*, (12 December 2010), http://codepoetics.com/octoblog/blog/2010/12/12/nova-criminals/

[9] Michel Foucault, *Discipline and Punish: The Birth of the Prison* (Penguin, 1991)

[10] Alex Williams, "On Negative Solidarity and Post-Fordist Plasticity", *Splintering Bone Ashes*, (31 January 2010), http://splinteringboneashes.blogspot.co.uk/2010/01/negative-solidarity-and-post-fordist.html

[11] Dave Osler, "Thrashing Royal Rollers: Some Public Relations Tips", *Liberal Conspiracy*, (10 December 2010), http://liberalconspiracy.org/2010/12/10/thrashing-royal-rollers-some-public-relations-tips/

Football/Capitalist Realism/Utopia

[1] k-punk, (6 July 2010), http://k-punk.abstractdynamics.org/archives/011626.html

[2] Chris Petit, "Review: The Damned United", *Guardian*, (19 August 2006), https://www.theguardian.com/books/2006/aug/19/sportandleisure.shopping

The Game Has Changed

[1] *The Visual Artists' News Sheet*, January/February 2011

Creative Capitalism

[1] *The Visual Artists' News Sheet*, March-April 2011

[2] Antonio Negri, *Art and Multitude*, (Polity, 2007), p. 9

Reality Management

[1] k-punk, (5 July 2011), http://k-punk.abstractdynamics.org/archives/011851.html

[2] See https://www.youtube.com/watch?v=wCem9EZb-YA

[3] Deterritorial Support Group, "Hari Kari/Hackery", (17 June 2011), https://deterritorialsupportgroup.wordpress.com/2011/06/17/hari-karihackery/

[4] Peter Preston, "Johan Hari's anonymous attackers have spun foolishness into dishonesty", *Guardian*, (3 July 2011), https://www.theguardian.com/media/2011/jul/03/johann-hari-quotes-honesty-foolish

[5] Dan Hind, "The Limits of Acceptable Controversy", *The Return of the Public* (25

October 2010), https://thereturnofthepublic.wordpress.com/2011/07/05/the-limits-of-acceptable-controversy/

UK Tabloid

[1] k-punk, (8 July 2011), http://k-punk.org/uk-tabloid/
[2] See the transcript of Cameron's press conference on phone hacking here: https://www.gov.uk/government/speeches/prime-ministers-press-conference
[3] Unemployed Negativity, "Clerks and Cynicism", (29 July 2006), http://www.unemployednegativity.com/2006_07_01_archive.html
[4] Adam Curtis, "Rupert Murdoch — A Portrait of Satan", *BBC*, (30 January 2011), http://www.bbc.co.uk/blogs/adamcurtis/2011/01/rupert_murdoch_-_a_portrait_of.html

The Future is Still Ours: Autonomy and Post-Capitalism

[1] *We Have Our Own Concept of Time and Motion*, (Auto Italia South East, 2011), pp. 5-7, https://monoskop.org/images/d/dd/Auto_Italia_eds_We_Have_Our_Own_Concept_of_Time_and_Motion.pdf
[2] Philip Blond, "The Ownership State", *ResPublica*, October 2009, http://www.respublica.org.uk/wp-content/uploads/2015/01/Ownership-state.pdf
[3] Gilles Deleuze, "Postscript on the Societies of Control", *October*, Vol. 59, Winter 1992, pp. 3-7
[4] Antonio Negri, *Art and Multitude*, (Polity, 2007), p. 9

Aesthetic Poverty

[1] *The Visual Artists' News Sheet*, September 2011
[2] Adrian Shaughnessy, "The Politics of Desire and Looting", *Design Observer*, (15 August 2011), https://designobserver.com/feature/the-politics-of-desire-and-looting/29508

The Only Certainties are Death and Capital

[1] *The Visual Artists' News Sheet*, May/June 2012
[2] Hari Kunzru, "Damien Hirst and the great art market heist", *Guardian*, (16 March 2012), https://www.theguardian.com/artanddesign/2012/mar/16/damien-hirst-art-market

Why Mental Health is a Political Issue

[1] *Guardian*, (16 July 2012), https://www.theguardian.com/commentisfree/2012/jul/16/mental-health-political-issue

[2] See http://calumslist.org/

[3] Isabel Hardman, "Welfare suicides are awful, but they're still a red herring", *Spectator*, (5 July 2012), https://blogs.spectator.co.uk/2012/07/welfare-suicides-are-awful-but-theyre-still-a-red-herring/

[4] Brendan O'Neill, "This exploitation of suicidal people is a new low for campaigners against welfare reform", *Telegraph*, (3 July 2012), http://journalisted.com/article/3xla7

[5] Helen Nugent, "Suicide on the rise among older men", *Guardian*, (15 July 2012), https://www.theguardian.com/society/2012/jul/15/suicide-rise-older-men

The London Hunger Games

[1] k-punk, (8 August 2012), http://k-punk.abstractdynamics.org/archives/011918.html

[2] Oliver Burkeman, "The Power of Negative Thinking", *New York Times*, (4 August 2012), http://www.nytimes.com/2012/08/05/opinion/sunday/the-positive-power-of-negative-thinking.html

[3] Charlie Brooker, "The Olympics: better than they looked on the tin", *Guardian*, (5 August 2012), https://www.theguardian.com/commentisfree/2012/aug/05/olympics-better-than-looked-on-tin

[4] Mike Marqusee, "London 2012: spare us the jingoistic Olympic hype", *Guardian*, (7 August 2012), https://www.theguardian.com/commentisfree/2012/aug/07/london-2012-olympic-hype

[5] Douglas Murphy, "Towers of Babble", *Frieze*, (1 May 2012), https://frieze.com/article/towers-babble/

[6] Juliet Jacques, "The ArcelorMittal Orbit: London's Eiffel Tower?", *New Statesman*, (11 July 2012), https://www.newstatesman.com/blogs/art-and-design/2012/07/arcelormittal-orbit-londons-eiffel-tower

Time-Wars: Towards an Alternative for the Neo-Capitalist Era

[1] *Gonzo Circus*, Issue 110, 2012, http://www.gonzocircus.com/exclusive-essay-time-wars-towards-an-alternative-for-the-neo-capitalist-era/

[2] Richard Sennett, *The Corrosion of Character: The Personal Consequences of Work in the New Capitalism* (Norton, 1998), p. 30

[3] Ibid., p. 31

[4] Federico Campagna, "Radical Atheism", *Through Europe*, http://th-rough.eu/writers/campagna-eng/radical-atheism.

[5] Carl Cederström and Peter Fleming, *Dead Man Working*, (Zer0, 2012), p. 2

[6] Franco Berardi, *Precarious Rhapsody*, (Minor Compositions, 2009), p. 41

Not Failing Better, but Fighting To Win

[1] *Weekly Worker*, (1 November 2012), http://weeklyworker.co.uk/worker/936/mark-fisher-not-failing-better-but-fighting-to-win/

[2] Mark Bolton, "Work isn't working", *New Left Project*, (31 August 2012), www.newleftproject.org/index.php/site/article_comments/work_isnt_working

[3] Kwasi Kwarteng, Priti Patel, Dominic Raab, Chris Skidmore and Elizabeth Truss, *Britannia Unchained: Global Lessons for Growth and Prosperity*, (Palgrave Macmillan, 2012)

The Happiness of Margaret Thatcher

[1] Verso blog, (8 April 2013), https://www.versobooks.com/blogs/1272-the-happiness-of-margaret-thatcher

[2] Toby Helm and Daniel Boffey, "Labour plans radical shift over welfare state payouts", *Guardian*, (6 April 2013), https://www.theguardian.com/politics/2013/apr/06/labour-plans-shift-welfare-payouts

[3] John Harris, "We have to talk about why some people agree with benefit cuts", *Guardian*, (31 March 2013), https://www.theguardian.com/commentisfree/2013/mar/31/we-have-to-talk-why-some-want-benefit-cuts

[4] Alex Williams, "On Negative Solidarity and Post-Fordist Plasticity", *Splintering Bone Ashes*, (31 January 2005), http://splinteringboneashes.blogspot.co.uk/2010/01/negative-solidarity-and-post-fordist.html

[5] Peter Walker, "Government using increasingly loaded language in welfare debate", *Guardian*, (5 April 2013), https://www.theguardian.com/society/2013/apr/05/goverment-loaded-language-welfare

[6] Ramona, "'The Revolution starts in the ATOS smoking area' — On Welfare, Addiction, and Dependency", *libcom.org*, (2 April 2013), https://libcom.org/blog/%E2%80%9C-revolution-starts-atos-smoking-area%E2%80%9D-welfare-addiction-dependency-02042013

[7] Wendy Brown, "Moralism as Anti-politics", *Politics Out of History*, (Princeton, 2001), p. 36

[8] Adam Kotsko, "Weaponised debate", *An und für sich*, (12 August 2012), https://itself.blog/2012/08/12/weaponiseised-debate-2/

Suffering With a Smile

[1] *Occupied Times*, (22 June 2013), http://theoccupiedtimes.org/?p=11586

[2] Tim Dowling, Laura Barnett and Patrick Kingsley, "What Time Do CEOs Wake Up?", *Guardian*, (1 April 2013), https://www.theguardian.com/money/2013/apr/01/what-time-ceos-start-day

[3] Gilles Deleuze and Félix Guattari, *Capitalism and Schizophrenia: Anti-Oedipus*, (Continuum, 2004), p. 254

How to Kill a Zombie: Strategising the End of Neoliberalism

[1] *openDemocracy*, (18 July 2013), https://www.opendemocracy.net/mark-fisher/how-to-kill-zombie-strategising-end-of-neoliberalism

[2] Mark Fisher and Franco "Bifo" Berardi, "Give Me Shelter", *Frieze*, (1 January 2013), https://frieze.com/article/give-me-shelter-mark-fisher

Getting Away With Murder

[1] k-punk, (9 January 2014), http://k-punk.org/getting-away-with-murder/

[2] Stafford Scott, "This perverse Mark Duggan verdict will ruin our relations with the police", *Guardian*, (9 January 2014), https://www.theguardian.com/commentisfree/2014/jan/09/mark-duggan-verdict-relations-police

[3] See http://www.telegraph.co.uk/news/uknews/law-and-order/10315329/London-Riots-Police-marksman-shot-Mark-Duggan-in-self-defence.html

[4] See http://www.telegraph.co.uk/news/uknews/crime/8687804/Tottenham-riot-bullet-lodged-in-officers-radio-at-time-of-Mark-Duggan-death-was-police-issue.html

No One is Bored, Everything is Boring

[1] *The Visual Artists' News Sheet*, (21 July 2014)

[2] Plan C, "We are all very anxious", (4 April 2014), https://www.weareplanc.org/blog/we-are-all-very-anxious/

A Time for Shadows

[1] *Visual Artists' News Sheet*, January/February 2015

[2] Jean Baudrillard, *The Ecstasy of Communication*, (Semiotext(e), 1998)

[3] Sherry Turkle, *Alone Together: Why We Expect More from Technology and Less from Each Other*, (Basic Books, 2011), p. 2. The full manifesto can be read and downloaded from: networkcultures.org

[4] Geert Lovink, Sebastian Olma and Ned Rossiter, "On the Creative Question — Nine Theses", *Institute of Network Cultures*, (20 November 2014), http://networkcultures.org/geert/2014/11/20/the-creative-question-nine-theses/

Limbo is Over

[1] k-punk, (26 April 2015), http://k-punk.org/limbo-is-over/

[2] Jonathan Jones, "Something new is happening in British politics. This image captures it", *Guardian*, (17 April 2015), https://www.theguardian.com/

commentisfree/2015/apr/17/tv-election-debate-new-british-politics-image

3 Plan C, https://www.weareplanc.org/about/#.VTkXhqbKbFI

4 Craig McVegas, "Last Night's Leaders' Debate Was a Vision of the Clusterfuck That British Politics Is About to Become", *Vice*, (17 April 2015), https://www.vice.com/en_uk/article/vd8pva/craig-election-leaders-debate-number-3-733

5 See the image here: https://www.theguardian.com/commentisfree/2015/apr/17/tv-election-debate-new-british-politics-image

6 The Free Association, "Talkin' 'Bout a Revolution", (2015), http://www.freelyassociating.org/wp-content/uploads/2015/02/talkin%27%20%27bout%20a%20revolution.pdf

7 Aditya Chakrabortty, "The three big election questions that all the parties are simply ignoring", *Guardian*, (20 April 2015), https://www.theguardian.com/commentisfree/2015/apr/20/three-big-election-questions-politicians-ignoring-real-challenges

8 The *Sun* ran a story that as a child Scotland's First Minister Nicola Sturgeon is said to have "devilishly hacked the hair from her sister's beloved doll". For the *Sun* this was "an early sign of the ruthlessness which propelled her to the top of Scottish — and potentially British — politics."

9 Eduardo Maura of Podemos interviewed by Andrew Dolan, *Red Pepper*, (22 February 2015), http://www.redpepper.org.uk/podemos-politics-by-the-people/

10 Plan C, "On Social Strikes and Directional Demands", (7 May 2015), https://www.weareplanc.org/blog/on-social-strikes-and-directional-demands/#.VTvv3qbKbFK

11 Mark Fisher and Jeremy Gilbert, *Reclaim Modernity: Beyond Markets Beyond Machines*, (Compass, 2015), http://www.compassonline.org.uk/wp-content/uploads/2014/10/Compass-Reclaiming-Modernity-Beyond-markets_-2.pdf

Communist Realism

1 k-punk, (5 May 2015), http://k-punk.org/communist-realism/

2 Jean Baudrillard, *Seduction*, (St Martin's Press, 1991), p. 66

3 See https://www.theguardian.com/politics/2015/may/01/david-cameron-election-career-defining-moment

4 Paul Krugman, "The Austerity Delusion", *Guardian*, (29 April 2015), https://www.theguardian.com/business/ng-interactive/2015/apr/29/the-austerity-delusion

5 Philip Mirowski, *Never Let a Serious Crisis Go to Waste: How Neoliberalism Survived the Financial Meltdown*, (Verso, 2013), p. 35

6 The Jam, "Funeral Pyre", (Polydor, 1981)

7 Ibid., pp. 35-6

Pain Now

[1] k-punk, (7 May 2015), http://k-punk.org/pain-now/

[2] See https://www.theguardian.com/uk/2010/jun/22/budget-2010-vat-austerity-plan

[3] Mark Fisher, "Good for Nothing", *Occupied Times*, (19 March 2014), https://theoccupiedtimes.org/?p=12841 (Also in this volume, pp. 747-750)

Abandon Hope (Summer is Coming)

[1] k-punk, (11 May 2015), http://k-punk.org/abandon-hope-summer-is-coming/

[2] Jeremy Gilbert, "3:00am thoughts on another General Election Defeat", (8 May 2015), https://jeremygilbertwriting.wordpress.com/2015/05/08/300-am-thoughts-on-another-general-election-defeat/?fb_action_ids=10155759772135314&fb_action_types=news.publishes&fb_ref=pub-standard

[3] Laura Oldfield Ford, "Seroxat, Smirnoff, THC", *Savage Messaish*, (9 October-29 November 2014), http://lauraoldfieldford.blogspot.co.uk/2014/09/seroxat-smirnoff-thc-9-october-29.html?q=seroxat

[4] Shaun Lawson, "The polls and (moots) the forecasts are wrong. Ed Miliband will not be the next Prime Minister", *Open Democracy*, (5 May 2015), https://www.opendemocracy.net/ourkingdom/shaun-lawson/polls-and-most-of-forecasts-are-wrong-ed-miliband-will-not-be-next-prime-min

[5] Paul Mason, "Labour haven't just failed to win — it's worse than that", *Channel 4*, (8 May 2015), https://www.channel4.com/news/by/paul-mason/blogs/labour-failed-win-worse

[6] Tim Burrows, "Meme Politics and Apathy in UKIP-on-Sea", *Vice*, (5 May 2015), https://www.vice.com/en_uk/article/qbx4qm/meme-politics-and-apathy-in-ukip-on-sea

[7] William S. Burroughs, *The Place of Dead Roads*, (Penguin, 2015)

[8] Jodi Dean, "The Lingering of the Party", *Open!*, (6 March 2014), http://www.onlineopen.org/the-lingering-of-the-party

[9] Gilles Deleuze, "Postscript on the Societies of Control", *October*, Vol. 59, Winter 1992, p. 5

[10] Benedict Spinoza, *Ethics*, (Moonrise Press, 2015), p. 144

[11] Ibid., p. 145

[12] David Smail, *The Origins of Unhappiness: A New Understanding of Personal Distress*, (Routledge, 2015), p. 45

[13] Jason Read, "The Order and Connection of Ideology is the Same as the Order and Connection of Exploitation: Or, Towards a Bestiary of the Capitalist Imagination", *Philosophy Today*, 59:2, Spring 2015, pp. 175–89 (Also available online at: http://www.academia.edu/11159929/The_Order_and_Connection_of_Ideology_Is_the_Same_as_the_Order_and_Connection_of_Exploitation_Or_Towards_a_Bestiary_of_the_Capitalist_Imagination)

[14] Mark Fisher, *Ghosts Of My Life: Writings on Depression, Hauntology and Lost Futures*, (Zer0, 2014)

[15] Simon Reynolds, *Retromania: Pop Culture's Addiction to its Own Past*, (Faber and Faber, 2010)

[16] Ewa Jasiewicz, "Our Commons are Being Privatised — it's Time for More Time", *Novara Media*, (10 May 2015), http://novaramedia.com/2015/05/10/election-reactions-our-commons-are-being-privatised-its-time-for-more-time/

[17] k-punk, "Communist Realism", (5 May 2015), http://k-punk.org/communist-realism/ (Also in this volume, pp. 559-566)

For Now, Our Desire is Nameless

[1] *European*, (20 May 2015), http://www.theeuropean-magazine.com/mark-fisher--2/8480-is-there-an-alternative-to-capitalism

[2] Francis Spufford, *Red Plenty*, (Faber and Faber, 2011), p. 4

[3] Michael Hardt, "The Common in Communism", *Rethinking Marxism*, 22:3, 2010, pp. 346-356

Anti-Therapy

[1] This is a previously unpublished English transcript of a 2015 talk, which was translated and published in German as "Anti-therapie" in Felix Klopotek and Peter Scheiffele ed., *Zonen der Selbstoptimierung: Berichte aus der Leistungsgesellschaft* (Matthes & Seitz, 2016)

[2] Kathryn Ecclestone and Dennis Hayes, *The Dangerous Rise of Therapeutic Education*, (Routledge, 2008)

[3] Jennifer M. Silva, *Coming Up Short: Working-Class Adulthood in an Age of Uncertainty*, (Oxford University Press, 2015), p. 19

[4] Ibid., pp. 16-17

[5] Gilles Deleuze and Felix Guattari, *Capitalism and Schizophrenia:Anti-Oedipus*, (Continuum, 2004), p. 53

[6] Wendy Brown, "Wounded Attachments", *Political Theory*, Vol. 21, No. 3, (August 1993), pp. 290-410

[7] Laura Kipnis, "Sexual Paranoia Strikes Academe", *Chronicle of Higher Education*, (27 February 2015), http://laurakipnis.com/wp-content/uploads/2010/08/Sexual-Paranoia-Strikes-Academe.pdf

[8] David Smail, *Power, Interest and Psychology: Elements of a Social Materialist Understanding of Distress*, (PCCS Books, 2005), p. 39

[9] Ibid., pp. 39-40

[10] Ibid., p. 46

[11] Silva, *Coming Up Short*, p. 142

Democracy is Joy

[1] k-punk, (13 July 2015), http://k-punk.org/democracy-is-joy/

[2] Plan C, "The Meaning of Oxi", (8 July 2015), https://www.weareplanc.org/blog/the-meaning-of-oxi/

[3] Plan C, "On Social Strikes and Directional Demands", (7 May 2015), https://www.weareplanc.org/blog/on-social-strikes-and-directional-demands/

[4] Media Mole, "What's this? Is Iain Duncan Smith visibly excited by prospect of hurting the poor?", *New Statesman*, (8 July 2015), https://www.newstatesman.com/politics/2015/07/whats-iain-duncan-smith-visibly-excited-prospect-hurting-poor

[5] John Lanchester, "The Robots are Coming", *London Review of Books*, Vol. 37 No. 5, March 2015), https://www.lrb.co.uk/v37/n05/john-lanchester/the-robots-are-coming

[6] Stewart Lee, "It's too late to save our world, so enjoy the spectacle of doom", *Guardian*, (5 July 2015), https://www.theguardian.com/commentisfree/2015/jul/05/too-late-to-save-world-heathrow-runway-stewart-lee

[7] Anna Kornbluh, "On Marx's Victorian Novel", *Mediations: Journal of the Marxist Literary Group*, Vol. 25, No. 1, Fall 2010, http://www.mediationsjournal.org/articles/on-marx-s-victorian-novel

[8] David Graeber, "Of Flying Cars and the Declining Rate of Profit", *Baffler*, No. 19. March 2012, https://thebaffler.com/salvos/of-flying-cars-and-the-declining-rate-of-profit

[9] See Barton, *Hidden Valleys: Haunted by the Future*, (Zer0, 2015)

[10] Nick Land, *Suspended Animation*, (Urbantomy Electronic, 2013)

[11] Graeber, "Of Flying Cars and the Declining Rate of Profit"

[12] @dpjhodges, 5 July 2015, https://twitter.com/DPJHodges/status/617775404049399808

[13] @simon_schama, 6 July 2015, https://twitter.com/simon_schama/status/617956623718449152

[14] From Ursula Le Guin's speech at the National Book Awards,2014, where she was accepting the National Book Foundation's Medal for Distinguished Contribution to American Letters. Watch the whole speech here: https://www.youtube.com/watch?v=Et9Nf-rsALk

[15] Lanchester, "The Robots are Coming"

Cybergothic vs. Steampunk

[1] Urbanomic, (2016), https://www.urbanomic.com/document/cybergothic-vs-steampunk-response-to-badiou/

[2] See http://www.bbc.co.uk/news/av/uk-politics-34991402/hilary-benn-is-hold-our-democracy-in-contempt

[3] Alain Badiou, *Our Wound is Not So Recent: Thinking the Paris Killings of 13*

November, (Polity, 2016)

4 Scott Atran, "Mindless terrorists? The truth about Isis is much worse", *Guardian*, (15 November 2015), https://www.theguardian.com/commentisfree/2015/nov/15/terrorists-isis

5 Ibid.

6 Karen Armstrong, "Wahhabism to ISIS", *New Statesman*, (27 November 2014), https://www.newstatesman.com/world-affairs/2014/11/wahhabism-isis-how-saudi-arabia-exported-main-source-global-terrorism

7 Mark Fisher and Jeremy Gilbert, *Reclaim Modernity: Beyond Markets Beyond Machines*, (Compass, 2015), http://www.compassonline.org.uk/publications/reclaiming-modernity-beyond-markets-beyond-machines/

Mannequin Challenge

1 k-punk's final, unfinished and unpublished post, (15 November 2016). There are some incomplete and fragmentary sections in the piece.

2 Gary Young, "How Trump Took Middle America", *Guardian*, (16 November 2016), https://www.theguardian.com/membership/2016/nov/16/how-trump-took-middletown-muncie-election

3 Simon Reynolds, "Is Politics the New Glam?", *Guardian*, (14 October 2016), https://www.theguardian.com/books/2016/oct/14/politics-new-glam-rock-power-brand-simon-reynolds

4 Ibid.

5 Francis Fukuyama, "American Political Decay or Renewal: The Meaning of the 2016 Election", *Foreign Affairs*, Vol. 95, No. 4, July/August 2016, https://ceulau.files.wordpress.com/2016/08/fa-politcal-decay-or-renewal-aug-2016.pdf

6 Martin Jacques, "The Death of Neoliberalism and the Crisis in Western Politics", *Guardian*, (21 August 2016), https://www.theguardian.com/commentisfree/2016/aug/21/death-of-neoliberalism-crisis-in-western-politics

7 Christian Parenti, "Listening to Trump", *Jacobin*, (22 November 2016), https://www.jacobinmag.com/2016/11/trump-speeches-populism-war-economics-election

8 Francis Fukuyama, "American Political Decay or Renewal? The Meaning of the 2016 Election", *Foreign Affairs Journal*, July/August 2016, p. 68

9 Joan C. Williams, "What So Many People Don't Get About the US Working Class", *Harvard Business Review*, (10 November 2016), https://hbr.org/2016/11/what-so-many-people-dont-get-about-the-u-s-working-class

PART FIVE

WE HAVE TO INVENT THE FUTURE: INTERVIEWS

They Can Be Different in the Future Too: Interviewed by Rowan Wilson for *Ready Steady Book* (2010)

[1] In 2010, Rowan Wilson interviewed Mark for *Ready Steady Book*
[2] Roy Mayall, "Not Nostalgia", *London Review of Books* blog, (3 December 2009), https://www.lrb.co.uk/blog/2009/12/03/roy-mayall/not-nostalgia/

Capitalist Realism: Interviewed by Richard Capes (2011)

[1] Mark Fisher interviewed by Richard Capes for www.moretht.blogspot.com, (14 October 2011)
[2] Mark Fisher and Jeremy Gilbert, *Reclaim Modernity: Beyond Markets Beyond Machines* (Compass, 2015), http://www.compassonline.org.uk/publications/reclaiming-modernity-beyond-markets-beyond-machines/

Preoccupying: Interviewed by the *Occupied Times* (2012)

[1] Mark Fisher interviewed by *Occupied Times*, (3 May 2012), https://theoccupiedtimes.org/?p=3454

We Need a Post-Capitalist Vision: Interviewed by *AntiCapitalist Initiative* (2012)

[1] Mark Fisher interviewed by *AntiCapitalist Initiative*, (11 May 2012), http://anticapitalists.org/2012/05/11/mark-fisher-we-need-a-post-capitalist-vision/
[2] Paul Mason, "These revolts have ended the period of capitalist realism", *Guardian*, (23 January 2012), https://www.theguardian.com/commentisfree/video/2012/jan/23/paul-mason-revolts-capitalist-realism-video
[3] Chris Harman, "Zombie Capitalism", *Socialist Worker*, (23 June 2009), https://socialistworker.co.uk/art/17914/Zombie%20capitalism
[4] Owen Hatherley, *Militant Modernism*, (Zer0, 2009)

"We Have to Invent the Future": An Unseen Interview with Mark Fisher (2012)

[1] Mark Fisher interviewed by Tim Burrows and Sam Berkson, posthumously published in *Quietus*, (22 January 2017), http://thequietus.com/articles/21616-mark-fisher-interview-capitalist-realism-sam-berkson

Hauntology, Nostalgia and Lost Futures: Interviewed by Valerio Mannucci and Valerio Mattioli for *Nero* (2014)

[1] Mark Fisher interviewed by Valerio Mannucci and Valerio Mattioli for *Nero Magazine*, Summer 2014, http://www.neromagazine.it/n/?p=20620

PART SIX

WE ARE NOT HERE TO ENTERTAIN YOU: REFLECTIONS

One Year Later...

[1] k-punk, (17 May 2004), http://k-punk.abstractdynamics.org/archives/002926. html

Spinoza, k-punk, Neuropunk

[1] k-punk, (13 August 2004), http://k-punk.org/spinoza-k-punk-neuropunk/

[2] Radar_Anomalous, "A Fragment of Badiou", (5 August 2004), http://radar_ anomalous.blogspot.co.uk/2004/08/fragment-of-badiou.html
[3] See http://hyperstition.abstractdynamics.org/archives/003698.html
[4] Rita Carter, *Mapping the Mind*, (Weidenfeld and Nicholson, 1998)
[5] See http://hyperstition.abstractdynamics.org/archives/003824.html

Why Dissensus?

[1] Mark Fisher writing on why the name "Dissensus" was chosen for the forum he co-founded with Matt Ingram (Woebot), (24 October 2004), http://www. dissensus.com/showthread.php?t=64

New Comments Policy

[1] k-punk, (5 September 2004), http://k-punk.org/new-comments-policy/

Comments Policy (Latest)

[1] k-punk, (10 September 2004), http://k-punk.org/comments-policy-latest/

Chronic Demotivation

[1] k-punk, (3 December 2004), http://k-punk.org/chronic-demotivation/

How to Keep Oedipus Alive in Cyberspace

[1] k-punk, (9 December 2004), http://k-punk.org/how-to-keep-oedipus-alive-in-cyberspace/

We Dogmatists

[1] k-punk, (17 February 2005), http://k-punk.abstractdynamics.org/archives/005025.html

[2] Kant, who begins as a Leibnizian rationalist, is famously "awoken from his dogmatic slumber" by Hume. The Kantian turn is away from dogma and into *critique*. Reason is not so much surpassed as *arrested*. Kant seeks to establish the *limits* of the thinkable, curbing Reason's alleged hubris, and laying the groundwork for the aporetic pathos-poetics piously peddled by the tragedians of deconstruction and postmodernism. Yet, Kant has himself been surpassed, by mathematics. Whilst it might appear that the mathematical paradoxes discovered by Cantor and Godel comfortably fit into Kantianism — the idea that "the Real itself is fundamentally unrepresentable; we can only become aware of "this outer limit of the symbolic" — Badiou allows us to see that the reverse is the case. For Badiou, that is to say, the mathematical paradoxes

demonstrate not that what we thought was coherent is actually not, but that what we thought was incoherent is actually rigorously understandable. Unconstructible sets, unique unnameable objects and unprovable statements all seem like they are impossible, but maths shows us that they're actually perfectly acceptable objects we can talk about without incoherence.

London Litened

[1] k-punk, (11 April 2008), http://k-punk.org/london-litened/

No Future 2012

[1] k-punk, (13 May 2008), http://k-punk.abstractdynamics.org/archives/010368.html "My presentation from yesterday's astonishingly successful Hauntology event at the Museum of Garden History. Thanks to everyone who attended..."

[2] Robert Macfarlane, "London Fields", *Guardian*, (8 December 2007), https://www.theguardian.com/books/2007/dec/08/photography

Ridicule Is Nothing to Be Scared Of (Slight Return)

[1] *Wire* Blog, (15 July 2008), https://www.thewire.co.uk/in-writing/themire/20640/ridicule-is-nothing-to-be-scared-of_slight-return_

Break Through in Grey Lair

1 k-punk, (16 August 2009), http://k-punk.abstractdynamics.org/archives/011269.html
2 Graham Harman, *Prince of Networks: Bruno Latour and Metaphysics*, (re:press, 2009), p. 120
3 Graham Harman, "Why Socrates Was Not a Grey Vampire", *Object-Oriented Philosophy*, (15 August 2009), https://doctorzamalek2.wordpress.com/2009/08/15/why-socrates-was-not-a-grey-vampire/
4 Graham Harman, "Another Quick Point on Trolls/Grey Vampires", *Object-Oriented Philosophy*, (3 August 2009), https://doctorzamalek2.wordpress.com/2009/08/03/another-quick-point-on-trollsgrey-vampires/

Real Abstractions: The Application of Theory to the Modern World

1 *Frieze*, Issue 125, (September 2009)
2 Louis Althusser, "Cremonini, Painter of the Abstract", *Lenin and Philosophy, and Other Essays*, (Monthly Review Press, 2001)
3 Benjamin Noys, *The Persistence of the Negative: A Critique of Contemporary Continental Theory*, (Edinburgh University Press, 2010), p. 168
4 Nick Cohen, "Why the Tate's posing curator is so passe", *Observer*, (1 March 2009), https://www.theguardian.com/commentisfree/2009/mar/01/tate-britain-bourriaud-art-market

No I've Never Had a Job...

1 k-punk, (6 August 2010), http://k-punk.org/no-ive-never-had-a-job/
2 Ivor Southward, "As if By Magic", *Screened Out*, (4 August 2010), http://screened-out.blogspot.co.uk/2010/08/as-if-by-magic.html
3 Digital Ben, "Writing Fiction", *Riding Third Class on a One-Class Train*, (6 August 2010), http://ridingthirdclass.blogspot.co.uk/2010/08/writing-fiction.html
4 k-punk, (18 November 2010), http://k-punk.abstractdynamics.org/archives/011723.html

Exiting the Vampire Castle

1 *North Star*, (22 November 2013), http://www.thenorthstar.info/?p=11299
This piece has proven to be one of the most controversial pieces written during Mark's lifetime. At the time of publication it attracted a large number of vociferous detractors, and it continues to do so to this day. The issues he was trying to address in the piece remain largely and sadly unresolved. However,

it is worth bearing in mind the extent to which this piece remains entirely in keeping with Mark's preferred rhetorical style and directions of thought, which is clearly evident when looked at within the context of the earlier k-punk posts reproduced here.

Good for Nothing

[1] *Occupied Times*, (19 March 2014), https://theoccupiedtimes.org/?p=12841

[2] David Smail, *The Origins of Unhappiness: A New Understanding of Personal Distress*, (Routledge, 2015), p. 46

PART SEVEN

ACID COMMUNISM

Acid Communism (Unfinished Introduction)

[1] This is the previously unpublished introduction to a proposed new book project, written in 2016. It is all that remains of this proposed work.

[2] Herbert Marcuse, *Eros and Civilisation*, (Routledge, 1987), p. 93

[3] Herbert Marcuse, *One-Dimensional Man*, (Routledge, 2002), p. 66

[4] Ibid., p. 63

[5] Herbert Marcuse, *The Aesthetic Dimension* (Beacon Press, 1979), p. 36

[6] Marcuse, *One Dimensional Man*, p. 62

[7] Ibid.

[8] Margaret Atwood, *The Heart Goes Last*, (Virago, 2016), p. 189

[9] Andy Beckett, *When the Lights Went Out: Britain in the Seventies*, (Faber and Faber, 2010), p. 209

[10] Ellen Willis, *Beginning To See The Light: Sex, Hope and Rock-and-Roll*, (Wesleyan University Press, 1992), p. 158

[11] Danny Baker, *Going to Sea in a Sieve*, (Phoenix, 2012), pp. 49-50

[12] John Foxx, "The Golden Section: John Foxx's Favourite Albums", *Quietus*, (3 October 2013), http://thequietus.com/articles/13499-john-foxx-favourite-albums?page=5

[13] Willis, *Beginning To See The Light*, p. xvi

[14] Ibid.

[15] Jonathan Miller, cited in *Life*, (25 November 1968), p. 100

[16] Michel Foucault, *The Order of Things*, (Routledge, 2001), p. xvi

[17] Michel Foucault, *Remarks On Marx*, (Semiotext(e), 1991), p. 121

[18] Michael Hardt, "The Common in Communism", in Costas Douzinas and Slavoj Žižek (eds), *The Idea of Communism*, (Verso, 2010), p. 141

[19] Greil Marcus, "The Myth of Staggerlee", in *Mystery Train: Images of America in Rock 'n' Roll Music*, (Penguin, 1997), p. 82

[20] Jefferson R. Cowie, *Stayin' Alive: The 1970s and the Last Days of the Working Class*, (The New Press, 2012), p. 46

[21] Ibid., p. 48

[22] Ibid.

[23] Franco Berardi, *After the Future*, (AK Press, 2011), p. 48

[24] Ibid., p. 23

acknowledgements

Sincere thanks to:

Tariq Goddard, Josh Turner, Tamar Shlaim and Johnny Bull (Repeater Books)

Zoe Fisher

Siobhan McKeown

Simon Reynolds

John Doran (*The Quietus*)

Tim Burrows and Sam Berkson

Tony Herrington (*The Wire*)

Joanne Laws (*Visual Artists' News Sheet*)

Richard Capes

Valerio Mannucci

Rowan Wilson

Repeater Books

is dedicated to the creation of a new reality. The landscape of twenty-first-century arts and letters is faded and inert, riven by fashionable cynicism, egotistical self-reference and a nostalgia for the recent past. Repeater intends to add its voice to those movements that wish to enter history and assert control over its currents, gathering together scattered and isolated voices with those who have already called for an escape from Capitalist Realism. Our desire is to publish in every sphere and genre, combining vigorous dissent and a pragmatic willingness to succeed where messianic abstraction and quiescent co-option have stalled: abstention is not an option: we are alive and we don't agree.

Repeater